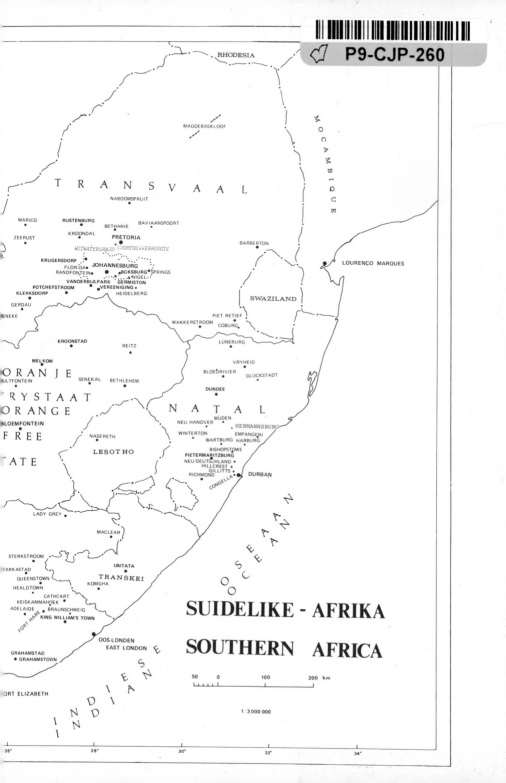

RHODESIA

MOCAMBIQUE

MAGOEBASKLOOF

T R A N S V A A L

NABOOMSPRUIT

MARICO
RUSTENBURG
BETHANIE
BAVIAANSPOORT
KROONDAL
ZEERUST
PRETORIA
WITWATERSRAND   VOORTREKKERHOOGTE
BARBERTON
KRUGERSDORP
LOURENÇO MARQUES
FLORIDA   JOHANNESBURG
RANDFONTEIN   BOKSBURG   SPRINGS
NIGEL
VANDERBIJLPARK   GERMISTON
POTCHEFSTROOM   VEREENIGING
KLERKSDORP   HEIDELBERG
GERDAU
ENEKE
SWAZILAND

PIET RETIEF
WAKKERSTROOM   COBURG
KROONSTAD   REITZ   LUNEBURG

WELKOM   VRYHEID
ORANJE   BLOEDRIVIER   GLUCKSTADT
ULTFONTEIN   SENEKAL   BETHLEHEM
RYSTAAT   DUNDEE
ORANGE   N A T A L
BLOEMFONTEIN   NEU HANOVER   MUDEN
FREE   NASERETH   WINTERTON   HERMANNSBURG
    WARTBURG   EMPANGENI
ATE   LESOTHO   BISHOPSTOWE   HARBURG
PIETERMARITZBURG
NEU-DEUTSCHLAND
HILLCREST
RICHMOND   GILLITTS
CONGELLA   DURBAN

LADY GREY

MACLEAR

O C E A A N

STERKSTROOM
ARKASTAD   UMTATA
QUEENSTOWN   T R A N S K E I
HEALDTOWN   KOMGHA
CATHCART
KEISKAMMAHOEK
ADELAIDE   BRAUNSCHWEIG
FORT HARE   KING WILLIAM'S TOWN

OOS-LONDEN
EAST LONDON
GRAHAMSTAD
GRAHAMSTOWN

ORT ELIZABETH

I N D I E S E
I N D I A N

SUIDELIKE - AFRIKA

SOUTHERN AFRICA

50   0   100   200 km

1:3 000 000

26°   28°   30°   32°   34°

SOUTH AFRICAN
MUSIC
ENCYCLOPEDIA

General Editor

DR JACQUES P. MALAN

VOLUME II

E — I

A publication of the
Human Sciences Research Council
Pretoria

1982

OXFORD UNIVERSITY PRESS
CAPE TOWN

Oxford University Press

OXFORD LONDON GLASGOW
NEW YORK TORONTO MELBOURNE AUCKLAND
NAIROBI DAR ES SALAAM CAPE TOWN
KUALA LUMPUR SINGAPORE HONG KONG TOKYO
DELHI BOMBAY CALCUTTA MADRAS KARACHI

AND ASSOCIATES IN
BEIRUT BERLIN IBADAN MEXICO CITY NICOSIA

INSTITUTE FOR LANGUAGES, LITERATURE AND ARTS
Director: *Dr K.P. Prinsloo*
Head, Research Centre for South African Music: *Prof. Dr J.P. Malan*

Logo by Elizabeth Couzyn
Music examples written and diagrams drawn by Stefans Grové

ISBN 0 19 570285 9
This publication is also available in Afrikaans (ISBN 0 19 570286 7)

Published for the Human Sciences Research Council by
Oxford University Press, Harrington House,
Barrack Street, Cape Town 8001, South Africa
Set, printed and bound by Citadel Press, Lansdowne, Cape

ABBREVIATIONS USED IN THIS ENCYCLOPEDIA

*		indicates date of birth
°		indicates date of death
**	(in the course of an article)	indicates that a separate article has been devoted to the person or matter thus marked.

Editorial team:

Full-time: Elizabeth Couzyn (secretary: 1969–1974), Mrs E.H. Snyman (1965–1968), Dr Lily Wolpowitz (1966–1969), Dr C.G. Henning (1970–1973), Mrs A.M. Wepener (from 1976) and Miss T. Smuts

Part-time: Mrs Eva Malan (1962–1964), Mrs M. Thomas (from 1977)

Typists (Part time): Mrs R. Eyssell, Mrs B. Auret, Mrs D.R. Bower, Mrs M.H. Wilmans

Supplementary information *1974–1979:* Dr C.G. Henning on behalf of the Music Documentation Centre, HSRC

Translators (Afrikaans/English):
Prof. L.H. Hugo
Dr G.S. Jackson
Prof. J.P. Malan

Language Editors:
Prof. A.C. Partridge
Mr Thys Uys
Prof. J.P. Malan

Advisory committee (1962–1974):
Dr A.C. Hartman *(Chairman),* Prof. P.R. Kirby, Dr. F.C.L. Bosman, Mr D.I.C. de Villiers, Dr Yvonne Huskisson, Prof. J.J.A van der Walt, Dr A.J. van Rooy *(Vice-president of the HSRC),* Dr P.G. du Plessis *(Director of the Institute for Languages, Literature and Arts),* Prof. Dr Jacques P. Malan *(General Editor)*

EAGAR, FANNIE EDITH STARKE (NéE WEBB), *4 August 1920 in Cape Town; at present (1977) in Port Elizabeth. Music teacher, composer and pianist.

Fannie Eagar studied at the South African College of Music** in Cape Town from 1938 to 1940, under Doris Lardner (piano) and Prof. W. H. Bell** (composition) and obtained the LUCT and UTLM diplomas. Whilst teaching in Sea Point between 1941 and 1945, she continued part-time study under Dr Alban Hamer.** She is also holder of the UTLM (harmony and counterpoint, 1944), LTCL (1963), FTCL (1964) and UPLM (1964) diplomas. — After teaching privately at Hermanus for some years, she joined the staff of the Oudtshoorn Girls' High School, working there from 1955 to July 1962. She has also taught at Kroonstad, Kuruman, Vryburg, and the Collegiate Girls' High School, Port Elizabeth. As a concert artist, she has given piano recitals in Kroonstad, Oudtshoorn and other centres.

WORKS
Hermanus School song (A. van Wyk). Ms., 1954. Laetitia, chorus for SATB (A.G. Visser). Ms., 1954. Die Pêrel se klokkies (A.G. Visser). Ms., 1954. Church anthem, chorus for SATB (St Francis of Assisi). Ms., 1954. Vreugdelied (F.E.S. Eagar). Ms., 1954. Seën Huis Naudè, song for SSA (J. de V. Krynauw). Ms., 1956. In die wonder van die berge, three-part chorus (J. de V. Krynauw). Ms., 1958. As die reënnimfe verdwyn, operetta for girls (libretto: I. Krynauw). Ms., 1959. Unielied, three-part chorus (J. de V. Krynauw). Ms., 1960. Psalm 121, two-part chorus. Ms., 1962. For eager fingers (Vir vurige vingers), a course for beginners, in two volumes. Ms., 1967.

– Ed.

EAMES, ARTHUR ('BANDY'), ° 12 February 1956 in East London. Bandmaster.

Eames joined the Royal Marines as bandboy in 1909, eventually became bandmaster and held the rank of lieutenant. Before going to East London in 1934, he had been in Cape Town where he conducted the RNVR Band. In East London he succeeded W.E.H. Kealey** as conductor of the Combined Bands of Kaffrarian Rifles and Comrades, and instructed the Selbourne College cadet band. During the Second World War he had a band of 60 members who played under his direction in the North. — In 1947 Eames revived the band of the Kaffrarian Rifles which had dispersed during the War and conducted it for a further two years. When the East London Municipal Band was formed in 1951, he became its bandmaster and in August 1952, also the conductor of the East London Municipal Orchestra. Despite the loss of his legs, he conducted the orchestra and the band until his death. Eames also had some experience as a choral conductor. On the sudden death of A.J. Ford** in 1937, shortly before an Eisteddfod performance of the East London Choral Society, he was in charge of the choir.

SOURCE
Daily Dispatch: 1934–1956.

– Ed.

EASON, W. Pietermartizburg

EASTERN PROVINCE THEATRE (PORT ELIZABETH) Port Elizabeth Amateur Theatricals

EAST LONDON

EAST LONDON ASSOCIATION OF ARTS AND ADULT EDUCATION
East London 4

EAST LONDON CHORAL AND ORCHESTRAL UNION   East London I

EAST LONDON CHORAL SOCIETY   Barratt, J. Tryal Beavan, W.J. Chapman,
East London 1, 3, A.J. Ford, F.E. Lee, E.R. Goodacre, J. Hyde, King William's
Town 5

EAST LONDON MUSICAL ASSOCIATION   H. Gwynne, F.B. Moeller, R.
Schneider, A.W. Woodcock

EAST LONDON MUSIC CLUB   East London 4

EAST LONDON OPERATIC AND DRAMATIC SOCIETY   A.J. Ford, E.R.
Goodacre, F.E. Lee

**EAST LONDON ORCHESTRAL SOCIETY (ALSO FRANZ MOELLER OR-
CHESTRAL SOCIETY, EAST LONDON MUNICIPAL ORCHESTRA, CA-
MILLO FIORE'S MUNICIPAL ORCHESTRA, EAST LONDON ORCHES-
TRA)**   East London 1, 2, Israel (Ferdinand), F. Hyde, F.B.M. Moeller

EAST LONDON PHILHARMONIC SOCIETY   East London 3

EAST LONDON STRING PLAYERS   East London II/2

EAST LONDON, MUSIC IN

  I. BEFORE 1920
  II. FROM 1920 TO 1960

  1. Brass bands
  2. Franz Moeller and the City Orchestra
  3. Choirs
  4. Opera and other concerts
  5. Music teaching and diverse artists

I. BEFORE 1920
East London came into being in 1847 as a military outpost on the western bank of the
Buffalo River. The original inhabitants were Scottish soldiers, but in the course of
time British traders, German soldiers, Boers and their families, Irish and Scots girls
and British railway workers settled there. When the railway line to King William's
Town was completed along the river's eastern bank in 1874, the town centre soon
shifted across the river. The population in 1875 was 2 134. — As at other military
outposts, such as King William's Town and Grahamstown, East London's early
musical life offered mainly military music. In addition, every population group tried to
retain its identity by practising its own national music. The programmes of the railway
brass band (1883 to 1894) bear witness to a period when brass bands and folk music
could satisfy the musical needs of a population centre. — The East London Choral

Society was formed on 22 May 1882 under the chairmanship of the mayor, John Gately; Sam Barratt,** who had conducted choirs in Bloemfontein and Kimberley, was appointed conductor at a salary of R100 per annum. Funds were to come from members' subscriptions (two guineas per person per annum), augmented by profits from concerts. But shortly after the first concert on 17 November 1882, Sam Barratt returned to Kimberley and Mr Green volunteered his services. There was a marked improvement under his leadership and the cantata *The merrie men of Sherwood Forest* (Birch) was sung by a choir of 24 women and 28 men. After a few successes the Society was in a position to buy a piano. — Green left for Port Elizabeth in 1883 and J. Humphreys-Jones succeeded him as conductor. The new conductor took considerable pains to familiarise the choir with notation and directed their singing of the cantata, *The wreck of the Hesperus,* by James Hyde,** who was then living in King William's Town. When Green returned in 1884, a new series of concerts, described as "popular entertainments", was initiated. This was more or less an acknowledgement of the fact that the quality of the programmes had deteriorated and that the demand had switched to lighter musical fare. The point was emphasised when a Grand Concert (with a serious programme containing excerpts from *Athalie* (Mendelssohn) and the complete *Wreck of the Hesperus*) turned out to be a failure. — In spite of popular programmes the choral society slowly disintegrated. No concerts were given for two years, but then the modest R.L. McDonald took charge and recommenced rehearsing. He also insisted on instruction in singing and sight-reading as had Humphreys-Jones earlier on. In September 1890 James Hyde came from King William's Town to rehearse and conduct the choir and they were able to give several performances of *The May queen* (Sterndale Bennett), *Messiah* (Handel), excerpts from *Maritana* (Wallace), *Trial by jury* (Sullivan), *Judas Maccabeus* (Handel) and *The building of the ship* (Lahee). A professional improvement that Hyde introduced was an "orchestral" accompaniment supplied by a piano, two cornets, two violins, a double bass, a clarinet and kettle drums. After Hyde's departure for Johannesburg at the beginning of 1892, the society remained inactive for a few months, and then Levy Howe** became the conductor. — Howe expanded Hyde's instrumental ensemble to such an extent, that from the beginning of 1894 the society was renamed the East London Choral and Instrumental Union. Under Howe's direction three vocal works by Birch (*The merrie men of Sherwood Forest, Vortigern and Rowena* and *Eveleen)* were performed, but most of the concerts offered orchestral items supplemented by soloists from the community. The choir found the shift of emphasis to orchestral work unsatisfactory and in 1895 this led to the formation of an independent East London Philharmonic Society. After two concerts and the death of their conductor, H.J. Winny, in July of the same year, the Philharmonic Society disbanded, but the division between vocal and instrumental resources remained. The two sections of the Choral and Orchestral Union were still separate in 1896, when L. Tryal Beavan** became their conductor. Under his guiding hand the two sections merged and the society began to rehearse operettas – *The Bohemian girl* (Balfé) and *The yeomen of the Guard* (Sullivan) – which were performed before the Society again dissolved because of Beavan's poor health at the end of 1898. — Meanwhile, in 1897, Levy Howe had become conductor of a newly-established East London Musical Association which performed *Elijah* (Mendelssohn) under his direction. Although his choir and orchestra exceeded those of the Choral Union in size, the Association was not remarkably active. At the beginning of 1899 Hugh Gwynne succeeded Levy Howe and eventually had *The Creation* (Haydn) performed. A.B. Woodcock directed the Association towards the end of 1899 in their performance of *Dorothy* (Cellier), and in their final concert six months later. Another short-lived choir was the Orpheus Glee Singers, a male-voice choir of 24 members formed by Hugh Gwynne in 1898. This group was fairly active for six months. — The following music teachers had settled in East London towards the end of the nineteenth century: Mr Hann, Mrs H. Howard Browne, A. Barfield, Mrs John Edwards, "Professor" H. Rabe, E. H. Marsh, T. H. Slater,** Laura Willetts, Mrs M. Robertson, J. Tryal Beavan, Mrs E. M. Humphries, Montague F. Young, Frank Hyde,** A.B. Woodcock and Franz Moeller.** Franz Moeller, who started teaching violin in East London in 1895, established a music school in 1899 that provided the city with violinists, viola players and 'cellists until the 1950s. His teaching inevitably led, in 1898, to the creation of an East London Orchestra which had 22 members. They frequently played independently, but they also supplied accompaniments to the vocal works studied by the choral societies. Their name was changed to East London Orchestral Society in 1899, but due to war conditions, it faded out towards the end of 1900. When the War was over, Moeller, in 1902, formed a school orchestra which grew into an ensemble of 20 players – violins, violas, 'cellos, drums and a piano. — From 1899 an annual choral competition was held between the schools of East London, Port Elizabeth and King William's Town. This competition, which alternated its venue between the centres, was organised by the music inspector, Fred Farrington,** under the aegis of the Education Department. It is interesting to note that, apart from the prepared pieces, choirs had to perform two sight-singing tests. Years later, in 1922, a similar competition for Africans, arranged by the Native Musical Association, was begun under the chairmanship of Col. E. Smedley-Williams; W.B. Rubusana was the secretary. The choirs competed for a shield, donated by Edmund Bryant, until 1939. In 1922 Farrington was one of the adjudicators of the competition. — In 1904, an East London Choral Society was formed which had a boom period under W.I. Chapman,** when the initial 100 members increased at one stage to 150. From 1906 onwards visiting British vocalists supported them as soloists. With an income derived from the proceeds of concerts and a membership fee of 50 cents for men and 25 cents for women, the society was financially selfsupporting, but it nevertheless disappeared after the outbreak of the the First World War. In the ten years of its existence the following works were presented: *Messiah, The creation, On shore and sea* (Sullivan), *Una* (Gaul), *Judas Maccabeus, Daughter of Jairus* (Stainer), *Elijah, Hiawatha* (Coleridge-Taylor), *Faust* (Gounod), *The revenge* (Stanford) and *The May queen* (Sterndale Bennett). Franz Moeller's school orchestra, which had grown in the meantime to include music lovers in the community, accompanied all these performances. — A Gipsy Orchestra came into being in 1916. They appeared in gipsy costumes at their concerts, the profits of which were intended for war funds. The first conductor was Robert Johnston-Wilson, who was succeeded by W. I. Chapman. The members were mainly drawn from Moeller's school orchestra. It is not mentioned after May 1921.

II. FROM 1920 TO 1960

1. Brass bands

As a popular holiday resort for the Free State and the Eastern Province, East London had a perennial interest in brass bands. A very active East London City Band conducted by W. Smith existed in 1920 and then there was, of course, the brass band of the Kaffrarian Rifles, which had started its career during the 1880s. It flourished, particularly before the First World War, when Robert Johnston-Wilson conducted a total of 32 players. — In 1922 George Freeman was appointed the city's first Director of Music and the leader of a new East London Municipal Band, which had succeeded the City Band. Players were mainly recruited from musicians outside East London and with their assistance the band was able to play on Orient Beach and in Marine Park during holidays. Freeman was also expected to form a Municipal Orchestra, but after this group of twenty players had given three concerts during the Easter holiday of 1923 and two more in September of the same year, the undertaking had to be abandoned. Freeman resigned as Director of Music in August 1925 and joined Lyell-Tayler's** orchestra in Durban. His successor, the former deputy conductor, Fred F. Hardesty,** had to be satisfied with the designation of "bandmaster". Although required only to supervise the 1925–1926 season, he remained band leader until 1929, when it was dissolved after the City Council had withdrawn its support, apparently for financial reasons. — The British Empire Service League (BESL) then stepped in and assumed control of the band, which was re-named Comrades' Band (occasionally Comrades' Military Band), with Hardesty as leader until 1931, when he left East London for Pretoria. Freeman who had returned to East London from Durban succeeded him. Meanwhile the Kaffrarian Rifles Band, having gone through a few lean years, was revitalized by the appointment of W.E.H. Kealey,** formerly deputy conductor of H.M. Brigade of Guards, who soon amalgamated the bands into a new unit called Combined Bands of the Kaffrarian Rifles and the Comrades (1932). The local newspaper described it as "second to none in the Union". When Kealey left East London in 1934 to become the first musical director of the South African Army, Arthur Eames,** formerly a conductor of the Royal Marines, succeeded him as conductor of the combination. — The Comrades' Band became inactive in 1935 and during the Second World War the Kaffrarian Rifles Band was also obliged to cease its activities; but in 1947 it was reassembled by Eames for the visit of the Royal Family. Alan G. Salmon was the leader in 1949 and Reginald Johnson in 1950, but at the beginning of 1951 it again lapsed into inactivity, when the Army announced that it would no longer provide uniforms or instruments for players who were not members of the Active Citizen's Force. However, in the same year and under the new name of the East London Municipal Band, it was reformed under Eames, and still exists as such today (1968).

2. Franz Moeller and the City Orchestra

By 1923 Moeller's school orchestra was so firmly established that when Freeman's Municipal Orchestra collapsed it quite naturally expanded into the Franz Moeller Orchestral Society. During the first year of its existence the orchestra gave eight Sunday evening concerts in the Vaudette Theatre, of which the first took place on 6 May 1923. A good standard was maintained throughout the series, with the sensational result that the initial membership of 31 doubled to 62 within a single year.

In October 1923 the City Council contributed to its upkeep by offering to make the City Hall available, free of charge, for six concerts a year, on the condition that the proceeds were donated to charity. This proposal was naturally refused, because members of the orchestra were themselves obliged to pay a monthly subscription to keep the orchestra going. But in 1926, when the orchestra had seventy members and enjoyed considerable fame, Moeller was again approached by the City Council, this time with the proposal that his Orchestral Society be renamed the City Orchestra. The proposal included benefits such as free use of the City Hall and its piano, the payment of advertising costs and a contribution of R30 per concert. Thus Moeller's dedicated educational work of many years was at last crowned with some success. This Eastern harbour city – like Durban and Cape Town – could henceforth boast its own municipal orchestra. The name was changed to suit its new status and it became known as the East London Municipal Orchestra. — The City Council's offer actually amounted to extremely little. No provision was made for salaries or for some form of compensation for members of the orchestra – it had to continue on a purely amateur basis and was consequently obliged to accept severe limitations in its repertoire. On the other hand, entirely dependent on its own resources as it was, the orchestra became the centre towards which professionals as well as amateurs and music students gravitated. It was in fact a genuinely communal institution which enjoyed satisfying support from the public. Its volunteer character necessarily made it subject to sudden changes in membership and, above all, entirely dependent on the continued availability of a Franz Moeller to maintain the standards. — The first concert of the renamed City Orchestra took place on 16 May 1926, with W.O. Fairbairn as leader of the orchestra and by December, 26 concerts had been given. After this auspicious start the rate dropped to an average of twenty concerts a year. Programmes were tolerably light to start with, but after 1927 there was a steady tendency towards symphonic literature. In 1928 the City Council took a decision that is possibly unique in the history of the troubled relationships between South African city councils and civic orchestras: the orchestra would thenceforth be "hired out" to the person who required the least financial support from the Council. This decision probably arose from a background of conflicting artistic and financial demands made respectively by Moeller and the Council. Camillo Fiore's** tender was accepted and the orchestra was entrusted to him. In 1922 he had attempted to gain a niche for himself in the city's musical life with a series of three Sunday evening concerts, presented by "Signor Camillo Fiore's Orchestra". This "Orchestra" was probably the ensemble he directed in the Vaudette Theatre to accompany the "silent" films. He himself played the piano in that group, but in Moeller's orchestra he acted as a harpist. After his take-over, probably because municipal support was now minimal, the orchestra was again re-named and from February 1928 to February 1929 was called "Camillo Fiore's Municipal Orchestra". To the disappointment of the public, the standard of the concerts dropped to the level of entertainment and when Fiore's contract expired in February 1929, Moeller, who had in the meantime calmly revived his Orchestral Society, again took charge of the Municipal Orchestra, after renewed negotiations with the City Council. There were no further incidents and he retained his position until 1946. — Late in the same year (1929) another orchestra, the Border Orchestra, came into being with Fred Hardesty as conductor. Although this group was under the aegis of the BESL and, as far as numbers were concerned, had nearly as many players as the city orchestra, it ceased to exist after a number of concerts in 1930. Other short-lived East London orchestras were the New Light

Symphony Orchestra (1930-1931), conducted by H.M. Calvé, and the East London String Players (1936-1947), conducted by, first, Marion Pobjoy** and later, Ann Jackson. Calvé also formed a string quartet and for three months in 1931 gave a series of weekly Sunday evening "Pop concerts" with his chamber musicians. All these activities indicate that the marked growth, particularly in the study of string instruments initiated by Moeller, was paying dividends in East London's musical life. — The City Orchestra reached its peak during the early years of the Second World War. Programmes at this time almost always included a symphony, an overture and a full concerto for a solo instrument playing with the orchestra. Concerts lasted two hours and also offered considerable opportunities for chamber music groups. The music critic of the local newspaper spoke at this time of its "good ensemble, fine technique and excellent variety of presentation", but during the last years of the war the orchestra went through a difficult time. Apart from the fact that membership shrank to 35, Moeller was again obliged to maintain his ensemble without financial support from the City Council, whilst attendance figures dropped and the local newspaper ignored its existence. But the orchestra continued to be active. — In 1945, financial support was again forthcoming in the form of R70 per concert from the Council; but the expense of each concert (R54,80) had to be paid out of the R70 plus the proceeds of collections taken at the doors. In 1946, surprisingly, Moeller's services as conductor were again terminated and Lionel Field became the new Municipal Director of Music and conductor of the East London Municipal Orchestra. This appointment caused quite an uproar, particularly when the City Council, undeterred by a protest meeting of rate payers, refused to grant Moeller compensation as a token of appreciation for many years of selfless service. On 10 March 1946 Moeller conducted the orchestra in the 722nd concert it had given under his direction and then he retired. At a farewell concert, held before his departure from East London in March 1953, he conducted the orchestra for the last time. The audience on this occasion was the largest in the city's history for a musical event of any kind. — Field had an uphill battle; three-quarters of the orchestra were former pupils of Moeller and could only be persuaded to rejoin the orchestra after Moeller had pleaded with them to do so; moreover, all the orchestral scores and many of the instruments belonged to Moeller! By 1948 the orchestra, with 30 members, was regaining its former strength and was giving fifteen concerts a year. Field began some new series entitled "First East London Performances", "Symphony Nights", "Music of the Masters Concerts" and "Popular Concerts", but in April 1952 the orchestra's activities were temporarily suspended, and when the regular concerts were resumed in August, Arthur Eames was the conductor. — The internal problems were evidently not yet resolved, as concerts were again suspended in February 1953 and then resumed in July, still with Eames as conductor, but with the orchestra now called the East London Orchestra. At the first concert, the audience numbered fifty, but by the seventh concert attendance had grown to three hundred. After that the orchestra was provisionally re-established as a factor in East London's musical life. Unfortunately, Eames, who had lost both his legs within a few years and conducted from a wheel chair, died early in 1956. He was succeeded by C.W. Hall who was still the conductor when the name was changed for the umpteenth time (May 1956) to East London Orchestral Society. L.A. Inskip became the Society's conductor in April 1962. The City Council had given (subject to revision and change) a modicum of regular support since 1929, and at present (1968) there is even provision (after the deduction of expenses) to pay compensation to members of the orchestra.

7

3. Choirs

Cambridge, a suburb of East London and until 1941 a separate municipality, enjoyed an active choral season from the nineteen-twenties onwards, with leading contributions by Robert R. Burns and his wife, both good singers. The Cambridge Musical Society's first concert was given by a few soloists in May 1922, but at the third concert they had a choir of fifty voices and a small orchestra of fifteen players giving account of diverse items. This established a pattern until December 1926, when excerpts from *Maritana* (Wallace) were given; this was followed by *The May queen* (Sterndale Bennett), *St Paul* (Mendelssohn), *A tale of old Japan* (Coleridge-Taylor) and other works. After Burns left the city in April 1930, the choir of thirty-five voices continued to exist until 1935 although they usually only sang at the East London Eisteddfod or in collaboration with other societies. The East London Eisteddfod, which had been held annually since 1922, contributed a good deal to the revival of good choral music in the city after the First World War. From 1923 a shield to the value of 100 guineas was awarded by the East London and Border Cambrian Society to the winner of the main choir competition. The Cambridge Musical Society won the coveted trophy in 1923, 1925, 1926, 1931 and 1932. — Edward Robertson Goodacre,** the organist of the Trinity Methodist Church, was particularly active in reviving choral music in East London. He enlarged his church choir in 1923 and renamed it E.R. Goodacre's Augmented Choir; it had sixteen sopranos, ten contraltos, seven tenors and six basses. They presented works such as *Ruth* (Gaul), *Elijah, Messiah* and *The daughter of Jairus* (Stainer), and at the 1924 Eisteddfod they won the shield. Goodacre's principal aim was the revival of the East London Choral Society. He achieved this ambition in 1927. The choir of 44 members worked hard and presented a concert performance of *Faust*, and excerpts from *King Olaf* (Elgar), *The Creation* (Haydn) and *Samson* (Handel) during the year that Goodacre was conductor. He was succeeded in 1928 by A.J. Ford,** who in turn was succeeded by F.E. Lee** in 1929. The choir won the "Cambrian" shield under Ford's direction in 1928 and when it appeared in 1929 that Lee was not willing to participate in choral competitions, a separate East London Eisteddfod Choir was formed, with Ford as conductor. This choir, in reality still the old East London Choral Society, was not only successful in East London, winning the shield in 1929, but also at the Port Elizabeth Eisteddfod, where they won another shield in May 1930. Shortly after their triumphant return to East London, Lee resigned – a few months before the termination of his appointment – and henceforth the East London Choral Society and the East London Eisteddfod Choir were reunited under Ford. The choir won the open competition at the Johannesburg Eisteddfod in 1934 and the "Cambrian" shield in East London on three occasions: 1930, 1934 and 1936. — Although the choir's repertoire consisted mainly of unaccompanied part songs, works such as *The miller's wooing* (Eaton Faning) and a concert rendition of *Il trovatore* (Verdi) were also studied. Ford remained conductor until his death in 1937. He was succeeded by the following conductors: Philip B. Preston (1938–1939), Jack Ford (1940), Cecil Winter (1941), Mrs Armour McMillan (1941), J.B. Williams (1942) and Hilbert Schmidt (1942– 1947). Preston introduced a small string orchestra for accompaniments and offered ambitious programmes, such as an abridged concert version of *Carmen* (Bizet). He also conducted performances of *Hiawatha* and a *Choral fantasia on Lohengrin*. Under Schmidt, a tenor who over a period of twenty years had frequently appeared as a soloist in East London, *The gondoliers* (Sullivan) and *Merrie England* (German) were performed, as well as an annual *Messiah*. In 1942 Schmidt acted simultaneously as tenor soloist and conductor of this work. — A particularly notable choir, the Orpheus Male Voice Party, was founded in June 1927. Although the initiative came from Tom Harries, its founding was strongly supported by the Cambrian Society. The choir consisted of 25 selected male voices; Hayden Matthews** (the composer Johannes Joubert) was its first conductor. They set and maintained a high standard from the beginning – a noteworthy feature was that throughout its existence the choir memorized its repertoire. To the city's disappointment, Matthews left for Johannesburg at the end of August 1928 and for a few months A.J. Ford bore the responsibility. After a period of silence the choir again emerged in September 1929 and continued to give concerts, John Corder conducting, until 1935. *Nursery rhymes* (Adam Carse), *The goslings* (John F. Bridge) and *The desert* (Felicia David) were among the works they performed. — Another choir in East London for several years, was the Rondo Choristers. E.J. Evans, Frank C. Gregg and S.B. Watson formed this group in May 1932, after a smaller choir with the same name had acquitted itself well at the 1931 Eisteddfod. The first conductor, E.J. Evans, had to withdraw in June 1933 because of ill health; he was succeeded by E. John Evans, who left East London in 1936. E.J. Evans felt obliged to resume control of the choir, but in 1944 his poor health finally forced him to resign and John Chiddick succeeded him. The Rondo Choristers won the Cambrian shield in 1933 and 1937. — In 1947 Schmidt offered to resign as conductor of the East London Choral Society in favour of Alan G. Salmon, on condition that the Rondo Choristers, of whom Salmon had become conductor early in 1947, and the East London Male Voice Choir, which Salmon had founded at the end of 1946, should amalgamate with his – Schmidt's choir – to form one large combined choir. Thus, on 2 June 1947, the East London Philharmonic Society came into being. Salmon was the conductor, supported by Schmidt, Chiddick and W.H. Smith. The choir of 71 sopranos, 35 contraltos, 18 tenors and 21 basses presented reasonably ambitious programmes, including works such as *Olivet to Calvary* (J.H. Maunder), *The pirates of Penzance* (Sullivan), *Elijah, Messiah* and smaller works by old masters (Dowland) and contemporary composers (V. Hely-Hutchinson).** They frequently broadcasted. Nevertheless, the membership dwindled, finally to forty. After Salmon's departure at the end of 1955, Brian H. Smith became the conductor. The tradition, started by Goodacre in 1920, of an annual Christmas performance of *Messiah,* was interrupted in 1957 for the first time in 37 years when there was a lack of singers. Hilbert Schmidt, who had again become the conductor only a few months before, was obliged to dissolve the Philharmonic Society. There have since been other choirs: the Bach Choir (1958–1960) the East London Male Voice Choir (1959–   ) and the Eureka-koorvereniging** (1949–   ), of which the conductors were respectively L.A. Inskip, T.H. Richards and Maria van Rooyen.**

4. Opera and other concerts

Not much was done in East London in the way of opera. There was an East London Amateur Musical and Dramatic Society, which in 1923 faded away for lack of funds and in 1928 was revived as the Amateur Operatic and Dramatic Society. It had a choir of sixty which presented *San Toy* under the direction of F.E. Lee; A.J. Ford produced *inter alia* Monckton's *Our Miss Gibbs,* E.R. Goodacre directed Monckton's *A country girl* and W.O. Fairbairn Monckton's *The Quaker girl,* but in 1945 the Society terminated its existence. During the 'forties and 'fifties there were far-reaching developments in the field of drama when the East London Repertory Theatre Society, the East London

Technical College Drama Club, the East London Music and Variety Club and the Dramatic Society of East London were established. In addition to plays, works such as *Lilac time* (conducted by P.J. Lemmer**), and *Yeoman of the Guard, Hit the deck* and *Merrie England* (all three conducted by Jean Fowler) were presented. When the Guild Theatre** was built and used for the first time in 1962, theatrical enterprise had acquired a permanent home in East London. — Beatrice Marx** founded the Federated Music Clubs of South Africa in 1926 and a branch was established in East London, which had May Rogers as its secretary. The East London Music Club gave its first concert in August, featuring the visiting artist May Mukle. The membership fee was R2,10 a season, for at least four concerts. To these the East London branch added concerts at which local artists performed, and arranged a series of lectures on Bach by Janet Allnutt, organist of the St Saviour's Church. The Club was discontinued and succeeded by the Melodic Society which was established in 1930 by a small group of music enthusiasts, one of whom was Mrs R. Burns, who also exerted herself on behalf of choral music in Cambridge. Their policy was to devote a meeting either to a specific subject, or to a single composer. Members gave lectures and the programme of the next meeting was arranged to serve as a practical illustration of a lecture. Members had to be performing artists and were required to take part in at least one concert a year. The meetings were held at the homes of members, a fact which limited membership to about twenty people. — In 1943 the Melodic Society was incorporated in the new East London Music Club which had been founded by Marion Pobjoy in February 1936. This club operated along the same lines as the Melodic Society, but membership was not limited to musicians only. An annual subscription fee of R1,05 was charged and they held between seven and twelve meetings each year. The main emphasis fell on the performance of music, and the music itself was considered to be more important than the performer. Critics were not invited to the Club's meetings. The standard of performance was high, especially at the early concerts when Marion Pobjoy was in control. From this society the East London String Players conducted by Marion Pobjoy, was formed. They were often the first to perform certain works in East London. Marion Pobjoy returned to England at the beginning of 1945, but others took the lead and continued the work until March 1963, when the Club dissolved. — In 1947 the East London Community Centre of Culture was established by members of the City Council – E.H. Tiddy, E.J. Evans, D. Lazarus and others – with the aim of encouraging lectures, art exhibitions, ballet, music and drama. During the following year the Centre broadened its scope and it was given a new name: the East London Association of Arts and Adult Education. Several South African artists gave concerts in East London under the auspices of this organisation. In 1950 a Subscribers' Club was inaugurated as part of the Association; its 440 members were granted special privileges in regard to concerts. From 1951 onwards the two divisions operated separately, the Subscribers' Club presenting each year at least five concerts by visiting artists. It still exists (1968), and has taken over several of the activities of the Association of Arts, although it still is a subsidiary of the Association.

5. Music Teaching and artists

The following music teachers have been active in East London this century: W.I. Chapman (organ, pianoforte, singing); E.R. Goodacre (organ, pianoforte, singing); Eugenie Vaux-Ellis (violin); F.E. Lee (singing, organ, pianoforte); Camillo Fiore; Ruth Oldman-Brownlee (singing, pianoforte); George D'Alessio (pianoforte); Elaine

Melvill (singing); Ann Jackson (violin); Sheila Starkey (pianoforte); Hayden Matthews (singing); Naomi Papé** (singing); Laura Palmer (pianoforte); Agnes Frances Scholl (pianoforte); Alan G. Salmon (organ, pianoforte); Robert Bilsbury (pianoforte, organ); L.A. Inskip (violin, pianoforte, singing); Nan Griffin** (singing); Maria van Rooyen (singing, pianoforte); Grace Edleman** (pianoforte); and Bruce Gardiner** (pianoforte). —Performing artists who at some stage played a prominent part in the music life of East London are – apart from those already mentioned – the following: the pianists Leslie Needham, Pat Keightley (later Mrs Gottgens), Doreen Moeller (also a soprano, later Mrs Vaughan-Hale), Phyllis Meine and Edith Griff-Jones; the violinists Ingaretha Lock, Dafne Keightley (later Mrs Walter Swanson**), Dr Felix Meine, Mary Rupus (later Mrs Lindsay), Edyth Wood (later Mrs W.F. Kirschman), Solomon Horwitz, Gerald Fainsinger and Fleetwood Howard; the cellists Arthur G. Swan, Daphne Moeller (later Mrs Coltman), Daphne Chavannes and Mavis Weaver; the sopranos Eileen Ryan, Violet Essenwein (later Mrs Stewart), Jennie Christie (later Mrs H. Goosen), Ethel Brown, Dorothy Hoskin, Marjorie Godding, Thelma Rundle and Mabel Fenney; the contraltos Kathleen Hall-Brown, Mrs G.R. Griffith, Doris Brown, Antoinette Williams, Edith Gell, Madame Zoe Ford and Hester Geddes; the tenors W.E. Dickie, Leslie McCullum, Ripley Evans, S.H. Weaver and Jack Ford; the baritones George Howe and Merwyn Hanau, and the basses G.R. Griffith, Reginald Beavitt and J.E. Lones.

BIBLIOGRAPHY
Van der Walt, E.H. (Snyman): *Musiek in Oos-Londen tot 1920.* B.Mus. script, UP, 1964.

SOURCES
The East London Dispatch: 1880–1897.   *The East London Daily Dispatch:* 1898–1901 and 1920–1924.   *The Daily Dispatch:* 1925–1960.   Programmes of the various societies.   Scrapbook of newspaper cuttings relating to W.I. Chapman in the possession of Mrs E.J. Evans, Cambridge, East London.   Minutes of the Rondo Choristers.   Correspondence with Franz Moeller, Hilbert Schmidt, Nora Rive and others.

– E.H.S.

EAST LONDON SCHOOLS' MUSIC AND DRAMA ASSOCIATION, THE was formed by a group of local teachers in 1941 to foster and encourage the development of music, drama and art in schools. Its chief function is the organisation of an annual schools' music festival on a non-competitive basis. Twenty-five of these festivals have been organised and for the past 7 years they have formed part of the City's Music Week in May. A feature of the festival is the singing of the junior and senior massed choirs of some 300 to 400 boys and girls. — It has arranged and subsidised lectures, recitals and performances for schools and local children, sometimes on its own initiative or in collaboration with other kindred bodies. In this way children were given the opportunity to see and hear artists such as Elsie Hall,** Cecilia Wessels,** Moira Lister, the Pro Arte Trio and many others. For the past two years the Association has also sponsored and organised an annual exhibition of school children's art. — Affiliated to the Schools' Music Association of Great Britain, the former South African Music Council** and the Border Theatrical Association, it has received no subsidy from Provincial or National Education Departments. Its sole sources of income have been several small grants from a local trust, in recent years, a small annual grant of R50 from the Municipality of East London and the proceeds of the festivals. — Over the past 25 years the Association has ploughed back into local schools more than R6 000 of its income, in the form of grants for the purchase of instruments, music, records, record-players and other equipment. It has also paid the fees of speech and music teachers for schools which could not otherwise afford the services of such specialised teachers. — In 1967 the Association launched a Junior Civic Orchestra which made its first appearance, appropriately enough, at the Association's Silver Jubilee Festival. The Schools' Art Centre, for which the Association has worked for many years, was approved by the Cape Education Department and was also established in 1967. It should be mentioned that over the years the Association has commissioned songs from the South African composers P.J. Lemmer,** G.T. Marnitz,** Arnold van Wyk** and G. Gruber.**

W.A.S

EAST LONDON STRING PLAYERS   East London II/2

EBERLEIN, CHARLES JOHN HERMAN, a violinist with a dynamic, though somewhat obstinate, personality who was prominent in the musical life of Port Elizabeth and Durban between the years 1874 and 1892. Equipped with a D.Phil. from a German university he came, via England, to South Africa, as organist of St Mary's in Port Elizabeth, and as music teacher at the Grey Institute. Perhaps his Christian names were Karl Johann Hermann which he anglicized either in England or in the Eastern Province; but in spite of this he was always known as Herr Eberlein, and in a description of him from Natal he is depicted as "the old singing master whose bald pate, white gingham and pith helmet were peculiarly characteristic".

The first advertisement concerning Eberlein, dated Port Elizabeth, 10 April 1874, has reference to a lecture which he was to deliver on "The mission and study of musical art", with vocal and instrumental illustrations. On 1 May he gave his first concert, in which a conductor (Cottmann), an accompanist (Denny) and a choir of 40 voices took part; he himself played De Beriot's *Sixth violin concerto* and (on the piano) Beethoven's *Sonata op. 10 no. 1* and Mendelssohn's *Rondo capriccioso in E.* Four weeks later he came before the public again in performances of De Beriot's *Eighth violin concerto* and the Gavotte from Bach's *Sixth violin suite,* the rest of the programme being made up of part-songs, glees and madrigals (including Eberlein's own arrangements). In this first year he presented three soirées, and divided the proceeds from the first two (R73) between the Ladies' Benevolent Society and the Band of the Prince Alfred's Guards.** —For the German Liedertafel in White's Road he sang his comic song *Katzennatur;* he also lectured before them, and on 27 December 1878, he conducted this group on the occasion of a big concert and dance in the Town Hall. In 1879 he played trios by Reissiger, along with the pianist Lagerwall and the cellist Kunze, and a year later he conducted the Liedertafel in a special concert for the dependants of the soldiers killed in the Basuto War. Among his lectures mention should be made of one on Wagner's "Music of the future", and another on "Composition and the study of music". In July 1886, he was the guest artist of the

Liedertafel when he played the Gavotte from Bach's *Second violin suite* and De Beriot's *Fantasia on the William Tell overture.* — During the year of his arrival, 1874, he resuscitated the Amateur Musical Society and directed it in performances of *The Creation* (in March), *Athalie* (in August) and *Messiah* (in December). This exceptional amateur effort was followed in 1876 by the *Hymn of praise* (Mendelssohn) and *Acis and Galatea* (Handel). About December, 1876, the society proudly changed its name to the Port Elizabeth Philharmonic Society. Weekly practices took place in the Grey Institute, the accompaniment being supplied by three pianos. Since this was inadequate, Eberlein opened a subscription list for R1 000 to order orchestral instruments, constructed to a pitch a semitone lower "for the benefit of the singers". Out of this fund he also acquired a grand piano for the Town Hall. Just as it began to appear that amateur music in Port Elizabeth was aspiring to new heights, there was friction with the Port Elizabeth Orchestral Musical Society over the use of the instruments. Apparently no compromise was possible, and in 1879 Eberlein resigned as conductor of the amateurs. — Since July 1874, he had also been music master at the Grey Institute. In the year of his resignation (1879), he advertised in the *Grahamstown Journal* that he was prepared to teach beginners and advanced students by a simplified method a way of solving their technical problems and to give them a "philosophical" concept of the musical classics. He also mentioned that for some years he had been "Professionally attending HRH the Princess Christian and Princess Helena of Great Britain". From 1 July until 1 October he was willing to give lessons in Grahamstown, and to continue if the response was satisfactory. Pupils would be able to enjoy the privilege of practising duets and trios in combination with string instruments. Perhaps the response was discouraging, since at this stage he did not start teaching in Grahamstown. On 30 May, however, he appeared in Grahamstown as accompanist for Mme E. Mendelssohn.** He accompanied her in works by Offenbach, Mozart, Verdi, Rossini, Meyerbeer, and he himself contributed piano and violin solos. The newspaper report was favourable, and Mme. Mendelssohn gave two more concerts, though they were not so well attended. — The association with Grahamstown did, however, bear fruit. In 1881 Eberlein became music master at St Andrew's College in Grahamstown. A product of these years was a pamphlet entitled *What everyone should know about music.* As a teacher, Eberlein was up-to-date and in many respects in advance of his Victorian environment. In a letter to the press in January 1880, he pointed out that just as mathematics is an exercise of the intellect, so music plays its part in exercising the emotions of the young. He deplored the abundance of "musical quacks" in the teaching profession, and set out those principles which should be put into practice: a child of ten years should be acquainted with the basic principles; children should be taught in small groups; singing and the piano should be studied simultaneously. He urged the establishment of an academy of music in Port Elizabeth, perhaps envisaging something on European lines: training for about 60 pupils, each to receive three 50-minute lessons per week, one for technique, one for theory and one for interpretation. As far as possible, he applied these principles in practice and strove to make mixed string and piano trios the basis of his teaching. — The six years Eberlein spent in Grahamstown, illustrate year by year the extent to which he identified himself with the musical life of the town by aspiring to higher standards and by his teaching, writings and example. Thus he presented a series of six lectures at the Wesleyan High School as part of his educational work. These were concerned with Beethoven, Schubert, Haydn, Music in France, Music – how it is composed, interpreted and played, and other subjects, all illustrated by examples played on the piano and the violin; towards the end of the series even with the addition of a flute and a cello. The girls were expected to make notes and had to write essays on the lectures they heard. The best effort was rewarded with a prize. — From 1881 to 1883 Eberlein also conducted a strong choral society in this town. This group was prominent with 15 concerts given in a period of 18 months, though some were repeats, often with the support of a "miniature orchestra". A memorable occasion was the inauguration of the Town Hall on 4 May 1882, when Spohr's *Last judgement* was sung, with instrumental and vocal items to complete the second half of the programme. Eberlein also contributed a violin solo. The as yet unravelled machinations of the organist Winney eventually forced the society to dissolve, after a last concert in December 1883. Until he left the town in Reményi's company in 1887, he was however in great demand to play on the violin at variety concerts, at times also to sing and once even to play the organ. — How long Eberlein remained at St Andrew's is not known (perhaps until 1887); but at the time of the South African Industrial Exhibition, which was held in Port Elizabeth from 10 December 1885 until 9 January 1886, Eberlein was appointed to supervise and direct all the musical functions. For the four weeks' duration of the exhibition, Eberlein arranged Irish, English and German concerts; glee singing, solo singing and piano recitals; excerpts from *Messiah, The creation* and the *Hymn of praise;* an operetta presented by the music pupils of Miss Peacock; and almost daily performances by the bands of a British ship, the *Raleigh,* and the Natal Inniskilling Dragoons. The newspapers complained that there was too much walking around, too much noise ("the soloists had to work hard to make themselves heard"), and that the lights faded out practically every night. Nevertheless, his efforts were regarded as a musical triumph, and at the close of the proceedings members of the chorus and orchestra presented Eberlein with a decorative ivory baton. — This useful career in Port Elizabeth and Grahamstown was interrupted in August 1887, by the violinist Reményi. When this celebrity arrived in Grahamstown, Eberlein became his most ardent admirer. In Grocott's *Penny Mail,* Eberlein wrote a glowing tribute to Reményi and criticized the first edition of Grove's *Dictionary of music and musicians* for not giving him the credit he deserved. After extolling his "most pure and ethereal ... sweetest and wildest Hungarian melodies", Eberlein went on to express the hope that the error in Grove's *Dictionary* would be rectified in future editions, and stated his conviction that this violinist "more than rivals the famous Herr Joachim, as the world will yet see, and I doubt very much if, for instance, his performance of Mendelssohn's *Concerto* or Paganini's *Carnival,* as heard on Wednesday night, has ever been equalled". This opinion was hardly confirmed by the derogatory verdicts of such masters of the violin as Henri Vieuxtemps and Henryk Wieniawski, but such a eulogy did demand corresponding action. In seven of the recitals given in Port Elizabeth, after the one in Grahamstown, Reményi's accompanist, Frl. Feddern, was summarily replaced by Eberlein, who acted as accompanist in King William's Town, and thereafter also in Johannesburg in 1887, at that time a bustling mining camp. In the same year Eberlein must have discovered the clay-feet of his idol, because their ways parted at Queenstown. Concerts advertised for 2 and 3 November had to be postponed until 11 November, and again until 6 December. Eberlein did not arrive to play the accompaniments and Sophie Birch** stepped into the breach. — After this debacle, Eberlein was hardly able to continue his career in the Eastern Province. He started anew in Durban in 1888, but arranged his first public appearance to coincide with Reményi's departure. With characteristic zeal he devoted himself to the musical life of Natal and started a Durban Orchestral Society.** He was a thorough, enthusiastic conductor, who deserves to be remembered in South Africa for his practice of giving the concert audiences short spoken introductions to the music on the programme. His livelihood in Durban arose also from teaching at different schools, where he encouraged a loftier conception of music as a form of cultural expression. One of his most successful pupils was Beatrice Stuart (Marx).** In August 1892, after the Orchestral Society had given subscription concerts over a period of three years, Eberlein was invited to take charge of the music organization for the South African and International Exhibition at Kimberley. In an ambitious programme, which far surpassed that of Port Elizabeth, a choir of 150 sang F.R. Statham's** specially composed festival cantata *Prosperity and praise.* There was a noticeable emphasis on Wagner, who was still relatively unknown in South Africa. The choir sang *Messiah, The ancient mariner,* Mendelssohn's *Psalm 95,* excerpts from *Tannhäuser* and *Rienzi,* Cowen's *St John's eve* and Haydn's *Creation.* - Eberlein was in Cape Town from January 10, 1893, when he advertised his "scientific method of music teaching" and referred readers to the London *Musical Opinion,* published in January and February 1892, in which his theories about voice production had been printed. His resolute attempt to take the musical bastions of Cape Town by storm remained without significant result. Until 1899, he was occasionally mentioned in the newspapers as a concert artist co-operating with other professionals.

BIBLIOGRAPHY
Bouws, Jan: *Geskiedenis van die musiekonderwys in Suid-Afrika (1652-1902).* Nasou Bpk., Cape Town, 1972.   Jackson, G.S.: *Music in Durban.* Publication series No. 6, Wits University Press, Johannesburg, 1970.   Marx, Beatrice: *She shall have music.* W.J. Flesch and Partners, Cape Town, 1961.   Radloff, T.E.K.: *Music in Grahamstown, 1863-1879.* B.Mus. script, RU, 1969.   Sparrow, M.J.: *Music in Grahamstown, 1880-1900.* M.Mus. dissertation, RU, 1978.   Troskie, A.J.J.: *The musical life of Port Elizabeth, 1875-1900.* M.Mus. dissertation, UPE, 1969.

SOURCES
Eastern Province Herald: Apr.-Dec. 1874.   *The Grahamstown Journal:* Aug. 1886.   *Grocott's Penny Mail:* Aug. 1886.   *Queenstown Free Press:* 6 Dec. 1887.   Research by Dr Jan Bouws, Dr C.G. Henning and Dr G. Jackson.

- J.P.M.

EBERLEIN, MIEMIE, *8 August 1884 in Prince Albert; resident in Worcester in 1969. Contralto.

The Eberlein family had strong musical inclinations, and four of the eight singers who made recordings as "Het Moeder Kerk Koor" in 1912, under the direction of Denholm Walker,** were Eberleins (see Discography). Miemie Eberlein studied voice-production under Walker and N.R. Ingleby,** and later won local recognition as a soloist in Cape Town.

SOURCE
Stegmann, Frits: Die musikale Eberleins van die Groote Kerkkoor. *Eikestadnuus,* 31 Jan. 1964.

- F.S.

EDLEMAN, GRACE, *30 January 1907 in Cairo; resident in Port Elizabeth in 1969. Pianist and music teacher.

Grace Edleman came to South Africa when she was 13 years old, matriculated two years later and in that same year obtained an LTCL. After study at the music faculty of the Cape Town University and in London, she went to Alexandria in 1932, where Queen Farida and two younger sisters of King Farouk were among her pupils. At the outbreak of the Second World War she joined an entertainment unit, but in 1943 returned to South Africa where she taught music at the Border High School and at the Selborne Boys' High School in East London. She also broadcasted for the SABC.

– Ed.

EDWARDS, CHRISTOBEL   Johannesburg Philharmonic Society, J.H.T. Schutte

EGEL, HANS WALTER, *14 June 1878 in Mannheim; °1914 in Germany. Musical director of the Huguenot Seminary, Wellington.

Hans Egel obtained his Ph.D. degree as a young man, probably in Leipzig, and came to South Africa in 1904 to manage the musical affairs of the Huguenot Seminary. Endowed with a well-developed tenor voice, he organised the teachers and pupils into a Wellington Choral Union and started quarterly concerts in the Seminary's Goodnow Hall. In 1905, with a choir of 100 voices, he presented a Handel festival which included *Samson* and excerpts from other works. This was followed by a Mendelssohn festival in 1906, in which 200 people participated, including Karl Metzler** and Hans Endler.** For this occasion he compiled a programme-book of nearly 20 pages. The accompaniment was undertaken by an "orchestra" which was established in 1905. In the winter of 1907 an organ of 1056 pipes was installed in the Goodnow Hall, and in 1908 Denholm Walker** used it for a recital in which he had the assistance of Egel, Metzler and Lena Malan. In this year Handel's *Joshua* and Mozart's *Twelfth Mass* were performed and in 1909 there was a performance of historical music in period costumes. In the second term of 1909 this energetic German returned to Germany for reasons of health. — Some of the works in the attached work list had been brought to South Africa by the composer and were published in Wellington together with other works which had their origin here. Opera 4, 8 and 10 were available for scrutiny. Egel had obviously received a thorough training in music, as his works are competently written in the romantic chromatic idiom, with facile modulations and ambiguous tonal relationships, more than tinged by Wagner. Memories of *Tristan und Isolde* are especially evident in his setting of the *1st Psalm.* — An interesting fact is that his *Mater dolorosa* was dedicated to Hans Endler and was actually written for cello and piano or organ. This argues more than cordial relations between the Stellenbosch musician and the newcomer to Wellington. It seems probable that Endler often came over from Stellenbosch to participate in Egel's productions of choral and orchestral works. Also of interest is that the South African singer, Nunez Holtzhausen,** translated Egel's *Ode to South Africa* into Dutch and that Egel compiled a *South African Music Calendar* which he dedicated to Professor F.W. Jannasch** of Stellenbosch. His relationship with prominent musicians in the Western Province needs further research.

WORKS

Drei Lieder (Avenarius), op. 1: 1. Gefunden 2. Gräber 3. Am Geburtstag. C.F.W. Siegels Musikalienhandlung (R. Linnemann), Leipzig, n.d. Drei ernste Sprüche (Geibel, Kerner, Sturm), op. 2: 1. Und ist auch der Himmel von Wolken grau 2. Wenn plötzlich in Dein Lebenslicht 3. Was Gott Dir gibt. C.F.W. Siegels Musikalienhandlung (R. Linnemann), Leipzig, n.d. Drei Charakterstücke für die Orgel, op. 3: 1. Abendruhe 2. Et incarnatus est 3. Idylle. C.F.W. Siegels Musikalienhandlung (R. Linnemann), Leipzig, n.d. Strong are the mountains about us! A Huguenot song (Miss Clark), op. 4. Arrangement for full orchestra and choir in unison by "Prof." Carl Metzler. Publ. by the composer; pr. Breitkopf & Härtel, Leipzig; distr. R. Müller, Cape Town, n.d. Sacred march of the early Huguenots, (for piano or organ) op. 5. Publ. Egel; pr. Breitkopf & Härtel, Leipzig; distr. R. Müller, Cape Town, n.d. Short valse in E major for piano, op. 6. Publ. Egel; pr. Breitkopf & Härtel, Leipzig; distr. R. Müller, Cape Town, n.d. Weisst Du es noch? (Sweetheart, you know? Weet je dat nog?) Song, op. 7. Publ. Egel; pr. Breitkopf & Härtel, Leipzig; distr. R. Müller, Cape Town, n.d. Mater dolorosa, for violoncello, violin or viola solo, acc. by piano or organ, op. 8, dedicated to Hans Endler. Publ. Egel; pr. Breitkopf & Härtel, Leipzig; distr. R. Müller, Cape Town, 1900. Berceuse d'Afrique in G major for piano, op. 9. Publ. Egel; pr. Breitkopf & Härtel, Leipzig; distr. R. Müller, Cape Town, n.d. Der erste Psalm (The first Psalm), op. 10, for tenor or soprano with piano or organ accompaniment. Publ. Egel; pr. Breitkopf & Härtel, Leipzig; distr. R. Müller, Cape Town, n.d. Gesang der Verklärten (Song of the glorified), op. 11. Publ. Egel; pr. Breitkopf & Härtel, Leipzig; distr. R. Müller, Cape Town, n.d. Oratorium: Die Aussendung der Jünger (Christ ordaining the disciples), op. 12. Publ. Egel; pr. Breitkopf & Härtel, Leipzig; distr. R. Müller, Cape Town, n.d. Ode to South Africa (Ode aan Zuid Afrika) (English: L. Herzberger; Dutch translation: Nunez Holtzhausen), op. 13. Publ. Egel; pr. Breitkopf & Härtel, Leipzig; distr. R. Müller, Cape Town, n.d. Roccocco-Suite (sic!) I, suite (G major) for string orchestra, op. 14. Publ. Egel; pr. Breitkopf & Härtel, Leipzig; distr. R. Müller, Cape Town, n.d. A simple melody, for piano, op. 15. Publ. Egel; pr. Breitkopf & Härtel; distr. R. Müller, Cape Town, n.d. Reformation anthem. Ms., n.d. South African music calendar for 1909, dedicated to Prof. F.W. Jannasch. Ms., 1909, South African Public Library, Cape Town.

BIBLIOGRAPHY

Oberholster, J.A.S.: *Na honderd jaar. Eeufees, Gemeente Wellington, 1840-1940.* Paarlse Drukpers Mpy. Bpk., Paarl, 1940.

SOURCES

Huguenot News Letter: 1905-1909. Research Centre for South African Music HSRC, Pretoria: Payne collection of sheet music. Information supplied by Miss Ella Malan of Wellington.

— J.P.M.

EICHLER, WERNER Evelyn Dalberg

ELIAS, OTTO H.G. Ketelbey

ELLIE MARX MEMORIAL SCHOLARSHIP Pierre de Groote (Philip), B. Marx, E. Marx

ELLIS, ARTHUR (COUSIN TO ALEC ASHWORTH) Castalides, L. Knobel

ELTON, E.A.   Johannesburg 1, 2, Touring Theatre Groups 4

EMMA RENZI (PSEUDONYM)   E. Scheepers

EMPIRE EXHIBITION, JOHANNESBURG   Durban Orchestra, South African Army Band

EMPIRE MUSIC HALL   Durban 5, Johannesburg 1

EMPIRE THEATRE, JOHANNESBURG   David Foote, Johannesburg 3(iii), Steele-Payne Bellringers

EMPIRE THEATRE ORCHESTRA   David Foote

ENDLER, JOHANN FRANZ (HANS), *1 January 1871 in Neudorf, Mohrau, Austria; °30 June 1947 in Stellenbosch. Versatile practical musician, composer, co-founder and second principal of what subsequently became the Conservatoire of Music of the University of Stellenbosch.**

Hans Endler possessed the typically Austrian *joie-de-vivre* and charm of the old school; but he was also dynamic and tenacious and able to vitalize large-scale music making in Stellenbosch. His endowments of personality, experience and musical talent, seemed to make of him the ideal man to partner the serious Protestant, F.W. Jannasch,** in the joint venture to create a significant Afrikaans music centre. But in practice, as it turned out, there could be no whole-hearted co-operation between two such people: both had strong personalities and their backgrounds, characters and religious convictions were too divergent. Each went his own way. Despite the inevitable clashes, however, they used their respective talents to benefit their common field of activity. — At the age of eight Endler was already playing violin, guided by the village teacher, and singing, as alto soloist, in liturgical masses and other religious vocal compositions; but not until 1884 did he receive differentiated training in cello, viola, double bass and trumpet under the military conductor, Ferdinand Czerny, in Sternberg, Lower Austria. During his compulsory military service (1890–1893) he was a member of the famous orchestra of the Fourth Mounted Regiment, "Hoch und Deutschmeister", conducted by Ziehrer. This orchestra was very popular at court functions and state banquets and the youthful Hans Endler was introduced to the carefree circles of a hedonistic world in which the elderly Johann Strauss was the musical leader. Nevertheless, during these years in Vienna, Endler seriously studied cello, violin and pianoforte, as well as the complementary theoretical subjects and, as a member of the Philharmonic Orchestra, had the privilege of playing under conductors such as Brahms, Grieg, Richter, Schalk and others. He was also one of Ferdinand Hellmesberger's pupils, and often played the cello in the Hellmesberger String Quartet. — The comprehensive festivals arranged for Queen Victoria's Diamond Jubilee in 1897 lured many European musicians to London, and Hans Endler was one of them. He remained in England for six years, occupying a variety of positions, enlarging the scope of his musical experience and acquiring a knowledge of English. During the summer of 1897 he played in Moritz Wurm's Viennese-Hungarian salon orchestra on the Folkestone strand; then he was a member of the Drury Lane Theatre Orchestra for six months; and from January, 1898 he taught music for two terms at the Uppingham Public School in Rutland County, where he became friendly with Karl Metzler** of Leipzig, a competent violinist, through whose agency he was to emigrate to South Africa in 1903. He returned to London from Rutland County, and became a member of the Haymarket Theatre Orchestra. During and after the Anglo-Boer War, he joined for different seasons the Carl Rosa Opera Company, the Harrison Orchestra and the Gottlieb Salon Orchestra. Shortly before his departure, he was a cellist in Sir Henry Wood's Queen's Hall Orchestra. — After meeting Rocco de Villiers** of Paarl in England, Karl Metzler was considered as his successor (presumably in 1896) and when Rocco died in May 1902, the idea was realised. Metzler left for South Africa in 1903 and when Mackay Brothers** launched their large-scale scheme of establishing a permanent opera orchestra and an active chamber music group, he interested the organisers in having Hans Endler as a participant. Metzler, the Mount Nelson Trio (Haasdyk,** Van Erkel and Luyt**) and some local musicians had already been recruited for the scheme. Three months after receiving Metzler's letter, Hans Endler arrived in Cape Town; but in the event nothing came of the plans to establish an orchestra, and the chamber music group was disbanded after five or six concerts, due to a lack of public interest. At the critical time following this disappointment, Endler stayed for a while with Metzler in Paarl, and here he met the youthful P.K. de Villiers,** who offered him an assistantship at his music school in Stellenbosch. But in December 1903, P.K. de Villiers left on a visit to England, and when he returned in April 1904, he settled in Worcester. It appears that De Villiers's offer had been made, in the first instance, with a view to Endler's taking over his practice in Stellenbosch. — From the beginning Endler, with his accumulated experience and comprehensive knowledge of the practical aspects of music, was able to influence the "sleepy" village (his own word) with the enthusiastic zeal which made of him a legendary figure in Stellenbosch. His activities during the first few years were characteristic of this musician. Shortly after his arrival, he and Metzler established the Germania String Quartet, which was for many years to give concerts in the Western Cape, and as far afield as Cradock and Colesberg. Meanwhile he acquired orchestral instruments, trained musicians and by August 1904, was able to present a programme consisting of ten items including Beethoven's *First symphony (!)*, with an orchestra of 47 members. During the same year he applied the experience gained in London with the Carl Rosa Company, and presented Gilbert and Sullivan's *Trial by jury,* repeated the performance of his symphony concert in Cape Town (including a Haydn symphony in the programme), and managed to establish a brass band. This became a regular feature in Stellenbosch, and even gave promenade concerts in De Laan. During the same tempestuously active year Endler gave his active support to a joint scheme of his colleagues in Stellenbosch to create one single conservatoire, capable of exerting a beneficial influence on music education in South Africa. The idea was realised in December of the following year and the Conservatoire was inaugurated in May, 1905. That first year in Stellenbosch, when Endler concentrated his enthusiasm for music, his knowledge and vital energy on the music of a village community, marks a climax in his career. In future years the Conservatoire steadily demanded more of his time and attention, but he never lost his enthusiasm for large-scale amateur performances, theatre productions and recitals of chamber music. — From 1907, when he presented *The Creation,* till his performance of *The seasons* in 1945, Endler was responsible for the practically annual performance of either an oratorio, or some other major choral work, or an operetta. Eight large-scale vocal compositions by Handel, Haydn, Mendelssohn and Peter Benoit** were performed several times; seven of Gilbert and Sullivan's works were presented; Léhar's *The merry widow* was performed; and, in addition to several minor works, he also presented his own works, *Pa se dogter* (text by Spiethoff,** an operetta in Afrikaans) in 1935, and the nostalgic *In old Vienna* in 1938. He maintained his own orchestra for these performances and, through his friendship with W. Pickerill** of the Cape Town Municipal Orchestra,** he was able to achieve much for his music students, and for the musical life of Stellenbosch as a whole. His friendship with Metzler led to sporadic mutual assistance: at times Endler assisted Metzler in Paarl and Metzler quite often played in Stellenbosch. He similarly maintained cordial relations with Egel** of Wellington and often exchanged services with him, playing in Wellington for Egel's concert productions and having Egel in Stellenbosch for his own efforts. — When Jannasch retired from the post of principal in 1921, to devote his time to teaching and playing the organ, Endler, at the age of fifty, took over the full responsibility of the Conservatoire – a burden he carried until 1934. Under his direction, the Conservatoire was re-fashioned, partly on the model of the Vienna Akademie für Musik und Darstellende Kunst, with the introduction of courses in speech, elocution and drama. Endler also introduced eurhythmics and painting as subjects, and continued to organise large annual concerts. He brought the Conservatoire to the notice of the public of Cape Town by repeating these performances in the Mother City, encouraged recitals of chamber music, invited scholars to give lectures on subjects relevant to the students' studies, organised memorial concerts for great composers, and arranged student concerts, with the emphasis in practical work steadily on high standards. The man behind these activities was, beyond doubt, a born musician, whose *raison d'être* was to make music and inspire others to join him in doing so. In the final analysis, his is the story of the thousands of students who sang and played under him, contributing to the fine reputation of Stellenbosch and its Conservatoire in this country. — Because of the financial pressures that are inevitable in such a large private institution, there had been repeated talk of a take-over by the University of Stellenbosch. After Endler had written a tactful, but firm letter, dated 8 November, 1933, in which he emphasised the advisability of such a course and hinted that the institution might be taken over by the Dominican Convent, the University bought the Conservatoire for R13 000. The official transfer took place on 2 April 1934 and Maria Fismer** was appointed to manage the University's new Music Department. Endler continued to do his work at the Conservatoire with undiminished zeal, until shortly before his death. — After a long illness, he died at the St Joseph's Hospital in Cape Town; the funeral took place on 2 July 1947 from the Roman Catholic Church in Stellenbosch. — In 1913 Hans Endler had married Enid Beryl Brughes-Briscoe (who died in November, 1968) in Paarl; she was from East London, and had been one of his cello students. In April 1925, one year after her return from England, where she had studied for several years, she left him, and in August 1926, the marriage was annulled. They had two children, Eric, who died as a Captain in the SAAF during the war (1944), and Yvonne** who is now living in Cape Town (1968). — In 1908 Endler revisited Austria, where Kaiser Franz Joseph conferred on him the Knighthood of the Franz Joseph Order for exceptional cultural services abroad. He was never accorded official recognition of his services in Stellenbosch or elsewhere in this country until recently.

WORKS

A. Vocal

Mass in B flat, dedicated to "His Apostolic Majesty Francis Joseph I, Emperor of Austria, King of Hungary, Bohemia, etc. etc." performed Stellenbosch, 1910.   Minnelied (Love song) (Hans Endler). Ms., 1914.   Drie Afrikaanse liedjies. Lowe & Brydone, London, 1923:   1.   Wiege-liedjie (E. de Roubaix) (also in *FAK-Sangbundel*)   2. Dis September (J.J. Smith)   3.   Blomme-spraak (H.A. Fagan).   As dew in Aprille (text: 13th century English Christmas Carol, tr. into old Dutch by Dr F. Malherbe). R. Müller, Cape Town, 1937. Also known as "I sing of a maiden".   Soos die windjie wat suis, song (H.A. Fagan). R. Müller, Cape Town, 1930. Sterrelied (Dr F. Malherbe). R. Müller, Cape Town, n.d.   Eerste Suid-Afrikaanse wynlied (Hans Endler). Cape Times Ltd, Cape Town, 1941.   Kinderliedjie (A.D. Keet). *Die Huisgenoot,* 22 May 1931.   Lentelied (Rita van der Merwe). Ms., 1935.   Pa se dogter, operetta (libretto Walter Spiethoff). Ms., first performance at Stellenbosch, 19–21 June 1935.   Sing weer vir my, a song for soprano with contralto *ad lib* (C.L. Leipoldt). R. Müller, Cape Town, 1937.   In old Vienna, operetta. Ms., performance Stellenbosch, 1938.   Een-stemmige liedjie (Else Lourens). Ms., n.d.   Legend (Hans Endler), based on "Elegy", for cello and piano. Ms., n.d.   Levenswysheid (W.B.). Ms., n.d.   Ou Afrikaans-Hollands lied uit Zoutpansberg, also known as "Twee bruin ogies" (words recorded by J.F.W. Grosskopf), with cello or violin obligato, dedicated to Mrs Grosskopf. Ms., n.d.   Rosemondjie (F.E.J. Malherbe) (same as "Blommespraak"). Ms., n.d.

B. Instrumental

1. Compositions for strings and pianoforte.
Albumblatt: 1. Lullaby 2. Yvonne's lullaby 3. Wiegenlied. Ms., n.d.   Berceuse (Schlummer-lied). Ms., n.d.   Elegy. Ms., n.d.   Gavotte. R. Müller, Cape Town, n.d.   Lorna polka (Always dainty), op. 7, comp. in London, 1900. C. Röder, Leipzig, n.d.   March. Ms., n.d.   Petite romance, for viola. Ms., n.d.   Petite valse. R. Müller, Cape Town, n.d.

2. Pianoforte compositions
Gavotte rococo. Ms., n.d.   Lullaby. Ms., n.d.   Petite valse. Ms., n.d.   The scout's patrol. Ms., n.d.   The second in command, comp. in London, 1903. Ms., n.d.   Valse antique. Ms., n.d.   Yvonne waltz. Ms., n.d.   La reine du bal, polka de concert, op. 8. C. Röder, Leipzig, n.d.

3. Orchestral works
Altvater Grüsse, military march comp. in Ober-Mohrau, Aug. 1898.   Always dainty (arrangement of the "Lorna polka" for violin and pianoforte). Ms., n.d.   Erinnerung an Sternberg, military march dedicated to his teacher, Ferdinand Czerny. Ms., March 1890. Overture Elfriede, for symphony orchestra. Ms., n.d.   Souvenir de regiment, military march. Ms., n.d.

WRITINGS

Uit die ou Weense dae – Die musieklewe in die stad van vrolikheid en skerts. *Die Huisgenoot,* 27 Jan. 1939.   Terugblik – Die musieklewe op Stellenbosch vyf-en-dertig jaar gelede. *Die Huisgenoot,* 3 Feb. 1939.   Musiekverwaarlosing in Suid-Afrika. *Die Huisgenoot,* 10 Feb. 1939.   Uit my Londense dae – Herinneringe aan die jare 1897–1903. *Die Huisgenoot,* 24 Feb.

1939.   Van twee vriende. *Die Huisgenoot,* 18 Aug. 1939.   What is wrong with music in South Africa? *The Outspan,* 19 May 1933.

BIBLIOGRAPHY
Grobbelaar, E.P.: *Die lewe en werke van Hans Endler en sy invloed op die musieklewe van Stellenbosch.* M.Mus. dissertation, US, 1967.   K., W.H.: *The arts in South Africa.* Durban, 1933.   Van der Merwe, F.Z.: *Suid-Afrikaanse musiekbibliografie, 1787–1952.* J.L. van Schaik, Pretoria, 1958.

SOURCES
Anon.: Hans Endler. *Die Brandwag,* 11 July 1947.   A.N.: Van twee vriende. *Die Huisgenoot,* 22 Aug. 1947.   Behrens, R.: *Gedenkblad, Konservatorium vir Musiek van die Universiteit van Stellenbosch 1905–1955.* Stellenbosch, 1955.   *Die Burger:* 1 July 1947; 4 Jan. 1971. *Conservatoire Minute Book:* 1905–1947.   *Council Minutes of the University of Stellenbosch:* Vol. VI (Dec. 1933, Apr. 1934); Vol. VII (June 1934, Dec. 1935); Vol. VIII (Dec. 1937); Vol. X (Dec. 1941); Vol. XIV (Apr. 1947).   *Die Matie:* I/3, 29 Oct. 1941; III/2, 5 Mar. 1943; V/2, 6 Apr. 1945.   *Ons Land:* 6, 12, 22, 24 May 1906.   *The Southern Cross:* A tribute, 9 July 1947; Obituary, 9 July 1947.   *Die Stellenbosse Oud-Student:* XVI/2, Dec. 1947.   *Die Stellenbosse Student:* XLII/5, Aug. 1941; IX/2, June 1951.   *Stellenbosch Student's Quarterly:* Vol. V (Sept. 1904); Vol. VI (Apr., Sept., Nov. 1905); Vol. VII (Apr., June, Nov. 1906); Vol. XVI (Apr., June 1915); Vol. XVIII (Apr. 1917).   Notes placed at the disposal of the writer by Dr E.P. Grobbelaar.   Research Centre for South African Music, HSRC, Pretoria.

In spite of the superficially impressive list of compositions, Endler was no composer. He made in music stereotyped ABA patterns, with a single sub-dominant modulation in the middle section. His songs have, at the most, melodic importance, and the harmony appears at times to be rather irresponsible. Neither the *Mass* nor the operettas show any sign of originality. In the last-named he tried to imitate the styles of Johann Strauss and Franz von Suppé. The orchestral works are predominantly in march style.

– J.P.M.

ENDLER, YVONNE (MRS RICHTER), *10 January 1919 in Stellenbosch; at present (1977) in Cape Town. Daughter of Hans Endler;** pianist and music teacher.

Yvonne studied pianoforte under Franziska Witt** and others, before becoming a pupil of Minnie Seabridge at the South African College of Music** in 1941. In addition to appearing at charity concerts and meetings of music societies in Cape Town, Stellenbosch, Bloemfontein and Pretoria, she did solo work for broadcasting, appeared as soloist at symphony concerts conducted by Pickerill,** Schulman** and Dodds Miller, and accompanied the violinist, Nella Wissema, on a concert tour of the country. — She eventually turned her attention to teaching and from 1960 until 1962 was music lecturer at Barkly House Training Centre. At present (1977) she is teaching at Wynberg Girls' Junior School, and acts as guest lecturer at Athlone Training Centre, Cape Town.

– Ed.

ENGELA, DAWID SOFIUS, *30 October 1931 in Florida; °25 November 1967 in a motor car accident near Laingsburg. Composer and versatile author on musical matters, especially in the service of the radio medium.

Mr Engela (sr.) (1895–1962), who was a schoolteacher and eventually a part-time lecturer in Philosophy at UNISA, and Mrs Engela (1903–   ), were both firm believers descended from Reformed (=Gereformeerde) stock, who tended music-making in the form of piano playing and singing. This imbued the boy with a veneration for the Christian religion and in a measure prepared him for his future vocation as a musician. His pianoforte training started in his seventh year and was continued sporadically until 1958 when he obtained, in London, the Associateship of the Royal College of Music. For Matriculation he submitted Music as a subject and obtained, in all, four distinctions, in Music and three other subjects. During his last years at school he also acted as organist in his church. It is a significant illustration of his religious and musical involvement, that when the congregation considered the purchase of a new organ, the young man prepared a comprehensive and painstaking memorandum on the type of instrument indicated by artistic and technical considerations, which he submitted to the church council. In spite of his obvious musical gifts, he enrolled for theological admission at the P.U.C. for C.H.E., although Music still featured as a first year subject for the B.A. During that year, however, the conviction grew that music should be his first choice and in 1949 he entered the University of the Witwatersrand for a B.Mus. course lasting three years. Partially as a gesture of independence, though it could be considered an expression of his restless and active intelligence, he took service with the SABC at the same time, at first in a part-time capacity as a programme compiler in the discotheque (December 1948–February 1950) and, after the completion of his academic studies, as an announcer-producer (November 1951–May 1953). — His meeting in 1952 with the singer, Mimi Coertse,** led to an active musical partnership and eventually to their marriage, which took place on 25 July 1953, with the attractive prospect of studying music in Austria during 1954. The grant of two small bursaries by the FAK, added to the proceeds of concerts they gave in collaboration with musical colleagues, enabled them to leave for London in September, proceeding via Holland and Germany to Vienna. Mimi Coertse entered the Academy of Music to be prepared as an opera singer and Dawid Engela enrolled at both the Academy and the Vienna University for studies in respectively practical music and musicology, the latter intended for the degree of D.Phil. After a year had passed, the couple were in financial straits and the obvious course was for him to seek financial support in South Africa, where he earned a basic salary by working for the Afrikaans programme of the SABC from 29 December 1954 to April 1955 (in the evenings also for Springbok Radio). To supplement this income he applied, at ministerial level, for government support, and when this proved abortive, he had the brainwave of submitting a scheme to the Head of the Rembrandt Organisation whereby he proposed to record Viennese celebrities for local broadcasting, with appropriate references to the sponsor. In the final event he earned and collected enough money to support themselves in Vienna for another two years. — After his return to Austria it became apparent that their marriage had taken an unfortunate turn and from May 1955 until its final dissolution in December 1957, their roads increasingly diverged, on a personal as well as a professional level, although there were efforts at a reconciliation. During the summer vacation of 1955

ENGELA

Engela worked for the BBC in London. In 1956 he was appointed to the permanent staff and served this organisation from September 1956 until September 1963, at the time when South Africa had left the British Commonwealth and the BBC terminated their broadcasts in Afrikaans. Concurrently he entered for composition and pianoforte playing at the Royal College, attended classes in music journalism and commenced working on a brand-new thesis for the degree of D.Phil. If one considers that he was at the same time an active composer and had accepted a commission from the SABC for a work based on selected Psalms, it becomes apparent that he was exceeding his capacities. He was in actual fact a "week-end composer", as he designated himself, but it seems to have been a characteristic of his career that he experienced difficulty in applying himself to the completion of an individual project. His active brain and diversified interests diverted his concentration from the ultimate object to themes sometimes closely and again distantly related to his main concern, which he had himself defined as being composition. This might serve to explain the attraction which the colorful mosaic of radio employment exerted on his career. On the other hand his concern over a period of four months (July–November 1960) with the London production of Bartho Smit's *The maimed,* can only be ascribed to cultural generosity. — A year after the dissolution of his first marriage, Engela was married to the Scottish contralto, Alison Ruth Morrison. They spent their honeymoon in South Africa (January 1959), returned again for the funeral of Mr Engela (sr.) in 1962 and at the end of the next year (after the cessation of the London broadcasts) they settled in South Africa, exactly ten years after his original departure. The years in London had been marked by important broadcasts, such as his interviews with prominent composers (including John Joubert**) and performances of his songs by the artists Joyce Barker,** Betsy de la Porte** and Dawie Couzyn.** It should also be mentioned that he had experienced a re-awakening of his early interest in the music of the Blacks (*Africa and the World of Music,* 1961). — Engela settled in Cape Town on 1 October 1963 as programme organiser to the local studio of the SABC. After a year and a half he resigned to become the Music Manager of CAPAB, a position he filled with characteristic verve and distinction up to the time of his death. In May 1967 he submitted to the Minister of Education the idea of an amphitheatre built against Table Mountain, between Devil's Peak and the Mountain, accompanied by a concert theatre on Signal Hill. This enterprising idea, like previous visions of an extensive choral symphony based on Van Wyk Louw's *Die dieper reg* for the Union Festival of 1960, or of a full-length opera based on Bartho Smit's *Don Juan onder die Boere* (1962–1966), was fated to be still-born. — His second marriage was dissolved in January 1967 and on 1 September of the same year he was married to Ansie Fouché, who died shortly after her husband as a result of the accident mentioned above.

WRITINGS

Protestantse kerkmusiek. *Gereformeerde Vroueblad,* Feb. 1951.   Musiek in Suid-Afrika. *Gereformeerde Vroueblad,* Dec. 1951.   Uit die oertyd van die opera. *Tydskrif vir Letterkunde* IV/3, Sept. 1954.   Agter die skerms van die opera. *Suid-Afrika,* Mar. 1955.   Probleme in die hedendaagse toonkuns. *Standpunte* 21, May/June 1958.   Staatsopera – sal ons Afrikaans sing? *Die Huisgenoot,* 27 Jan. 1961.   *Stories uit die Italiaanse operas.* Human & Rousseau, Cape Town, 1963.   Jean Sibelius. *Lantern* XV/2, Dec. 1965.   Nagelate gedigte en vertalings. *Tydskrif vir Letterkunde* XVI/2, May 1978.   *Dagbreek en Sondagnuus:* 4 May

1956. *Die Burger:* 16 Sept. 1964; 1 Jan. 1965; 9 Jan. 1965; 22 May 1965; 23 Oct. 1965; 2 Nov. 1965; 10 Nov. 1965; 18 May 1966; 2 July 1966; 24 July 1967. *The Radio:* 9 June 1950; 25 Aug. 1950. Numerous radio scripts.

WORKS

A. Vocal

1. Songs
Twee klein konsertarias, comp. 1949 and 1952. DALRO 1979: 1. Opdrag (N.P. van Wyk Louw) 2. In die Hoëveld (Toon van den Heever). Sewe Afrikaanse liedere, comp. 1955/56 and no. 7 in 1964, English transl. by D.E. de Villiers – Seven South African Songs (N.P. van Wyk Louw). Pr. Studio Holland, distr. DALRO 1969: 1. Voordag (Daybreak) 2. Die verslaene (The dazed one) 3. Die nagwaak (Restless night) 4. Paniese angs (Wild terror) 5. Omdat jy self (Since you yourself) 6. Jy was 'n kind (You were a child) 7. Nog in my laaste woorde (In my last words). Liedere van 'n vergeefse liefde (I.D. du Plessis), comp. 1955, 1956 & 1958, pr. Studio Holland, distr. Human & Rousseau: 1. Ek het my aan jou oorgegee (1958) 2. Droom nou op die boesem van die teerbeminde (1958) 3. Ek het my van jou losgeskeur (1958) 4. Ons het mekaar gegroet (1955) 5. Al wat ek het is joune (1956). Two songs, for baritone and orchestra (Roy Campbell), comp. 1964. DALRO 1978: 1. The Zulu girl 2. The serf.

2. Choir
Koraaltoonsetting (! = choral setting) uit die Lofgesange (Rom. XI: 33–36), for four-part choir and organ, 1950. DALRO, 1974. Wedding cantata, for baritone, mixed choir, organ and orchestra. Ms. (lost), 1952/53, for his wedding. Motet on a Voortrekker tune, for choir, organ and soloists (or children's choir), comp. 1954. DALRO, 1976: parts 3 & 4 of the Motet were adapted to a selection of verses from Ps. 38 and performed separately in Cape Town as *Lied van Boetedoening* (1966). Only the Motet has been published. Two Afrikaans Psalms, for unacc. choir, based on Pss. 63 and 96, comp. in 1964. DALRO, 1975.

B. Instrumental
Sonata, op. 5 (two completed movements). Ms., ca. 1946. Rondo. Ms., ca. 1946. Introduction and scherzo capriccio, from an incomplete sonata in F. maj. Ms., 1946/47. Twee klavierbrokkies (also called Two Preludes). Ms., 1948/49: 1. Prelude 2. Notturno. Sonata (Sonatina), for violin and piano (1st and 3rd movements complete). Ms., 1951. Divertissement, for three wind instruments, comp. 1954 as *Bläsertrio,* rev. 1958, with the addition of two parts (nos. 1 & 5), and again in 1962 as a *Divertimento for five wind instruments.* DALRO, 1976: 1. Praeludium 2. Capriccio 3. Pastorale 4. Scherzo 5. Chorale, variations and fugato (fuguetta!).

C. Incidental music (only one piece has been preserved)
The cloak, trans. as *Die mantel,* for instrumental trio. Ms., 1966: 1. The angel 2. The unborn child 3. Death 4. Death passes by 5. Birth of the child.

D. Incomplete works. Engela was a slow composer, who often lacked the time or the energy to complete works, a point illustrated by the following summary of fragments and pieces:

1. Instrumental
1. Rhapsody, for pianoforte, comp. approx. 1946 2. Sonata, for pianoforte, comp. approx. 1946 3. Twee Afrikaanse volkswysies, for pianoforte, comp. approx. 1956 4. Quintet, for strings, comp. 1956 5. Praeludium, Chorale, Variations and Fugue, comp. approx. 1957 6.

ENGELA

Concerto, for pianoforte and orchestra, comp. 1958/59   7. Five motives, for 11 brass and percussion, comp. after 1960   8. Suite, for flute, bassoon and strings, comp. approx. 1956/66.

2. Vocal

1. Vroegherfs, song for soprano and pianoforte, comp. before 1953   2. Abélard, for baritone and orchestra, comp. 1956/57   3. Die ontwaking and Die geskenk (E. Eybers), comp. 1956/1958   4. Hälfte des Lebens (Hölderlin), comp. 1957   5. Quatre mélodies (Michaux), comp. 1957/58   6. Vier Slampamperliedjies, started in 1959   7. Drei Stimmungslieder (Nietzsche), n.d.

3. Choir

1. Trio Prelude, for choir or solo with organ, comp. 1952   2. Die dieper reg, comp. 1954–1958   3. Feeskantate (Ps. 105), comp. 1959/60   4. Don Juan onder die Boere (B. Smit), sketches for an opera, comp. 1962–1966.

E. Arrangements

1. Das musikalische Opfer (Bach)   2. The snow queen (Tchaikovsky)   3. Tales from the Vienna woods (Strauss)   4. The St Matthew Passion (Schütz)   5. Cantatas 207 and 208 (J.S. Bach).

BIBLIOGRAPHY
De Wet, Wouter: *Onse Mimi*. Perskor-uitgewery, Johannesburg, 1976.   Greyling, J.D.: *Die musiek van Dawid Engela (1931–1967)*. M.Mus.dissertation, UNISA, 1980.   Paxinos, S.: Dawid Engela and his songs. *Ars Nova* V/2, June 1973.

SOURCES
Rooi Rose: Apr. 1953.   *Die Brandwag* XXV/12: 19 May 1961.   *Die Burger:* 25 May 1964; 22 June 1964; 6 Jan. 1965; 25 Jan. 1965; 3 June 1965; 31 May 1966; 27 Nov. 1967 (obituary).   *Dagbreek en Sondagnuus:* 17 Feb. 1957.   *Die Transvaler:* 19 Sept. 1957. Research Centre for South African Music, HSRC, Pretoria.

– JPM.

ENSLIN, J. – J.W. van der Merwe

EOAN GROUP
I. INTRODUCTION
II. HISTORY

1. To 1956
2. The arts festival of 1956 and afterwards

I. INTRODUCTION

Since its inauguration in 1933 by Helen Southern-Holt, the Eoan Group (Gr: Eos = Dawn) has become South Africa's most important cultural and welfare organisation for the Coloured community. With a membership of approx. 2 000, a total of over 50 000 Coloureds have benefited through its activities. There have been attempts to establish it on a national basis, but it remained a product of Cape Town. The administration is conducted by an Executive Committee elected each year at an annual general meeting of members; it is responsible for general management and policy. In addition, there are two permanent sub-committees, for finance and planning, and for branch management. Up to March 1956 the Group had a financial grant from the Department of Education, Arts and Science. — Apart from an annual R2 000 grant donated by the Municipality of Cape Town, and a substantial subsidy from the Administration of Coloured Affairs, the Group is dependent on profits from performances and donations from the public. Despite the inevitable tightness of its budget, the Group has grown phenomenally and established a national reputation; this is in no small measure due to the efforts of a number of artists and professionals from the White community, and the gratuitous services of the members themselves. The policy has been to discover and promote exceptional talent among the Coloureds, and in recent years Una Scholtz (producer) and a variety of singers, actors and dancers have come to the fore and established reputations: May Abrahamse, Ruth Goodwin, Lionel Fourie, Richard Manuel, Caroline Rijker, Gwen Michaels, Joan Boonzaaier, Didi Sydow, Dan Ulster, Winifred Clarke and Josef Gabriels, to mention only a few names. The establishment of bursaries for music, drama and ballet has enabled talented dancers like Gwen Michaels, Joan Boonzaaier, Didi Sydow, some 20 singers and the pianist, Gordon Jephtas, to study at recognised institutions in Cape Town and London, and to carve out careers in their respective fields.

II. HISTORY

After its establishment the Group started in a small way, with instruction in speech-training and remedial exercises; these were extended to include dancing, public-speaking and play-reading. Since then the Group has grown steadily and quickly. Some ten or more branches have been established in and around Cape Town, and their activities have blossomed out in a variety of spheres. This may be conveniently surveyed in two periods: to 1956, when the first Arts Festival was presented; and the period from then to 1969.

1. To 1956

(i) *Ballet.* Tuition in physical education and simple dancing provides recruits for the central ballet class, from which the principal dancers and corps-de-ballet are drawn for the productions of the Group. Two permanent, paid teachers provide the instruction. The first Coloured dance display with the Cape Town Municipal Orchestra** took place in 1937, and was followed by a physical education display by 1 000 children in 1940. After that there were regular ballet performances (operatic and Greek), divertissements (classical, comedy and tap) and physical education displays each year.

(ii) The *drama section* was launched in 1934 with a production of *Thirteenth chair,* and since then has appeared fairly regularly each year with productions of a sometimes ambitious nature, such as *The rivals* (Sheridan), *The late Christopher Bean* (E. Williams), *A midsummernight's dream* (Shakespeare), *Escape* (Galsworthy) and other plays.

(iii) The *music section* came into its own in 1943, when Joseph Manca** was approached to take charge of the small choir that existed at the time. After the first choral concert by 35 choristers (1944), the choir presented annual performances of smaller cantatas and works for children's voices, and there were two performances of *The Redeemer* (Martin Shaw). In 1949 this section ventured on its first complete operetta, *A slave in Araby,* in which 75 performers took part, assisted by the Municipal Orchestra. This was a milestone in the Group's musical section, which began to expand and to establish its present reputation. Other operettas followed, including

EOAN GROUP

Hong-Kong (1950), *Maid of the mountains* (1950), *Gipsy princess* (1953) and *Magyar melody* (1954). Large-scale choral works, such as *Messiah, Elijah* and the Finale to Beethoven's *Ninth symphony,* were studied and performed with the Municipal Orchestra. — In addition to these three main activities, the Group also organised a Boys' Club for youths interested in body-building and weight-lifting, and a Nursery Play Centre run on the lines of a crèche, to assist working mothers in the care and education of their small children.

2. The arts festival of 1956 and afterwards
The idea of an extended Arts Festival was proposed by Joseph Manca early in 1955, and a year was devoted to its preparation. The festival lasted from March to August 1956, and included *La traviata* (sung in Italian), *The mikado* in a children's version, the play *Johny Belinda,* a variety of ballet offerings in various styles, the oratorio *Elijah,* the operetta *Zip goes a million,* a photographic and a poster exhibition, and a floral arrangement competition. The scope and magnitude of the festival can only be grasped, if it is realized that this was the first of its kind undertaken by the Coloured community and that the entire scheme was put into effect by a cross-section of the population of labourers, housewives, factory workers, artisans, teachers and one or two principals of schools. This is believed to be the first time a complete opera in Italian was sung by a Coloured community anywhere in the world. The festival was the climax of years of unremitting and devoted labour, but it also marked a point of departure in the cultural development of the Cape Coloured people. After *La traviata* followed *Cavalleria rusticana, Rigoletto, La Bohéme* and *Madame Butterfly,* all produced in Italian by Gregorio Fiasconaro,** who had previously handled the production of *La traviata.* The Ballet Section extended its activities under the direction of David Poole,** to include a complete ballet, *Pink lemonade,* featuring Johaar Mosaval,** who had become a leading member of the Royal Ballet, London. — In 1960 the Group took its next great step, when it toured the Republic for three months, with four operas and six ballets. The tour was a triumphant success and realized a profit. Two years later the Second Arts Festival was held, with the addition to the repertoire of *Die Fledermaus* and a completely South African ballet, *The square.* The music for *The square* was composed by the South African, Stanley Glasser;** David Poole was responsible for the choreography, and Johaar Mosaval returned to dance the principal part. In addition, Verdi's *Requiem,* two children's musical plays, and a comedy were presented. In 1964 the group notched another important mark in its history, when it was invited by the Johannesburg Operatic and Dramatic Society** to participate in their production of *Show boat* in the Alhambra Theatre, Cape Town. — In 1964 the EOAN Group Trust was formed to look after the Group's financial affairs. Its deeds provide for a Board of Trustees of 13 members, who accepted the responsibility of providing the Group with a regular income to supplement its limited earning capacity, to expand cultural activities, and to assist and advise in the administration of its affairs. The Trust has been so successful in its efforts that an Athlone Cultural Centre, including the Joseph Stone Auditorium, built on a freehold grant of $3\frac{1}{4}$ acres by the Cape Town Municipality, could be handed over to the Group on 21 November 1969. The former Department of Coloured Affairs contributed R120 000 to the cost of the scheme. A considerable portion of an Endowment Fund to subsidise the efforts of the Group was realized in the same year. The result is that it now enjoys a greater measure of stability than ever before. — In the interim between the creation of the Trust and

the inauguration of what is now known as the EOAN Group Cultural Centre at Athlone (near Cape Town), the Group presented a sixth opera season in the City Hall, Cape Town (1965), and went on a second tour of the Republic with successful productions of *Oklahoma* (1966) and *South Pacific* (1968). In addition, it contributed a performance of *La traviata* to the 1966 Republic Festival in Cape Town, gave a protocol performance of the same work for an audience of Members of Parliament, the Diplomatic and Consular Corps, and other distinguished guests (1967), and held operatic concerts in Cape Town and Worcester. The seventh opera season (September 1967) saw productions by Alessandro Rota of *Madame Butterfly, La traviata* and *l'Elisir d' amore*, which included 19 principal singers, a chorus of 50 members, and a corps-de-ballet of 21 dancers. The eighth opera season (1969) consisted of four Italian works from the Group's operatic repertoire. — Since the production of *A slave in Araby* in 1949, the Group has produced no less than 11 operettas and musicals; and since the production of *La traviata* in 1956, seven Italian operas by Verdi, Puccini, Mascagni, Donizetti and Rossini, as well as Bizet's *Carmen* and *Fledermaus* by Johann Strauss. It has also given concerts, under the title *A night at the opera,* in which excerpts from popular Italian operas are presented in costume and decor. Of the major choral works, they have sung Handel's *Messiah,* Mendelssohn's *Elijah,* Martin Shaw's *Redeemer* and Verdi's *Requiem.* All these were sung with the Cape Town Municipal Orchestra, conducted by Joseph Manca.

(Also read article on Joseph Manca in Vol. 3 of this Encyclopedia.)

SOURCES
Die Burger: 27 Feb. 1956; 24 Mar. 1956; 15 Mar. 1958; 22 Mar. 1969.   *Cape Argus:* 10 Nov. 1969; 8 Mar. 1970; 1 Aug. 1970; 19 Oct. 1971; 8 Nov. 1971.   *Cape Times:* 2 Mar. 1970; 22 Nov. 1969.   *Pretoria News:* 1 Nov. 1969.   *Sarie Marais:* 9 Sept. 1970.   Research Centre for South African Music, HSRC, Pretoria.

– J.S.M. (amplified)

EPSTEIN, ISADOR, *1883 in The Hague; residing in Johannesburg in 1975. Concert pianist and teacher, who trained several generations of pianists in Johannesburg.

Isador was the fifth of six children, who were all very musical. Three of his brothers, Samuel ("Hugh Marleyn"),** Edward and Randolph ("Eric"), became professional musicians. When Isador was taken to England as a child, he at first had (in his own words) "inefficient, old-fashioned teaching"; nevertheless, he performed in public before he was seven years old. Bursaries enabled him to receive superior teaching at the Guildhall School of Music, and when he was seventeen he won a further scholarship to the RCM where he obtained the ARCM Diploma, after four years. His adult training as a pianist was completed by Tobias Matthay and Arthur Friedheim. — A year or two later Epstein started his concert career in London and other centres in England. At the same time he built up a teaching practice in London. A few prominent British musicians had their pianistic training from him. In September 1929, he emigrated to South Africa for health reasons, recuperated completely, and became one of the most important pianists in the country. After a concert tour, he settled in Johannesburg, where he established a teaching practice that developed into a private school of music, his most gifted pupils acting as his assistants. — Epstein's career in

South Africa has been that of a concert pianist known throughout the country; and he is a much sought-after piano teacher. The names of Bedana Chertkow,** Anna Bender,** Glyn Townley,** Leslie Riskowitz, Anton Hartman,** Melanie Vale and Leo Quayle,** may be mentioned as representative of the South African musicians who have studied under his guidance at some time in their careers.

WORKS

Vocal

The dream pedlar (unfinished operetta). Ms., n.d.   The haven of memory, song (Margaret Pedler). G. Ricordi & Co., London, 1920.   In Karooland, song. Ms., n.d.   Slampamper-liedjie, song. Ms., n.d.

Instrumental

Suite for Orchestra. Ms., n.d.   Fantasia for piano. Ms., n.d.   Five preludes for piano. Ms., n.d.   Sarabande, gavotte and musette for piano. Augener Ltd, London, 1922.   Elysium for piano. Ms., n.d.   Lighter, unidentified pieces for piano. Ms., n.d.   Trio for piano, violin and cello. Ms., n.d.   Trio for strings. Ms., n.d.   Monologue for pianoforte and a narrator (E.A. Poe). Ms., n.d.

PUBLICATION

The evolution of pianoforte technique. *The arts in South Africa.* Knox Printing Co., Durban, 1933.

BIBLIOGRAPHY

Dictionary of modern music and musicians. J.M. Dent & Sons Ltd, London, 1924.   *Grove's dictionary of music and musicians* (ed. J.A. Fuller – Maitland). Macmillan & Co., London, 1910.   *Who's who in music.* Love & Malcolmson, Surrey, England, 1949–1950.

SOURCES

Bandstand, South Africa, Nov. 1953.   *Daily Graphic:* 8 Mar. 1921, England.   *The Gentleman:* Spring number, 1921, England.   *SAMT:* 15, Oct. 1938.   *Opus,* new series V/I, Oct–Nov. 1973.

– M.Kl.

EPSTEIN, LOUIS, *29 March 1903 in Springs; °22 October 1953 at St James, Cape Town. Baritone, composer of light music.

Although he gave early proof of musical ability, Louis Epstein had to share his father's business interests (1921–1932), but in 1933 he eventually left for London to prepare himself for a musical career. He studied piano and singing and interpreted a few parts in films and theatrical entertainments until 1935 and returned to South Africa to become professionally engaged in entertainment as an actor, singer, composer, pianist and radio performer, alone and in conjunction with established artists like Dean Herrick, Roy Martin, Gwen Frangcon-Davies and others. During the War he scored a particular success with his *Springbok frolics,* an entertainment devised for the South African troops and presented by ACT and the Potchefstroom Military Camp Concert Party. This was in effect a revue in two acts and thirty-two episodes. It was produced with the co-operation of Frank Rogaly. After a serious illness in 1946, he went to

America for treatment and had his *First symphonette* performed in Boston (1948). In 1948 he retired in South Africa and spent the rest of his days in St James. — Melodies which achieved publication are: Oh how I miss you. W. Paxton & Co., London, 1926; England, home of the mighty. Alex White & Co., Johannesburg, 1940; Monarchs of the air. Alex White & Co., Johannesburg, 1940; Liberty cavalcade. Johannesburg, 1942; Roll up and cheer for your Golden City. R.L. Esson, Johannesburg, 1942. Twenty-three other lyrics, still in manuscript, are in the files of the Research Centre for South African Music, HSRC, Pretoria.

SOURCES

Sunday Times: 22 Dec. 1940.   *Springs and Brakpan Advertiser:* 30 Oct. 1953.   *Around Springs in war-time, a commemorative publication (1939-1945).*   Research Centre for South African Music, HSRC, Pretoria.

– C.G.H.

EPSTEIN, SAMUEL FEINSINGER   Johannesburg 2, H. Marleyn

ERATO CHOIR   G. Bon (sr.), Pretoria 3

ERLANK, DR. W. DU P. (EITEMAL)   S.H. Eyssen, FAK, FAK-Volksangbundel, R. Mengelberg, D. van den Heever

ERROL, SLATTER CHORALE   E.M. Slatter

ESPEN, KEN, *14 February 1917 in Marienburg, Germany; at present (1977) in Johannesburg. Music teacher, pianist and organist.

Espen studied in Freiburg (Germany), before arriving in South Africa in 1938. Here he has been active as a soloist with the SABC Symphony Orchestra, as bandleader, arranger and orchestrator, musical director for theatrical productions, and accompanist. From 1948 to 1958 he was the Resident Organist for African Theatres; he practised the profession of cinema organist right up to the time when it had ceased to exist elsewhere. A large number of his recordings are well-known, including classical works (with Kathleen Alister,** Walter Mony** and others), light classical, religious, dance and popular music. The majority of these recordings were made on or with the organ. Espen runs his own School of Music in Johannesburg, and is well-known as a broadcaster. — Melodies: Ken's tune; Ken's polka; Fris en vrolik; Hawaiian serenade; Scaler's waltz, etc.

– Ed.

ESPINOSA, E. AND J.   Ballet I, II, VIII, Ivy Conmee, J.H. Seaborne, Spanish dancing

ESSEX, ALFRED   H. Bolus, Graaff Reinet 7

ESTERHUYSEN, ABRAHAM MATTHYS DE VILLIERS, *5 December 1888 in Caledon; ° 17 October 1959 in Pretoria. Minister of the Dutch Reformed Church and a mainly autodidactical organist.

31

ESTERHUYSEN

Abraham Esterhuysen was the second son of J.J.C. Esterhuysen** and Maria de Villiers, daughter of Rocco Catorzia de Villiers.** His father was an organist and a band leader in Caledon, Montagu and Paarl, who took care of the early musical training of Abraham, whilst his uncle Dirk Izak de Villiers,** assisted his organ, pianoforte and violin playing at his Music Institute when Abraham was a student in Wellington for the school teacher's diploma. To the home and institute concerts arranged by his uncle, he often contributed items. — Abraham Esterhuysen was a teacher for only one year, and then went to Stellenbosch to be trained for the ministry (1911–1917). During the years at Stellenbosch he collected a group of student string players including Stephen Eyssen.** Members of this ensemble sometimes went across to Robben Island to give a concert at the leper hospital, taking a little harmonium along with them. He was ordained in 1918 and in 1937 he was delegated to the Dutch Reformed Church in Rhodesia where he served in the ministry until his retirement in July 1955. In Free State and in Rhodesian congregations the Rev. Esterhuysen sometimes conducted the services and played the organ as well. For the Ox Wagon Trek of 1938 he composed two trek songs and when the Monument was inaugurated in 1949, he brought a choir from Northern and Southern Rhodesia, which sang in the amphitheatre. One of their contributions was his own composition, *Noordwaarts*. — After his retirement, he worked in Salisbury and in Bloemfontein (1956–1959), where he was organist at sittings of the Free State Synod.

PUBLICATION
Corneels Kanniedood, lewensgeskiedenis van kolonel Du Preez, persoonlike adjudant van pres. M.T. Steyn. APB, Johannesburg, 1953.

WORKS
School song of the Jongens Hoër Skool ("Boys' High"), Paarl. Ms., 1911.   Die Boland, rowers' song (G.C. Tomlinson). *Ons Moedertaal,* Stellenbosch, 15 Aug. 1914.   School song of the Malmesbury High School (G.C. Tomlinson). *Ons Moedertaal,* Stellenbosch, 15 Sept. 1914. Wiegeliedjie van 'n trekkerkindjie. Ms., 1938.   Noordwaarts (C.F. Visser). Ms., 1949(?). Ps. 42:1, 2, 3. Ms., n.d.   Research Centre for South African Music, HSRC, Pretoria.

– J.M.

ESTERHUYSEN, JACOBUS JOACHIM CHRISTOFFEL, *13 September 1860 on Paarden Island; *14 June 1940 in Sea Point. Amateur organist.

"Kobie" Esterhuysen was a young man with musical inclinations which became evident in his fifth year when he attempted hymn tunes on the stable boy's concertina. His ambition to become a medical doctor was thwarted by the death of his father – he became a business man instead – but his love of music led him to the music school of Rocco de Villiers** in Caledon (November 1, 1882). After one month's tuition, Rocco insisted that he should interpret Hymn No. 11 on the church organ before he gave his consent to Kobie's marriage to Rocco's daughter Maria de Villiers. Their marriage was duly solemnized on 1 October 1883, to the strains of a wedding march composed by the bride's father. — When Rocco became organist in Paarl in 1887, Esterhuysen succeeded him in Caledon. In September 1892 the town planned its first large flower show and the organisers invited a brass band from Worcester to provide appropriate music. This caused an immediate Caledonian reaction – Esterhuysen was instructed to establish a brass band, and to order the instruments from Germany. A number of his players were artisans; to acquaint them with staff notation, Kobie used artisan terminology – a crotchet being represented as one inch, a quaver as a halfinch, etc. The results were satisfactory and the band played at the consecration ceremony of the rebuilt vicarage, barely three months after the first rehearsal. In time it became customary to use the band in church with the choir and organ at the annual Reformation Festival, and to entertain visitors to the mineral springs. — Esterhuysen's patriotism at the time of the Boer War earned him house arrest for 10 months – he played *Kent gij dat volk* at a christening when a child was baptized Stephanus Johannes Paulus Kruger. After a short stay at Montagu (1909–1910?), where Esterhuysen also played the church organ, he returned with his family to Paarl in 1911 and succeeded Rocco de Villiers (jr.) as organist of the Thatched-roof Church. Here he again employed a brass band at the Reformation Festival, but his position was only temporary. After the post had been advertised, the blind A.C. van Velden was chosen to become the organist and assumed his duties on 31 August 1913.

WORKS
Grey College Song (J.J.C. Esterhuysen). Ms., n.d.   Slapedoe (J.J.C. Esterhuysen). Ms., n.d.   Goeienag (T.W. Jandrell). Ms., n.d.   Geeft Gode sterkte, for four-part choir and organ. Ms., n.d.   De God van Israel, for four-part choir and organ. Ms., n.d.   Ere zij God, for four-part choir and organ. Ms., n.d.   Houdt Christus (Hymn 156). Ms., 1916.   Helpmekaar. Ms., n.d.

SOURCE
Research Centre for South African Music, HSRC, Pretoria.

– J.M.

EUNICE LADIES' INSTITUTE (EUNICE HIGH SCHOOL) BLOEMFON-TEIN Bloemfontein, M. Barlow, D. Bosman, G. Butler, F. Fraser, I.H. Haarburger, Israel (Charles Wilhelm), E. Leviseur, Port Elizabeth I/5, S. Sullivan

EUREKA CHORAL SOCIETY, THE was formed on the recommendation of Lionel Field in East London in December 1949, to provide for the musical needs of the Afrikaans community. It was known as the Eureka Choir until 1956, but when they accepted parts in theatrical productions they changed their name.

The first leader was Maria van Rooyen,** who in 1959 was succeeded by Louis van der Westhuizen. In 1963, however, she was again chosen as conductor. After 1951 the choir received an annual subsidy from the City Council for two concert performances, but the number of subsidised concerts was increased to three in 1954, and to four in 1966. Works presented by the choral society included *The crucifixion* (Stainer), *Messias,* and six operettas. The choir gives frequent performances at national festivals, cultural and local functions. — Apart from East London, the choir has appeared in a number of other centres, namely King William's Town, Komgha, Umtata, Adelaide, Queenstown, and also in Cape Town during the Van Riebeeck festival.

SOURCES
Die Oosterlig: 26 Feb. 1971; 26 Mar. 1971.   Research Centre for South African Music, HSRC,
Pretoria.

– W.v.d.N.

EUTERPE SOCIETY FOR THE PROMOTION OF ART, THE, was founded in Pretoria in September 1925 with a broad committee representative of the English, Dutch and Afrikaans communities under the chairmanship of Edw. Rooth, with Willem Gerke** as director of musical matters. Among those who were active as committee members during the early years of the Society, the following may be mentioned: Mrs H. Greenlees, P.V. Pocock, S.F. Naude, Mrs F. Gerke, Miss A. Lansdorp, W. Kat and Dr S. de Moor. Active members were enrolled on the payment of a subscription fee of R1,10 and ordinary members paid double that amount. At the foundation meeting there were 50 members. The Society aimed at concentrating the musical talent of the Capital City, by creating a choir and an orchestra and by giving regular monthly concerts, so that the musical life could be stabilised. This would in effect have amounted to a musical education of the public, with a view to the ultimate object of launching a permanent municipal orchestra. Starting with a chamber music evening presented in the Memorial Hall on 6 May 1926, the committee succeeded over a period of eight years in organising 65 concerts given by the talents available in Johannesburg and Pretoria. The programmes were usually diversified and included assortments of orchestral, pure chamber music and vocal items. Artists who contributed to the programmes included well-known Johannesburg and Pretoria personalities, such as Erwin Broedrich,** Isador Epstein,** Ada Woolfson, Stephen Eyssen,** Hester Boshoff,** Pattie Price,** Nunez Holtzhausen,** Ada Cruse, Otto Menge,** Lorenzo Danza** and Willem Gerke himself. — As early as 1926 Gerke had conceived the ambitious notion of producing Gluck's *Alceste* with his apparently unbalanced choir and a small orchestra. Other highlights were a Beethoven Memorial Concert in 1927, two similar concerts devoted to Schubert in 1928, and a performance in April 1929 of eight scenes from Ibsen's *Peer Gynt,* with the incidental music of Grieg. This programme concluded with a performance of this composer's *Pianoforte concerto* played by Mme D. Wedlake-Santanera and the Euterpe Orchestra. Membership increased rapidly, and by 1929 exceeded four hundred. This growth encouraged Gerke to launch his own magazine, the *Euterpe Journal,* which appeared periodically from 1926 (as a monthly magazine from 1929) and included the programme of the next concert, appreciations, society news and elucidatory – at times polemical – articles by Gerke himself. When membership had reached 600 by 1930, it became necessary to repeat some concerts as the old City Hall could not seat all the members. The expanding size of the orchestra was equally gratifying. In 1928 Schubert's *Unfinished symphony* was performed by an orchestra consisting of between 40 and 50 musicians, mostly amateurs; in later years, however, its register included the names of leading professional musicians like E. Broedrich and G. Bon.** — Repeated attempts to obtain financial support from the City Council failed. In a memorandum dated 24 June 1929, supported by a petition signed by 500 people including members of Euterpe, the Chamber of Commerce, the Women's Council, the Publicity Association and the Students' League, the achievements of the Society, the work which it had done, its growth from 50 to 500 members and its future possibilities were put forward as arguments justifying a proposed subsidy of R2 000 from the City

Council. According to Gerke's annual report in the Journal, the Society's expenditure in that year amounted to R1 251. In 1930 the Council announced that it was prepared to meet a deputation from the Society, but the negotiations finally broke down and the Council's annual contribution remained in the region of R180. The Council was at the time in the planning stage of a new City Hall with a gigantic organ, and was also considering the idea of appointing a municipal Director of Music. These factors possibly influenced their decisions. According to the *Pretoria News*, it was moreover felt that the Society was too sectional – strongly Dutch in character – and that Gerke constituted the pivot of the Society's life, so that the subsidising of the Society would have amounted to the subsidising of an individual. It appears that whilst considerable development of Pretoria's music life was being planned, the time was not yet considered ripe for large-scale schemes such as the one put forward by Gerke. His ultimate aim, according to his own testimony, was the founding of a permanent orchestra with himself as conductor. In view of the problems encountered in Cape Town, Durban and Johannesburg in founding and maintaining a municipal orchestra, the Pretoria authorities were no doubt justified in their decision not to embark on such an adventure. — Nevertheless, Euterpe perservered with its works, but when the effects of economic depression were felt towards the end of 1931 and in 1932, the Society was obliged to retrench and give less concerts. A notable achievement in 1931 was the performance of *Die mieliedogter*, an operetta composed by Charles Nel** to a libretto by Mrs M.E. Rothman, who was to achieve fame as an author. This undertaking might be regarded as an artistic reply to critics who regarded the Society as being "too sectional in character". After the failure of an attempt in 1933 to unite all the available choir and orchestra potential in Pretoria – including that of Euterpe – and to co-operate instead of opposing one another, the music life of the Capital suffered, and Euterpe – for all practical purposes – disappeared from the scene, although it was not dissolved. The ideal of amalgamation miscarried for purely practical reasons: it transpired that four of the six Pretoria conductors had to appear on the stage during one single evening. The inevitable friction which this multiple responsibility caused, doomed the plan to failure. — By 1935 the country's economy was recovering, and in 1937 Gerke was beginning to reassert his authority to the extent of again organising concerts. To place the Society on as firm a footing as before, he began preparations in 1939 for a performance of *Fra Diavolo* (Auber), but the plan was thwarted by the outbreak of the Second World War, which, in effect, gave Euterpe its deathblow. — Euterpe was essentially the creation of one man, who was qualified through background and training to make a dynamic impact on, and to impart stability to the Pretoria music life, so that the ideal of a permanent municipal orchestra might be realised. The optimistic expectation that sheer achievement would make the necessary funds available, for the sake of the value of music to the community, was not realised; and the adverse effects of the economic depression, followed by the World War, finally frustrated Euterpe's plans. In the musical history of Pretoria these plans represent the most determined and the most comprehensive individual effort ever made to enrich the city's cultural life with an urban orchestra – and as such they demand respect.

SOURCE

Zaidel, Jeanne: *Music in Pretoria, 1926–1931, with special reference to Prof. Willem Gerke and the Euterpe Society*. B.Mus. script, UP, 1969.

– J.P.M.

EVANGELICAL-LUTHERAN CHURCH MUSIC IN THE CAPE PROVINCE

According to Kolb, an early eighteenth-century custom on ships of the Dutch East India Company was a trumpeter's sounding of *Aus meines Herzens Grunde* at dawn, and *Nun ruhen alle Wälder* at nightfall. The same authority states that ministers of visiting ships occasionally conducted German services at the Cape. Lutheran church music in the true sense of the word, however, dates back to 10 December 1780 when, with the granting of religious liberty at the Cape, the first Evangelical-Lutheran minister – Andreas Lutgerus Kolver – delivered his inaugural sermon in the Strand Street church: "Voor een ontzaggelijken toevloed van menschen, wordende de Godsdienste begonnen-geeindigd met Vocaal-instrumentaal Muziek" (In the presence of a large gathering of people, public worship was commenced and concluded with vocal-instrumental music). The service began with Luther's translation of the *Te Deum (Herr Gott dich loben wir, Herr Gott wir danken dir)*, sung by a choir of young people led by the precentor, Johannes Esler, and accompanied by the organ and other musical instruments. Notwithstanding objections raised by Amsterdam, the community decided to maintain the traditional singing in German ("as has always been customary"). Since "no common hymn-books were available, the one possessing this and another that" (cf. hymn books of this period in the Dessinian Collection, South African Public Library, Cape Town), the congregation in 1783 adopted the *Gesangbuch der evangelischlutherischen (sic!) Domgemeinde zu Bremen.* This, however, was a hymn book without music, and after 1830 the *Christelijke Gezangen voor de Evang. Luthersche Gemeenten in het Koningrijk der Nederlanden* (1826), in which the tunes were provided, was used. But since the tunes were frequently not printed exactly as they were customarily sung by members of the congregation, uncertainty and disputes arose which had an adverse effect on communal singing. — As far as can be ascertained, the German hymn book fell into disuse at the Cape after the turn of the century, since the partial switch to English as a language medium in churches (1891), brought various new hymn books into use, e.g. *Hymns for the use of the Evangelical Lutheran Church, Cape Town* (Cape Town, 1898) and, after 1960, the *Australian Lutheran Hymn Book.* Eventually Afrikaans services replaced the Dutch services (which still persisted) and the Afrikaans Hymn Book of the Berlin Mission, *Cantate,* was adopted. — The St Martini congregation of the Evangelical Lutheran Church in Cape Town (est. 1861), as well as the seceded communities in the Western and Eastern Cape, used a variety of books in their services. The Mother Church sang from the above-mentioned Dutch hymn book and, when there proved to be insufficient copies, also the *Geestelijke Gezangen ten Gebruike van Evangelische Gemeenten in Zuid-Afrika* (published by the Berlin Mission Society). The hymn book of the Lutheran Church in Bavaria, together with other anthologies, was used to supplement the Dutch compilation; it had a special title page reading: *Gesangbuch der deutschen evangel.-lutherischen St Andreas-gemeinde zu East London und Umgegend,* or: *Gesangbuch für die deutsch-lutherische Kirche am Kap der guten Hoffnung.* — Before the St Martini congregation was formed, the Lutheran services were held in accordance with the strict and simple, almost Reformed, order of service observed by the Netherlands Lutheran Church. This however, was as foreign to many German-speaking immigrants as it was to Pastor J.L. Parisius, and in 1861 it eventually became one of the main reasons for the establishment of a German congregation employing the German language. To begin with, the pastor and the organist, F. Clüver (1829–1898), attempted to remedy the situation by compiling an album of *Gesangen en liederen ten behoeve van scholen verzamelt,* of which a second edition copy (1860) is preserved in the Parliamentary Library in Cape Town. In this volume parts of the German Lutheran service are published in English and Dutch, e.g. *Gloria patri, Gloria in excelsis* (complete text), *Sanctus* and *Agnus Dei.* Probably it was intended for use in the Lutheran church school in Cape Town, but in effect it hardly delayed the threatening schism in the church. In 1861 the St Martini congregation seceded and invited Parisius to act as minister. This congregation, and others which followed it, conducted their services in accordance with the strict Lutheran order which provided for liturgical singing by the pastor, choir and congregation, as prescribed by the *Calenbergische Kirchenordnung* of the kingdom of Hanover. — Friedrich Clüver, who came to South Africa from Germany in 1859 as a teacher and as the organist for the Strand Street congregation, was ordained as minister of the new St Martini congregation in King William's Town in 1864. He introduced the St Martini order of service to Lutheran churches in the Eastern Province area and thus brought about a measure of uniformity during the early years of the German communities. — Collaboration between the majority of the Lutheran churches in the Cape Colony led to a synod in 1895. In time, they all adopted the Hanover hymn book (e.g. the Philippi community, in 1913). It is interesting to note that this hymn book was originally also printed with a special title page: *Gesangbuch für die deutsche evangelisch-lutherische Kirche Süd Afrika.* They published their own order of service in 1922 and accepted the recent German *Evangelisches Kirchengesangbuch* for use after 1953, St Martini as early as 1953 and St Andreas in East London as recently as 1962. In 1959 it was possible to print and apply a uniform order of service, practically identical to that of the liturgically and musically excellent order of the Evangelical Lutheran Church in Germany. Since the foundation in 1965 of the United Evangelical Lutheran Church of Southern Africa, this order has become the basis for the common liturgy which is at present (1970) in preparation for use in German-, English- and Afrikaans-speaking communities in South Africa and South West Africa. The hymn books intended for Afrikaans and English services are identical to those used in the Strand Street congregation since 1960. — Some of the best-known music personalities in the Cape during the first half of the nineteenth century have been organists of the Lutheran Church in Strand Street: A.H. Heyns (1780–1793), J.C. Wahl (1793–1814), C.F. Lemming** (1814–1817), F. Osmitius** (1817–1820), W. Brandt** (1820–1838), F. Logier** (1838–1839), Ludwig Beil** (1839–1870). During this time the Strand Street church was an important centre for good music, especially church music. It had a good organ and a permanent choir and on special occasions, like the presentation of the Augsburg Confession at the end of June, there was the possibility of an additional instrumental ensemble. But the mounting tension in the congregation and the eventual schism of 1861 had an adverse influence on the practice of church music in Strand Street. Since that year neither this church nor the St Martini Church, which had initially to dispense with an organ, played a part of any significance in the musical life of Cape Town. In the new church musical circumstances gradually improved as a result of the significant contributions made by the organists G.W. Kühn** (1878–1924) and Walter König** (1936–1948). Both these musicians were also prominent in the City's music. Margot Scherz became the organist in 1950. Her untiring zeal and infectious enthusiasm has raised the standard of church music at St Martini. It has again become a factor in Cape Town's musical life. — Nineteenth-century revival hymns had an adverse effect on Lutheran church music, especially with regard to the repertoire of church choirs. On the other hand the German Singbewegung after the First World War contributed to an improvement in this connection. The Posaunenchöre (church brass bands), a characteristic feature of Lutheran church music, played an important part in the Cape congregations until the outbreak of war in 1914. Then they were either forbidden or subverted, and practically vanished from the Lutheran sacred music. At present there is a revival of church music in the Western Cape congregations. Evidence of this fact is the tendency to follow the organ reform in Germany. Two mechanical action organs have been acquired, one for the St Petri Church in Paarl (1961) and another for the new Stellenbosch Church (1965). — The mission churches in Cape Town, originally started by the Berlin Mission Society (since 1963 included in the Evangelical-Lutheran Church of Southern Africa, Cape-Orange River), have their own order of service which differs from the European one, especially on the musical side. It is still tied to the Bortnianski tradition of the nineteenth century. The hymn book *Cantate* (mentioned above), is widely used in the mission church, although they have an exceptionally lively tradition of church choir and brass band music.

BIBLIOGRAPHY

Bouws, Jan: *Die musieklewe van Kaapstad, 1800–1850, en sy verhouding tot die musieklewe van Wes-Europa.* Doctoral thesis, US, 1965. Hoge, Dr John: *Die Geschichte der ältesten evangelisch-lutherischen Gemeinde in Kapstadt.* Munich, 1939. Kolb, Peter: *Caput Bonae spei hodiernum, Das ist: vollständige Beschreibung des Africanischen Vorgebürges der Guten Hofnung . . .* Nürnberg, 1719. Naumann, Dr Theol. Kurt: *Deutsche Evangelisch-Lutherische Kirche St Martini Kapstadt Festchrift zum 100 jährigen Jubiläum.* Cape Town, 1961. Ottermann, Reino Ernst: *Die kerkmusiek in die Evangeliese Lutherse Kerk in Strandstraat, Kaapstad, tussen 1780 en 1880.* M.Mus. dissertation, US, 1963.

– R.E.O.

EVANGELICAL LUTHERAN CHURCH OF SOUTHERN AFRICA (HER-MANNSBURG), MUSIC IN THE
1. Introduction
2. Brass bands
3. The choral societies
4. The choral weeks
5. The church's advisory committee
6. Training
7. Christopherus choir

1. Introduction
When the ship *Kandaze* entered Durban harbour in March 1854, a group of men with brass instruments were on board, playing a Lutheran chorale and thus heralding the distinctive arrival in South Africa of the first missionaries and German colonists of the Hermannsburg Mission. Since that time, music has remained prominent in their ecclesiastical life and mission work. According to Haccius II, p. 217, their missionary duties were summarized under three headings: "Three things you have experienced should be communicated to the heathen: the glory of our faith, the true doctrine and true sacrament, and the power of our singing." This mandate was carried out to the

last letter. When the colonists built a house for the Zulu king Mpanda, they sang chorales at their labour whilst the Blacks stood by and watched them, more astonished at the singing than by the construction work. Even today, legends still circulate about the blacksmith Gathmann who started his daily labours at the forge with chorale singing. — Eight years after their arrival the colonists had established a mixed choir which included converts of the Hermannsburg Mission Station, a brass band at Elim and, by 1869, they had printed the first hymn book in the Batswana language. In this hymnal a weakness often encountered in missionary music was apparent. The hymns were translations of German chorales, mostly of a pietistical nature, which simply ignored the musical traditions of the heathen. These were dismissed as "hellish bleatings" and the sounds of nineteenth century religious Romanticism were directly superimposed upon the powerful originality of the Bantu languages. — By 1900 German congregations began to secede from the mission community, but they retained their traditional love for music and each had its own brass band and its own vocal group. The liturgy was based on the *Kantionale Lüneburg,* whilst the *Lüneburgische Kirchen-Gesang-Buch* of 1176 hymns was generally used. Much later (1930) *Das singende und betende Zion,* the *Evangelisch-Lutherische Gesangbuch der Hannoverschen Landeskirche* and eventually, in 1960, the *Evangelische Kirchengesangbuch* followed. The accompaniments were generally played on an harmonium, eventually on an organ; the chorale books of Enckhausen and Hille were used for this purpose. — The White congregations were scattered in the vicinities of Pietermaritzburg, Vryheid and Rustenburg and the settlements were usually named after German owns – Wartburg, Harburg, Müden, Braunschweig, Lüneburg, etc. In course of time they were all joined together to form the Evangelical Lutheran Church of Southern Africa (Hermannsburg). They have remained true to their church, to the German language and to their own cultural tradition right up to the present time (1970). The schools established by the congregations and maintained by the ample generosity of the church members, have undoubtedly played a major part in keeping the Hermannsburg music traditions intact.

– H.B.

2. Brass bands

The bands have remained a mighty factor in the Hermannsburg congregational life. They originated in Hermannsburg, Germany when Pastor Theodor Harms and his brother and colleague, Ludwig Harms, founded the first band at the Missionary Training Institute. Members of the band had come to South Africa as missionaries and they brought their instruments along to sound the praise of God among the heathen. Soon they had taught their converts to play on these and, before long, brass bands were constituted which consisted entirely of converts. The first one was formed at Bethany in the Transvaal by the missionary W. Behrens (sr.); there were similar groups in Natal at Enhlanzeni and mixed groups at Müden and Nazareth. — As White congregations were founded, each one formed a brass band which played on festival days and during the services to enhance the spirit of communal worship and joy. At first there was no connection between the various groups and not until the 75th Jubilee Festival of the Hermannsburg Mission on 28 October 1924, did Hermannsburg, Wartburg, New Hannover and Verden combine to add a splendour of sound to the occasion. Thirty-two players led by the missionary Otto Dedekind of Verden, opened the festival early that morning with a rendering of the chorale *Jerusalem, du*

39

hochgebaute Stadt. From this combination of bands came the idea of a special brass band society of the Hermannsburg Synod and of communal bi-annual festivals. — These have been held regularly since that time, with a single interruption during the Second World War and one or two years afterwards (1940–1947). The directors of the combined bands have through the years been Otto Dedekind (1926-1932), Pastor Reinhardt Drews (1932–1954) and Walter Dedekind, a schoolmaster and a nephew of the first conductor (since 1954). At the first performance in 1924 there were four groups and 32 players – today the society incorporates 24 groups and 520 players. They have remained true to their early traditions, still feel themselves dedicated to the praise of God, to support missionary work and to participate in parish life, as on festival occasions, at confirmations, marriages, birthdays of elderly church members, also in cases of severe illness and at funeral services. But they also serve a social function and oblige by playing convivial music at secular meetings. In later years they have made their services available in a wider and more national context by playing at festive occasions, such as the Day of the Covenant (since the festival year of 1938). — The usual band complement is: trumpets, valve horns, trombones, tenor horns, French horns, bombardons and helicons; since 1924 these have been imported from Germany and tuned to a common pitch to facilitate combined performance. There are ties with Germany's large brass band associations – consisting of altogether 65 000 members – and these are maintained by mutual visits, the distribution of common periodicals *(Spielet dem Herrn* and *Zu Gottes Lob und Ehre)* and the provision of appropriate music. Originally the repertoire of the South African bands was drawn from the four volumes compiled by Pastor D.J. Kuhlo and from the three volumes of Schultz's *Lobopfer.* In time more idiomatic anthologies were compiled which are now widely used. These are *Lass Dir unser Lob gefallen, Zu Gottes Lob und Ehre, Lobt Gott, An hellen Tagen* and *Wachet auf* (an anthology of folk songs). There are also a good many individual pieces which have not been collected in anthologies. — Rehearsals are held without fail every week and great efforts are made to encourage young boys – more recently girls as well – to participate in the ensembles from their eighth year on. This policy ensures a constant succession of young talent. The rehearsals are characterised by an atmosphere of jovial cameraderie and a friendly spirit enthused by a common passion for music. A typical phenomenon is the fact that players retain their membership for as long as they live. — The present members of the brass band society in 1970 are those representing the congregations of Augsburg, Bishopstowe, Braunschweig, Glückstadt, Hermannsburg, Hillcrest – Neu-Deutschland, Coburg near Piet Retief, Neu-Hannover, Vryheid, Winterton, Bethany, iMpangeni, Gerdau, Harburg, Kroondal, Verden, Wartburg, Pretoria and Johannesburg. In addition teachers, students, university lecturers and officials have become active members and receive – as do the members of the groups – monthly news letters and suitable band music.

– W.D.

3. The choral societies

In the South African Lutheran communities, as in Germany, choral music is an essential part of Divine Service. Since approximately 1936, the reform of Evangelical church music in Germany has caused a certain amount of tension in the South African church choirs. Some of these favoured the pietistical choral works of Romanticism (as represented by the anthologies *Zion's Perlenchöre, Missionsharfe, Dölker* and *Heim*) while others appreciated the need for regeneration and for artistic work on a higher level. Eventually, in 1956, the Hermannsburg choirs led by Hans Bodenstein,** decided to found a new society which has since then acquired 16 Natal choirs as members, with another five from the Transvaal and one from South West Africa. — The emergence of this society emphasized the need for common choral anthologies of a high standard. Gölz's *Chorgesangbuch* was adopted for public worship and Baum's *Geselliges Chorbuch* was approved for secular purposes. Other anthologies have been adopted since then and do justice to the choral music of the Reformation, the Baroque period and to contemporaries. The choirs meet every second year during July for a choral festival which commences on a Saturday evening with a large joint rehearsal and reaches a climax on the following Sunday with Divine Service and a festival gathering. The programmes are provided approximately one year in advance, leaving the choirs ample time to study the nearly 30 chorales, Psalms, Evangelical motets and folk songs. The purpose of these communal gatherings is stated to be the communal experience of praising God in song, the promotion of unity in the church through the acceptance of the same choral music and choral standards by all and the encouragement of choirs to venture on new works and to tackle more ambitious works in the repertoire.

– H.B.

4. The choral weeks

Every year – occasionally every second year – the Choral Society, collaborating with the Church's Youth Society, organises a choral week to take place during a school vacation. On these occasions 30 to 60 generally teenage singers gather for choral practices which last up to eight hours every day. Usually they work at the larger compositions of Bach or Schütz, but folksong arrangements, domestic instrumental music and folkdancing are practised for variation. The idea behind these gatherings is the intense experience of words set to music and the constructive influence of brief, happy periods of association and shared experience. The tradition was established by Cantor Stache, who visited South Africa from Germany shortly before the outbreak of the Second World War, to organise a number of these choral weeks in Natal. At that stage the German Youth Movement was important in advancing a national awareness among German communities in all parts of the world by the emphasis it placed on folk songs associated with nature and the culture of the German people. — After Stache's departure, the choral weeks have been directed by Maria Fricke, Pastor A. Engelbrecht, Emanuel Haller,** Hans Bodenstein** and Cantor Meyer. By degrees the original national attachment receded and the study of the choral repertoire from the period preceding Bach became the main concern. This meant that the aims of the choral weeks were henceforth directed to the work of church choirs, to integrate them as a functional part of public worship and the liturgy and in this way to aid the proclamation of the Gospel. Attention was also given to a revival of interest in the original, rhythmical forms of the chorale melodies, which had become adulterated in the previous century. Apart from these aims the simple pleasure of participating in choirs on a secular basis and without any ambition to give a public performance, has been maintained.

– H.B.

5. The Church Advisory Committee

This committee was formed in 1961 to co-ordinate the work being done by brass bands and choral societies and to give guidance in respect of choral music, community singing, organ music, the training of organists, the building of organs, the testing of organs, church architecture, living contact with new trends in church music and liturgy and finally the guidance of young people in all matters concerning church music. All congregations of the Hermannsburg Church are obliged to consult this commission when building or rebuilding churches and parsonages. — An important sector of the work is devoted to advice on organ building. Organs are well-cherished in the Lutheran service and fulfil important functions. Thus it came about that Adam Lauterbach and his brother ventured into organ building in Hermannsburg in 1870. According to the accounts of the first colonists, every part of the instrument was manufactured through the joint efforts of the smithy, the joinery and the tannery of the first settlers. The last organist to play on this instrument was Mrs G. Kassier and she stated that it had two manuals with pedals, with respectively three, three and two registers. It was inaugurated in 1872 and the congregational minutes aver "that this instrument was the first organ to be built in South Africa". But it had numerous weaknesses and had to be replaced in 1910. Since that date all traces of the instrument have been lost. Shortly after 1880 the same two brothers built a second organ for Wartburg, which for many years was stored, unused, in a barn on their farm. In 1907, however, the congregation decided to buy it and had it erected in their church where it is still in use. The specification of this historical instrument is as follows:

First manual:
Principal 8′; Salicional 8′; Gedeckt 8′; Flöte 4′; Hohlflöte 4′; Octav 2′

Second manual:
Aeoline 8′; Dolce 8′; Lieblich Gedeckt 8′; Fugara 4′
Pedals: Sub-bass 16′; Octav-bass 8′; Octav 4′
Manual couplers; wind pressure by water column of 80 mm; mechanical action.

The organ advisory service is quite prepared to serve all South African churches with specialised advice regarding matters such as new tendencies in organ building as exemplified by the movement launched by the "Organistentagung in Hamburg-Lübeck" (1925), which held up the Arp Schnittger organ of 1683 in the church of St Jacobi as a model for contemporary organ building. The following principle is kept to the fore in the committee's work – the organ has to serve the simple proclamation of the Gospel and the religious meditation it implies. The necessary adjuncts of this function are a clear projection of sound, sharply contoured registers, a concentrated sound effect and a predilection for linearity. On the other hand, the imitation of orchestral instruments, blurred sound effects, a vertical, harmonic predisposition and all the ways and means of delicate nuances and dynamic effects are regarded as undesirable. Taken together, these various points form a protest against music which is aimed at stirring emotional reactions in the listeners. From a practical and technical point of view they indicate that the dispositions, mensurations, slider chests, mechanical tractions, durable materials and proper organ fronts of the Baroque are reinstated, whilst dubious inventions such as the multiplex system, the crescendo pedal, and free standing fronts are disapproved of. As a result of the efforts of the advisory committee under the chairmanship of Pastor G. Scriba of Braunschweig, which has H. Bodenstein as secretary, a considerable number of organs produced in accordance with these principles have been imported from Germany since 1955. In this connection the co-operation of some university music departments should be mentioned.

– H.B.

6. Training
In the light of the foregoing summaries, the training of choral leaders and organists can be regarded as an urgent responsibility of the Hermannsburg denomination. Led by Maria Fricke, the first course for part-time church musicians took place at Hermannsburg in 1938. The work was subsequently continued under the auspices of the choral society by Kantor F. Meyer and Hans Bodenstein. Usually the course lasts a single week and includes lectures and practical work in the following subjects: hymnology, musical theory, choral training, voice production, form, repertoire, etc. — The Hermannsburg School in Natal is responsible for a basic course offered for organists and choral leaders. Included in this are organ playing, choral training, liturgy and hymnology; a condition is that participants should have a fair facility in playing the organ. It lasts for a year and is offered in conjunction with the pupils' school education. They are examined at the end of the year and the successful candidates are equipped with a certificate stating their competence to act as organists and choral leaders of Hermannsburg congregations.

7. Christopherus Choir
This is a school choir which was started by Hans Bodenstein at Hermannsburg in 1956. The exceptional quality of their singing and the comprehensive nature of their repertoire, which included music by pre-classical, but also contemporary composers, gave the choir a national reputation. They toured in all four provinces of the Republic, were frequently heard on radio and made some gramophone records. The example set by this choir has since been followed by a number of similar enterprizes in the other provinces.

– H.B.

EVANS, BOBBY   H. Becker, L. Danza, M. Doré, Johannesburg 3(ii)

EVANS, G.   Ballet III, Johannesburg Philharmonic Society

EVANS, HARRY *1874 in Tredegar, South Wales; °8 July 1962 in Durban. Tenor and choir conductor.

Starting as a 12-year-old pit boy in a Welsh coal mine, Harry Evans at 18 was well-known as a boy alto; when only 19 he conducted a Welsh church choir of 40 voices. A namesake of his was city organist of Liverpool, and probably assisted the young singer, who won in all about 70 first prizes at Eisteddfodau in Wales. After he had decided to emigrate to South Africa, Harry Evans travelled in the same ship as the D'Oyly Carte Opera Company and was invited to sing tenor parts on their South African tour. He was in Johannesburg for five years and became conductor of the Plein Street Baptist Church Choir, before leaving for Durban in 1907. In 1909 he became choirmaster of the Aliwal Street Congregational Church and remained their choral leader for most of his active musical life. — Evans sang in opera, operetta and oratorio, and performed popular ballads; but he is best remembered for the Durban Male Voice Choir of 40–50 voices, which he formed in 1910. This choir was generally known as the Durban Male Voice Party, and it sang under his leadership for nearly fifty years. During the two wars it worked in the interest of public charities, and for the preservation of the best Welsh vocal tradition. A few of the original members were still with the choir when it gave one of its last concerts in the Wesley Hall, West Street, in February 1957. In 1938, while on a visit to Britain, Harry Evans was made a Welsh bard, with the name of Harri Natal. He had married a girl from his home town, and soon after their 65th wedding anniversary in 1961, she died in Cape Town. Of their two sons, Cyril is a singer in that city.

– G.S.J.

EVERSON, O. CROMWELL   Higher Educational Institutions I/8

EWINS, BERNARD JAMES, *June 1863 in Newport, England; °19 August 1955 in Pretoria. Organist and music dealer.

An advertisement of a choral concert to take place in St Michael's contains the earliest reference to Ewins (*Queenstown Free Press*, 15 September, 1893). He was organist at St Michael's and All Angels until 1895, gave recitals in July 1894 and March 1895, and played the organ when the *Dettingen Te Deum* (Handel) and Gaul's *Holy city* were performed in November and December 1895 respectively. Advertisements announce Ewins as an organist and as a teacher of pianoforte, organ and singing, also stating that he was a professional piano tuner. — His name is remembered in South Africa for a music shop which was still in existence in 1958, although Ewins himself was only concerned in the trade for a few years. His shop in Queenstown was advertised for the first time on July 5, 1898, but by 1904 he had sold it to F.R. Bartlett and from Bartlett it went to T.D. Charteris and Peter Barnes. Barnes eventually became the sole owner and was declared bankrupt at some time before 1960. In the meantime Ewins had started another music shop in East London, on the corner of Oxford and Terminus Streets (October 1917). This shop was sold to C. Bartlett, a brother of the man who had bought the Queenstown shop. "Ewins" was retained as the trading name of the concern, until it was absorbed into the Bothner-Polliack group of companies (1958). — Bernard Ewins married twice and lived in Pretoria after 1952.

SOURCES
Queenstown Free Press: 15 Sept. 1893–1895; July 1898.   *EL Daily Dispatch:* 10 Dec. 1953; 24 Jan. 1959.   State Archives, Pretoria: Estate B.J. Ewins, No. 5125/55.   Information supplied by John W. Dowar, attorney in Queenstown.

– C.G.H. (amended)

EYSSEN, STEPHEN HARRY, *23 May 1890 in Montagu; °11 April 1981 in Pretoria. Leader of folk singing, baritone and composer, who contributed significantly to the cultural development of the Afrikaner.

Stephen Eyssen spent the main part of his formative years in Stellenbosch, where the enthusiasm for Afrikaans and the influence of ATV leaders such as Gordon Tomlinson and Dr Tobie Muller became decisive in shaping his career. After matriculating at the Jongens Hogere School in Stellenbosch, he entered the Normal College in Cape Town as a student for the teacher's diploma (1910–1911). He taught for a while before returning to Stellenbosch in 1914 with the intention of studying at the Victoria College. After again teaching from 1915–1917 he entered for the BA degree at the newly-constituted University of Stellenbosch in 1918. He graduated in 1920. During the early years he was also trained in music at the Stellenbosch Conservatoire of Music,** resuming an interest which had been rooted in his boyhood through the example of his parents. Nancy de Villiers** (piano), Denholm Walker** of Cape Town (organ) and Walter Spiethoff** (singing), were among those who contributed to his musical development. — The prevalent enthusiasm for Afrikaans found a musical outlet in Eyssen's case. In 1914 the Werda Commission organised a festival of Afrikaans culture in the Cape Town City Hall and he was approached for a vocal contribution. There were no suitable songs in Afrikaans, so he composed what became known as his *Segelied* for the occasion. At a later date (1920) he acted as the leader of a concert group of students who toured in aid of charity and Eyssen had all the items on their programme as well as the advertisements, printed in either Afrikaans or Dutch. For this tour Jan Celliers had translated the text of Brahms's *Wiegenlied* into Afrikaans and dedicated it to the singer Miss A. Bartels, whom Eyssen married in 1921. — From 1921 to 1933 he was the teacher of Afrikaans at the Hoër Volkskool in Heidelberg (Transvaal) and from 1934 until 1948 he was the principal of this school. During the Second World War he was interned under the Emergency Regulations, but on 1 June 1945, the school had the pleasure of welcoming him back again. Three years later he resigned to enter politics and became, for the next ten years, the member of Parliament for the Heidelberg constituency (1948–1958). In the latter year he surrendered his seat to Dr H.F. Verwoerd and then settled near Pretoria where he occasionally acted as *locum tenens* in the teaching profession and became an honoured personality in cultural circles. — Folk singing was his particular forte. He was well-known in South Africa as a leader of mass singing at Kruger Festivals, at the inauguration of the Voortrekker Monument in 1949, at the courses organised by the *Lenteskool*-movement and at numerous cultural and patriotic gatherings. This identification with the Afrikaner cause is reflected in many of his own songs and large-scale compositions. As a baritone – singing solo or at times in duets with his wife – but also as a public speaker and lecturer, he championed the cause of South African composers and of the emerging art song in Afrikaans. — The radio made much use of his vocal gift and in Pretoria he was in continual demand to sing solo parts in G. Bon's** performances of *Judas Maccabeus, Des geestes bruid* (Dvorak), *Deutsches Requiem* (Brahms) and Bach's *Johannes passie* (five times in all!). In 1930 and again in 1932 he recorded Afrikaans national music for the companies Columbia and His Master's Voice (see Discography). Eyssen served on the Music Commission of the FAK** from 1932 to 1962 and was an obvious choice to act as co-editor of the first *FAK-Volksangbundel* (1937), collaborating with Dr H. Gutsche** and Dr W. du P. Erlank (Eitemal). He was also actively involved in the preparation of the *Nuwe FAK-sangbundel,* which was published in 1961. In this connection the interesting fact should be mentioned that during his student days he had collaborated with others in compiling a first album of student songs in Afrikaans. — In Heidelberg he was organist and choral conductor of the Dutch Reformed congregation, from 1921 until he left the town. The school's Orpheum Choir and, after Otto Menge's** departure in 1922, also the Orpheum Orchestra were both directed by him, children and amateurs combining to give bi-annual concerts and an occasional performance of an operetta or a light cantata. Artists of renown such as Nunez Holtzhausen,** Gladys Daniel** and Sydney Rosenbloom** performed under the auspices of these Societies in his time. In 1947 he even organised a performance of Arnold van Wyk's** *String quartette.* The establishment of the Heidelberg Eisteddfod was another of his achievements in the field of music. After 1958 he continued his musical work in Pretoria, where he conducted the choirs of the Afrikaanse Musiekklub** and the Sangluskoor** on several occasions. — In 1964 Eyssen settled in East London but he returned to Pretoria in 1972. In 1969 the Suid-Afrikaanse Akademie vir Wetenskap en Kuns** awarded him a medal of honour for his musical contributions to Afrikaans culture.

WORKS

A. Published
Normal College students' song (Ronald Graham: Latin and English). R. Müller's Music Warehouse, Cape Town, 1911; pr. C.G. Röder, Leipzig.   Segelied (A.B. Wessels). Aan ons Afrikaner Volk opgedra. Cape Times Ltd, Cape Town, 1914. Second Edition, J.H. de Bussy, Pretoria, n.d. *Nuwe FAK-sangbundel,* Nasionale Boekhandel Bpk., Johannesburg, 1961.   Memoria, gewy aan die nagedagtenis van die epidemieslagoffers van Swart Oktober 1918 (own words). De Nationale Pers, Bpk., Bloemfontein, 1919.   Die Stem van Suid-Afrika (C.J. Langenhoven). Lowe & Brydone London, 1931; arranged for mixed voices by Arthur Ellis. Die Elsmy Musiekverspreiders, Johannesburg, n.d.; with new words: Uit die chaos van die eeue (D.F. Viljoen). *FAK-Volksangbundel,* 1937; *Nuwe FAK-sangbundel,* Nasionale Boekhandel Bpk., Johannesburg, 1961.   Komaan (J.F.E. Celliers). Gestetner, S.H. Eyssen, Heidelberg, 1932. Die murasie, two part song (J.F.E. Celliers). Duplicated S.H. Eyssen, Heidelberg, 1937. *Nuwe FAK-sangbundel,* Nasionale Boekhandel Bpk., Johannesburg, 1961.   Saam met die wa (Die baardlied) (J.C. Eyssen). *Eeufeesliedjies,* Nas. Pers Bpk., 1938; *Nuwe FAK-sangbundel,* Nas. Boekhandel Bpk., Johannesburg, 1961.   Fugit Imago (D.F. Malherbe), comp. 1942. L & S Boek- en Kunssentrum, printed by Paul J. Gerber, Johannesburg, 1947.   Wiegeliedjie (R.H. Rautenbach). Ms., 1942. *Nuwe FAK-sangbundel,* Nasionale Boekhandel Bpk., Johannesburg, 1961.   Ons Boerwording, 1486-1949, 'n sangbeeld (Dr J.H. Pienaar). Gestetner, FAK, Johannesburg, 1942; first performance: inauguration of Voortrekker Monument, 1949; bilingual second ed., pub. Dr J.H. Pienaar and S.H. Eyssen; pr. Nirota, Amsterdam, 1952.   Bybelkantate (own compilation from the Bible and hymn book), comp. 1943. Voortrekkerpers Bpk., Johannesburg, 1944. First perf., Pretoria, 12 November 1944.   Goue vrug (own words), comp. 1944. Pub. L & S Boek- en Kunssentrum, Johannesburg-Amsterdam; pr. Nirota, Amsterdam, 1947.   Van der Stel se verjaarsdagfees (Dr Jan Pienaar). Dupl., 1946; one section for tenor and choir from *Ons Boerwording.*   Die Veepos, three-part song (Totius). L & S Boek- en Kunssentrum, Johannesburg, 1947.   Die Lewerkie (Dr Jan Pienaar). L & S Boek-en Kunssentrum, Johannesburg, 1947.   —

B. Unpublished
Bede vir elke dag (words and music). Ms., 1962.   Bid en werk, for two voices (Totius), written for Geref. Sustersvereniging, Potchefstroom. Ms., 1947.   Dit is nag (Totius). Ms., 1942. Gebed, for choir. Ms., 1961.   Heil ons Republiek! (P.H. Langenhoven). Ms., 1961.   Heil ons Universiteit Stellenbosch! (J.J. Pienaar). Ms., 1944.   Heil Suid-Afrika, ons land! Ms.,

n.d.   Kappielied. Ms., 1938.   Die Kappietuit (J.C. Eyssen). Ms., 1945.   Koffiefontein-kamplied (J. Engelbrecht). Ms., 1942.   Kom na die velde (A.B. Wessels). Ms., 1917.
Lokstem van die Laeveld (R.G.P. Pretorius). Ms., 1946.   Montagu, 1854–1954 (J. Powell).
Ms., 1954.   Monday prayer, for choir (words and music). Ms., 1962.   Mijn Vaderland
(Hofmeyr/J.H. Pienaar). Ms., 1942.·   Mynwerkerslied (J. Bronkhorst). Ms., 1962.   Nasi-onale Party-lied (J. Pienaar). Ms., 1956.   Ons Bondslied (J. Pienaar). Ms., 1956.   Prelude
to *Paul Kruger,* arranged for piano, also for brass band. Ms., 1954.   Roepstem van die môre,
for choir (J. Pienaar). Ms., 1942.   Volkskas-lied (J. Pienaar). Ms., 1956.   Voortrekkeros,
vergete held (J. von Moltke). Ms., 1957.   Waar Tafelberg begin. Ms., 1915.   Wiegeliedjie
(R.H. Rautenbach). Ms., 1942.   28 School songs.

C. Arrangements
8 picnic songs in collaboration with C.J. Langenhoven.   Assistant-editor FAK-Volksang-bundels,** 1937 and 1961.   Editor of *RDB Volkspele Handleiding,* collected and arranged by
A.M. Köhler. Nasionale Pers Bpk., Bloemfontein, 1941.

D. Writings
Dr A.G. Visser. *Die Christelike Skoolblad,* Sept. 1929.   Kultuurvak op skool. *Tydskrif vir
middelbare onderwys,* Mar. 1935.   Afrikaanssprekendes in die Unie se musiekwêreld. *Die
Transvaler,* 3 Oct. 1938.   Die orrelis en die gemeente. *Jaarboek, N.H. Sustersvereniging,*
1946.   Musieklewe in die Boerekamp. Ms., 1949.   Die singende Kaapstadse Maleiers.
Jaarblad, Hoër Tegniese Skool John Vorster, 1963.   Uit my herinneringe, articles published
in *Die Oosterlig,* 14 Aug.–13 Sept. 1968.

BIBLIOGRAPHY
Hamman, B.M.: *Stephen Eyssen.* B.Mus. script, UP, 1965.

SOURCES
(a) Newspapers
Die Burger: 5 May 1961; 23 May 1970; 28 Jan. 1972.   *Cape Fayre:* 2 Oct. 1948.   *Daily
Dispatch:* 24 June 1965.   *Evening Post:* 18 Sept. 1969.   *Heidelberg Weekblad:* Series of
articles on music in Heidelberg by P.H. Langenhoven, 1965–1966.   *Hoofstad:* 2 Jan. 1969; 23
July 1970.   *Die Oosterlig:* 22 Nov. 1963; 31 Oct. 1969; 3 Nov. 1969; 17 July 1970; 26 May
1975.   *Paarl Post:* 25 Oct. 1955.   *Die Perdeby:* Oct. 1944.   *The Star:* 16 Aug. 1930; 5
June 1931.   *Sunday Times:* 23 Nov. 1941.   *Die Transvaler:* 3 Nov. 1941; 31 Mar. 1942; 11
Nov. 1944; 13 Nov. 1944; 31 May 1945.   *Die Vaderland:* 19 Oct. 1945.

(b) Periodicals
Afrikaans-Nederlands Maandblad: 19 Aug. 1957.   *Die Dienares:* Jan. 1950.   *Fleur:* Nov.
1947.   *Jaarboek van die SA Akademie vir Wetenskap en Kuns:* 1969.   *Kultuur:* Jan.
1945.   *Ons Skoolblad: Hoër Volkskool, Heidelberg: 1921–1948,* 1963.   *SABC Bulletin:* 14
Jan. 1947; 23 Mar. 1970.   *Zuid-Afrika* XXV/7, Amsterdam, July 1948.   Information
supplied by S.H. Eyssen.
The Stephen Eyssen collection in the Research Centre for South African Music, HSRC, Pretoria.
                                                                                – J.P.M.

FACER, C.W.   Port Elizabeth I/5

FAGAN, GIDEON, *3 November 1904 in Somerset West; ° 20 March 1980 in Cape Town. Conductor and composer.

Fagan's musical education began under supervision of his brother, Johannes Fagan,** who engaged private tutors in pianoforte and the theory of music and harmony, as Gideon progressed. From 1916 to 1922 he attended the South African College of Music,** not taking a degree course, but specializing in counterpoint, harmony, composition, score-reading and orchestration, under the guidance of W.H. Bell.** Adolph Hallis** and Mrs Bell shaped his pianoforte playing. There followed further study, lasting four years, at the RCM, where Gideon had the privilege of being trained by prominent men (1923-1926). With conducting as his principal subject, Fagan obtained the highest ("seven-star") degree. He was at the time the youngest student to conduct opera in the Parry Opera Theatre, and the first to conduct professional orchestras at the RCM Patrons' Fund concerts: the Royal Philharmonic, the Royal Albert Hall, the Queen's Hall and the London Symphony Orchestras. He was clearly destined to become the first professional conductor born in South Africa. — Fagan returned to South Africa in 1926, but he left again for London a year later, because at the time there were only limited opportunities in his chosen profession in South Africa. His second stay in England lasted until 1949. During this time he held a variety of conducting posts and acquired experience of all aspects of orchestral work. His long association with Ernest Irving began soon after his arrival in England in 1927. This afforded him valuable experience of musical practice in the theatre, including conducting, musical arrangements, orchestration and the composition of incidental music for film and theatre productions. — Music publishers were eager to make use of Fagan's services in these various accomplishments. Using the *nom de plume* of Albert Diggenhof, he made arrangements of traditional Afrikaans folk songs for HMV as well as for the BBC (see Discography). After 1936 he enjoyed a firm reputation as a guest conductor, as a popular composer of incidental music for films and documentaries and as musical director during recordings, also of his own music. *The two bouquets, The glass slipper* by H. and E. Farjeon and the successful *Song of Norway* are a few of the works which were performed under his direction. When the appointment of a new conductor for the Northern Orchestra of the BBC in Manchester was discussed in 1939, a committee of 12 specialists, including Adrian Boult and Hamilton Harty, were unanimous in appointing Fagan. He conducted this orchestra for three years running, in broadcasts and public concerts, and then he tendered his resignation. Until his departure from England he conducted only as an independent artist in symphony concerts, broadcasts, ballet productions and film music. — He signed a contract with the Johannesburg City Council in 1949 to conduct the City Orchestra for two years, as second conductor to Frits Schuurman.** The time limit was eventually extended to three and a half years. Since 1926 there had been considerable changes in South African musical life and Fagan often had the opportunity of conducting concerts, operas, school concerts and on tours of the orchestra in the country districts. When the Voortrekker Monument was inaugurated in 1949, he was the conductor of the combined SABC and City orchestras, and also of massed choirs who sang in the amphitheatre at the Monument. Three years later he was again prominent during the Van Riebeeck Festivals in Johannesburg and Pretoria. The popular lunch-hour and Saturday concerts in Johannesburg were originated by Fagan at this time. When the City Orchestra was terminated in 1953 and his contract with the City Council was ended, he became the organiser of music during the Golden Jubilee Festival of African Consolidated Theatres. — The SABC appointed Fagan as manager of their music department in Johannesburg in 1954. He was in succession manager, then music advisor, manager of music planning, acting Head of Music and after 1964, Head of Music. During his thirteen years with the SABC Fagan consistently exerted himself to advance the cause of South African music. He commissioned the first South African radio opera, *The coming of the butterflies* by Stephen O'Reilly, libretto by Cecil Jubber, founded the SABC Junior Orchestra and conducted, on occasion, the National Symphony Orchestra of the SABC and other SA orchestras. In 1967 he became senior lecturer at the South African College of Music,** chiefly for orchestration and composition, remaining in this position until the end of 1972. He then retired to his seaside home at Betty's Bay where he devoted himself to original work. In 1973 and again in 1976 the National Education Department awarded Fagan their triennial prize for "the best concert work written in South Africa". His achievements and his services to music were acknowledged in 1963, when the Swiss International Institute of Arts and Letters awarded him a life Fellowship (FIAL).

WORKS

A. Vocal

1. Songs with pianoforte accompaniment
I had a dove (Keats). Schott & Co. Ltd, London, 1929.   Die nag (G. Fagan). Ms., 1929.   Klein sonneskyn (A.G. Visser). Ms., 1930.   Lied van die Wonderboom (A.G. Visser). Ms., 1930.   Omdat die dood . . . (A.G. Visser). Ms., 1930.   Die bergblommetjie (H.A. Fagan). Ms., 1935.   She walks in beauty (Byron). Ms., 1935.   Elegy (Byron). Ms., 1937.   Slampamperliedjie no. 2: Eis van die vonk (C.L. Leipoldt). Ms., 1941.   Ek sal opstaan (W.E.G. Louw). Ms., 1972.

2. Songs with orchestral accompaniment
Wagter op die toring (H.A. Fagan). Ms., 1926.   Slampamperliedjie no. 1: Wys my die plek (C.L. Leipoldt). Ms., 1941.

3. Solo voices, chorus and orchestra
Tears (Walt Whitman), a symphonic poem based on an incomplete work by Johannes Fagan.** Ms., 1954.   Een Vaderland, oratorio commissioned by the National Education Department. Ms., 1977–1978.

B. Instrumental

1. Orchestra
Nocturne, for woodwind and strings. Ms., 1926.   Jungle music, pastoral and lion hunt, from the film music for *David Livingstone,* subsequently superseded by the tone poem *Ilala,* written on the same thematic material. Ms., 1937.   Ilala, tone poem. Ms., 1941.   South African folk-tune suite, commissioned by the BBC. Ms., 1942.   Five orchestral pieces, mood music commissioned by the Chappell Library, London. Ms., 1948–1949: 1. Pastoral montage   2. The haunted house   3. Playtime waltz   4. Motif for murder   5. Kampala kraal-dance.   Concert overture in D, commissioned by the SABC. Ms., 1954.   Heuwelkruin, suite for pianoforte and

FAGAN

orchestra. Ms., 1954.   SABC anniversary overture, commissioned by the SABC for its 21st birthday celebrations. Ms., 1957.   Fanfare for Radio South Africa, commissioned by the SABC for use as opening to its "A", "B" and "RSA" services. Ms., 1966.   Albany, overture dedicated to the British Settlers in South Africa, commissioned by the SABC for the 150th Settlers' anniversary. Ms., 1970.   Ex unitate vires, symphonic sketch, commissioned by the Republic Festival Committee for the 10th anniversary of the Republic. Ms., 1970.   R–10 march, as Ex unitate vires above. Ms., 1971.   Suite for strings, commissioned by the Brussels Chamber Orchestra, awarded the National Education Department's triennial award in 1976. Ms., 1974.   Miniature overture – fanfare for a festival, for 22 brass, 8 percussion and 6 harps, commissioned by the SABC for the 10th anniversary of the SABC Junior Symphony Orchestra. Ms., 1976.   Karoo-simfonie, commissioned by the SABC. Ms., 1976.

2. Chamber music
Nocturne, transcription of the work for woodwind and strings, for violin and pianoforte. Ms., 1930.   Nonet, commmissioned by the Czech Nonet. Ms., 1958.   My lewe, a continuous work based on six poems by Totius, for baritone and chamber music ensemble, awarded the National Education Department's triennial prize in 1973. Ms., 1970.   Little suite – memories of Jojo's visit, for violin and piano. Ms., 1973: 1. Happy meeting   2. Fond greeting   3. Contentment   4. Parting.   Quintics, "a five-time frolic for five brass". Ms., 1975.

3. Pianoforte
Danse des harpies. Ms., 1929.   Two mood sketches, commissioned by the Kingsmead College for the inauguration of the extention to the building for Music. Ms., 1968.   Children's pieces, six little pieces for Jojo. Ms., 1973: 1. Prelude for Button-nose   2. G.P.P. (Guppy, Puppy, Pluto)   3. Cheeky aristobrats   4. Pawns and pieces   5. Weaving   6. Mimoff's march.

Film music
(i) British films: *David Livingstone, The captain's table, The last rose of summer , Auld lang syne.* Shorts and documentaries: *The music-master series, Quaint Quebec, Highlights of Cape Town, Irish interlude, Dangerous journey, Mrs Worth goes to Westminster.*   (ii) South African documentaries: *Vaal River story, Fishermen of Skeleton Coast, They came to stay, South African mosaic.*

BIBLIOGRAPHY
Blume, Friedrich: *Die Musik in Geschichte und Gegenwart* IV. Kassel, 1957 ff.   Bouws, Jan: *Suid-Afrikaanse komponiste van vandag en gister.* Balkema, Cape Town, 1957.   Brook, Donald: *Conductor's gallery.* Rockliffe, London, 1946.   *The concise Oxford dictionary of music,* 5th impression. OUP, Oxford, 1960.   *Grove's dictionary of music and musicians,* 5th ed., 1954.   *Riemann's Musiklexicon* II. Mainz, 1959.

SOURCES
The Argus: 9 Jan. 1974.   *Die Burger:* 26 Mar. 1949, 19 Jan. 1957, 9 July 1963, 22 Aug. 1966, 1 Nov. 1974.   *Capab News:* 22 Feb. 1974.   *The Cape Times:* 27 May 1971.   *Daily News:* 3 May 1971.   *Eikestadnuus:* 21 Mar. 1975.   *Natal Mercury:* 29 April 1971.   *Res Musicae:* Mar. 1957, Mar. 1961, Dec. 1962.   *SABC Bulletin:* 23 Jan. 1961, 27 Mar. 1961, 30 Sept. 1962, 13 Oct. 1965.   *Die Vaderland:* 18 Mar. 1949, 22 Aug. 1964.   *Vita Musica:* I/1, Oct. 1962.   Research Centre for South African Music, HSRC, Pretoria.

– Ed.

FAGAN, JOHANNES JACOBUS, *22 February 1898 in Tulbagh; ° 13 July 1920 in London. Composer.

Johannes Fagan's gifts as composer came to light at an early age, while he was studying pianoforte with a private tutor at Somerset West, where the family took up residence a few years after his birth. In 1914 he became a student at the South African College of Music** and entered for a general musical course, though he concentrated mainly on composition under W.H. Bell.** In 1916 he won a scholarship for piano playing, performing for the examination a sonata of his own composition, besides the prescribed pieces. —The scholarship provided for three years' tuition at the RCM, where Fagan again took a general course, devoting himself to composition under Vaughan Williams. His health had been poor for some years, and in 1918 he returned home in need of regular care and treatment. In South Africa he resumed studies with W.H. Bell, and in 1919 his *Prelude for orchestra* received its first performance in the City Hall, Cape Town, at a symphony concert of the Cape Town Municipal Orchestra,** conducted by Theo Wendt.** — A few weeks later, in better health, he returned to London to complete his scholarship course under Vaughan Williams. Both in Cape Town and London high hopes were held for Fagan's future, but before long his health deteriorated again, and at the age of twenty-two he committed suicide while still a scholar at the RCM. — He left behind him a variety of manuscripts in different stages of completion and varying degrees of maturity; but in all of them there is evidence that the hopes entertained for him were well-founded, and that his death deprived South Africa of its first home-born composer with a potential for large-scale works.

WORKS

1. Orchestra
Prelude. Ms., 1918–1919.

2. Baritone and orchestra
Tears (Walt Whitman). Not completed; thematic material used by his brother, Gideon Fagan,** for a tone poem of the same title for solo voice, mixed choir and orchestra. Ms., n.d.

3. Chamber music
Trio for piano, violin and cello (last nineteen bars of piano part missing). Ms., nd.   String quartet (two movements completed). Ms., n.d.

4. Mixed chorus (or vocal quartet)
Love-sick am I (Robert Herrick). Ms., n.d.   Kyrie eleison. Ms., n.d.

5. Solo voice and piano
Soos die windjie wat suis (H.A. Fagan). *Die Nuwe Brandwag,* 1931, p. 240.   Die soekende moeder (Jan F.E. Celliers). Schott & Co. Ltd, London, 1931 (revised by Gideon Fagan in 1929).   I saw a cherry weep (Robert Herrick). Ms., n.d.   The vision to Elektra (Robert Herrick). Ms., n.d.

6. Piano solo
Sonata in C sharp minor, in three movements. Ms., 1915–1916.   Intermezzo in D flat. Ms., 1918.   Etude in A flat. Ms., 1919.   Notturno. Ms., n.d.   Cadenza for Mozart's pianoforte concerto in B flat major (K 450). Ms., 1917.

FAGAN

BIBLIOGRAPHY
Bouws, Jan: *Suid-Afrikaanse komponiste van vandag en gister*. A.A. Balkema, Cape Town, 1957.

SOURCE
Quarterly Bulletin of the S.A. College of Music, July 1920 (obituary).

– G.F.

FAINSINGER, ETHEL   Israel (Charles W.), Touring Theatre Groups 3

FAINSINGER, GERALD   Windhoek 3

FAIRLESS, M.   L. Danza, G. Sharp

FAK AND AFRIKAANS MUSIC, THE. When the Federation of Afrikaans Cultural Societies (FAK) was formed at a congress in Bloemfontein in 1929, it was clear that the promotion of Afrikaans music was to be one of the tasks of the organisation. With others, Willem Gerke** made a special appeal to the congress about this matter. The first indication that the executive committee of the FAK had been giving Afrikaans music its serious attention, was the establishment of a committee (March 7, 1931) to investigate the possibility of publishing a volume dedicated to Afrikaans musical folklore. The following were invited to serve on this committee: Dr M.L. du Toit (Pretoria), Prof. W. Arndt (Bloemfontein) and S.H. Eyssen,** P. de la R. Prinsloo, J.J.F. du Toit and Miss J. de Villiers, all of Heidelberg, a town which at that time was a focal point of Afrikaans culture and folk song. The committee compiled a list of about 200 songs and recommended that an editorial committee consisting of Dr Hugo Gutsche,** Dr W.J. du P. Erlank and S.H. Eyssen be given the task of adding to the collection and of preparing an album for publication. The work was completed in 1937 with the publication of the first *FAK-Volksangbundel*. This was thoroughly revised twenty years later: out-moded songs were removed and indigenous Afrikaans songs were more widely represented. The revised edition was published in 1961. — Other matters pertaining to music to receive the attention of the executive committee during the nineteen-thirties were: (a) organisation of attempts to reach unanimity among Afrikaners on the question of a national anthem (this led to the official recognition of *Die Stem van Suid-Afrika* (M.L. de Villiers)**); (b) appeals to manufacturers of gramophone records to distribute Afrikaans records of higher quality and to finance a number of recordings of outstanding Afrikaans songs (see Discography); (c) the appointment of South African musicians to collaborate with examiners of the London Associated Board in music examinations conducted in South Africa. — A result of the work done during the thirties was the realisation that a permanent music commission was desirable and on June 19, 1941 the FAK Music Commission met for the first time. The meeting took place in Johannesburg under the chairmanship of I.M. Lombard. Other members present were Hugo Gutsche, S.H. Eyssen, Rosa Nepgen** and J.H. Coetzee. P.J. Lemmer** was co-opted to serve on the commission and later Mrs J.E. Fourie** and A.C. Hartman** came in as additional members. The Music Commission is appointed biennially by the Executive Committee with the following terms of reference: (a) to make Afrikaans music known and to encourage the performance and use of Afrikaans art songs; (b) to assist young Afrikaans composers by appraising their work and to ensure that selected works are published; (c) to promote Afrikaans as the medium of instruction in music teaching and lecturing; (d) generally to protect and promote the interests of Afrikaans composers. — The Commission has recommended the publication by the FAK of church choir books, piano teaching manuals, school operettas and songs in Afrikaans and took the initiative with regard to the special congress devoted to folk music and singing which was held in Stellenbosch between 30 September and 3 October 1957. An important result of this congress was that negotiations were conducted with various authorities to establish an institute for folk music at an Afrikaans university. This was created at the University of Stellenbosch in 1960, with Jan Bouws** of the Netherlands (later Dr Jan Bouws) in charge. Other tasks of the Commission include the compilation of programmes for Afrikaans festivals, language festivals and Republican thanksgiving festivals, and the distribution of circulars and lists of select titles providing information and advice on folk-songs, recordings of Afrikaans music and published compositions by Afrikaans composers. In 1950 the FAK took the lead in publishing a first Afrikaans Music Terminology drawn up by M.C. Roode.** The Federation also grants annual bursaries for music to candidates recommended by the Commission. — The following people have served on the Commission since its formation in 1941: I.M. Lombard, Hugo Gutsche, S.H. Eyssen, Rosa Nepgen, P.J. Lemmer, J.E. Fourie, A.C. Hartman, Nunez Holtzhausen,** M.C. Roode, C.E. Lamprecht,** G.G. Cillié,** B. Kok,** D.I.C. de Villiers,** P.J. de Villiers,** H.J. Moolman, P. McLachlan,** J.P. Malan,** J.J. Pauw, Jan Bouws and W.E.G. Louw.

– W.S.J.G.

FAK-VOLKSANGBUNDEL, DIE. The first copies of this publication were handed to the chairman of the FAK (Dr N.J. van der Merwe), the General Secretary of the FAK, and the chairman of the ANS (successor to the ASB) by Dr A.J.R. van Rhyn on behalf of the FAK, on the occasion of the fourth FAK Congress held in the Clarendon Hall in Bloemfontein on 7 July 1937. — The idea of an album of Afrikaans songs originated with the Afrikaanse Studentebond (ASB). During 1929 and 1930 this organisation started collecting Afrikaans songs with the intention of compiling them in a volume, but progress was slow. In 1930 the ASB turned to the FAK with the request that the FAK undertake the publication of an Afrikaans song book. On 7 March 1931, it was decided that the FAK would definitely publish such a volume and the songs already collected by the ASB were catalogued by Mr (later Prof.) L.J. du Plessis and sent to the FAK on behalf of the ASB. On 30 July 1932, the FAK set up a commission to consider the *modus operandi* of compiling a folk-song anthology. This commission consisted of Messrs I.M. Lombard (chairman), J.J.F. du Toit (secretary), Stephen H. Eyssen** (editor), P. de la R. Prinsloo (secretary to the editor), Prof. Dr W. Arndt, Dr M.L. du Toit and Miss J. de Villiers. The first meeting was held on 5 November 1932 and after that a start was made in increasing the size of the collection. — In 1918 Dr Hugo Gutsche** and Dr A.G. Visser had fostered the idea of an anthology of Afrikaans songs. However, it was only after the death of Dr Visser in 1929 that Dr Gutsche and Mr (later Dr) W.J. du P. Erlank (Eitemal) decided to compile such a volume and in 1933 they approached the firm of J.H. de Bussy to act as publishers. This firm realised that there could be duplication and approached the FAK with the suggestion that the parties work in collaboration. They offered to bear the costs of printing and distribution and suggested that Stephen Eyssen, Dr Gutsche and Eitemal work together as joint editors. These proposals were accepted by the FAK on 8 August 1934. — The purpose of this volume of national songs was to strengthen the feeling of solidarity among Afrikaners and to inspire them with a love of singing. The tunes used were those which originated in South Africa, or those with a Pan-Dutch origin. The words to these tunes were supplied by W.J. du P. Erlank, F.J. Eybers, Dr G. Mes, Rev. J. Baumbach, P.H. Langenhoven, D.F. Viljoen, Theo Jandrell and others. Included in this first *FAK-Volksangbundel* were 314 songs of which about 15% are traditional. By 1961 about 70 000 copies of this volume had been sold and of the tonic solfa edition of May 1938 about 30 000. — When South Africa became a republic in May 1961, the *Nuwe FAK-sangbundel* appeared, with 388 songs of which about 42% are traditional. A new editorial committee: Dirkie de Villiers** (Chief Editor), Anton Hartman,** Prof. G.G. Cillié,** Prof. B. Kok,** S.H. Eyssen, I.M. Lombard, P. McLachlan,** P.J. de Villiers,** C.E. Lamprecht,** H.J. Moolman, G.L.H. van Niekerk, T.W.S. Meyer, W.S.J. Grobler, was responsible for the corrections, additions and excisions in the new and enlarged volume. The printers were the Nasionale Boekhandel Beperk.

– S.H.E.

FAKTOR, LUCY (MRS CHARLES KREITZER), *1922, in Latvia; at present (1977) in Cape Town. Violinist.

Lucy Faktor was brought to South Africa when her parents emigrated from Europe in 1926, and two years later she commenced violin lessons under Thomas Baker in Paarl. During subsequent studies at the South African College of Music,** Cape Town, where her violin teachers were Ellie Marx** and Editha Braham, she won awards, including the Van Hulsteyn Scholarship and the Percy Ould Prize.** — After completion of her studies, she became a member of the SABC Studio Orchestra** in Cape Town, and has frequently played as an extra first violinist in the Cape Town Municipal Orchestra** during the past twenty years. On several occasions she has also appeared with this orchestra as violin soloist. — In 1943 she married the violinist Charles Kreitzer,** and has been a member of his Chamber Music Ensemble** since its inception in 1945.

– C.K.

FALLOWES, G. Johannesburg 1, E. and C. Mendelssohn, Theatres and Concert Halls II/2, IV/3, Touring Theatre Groups 3, 4

FARRELL, TIMOTHY WILLIAM, *13 July 1892 in Birmingham; ° in late sixties in Kent, England. Baritone and lecturer in singing.

Farrell began his musical career as an instrumentalist, playing cello in the Harrogate Symphony Orchestra and euphonium in different bands. After the First World War he resumed his singing career, which had begun when he was a choir boy at St Martin's Church, Birmingham. He studied under R.A. Clark and F.J. Clifford, as well as in Germany during short visits; after 1922 he was with Robert Parker for three years. During this time he was a member of the British National Opera Company, where he became acquainted with Leslie Heward.** — While calling at Cape Town in 1925 *en route* to Australia, he was persuaded by Heward and Prof. W.H. Bell** to become a lecturer in singing on the staff of the South African College of Music** (1925–1943). In 1944 he opened his own studio in Cape Town, at which he taught until leaving for England on an extended visit in 1962. During his stay in South Africa, Timothy Farrell was often heard in song recitals, and as a soloist in opera and oratorio, over the radio and on the concert platform. His most outstanding operatic roles were Scarpia in *Tosca* and Figaro in *The Barber of Seville*.

BIBLIOGRAPHY
K., W.H.: *The arts in South Africa*. Durban, 1933.

– Ed.

FARRER, BERNARD ERIC, * 1879 in Hampstead; ° May 1916 on active service in East Africa. Violinist.

Farrer's first teacher at the old Hampstead Conservatoire was Hans Wessely. At a later stage he studied at the RAM and in 1903 he came to South Africa as organist in Port Elizabeth and as music teacher at Riebeeck College Girls' High School, Uitenhage. He was more than welcome in Port Elizabeth, often had to play the violin at concerts and occasionally acted as replacement organist for Roger Ascham.** On one occasion (at Ascham's 177th concert) he played the pianoforte. He left Port Elizabeth at the end of 1904 to work in Grahamstown, and later in Beaconsfield, Kimberley. In 1910 he was organist in King William's Town and music teacher at Dale College. Farrer joined the army in 1914. — Since 1905 he had been married to a music teacher, Margery Wakefield, who took his place at Dale College whilst he was absent on active service. She played a major part in the town's musical life. One of their children, a daughter (now Mrs Rosemary Cloete),** chose music as her profession.

WORKS
Onward, ever onward (Decor integer aevi), school song of the Diocesan Grammar School, KWT. Ms., between 1910 and 1914.   Saltarello for violin. Ms., before 1904.

SOURCES
EP Herald: Sept. 1903–Nov. 1904.   Information supplied by Mrs Rosemary Cloete.

– Ed.

FARRINGTON, FREDERICK, *31 October 1869, near Chester; ° 20 June 1931 on board the *Kenilworth Castle* between East London and Port Elizabeth. A school inspector of music who pioneered the tonic sol-fa system in the schools of the Eastern Cape.

Fred Farrington was the seventh of eight children born to an English father and a Welsh mother, Mary Evans, from whom he probably inherited his love of music. He had a fine tenor voice but was trained to become a school teacher. After a few years he found that opportunities in England were few and far between and in 1893 he emigrated to South Africa, just at the time that Sir Thomas Muir, Superintendent-General of Education in the Cape Colony, aimed at introducing the tonic sol-fa system into Cape Colonial education. He was appointed a music inspector of schools on 26 September 1894, but when the circuit became too large for one man, the Colony was divided into an Eastern and a Western Province (1897), of which the former was placed under Farrington and the latter under Arthur Lee. — In the Port Elizabeth-Uitenhage area, Farrington had the responsibility for music in 20 schools and in addition used his Saturday mornings to instruct teachers and pupil teachers in Port Elizabeth. By the end of the first year, 3 500 children were being musically instructed through tonic sol-fa, the London Tonic Sol-fa College had conducted its first examination in Port Elizabeth and 15 candidates had passed the elementary theory examination. During the next two years he supplemented this work with school choir competitions held in the Feathermarket Hall. The major award was a shield donated by the municipality, winning choirs received medals and each member of the winning choir was given a book prize. At the close of the competition, Farrington led the combined choirs in a series of tonic sol-fa exercises to illustrate the advantages of the method. For a period of about two years he was occupied in the East London–King William's Town area, but in 1902 he conducted a coronation concert in Port Elizabeth with 14 schools participating. Local singers assisted the effort, Roger Ascham** was at the organ and an orchestra conducted by Sign. Tardugno** contributed to the concert. — In this same year the Department of Education instituted book prizes for ear training in the schools of Port Elizabeth and Uitenhage. Competitions were held in 1903 and 1904. Farrington's attention was then diverted to the country districts, but in April 1910 he conducted about 400 children's voices in P.E., accompanied by an amateur orchestra and again assisted by Roger Ascham and vocalists. The programme consisted of 16 items. In September of the next year, the press announced that the Municipal Shield Competition would be revived and that Edward Sangster** would conduct the choir, but the interest in the competitions was waning. In July 1912 only three schools took part, and during 1913 and 1914 an eisteddfod took the place of the competition. The whole movement was eclipsed by the outbreak of Word War I. The last known occasion when Farrington conducted a children's choir was on 15 June 1915, when he directed a patriotic concert with a chorus of 550 voices. — As early as 1899, Farrington had established an annual schools' choral competition between East London and King William's Town. This was sponsored by the Education Department and was subsidised by the two municipalities. On 7 October at King William's Town, Frank Hyde** conducted a choir of 100 children who sang inter alia, James Hyde's** *Land of Good Hope*. The choir was accompanied by an orchestra conducted by E.J.C. Woodrow.** When the competition was held in East London, the orchestra of Franz Moeller** assisted. — For about four months in 1898 Farrington taught on the staff of the Midlands Seminary in Graaff Reinet, and introduced the sol-fa system; he also had considerable success in Queenstown. Between 1902 and 1904, when the Municipal Shield Competition was getting under way, Farrington started the District Challenge Shield Competition in which schools from Queenstown, Tarkastad, Cathcart and Sterkstroom competed. The Girls' High School at Queenstown appears to have won this shield quite regularly. — Part of his work was done in the Transkei, where he travelled on horseback or in a horse cart, on tracks instead of roads, and often through flooded rivers – at least three times he was washed along and once his horse was drowned. Another time he was thrown out of his cart on a very bad road and a wheel passed over him. During the last years of his service in the Department Farrington also interested himself in Black music education; in collaboration with Col. E. Smedley-Williams, he organised a Native Musical Association in East London and acted as adjudicator at the first competition. At St Matthew's College in Keiskama Hoek he stimulated a Black composer, J.T. Mtyobo. The development of Black choral music and the institution of choral competitions among the Blacks are movements with which he was closely associated. — He married in December 1909 and built his home on two adjoining farms which he had previously bought in the district Maclear. He retired in December 1924 to live there permanently and became an active member of the Divisional Council. In 1931 he decided to visit his surviving brothers in England, but died at sea shortly after his departure.

BIBLIOGRAPHY
Troskie, A.J.J.: *The musical life of Port Elizabeth, 1875–1900.* M.Mus. dissertation, UPE, 1969.

SOURCES
Henning, C.G.: The introduction of the tonic sol-fa system into the Eastern Cape. *Musicus* IV/1,2, 1976.   *Eastern Province Herald:* 1900–1920.   *East London Daily Dispatch:* 1900–1905.   *Queenstown Free Press:* Centenary issue, 1953.   Programmes in the KWT Museum.   Records of the School Board, Cape Colony.   Register of estates, Cape Province: No. 30875 of 1932.   Correspondence with Margaret de Wet (née Farrington) of Newlands, Cape Town.

– C.G.H.

FAUL, LOURENS ABRAM, *23 October 1931 in Johannesburg; now (1977) in Johannesburg. Head of the Music Department of the Johannesburg College of Education,** singer and composer.

During his schooling, Lourens Faul won the Joyce Behrman cup, the Trinity College cup and several diplomas and medals at Afrikaans eisteddfodau for singing and for choral work. In 1948 he became a student at the University of the Witwatersrand, where, three years later, he obtained the B.Mus. degree and in 1958 the M.Mus. degree. Meanwhile, he also qualified as a school teacher, obtaining the THED. From 1958–1961, aided by the Melanie Pollak Scholarship,** he studied at the Vienna State Academy of Music, concentrating on singing, pianoforte accompaniment and composition. After his return, he obtained the LTCL, LRSM, ULSM, and UTLM diplomas in singing after a period of study under Betsy de la Porte.** In Vienna he had gained considerable experience as co-repetitor, which he put to good use after his return by collaborating with the Operavereniging van Suid-Afrika** and the South African Federation for Opera** and by acting as choirmaster to the SABC. He founded the Lyra Sangkwartet (1962–1964) and was a member of the Boere Sangers and other SABC choirs and song groups. —From 1952 to 1955 he taught music at the Fakkel High School in Johannesburg and was organist to the Forest Hill DR Congregation (1949–1958). In 1961 he became senior lecturer in music at the Johannesburg College of Education and until 1963 he was also a part-time lecturer in singing and pianoforte at the University of the Witwatersrand. In 1968 he became Head of the Music Department of the Johannesburg College of Education. He has since obtained a D. Mus. degree at the University of Pretoria for a number of major compositions (1970). After attending a course on electronic music by Henk Badings at the SABC (1971) he was commissioned by the SABC to write an electronic study, which he did to words by Boerneef. This composition, *Malkopwoorde,* was broadcast on 23 March 1972. His musical comedy, *Lekkerleefland* (libretto Fanus Rautenbach), won second prize in R. Müller Ltd's** country-wide Otto Bach competition in 1971.

WORKS
A. Vocal

1. Works for theatre
Legend of the last miracle, opera. Ms., 1969.   Lekkerleefland, musical comedy (Fanus Rautenbach), awarded a second prize in Otto Bach's 1971 competition. Ms., 1971 (?).

2. School operettas
Prins van Monakatoo (Sophie Faul), 1957. DALRO, 1970.   Skoenmaker Stillewater (Sophie Faul), 1960. DALRO, 1971.   Die seemeeu roep (Sophie Faul), 1962. DALRO, 1970.   Mooifontein se meisies (Sophie Faul), 1964. DALRO, 1970.   Ons vir jou (Mike Heine). Ms., 1965.   Ponkie en sy donkie (Sophie Faul), 1974. DALRO, 1975.

3. Songs
Waar die wind die goue gras, four-part song (Sophie Faul). Ms., 1949.   Toera loera la, die winter is verby, three-part round (C.L. Leipoldt). Ms., 1952.   Al die veld is vrolik, three-part round (C.L. Leipoldt). Ms., 1952.   Kersliedjie (D.J. Opperman). Ms., 1961.   Man wat mal word, song (Peter Blum). Ms., 1963.   Banjo lullaby, carol (Brian Rose). Ms., 1964.   Daar's 'n oulike witkop kannetjie, song (Boerneef). Ms., 1964.   Hoe's dit nou met die jawoord? Four-part song (Boerneef). Ms., 1964.   Laat bokspring die kram, four-part song (Boerneef). Ms., 1964.   Die moed ontbreek my, song (Boerneef). Ms., 1964.   O Father, for our daily bread, two-part canon. Ms., 1964.   Wyn rym met pyn, four-part song (Boerneef). Ms., 1964.   Psalm 150, for tenor, soprano and organ. Ms., 1965.   Terugtog, four songs (W.E.G. Louw), awarded first prize in the national competition of the SA Composers' Society. Ms., 1965.   Dit is en bly nou emalso, song (Boerneef). Ms., 1966.   Twee slampamperliedjies, for a high voice with piano (C.L. Leipoldt), 1966. DALRO 1970: 1. Op my ou ramkietjie   2. Wys my die plek.   Christmas bells are ringing, carol. Ms., 1967.   Engele bring die blye tyding, four-part carol (composer and Sophie Faul). Ms., 1967.   Hoor hoe lui die vreugdeklokke, four-part carol. Ms., 1967.   In Bethlehem lui weer die klokke, four-part carol (Sophie Faul). Ms., 1967.   Ons velde is groen, unison carol. Ms., 1967.   Onder helder Suiderkruis, carol (composer and Sophie Faul). Ms., 1967.   Pennyworth of praise, three-part carol (Brian Rose). Ms., 1967.   Sing, vinkie, sing, three-part round (C.L. Leipoldt). Ms., 1967.   Vyf palissandryne, for mezzo-soprano, baritone and piano (Boerneef), 1967. DALRO, 1972: 1. My blokfluit   2. Die tortelduif   3. Die kwikkie   4. Van al my land se Tafelberge   5. Die bloedrooi kapokhaan.   Drie passieblomme, for solo voice and piano. Ms., 1968.   Fluit windswael, song (C.L. Leipoldt). Ms., 1968.   Met transistor innie hand, four-part song (Boerneef). Ms., 1972.   Pierambamba, four-part song (Boerneef). Ms., 1972.   Vir hierdie vygieplate en kleur heb dank, four-part song (Boerneef). Ms., 1972.   Ek het 'n vreemde voël hoor fluit, four-part song (Boerneef). Ms., 1973.   Praat van die ding, four-part song (Boerneef). Ms., 1973.   —

B. Instrumental

Phantasy for orchestra. Ms., 1965.   Sonata for two pianos. Ms., 1967.   Malkopwoorde, electronic composition (Boerneef), commissioned by the SABC. Ms., 1971.   Paradise lost, electronic ballet. Ms., 1973.

ARTICLE
Elektroniese musiek in Suid-Afrika. *Opus* 2/1, Nov.–Dec. 1970.

SOURCES
Otto Bach musical play competition. *Opus* 3/1, Sept–Oct. 1971.   *SAMT:* 81–87, 1971–1975.   Research Centre for South African Music, HSRC, Pretoria.

– Ed.

FEATHER MARKET HALL   R. Ascham, W. Baker, F. Bradley, J. Bredell, F. Farrington, E. R. Goodacre, Port Elizabeth II/2, II/7, Port Elizabeth Music Society, T. Robinson, R. Tardugno, J. S. Yates

FEDERATED MUSIC CLUBS OF SOUTH AFRICA   Durban Philharmonic Society, East London II/4, A. Hallis, Kimberley 2, King William's Town 2, B.M. Marx, Vryheid Musical Society

FEDERATION OF MUSIC SOCIETIES (EASTERN CAPE), THE. Before the inauguration of the Federation of Music Societies of the Eastern Cape at a meeting held at Rhodes University College (now Rhodes University) on 27 February 1949, there had been a loose arrangement between the Music Clubs of Port Elizabeth, Queenstown, East London, King William's Town, Cradock, Grahamstown, Graaff Reinet and Umtata to engage artists for tours of the Eastern Cape. Barend Smulian, who was then President of the Port Elizabeth Orchestral Society, took the initiative. — In about 1940 he called a meeting at Rhodes University College to form a Federation. Dr Smeath Thomas, then Principal of Rhodes University College, and Prof. F.H. Hartmann** submitted a proposal under which artists would be engaged by Rhodes, and tours be organised to cover the Eastern Cape. This arrangement, with Prof. James Irving as organiser, was carried on until about 1948, when the University decided it could no longer participate in the scheme. — A meeting to form a new Federation was held and the following Clubs became affiliated: the Port Elizabeth Orchestral Society (now the Music Society of Port Elizabeth),** the East London Association of Arts, the Queenstown and District Music Club, and the music clubs of King William's Town, Grahamstown, Cradock and Umtata. Barend Smulian became the first Chairman of the new Federation. — Plans were immediately set afoot to engage artists for 1949. Their tours were arranged through the headquarters of the Federation in Port Elizabeth. Amongst the artists who were engaged in the first year were Lili Kraus,** Tito Schipa and Harold Rubens; in subsequent years there were Pierre Fournier, Kathleen Long, Julius Katchen, the Loewenguth Quartet, Philippe Entremont and others. The subscriptions of the affiliated clubs made funds available at the beginning of each year, by means of which the Federation could present leading South African, as well as overseas artists for their concerts. — For lack of support, the music clubs at Umtata and Graaff Reinet ceased to function, but the other clubs are still

FEDERATION
active, particularly those in Port Elizabeth and Queenstown. With the exception of the Music Society of Port Elizabeth, all the clubs are now (1969) affiliated to CAPAB's concert organisation, although additional recitals by overseas artists are still arranged by the Clubs, depending on their resources. Usually a choice of 8 to 10 artists every year is offered to each of the federated clubs.

– B.S.

FEINHOLS, BERTHA Durban 5, Potchefstroom 2, Pretoria 2

FELDMAN, ANNE (Née TREGER), *28 December 1927 in Latvia; now (1977) in Johannesburg. Soprano and singing teacher.

The dancer Mitsava trained Anne Feldman in ballet from the time she was three years old. This continued until she was brought to South Africa in 1939. During her school days in Cape Town Anne had pianoforte tuition from Miss L. Brunt (1940–1948), and matriculated with distinction in Music. Subsequently she obtained the ATCL Diploma (pianoforte); but in the meantime she had begun her study of singing (1944), first under Sign. Paganelli in Cape Town, then under Francis Russell** in Johannesburg, and eventually under Helena Isepp in London (1953–1954). — In 1959 Mrs Feldman coached a Black choir in Johannesburg for a performance of *Elijah,* and appeared with them as soloist. The next year she was appointed singing teacher at the Joseph Edward Singing School (also known as the African Music and Drama Association – AMDA). Since then she has been active as soloist and coach of the Johannesburg African Music Society (JAMS), and in the productions of Union Artists. She was consequently involved in the productions of *King Kong* (1961) and *Sponono* (1963) and in the choral work of the Messiah Choir under the auspices of JAMS. Since 1963 she has also acted as musical director of the Insholo Civic Theatre. She has been a soloist with the symphony orchestras of Johannesburg and Cape Town, in chamber music programmes, and in concerts of Spanish and Jewish folk songs. For the South African Opera Federation** she sang the part of Norina in *Don Pasquale* (1961). The institution of the Regional Councils for the Performing Arts has led to engagements by CAPAB and PACOFS. Latterly she has been teaching music privately and at schools in Johannesburg.

– Ed.

FELLOWES, J. Johannesburg Philharmonic Society

FENTON, A. AND B. Barberton, Johannesburg 1, L. Searelle, Touring Theatre Groups 4, K.E.O. von Booth

FERGUSON-BROWN, J. Durban 3, 5, 6, Durban Amateur Operatic Society, Organs 2, Touring Theatre Groups 4

FEROS, CHRISTIE GEORGE, *9 April 1928 in Cape Town; now (1978) in Cape Town. Pianist and mathematician.

60

Feros commenced taking lessons in pianoforte in Cape Town, continued his studies in King William's Town (1940-1943), and was prepared for the performer's licentiate in music by Archie H. Iliffe-Higgo in Grahamstown (1944-1948). On the strength of his competence in this examination, he was awarded the overseas scholarship of UNISA and studied at the RAM under Leslie England. There he won the Matthew Phillimore and Kate Steele Memorial Prizes. — On his return to South Africa in 1952, Feros taught at the South African College of Music** until 1957, giving solo recitals for the University Music Society and also acting as accompanist to Noreen Berry, Emily Hook, Adelheid Armhold** and other prominent vocalists. He soon established a reputation as an exceptionally competent and sensitive accompanist and was often called upon by singers for recital tours in the Cape area. When the College of Music undertook its historic tour to England in 1956-1957, he was the accompanist in songs of Arnold van Wyk** Hubert du Plessis** and John Joubert,** sung in the Wigmore Hall, London. Apart from these activities, he is a radio recitalist, and has performed concertos with the Cape Town City Orchestra** and the Symphony Orchestra of the SABC. With Howard Ferguson and Arnold van Wyk, he has given duet recitals, also recording for HMV duets written by Arnold van Wyk and John Joubert, with Van Wyk as his partner. Since 1962 he has broadcast works for violin and piano with Artemisio Paganini. — Divided between his talents in mathematics and music, Feros became a lecturer in the Department of Applied Mathematics in the University of Cape Town, when he resigned from the teaching staff of the South African College of Music in 1957.

– Ed.

FERRAMOSCA, E.   Stella Blakemore, L. Danza, Johannesburg 3(ii)

FERRANTI, M.   Pietermaritzburg

FERRI, E.   F. Dalberg

FESTIVAL CHOIR   Port Elizabeth II/3, Port Elizabeth Amateur Choral and Orchestral Music

FESTIVAL ORCHESTRA   J. Connell, Johannesburg

FIASCONARO, GREGORIO, *5 March 1915 in Palermo; now (1977) in Cape Town. Baritone, opera producer and Director of the University Opera School of the University of Cape Town.

Son of the soprano, Rosalia Calderoni, Fiasconaro appeared on the operatic stage for the first time when he was 7 years old, singing the child's phrase in Act II of *La Bohème*. Serious musical study started four years later, and in 1932 voice training commenced at the Paganini Conservatoire in Genoa. In 1935 this was continued at the Academia Santa Cecilia in Rome, now supplemented by classes in drama and opera production. Since his debut in the role of Germont (sr.) in *La traviata,* he has interpreted in all some 38 roles in 34 operas. The majority of these were leading roles in the mainly Romantic Italian repertoire. — During the war he was a pilot in the Italian Air Force, until he was taken prisoner in 1942 and interned in South Africa. After the war he became known in this country by his singing with the orchestras in

Cape Town, Durban and Johannesburg and in radio recitals. Aware of his potential, Prof. Chisholm** appointed him as teacher of singing at the S.A. College of Music** in Cape Town in 1949, anticipating a considerable expansion of training in opera to come. John Connell** also made use of his singing in the opera season at His Majesty's Theatre** when *La Bohème, Madame Butterfly* and *Faust* were produced in 1951. The next year Chisholm established his Opera School and University Opera Company at the College of Music and appointed Fiasconaro as its director. — From 1952 to 1977 he has produced with his School, in two seasons a year, more than 40 operas in close on 100 productions; in addition he has supervised about 18 student productions of mainly one-act theatre pieces. Many of his University productions were also seen outside Cape Town, ranging as far afield as Durban, Johannesburg and Bloemfontein. — With the establishment of the Regional Councils a new era started in which the University Company co-operated with CAPAB in joint productions or in providing CAPAB with operas which were staged in Cape Town, or sent on tours in the Cape and at times in other provinces. This fruitful co-operation was brought to its logical conclusion in 1971 when the Nico Malan Theatre was inaugurated in Cape Town. Fiasconaro produced *Aïda* for this occasion and, in the same year, also *Madame Butterfly*. The next year he became a member of CAPAB'S Opera Committee and produced four operas for this Council in 1972, and five in 1973. Since these two peak years he has averaged two operas per year. Some of these were also staged in Durban and Bloemfontein as well as in Windhoek for SWAPAC and in Johannesburg/Pretoria for PACT. In all, Fiasconaro has been responsible for the staging of 125 productions of 51 operas, which entitles him to be called the most active opera producer in South Africa. In 1952 he was distinguished by being asked to act as co-producer of *The Trojans* (Berlioz) and in 1953 the Cape Tercentenary Foundation's Award was conferred on him for his contributions to opera during the period 1950–1952. The University of Cape Town acknowledged his contributions to the educational establishment of training in opera by promoting him to an Associate Professorship in 1972. — His association with the EOAN Opera Group** started in 1957 when he produced the sensational performance of *La traviata* in Italian, with a complete cast of Coloured singers. He assisted them until 1962 and directed their productions in Cape Town, Johannesburg, Port Elizabeth and Durban. — In 1960 the Carnegie Foundation awarded him a travelling scholarship for the study of opera production in the United States of America. A year later he was responsible for the world première of John Joubert's** *Silas Marner* in the Little Theatre** in Cape Town. A highlight of his career was the visit of the University Company to England under the direction of Eric Chisholm. They sang *The consul* and treated London to the first stage performance of *Bluebeard's castle* (Bartok), with Fiasconaro singing the title role in his own production of the Bartok. This was the first time that a South African opera company had ventured to reverse the usual procedure of British companies visiting South Africa.

SOURCES
Cape Argus: 14 May 1969.   *Cape Times:* 6 Aug. 1960; 4 Apr. 1964; 30 May 1964; 20 Mar. 1965: 19 June 1965.   *Personality:* 7 Mar. 1963.   *Res Musicae:* VI/1, Sept. 1959. Numerous reviews in various newspapers.   Research Centre for South African Music, HSRC, Pretoria.

– J.P.M.

FICK, F.E. (MRS ROODE)   D.J. Roode

FIELD, LIONEL   E.G. Draycott, East London II, F.B.M. Moeller, Port Elizabeth, Port Elizabeth Amateur Choral and Orchestral Music, Port Elizabeth Music Society

FILLIS, LEONARD MILFORD (LEN), *in 1903 in Cape Town; ° 19 June 1953 in Johannesburg. Player of banjo, guitar and Hawaiian guitar.

At the age of ten Len Fillis began to play the banjo and four years later toured through South Africa with his brother and his sister as the Fillis Trio. After two years of vaudeville he joined the dance band of Edgar Adeler** in Johannesburg. In 1923 he went to England where he stayed for fifteen years, actively engaged, first as a member of the bands of Jack Hylton and Fred Elizalde, and subsequently as a free-lance musician. He made several records and featured in radio programmes. In 1938 he toured Australia, where he remained until 1946 on account of the Second World War. He moved to England after the war, but his health was so poor that he returned to South Africa some months later. During the last seven years of his life he was able to give occasional performances in Johannesburg (see Discography).

PUBLICATION
The plectrum guitar method. Lawrence Wright, London, n.d.

– C.G.

FINCH, THELMA (MRS DENNIS)   E.J. Dennis

FINCKEN, MARY EVELINE, *27 April 1882 in the village of Hoyland, near Barnsley in Yorkshire; ° 15 June 1955 in Cape Town. Contralto and eminent teacher of singing.

Eveline Fincken was the eldest daughter of Christopher William Fincken of Hoyland Hall. The family was of Swedish-German stock and settled in Bristol as sugar-refiners at the beginning of the reign of George I. Her grandfather and his sons were enthusiastic amateur organ builders and musicians, and her father became an able amateur organist. On her mother's side there were a number of singers in the North of England Choral Societies, one of her aunts being a teacher of Clara Butt. An early environmental influence was choral singing on Sunday afternoons and evenings at Hoyland Hall, where local Prize Bands often treated the little community to open-air concerts. — These pleasant days ended when Miss Fincken's father died in 1894; her mother had preceded him by five years. Handicapped by poor eyesight and a rheumatic heart, Eveline attended school at Sheffield and Manchester, where she distinguished herself with a beautiful voice and a talent for organizing her companions into concert parties, charades and the like. When she was 17, she was awarded a gold medal for singing at an eisteddfod in Manchester, and this decided her on a singing career. An appointment in 1903, as assistant teacher at Gunnusbury High School in London, paved the way and provided a means of subsistence. In this year, she won a scholarship to the RAM, where she studied singing under the direction of

FINCKEN

William Shakespeare, obtaining the LRAM in 1905. — Still in 1905, Miss Fincken made her debut in a concert with the Queen's Hall Orchestra, conducted by Henry Wood, after which she was soloist at a performance of *Elijah* in Rochdale. This was followed by engagements in London and other parts of England, and an appointment in London as singing mistress at Wentworth Hall, a ladies' finishing school. The London climate was seriously affecting her health, however, and she was advised to visit South Africa, where she arrived in 1908. This recuperative visit turned into permanent residence. — Shortly after her arrival, Eveline sang in the City Hall in Cape Town, and later also in the principal cities of the interior. Thus she visited Bloemfontein during October and November of 1911, and gave two song recitals, also a lecture recital in the hall of the Normal College. On the latter occasion she analysed a variety of songs before interpreting them for the audience. In Cape Town, she was one of the initiators of the South African College of Music,** and when this college was incorporated in the University of Cape Town, she became senior lecturer in singing (1912). She devoted herself more and more to education, which she had come to recognise as her true vocation, engaged in music educational tours under the aegis of the Education Department, and later arranged University extension courses in music, coupled with tours to various Cape centres. From the proceeds of these concerts she established the first overseas scholarships for students at the College. Among Miss Fincken's pupils were prominent singing personalities such as Cecilia Wessels,** Mabel Lewin (Mabella Ott-Penetto**), Jessie Sonnenberg** and Albina Bini.** — Closely related to her educational work was the founding of the Melodic Society (1911), of which she was Life President, and the creation of the Eveline Fincken Ladies' Choir, which she conducted personally. She was also co-founder of the Women's Business and Efficiency Club. Her work for the advancement of musical culture in South Africa was recognised by the RAM, when in 1920 they conferred on her an honorary ARAM. She also became a member of the New Education Fellowship, and was responsible for the organization of the music section during the World Conference in South Africa in 1932. — When in 1935 her health started failing, Miss Fincken retired from the College of Music. After a farewell concert at the City Hall, she left for London, where she was a founder of two Clarendon Clubs, hostels for overseas' students. The clubs were severely damaged during air raids. In 1943 she returned to South Africa, and once again became prominent as a teacher and organiser of concerts. She even revived her ladies' choir. — This greatly respected woman and inspiring personality had a wide circle of interests and friendships among many sections of the Cape community. At her death, the South African Broadcasting Corporation paid her a tribute, as a pioneer artist of the microphone when a Cape service was instituted in 1924. She bequeathed her valuable collection of music to the Non-White section of the Public Library in Cape Town. — Miss Fincken is survived by a sister in England, Irene Alice Fincken, who had a reputation as a teacher of pianoforte and as a conductor of female choirs, and by a brother, Vernon S.T. Fincken, a past conductor of military bands and choirs; who lives in South Africa and is known as an organist.

SOURCES
The Eveline Fincken vocal library foundation. *SAMT* 41, Dec. 1951.   In memoriam. *SAMT* 49, Dec. 1955.

– V.S.T.F.

FINCKEN, V.S.T.   E. Fincken

FINE, TOBY, *6 October 1932, in Johannesburg; now (1977) in Cape Town. Ballet dancer.

While she studied under Marjorie Sturman** in Johannesburg, Toby Fine won the Transvaal Ballet Championship four years in succession and the South African Ballet Championship three years in succession. In 1949 she was awarded a bursary to study overseas. She studied in Europe with Vera Volkova, Mary Skeaping and Preobrajenska, before becoming a member of the New York City Ballet. During her two years with the company, she had George Balanchine, Jerome Robbins, Vladimiroff and Oboukhoff as her mentors. — On her return to South Africa in 1952, Toby Fine danced leading roles with the Johannesburg Festival Ballet Company, and later with the University of Cape Town Ballet.** She has also appeared with Fonteyn, Markova, Dolin, Gilpin, Poole** and Wright.

– M.G.

FINE, WENDY MARION,*19 December 1938 in Durban; at present (1978) connected with the Opera in Munich. Lyric soprano.

With all the advantages of a musical home (her father is an amateur tenor singer and her mother an enthusiastic amateur opera singer), Wendy Fine exhibited her natural talent for singing at an early age. Starting in her twelfth year, John van Zyl** took her voice production in hand, after which she became a regular competitor in Eisteddfodau, winning medals and other prizes for her interpretations of songs and extracts from oratorios. In 1958 she won the Gustav Hallé bursary for the most polished vocal performance in any section of the Durban Eisteddfod. She also sang with the Durban City Orchestra** in a programme devoted to opera extracts and Afrikaans songs, and broadcast a number of radio programmes. — In the year in which she became of age, she left South Africa for voice training at the State Academy in Vienna. Maria Hittorff took charge of her voice and she gained theatre experience by participation in the Academy's chamber opera class and their productions in the Schönbrunn palace theatre. She was awarded a bursary for performance in the Master class for the Lieder-art and in 1961 she completed the course with distinction. On this occasion she received a special diploma for "exceptional artistic merit". During and after these years of study she was given parts in TV as well as radio productions. In 1962 she sang the female lead in Stravinsky's *Mavra* and in the following year she was awarded a prize during the International Mozart Festival. — Embarked on a professional career since 1963, Wendy Fine was engaged as a lyric soprano by the opera in Berne (1963–1965), Wiesbaden (1965–1968; another South African, Hans van Heerden,** was engaged by the same opera at the same time), and Cologne (1968–1971). In Cologne she soon gained a reputation as an exceptionally gifted singer and the circle of her engagements spread to include eventually Hamburg, Frankfurt, Stuttgart, Munich, Berlin, Paris, Zürich, Madrid, Lisbon, London, Amsterdam, Bayreuth (Wagner Festivals), Prague and La Scala in Milan. New demands were continually made on her; consequently her repertoire of operas grew steadily and now (1978) comprises about 200 roles, including works sung in Czech (*Jenufa*) and Russian *(Boris*

FINE

Goudonov). In this total there are the *Ring* (Wagner), *Rosenkavalier* (Strauss), *The bartered bride* (Smetana,), sung in Czech and also a film success; further, the standard Italian operas, the works of Mozart, and numerous contemporary operas like *The rake's progress* (Stravinsky), *Aufstieg und Fall der Stadt Mahagonny* (Křenek), *Die Hexenjagd* (Robert Ward), *Wozzeck* (Alban Berg – a splendid production in Munich), *Der junge Lord* (Henze), *Hamlet* (Sándor Szokolay), *Delilah* (Sándor Szokolay – composed for her voice after the composer had experienced it in *Hamlet*). Since her debut in Covent Garden in 1971, she has repeatedly been a guest artist in this theatre. An exceptional occasion was in 1977 when she sang before the Queen in a jubilee production of Janácek's *Jenufa*. Her American debut took place in 1973 and in 1978 she again sang in *Jenufa,* but this time in Prague and in Czech. She was booked in 1978 by CAPAB for *Eugen Onegin* staged in Cape Town in 1979. This was her first appearance in South Africa since her departure in 1959. — She rarely sings in concert recitals, because she regards herself as a "singing actress" and not as a solo singer. She has nevertheless sung over 100 times with orchestras: in Cologne (very often with the conductor Carlos Kleiber), Paris (Georg Sholti conducting) and London (i.a. with Pierre Boulez, conducting the BBC Orchestra). In Zürich, Amsterdam and Berlin she has taken part in TV productions of operas and, also in Berlin, has herself staged TV programmes in which narrative is combined with vocal performance in costume.

SOURCE
Serfontein, Pieter: Wendy Fine, Suid-Afrikaanse sopraan van wêreldformaat. *Lantern,* Mar. 1972.

– J.P.M.

FIORE, CAMILLO, *26 October 1884 in Gallichio, near Naples; ° 11 September 1929 in East London. Pianist, conductor and author of a few slight works.

Camillo Fiore received his musical training at the Royal Academy of Music in Naples, and at the age of sixteen qualified as pianist, with harp as his second instrument. He subsequently conducted orchestras in Italy and Egypt, and settled in Pretoria in 1905. He moved to Lourenço Marques after his marriage in 1909, but returned to Johannesburg in 1912. His wife, Esther Lombard, was sent to Gallichio in 1915, where she died in 1917, survived by a five-year-old son. Fiore married again in July, 1921, and settled in East London in July, 1922. As local musical director of African Theatres, he conducted the "orchestra" and played the piano in the Vaudette Theatre, until 1929. An "orchestra" bearing his name gave a series of three concerts in East London in 1922, and performed in The Lounge Tea Rooms during the holiday season of 1923–1924. — As a harpist, Fiore was a member of the East London Municipal Orchestra under Franz Moeller.** In 1928 he was appointed conductor of this orchestra, which gave about sixteen concerts under his direction, generally providing music of a light character. At a concert on 13 January the programme included three of his own compositions. In 1927 he conducted incidental music for the stage performances of Sybil Thorndike and Fay Compton. (Also see Music in East London, II/2)

WORKS
The fighting port, march. Ewins & Co., East London, 1929.   Two pieces. Ewins & Co., East London, 1929: 1. On the lake   2. The white dove.

BIBLIOGRAPHY
Van der Merwe, F.Z.: *Suid-Afrikaanse musiekbibliografie,* 1787–1952. J.L. van Schaik, Pretoria, 1958.

SOURCES
Daily Dispatch: 1922–1929.   Information supplied by Mrs A.M. Richardson of Johannesburg.

– Ed.

FISCHER, MRS C.   Piano Music II/2

FISCHER, FREDERIK S. (FRED), *11 November 1917 in Senekal; resident in Germiston in 1970. School principal, singer and leader of a "Boereorkes".

Since his seventh year Freddie Fischer had musical tuition which was continued after 1927 in Schweizer-Reneke. In 1930 his schoolteachers insisted that he be given the opportunity of appearing on the stage with the boy soprano, Philip (Flippie) Theunissen. This led to a tour of South Africa (excepting Natal) with Theunissen, and to the distinction of singing with the Municipal Orchestra of Cape Town conducted by William Pickerill.** From 1938–1940 he was a student at the Teachers Training College at Potchefstroom and in great demand as a solo vocalist with choirs and as a pianist in the College orchestra. — His career as a teacher started in Johannesburg in 1942, but he often appeared as a pianist and singer with the "Boere"-dance bands of Jock du Toit, Sam Petzer, Arnout Malherbe, Hansie van Loggerenberg,** Hendrik Susan** and Freddie Luyt. He recorded for the firms of Gallo, Trutone and Teale. Freddie Fischer started his own ensemble in 1950 and in 1954 won the SABC trophy for the best national broadcasting ensemble. It was regularly engaged for variety programmes; Fischer himself acted as substitute pianist at broadcasts of early morning physical exercises. — As a teacher, Freddie Fischer exerted himself to advance music at the Kensington High School and by training choirs. He is now principal of a primary school in Germiston.

– Ed.

FISCHER, PETA   Musica Viva Society

FISMER, MARIA VAN DER LINGEN (NéE VON WIELLIGH), *7 July 1889 in Pretoria; °3 June 1953 on her farm in Magoebaskloof. Musical pedagogue and third principal of the Conservatoire of Music of the University of Stellenbosch.**

Maria Fismer's father was Surveyor-General of the Zuid-Afrikaansche Republiek and one of the first Afrikaans writers; her mother was a talented daughter of Jan S. de Villiers** of Paarl. When the Anglo-Boer War broke out, Mrs Von Wielligh** moved to the Boland with her children and when, shortly after the war, her husband was virtually blinded in an accident, she and her sister Nancy de Villiers** established the Villieria School of Music in Stellenbosch. In 1905 this school was incorporated into the new Conservatoire of Music.** When Maria's talent became evident she received lessons from F.W. Jannasch** and by the time she was eighteen years old, she had obtained all the certificates for piano and organ playing available at the time. She started her music career in Britstown in 1907. During the same year her mother retired from the Conservatoire and settled in Robertson where she was organist and taught music until her death a few months later. Maria then left Britstown to take up her mother's post as organist and teacher of music, so successfully, that she drew pupils to Robertson from other parts of the country. Meanwhile she continued her own studies, supplemented with journeys to London, where she obtained the LRAM and ARCM diplomas of the Royal Colleges. — In 1917 she married Walter Fismer, a surveyor who was also a good violinist, but she kept her music practice going until her husband's death in 1933. In 1934 the University of Stellenbosch bought the Conservatoire from Hans Endler** and invited Maria Fismer to join the staff. She remained at the Conservatoire from 1935 until she retired in 1951, initially as a member of the staff, while the administration of the Conservatoire was controlled by the University, and from 1939 onwards as Professor and Principal of the institution. — The thoroughness and meticulous devotion to duty that had distinguished her music practice in Robertson, made Maria Fismer consider the training of organists and music teachers in the Stellenbosch Conservatoire a vocation. Under her guidance the educational work in Stellenbosch was consolidated and given a purposiveness which achieved a fine reputation in all parts of the country through the dependability and enthusiasm of the students. It is no exaggeration to say that Maria Fismer became the Afrikaans woman who exerted the greatest influence on the training of organists and music teachers in South Africa until 1950. — Her meritorious service to the country was duly recognised when the Suid-Afrikaanse Akademie vir Wetenskap en Kuns** awarded her an honorary medal (1952), and when the University of Stellenbosch conferred on her an honorary doctorate in music (1951). While Jannasch and Endler were the pioneers who provided the conditions for establishing a musical centre, Maria Fismer consolidated their work within the framework of the University.

BIBLIOGRAPHY
Behrens, R.: *Gedenkblad.* Conservatoire of Music of the University of Stellenbosch. Pro Ecclesia Printers, Stellenbosch, 1955.

SOURCES
Grootgeword met musiek. *Sarie Marais,* 17 Jan. 1951.   Kotzé, D.J.: Sy het gelewe vir musiek. *Die Huisgenoot,* 24 July 1953.   *Die Burger:* 5 June 1953 (obituary).   Research Centre for South African Music, HSRC, Pretoria.

– J.P.M.

FISMER, W.   M. van der L. Fismer

FLAMAND, YVONNE (NéE CORKE), *29 August 1907 in Croix, France; living in Johannesburg in 1970. Mezzo-soprano.

Yvonne received her musical education at the Paris Conservatoire of Music, and made her debut as a soloist on the Radiodiffusion Française. Her operatic career commenced in 1936; ten years later she was engaged at the Paris Grand Opera. Subsequently, under the French conductor, Albert Wolff, she sang in *L'Enfant et les sortiléges* (Ravel) and *Pelleas et Melisande* (Debussy), and at the Teatro San Carlo in Naples, the Opera House in Rome and the Teatro Communale in Bologna. In 1948 she accompanied the Paris Opera to London, where she sang under Thomas Beecham in *Les Troyens* (Berlioz). — Yvonne Flamand came to South Africa in 1950. Here she has sung with the SABC Orchestra and, during the Van Riebeeck Festival in Cape Town in 1952, again interpreted her part in *Les Troyens*. In France she sang under her maiden name, Yvonne Corke, but in South Africa Yvonne Flamand has adopted her husband's name.

— Ed.

FLINK, MAISIE (MRS ALEC SILVER), * in Zeerust; living in Johannesburg in 1967. Pianist.

Maisie Flink was started on her musical career by her mother, followed by tuition at a convent school in East London, which she entered when she was twelve. Good results in music examinations earned her bursaries and when she was sixteen she had obtained the LTCL diploma. After her matriculation she became in succession a pupil of Horace Barton** in Johannesburg, P.J. Lemmer** in Bloemfontein and finally of Adolph Hallis** in Johannesburg. In 1947 she studied for a further year under Nadia Riesenberg in the USA. — From 1944 to 1946 she partnered Harold Ketelbey** in his broadcast series devoted to the sonata, also participating in his chamber music series in the Library Theatre. Among the South African "firsts" which she performed, are the *Pianoforte concerto in G minor* by Kabalevsky and the *Preludes for pianoforte* by Schostakovitch. She is also well-known as a radio recitalist and as a teacher.

— L.W.

FOCKENS, W. Pretoria 1, P. van den Burg

FOLI, SIGNOR (ALLAN JAMES FOLEY), *7 August 1835 in Cahir, Tipperary, Ireland; °20 October 1899 in Southport, England. Bass.

Before making his debut in *Othello* in 1862, Allan James Foley had lived in America and had studied singing in Naples. For his first performance in Paris in 1864 he changed his name to Signor Foli. Thus Italianated he became famous in opera houses and concert halls in Europe, England and America. Six years before his death, he came to Cape Town where, on 22 June 1893, he gave a recital of arias and songs by Meyerbeer, Gounod and Mendelssohn (accompaniment: T. Barrow-Dowling).** After that he went to Kimberley to sing the bass part in Haydn's *The Creation,* and then on to Johannesburg and Pretoria for a series of six concerts. His concert tour also included the Eastern Province and Natal, and ended in Cape Town where he took part in a performance of *Messiah* with a choir consisting of 300 members and an orchestra conducted by Barrow-Dowling. — On 6 September 1893 he left South Africa *en route* to England.

FOLI

BIBLIOGRAPHY
Wolpowitz, Lily: *James and Kate Hyde and the development of music in Johannesburg up to the First World War.* D. Mus. thesis, UP, 1965.

SOURCE
The Cape Argus and Cape Mercantile Advertiser XXXVIII: 8307 (19 June 1893) to 8378 (9 Sept. 1893).

– J.B.

FONTEYN, M.   Ballet I/11, M. Sturman

FOOTE, DAVID, *7 February 1873 in London; °17 June 1927 in Johannesburg. Conductor and composer.

His father, Samuel Foote** (originally Dutch, Voet, anglicized to Foote), settled in Johannesburg with his family in 1889. David was articled to a Johannesburg attorney, Charles Leonard, but exchanged the legal profession for music. "I soon found out that the only bar that suited me, was a bar of music", he wrote in later days. Completely self-taught, he was particularly gifted in the art of improvisation and extempore harmonization. When the Old Empire, later known as the New Empire, was re-opened as a vaudeville theatre in 1894 (on the site of the first Globe Theatre), Foote became conductor of the orchestra. In approximately 1913–1914 this led to his appointment as Chief Musical Director of African Theatres, so that practically his whole adult life was spent in conducting theatre orchestras. He was largely responsible for bringing the orchestra of the Empire Theatre to a pitch of excellence commended by local and visiting artists. — During World War I Foote organised and conducted a continuous series of Sunday-evening orchestral concerts at the Orpheum Theatre. The orchestra of 45 members presented to the public "the kind of music you love", and it became extremely popular. This was the first attempt after 1914 to maintain an orchestra in Johannesburg. On 3 October 1926, tribute was paid to Dave Foote** and James Hyde,** when these two pioneers of orchestral music in Johannesburg were invited to conduct items at a concert in the Orpheum; afterwards they were crowned with laurel wreaths. This particular concert was one of a new series begun by Theo Wendt** on 6 June, featuring his newly created Johannesburg Symphony Orchestra. A second series was given in 1927, with Lyell-Tayler,** P.R. Kirby,** Harold Ketelbey** and David Foote** conducting in turn. — Described by Beatrice Marx** as an "accomplished musician . . . (whose) . . . modest bearing belied his talent as a composer, and first-class director of his fine band of players", David Foote quietly and expertly devoted his talents to the advancement of music, always ready to assist individuals as well as groups.

WORKS
Egyptian serenade, revised and orchestrated by P.R. Kirby. Ms. in SABC Music Library, n.d.   As ek in jou twee ogies kyk, song for soprano and orchestra. Ms., n.d.   Chanson de la deux, song for soprano and orchestra. Ms., n.d.   Ek het gedroom, song for soprano and orchestra. Ms., n.d.   Serenade, for soprano and orchestra. Ms., n.d.   A woman's last word,

for soprano and orchestra. Review in *The Star,* 2 May 1904.   Captain Arminie's song, for soprano and orchestra. Review in *The Star,* 2 May 1904.   Follow my leader, prologue for orchestra. Ms., n.d.   Merchant of Venice, intermezzo for orchestra. Ms., n.d.   The wrath of Ra, dramatic scena, produced at the Empire Theatre. Verbal communication, unratified.   The magic key, musical fantasy on a libretto by L.E. Salomon. Produced by Muriel Alexander at the Palladium Theatre, 24–29 Oct. 1921.

BIBLIOGRAPHY
Aronowsky, S.: *Performing times of orchestral works.* Ernest Benn Ltd, London, 1959.   Chilvers, H.A.: *Out of the crucible.* Cassell, London, 1929.   Marx, B.: *She shall have music. The memoirs of B. Marx.* W.J. Flesch & Partners, Cape Town, 1961.

SOURCES
The Star: 2 May 1904; 17 July 1927 (obituary).   Papers and notes concerning the Foote family in the Strange Library of Africana, Johannesburg Municipal Library.

– L.W.

FOOTE (VOET), SAMUEL, *1848 in Amsterdam; °5 March 1905 in Johannesburg. Baritone.

After living in London for several years, Foote decided to try his luck on the diamond fields of Kimberley (1888), but eventually he settled in Johannesburg (1889) where his home became a popular venue for musical evenings. Said to have been a concert singer in Holland, Foote had an excellent baritone voice and some acting ability. On 28 April 1889 he sang in public for the first time at a vocal and instrumental Sunday evening concert which he had organised to take place in the Globe Theatre. This vogue of having concerts on Sunday evenings was continued in Johannesburg for many years. He also took part in opera productions staged in the golden city after 1890.

SOURCES
The Star: Apr. 1889–Mar. 1905.   Papers and notes on the Foote family in the Strange Library of Africana, Johannesburg Municipal Library.

– L.W.

FORBES, D.J.   Potchefstroom 1

FORD, ARTHUR JAMES, *11 February 1877 in England; °27 July 1937 in East London. Conductor.

Ford arrived in South Africa from England in April 1896 and was subsequently trained in the Railway Training College in Cape Town. Equipped as a clerk, he accepted an appointment in the office of the System Manager in Port Elizabeth and served there until 1899, after which he was employed with the rank of station master in a succession of towns till 1908. In February 1926 he finally became a special grade station master in East London and occupied this position until November 1929 when he had to retire, probably on account of uncertain health. — This railwayman became a very popular figure in musical circles, on account of his useful tenor voice and conducting ability. He sang roles in performances of oratorios and concert versions of operas and played a prominent part in the creation of the Orpheus Male Voice Party, which he conducted after 1928, and of the East London Choral Society. He conducted this group in 1928–1929 and again for the last seven years of his life. Under his guiding hand they won the Challenge Shield of the Eisteddfod Society for three years running (1928–1930) and again in 1934 and 1936. With Ford conducting, they were also successful at eisteddfodau in Port Elizabeth and Johannesburg. When the East London Operatic and Dramatic Society produced *Our Miss Gibbs* in 1931, he acted as music director and in 1933 he again took the lead when *Il trovatore* was produced in a concert version, with the Choral Society co-operating. Apart from his choral work, Ford also played the viola in Franz Moeller's East London Municipal Orchestra, of which he was for a while the second conductor. — To commemorate his work in East London the Choral Society presented a silver shield to the Eisteddfod Committee for competition by ladies' choirs.

SOURCE
Daily Dispatch: 1926–1938.

– Ed.

FORD, DOROTHY, WIFE OF   Hermann Becker

FORESTA, BERTHA   Krugersdorp

FORREST, ADA (MRS CHERRY KEARTON), *17 July 1877 in Congella, Natal; ° 19 January 1966 in London. South African soprano who achieved international recognition.

Ada Forrest was instructed in music by Rabbi Woolfe in Barberton and by Sister Mary Gertrude in a Durban convent until 1898, when she left for the RAM where she studied for two years under Arthur Oswald. During her first year in London she won the Sims Reeves bursary for solo singing. In October, 1900, she returned to Durban and gave several recitals, before she decided to make England her permanent home. — On the recommendation of Dame Clara Butt, she made her debut in the Royal Albert Hall in 1906. She concentrated on oratorios, but also became a noted concert singer, who performed with conductors such as Hans Richter, Thomas Beecham and Henry Wood; composers such as C.H. Parry, Amy Woodforde-Finden, Eric Coates and Coleridge-Taylor wrote songs for her. In addition to a visit to the Continent, she undertook a few concert tours of South Africa, but her finest achievement was in England (see Discography). — She was married twice. Her first husband was Allen Hawes, an able amateur actor and singer, who contributed a good deal to music in Durban in the form of choir-training. He died in 1914. She married the famous explorer and nature-photographer, Cherry Kearton, in 1923, relinquished her singing career and accompanied her husband on his journeys. He died in 1940 but she preferred to remain in London, where she wrote her two books and a few articles dealing with their journeys.

PUBLICATIONS
My life as the Natal nightingale. *The Outspan,* 13 Feb. 1948. *Under African skies. On safari.* Robert Hale, London, 1956. *Penguin island.* Hutchinson, London, 1960.

BIBLIOGRAPHY
Jackson, G.S.: *Music in Durban from 1850 to 1900.* D.Phil. thesis, UWits, 1961.

SOURCES
Stegmann, Frits: Ada Forrest, die nagtegaal van Natal. *Die Burger,* 29 June 1961. *Daily Dispatch:* 3 Sept. 1898.

– F.S.

FORSTER, E.A.   S. Whitehouse

FORTESCUE, VIRGINIA, *20 May 1922 in Marycueter, Scotland; now (1977) in Port Elizabeth. Pianist and lecturer.

Virginia Fortescue studied with Frederick Moore at the RAM (1940–1943), obtaining the LRAM diplomas for performance and teaching. During the latter part of World War II she accompanied ENSA on their tours of Ceylon and India and when peace came she studied for six years (1946–1951) with Frieda Kindler, a pupil of Busoni and the widow of the composer, Bernard van Dieren. In 1948 she made her debut as a concert artist in the Wigmore Hall, London, where she has appeared many times since then. In Britain she toured with orchestras, and in 1956 left for South Africa at the invitation of Prof. Chisholm, to become a lecturer in piano at the South African College of Music.** She obtained the B.Mus. degree at the College in 1958. — Since then she has become known in Southern Africa as a soloist in concert and radio recitals. Together with Pierre de Groote** and Granville Britton** she maintained for a while the Virginia Fortescue Trio. In 1970 she accepted a senior appointment as lecturer in pianoforte at the University of Port Elizabeth.

PUBLICATION
An open letter to a young artist. *SAMT* 77, Dec. 1969.

SOURCES
SABC Bulletin, 21 Oct. 1957.   Who's who. *SAMT* 85, Jan. 1974.

– Ed.

FORT HARE INSTITUTION   Bantu Composers of South Africa, R. Mngoma, J. Mohapeloa, B. Tyamzashe

FOSTER, the name of four musically gifted brothers who were prominent in Johannesburg's musical life.

FOSTER

Francis Foster (Frank), harpist and pianist, arrived with his brother **Edgar,** a cellist, in 1903. Edgar's health failed, and he died shortly after their arrival. In 1912 **Lorenzo,** an accomplished violinist, joined Francis in Johannesburg, followed shortly after- wards by their parents and two other brothers: **William,** who played double bass and pianoforte, and eventually the experienced and widely travelled violinist, **Edward.** During and after the 1920s the names of these four brothers occur variously as soloists, accompanists and members of chamber-music groups and orchestras, as well as in light musical entertainments. The father, William Crump Foster, died in Johan- nesburg in 1924 at the age of 83 years.

– Ed.

FOSTER, FRANCIS, *2 December 1878 in Sheffield, England; °9 December 1959 in Johannesburg. Pianist, harpist and music teacher.

Francis Foster was instructed in pianoforte playing by his brother, William, but his real interest was centered on the harp, an instrument which he taught himself to play. He progressed so well that, still in his teens, he earned his first professional fee by playing the harp in the Oswald Stoll Theatres in Wales. In 1903 he and his brother Edgar (cellist) came to South Africa and joined Madame Cheron's** Concert Party. Other members of the party were Avon Saxon (baritone) and Rodine (violinist). The two brothers should have gone on to Australia with the party, but Edgar's health failed, and Francis remained in South Africa with his brother who died shortly afterwards. — For a while Francis acted as pianist-conductor to Fillis's Circus, but when the Moody-Manners Opera Company arrived in Durban in August 1904, he joined them as harpist, touring the country until April 1905, when he settled in Johannesburg. Here he was associated with many concerts in the old Wanderers' Hall, and also became well-known as a teacher of pianoforte and harp. In the 1920s he was engaged by African Consolidated Theatres as pianist-conductor for the Apollo Theatre in Germiston, and also for a South African tour. With the advent of "talkies" he had to devote himself more to teaching, although he continued to play the piano in a trio at the Palm Court of the old Carlton Hotel for many years. As a harpist he was in demand for shows (*Land of Smiles* and *Rose Marie*) and as a member of companies, such as that of Ivor Novello. During the Second World War he played French horn and pianoforte in the military band at Roberts Heights (now Voortrekkerhoogte). Kathleen Alister** was his pupil for a while.

– K.A.

FOURIE, GEORGE KARL, *25 October 1929 in Johannesburg; living in Europe in 1970. Baritone.

George Fourie was a member of the Asaf Choir** and sang in choirs participating in the Johannesburg opera season from his 16th year onwards. In 1947 he sang in *The magic flute,* after which Olga Ryss** and Bruce Anderson** became responsible for his vocal training. He continued his study in London in 1955 and for two seasons took part in productions of the Sadler's Wells Opera Company. There, in 1957, he won the Richard Tauber Memorial Award which he spent on the study of singing at the State

Academy in Vienna. In due course he obtained the Academy's diploma for opera. — From 1958 onwards he was baritone in the Graz opera, but in 1963 Walter Felsenstein engaged him to sing in the Comic Opera in Berlin (1963-1967). He visited Moscow as a member of this company in 1965, to interpret the role of Oberon in Britten's *A midsummer night's dream*. His American debut came in 1966 when he took part in two Boston productions of *Boris Godounov* (Moussorgsky) and *Hippolyte et Arice* (Rameau). Afterwards he toured America with the American National Opera Company and, on another occasion, with the Boston Opera Company (1967-1968). Since 1967 he has also sung in Munich, Stuttgart, Berlin and Bremen; in June 1969 he had the privilege of taking the leading baritone part in Penderecki's new opera, *Die Teufel von Loudon*. — He returned to South Africa in 1960 for the Union Festival to sing the title role in *Rigoletto*. He visited the country again in 1961, 1963 and 1964. His repertoire includes more than 60 roles, ranging from Offenbach to Mozart, Italian opera (especially Verdi), Moussorgsky and Wagner to Stravinsky *(The Rake's progress)*, Schönberg *(Jacobsleiter)* and Penderecki.

SOURCES

Sarie Marais: 19 Jan. 1962.   *Die Burger:* 8 Dec. 1955; 23 Mar. 1956; 9 July 1958.   *Die Transvaler:* 28 Jan. 1971.   Research Centre for South African Music, HSRC, Pretoria.

– Ed.

FOURIE, JOANNA EVERHARDA (NéE RIVIÈRE), *17 September 1884 in Zwolle, the Netherlands; °12 March 1973 in Pretoria. Expert on South African folk songs.

Jo Fourie was trained in the Netherlands where she obtained a diploma in pianoforte from the Koninklijke Nederlandse Toonkunstenaarsvereniging. She came to South Africa in 1911 with her husband, the Rev. (subsequently Dr) H.C.M. Fourie. During a stay in Indonesia (then known as the Dutch East Indies), she happened to listen in 1934 to a broadcast of folk songs from different countries and the Afrikaans songs appealed to her for the first time – they seemed so unspoilt and natural. This interest grew with the revival of Boeremusiek in the years preceding the Commemorative Trek of 1938 and in 1937 led to the creation of her own "Boereorkes" in Marico, where she was living at the time. —Her son, Mr Hugo Fourie, supported and encouraged her endeavours and played an important part in the jotting down, arrangement and publication of the melodies. Dr Fourie, her husband, died on 5 August 1939; Mrs Fourie soon engaged in obtaining an acknowledged diploma in music education (LTCL in 1942) and music became her professional occupation. The first tunes published in 1944 and 1945 were all written down in Great Marico and Zeerust. Largely this was a labour of love, but it suddenly achieved public recognition when in 1952 the SABC appealed to its listeners for folk melodies suitable for the program series *Uit die jaar vroeg* (presented by Bosman de Kock** and Anton Hartman,** with the co-operation of Hendrik Susan's** Boereorkes). There was considerable excitement when Mrs Fourie reacted with a collection of more than 300 melodies. — This enthusiasm stimulated her own endeavours and in 1952-1953 she covered South Africa systematically, writing down songs and dance melodies performed by old singers and players of the concertina, the harmonium or the violin. In the end her labours amounted to some

1155 melodies written down in 68 manuscript books. Besides the actual music, the collection also includes 5 diaries, 7 books with written notes, 5 concerning the people who sang or played the music, and her correspondence on the subject. Much of this material is of some folkloristic importance. The whole collection was finally acquired by the SABC, which had been intimately concerned with the work of discovering these musical expressions of Afrikanerdom. The SABC compensated Mrs Fourie for her work and in 1973 they presented the whole collection to the Research Centre for S.A. Music. — The collection contains vocal as well as instrumental music, with the second category well to the fore. It consists almost exclusively of dance tunes based on the popular rhythms of the 19th Century, such as the waltz, polka, settees (schottische) and mazurka. A number of the songs have retained, or partially retained, the original Dutch words, an example of the conservatism which characterises all folk art. A number of the tunes also occur in the collections of other folksong specialists, usually in a varied form.

PUBLICATIONS
(All the items listed below have the same sub-title: Old and new Boer-tunes collected and arranged for Boer dance band by Mrs J.E. Fourie . . . and Hugo Fourie).

Die Bosveld mazurka. Gallo (Pty) Ltd, Johannesburg, 1944.   Die kat kom terug. Gallo (Pty) Ltd, Johannesburg, 1944.   Die Marico seties. Gallo (Pty) Ltd, Johannesburg, 1944.   Marico-wals en Rietskraal Pollie. Gallo (Pty) Ltd, Johannesburg, 1945.   Mymering. Gallo (Pty) Ltd, Johannesburg, 1944.   Natie se seties. Gallo (Pty) Ltd, Johannesburg, 1944.   Polka: Die jonk mans kom van verre. Gallo (Pty) Ltd, Johannesburg, 1944.   Vastrap mazurka. Gallo (Pty) Ltd, Johannesburg, 1945.   Vriendskap-wals en Kalfie-wals. Gallo (Pty) Ltd, Johannesburg, 1944.

BIBLIOGRAPHY
Bouws, Jan: *Die Afrikaanse volkslied*. Johannesburg, 1958.   Bouws, Jan: *Suid-Afrikaanse komponiste van vandag en gister*. A.A. Balkema, Cape Town, 1957.   Bouws, Jan: *Woord en wys van die Afrikaanse lied*. HAUM, Cape Town, 1962.   Van der Merwe, F.Z.: *Suid-Afrikaanse musiekbibliografie, 1787–1952*. J.L. van Schaik, Pretoria, 1958.

SOURCES
Bouws, Jan: Mevrouw Fourie en de Afrikaanse volksmusiek.   *Zuid-Afrika*, Sept. 1948, Amsterdam.   Bouws, Jan: Mev. Jo Fourie – haar onverganklike glorie. *Handhaaf* II/1, Johannesburg, Sept. 1964.   Bouws, Jan: Südafrikanische Volksmusik. *Schweizerische Musikzeitung* 99, Zürich, 1959.   Bouws, Jan: Sy het ons volksliedere help bewaar. *Die Burger,* Cape Town, 21 Sept. 1964.   Bouws, Jan: Zuid-Afrikaanse volksmuziek. *Mens en Melodie* V, Utrecht, 1950.   Fourie, J.E.: Mineur en majeur in die Psalm- en Gesangbundel. *Tydskrif vir volkskunde en volkstaal* I, Johannesburg, May 1945.   The Jo Fourie Collection in the Research Centre for South African Music, HSRC, Pretoria.

– Ed.

FOURIE, LOUIS J., *2 November 1932 near Reitz; living in Welkom in 1963. School music teacher and organist.

Louis Fourie received lessons at irregular intervals in piano, violin, organ and singing from I. Bloch, Victor Pohl,** G.W. Koornhof, G.Z. van der Spuy,** T. van

Huyssteen** and others, and reached the level of the UTLM in all the above instruments, with the exception of the violin. During the Union Festival celebrations in Bloemfontein in 1960 he conducted a large children's choir. He regularly enters both children's and adult choirs for the eisteddfodau. — In addition to his musical activities at schools, Louis Fourie gives private lessons in piano and is the organist of the Dutch Reformed Bedelia parish.

WORKS

Alles is joune, song for tenor (I.D. du Plessis). Ms., 1960.   Lenteliedjie, song for soprano (H. van der Merwe). Ms., 1961.   Die lewe is 'n spotter, song for baritone (I.D. du Plessis). Ms., 1961.   Nerina van Bosvallei, operetta (libretto by composer). Ms., 1962.   The above three songs were incorporated in the operetta.

– Ed.

FRAMES, POPPY, *1903; living in Johannesburg in 1966. Choreographer, ballet dancer and teacher.

Poppy Frames received her early training from Vivien Tailleur** and later continued under Madame Ravodna.** Until 1930 she arranged and took part in a large number of dancing displays presented in Pretoria, Johannesburg and various centres along the Reef. During 1926 she and Dorothy Morrison toured the principal cities of South Africa under the title of *Daye and Dawn,* presenting a programme of dances as part of vaudeville interludes in the cinemas of African Consolidated Theatres. At the inception of the South African Dancing Teachers' Association, she became an active member, assisting in the presentation of dancing displays and taking part as a dancer in some of them; but later she dissociated herself from this organisation. — In 1933, after her return from London, where she had received tuition from Judith Espinosa, she assisted John Connell** as choreographer and producer of ballets and dances which formed a part of his Musical Fortnights. This was the beginning of a collaboration which was to last for two decades. During this period she was also associated with the Johannesburg Operatic and Dramatic Society** as choreographer and dance producer. In 1943 she collaborated with Marjorie Sturman,** Ivy Conmee** and Lesley Hodson in the establishment of the Johannesburg Festival Ballet Society, for whom she choreographed and produced a number of ballets. — Poppy Frames is a leading adjudicator of dancing in Southern Africa. She was one of the first to pass in all the examinations of the Royal Academy of Dancing (RAD) and the Cecchetti Organisation, and also one of the first to be appointed as examiner for the Association of Operatic Dancing of Great Britain and later of RAD. She was made a member of the Overseas Advisory Council of RAD in 1938. — Amongst the ballets she has choreographed, are *The willow pattern plate, Petite suite, The yellow mask* and *The judgement of Paris.*

– H.D.

FRANCKE, C.F.   Brüderkirche

FRANK, GEOFFREY   Durban 8, V.L.E.M. Schelpe

FRANKEL

FRANKEL, BERTHA   Johannesburg 3 (ii), E. Mann

FRANKLIN, J.G.   Grahamstown 2, Organs 5

FRANZ MOELLER'S MUSIC WAREHOUSE   F.B.M. Moeller

FRASER, FLORENCE DOROTHEA, *29 August 1868 in Philippolis; °13 July 1928 in Johannesburg. Free State soprano.

Florence Fraser was the first child of Sir John G. Fraser, Member of the Free State Volksraad (1880–1899) and Senator of the Union of South Africa (1910–1920). While she was at school at the Ladies' Institute Eunice, the possibilities of her voice were discovered by the music teacher, Miss Hamma. Miss Hamma was so insistent on an overseas training, that Florence Fraser was taken to Munich in 1884 by Miss Hamma herself, who arranged for accommodation for Florence with her parents. Mr Hamma was professor of singing at the Conservatoire in Munich and handled all the arrangements in connection with her vocal training. For the next five years she stayed in Germany (1884–1889) and then returned to South Africa, where she sang with great success up to 1894. Starting her career in Bloemfontein on 20 February 1889, she visited the Transvaal and Natal and finally Cape Town, where she sang at a Mozart centenary festival held on 9 December 1891. After this tour the newspapers started referring to her as the Free State Nightingale – a fitting appellation for a coloratura singer. But her voice gradually began to change, took on depth and eventually became a soprano with an exceptionally wide vocal range. Her programmes indicate that she was equally at home in opera, oratorio and songs, especially those of English origin. — In 1894 she left for a second period of study in Europe, this time in Stuttgart, where for about two years she was a pupil of Mme Niklas-Kempner, and then in London, where Sir Charles Santley guided her interest towards oratorio. She returned to South Africa in 1898 and her second tour of the country was a triumph. Shortly before the outbreak of war, she was still singing at concerts in the Western Transvaal, at Klerksdorp and Potchefstroom. She was befriended by Barrow-Dowling** and often sang with his Choral Society in Cape Town in performances of e.g. *Messiah* and *Elijah.* — Florence Fraser was the gifted child of a prominent and well-to-do family and, practically without exception, employed her vocal gifts to benefit charities or to support meritorious causes. This was especially apparent after the British troops had occupied Bloemfontein, when she used her voice to support funds for widows and orphans, or to solace wounded soldiers. From the public's point of view, each occasion was regarded as a special and a fashionable affair. At the farewell reception to Miss Fraser and on the occasion of her forthcoming wedding (1905), the Mayor of Bloemfontein handed her an address in which much was made of the selfless way she had placed her vocal gifts at the disposal of her fellowmen. Apart from this aspect, Dr J. Human finds much to praise in the integrity and good taste which marked her programmes. — In May 1905 she married Thomas Burnham-King of East London and checked her public career. Instead, she devoted herself to charity. In later years she was president of the Presbyterian Church's women's association (1919–1922). She died in Johannesburg where she had gone for medical treatment, but is buried in Bloemfontein. On her gravestone are the words: "Whose I am and whom I serve".

FRASER

BIBLIOGRAPHY
Human, J.L.K.: *Musiek in die Oranje-Vrystaat vanaf 1850 tot aan die begin van die Anglo-Boereoorlog.* M.Mus. dissertation, UOFS, 1963.   Human, J.L.K.: *Die musieklewe in Bloemfontein, 1900–1939.* D.Phil. thesis, UOFS, 1976.

SOURCES
Daily Dispatch: 16–19 July 1928.   *The Friend:* 1904–1905.

– Ed.

FRASER, W.A.   Piano Music III

FREE STATE MUSIC SOCIETY, THE, was active in Bloemfontein between 1944 and 1963. The Society was founded on May 15, 1944, on the initiative of Dr Benedictus Kok,** who was chosen as Chairman. In 1957 he was followed by Lotte Pretorius who still occupied the chair when the society dissolved at the end of 1963.

The aims of the society were to cultivate the taste for and interest in music among Bloemfontein residents. Country members were accepted after 1952, if they paid one half of the usual annual subscription. Members enjoyed the privilege of attending most of the society's concerts without paying admission fees, or paying at times only a small percentage of the admission charge. Other privileges were advance booking for concerts and, eventually, members could bring guests along for whom a reduced rate was charged. The society was subsidised by the Department of Adult Education, the Free State Administration and the Bloemfontein City Council. When funds became depleted, an effective counter measure was usually the performance of an operetta by members of the society: *Lilac time* (directed by P.J. Lemmer**), *Victoria and her hussar* (under the direction of D.J. Roode**) and *Die graaf van Luxemburg* (directed by Mary Rousseau**) were some of them. — Initially, local talent was responsible for the concerts, or there were lecture evenings and variety concerts organised by committee members such as Dr Kok, D.J. Roode, O.A. Karstel** and P.J. Lemmer. In due course the society also offered performances by overseas as well as South African artists. When PACOFS was created in 1963, the society became practically redundant and was dissolved. Interest on the funds of the society is now used for the financial support of promising Free State music students.

SOURCES
Minutes of the Free State Music Society.

– J.L.K.H.

FREE STATE SCHOOL OF MUSIC   Higher Educational Institutions I/1, D.J. Roode.

FREE STATE STRING QUARTET, THE,   was established in 1960 with the aim of furthering music in Bloemfontein and in the Orange Free State. The establishment was made possible through the collaboration of the OFS Provincial Administration, the Bloemfontein City Council and the Council of the University of the OFS, each of whom contributed towards its maintenance. Until 1967 the quartet had obligations towards each of these patrons: for the OFS Provincial Administration the quartet gave 24 concerts a year in country towns coupled with a school concert in each centre and, in addition, each member of the quartet gave lessons on his particular instrument at schools in Bloemfontein; for the Bloemfontein City Council the quartet had to give a number of concerts in Bloemfontein each year; but from 1968 onwards, the quartet became permanently attached to the University of the OFS and its members were required to teach and to promote ensemble work in the Music Department. Its existence has since been terminated. — The members of the quartet were Jack de Wet** (first violin), Jonas Pieters (second violin), François Bouguenon** (viola) and Harry Cremers** (cello). Initially Noel Travers** played the second violin. Michael Haller succeeded Harry Cremers as cellist. Jack de Wet left for Port Elizabeth in 1974.

– Ed.

FREE STATE YOUTH CHOIR. This choir, an official, subsidised body under the protection of the Free State Provincial Administration, was established in 1965. It gives about twenty performances a year and has appeared in all four provinces and in South West Africa. In 1968 it was invited to sing with the Stellenbosch University Choir** at the State President's induction in the Groote Kerk, Cape Town, and to present a programme at the ensuing state banquet. In 1971 the choir was invited to sing at the OFS Republic Day celebrations as well as at the main celebrations in Cape Town and Stellenbosch. These concerts were part of a tour which included twelve cities and towns (19 March–24 July). The choir conductors were Philip McLachlan** (guest conductor) and the two permanent conductors, Dirkie de Villiers** and Tersteegen van Huyssteen.** The programmes included works by Bach, Handel, Scarlatti, Di Lasso and Gastoldi, early European church music, Christmas carols and folk songs of different lands. Two items, *Hoe stil kan dit word as Sedoos gaan lê* and *Jankemalanke Langklaas-franke* (Boerneef) were commissioned from Hubert du Plessis,** who set the words to music under the title *En Boplaas sing koortaal* (opus 32). — The choir has sixty voices and the ages of members range from 15 to 18 years.

– D.deV.

FREE STATE YOUTH ORCHESTRA, THE, consists of two ensembles – a Senior Orchestra of more advanced players and a Junior Orchestra which also serves as a training ground for the Senior Orchestra.

It was created by Jack de Wet** in 1962 and since 1963 it has been managed by the Regional Council for the Performing Arts of the Free State. The programmes consist of *concerti grossi* and other orchestral forms, including modern works for string orchestra. The latter items were generally appreciated by the audiences, since they abounded in technical problems and the players were so very youthful! The annual youth festival in Bloemfontein is an important occasion in the city's musical life. A programme of the year's best works are played and a trophy is awarded to the "player of the year". This presentaton is on behalf of the orchestra to the string player who has progressed particularly well and has approached a superlative standard. — A climax in the history of this ensemble was their participation in the International Musical Youth Festival held at St Moritz in Switzerland in 1970. At the end of the festival, seven of the thirty-four Free Staters were chosen to play in the final concerts of an International Youth Orchestra and, in addition, the leader of the Free State ensemble was awarded a bursary for excelling as the most promising violinist at the festival. Since 1974, when Jack de Wet left Bloemfontein for Port Elizabeth, the conductor of the group has been Pierre de Groote** (1974-1978). The orchestra commissioned a Concerto Grosso from Stefans Grové** in 1976.

– J.deW.

FREWER, WILLY, *19 December 1911 in Essen; °22 December 1969 in Windhoek. Conductor, pianist and organist.

Frewer received his musical training at the People's Singing School in Essen, studying a variety of musical instruments: cello, clarinet, pianoforte and organ, as well as orchestral conducting and theory of music. In February 1935 he came to Windhoek as a member of a trio, which played in the Zoo Café. The other members of the trio were W. Kehrmann** and C. Hatterscheidt. After presenting a series of chamber music concerts the trio dissolved, though all three eventually settled in South West Africa. Frewer remained in Windhoek, where he developed his gifts as a conductor. When Hans Müller** was repatriated in 1939, Frewer succeeded him as organist at the Christus Kirche and as director of his orchestra and choir. Within a year (1940) they were able to present a performance of Schubert's *Stabat Mater,* but in 1941 Frewer was interned in Andalusia and became one of the musical leaders in that camp. — He formed a large male voice choir, created an orchestra, organised evenings of chamber music, took part in piano performances, delivered a series of 14 lectures on piano music of the Romantic period, inaugurated a course in harmony, and acted as accompanist at song recitals. He was interned for an additional year, from 1945 to 1946, at the camp at Baviaanspoort, but returned to Windhoek in the latter year, formed the Windhoek Music Society and shortly afterwards revived the Windhoek Symphony Orchestra (1947). Frewer conducted this orchestra in a large number of symphonic concerts over a period of 20 years (1947-1967), and increasingly presented symphonic works worthy of the name. Peaks of his career were the Windhoek Festival Concert in 1965 and the Republican Festival Concert in 1966, when he invited artists to augment his orchestra to 51 players. — Back in 1947 he had pioneered the music trade in SWA by opening a music shop in Windhoek; in 1956 he was able to open a branch of this business in Keetmanshoop.

– H.H.M.

FRIEDLAND, J. Johannesburg 4, Johannesburg Philharmonic Society

FRIEDMAN, MARIAN, *25 December 1952 in Johannesburg; now (1977) in the USA. Pianist.

Marian's extraordinary talent for pianoforte playing became manifest at an early age; she was taught and encouraged at home and was able to make her first broadcast in the Young South Africa Programme of the SABC when she was seven years old. On 21

81

May 1963, she made her concert debut in Beethoven's *First piano concerto* with the Cape Town Municipal Orchestra.** This was followed by a number of recitals in major centres of the Republic. Alexander Cherniavsky** became interested and, during the next four years (1964–1967), promoted her concerts in South Africa. In 1965 she became a pupil of Adolph Hallis,** and had lessons in harmony and counterpoint with Stephan Zondagh** (from 1966). For the Republic Festival in 1966 she was asked to perform with the SABC Orchestra, and furthermore in Rhodesia and for educational bodies such as the South African Teachers' Association and the University of Pretoria. — In 1970 Marian Friedman was awarded the first prize in a Beethoven Competition sponsored by the SABC which enabled her to study with Abbey Simon at the Indiana University from 1971 to 1974. Whilst a student there, she won a number of competitions and awards and in 1973 she passed in the examination for the University's Performer's Certificate. She received the B.Mus. degree with distinction in 1975 and is currently (1977) preparing herself for the examination leading to the M.Mus degree. Her present teacher is Menahem Pressler of Indiana University. During visits to South Africa in 1972, 1974 and 1977 she played in concertos with the National Orchestra of the SABC, winning another SABC music prize in 1974.

SOURCES

Opus: I/1, *Dec. 1969;* II/4, *July/Aug. 1971;* V/1 *Oct./Nov. 1973.*   *Panorama: Oct. 1963.*
Die Burger: 25 May 1963.   *Rand Daily Mail:* 12 Feb. 1970.   *SABC Bulletin:* 12 Nov. 1962;
27 May 1963.   *SA Jewish Times:* X/19, 2 July 1971.   *The Star:* 18 May 1963.   *Sunday
Times:* 9 Aug. 1970.   *Die Transvaler:* 27 May 1963.   Research Centre for South African
Music, HSRC, Pretoria.

– Ed.

FRIENDS OF MUSIC SOCIETY   Johannesburg 3(iii)

FRITTELLI, JOSEPH   V.E. Frittelli

FRITTELLI, VINCENT E., *7 December 1940 in Johannesburg; now (1978) in Johannesburg. Violinist.

Vincent Frittelli studied under Max Weinbrenn,** Pierre de Groote** and his father, Joseph Frittelli. After a series of concerts, and a recommendation from Pierre Fournier, he was sent in January 1956 to the Juilliard School of Music in New York, where he studied under Ivan Galamian. Two years later he won the Ellie Marx** Memorial Scholarship which enabled him to study at the Brussels Conservatoire for nine months under Carlo van Neste. After a short tour of his home country, Frittelli returned to New York in January 1959. There he won a four-year scholarship and resumed his violin lessons under Galamian at the Curtis Institute of Music in Philadelphia. — For a time Frittelli was the leader of the Cape Town Municipal Orchestra** (1966–1967); but after an even shorter association with the PACT Orchestra, he returned to the USA in September 1967 to act as sub-leader of the New Orleans Orchestra until his appointment as professor of violin and assistant conductor of the Akron Symphony Orchestra at the University of Akron in Ohio (1969–1972).

He returned to South Africa in the latter year and acted successively as leader of the CAPAB Orchestra in Cape Town and of the National Symphony Orchestra in Johannesburg. Whenever possible, he still plays in public and has performed as soloist with all the symphony orchestras in this country.

SOURCES
Opus: III/1, Sept./Oct. 1971.   *Res Musicae:* III/3, Mar. 1957; VII/1, Sept. 1961; VIII/5, Sept. 1962; IX/1, Dec. 1962.   *SABC Bulletin:* 13 Oct. 1958.   *Die Burger:* 4 May 1967.   *Rand Daily Mail:* 9 July 1971.   Research Centre for South African Music, HSRC, Pretoria.

– Ed.

FROHNE, E.   German Male Voice Choir, Vanderbijlpark

FRYER, J.   E.J. Scotcher

FRYLING, B.   Johannesburg 3(iv), A. Solomon

FULTON, THOMAS ARNOLD, *16 January 1896 at Saltcoats, Scotland; now (1978) in Johannesburg. Conductor and teacher of singing.

Arnold Fulton studied music privately (1905–1914) before the First World War, during which he served in the Forces. When peace came, he entered the RAM (1919–1924) and obtained an Associateship in 1924, as well as an Associateship of the RCO in the same year. He taught singing and had pupils who became prominent in Washington and Canada; he was also organist at the Cathedral Church of Scotland in London, until 1941. In 1924 he founded the London Select Choir, which he conducted at the Royal Albert Hall, Queen's Hall and Wigmore Hall, as well as in Edinburgh and Glasgow. — In 1926 Fulton came to South Africa to marry the South African contralto Isobel McLaren,** who had also been a student at the RAM from 1919 until 1922. In England he led his Select Choir until the outbreak of war in 1939, acted as organist and choirmaster and at times conducted the orchestras of the City of Birmingham and of the BBC, the latter at international festivals of music in 1931 and 1937. He was associated with Sir Thomas Beecham in the Delius Festival, held in 1929, which led to a new understanding of Delius and set new standards of choral singing in Britain. Fulton became a member of the Royal Philharmonic Society in 1937, a Fellow of the RAM in 1949 and eventually also a Fellow of Trinity College. — After demobilisation from the British Army, Fulton came to South Africa, where his wife and children had been resident since 1940. The family settled in Johannesburg where Fulton taught voice-production and vocal interpretation, also acting as adjudicator and examiner. He came very opportunely for John Connell,** with whom he was associated as a conductor of opera productions in 1946, 1947 and 1948; he also conducted operas produced by Volksteater in Pretoria in 1950, 1951 and 1952. —The SASMT elected him as their President in 1953 and he became Vice-chairman of the Johannesburg Musical Society in 1971.

SOURCES
Opus: I/3, Mar. 1970.   *SAMT:* 37, Nov. 1949; 41, Dec. 1951; 44, June 1953; 46, June 1954.   Research Centre for South African Music, HSRC, Pretoria.

– L.W.

GAFNER, OTTO CHRISTIAN, *10 March 1899 in Johannesburg; °26 June 1973 in Pretoria. Music teacher.

Otto Gafner's parents were Swiss who had settled in Johannesburg before the Anglo-Boer War. The family moved to Pretoria in 1904 and in due course Otto entered the Gymnasium School. His first steps in music were guided by a Mrs Negro and at a later stage by Henry Newboult.** In the Advanced pianoforte examination taken in 1915, he did so well that he was awarded an exhibition cash prize and the examiner seriously suggested that he choose music as his profession. He became a licentiate of Trinity College in 1917, saw military service in 1918 and returned to Pretoria after the cessation of hostilities to continue his musical studies, now supervised by Lorenzo Danza.** He acquired a licentiate of UNISA in 1920 and 6 years later another one in Harmony and Counterpoint. It should also be mentioned that he studied in England in 1935 and obtained the LRAM. During this stay he was introduced to the Matthay pianoforte method. — As a music teacher Otto Gafner had a private studio in Pretoria, taught at the Pretoria Boys' High School (1923–1960) and at Christian Brothers' College (1969–1971), but also maintained a studio in Kroondal where he had a few pupils among the German community (1936–1970). Among his pupils were Reino Ottermann,** Derek Lewis,** Bernard Riley and Claudia Strauss. At different times he performed in Rustenburg and Pretoria, his repertoire drawn mainly from the Romantic composers, but also including some classical and a few modern works. — During the '30s Otto Gafner's interest in composition was stimulated by a competition for a patriotic song launched by *Die Huisgenoot.* His *Komaan!* was awarded the first prize. This was followed in 1939 by two South African songs written to his own words, and then he ventured into orchestral work and opera. His compositions were neither numerous nor extensive, and probably served as an occupational recreation, though he took considerable trouble with his operas. In 1971 he even visited the Swiss opera composer, Sutermeister, to obtain assistance in connection with *Oranje,* subsequently revised as *A visitor to the vineyard.* Some of the orchestral works were performed by the Iscor orchestra during the 1950s. — From 1923 to 1934 Gafner was the organizing secretary of the Pretoria Musical Festival. During these years he saw it grow from a small musical festival to a large organization offering competitions in vocal and instrumental music, choral work, elocution and dancing. It had the active co-operation of the most prominent English-speaking teachers in Pretoria, including Rosita Gooch, Ellen Norburn** and Henry Newboult.**

WORKS

Komaan! (J.F.E. Celliers). *Die Huisgenoot,* 2 Sept. 1938 and Nasionale Pers, Cape Town, 1938.   Two South African songs. Chappell & Co., London 1939: 1. Jacarandas 2. The reeds (O.C. Gafner).   Phantasmagoria, four phantasy pieces for orchestra. Ms., performed by Iscor Orchestra, Mar. 1954: 1. Prelude   2. Scherzo   3. Serenade   4. Waltz movement.   Andantino, for strings. Ms., n.d.   Gold mine, symphonic poem. Ms., n.d.   Concerto piccolo baroque, for piano and chamber orchestra. Ms., n.d.   Oranje (A visitor to the vineyard), opera on a libretto by the composer. Ms., n.d.   Die swart tulp, opera based on Alexandre Dumas' story. Ms., n.d.

BIBLIOGRAPHY
Viljoen, A.W.: *Drie Pretoriase musici: Blakemore, Yates en Gafner.* B.Mus. script, UP, 1973. (This supplies a detailed bibliography).

SOURCES
Die Eeufeeslied. *Die Huisgenoot,* 2 Sept. 1938.   *SAMT:* 85, Jan. 1974 (obituary).
– Ed.

GAILLARD, MR AND MRS RODOLPHE   Johannesburg 3(ii)

GALE, A.H.   Queenstown 7

GALEFFI, A., *1858 or 1859 in Italy; °11 September 1918 in Johannesburg. Conductor and singing teacher.

Galeffi received his training in Milan and at the Instituto Musicale in Florence, came to South Africa in 1904 as the conductor of the Moody-Manners Opera Company and after completing a tour of the country with this group, settled in Johannesburg and was appointed conductor of the Johannesburg Philharmonic Society** (1905). He conducted them on a high artistic level in Sunday-evening concerts in Johannesburg and Pretoria, his programmes at times including complete symphonies by Mozart, Schubert, Haydn and Beethoven. — In August 1906, Galeffi settled in Pretoria and tried to establish a local orchestra in collaboration with the Pretoria Philharmonic Society. In October 1907, their attempts were successful and the new orchestra made its debut in April 1908; but in 1909, after only a few concerts, the enterprise came to an end. He also trained the choir of the St Andrew's Presbyterian Church and gave instruction in singing which contributed significantly to the development of Pretoria's singing talent during the four years he stayed in the city. With his opera class he staged performances of Wallace's *Maritana* and Bizet's *Carmen.* More notable was his production of *Faust* in April 1909, which earned him the reputation of being a knowledgeable opera producer. Financial difficulties forced him to relinquish his projects and in May 1910 he left Pretoria to return to Johannesburg where, in August 1910, he produced *Il trovatore* in His Majesty's Theatre.** This production was repeated in the Opera House** in Pretoria in November of the same year. — In 1916, in collaboration with Alberto Terassi, he attempted to revive interest in operatic music with a series of "Grand Opera Concerts", but he was handicapped by a disease which eventually caused his death.

BIBLIOGRAPHY
Vermeulen, Elizabeth: *Die Musieklewe in Pretoria tussen 1902 en 1926.* M.Mus. dissertation, UP, 1967.
– Ed.

GALEFFI, MADAME   A. Galeffi, Johannesburg 2

GALLO (AFRICA) LTD   Discography, H.T. Tracey, R. Trewhela

GARDNER, DOROTHY   Johannesburg 3(iv)

GARRATT, T.   C.A. Blignaut, L.H. Rees

GARRISON THEATRE   King William's Town 2

GARVIN, HENRY (HARRY), *1871 in Chesterfield, Derbyshire; °25 March 1932 in Johannesburg. Violinist, music teacher and composer.

Garvin studied at the Guildhall School of Music before coming to South Africa in 1891 as leader of the orchestra of the Standard Opera Company, which had been created by A. Bonamici** to play at the opening of the Standard Theatre** in Johannesburg. One of the first professional violinists to arrive in the town, Garvin was in turn leader of the orchestra of the Lyric Company (1892), of Von Himmelstjerna's** orchestra (1895), and of the Wanderers Orchestra conducted by James Hyde**. He helped to form the Musicians' Club in 1895, and held office as first President until 1907. — During the South African War Garvin was in Cape Town, where he became the leader of an orchestra consisting of many refugee members of the Wanderers group, assembled by James Hyde. By March, 1902, he was back in Johannesburg, where he re-established his teaching connections, and was appointed on the staff of St Mary's College. When the Lyric Club was founded in May 1902, he became its musical director. A year later he became one of four violin teachers on the staff of Tressi's South African College of Music in Johannesburg; when this closed down in 1911, he was appointed to the staff of Maude Harrison's Conservatoire of Music, which flourished until 1930. — The Rand Society of Music Teachers (later the South African Society of Music Teachers**) was formed in 1919, and Garvin became its first President. In 1922 branches were formed in other parts of the Union, and Garvin was also elected Chairman of the Johannesburg Centre, a position he held until 1931. While overseas in 1931, he attended the Anglo-American Conference on Musical Education in Lausanne, in the dual capacity of delegate from the Union of South Africa and representative of the South African Society of Music Teachers. Shortly after his return his health failed. — Garvin was conductor of the Catholic Cathedral Choir in Church Street for about twenty years, and until 1931 choral and music instructor at Parktown High School for Boys, King Edward VII School, Marist Brothers School for Boys, and Athlone High School.

WORKS
Berceuse, for violin with pianoforte accompaniment. Darter & Sons, Cape Town, n.d.   Reverie, for violin with pianoforte accompaniment. Charles Vincent, London, n.d.   Romance and Bolero, for violin with pianoforte accompaniment. Charles Vincent, London, n.d. Tyrolienne, for violin with pianoforte accompaniment. Darter & Sons, Cape Town, n.d.

BIBLIOGRAPHY
Van der Merwe, F.Z.: *Suid-Afrikaanse Musiekbibliografie, 1787–1952.* J.L. van Schaik, Pretoria, 1958.

SOURCES
The Standard and Diggers News: 15 Aug. 1893.   *The Star:* 2 Mar. 1895.   *SAMT:* 2, Apr. 1932 (obituary).   Material in the Strange Library of Africana, Johannesburg Municipal Library.

– L.W.

GAUCHE, H.S.   R. Müller (Pty) Ltd

GEMENGD KOOR ZANGLUST, THE, was founded in Pretoria on 1 September 1926 to replace the Christelike Sangvereniging Asaf** which had dissolved in April 1926. During the seventeen years of its existence, this choir was led by Prof. Gerrit Bon.**

Its aim was the practice of vocal music in Dutch and Afrikaans. It consisted of active members who contributed twenty cents per month, of music lovers who contributed R2 per annum, and of honorary members. Among the performances given by this choir were the following: Mendelssohn's *Lobgesang,* 1929; Handel's *Judas Maccabeus,* 1930; Dvořak's *Stabat mater,* 1933; Brahms's *Ein deutsches Requiem,* 1933; Bach's *Gottes Zeit ist die allerbeste Zeit,* 1934; excerpts from Bach's *Ich hatte viel Bekümmernis,* 1934; Mendelssohn's *Elijah,* 1934 and 1936; Haydn's *Die Seisoene,* 1935; Cherubini's *Anacréon,* 1935; Dvořak's *Die Geisterbraut,* 1937; and Haydn's *Die Schöpfung,* 1941. The choir also presented jubilee programmes to commemorate Schubert (1928), Haydn (1932) and Brahms (1933) and was responsible for other instrumental and vocal concerts. The concerts were presented in collaboration with orchestras, such as the Pretoria City Symphony Orchestra or the SABC Symphony Orchestra. Prominent singers and instrumentalists from Johannesburg and Pretoria were often invited to perform with the choir. — Membership remained fairly constant: usually about 45 members. In 1940 there were 79 art-loving members, but during the War people tended to lose interest and in 1942 the choir could not give a concert at all, due to the sporadic attendance of members at rehearsals. At the beginning of 1943 the choir temporarily discontinued its activities, but in 1954 it officially ceased to exist and its assets were distributed among charity organisations.

SOURCES
Minutes, programmes and other documents connected with the Gemengd Koor Zanglust in the Nederlandse Kultuur-historiese Instituut, UP, Pretoria.

– Ed.

GENADENDAL   Brüderkirche, C. Murray, Sacred song books with Dutch words

GERKE, WILLEM, *3 August 1876 in Amsterdam; °27 March 1953 in Pretoria. Conductor and violinist.

At the age of six, Willem Gerke commenced violin lessons under the guidance of a teacher named Tak. It soon became apparent that he was exceptionally gifted and in 1890 he was allowed to enrol at the Amsterdam Conservatoire, where Bernard Zweers was prominent in his musical education. A violinist in the Conservatoire orchestra (1900–1909) he had a good friend in Willem Mengelberg. His days as a student also marked the beginning of his relationship with the Norwegian composer Grieg, whom he visited in Norway in 1901. — At the age of 30 Gerke had developed a lively interest in the possibility of doing constructive musical work in the Transvaal, especially as a conductor, and in a letter to the Netherlands Society in Johannesburg he enquired about the prospects for a musician. The secretary replied in a letter dated 19 November 1906, in which he referred to information gained from a Dutch musician in

Johannesburg and then goes on to paint a sober and discouraging picture of uneducated taste and opportunistic dilettantism. He made it clear that Gerke was running a risk in emigrating to South Africa and the Dutchman accordingly shelved the idea of exchanging Europe for the Transvaal. Another argument against his emigration was the fact that he had become director of the Amsterdam Students' Music Society called J. Zweelinck (established in 1878). He conducted this company in a successful performance of his own *Symphonic overture,* during the 55th Lustrum of the University of Amsterdam (1907). The next year he married Francina van Rossum and in 1909 he was appointed assistant director of Amsterdam's Wagner Society. This position he held until he eventually came to South Africa. Musicological studies during this period led to new productions of Beethoven's *Die Geschöpfe des Prometheus* (1909) and of Gluck's *Iphigenie in Aulis* (1914). Both performances were given by his student company and both were accompanied by printed, detailed listeners' guides. — In the second half of 1921 Gerke was again corresponding with people in the Transvaal who cherished the ideal of establishing a permanent orchestra in Pretoria. Although offered the conductorship of an orchestra in Utrecht in the same year, he decided to accept the offers made by the South African group and on March 1, 1922, he and his family arrived at Cape Town. The proposed orchestra was wrecked by the unrest attendant upon the strikes in Johannesburg, but Gerke nevertheless decided to settle in Pretoria with the laborious prospect of carving out a career for himself. He was to remain in Pretoria for the rest of his life. — During the first two years he collaborated with Dolores Wedlake-Santanera in presenting series of sonata concerts in Pretoria and Johannesburg, at which both the classical and the more contemporary repertoires were presented with elucidatory programme notes. The last known concert in these series was given in October 1924. But in the meantime Gerke had extended his activities; in 1923 he started organising Sunday evening concerts, at which sacred music was presented in the old Pretoria Town Hall, and he also revived the Dutch Male Voice Choir. From 1925 he achieved greater personal financial stability by training choirs at several Afrikaans primary and high schools, extending his educational work by giving illustrated appreciation classes on music. The great depression that lasted from 1931 to 1933 had an adverse effect on the different posts that he held at these schools and, as far as can be ascertained, he never again held a permanent position at Pretoria. His choral work at the Afrikaanse Hoër Meisieskool had been particularly successful. — In September 1925 Gerke was elected Artistic Director of the newly-established Euterpe Society for the Advancement of Art.** Until the 1930s, his career was closely associated with this Society, which had memorable successes in the Schubert memorial festival (1928), the production of Gluck's *Alceste* (1926) and the presentation of scenes from *Peer Gynt,* with the music of Edvard Grieg (19 April 1929). During the eight years of its uninterrupted existence, the Society organised 64 monthly concerts of mainly chamber music, although the more accessible symphonic works were also presented to Pretoria audiences. A few concerts were given in Johannesburg. The Society had its own monthly periodical which announced coming programmes, presented discussions of works to be performed and included general essays on musical matters by Gerke, as well as news items concerning the activities of the society. Their ultimate ideal was the establishment of a permanent symphony orchestra in Pretoria. To gain the sympathy of the local authorities for this scheme, Gerke had created an amateur orchestra of 50 members with a sprinkling of professional players, which he presented as a practical example and as an argument in favour of his intentions. But the financial difficulties of the early 1930s, coupled with inability on the part of the Town Council to grasp the scope and significance of Gerke's ideal, eventually caused the scheme to collapse. To a man who had contributed so significantly to the Capital's music and who had succeeded in maintaining a society of nearly 600 paying members by sheer self-sacrificing devotion to an ideal, this was a bitter disappointment. Gerke was fated to be the right man at the wrong time. This is proved by the high standard of Euterpe's programmes, to the majority of which Gerke contributed actively as violinist or as conductor, as well as by the esteem in which he was held by professional musicians in Pretoria and Johannesburg who supported his ventures. In addition he became the victim of unfair insinuations that he was in fact propagating a pro-Dutch policy in Pretoria's musical life. Despite all his exertions, the realisation of his ideals proved to be impossible. — By 1933, Euterpe had begun to crumble, but the economic revival which started in 1937 caused Gerke to come to the fore again. He was preparing a large-scale production of Auber's *Fra Diavolo* in 1939, when the war broke out. This was the final blow to a career frustrated time and again, and prevented from coming to fruition. At the age of 63, Gerke increasingly distanced himself from Pretoria's musical life, but he continued giving private lessons until ill health in 1949 put an end to his career.

WORK
"Lustrum" overture for choir and orchestra, composed for the 55th Lustrum of the Amsterdam University. Ms., June 1907.

PUBLICATIONS
Leiddraad voor Die Geschöpfe des Prometheus. Amsterdam, 1909. *Leiddraad van de opera Iphigenia in Aulis . . . volgens de bewerking van Richard Wagner*. Amsterdam, Mar. 1914. Toonkuns, in the series *Kuns deur die Eeue*. J.L. van Schaik Bpk., Pretoria, 1935. Richard Strauss. *Handhaaf*, 1935. Ons Afrikaanse komponiste. *Die Taalgenoot*, May 1936. Edvard Grieg. *Die Huisgenoot*, 11 June 1943.

BIBLIOGRAPHY
Bentum, A.: *Professor Gerrit Bon*. B.Mus. script, UP, 1965. Matthews, G.: *Ellen Norburn and her son Charles*. B.Mus script, UP, 1966. Vermeulen, E.: *Die musieklewe in Pretoria, 1902-1926*. M.Mus. dissertation, UP, 1967. Zaidel, J.: *Music in Pretoria, 1926-1931, with special reference to Prof. Willem Gerke and the Euterpe Society*. B.Mus. script, UP, 1969.

SOURCES
Euterpe Journal: 1926-1933. *Pretoria News:* 1926-1931. Personal documents in the possession of Dr F. Gerke of Pretoria.

– J.P.M.

GERMAN MALE VOICE CHOIR, VANDERBIJLPARK, THE, was formed by German immigrants associated with the steel industry of Vanderbijlpark. After preliminary discussions, the first meeting was held on 1 September 1951, under the chairmanship of Heinrich Hahn. The first choirmaster was Emil Frohne. — After its first concert performance on 17 October 1951, the choir became known not only through concerts, but also through radio broadcasts. It won a shield for the most outstanding male voice choir participating in the Vereeniging Eisteddfod in 1953. Its membership increased to fifty after Anton Kratz became the conductor in February 1956; under his leadership concert performances were given also in Johannesburg, Pretoria and other Transvaal centres. The choir was temporarily without a choirmaster after Kratz's departure from Vanderbijlpark at the beginning of 1958 and the rehearsals were conducted by Messrs Burry and Stepp, until Jan Coljee became the leader in the latter half of 1958. Under his guidance the German Male Voice Choir has given frequent performances in collaboration with the Iscor and Sasol choral societies.

BIBLIOGRAPHY
Armer, Heinrich C.: *Die musieklewe van Vanderbijlpark ten opsigte van musiekopvoeding en koor- en orkesverenigings.* B.Mus. script, UP, 1967.

SOURCE
Commemoration programme of the tenth anniversary of the German Male Voice Choir, Vanderbijlpark, 7–9 July 1961.

– Ed.

GERSTMAN, BLANCHE, *2 April 1910 in Cape Town; °11 August 1973 in Cape Town. Composer, double bass player and accompanist.

Blanche Gerstman was born in South Africa of English stock and brought up by foster parents whose name she adopted when she was 12 years of age. She had a strict religious education, and when her musical talent became evident, was given every encouragement, often at great personal sacrifices to the Gerstmans. She evinced a tremendous desire to be a missionary doctor ("I have always loved the idea of 'making people better'"); but music prevailed, and at the age of 13 she wrote her first composition, a Voluntary for the church where she played the organ. This was followed by a *Minuet* dedicated to Victor Hely-Hutchinson,** who instructed her in harmony at that time. He was impressed and brought it to the attention of Prof. W.H. Bell**, Dean of the newly-created Faculty of Music of the University of Cape Town. — After completing her matriculation with distinctions in Mathematics and Music, Blanche considered a career in Actuarial Science; but Prof. Bell obtained for her a university scholarship, and advised her to study for the degree of B.Mus. in his Faculty (1928). He himself supervised her work in composition and Colin Taylor** became her teacher in advanced pianoforte playing, strongly influencing her conception of music and her emotional attitude to the beauty of sound. In the initial year of her graduate study, she wrote her first significant composition, a choral work, *Hellas,* which was performed at a symphony concert in the City Hall, Cape Town. In 1932 she became the first student to graduate in Music from the University of Cape Town, and was appointed official accompanist and pianist to the broadcasting studios of the SABC in Cape Town. During the 'thirties she was brought to public notice through concerts organised by Charles Weich,** at which some of her work was performed — After ten years of active music-making in broadcasting, Blanche Gerstman became lecturer in harmony and counterpoint at the SA College of Music,** and interested herself in playing the double bass (1942). Her study of this rare instrument for a woman went forward rapidly, and in 1950 she left the University to become principal double-bass player in the Cape Town Municipal Orchestra.** In the same year, however, she was awarded the scholarship of the Performing Right Society, which enabled her to study at the RAM, where Howard Ferguson supervised her work in composition (1950-1952). — During this period in London, Miss Gerstman completed the first and second movements of her *Sonata for violin and piano;* the third movement was completed in Cape Town after her return. In 1953 she resumed her duties in the City Orchestra and remained a member until 1961, when she was appointed lecturer in harmony and counterpoint to the newly-formed Academy of Music of the University of Pretoria.** She resigned in June 1963, and returned to orchestral playing. For a short period she played double bass in the Durban Civic Orchestra,** and then returned to Cape Town as a part-time lecturer in harmony and counterpoint at the College of Music (1964). Eventually, in 1969, she again became double-bass player in the Cape Town Municipal Orchestra. — Blanche defined her artistic credo in a radio talk, as follows: "The essential things for a composer are a high measure of intelligence, a sensitive and selective self-criticism, a feeling for beauty in all its aspects in nature and humanity, logic, balance, the whole gamut of emotions and, of course, a warm-hearted, all-enveloping love". These elements characterize her original work, which exhibits a personal relationship to the emotional beauty of sound; her compositions are free from the constraints of system, and obedient only to the dictates of her strong, sound feeling and warm humanity.

WORKS

A. Vocal works

1. Choral

Hellas, for female chorus, solo soprano and orchestra (Shelley). Ms., 1928.   The Lord's prayer, for unaccompanied female chorus. Ms., 1934.   Uit die Passie, Easter cantata for mixed chorus and orchestra, commissioned by the SABC (W.E.G. Louw). Ms., 1941-1946: 1. Avondmaal 2. Getsèmane 3. Verraad 4. Golgotha 5. Begrafnis 6. Opstanding.   Die boodskap aan Maria, Christmas cantata, commissioned by the SABC. Ms., 1945: 1. Die boodskap aan Maria, for mezzo-soprano, mixed chorus and organ (N.P. van Wyk Louw) 2. Maria, for mezzo-soprano and orchestra (W.E.G. Louw) 3. Maria, for mezzo-soprano and orchestra (Elizabeth Eybers) 4. Heilige nag, for female choir, strings and harp (Elizabeth Eybers). Ode aan Suid-Afrika (Ode to South Africa), for solo soprano, mixed choir and orchestra, commissioned by the SABC (I.D. du Plessis; English by Gideon Roos). Ms., 1948: 1. Waarheen? (Whither?) 2. Gebed (Prayer) 3. Ontwaking (Awakening) 4. Samewerking (Co-operation) 5. Die nuwe dag (The new day) 6. Eenheid (Unity).   O Lord, God of Israel, anthem for two- and three-part soprano voices and organ (Biblical). Ms., 1953.   A song for St Cecilia's day 1687, for women's voices and piano (John Dryden). Ms., 1956.   Book of choruses, for Sunday School (Blanche Gerstman). Ms., 1957: 1. Won't it be wonderful 2. Put your hand into the hand of God 3. Kept by the power of God 4. Best of all 5. The fruits of the Spirit 6. There'll come a time 7. Come unto me 8. Whitsuntide 9. Rejoice in the Lord always 10. Stay tuned-in to Jesus 11. Put a bridle on your tongue 12. Slow to anger 13. Good Friday 14. Easter day.   Thuismarsch, for double quartet with piano accompaniment (Heurkes) Ms., n.d.

2. Songs

Have you seen but a white lily grow? For soprano and pianoforte, also with orchestral accompaniment (Ben Jonson). Ms., 1928.   Epitaph, for soprano and orchestra (Walter de la Mare). Ms., 1928.   Requiem, for mezzo-soprano and orchestra (R.L. Stevenson). Ms., 1928.   Frühlingslied, for soprano and piano (Hölter). Ms., 1930.   The toad and the star, for soprano and piano (J. Wood). Ms., 1933.   Song cycle, for soprano and piano, also with orchestral accompaniment (C.H. Weich). Ms., 1934–1935: 1. Ek ken jou skaars   2. Ek ken jou nou   3. Waarom?   Vaalvalk, for soprano and pianoforte, also with orchestra (W.E.G. Louw). Ms., 1934.   Branders, for soprano and piano, also with orchestral accompaniment (Jan F.E. Celliers). Ms. in SABC Music Library, 1937–1938.   Five songs for voice and pianoforte, also with orchestral accompaniment. Ms. in SABC Music Library, 1937–1938: 1. Caprice, n.d.   2. Farewell my lute, for baritone with woodwind and strings (Boleyn)   3. May sweet oblivion lull thee, for mezzo-soprano (anon.)   4. Scherzo   5. Swayeth my Linden, for soprano (from *Marriage with genius* by Freda Strindberg).   Voice in the night, for soprano with orchestral accompaniment (from *The modern comedy,* by Galsworthy). Ms., 1942.   To . . ., for mezzo-soprano and piano (Shelley). Ms., 1942.   Only in dreams, for soprano and orchestra (Wilbraham Leftwich). Ms., 1942.   The country faith (God op die veld), for mezzo-soprano or baritone with orchestra (Norman Gale). Ms., 1943.   As those we love decay, for mezzo-soprano (or baritone) and piano (James Thomson). Ms., 1943.   Summer night, for mezzo-soprano (or baritone) and piano (Tennyson). Ms., 1944.   Songs (Ariel) from *The tempest,* for soprano with celesta (Shakespeare). Ms., 1946: 1. Come unto these yellow sands   2. Full fathom five   3. While you here do snoring lie   4. Where the bee sucks.   To sleep, for mezzo-soprano (or baritone) and piano (Wordsworth). Ms., 1947.   How sweet the moonlight sleeps upon this bank! For mezzo-soprano (or baritone) and piano (from *The merchant of Venice,* by Shakespeare). Ms., 1947.   Nag-rit, for soprano and piano (N.P. van Wyk Louw). Ms., 1948.   Thou art the sky, for mezzo-soprano (or baritone) and piano (Tagore). Ms., 1948.   Sonnet no. 29, for soprano and piano (Shakespeare). Ms., 1953.   The Lord's prayer, religious solo for mezzo-soprano (or baritone) and piano, also for unaccompanied women's voices. Ms., 1957.   23rd Psalm, religious solo for contralto (or baritone) and piano. Ms., 1957.   Die lied van 'n vrou (The quiet adventure), for soprano and piano (Elizabeth Eybers). Ms., 1958: 1. Die ontmoeting (The meeting)   2. Ek was so arm (In my poverty)   3. Die geskenk (The gift)   4. Voorbereiding (Preparation)   5. Vervulling (Fulfilment)   6. Die eerste nag (The first night).   Oop wêreld wat verwagtend lê (The virgin soil) (I.D. du Plessis). *Die Burger,* 8 Mar. 1960.   Elizabethan melodies arr. for voice and orchestra, for Shakespeare birthday concert at Hiddingh Hall, Apr. 1964. Ms. in Jagger Library, UCT.   Three South African Carols (Drie Suid-Afrikaanse Kersliedere), in *South African Christmas Carols (Kersliedere uit Suid-Afrika).* Voortrekkerpers, 1968: 1. Bethlehem's star (Tienie Holloway)   2. Did the wise men know? (Jo Ross)   3. Christmas bells (Jo Ross and composer).   Come, ring the merry bells, first prize in SA competition for a radio carol. *SABC Bulletin,* 24 Nov. 1969.   Africana. Ms., 1968–1969: 1. Die fonteine (Francois Marais)   2. For Elsie Hall (Dorothea Spears)   3. Himne aan die aarde deur die eerste maanreisigers (Francois Marais)   4. Groote Schuur, dedicated to Chris Barnard (Jessie Priman)   5. Weep for ourselves, dedicated to Mrs B. Verwoerd on the day after the death of Dr H.F. Verwoerd (Dorothea Spears)   6. Oom Paul, dedicated to Etienne and Joubero Malherbe. ATKV Prize   7. Pinkfaced monkey with the big ears, for Retha-Louise (see Instrumental).   Dierereeks, for the Afrikaanse Musiekklub in Pretoria. Ms., 1970: 1. Seemeeu (Uys Krige)   2. Ma en Pietjie (Jan Celliers)   3. Steenbokkie (S.J. Pretorius).   Psalm VIII, for 4 voices. Ms., 1970.   Song of the water year (Die waterjaarlied) (G.A. Watermeyer). Studio Holland, Cape Town, 1970. Blow,

blow, thou winter wind, for soprano and piano (Shakespeare). Ms., n.d. The donkey, for mezzo-soprano (or baritone) and piano (G.K. Chesterton). Ms., n.d. Hoor jy my? With harp and strings (Jacques Malan). Ms., n.d. Huweliksgebed, for mezzo-soprano (or baritone) and piano or organ (C.H. Weich). Ms., n.d. Juno, Ceres' song from *The tempest* (Shakespeare). Ms., n.d. Kruger song 1968, for baritone and piano (Jan F.E. Celliers). Ms., n.d. Let's march into the future, for four voices and piano (Eric Rosenthal). Ms., n.d. Lied van die stem, with harp and strings (Jacques Malan). Ms., n.d. Little Babe of Bethlehem (Kindjie van Bethlehem), Christmas carol (Jo Ross and composer). Ms., n.d. Maria, for voice and piano, also with orchestra. Ms., in SABC library, n.d. Maria en die engel, with piano (anon.). Ms., n.d. May sweet oblivion lull thee, for mezzo-soprano and piano (anon.). Ms., n.d. O mistress mine, for mezzo-soprano (or baritone) and piano (Shakespeare). Ms., n.d. Song cycle, for mezzo-soprano and piano (Xander Haagen). Ms., n.d.: 1. Ontmoeting 2. Kontras 3. Wense. Sonnet no. 18, for mezzo-soprano (or baritone) and piano (Shakespeare). Ms., n.d. South African Republic, for 4 voices and piano (Composer). Ms., n.d. The source of love, for mezzo-soprano (or baritone) and piano (Robert Bridges). Ms., n.d. Vreugdeboodskap aan Maria, for voice and piano, also with orchestra. Ms. in SABC Musical Library, n.d.

B. Instrumental
Prelude and fugue in A minor, for piano. Ms., 1928. Bagatelle, for violin. Ms., 1928 or 1929. Study, for piano. Ms., 1928. Romance, for violin solo with piano. Ms., 1929. Caprice, for piano. Ms., 1929. Scherzo, for piano. Ms., 1932. Suite for two pianos: 1. Prelude 2. Minuet 3. March. Arnold van Wyk wrote the part for Piano I; perf. by Gerstman and Van Wyk at a concert of the Oranje Club, Cape Town, 26 Nov. 1937. Paraphrase on Grieg's *Ich liebe dich,* for small orchestra. Ms., 1937. Out of the Christmas stocking, for string orchestra (also for piano solo) to illustrate various styles. Ms., 1937: 1. Sonatina (Scarlatti) 2. Arioso (Bach) 3. Minuet (Court elegance) 4. Lullaby (Brahms) 5. Scherzo (Aunt Blanche). Three intermezzos in D, A flat and F major, for piano. Ms., 1947. Prelude, for small orchestra. Ms., 1949. Variations on a theme by Righini (Vieni amore), for piano. Ms., 1950. Serenade and scherzo, for woodwind trio. Ms., 1951. Sonata no. 1, for violin and piano. Ms., 1951–1952. Fanfare for the Van Riebeeck Festival. Ms., 1952. We shall endure, dance drama for two pianos; or small orchestra; or violin, viola, cello and piano (composer). Ms., 1952: 1. Minuet for Sally 2. Melody for Mary 3. A story for Jonathan. Pieces for ballet, children's pieces for piano solo. Ms., 1953: 1. Dance of the Primroses 2. Forget-me-nots 3. Bluebells. Three ballet pieces for school orchestra or string trio. Ms., 1957: 1. Minuet 2. Melody 3. A story. (Possibly the same as "We shall endure"). Table Mountain overture, for full orchestra. Ms., 1958–1961. Greensleeves, arr. for orchestra for Shakespeare birthday concert at Hiddingh Hall, Apr. 1964. Ms. in Jagger Library, UCT. Pink-faced monkey with the big ears, for Retha-Louise (see Africana), for piano solo. Ms., 1969. The flute player, for flute and piano. Ms. in Jagger Library, UCT, n.d. The ox and the ass at the crib, radio music for strings. Ms., n.d. Serenade and minuet, for strings. Ms., n.d. Serenade to starlight, for orchestra and piano. Ms., n.d. Vorausnahme, song prelude for violin and strings. Ms., n.d.

SOURCES
Anon.: Blanche Gerstman. *Opus* V/I, Oct/Nov. 1973. Bourdon: Ons onbekende komponiste. *Die Burger,* 28 Oct. 1935. Malan, J.P.: Blanche Gerstman. *Res Musicae* VII, June

1961. Stegmann, Frits: Suid-Afrika verloor toonskepper. *Die Burger,* 15 Aug. 1973. Research Centre for South African Music, HSRC, Pretoria.

– J.P.M.

GERTRUDE BUCHANAN MEMORIAL PRIZE D.B. Coutts, P. de Groote (Oliver), M.J. Heiberg, Higher Educational Institutions VIII/2(ii)

GHOEMA SONGS Cape Malays

GIBBS, ALFRED J. Luyt (sr.)

GIBSON, GILBERT, *20 January 1928 in Naboomspruit. Composer of light music, author and company director.

Gilbert Gibson was the son of a musically gifted mother – he had hardly turned five when he was picking out tunes on the piano and improvising songs. This led to musical training during his years at school, after which he was a student at the University of Pretoria for three years and the editor of a periodical who tried his hand at writing novels. At the same time he was a critic of light music for local and overseas newspapers, also for the SABC, and had a record collection comprising more than 14 000 titles. — In 1962, partnered by Taffie Kikillus,** he started publishing music as Sun-Pacific Music, a firm which also included his own compositions. Some of his numbers were published overseas by Tuckahoe Music, Nashville, America; Sydney Bron Music; and One Four Two Music in England. His first composition was the well-known *Vaal ou Karooland* which was recorded by Hendrik Susan and six other groups. Though he had started writing music in 1952, he only devoted himself to creative work after 1962, when he had been encouraged by Hendrik Susan to do so. For Jim Reeves, who sang three of his tunes in *Kimberley Jim,* he composed a further number, *I'm crying again,* which also became a song-hit. Besides his work in film music, he has also written two musical comedies in collaboration with Nico Carstens and Anton de Waal.

A SELECTION OF HIS TUNES
Vaal ou Karooland; Ek verlang na jou; Neem my terug na die Bolandse berge; Kleindraai se mense; Tokoloshe man; Insecure; My summer is gone; Drommels in nood; Sing weer vir my; Miranda, waarom het jy my verraai?; Sands of the Kalahari; The moment for love; Lolita; Bokkapater; I'm crying again.

FILM MUSIC
Kimberley Jim: A stranger's just a friend; Diamonds in the sand; Dolly with the dimpled knees.

MUSICAL COMEDIES
Sarie van Mooifontein; Janewariebaai.

– Ed.

GIBSON, PERLA SIEDLE, *30 April 1888 in Durban; °5 March 1971 in Durban. Pianist, painter and singer, who became well-known during the Second World War as "The lady in white".

Of musical parentage, Perla was given every opportunity of studying under the direction of prominent artists, at home and abroad. After South African training in pianoforte playing, under artists such as Theo Wendt** and Gertrude Kind, she continued her studies in Berlin under the tuition of Martin Krause, the principal of the Stern Conservatoire. On her return, she made her debut in 1909 as a pianist in the last concert to be held in the old Durban Town Hall (now the General Post Office). Her interest was not confined to music, for she also undertook a study of the fine arts in Berlin and exhibited successfully in various galleries and salons. — Since she was also the possessor of a good voice, Perla was invited to sing parts in concert versions of grand opera in Durban and this led to studies in voice production in London and New York. During and after these studies she performed in song recitals and appeared with Dan Godfrey's Bournemouth Orchestra and with famous British military bands. As a singer she also represented this country on South Africa Day at Wembley. Performances in programmes presented by the SABC, BBC and television were frequent. — Although invited to sing Wagnerian roles in Covent Garden, Miss Gibson elected to return to South Africa before the outbreak of the Second World War. During the War, clad in white, it was her practice to sing from the North Pier in Durban harbour to convoys passing through the port and became a well-known figure to all the services entering or leaving the harbour. This voluntary service was publicly acknowledged by her presentation to Queen Elizabeth II in 1949, at a Buckingham Palace Garden Party, and again when she was invited as the guest of honour to a military rally in London in 1963.

SOURCE
Everwyn, Ingeborg: Lady in white sing in hawe. *Die Burger,* 15 Sept. 1964.

– Ed.

GILCHRIST, G.   Piano Music IV/3

GILFILLAN, BEATRICE (TRIXIE) AND ZOE, Mr and Mrs Gilfillan were early settlers in Queenstown. Mr Gilfillan, who was a violinist and a singer, and Mrs Gilfillan, who was a pianist, are mentioned in 1869 and afterwards in connection with concerts arranged by the Rev. H. Dugmore** and others arranged by Mrs Stier.** They had two daughters who practised music professionally, Beatrice (Trixie) and Zoe. The Lyric Opera Company, formed in Johannesburg in the latter half of 1892, went on a South African tour in 1893 and came to Queenstown in June. Trixie became a member of the company and sang parts in *Iolanthe* and *La cigale.* Zoe again, assisted in staging musical sketches produced by Nellie Ganthony in February 1894 and left for Great Britain in 1895. There she became a member of the Moody Opera Company and then of the D'Oyly Carte Opera Company. Both sisters were mentioned in connection with concerts in Bloemfontein before 1895, but it was Beatrice who actually lived there for a while and taught at the Eunice Girls' High School. She eventually became a member of the Rand Grand Operatic Company.

BIBLIOGRAPHY
Human, J.L.K.: *Musiek in die Oranje Vrystaat vanaf 1850 tot aan die begin van die Anglo-Boereoorlog.* M.Mus dissertation, UOFS, 1963.   Wolpowitz, L.: *James and Kate Hyde and the*

development of music in Johannesburg up to the First World War. NCSR Publications series no. 31, J.L. van Schaik, Pretoria, 1969.

SOURCE
Queenstown Free Press: 1869, 1893, 1894.

– J.L.K.H. (amplified)

GLASSER, STANLEY, *28 February 1926 in Johannesburg; living in London in 1966. Composer, pianist and lecturer in music.

The son of Joe Glasser, a Jewish violinist who came to South Africa before the First World War, Stanley was at first a pupil of Isador Epstein** and later of Adolph Hallis.** After matriculation at the King Edward VII School in 1945, he studied for the B.Com. degree at the University of the Witwatersrand, but he maintained music as a hobby, wrote some pianoforte music, and received guidance in composition from Prof. P.R. Kirby** and S. Hylton Edwards.** — Glasser graduated in 1949, and left for England in April, 1950, to study composition at the Guildhall School of Music under Benjamin Frankel and, privately, under Matyas Seiber. He won various musical prizes, among them the Royal Philharmonic Society Prize for composition in March, 1952 *(Sinfonietta concertante).* After a visit to South Africa in 1954, he returned to England in 1955 to continue his study at King's College, Cambridge, where he graduated (first class) in June 1958 in the Music Tripos examination. At Cambridge he won the George Richards prize for academic distinction, and wrote articles on music for the *Cambridge Review* in 1957 and 1958. — Glasser was appointed to the staff of the South African College of Music** as lecturer in music in 1958, and was promoted to the position of Assistant Director to Prof. Chisholm** in 1960. A trustee of the African Music and Drama Association of Johannesburg, he was the obvious choice to act as musical director of the musical, *King Kong,* presented in London early in 1961. With Hugh Tracey** he has on two occasions also carried out research in African folk music (1948–1950, 1954–1955). — From 1952 to 1962 Glasser was a member of the Presidential Council of the International Society for Contemporary Music, acting as an executive member from 1952 to 1955. Since 1960 he has been a member of the Composers' Guild of Great Britain, the Songwriters' Guild of Great Britain and the Performing Right Society of Great Britain. He acted as record reviewer for the *Cape Times* in the years between 1960 to 1962, and also as music critic for several papers. — After leaving Cape Town at the end of 1962, Glasser was appointed Lecturer in Music in the extra-mural department of the University of London (1963), and also Lecturer in Music to evening classes arranged by Goldsmith's College, of the same University. Since 1969 he has been Head of Music at this College.

WORKS
Opus 1: Four Inventions, for violin and viola. Ms., 1954.   Opus 2: Three pieces, for piano. Ms., 1955.   Opus 3: Four simple songs, for baritone and piano (Adolf Wood). Ms., 1956.   Opus 4: Trio, for brass instruments. Musica Rara, London, 1957.   Opus 5: Four madrigals, for SSATB a capella (Adolf Wood). Novello and Musica Rara, London, 1958.   Opus 6: Three dances, for trombone quartet Musica Rara, London, 1961.   The square, ballet for symphony orchestra and jazz ensemble. Ms., 1962.   Opus 7: Movements, for strings. Ms., 1964.   Opus 8:

Casino-concertino, for violin and strings. Ms., 1964.   Opus 9, Soho sketches, for dectet. Ms., 1964.   Opus 10, Te Deum, for SATB and small orchestra. Ms., 1965.   Opus 11, Dances, for dectet. Ms., 1965.   Opus 12, String quartet no. 1. Ms., 1965.   Bric-a-brac. Ms., 1963: 1. Three piano pieces   2. It is like the flowers, for baritone and piano   3. Two pieces for piano, for children   4. Lullaby, for viola and piano   5. The adventures of Bomvu, for school recorders and piano.   The chameleon and the lizard (based on an old Zulu legend by Lewis Nkosi), for double choir and 16 instruments. Ms., 1971.   Incidental music to the following BBC television plays: *A dragon to kill; The unknown citizen; Try for white; Hermit crabs*. Ms., 1964–1965. Incidental music to the following plays: *Antony and Cleopatra; A midsummer night's dream; Oedipus rex; Lady Precious Stream and Emperor Jones*. Ms., n.d.   Incidental music to the film, *Last of the few*. Ms., 1960.

BIBLIOGRAPHY
International who's who in music, 8th edition. Melrose Press, Cambridge.

SOURCES
The square. *Vita Musica* I/1, Oct. 1962.
Research Centre for South African Music, HSRC, Pretoria.

– Ed.

GLEE SINGING   W. Bolus, A.G. Dixon, Durban 2, 4, 6, 8, Durban Philharmonic Society, C. Hoby, Military Band of the CMR, Pietermaritzburg Philharmonic Society, Port Elizabeth, C.N. Thomas

GLEN'S MUSIC SHOP   Jackson Brothers

GLENTON GIRL CHORISTERS, THE.   This choir was started in Johannesburg by Mauryn Glenton** in 1949. It had, on an average, 20 members, including well-known artists and a variety of members from other professions, such as teachers, nurses and office workers, from both the English and the Afrikaans sections of the community. — The group has repeatedly won the trophy for the best choir at the National Eisteddfodau of South Africa (1949, 1963, 1964, 1967), and has participated in performances of works such as *L'Avvento,* by Franco Chioni, who conducted the first performance in Johannesburg in 1952, *Les sirénes* (Debussy) and *The planets* (Gustav Holst), conducted by Sir Malcolm Sargent. — An extensive repertoire includes two- and three-part songs in various languages, including Afrikaans.

– M.Gl.

GLENTON, LAURENCE ROBERT, *1880 in Doncaster, Yorkshire; ° 11 August 1935 in Johannesburg. Choral conductor and organist with a distinguished career in Johannesburg.

Gifted with a beautiful soprano voice, Laurence was a boy-chorister at New College, Oxford. In due course he was trained as an organist, serving in Richmond, York-minster and in Christ Church, Fenwich. At the outbreak of the South African War Glenton came to South Africa with the Irish Yeomanry and afterwards decided to settle in Johannesburg in the service of the Railway Administration. — Glenton's musical career in Johannesburg dates from the early part of 1900, when he appeared at concerts given at the mines as conductor, pianist, organist and humorist. Beatrice Marx** remembers him as an accompanist, "throwing in numerous songs at the piano, in a not-too-wonderful but adequate tenor". His competence as organist was recognised, and in 1908 he became organist and choirmaster to St Augustine's in Doornfontein. In 1933, after 25 years' service, he transferred to St Aidan's in Yeoville. — Largely owing to his efforts, talent and organising ability, the Johannesburg Philharmonic Society** and the Johannesburg Operatic Society** were created and achieved a prominent place in the musical life of the city. His greatest personal contribution was, however, as choral conductor. In 1903 he succeeded Hugh Gwynne as leader of the Johannesburg Male Voice Choir, which he conducted until 1929. In addition, he organized various scattered choral units and formed the Rand Choir in 1905, which performed *Messiah* on 4 April; and the Apollo Male Voice Choir, which made its debut at a grand concert in the Masonic Hall on 2 November. — Glenton gathered more and more influence and prestige as the years went by. His Philharmonic Society came into being on 20 August, 1909, with himself as Musical Director, and Sir Willem van Hulsteyn as its first president. Glenton now had at his command a choir of 200 voices and an orchestra, which performed *Messiah* in the Wanderers' Hall on 9 December. From that time the performance of this work became an annual event. In addition, the Society presented Haydn's *Creation,* Mendelssohn's *Hymn of praise,* and choral works by British composers, such as *The ancient mariner* by Barnet (1912), *A tale of old Japan* by Coleridge-Taylor (1911), *The revenge* by Stanford (1911), and *King Olaf* by Elgar (1911). — The war interrupted Glenton's work in 1914. When he returned from active service, the Philharmonic Society was directed by another conductor. Glenton formed a new group, the Johannesburg Choral Union (1917), which sang *The creation* in the Orpheum Theatre on 3 March, 1918. This was followed by other choral works including the inevitable *Messiah.* From 1920, for fifteen years, he also directed the Johannesburg Operatic Society** in their performances of the Savoy operas. In 1924, during John Connell's** absence overseas, he gave organ recitals in the City Hall on Sunday evenings, and again conducted the Philharmonic Society in its annual performance of *Messiah.* — In addition to these responsibilities, Glenton had exceptional success with his Johannesburg Male Voice Choir and Apollo Male Voice Choir and stimulated choral music outside Johannesburg by creating an East Rand Male Voice Choir. — The South African adjudicator, C.A. Duggan,** was impressed by the high standard of choral singing provided by the Johannesburg Male Voice Choir, and described Glenton as "a great choir trainer, a wizard of juvenile choirs, and a true master of choral detail and interpretation". Johannesburg had never before had a musician with such a complete command of choral techniques and repertoire. He created a tradition that remains one of the proudest of the City. Glenton's wife was Blanche Thomas. They had two daughters, of whom Mauryn** continued her father's work.

– L.W.

GLOBE COMEDY COMPANY   Johannesburg 1, Touring Theatre Groups 4

GLOBE THEATRE   S. Foote, K.C.C. Hyde, Johannesburg 1, E. and C. Mendelssohn, Touring Theatre Groups 4

GLUCKMAN, JEAN, *18 November 1909 in Randfontein; living in Johannesburg in 1966. Mezzo-soprano.

After graduating BA at the Witwatersrand University in 1929, with History, English and the History of Music as her main subjects, Jean Gluckman studied at the RAM (1931–1934), where she obtained the LRAM and won the Parepa Rosa scholarship for overseas students. She is also an Associate of the RCM, and holds the LTCL diploma. — An experienced opera singer, Jean has sung main roles since the early Johannesburg productions of John Connell** in works such as *Tales of Hoffman* (Offenbach); *Madame Butterfly* (Puccini); *Il trovatore* (Verdi); *The consul* (Menotti); *Hänsel and Gretel* (Humperdinck); *Faust* (Gounod); *Die Fledermaus* (J. Strauss). It is, however, for interpretations of art songs in concerts and broadcasts that Miss Gluckman was appreciated in South Africa. For the SABC Transcription Library she has recorded works by South African composers in both Afrikaans and English, notably the song cycle by Joyce Loots,** *The golden threshold* (1942). During 1966 she was engaged by PACT for a concert tour of the Transvaal with Lessie Samuel,** Gerrit Bon** (jr) and Jos de Groen.**

– Ed.

GODFREY, DAN(IEL), *21 May 1893 in England; °23 April 1935 in Durban. Conductor.

Dan Godfrey was the eldest son of Sir Dan Godfrey, founder and conductor of the Bournemouth Municipal Orchestra and Director of Music to the Bournemouth Corporation. He was educated at Sherborne School from 1907 to 1910, saw active service during World War I, and was demobilised in 1919. Although it had been his original intention to qualify as an army bandmaster, he entered the RAM, where he obtained the ARAM in 1923, his two main instrumental studies being violin and clarinet. He also studied under his father, played under him in the Bournemouth Orchestra and acted as assistant conductor to the Corporation of Harrogate between the years 1919 and 1922. He next joined the BBC (then called "2LO") and held the post of Musical Director from 1924 to 1926. He was appointed Musical Director to the Durban Corporation in May 1928, in succession to H. Lyell-Tayler.** His link with the city was through his Durban mother, Jessie Stuart (died 1926), who was married to Sir Dan Godfrey during his first visit to South Africa, when he directed the Standard Opera Company (1891). — Dan Godfrey made his first concert appearance in Durban on 24 June 1928, as conductor of the Durban Orchestra, with the British baritone, Percy Heming, as soloist. He remained with the orchestra until his death in 1935 and also conducted choirs. As an ex-soldier, who had joined the Coldstream Guards in 1913, he never really abandoned military connections, and became closely associated with the Durban Light Infantry. Towards the end of his life he gave much thought to the formation of a stock company for the performance of operettas and musical comedies. He enjoyed immense popularity as a conductor, being well-liked by both the public and the musicians who played under him.

BIBLIOGRAPHY
Grove's dictionary of music and musicians, 5th edition, 1954.   *International cyclopedia of music and musicians,* (ed.) O. Thompson, 9th edition, 1964.

GODFREY

SOURCES

Natal Witness: 29 May 1928.   *Cape Argus:* 11 Mar. 1934 (address to Rotary Club).   *Natal Mercury:* Mar. and Apr. 1935.   *Res Musicae III,* Mar. 1961.   Information supplied by Mr Patrick Chambers.   Research Centre for South African Music, HSRC, Pretoria.

– G.S.J.

GODFREY, SIR DAN   Bloemfontein, Cape Town Municipal Orchestra, P.J. Chambers, E. Dunn, Durban 7, D. Godfrey (jr), C. Hoby, Johannesburg 1, L. Searelle, Theatres and Concert Halls IV/3, Touring Theatre Groups 4

GODFREY, LOUIS, *29 October 1930 in Johannesburg; living in Johannesburg in 1970. Ballet dancer.

Godfrey was one of Ivy Conmee's** and Marjorie Sturman's** pupils who eventually became a member of the Johannesburg Festival Ballet Society. When Anton Dolin and Alicia Markova performed with this society in 1949, they invited Louis Godfrey to join their company on a tour of England. This touring company later formed the nucleus of the London Festival Ballet, for whom Godfrey, in the course of thirteen years, danced all the leading classical parts. He left the London Festival Ballet in 1962 to do television and theatre work, but at the same time he did the choreography and acted as ballet master for several musicals. — Louis Godfrey returned to South Africa early in 1970 to become ballet master and teacher of the PACT ballet company.

– H.D.

GOLDBERG, REUBEN   H.G. Ketelbey

GOLDEN RECORD   Discography

GOLLMICK, KARL, *19 March 1796 in Dessau; °3 October 1866 in Frankfurt-am-Main. Composer.

Gollmick studied music and theology in Strassburg and from 1818 onwards was attached to the City Theatre of Frankfurt for forty years. One of his songs was included in the *Afrikaner Volkszang,* a setting of C.W.H. van der Post's Dutch text, "Slaapt het Afrikaner volk?" as two duets with piano accompaniment, followed by a four-part choral song on the melody of Hymn 156. The *Afrikaner Volkszang* is included in both the *Hollands-Afrikaanse liederbundel* (1907) and the *Groot Afrikaanse-Hollandse liederbundel* (1927).

SOURCES

Mansvelt, N. (ed.): *Hollands-Afrikaanse liederbundel.* Amsterdam/Cape Town/Pretoria, 1907.   Van Niekerk, Joan (ed.): *Die Groot Afrikaanse-Hollandse liederbundel.* Cape Town/Pretoria, 1927.

– J.B.

GOOCH, ROSITA   O. Gafner, J.M. Imrie, Pretoria 3, O.F. Rorke, L. Samuel, S. Smuts, B. Taylor, L. Wolpowitz

GOODACRE, EDWARD ROBERTSON, *16 February 1879 in Leeds; °28 August 1940 in East London. Organist and conductor who composed a small amount of sacred music.

Goodacre was trained as a chorister and became deputy organist at Yorkminster where he was an organ pupil of John Naylor. Subsequently he obtained the ARCO and an LRAM and acted as music critic at the Three Choirs' Festivals held in Gloucester and Hereford. He came to South Africa before the First World War and at first played the organ in St Alban's Cathedral, Pretoria, and then in the Lutheran Church, Strand Street, Cape Town. Goodacre also performed on the organ in the City Hall, accompanied singers and contributed articles on musical subjects to an unnamed newspaper in Cape Town. At the outbreak of the war he was sent to South West Africa on military duty, but was demobilised early in 1916 when he returned to become the organist of the St John's Methodist Church in Port Elizabeth and conductor of a cinema ensemble in the Grand Theatre. — The other posts of organist which he held were those in the Wesleyan churches of Russell Road and North End and the Baptist Church in Queen Street, where he gave a monthly series of recitals from January to June 1920. His association with the Grand Theatre ended in 1917, when he started conducting a small ensemble for Messrs Cleghorn and Harris at tea time. His ensemble also played at Marshall's, at Humewood beach concerts in November 1918 and in the Roof Gardens of the Grand Hotel from January 1919. This must have been frustrating work for a trained musician, but there were compensations in the accompaniments he played for singers and violinists during 1918 and 1919. — After these and other rather scattered activities in Port Elizabeth, Goodacre went to East London in June 1920 to become the organist and choir master of Trinity Methodist Church. During his twenty years as organist there, he gave about 200 organ recitals and arranged choral performances of works by Gaul, Stainer and Mendelssohn (*Elijah*). Until the advent of talkies, he had a small cinema orchestra in the Vaudette Theatre. In addition, he taught organ, pianoforte and singing privately, acted as music director to the East London Operatic and Dramatic Society (*A country girl,* 1939), accompanied singers and instrumentalists, adjudicated choir competitions of the Native Musical Association and gave lectures on sacred, vocal and instrumental music. Under the heading "Music Jottings", he published a weekly article on music in the *Daily Dispatch* from August 1923 until April 1930. These he usually signed with the pseudonym Legato. He propagated the formation of a municipal orchestra, pleaded for an organ in the City Hall, and supported the revival of the East London Choral Society. His reviews of concerts were still published in the local press after 1930. — He formed Goodacre's Augmented Choir in 1923 (in 1927 this became the East London Choral Society) and conducted it in *Messiah* and works by Gounod (*Faust*), Elgar (*King Olaf*), Haydn (*The creation*), Handel (*Samson*), Gaul and Stainer. After 1920 an annual performance of *Messiah* became a tradition in East London, through Goodacres's initiative, and was carried on after his death, first by the East London Choral Society and then by the East London Philharmonic Society. — For his compositions, Goodacre sometimes used the pseudonym "G. Edward Robertson".

WORKS
Four-part songs. R. Müller's Music Warehouse, Cape Town, n.d.: 1. Peace, perfect peace   2. Light after darkness   3. A prayer   4. Nearer my God, to Thee   5. Crossing the bar   6. Zijt gij

GOODACRE

moede. (In Müller's *Kerkkoorboek*, part I, there is a translation of this work with the words "Sondaar, voel jy moeg en treurig"). Lead kindly Light, sacred song (Cardinal Newman). R. Müller, Cape Town, n.d. The light of eternal day, song (C.M. Haddock). Mackay Bros, Johannesburg, n.d. Mizpah, a song (A.E.G.). Mackay Bros, Johannesburg, n.d. My Queen of Roscrae, song. Ms., n.d. O perfect love, song. Ms., n.d. Rock of ages, sacred song. Ms., n.d. The storm, for organ. Ms., n.d. Three greetings, song (P.D.R.). R. Müller, Cape Town, n.d.

BIBLIOGRAPHY
Van der Merwe, F.Z.: *Suid-Afrikaanse musiekbibliografie, 1787–1952.* J.L. van Schaik, Pretoria, 1958.

SOURCES
Daily Dispatch: 1920–1940. *Eastern Province Herald:* 1916–1920.

– E.H.S. (amplified)

GOOD HOPE HALL, CAPE TOWN   P. Ould

GOODNOW HALL, HUGUENOT SEMINARY   H.W. Egel, Wellington

GOODWIN, R. BRIAN, *27 June 1924 in Pietermaritzburg; living in Pietermaritzburg in 1962. Organist and music teacher.

On his mother's side a descendant of William Sterndale Bennett, Brian Goodwin had lessons since his ninth year in pianoforte, organ and theory from his uncle, J. Withers Carter,** the borough organist of Pietermaritzburg. His apprenticeship ended in 1949 when he was awarded the Elizabeth Allen Bursary. He left for England, where he was an articled pupil of Dr Gordon Slater of Lincoln Cathedral and then entered the RAM where he had tuition in organ, pianoforte, harmony and counterpoint, choral conducting and, under Aubrey Brain, in the French horn. During these years he gave some seven organ recitals in various churches in London and was an assistant organist at a church in Gipsey Hill from 1950 to 1952. — In South Africa he gave organ recitals in various centres, including the town halls of Durban and Pietermaritzburg. He was music master at Cordwalles School in Pietermaritzburg from 1954 to 1958 and in 1959 he became Director of Music to Hilton College in Natal. There he has been engaged in extending the musical life of the school by creating a choral and an opera society and giving the first Natal performance of a *Passion according to St Luke* (ascribed to Bach) in Hilton College Chapel in 1962. Since the latter year he has also been a music examiner of the Natal Education Department and an adjudicator at music festivals; 1962 was also the year in which the Italian government awarded him a bursary to study organ and school music in Venice.

– Ed.

GORDON BELL, E. AND I.   Barberton, Bloemfontein, Johannesburg 2, Port Elizabeth, Touring Theatre Groups 3

GORDON, LADY DUFF   Cape Malays

GORRIE, ROBERT (BOB)   Potchefstroom 2

GOULD, MICHAEL   Colonial Cape Mounted Riflemen, Military band of the

GOUWS, HANSIE, *1920 in the vicinity of Wakkerstroom; now (1977) in Johannesburg. Composer of light Afrikaans music.

A pianoforte pupil of S. le Roux Marais** during his school years in Ermelo, Hansie Gouws became a student at the Potchefstroom Teachers' Training College in 1938 and formed a band for light Afrikaans music. Shortly after he had accepted his first teaching appointment in Alberton, he formed a Rhythm Group, which has been heard on radio since 1950. In 1962 he became music adviser to the Transvaal Education Department, with the responsibility for vocal and instrumental music in the Johannesburg-Central, Heidelberg and Vereeniging areas.

TUNES
Rietdakhusie (1948), Hier (1948), Eensame aande (1948), Danie (1948), Herfsblare (1948), Dag na dag (1949), Jy is bekoorlik (1949), Laat in die nag (1949), Wat help dit? (from the operetta *Afskeidsdans* (1950), Die rooikop (1950), Ek wens (1950), Is dit maar net (1950), Lugkastele (1950), Daardie oomblik (1950), Kommandolied (1951), Skemermelodie (1951), Wit satyn (1951), Laat my los, kêrels (1951), 'n Ruiker (1951), Waarom? (1951), Ver, ver van hier (1952), Sawens in Desembermaand (1952), Sekelmaan (1952), As die windjie waai (1952), Dit is die maanlig (1953), Trippens, sikspens (1953), Daar anderkant die bult (1953), Kom ons wandel (1954), My hart behoort aan jou (1954), Iemand soos jy (1954), Vonkeloognooi (1961).

OPERETTA
Vrolike feesdae, school operetta (Ela Spence). Van der Westhuizen & Grobler, Pretoria, n.d.
– Ed.

GRAAFF REINET DRAMATIC AND ORCHESTRAL SOCIETY Graaff Reinet 5

GRAAFF REINET, MUSIC IN (1786–1960)

1. Introduction
2. Music education, 1850–1921
3. Communal music, 1856–1886
4. Professional touring companies
5. The Dramatic and Orchestral Society
6. Church music
7. Music education, 1921–1970
8. A few Graaff Reinet composers

1. Introduction
Founded as a lone outpost of European civilization in the 18th Century, Graaff Reinet lost its rugged frontier character when law and order became established under the two Landdrosts Stockenström, father and son (1804–1828), and when the influence of Christian worship radiated out over the Midlands through the work of the Rev. Andrew Murray (sr) (1822–1866). The Great Trek of 1838 created a vacuum in the Graaff Reinet area, which was filled by an influx of English and German farmers,

103

businessmen and artisans. Owing to its strategic position on the route from Port Elizabeth to the North and North-East, the town became the second most important commercial centre in the Cape Colony after the middle of the century, reaching the peak of its commercial and cultural development in the '80s. During this period, Graaff Reinet was sometimes referred to as "The Athens of the East". With the subsequent decline of prosperity, the once buoyant musical life also waned, although the town has retained its ecclesiastical and educational lead in the Karroo area.

2. Music education (1850–1921)

Education in music is mentioned for the first time in April, 1861, when Mr Geo. Kidd, the Government schoolmaster, had a Juvenile Singing Class which he instructed through the tonic sol-fa method. He presented the fruits of his labours in a concert on August 20, but was severely criticised in the press for the "unschooled" singing and a sad lack of balance in his choir. Part songs were sung, such as *The lark* and *The nightingale* (Mendelssohn) and Morley's sprightly madrigal, *Now is the month of Maying*. Kidd's choir did not survive, and in 1864 the government school closed down. Twenty years were to pass before state schools were again established in Graaff Reinet and in the meantime private schools prospered. There were no less than 50 private schools in this town, all established between 1850 and 1886. — The teaching of music was limited before 1858, and up to 1875 music was always offered as a secondary branch of education, for which additional payments were due. In 1858 Miss Grubb's School, for example, charged R4 per quarter for general education, and R2 extra for tuition in pianoforte or singing. That there was a demand for this type of extra tuition is proved by a continuous succession of teachers. A Mrs and Miss Teubes taught pianoforte in 1858, and they were followed by Miss Brooks (1859), Mrs S.J. Naude and Miss Vos (1868), Mrs and Miss Brown (1869), Mrs Roach (1869) and Miss Arderne (1879). Miss Purdon taught harp and guitar in 1884, and Mrs Maude pianoforte and singing in 1886. The press mentions that some schools gave concerts at the annual prize-giving ceremony. Thus Auret's Primary School, which existed from 1860 to 1911, had an annual social gathering of parents and children at which music items were presented, and from 1867 to 1872 the so-called English Choir of Mr Atkinson and some adult amateurs contributed numbers to the programme. The nature of these gatherings is indicated by oblique references in the press, such as a discreet warning to a mother that "Belinda should not appear more than once!" — The Jesuit School (1852–1894) was more ambitious, and performed *The rose of Savoy* (1883) and *The flower queen* (1884). Miss Purdon assisted in their musical direction. This lady, likewise Miss Arderne and Mrs Kidd, ran a dancing school between 1879 and 1886. In typical Victorian fashion, there was quite a demand for this type of instruction: John Humphreys, who came from Jamaica, had a shortlived Dancing Academy in 1855, the Misses Melville had another one in the '90s, whilst the bandmaster, James Saunders, enjoyed an enviable reputation with his "quadrille parties" in the years between 1883 and 1890. — Independent tuition in music seems to have started with John Lewis Viner,** who came in 1859 and taught pianoforte, organ and singing. He is of considerable importance as the owner of the first music shop in Graaff Reinet, which existed until after the turn of the century. About the middle of the century much attention was paid to the training of adults in choral singing. Apart from his efforts with the juvenile singing class, the government schoolmaster, Geo. P. Kidd, applied the tonic sol-fa method in training choral singers. He left Graaff Reinet in 1863, but returned in 1875 as a teacher of singing, theory and commercial subjects. Two years later this educationist formed a glee class, and advertised evening lessons in singing for young men. — When the Athenaeum was created in 1862, the prominent Harry Bolus** and the previously mentioned Joseph Atkinson organised choral classes to discipline the untrained frontier voices, with the object of starting a choral movement. Atkinson led the "English choir", which sang at the English services held in the Dutch Reformed Church; he also assisted at the Auret's Primary School, and acted as a part-time gymnastic instructor at Graaff Reinet College, which was established in 1861 and became the Boys' High School in 1884. This important institution was financed by local interest, but also enjoyed the privilege of a State grant of R800 per annum. The College does not seem to have been very active musically, but its first two "professors", F. Guthrie and J. Gill, strongly advanced the cultural cause among the townsmen. — After years of economic depression (c. 1862–1870), the discovery of diamonds at Kimberley stimulated revival, and when the railroad from Port Elizabeth to Graaff Reinet was completed in 1879, the town entered a period of expansion and prosperity. Among the various interests attracted to the town, trained musicians arrived and assisted in changing the pattern of musical life. There were the adventurer Z. Lionarons,** a violinist who came and left in 1875; the conductor, M. Kennedy (1878–1879); Thomas Ross, a flautist and ex-bandmaster from Cape Town, who came in 1880; the bandmaster, Mr Moore, who died in Graaff Reinet in 1879; James Saunders, who conducted the Graaff Reinet Brass Band (1879–1883), and James Liebmann, Professor of Classics at the Graaff Reinet College, who had been trained in music at the Brussels Conservatoire. They were not only active in organizing and training groups, but also taught music individually. — The prosperity of Graaff Reinet led to the establishment of a number of new schools. Miss Armstrong started her school in 1873, and a year later Miss Hall's Establishment for Young Ladies, advertised as a "finishing school", opened its doors. Miss Hall was enthusiastic about musical training and engaged a number of qualified overseas teachers as full-time members of her staff. Alice Hart,** a licentiate of the RAM, taught music at the establishment from 1880 to 1881, and Fräulein Reimar from 1881 to 1882. Miss Hall subsequently became principal of the Collegiate Girls' High School in Port Elizabeth (1886–1889), Miss Hart left for Durban, and Miss Reimar re-appeared at the Collegiate GHS in Port Elizabeth and again in Bloemfontein. — The most important new establishment was the famous Midland Seminary (1876–1921), which came into being as an institute for young ladies under the aegis of the Dutch Reformed Church, with the Rev. Charles Murray** as the leading spirit. It was modelled on the lines of the Huguenot Seminary at Wellington, and was for many years nick-named the "American Seminary", on account of the strong American influence on its staff and educational pattern. Helen Murray, sister of the Rev. Charles Murray, was the principal for no less than forty years (1876–1916). The fame and undoubted success of the Seminary were largely due to her untiring efforts and to the firm Christian discipline with which she guided its destinies. Music was prominent in its educational programme. In 1910 it had no less than five music teachers, and a separate building devoted to music, with studios and practising rooms. — The Seminary unfortunately burnt down in 1921, and all the school's records were lost in the fire. The following teachers are, however, known to have taught music at the school: Fräulein Bau (pianoforte, organ, singing, 1882–1893); the Misses Van Reenen (pianoforte and singing), R. du Toit, Davidson, Phillips and Müller during the '80s; Miss Hayden (violin, c. 1896–1900); Mrs Abercrombie-Dawes (pianoforte), Miss Angeron (piano-forte), Miss Craig (singing), Mary Dawson (singing), all the latter serving between 1900 and 1921; Gladys Fendick (violin, c. 1896–1911); Miss Luke (pianoforte and organ, c. 1907–1912); Miss Thring (violin, c. 1905–1912); and Mrs Jack Priest (pianoforte). Gladys Fendick, who had studied in England and Germany, made her debut at Port Elizabeth's Municipal Sunday Evening Concerts on 11 July 1909. The active music inspector, Fred Farrington,** was a guest teacher at the school in 1898, for about four months, to give instruction in the tonic sol-fa method. — The outstanding music teacher at the Seminary was Miss Bau, an able pianist who was also a fine choral conductor. After 1883, the concerts she gave became more frequent, more ambitious and also lengthier; progressively she drew upon the interest and assistance of colleagues on the staff, local amateurs, and even professional musicians, such as bandmaster Saunders. During 1884 she presented no less than five concerts, including a performance of Franz Abt's *Cinderella* (June 6), which attracted so much support that her "Grand Concerts" had to be presented in the largest available halls, either the Town Hall or the Market Hall. In 1885 there were four concerts: the first on 17 June was devoted to part-songs by Mendelssohn and Schubert; the second and third included *The lady of the bell* (Romberg); and on 17 December she surpassed herself with a programme containing no less than 17 items, including readings from Shakespeare by the Rev. Tearle. — During her last year at the Seminary, Miss Bau presented a magnificent concert lasting three hours, probably the longest school concert on record; it was criticized on this account by no less a person than The Rev. Charles Murray himself. The programme included the *42nd Psalm* (Mendelssohn), *The Lord is my Shepherd* (Schubert), *Hear my prayer* (Mendelssohn) and Handel's *Halleluja chorus*. At her final concert in December, the astounded public was informed that this dynamic woman was leaving for Cape Town. She was fortunately prevailed upon to return to Graaff Reinet at a later date. — From 1894 to 1969, the Convent of the Sacred Heart did much to foster music. Another church school, the short-lived "St James School for Young Ladies", sponsored by the Anglican Church (1894 to c. 1909), employed music teachers such as Miss Wiltshire (1904) and Mrs and Miss Leslie (1905). — Since music was at this time considered to be mainly an accomplishment for young ladies, the majority of the students was concentrated in the ladies' schools, where they were taught by a salaried and capable staff. This resulted in a decline of private tuition, and at the turn of the century only four private teachers managed to survive the organized teaching at schools. They were P.B. de Ville** (1894–1947), A.O. Wagner** (1905–1922), Mrs H.G. Viner (who was active up to 1903), and Frank Hyde** (circa 1908–1911). Of lesser importance were Mesdames Knox-Davies, Von Abo and Watermeyer.

3. Communal music

(i) 1856–1879

The first recorded musical concert took place on 4 April 1856. It lasted for three hours, 21 items were offered, and it took place in the library under the direction of Herman Mosenthal. Vocal items predominated, including glees, sung by a company of seven gentlemen and nine ladies! Herman Mosenthal played a pianoforte fantasia on airs from Meyerbeer's *The prophet,* and the two friends Harry Bolus and A. Essex (jr) presented two marches arranged for flute and seraphine. The Graaff Reinet Choral

Society was created soon afterwards, and sang in public for the first time on 29 May, under Mosenthal's direction. The choir was responsible for five glees and a madrigal; there were three vocal duets and three songs, and Mosenthal gave another spirited rendering, now of a fantasia on airs from Donizetti's *Daughter of the regiment,* as well as an arrangement of the *Zampa overture.* The German-Jewish family of Mosenthal were at the time successful merchants in Graaff Reinet; in the course of time they extended their interests to other centres, such as Port Elizabeth, Richmond and Murraysburg. In each of these towns members of the family stimulated amateur talent to musical expression. — Harriet Rabone records that the Choral Society continued to meet regularly until 1859. In this year, it rehearsed Mozart's so-called *Twelfth mass,* in addition to glees and madrigals, for all of which she played the accompaniments. Concerts were given on 2 August 1859, and again on 27 March 1860; they were organized by Edward Nathan, and directed by J.L. Viner. According to the press, these functions were marred by the unruly behaviour of several "gentlemen farmers", who "occasionally mimicked the conductor and the singers for their own amusement". The Choral Society seems to have gone into recess, but in the meantime, in March 1858, the G.R. Amateur Dramatic Club had been founded. Between 1858 and 1868 the Club gave 58 performances, generally of comedies and farces, with light music provided during the intervals. Initially, Harry Bolus was the Secretary, but in August of the first year he was succeeded by S. Weinthal. The performances took place in the new Steam Mills, which accommodated 300 people, or in the stores of either Dixon, Schimper or C. Rubidge. They generally had capacity audiences and became a prime factor behind the municipal purchase of the store of Meintjes and Hendrikz, on the corner of Bourke and Caledon Street, for R3 090 (1862). Liberal donations by members of the Athenaeum Club and the public, together with proceeds of performances and concerts, enabled the Club to convert this store into a town hall *cum* theatre. The Gem Bioscope now stands on this historic site. In the lighthearted fashion of pioneering amateurs, the Club had no scruples about supplementing sketchy variety programmes with musical items, which must at times have provided the major part of the programme. The band of the Rifle Corps and the German Brass Band were regular attractions, and in 1858 the Club even went so far as to engage a singer from Port Elizabeth. — The cultural movement gained impetus when the more enlightened leaders, such as Harry Bolus, the Rev. Steabler and W.H. Rabone, editor of the *G.R. Herald,* established a Mechanics Institute in 1859. The venture failed, so in 1862 they fathered the Athenaeum Club (1862–1865). Though shortlived, it was a significant contribution to the development of a more enlightened way of life, with new aims and desires. This Club may be described as an open club where men could gather for recreation and education. Mosenthal was apparently involved in its formation, since he organized a concert for funds at Graaff Reinet on 4 August 1862. Nine days later, the Club held the first of its *conversaziones* or *musical soirées.* In a brilliant lecture, entitled *The science of recreation,* Bolus expounded on the cultural and educational principles of the Athenaeum, as embodied in projected classes for debating, dramatic reading and choral singing. About 170 people crowded into a schoolroom which normally seated 85; the choir sang a few glees; Prof. Gill supplied readings from *Pickwick Papers;* the dialogue between Brutus and Cassius from *Julius Caesar* was read by Prof. Gill and Mr Hurford; Messrs Tweed, Benjamin and others performed literary and musical satires; and to conclude, Mr Hune's concertina wailed variations on *The last rose of summer.* — By 5 June 1964, five meetings of the Club had been held, each an important social occasion with a capacity audience; but in 1865 a long drought and the consequent economic depression brought this enterprise to an end. Although the Club as such became extinct, it seems to have lived on in the Choral Society, which was revived at this time by Harry Bolus. It gave three concerts of sacred and secular music between 1864 and 1866, reaching a reasonable standard in its repertoire. The programmes contained choruses by Handel and Haydn; anthems and sacred works by the contemporary British composers G.B. Allen, G.J. Eluey and McEwan; selections from Mozart's *Twelfth mass;* choruses from Gounod's *Faust;* glees and part-songs by the contemporary British composers Sir Henry Bishop, Macfarren, Barnby, Wallace and Hatton; one or two madrigals by Wilbye; and operatic duets and arias by Mozart, Bellini and others. Bolus himself performed as a vocal soloist. It is recorded that he sang a setting of *The village blacksmith* (Longfellow) by Weiss. His eager enthusiasm for music in this early period has not been acknowledged in biographies. After the death of his eldest son in 1865, Bolus rested from his social exertions, although he was probably still an active supporter of musical ventures. He devoted himself increasingly to other interests, of which Botany was to make him famous. — The successor to Bolus was an able young violinist, John Oliver Reeve, who led the Choral Society in a programme presented on 10 October 1867. This included *The lay of the bell* (Romberg), vocal solos and duets by Mendelssohn and Rossini, and a few violin pieces by De Beriot, played by the conductor. This talented young man died in Graaff Reinet in 1872, when he was only 30 years old. The economic depression had become severe, and when diamonds were discovered, many inhabitants left to seek their fortunes on the diggings. A further result was the continuous passage of foreign adventurers through the town and the consequent revival of business life. Cultural life had, however, stagnated, and even the popular Christy Minstrels temporarily vanished from the scene. — These entertainments had appeared in Graaff Reinet for the first time in 1858. As elsewhere in South Africa, their costumes and programmes soon made them extremely popular, apart from the opportunity they offered local poetisers and music makers for fabricating parodies on the town scene in a jesting but good-natured way. When cultural life revived during the seventies, minstrel entertainments were again offered, stimulating local creative talent and activating an interest in the theatre. The brightest fruit of their efforts was the production of *Robinson Crusoe* in December 1873. This work was a burlesque, with dances and a hodge-podge of smoothly written rhymes, full of fun and merry ideas, of topical parodies and inoffensive, witty gibes. According to the press, "it took everyone by surprise, and kept the house in a roar of laughter from beginning to end". The author is unknown; the show was proabably the combined effort of some lively young men bubbling with ideas. — In the same year people interested in theatricals formed a Midland Amateur Dramatic Club. It had 100 members, who produced *twelve* (!) works between 26 August 1873, and 13 August 1874. Despite their enthusiasm, they were defeated by the lack of an adequate hall and the unco-operative attitude of the Town Council. The commissioners often refused to let the Town Hall for theatrical purposes, or imposed impracticable restrictions on rehearsals, stage properties, lighting facilities, etc. This led to heated controversies in 1874, between what was fundamentally the cultured class and a stodgy, uncultured officialdom. Besides, the prospect of easy fortunes on the diamond fields enticed professional companies to South Africa, and most of them at that time had Graaff Reinet on their itineraries. This competition defeated the amateurs, who had too many difficulties of their own. In March 1876 they put all their properties up for auction, and another local venture had become extinct. *Robinson Crusoe* was, in a sense, a laughing protest against the indignities suffered at the hands of an ignorant Town Council. — "Professor" Zacharias Lionarons invaded Graaff Reinet in 1875, and brought a temporary revival through his ability as a composer, conductor and violin teacher. There was some choral and instrumental activity, and even the Christy Minstrels were fleetingly resuscitated. After four months and six concerts, the frustrated Professor departed. By 1879 the amateurs had become almost totally inactive. Two charity concerts, one in October 1878, to gather funds for the Dutch Reformed Church cemetery, and one in March 1879, in aid of distressed persons in the Zulu War, were merely isolated ventures that, for a while, brought them together again. — Scattered newspaper reports indicate that an amateur band existed as early as 1850, probably playing for fun rather than for any artistic reason. Its vague existence crystallized into organized reality in 1856, when the group became associated with two volunteer defence units and performed at the monthly musters. In May 1860 J.L. Viner became the bandmaster, but apparently held the appointment for only a few months. In July 1860, six ex-German legionnaires were engaged for twelve months, each to receive a meagre sum of R6 per annum. One of them soon became bandmaster in Viner's place, and received R12. This tentative step into professionalism had a beneficial effect on the morale of the other members, who decided to double their monthly subscriptions to 50c, in order to meet the cost. The reconstituted band offered proof of their existence when they performed in Cradock in August 1860, and again in October in their home-town, but when the depression made itself felt in 1861, their slender budget collapsed irremediably, and there is no further mention of band activity in Graaff Reinet until 1878.

(ii) 1879–1886
The prosperous conditions that prevailed in the late 'seventies stimulated the optimism of band enthusiasts for this form of amateur entertainment. The revival must have infected the public too, since there were liberal donations, and the players were willing to pay regular subscriptions to cover the purchase of instruments and uniforms. No less a person than the Town Clerk, J.C. Naude, consented to act as Honorary Secretary. A significant indication of this prosperity is the considerable salary of R200 p.a. that was set aside for the bandmaster. — Mr Moore assumed these duties in September, 1878, and led the band until his death in June 1879. This setback was overcome in August of the same year, when James Saunders, ex-bandmaster of the Philharmonic Society at Kimberley, arrived in Graaff Reinet and stepped into the vacant position. In the same month the PAVG Band of Port Elizabeth visited the town, and gave some excellent performances, which fired the enthusiasm of the Graaff Reinet amateurs. By December they had reached an efficiency that justified their collaboration at a concert of the Choral Society (11 December); and six days later their first promenade concert was given in the Botanical Gardens. — The open-air concerts soon became a regular institution. They were generally held in the evenings during summer, and at 3 o'clock in the afternoon during winter. Adults paid 10c for admission, and children 5c. Saunders proved to be an excellent and experienced conductor and an indefatigable teacher. By maintaining rigid discipline and providing the musicians with skilful arrangements, he developed his band into an efficient unit. During his term as bandleader (August 1879–August 1883), it acquired a repertoire of over 90 pieces, including marches, selections, overtures, quadrilles and a variety of

dances by composers such as Auber, Bonnisseau, Coote, Donizetti, Flotow, Harmann, Lecocq, Mendelssohn, Offenbach, Johann Strauss, Verdi, and others. Saunders's efforts and successes were properly recognised in the form of gratuities, and in 1880 his salary was increased by 50 percent to R300 p.a. — The band became a feature at every public, social and sporting function. One big occasion was on 9 March 1883, when it performed at the Agricultural Show and concluded a successful day with a grand promenade concert in the Market Hall. As its reputation spread, there were invitations from neighbouring towns. By the middle of 1883 the band had reached a respectable level of artistic achievement, but the sad fate of all amateur bands in South Africa overtook it in August 1883: it petered out owing to the lack of financial support. At that stage there were 21 musicians in the group, and the list of members contains a sprinkling of Afrikaans names, showing that the endeavour had the support of both sections of the White population.

(iii) The Choral Society
At the time when the band had become the pride of the town, M.P. Kennedy revived the Choral Society; they gave a concert in September 1879 at which 19 items from Haydn's *Creation* were sung. George Hurford and Maurice Nathan** succeeded Kennedy as conductors of the Society, and during the next four years choral singing was quite general in Graaff Reinet. — Alone, and in association with other musical, literary and dramatic groups, the Society strove to engage the available local talent, enjoyed constructive press criticism, and provided its public with such hearty entertainment that encores had to be forbidden. It often performed for charities and at benefit concerts, e.g. for bandmaster Saunders, for conductor Nathan, and for the widow of President Burgers, who had been prominent in a theological controversy in Graaff Reinet in earlier days. The repertoire included lesser cantatas by composers such as Franz Abt, Gibson, Sterndale Bennett (*The May queen*), and James Hyde** (*The wreck of the Hesperus*); operatic choruses, part-songs and glees. In December 1882, the Society ventured into the domain of operetta, with a performance of *Trial by jury* (Gilbert and Sullivan). Professors Liebmann and Bristow, Messrs Jordan Dexter and Sutton, and Miss Bigg sang in the cast. — The Choral Society's accompaniments were served by the band of J.A. Saunders, whose cornet and violin playing was a feature of the concerts. He also took the initiative in encouraging the inclusion of chamber and orchestral groups in the programmes. In September, 1880, the little "orchestra" consisted of two violins, two flutes, cornet, baritone-brass and pianoforte, played by Maurice Nathan; in addition there were a brass quartette consisting of two cornets, baritone-brass and sax-horn, all members of the amateur band, and a flute trio, accompanied by Dr Arenhold. Prominent among the soloists were Alice Hart, who was highly rated as a pianist, and Miss Reimar. — A notable feature of musical life was the number of concerts presented for charity, or in aid of institutions. On 21 November, 1882, a large programme consisting of nineteen items was performed in aid of funds for the Graaff Reinet College. Two polonaises of Chopin were played by Prof. Liebmann and Mrs Burgers respectively, and Fräulein Bau contributed the *Variations serieuses* by Mendelssohn. Other artists were Miss Van Reenen and Mrs Eady, who interpreted an aria by Meyerbeer; Dr Te Water offered readings from Shakespeare and there was a variety of vocal solos, duets and trios. The College was apparently in financial straits at this time and during 1883 no less than four programmes in aid of College funds were arranged by the 100 amateurs who rallied to

its assistance. Prominent soloists were invariably Prof. Liebmann, Master Adolf Arenhold and Mrs Eady; part songs and glees were sung by a group of 15 vocalists, and two performances of *Trial by jury* and one of selections from *HMS Pinafore* were staged. — The Society's efforts were sadly handicapped by the lack of an adequate concert hall. The first Town Hall, originally a store purchased in 1862, was still in use, but for more ambitious efforts the Market Hall had to be hired. Towards the end of 1883, Graaff Reinet had the misfortune to lose the services of both Hurford and Nathan and the Choral Society came to an end. It had elevated musical taste to a quite respectable standard. At the end of 1882 the *Herald* wrote, with justifiable pride, that the amateurs of Graaff Reinet could challenge the smaller professional companies: "Let GR develop as far as possible upon itself and upon its neighbours. Let us welcome as far as possible foreign talents whenever available; but never neglect what can be done to utilize and encourage similar talents close to our own doors; and especially when all the benefits from this amateur talent are freely given for the benefit of local charity." — By this time the schools had risen to musical prominence, and Miss Bau and James Saunders sometimes joined forces to present concerts based upon the organized music of the Seminary. Complete collapse of choral activity was also counteracted by the work done in the various churches.

(iv) The Music and Literary Society
This Society, with a membership of approximately 200, had been promoted by Maurice Nathan and James Saunders in March 1881. It more or less had the same ideals as the earlier Athenaeum. Musical items were included at the monthly meetings and, with the passage of time, they advanced to regular quarterly concerts. At the first of these on April 23, 1883, the programme contained 16 items, including a part-song for eight voices, a trio (for violin, cornet and pianoforte), five solo songs, three pianoforte solos, three vocal duets, a violin solo, a comic reading and a scene from *The school for scandal*, read by Emma Burgers and F. te Water. On 11 June of the same year, Saunders conducted a performance of the *Toy symphony* and Prof. Liebmann's lecture on Goethe's *Faust* (July 4, 1884) was illustrated by selections from Gounod's opera, at which an instrumental sextet of four violins, a cornet and a pianoforte supported the singers. Possibly as a result of the gradual shifting of interest to music, a purely literary society was formed in June, 1883, to compensate for the neglect of literary interests. The College professors, and the Revs. Rawlings, Philip and Doke, were especially prominent at its meetings. — Mainly as a result of the initiative of Nathan and Saunders, "Negro" minstrels were revived in a group called the Midland Minstrels, who appeared periodically at concerts in aid of charity. Whenever there was a need for fund-raising in aid of the College, the hospital, or the Ladies' Benevolent Society, these gentlemen were available. This spirit of benevolence was one of the main characteristics of the English and German sections of the community, who gave their services willingly, with the incentive of bringing enjoyment and laughter to the public. Between September and November, 1883, the Minstrels gave no less than four performances, and the same number between June and December, 1886. Bertie Phillips,** who played the banjo, was the most popular and successful member of this group. He often gave solo concerts in Graaff Reinet, and also in neighbouring towns, for the benefit of charity. — The active Saunders was furthermore responsible for the creation of a professional dance band, called the Quadrille Band, which became the mainstay at dances, and provided popular items at variety concerts. Professors Bristow

111

and Liebmann were successful in reviving the old Amateur Dramatic Society, and produced *Our boys* (Byron) in October 1883, *Glitter* in May 1884, *Weak women* (Byron) in October 1885, and *Not such a fool as he looks* (Byron) in June 1886. The next year the Society ventured on a Shakespearian play. A feature of these productions was the lively co-operation of the Quadrille Band. The two professors tried to start an oratorio society, with the aim of performing Mendelssohn's *Elijah*, but the Choral Society was suspicious of this attempt, and personal animosities among the female singers caused it to collapse. — After 1882, when the Young Men's Christian Society was established in Graaff Reinet, the churches of English-speaking denominations favoured adult education. Under the patronage of the mayor, five lectures were given in 1883 by three clergymen and Prof. Bristow, with musical items as an added interest. These functions must have been quite popular: when the Rev. Doke lectured on Oliver Cromwell on 27 June, he had an audience of over 400 people! This exemplary work was emulated by the Free Protestant Church in 1884, which held monthly *conversaziones*, with lectures as the main feature, and choral or other musical items to supplement the speeches. The Rev. Rawlings lectured on *Silas Marner* and the "History of Civilisation" and the German-born Mrs Rawlings on the "Oberammergau Passion Play", "Lessing" and "The Black Forest". On the latter occasion, Mendelssohn's *Hymn of praise* was sung. The Free Church's efforts seem to have dwindled before the Church closed in 1891; but in the meantime the Baptists and the Methodists had followed suit. Ministers gave travel lecturers (e.g. the Rev. Doke: "The Wonders of Egypt" and "Right Across India", in 1886); or spoke on subjects such as Literature (the Rev. Rogers: "Charles Dickens"), Electricity (Dr Richards DD), or "Brains, what they are and how to use them' (the Rev. J. Smith-Spenser). No admission fee was charged for these lectures. — This emphasis on adult education led to the creation of the Midlandsche Debats Vereeniging, led by the school teacher, B.J.S. Dippenaar. This move marks the independent entry of cultured Afrikaners into the cultural life of Graaff Reinet. The Society held monthly meetings, at which debates were conducted; also included were performances of Dutch dramas and music. — After the departure of Hurford, Nathan and the Professors Bristow and Liebmann (1883–1884), Saunders had to keep the music going, often with the aid and support of Fräulein Bau. In August 1886, he conducted choruses from *Norma* and *Anna Bolena*, in a programme that also included a variety of vocal ensembles and solos by members of the younger musical generation. Dr Adolf Arenhold did good work for the St James Church, and directed a programme on 3 September 1886, at which he himself, two members of his family, and seven other Graaff Reinet artists co-operated. When the town celebrated its centenary in 1886, it had to its credit a considerable tradition of communal music and a record of sustained effort in promoting education and culture. — Industry and commerce stimulated the cultural links between Port Elizabeth and Graaff Reinet at this time, since there were firms with branches or agents in both towns. Mosenthal Brothers and Bolus Brothers are examples. In 1873 the Graaff Reinet Chamber of Commerce allied itself in matters of common interest with the Chamber in Port Elizabeth. The establishment of the Athenaeum, the Mechanics' Institute and the Brass Band (1856) were virtually parallel developments in the two centres. For instance, the Graaff Reinet College was modelled on the Grey Institute; the Graaff Reinet Amateur Theatre had the same taste in plays as the PE Amateur Theatre; the musical, *Robinson Crusoe,* was probably modelled on a Port Elizabeth production; and with the opening of the Graaff Reinet-PE Railway in 1879 the PAG

Band set new standards for Graaff Reinet's amateur bandsmen. The essential difference was that, whereas these cultural exertions were rather evanescent in Graaff Reinet, most of their counterparts, the Athenaeum, Grey Institute and the PAG Band, existed for many years in Port Elizabeth.

4. Professional touring companies (1854–1886)

About a third of these companies devoted their performances to music. The most important companies were: Ali ben sou Alle (1858); Bailley-Poussard** (1868); Ohio Christies (1868); Mr and Mrs D'Arcy Read** (1868 and 1874); Miranda-Harper** (1869); Harper-Leffler** (1873); Mr Sinclair and Miss Clifford (1874 and 1876); Harvey-Turner Opera Company** (1876); Madame Anna Bishop** and Charles Lascelles** (1876); Mr and Mrs E. Palmer (1877); Geo. Case and Grace Egerton (1878); Mme. Mendelssohn** and Sign. Orlandini (1879); Paulton Daws and Seaton (1880); Victoria Loftus Troupe (1882); Madame Pauline Bredelli** (1882); Albert Thies and Norman Henry (1882). — In common with other centres in South Africa, Graaff Reinet owed much to these companies, which although artistically threadbare and compelled to extemporize, introduced rarely-heard works, especially in the field of opera and operetta. Local amateurs had reason to welcome their visits, since they were engaged to sing or play with the professionals. Paulton, for example, engaged the local brass band in 1880, and Daws the services of Messrs Saunders (cornet) and Hind (clarinet). — During the '80s the discovery of gold in the Transvaal speeded the building of railways to the North, from the terminal points at Cape Town and East London; whereas Graaff Reinet, despite all protestations, remained dependent on a short railway line from Port Elizabeth. The natural result was that touring companies and artists, attracted by the prospects of gain in the Transvaal, tended to by-pass Graaff Reinet; this caused a sharp decrease in the number of professional concerts. Conversely it was responsible for a revival of amateur culture. The interesting pattern that evolved, clearly relates professional and amateur music-making in Graaff Reinet to economic development in South Africa, especially to the rapid extension of railway connections. This is reflected in the following summary:

PERIOD	AMATEUR CONCERTS	PROFESSIONAL CONCERTS	TOTAL
1854–1865	138	14	152
1866–1871	42	52	94
1872–1877	21	134	155
1878–1883	155	94	249
1884–1886	141	9	150

An increase in amateur presentations coincides neatly with a corresponding decline of professionalism, and *vice versa*.

5. The Dramatic and Orchestral Society and amateur activity

The cultural townsmen took up this challenge, deploying their resources in a Dramatic and Orchestral Society, which came into being in the nineties and lasted until at least

113

1930. Unlike King William's Town, the town had no British Military Bands to support its endeavours, and was entirely dependent on its own talent. — The Dramatic and Orchestral Society was created for the special purpose of performing the fashionable works of Gilbert and Sullivan, or for presenting musical comedies of the easygoing, humorous and dancing type, which dominated the theatre world in London during the nineties. In 1896 its committee was composed of Mesdames Viner, Watermeyer, Knox-Davies and Miss R. du Toit; Messrs. H. Urquhart, P. de Ville, Penny, H.G. Viner and Dr Spencer. For its performance of *Iolanthe* on 4 and 5 August, it had at its disposal a chorus of 18 and an orchestra conducted by De Ville, with Mrs Viner as pianist and Mrs Watermeyer playing a small organ. It is to the credit of De Ville's enthusiasm that he managed to assemble seven violins, a violoncello, one flute, two cornets, a clarinet, a horn and two percussionists to play in his "orchestra". This capable musician also had a children's "orchestra" in reserve; this served as a training ground for more ambitious ventures. Besides a great variety of musicals and dramas, with or without music, the Society presented before 1914 six works by Gilbert and Sullivan and three other operettas. During the South African War, and for a year or two afterwards, Graaff Reinet had the benefit of the band of the Coldstream Guards who were stationed there. It gave regular promenade concerts in the Botanical Gardens on Sunday afternoons. In 1903 the Wiltshire Regiment was temporarily stationed in Graaff Reinet; its band was in attendance at the Botanical Gardens when a great garden party, with 3000 guests, was arranged for the Rt Hon. Joseph Chamberlain, British Secretary for Colonies since 1895. — A significant addition to the facilities of the amateur musicians was the opening of the new town hall, the Victoria Hall, on September 5, 1911, by the Hon. Henry Burton, Minister for Native Affairs. This long-awaited event was fêted in great style during a week of festivities, which included a Grand Concert, a ball, theatre productions, and other entertainments. A.O. Wagner** conducted the *Halleluja chorus;* solo items were presented by the Misses Marriott (pianoforte) and Goldman (violin); Peter Pohl offered a reading; and Miss M. Craig, supported by Messrs G. Hawkins, R.F. Simmonds and M.C. Roberts, was responsible for vocal items. Mrs Roberts sang a song especially composed by Frank Hyde** to words by the wine merchant, Henry Heugh *(Sons of South Africa)*. Frank Hyde was at the time a piano teacher and tuner, resident at 112 Cradock Street.

6. Church music

In an early reference (1797) to Graaff Reinet, John Barrow wrote that children were taught to "read, write and sing Psalms"; and Burchell recorded in 1811 that hymns were accompanied simply on an organ (probably a harmonium) in a musically deficient condition: "This person, who merely played psalm tunes in a plain manner and made no pretensions to a voluntary was glad to accept, in addition to his music, a trifling salary as assistant to the village school". Of the first (1792) and second (1798) Dutch Reformed Churches there is musically little to record. The completion of the third DR church in 1822 coincided with the arrival of the Rev. Andrew Murray (sr) whose ministry was again conspicuous for its lack of organized church music; no records of the instrument used or of musical practices in the church have come to light. The Rev. Dreyer names Dag Brummer as "organist" in 1822; and it can be assumed that, up to 1849, the offices of clerk, sexton, organist precentor and school teacher were combined in some way or another. M.C. Luttig, a school teacher, became organist in 1849, and was succeded by J.L. Viner** in 1860; he was followed by Miss Luttig in 1865. Until 1867 there was no choir, but thereafter a Miss Auret organized and led a group known as the "English Choir", which sang at the English services held in the Dutch Reformed Church on Sunday evenings. Joseph Atkinson coached this choir gratuitously for about five years, and then, in 1872, it was discontinued for some unknown reason. "Professor" Jan de Villiers** (Jan Orrelis) "astounded" the congregation with an organ recital in 1873; but, as with the English Choir, his kind of "complicated" music was not acceptable to the older and more conservative church members. — The fourth DR Church was inaugurated on Saturday, 10 September 1887, in the presence of over 2 000 people. Miss Bau, who had left Graaff Reinet at the end of 1886, was prevailed upon to return, and trained a choir whose singing was a highlight of the occasion. It sang *Psalm 95* by Mendelssohn; *How lovely are Thy dwellings* (Spohr); *How lovely are the messengers* (Mendelssohn's *St Paul*) and *The heavens are telling* (Haydn's *Creation*). There was another impressive ceremony in 1894, when a two-manual organ was inaugurated by the Rev. Hofmeyer of Prince Albert, the organist being P. de Ville. The instrument was installed by the organ-builders Messrs Hatfield, at a cost of R1 924. As far as can be established, the following persons have played the organ since then: Miss Bau (1887–1894?); P.B. de Ville (1894–1904, assistant organist 1905–1947); A.O. Wagner (1905–1922); Amy Asher (née Murray) (c. 1922–1930); probably P.B. de Ville (1930–1939); George Z. van der Spuy** (1939); Mrs A.C. Labuschagne (1940–1970). — The Anglican Church of St James (established 1845) had an harmonium in use in 1856, possibly the instrument that had been jointly owned by Harry Bolus and Alfred Essex. It was played by Harriet Rabone. About 1866 Dr Adolf Friedrich Karl Arenhold, physician to the German immigrants of Kaffraria, became the "organist". He was an outstanding musician and led a church choir composed of English and German residents, which played a part on festival occasions, such as the laying of a foundation stone in the chancel (November 30, 1868) and the consecration of the chancel by Bishop Merriman (October 7, 1870). On Sunday, October 5, 1873, Arenhold had the privilege of inaugurating Graaff Reinet's first pipe organ, erected to the memory of J.O. Reeve. This little one-manual organ with seven stops, one pedal stop, a coupler and two composition pedals, was erected by the music-shop owner, Viner, who also had the contract for repairing and tuning it at R10 per annum. The instrument was enlarged in 1883, and remained in use until 1945. Dr Arenhold remained the organist until 1887, and established a dedicated tradition by declining payment for his services. Shortly before his death he climaxed his work at St James by presenting a choral festival. Succeeding organists have been: Miss Steabler (1887– 1892); Mrs H.G. Viner (1893–1903); W.J. Clegg (1904–1954), and Mrs J. Fiveash (1955–1966). Assistant organists have been: William te Water (1895); Emily Luscombe (1896); W. Clegg (1893–1903), and in more recent times U.V. Schneider** (c. 1950), a pupil of Mr Clegg. — Little is known about sacred music in the Methodist Church, the Baptist Church and the Roman Catholic Church. The Free Protestant Church (1872–1891) was very active musically, especially in 1884. — The new Dutch Reformed Church of 1926 had an organ from the outset, through the beneficence of Mrs P.A. Luckhoff who donated R3 000 towards the instrument. The following organists have served in this church: Stephanus van Zijl (1926–1933); Marie Nel (Blignaut)** (1933–1941); S. le Roux Marais** (1942–1944); Marie Blignaut (1944–1946); Philip McLachlan** (1946–1954); Dirk de Villiers** (1954–1956); Theo Wendt (not the Cape conductor) (1957–1958); H. Babst (1959–1960);

Mrs A. Terblanche (1961– 1970). During his period as organist in Graaff Reinet, Philip McLachlan conducted part I of Haydn's *Creation* when the church celebrated the 25th anniversary of its establishment.

7. Music education, 1921–1970

The fire that burnt down the Midlands Seminary in 1921 concluded an important chapter in Graaff Reinet education. With the exception of the Convent School (which existed until 1969) the Seminary was the last of the private schools of the 19th Century. The loss was great from a musical point of view, since the Seminary had played a beneficial role in the instruction of the town's youth. After this date schools came increasingly under the jurisdiction of the Cape Department of Education, which made little provision for instruction in music. — As in the rest of South Africa, the position in Graaff Reinet has improved since then and educational institutions have again become the pivot of regular music-making. Among the teachers who have served with distinction at schools was S. le Roux Marais (Union High School: 1957–1960; Hoër Volkskool: 1961–1964). Since its establishment in 1917, the Graaff Reinet Training College has at different times been prominent musically. The following have been lecturers at this institution: Jan Coetzee** (1954–1961); Cosmo Henning** (1963–1967); Philip McLachlan (1945–1954); Dirk de Villiers (1954–1956); Mrs A.C. Labuschagne (1958–1970); and Robin Radue** (1965–1966). — The Training College has also embarked ambitiously on opera production, with Mrs Labuschagne especially prominent. She produced Gluck's *Alceste* in 1962; a reduction of *The magic flute* called *Papageno* in 1963; *The merry widow* in 1965; and *Fledermaus* in 1967. Cosmo Henning conducted a choir and orchestra in a performance of Faure's *Requiem* in 1963. Masha Arsenieva** and Boris Igneff** settled in Graaff Reinet in 1960. Since then the teaching and production of ballet have become established in this town; the pair have extended their teaching practice to other towns in the vicinity. — With its record of musical education in private schools and of music-making by amateurs, Graaff Reinet supported a number of music shops, which supplied not only the town but the Midlands generally. A book-shop owned by the *Graaff Reinet Herald* (est. 1852), with premises on Market Square, carried fairly extensive stocks of sheet music, including pianoforte works of the educational type, popular music, operatic arrangements, dance music, minstrel songs and English folk songs and ballads. Popular new works such as *La traviata* were available in the town, only eight years after the première in Italy! The early proprietors were the owners of the *Herald,* Alfred Essex, William Rabone and Harry Bolus (c. 1860). — John Lewis Viner came to Graaff Reinet in 1859 as a music teacher and established a Music Saloon and Warehouse which became the largest establishment of its kind in the Midland area. In the '70s Viner advertised every type of sheet music (vocal, instrumental, classical, popular, operatic and sacred), as well as instruments and accessories such as metronomes, music stools, digitoria (for strengthening the fingers), canterburies (stands for storing music); in fact, "everything connected with the music trade". In 1879 his son Harry was in partnership with his father, and in the same year they acquired the services of Mr Eade, a piano tuner who had been trained in London. Between February and June 1881, Maurice Nathan provided a measure of competition, but as he made little headway, Viner took over all his stock. In 1881 Viner was so up-to-date that he offered for sale the music of Sullivan's *Patience,* six months after its première in London! His establishment at that time extended for about 100 metres from Caledon Street to North Street. In 1896, at the height of his prosperity, Viner advertised that he had over 40 000 items in stock. Between 1882 and 1890, only James Saunders offered some competition by selling brass and stringed instruments in his tobacco shop, next to the Cape of Good Hope Bank. — Towards the end of his life J.L. Viner drastically reduced his stock, and after his death in 1904 his son Harry sold the business to Sidney Rabone, who bought the remainder of the sheet music for R150, and converted the business into a book-shop and news agency. P.B. de Ville established a new music shop in 1910, and traded until about 1930 at 28 Church Square, which in olden days had been Auret's Primary School; to-day it is a surgery. De Ville also undertook some publishing, and printed at least one song, *Sons of South Africa*, by Frank Hyde. On a smaller scale C.G.C. du Toit conducted some musical trade in Caledon Street from 1930-1940. To-day Graaff Reinet offers no commercial facilities of this kind at all.

8. A few Graaff Reinet composers

The best-known composers who have lived in Graaff Reinet have been Maurice Nathan, P.B. de Ville, Frank Hyde, S. le Roux Marais and Boris Igneff. The primary concern in this section is with resident musicians who only wrote one or two pieces; the others are dealt with in the alphabetical section of this encyclopedia. — **Max Wertheim** (*13 December 1882) was an engineer who wrote a number of salon pieces for pianoforte. Of these, *African sunbeams* (a waltz) and *The gem barn dance* have been traced. They were published by Darter & Sons in Cape Town, and printed by C.G. Röder of Leipzig. — **Ina Tozer Melvill** (*2 August 1874 ° 12 November 1941) wrote a piece for pianoforte entitled *Impatience,* and two songs which were published by De Ville & Co., and printed by William Reeves of London. — **Jan Pohl** (* 5 April 1917) enjoys a national reputation as a composer of light Afrikaans songs. — **Lilian du Toit** (née Ziervogel) wrote a pianoforte waltz called *Secrets,* and two songs which were published in London in 1929. — **Johanna Schonland** (née Nathan) (*20 April 1864 ° 10 March 1938) wrote a *Bushveld waltz* for pianoforte, which she dedicated to Sir Percy and Lady Fitzpatrick. — In the field of theoretical music, Catherine Mary Thornton had her *Easy lessons in the theory of music* published by De Ville & Co. while Darter & Sons, Cape Town, published A.O. Wagner's *Technique, a handbook for pianists and pianoforte teachers.*

BIBLIOGRAPHY

Essex, A. and Rabone, H: *The letters of a pioneer family.* Struik, Cape Town, n.d.   Henning, C.G.: *A cultural history of Graaff Reinet, 1786-1886.* D. Phil. thesis, UP, 1971; publ. as *Graaff Reinet, a cultural history (1786-1886).* T.V. Bulpin, Cape Town, 1975.   Van der Merwe, F.Z.: *Suid-Afrikaanse musiekbibliografie, 1787-1952.* J.L. van Schaik, Pretoria, 1958.

SOURCES

De Graaff Reinetter: 1884-1890.   *Eastern Province Herald:* 1845-1920.   *G.R. Advertiser:* 1860-1960.   *G.R. Herald:* 1852-1884.

– C.G.H. (adapted)

GRAHAM, ALAN, *17 July 1910 in Johannesburg; living in Stellenbosch in 1977. Lecturer and pianist.

Alan Graham initially received piano lessons from Barclay Donn, continued his studies at the RAM under Claude Pollard (1928–1930) and obtained the LRAM and ARAM. At the beginning of 1931 he was appointed lecturer in pianoforte at the Stellenbosch Conservatoire of Music,** where he taught both Arnold van Wyk** and Hubert du Plessis.** In 1948 he accepted a post as lecturer in the Department of Music of the Rhodes University College in Grahamstown, remaining there until the end of 1952. Since then he has taught music at St George's College in Salisbury. During the 'thirties he was soloist with the Cape Town Municipal orchestra,** conducted by William Pickerill,** acted as examiner for the annual music examinations of the University of South Africa, and gave a recital of two of his own compositions for pianoforte at a concert arranged by the Oranjeklub (15 November 1935).

WORKS
Waltz. Ms., n.d.   Theme and variations. Ms., n.d.

– H.duP.

GRAHAM LAWRENCE, A.E.   Barberton III/2, IX

GRAHAMSTOWN, MUSIC IN (1812–1900)
1. Introduction
2. Military bands
3. Amateur and church music
4. Visiting musicians
5. Music education
6. Music shops, printers and publishers
7. Composers

1. Introduction
The history of Grahamstown is intimately connected with the colonization of the Eastern Province and with the Frontier Wars. Established by Col. Graham immediately after the 4th "Kaffir" War (April 1812), Grahamstown remained the headquarters of British regiments for the next 50 years, to be superseded as a military centre when King William's Town was founded after the 7th "Kaffir" War (1848–1850). The 1820 Settlers, of whom the majority settled in the Albany district, including Grahamstown, Bathurst, Salem, and other places, augmented the civilian population and changed the pattern of life in what had in the main been merely a military outpost. The building of churches was a sign of the profound change in Grahamstown's way of life. The foundation stone of the Wesleyan Chapel was laid on 10 November 1822; the Cathedral of St Michael and St George was started in 1824 and completed in 1830; the Baptist Church was started in 1823 and, with additions and changes, reached completion in 1854; the Roman Catholic Church of St Patrick and the Presbyterian Church were both completed about 1840. Frontier life, agriculture and trade under periodically unsafe conditions demanded initiative and an intrepid spirit. On Christmas Day 1834, during the disastrous "Kaffir" War, no services could be held at St George's, because the church had been commandeered as a magazine for

arms and ammunition, and to serve as a refuge for those who had to desert their farms.
— Further monuments to their cultural endeavours were the *Grahamstown Journal*
(1831), the Library (1832), St Andrew's College (1855), a Museum (1855) and a
Botanical Garden. Many had brought musical instruments and traditions of choral
singing with them, and there was considerable though modest music-making in their
homes. Many of the regiments had bands led by professional musicians, and a variety
of talents flowered among the officers and men. An exceptional case was that of Mrs
Somerset, the wife of the commander on the frontier, who must have been an
accomplished musician, since she ensured that two pianos, a harp and a pipe-organ
were brought in their military train to offer her musical consolation in the wilderness.
The pipe-organ was a noteworthy instrument and is described by Prof. P.R. Kirby**
in *Organs of South Africa*.

2. Military bands

The 19th-Century tradition of attaching military bands to British regiments exercised
an important influence on South African musical history. These bands were at times
almost "orchestras" including woodwind and even stringed instruments. The leaders
were often aliens who had entered British military service – in Grahamstown the
names of bandmasters Becker, Crozier, De Staab, Faccioli, Rupel, Willemse and
Wiesbecker were indicative of non-British origins. The repertoire of the bands was
not confined to marches, but included overtures, excerpts from operas, arrangements
of popular arias, fashionable salon pieces, as well as the production of musical
comedies and even operettas. Traditionally, these musical units played in public
gardens and at civic functions and co-operated gladly, sometimes enthusiastically, with
civilians in staging theatrical productions. Rather surprisingly, bandmasters acquired
their discharge from the army quite easily, and it often happened that they left the
service to establish themselves independently as teachers of music, tuners and
repairers of instruments, or as conductors of amateur bands and societies. — In
Grahamstown military bands provided the music for the Queen's birthday celebrations; they played at subscription, regimental and other balls, often into the early
hours of the morning; or were in efficient attendance on occasions such as the laying of the foundation stone of the Commercial Hall in 1833, or at the official
opening of the library. — After 1853 they played in the newly laid-out Botanical
Garden on Saturday afternoons. These were pleasant social occasions, which became
so popular that, from 1857, there were two concerts each Saturday, each of two hours
duration, presented by two different bands. The four hours of music added colour and
excitement to the simple elegance of frontier life. And wherever the British went, a
Turf Club was sure to be found. Grahamstown had its own, and enjoyed the additional
privilege of having the band of the Imperial Cape Mounted Riflemen** playing
between races on Thursday afternoons. — Quite a brilliant concert was the one given
in the Drostdy grounds in August 1852, when a military band presented a programme
of sixteen items including the Overtures to *Semiramide* (Rossini) and *La cenerentola*
(Rossini). Unfortunately, these musical amenities were not destined to last very long.
From 1857, there was a steady withdrawal of regiments from the Eastern frontier for
service in India. By 1862 all were gone, either stationed in King William's Town or in
foreign countries. The *Grahamstown Journal* was led to comment rather nostalgically
"that the streets are now as dull as the middle of the Kalahari". — This did not mean

that Grahamstown was entirely denuded of bright uniforms and martial strains. At intervals regiments still passed through the town and often stayed a couple of weeks and even for months on end. Thus the band of the 5th Fusiliers, bandmaster F.A. Moran, played in the Botanical Gardens for the greater part of 1866 and the first half of 1867. On the 31st October they gave a Grand Concert at which Mrs Stier** sang and in March and July following they assisted at choral performances given in the church. The band of the 2–11th Regiment co-operated with the Poussard-Bailey Company and was involved in a Grand Choral Fête and Promenade Concert in the Albany Hall on 9 January 1868. Chris Glennon and the band of the 32nd Light Infantry performed in the Botanical Garden, at cricket, in plays and at festival services in the Cathedral. This band was in attendance during the week-long 1820 Settlers Grand Jubilee Celebrations. Starting on the 22nd May 1870 with anthems and selections from Haydn's *Imperial mass,* sung by the Cathedral choir at a festival service, there was bell-ringing on Monday, sports and a ball on Tuesday and on Wednesday an address by the Rev H.H. Dugmore** in the crowded Albany Hall. This lasted four hours, was introduced with a choral march, ended with a Jubilee Ode and had two choral interludes during its course. The words and the music were by the Rev. Dugmore himself, orchestrated for the band of the 32nd Light Infantry. On Thursday there was a music festival at which selections from *Elijah* were sung to the support of an organ (played by Mr Griffiths) and of the orchestra. The functions on the other two days were not reported in the press. — Local efforts at forming a band were not lacking: a Volunteer Band is mentioned in 1863 and again in 1864; Mr Ainstree's Amateur Band played an introduction to a lecture given by the advocate Mr Barry on *Reminiscences of Italy* (1864); a New City Band conducted by J. Leonard is mentioned in 1872. For this and the following years there is a plethora of titles such as Grahamstown Instrumental Band (1873); Grahamstown Brass Band (1874); Volunteer Brass Band (1876): probably all one and the same group, since they were all conducted by Mr Leonard. Then there was the Grahamstown Volunteer Artillery Band conducted by Mr Lennon, "late of the Prince Alfred Guards", and the First City Volunteers, conducted by Mr Glennon, "late of the 32nd Light Infantry". According to press reports there must have been at least two bands in 1877, since the First City Volunteers played "Moodie and Sankey's Airs whilst the Rifles had their fife and drum band playing a very different style of airs" at the same time. On resigning the conductorship of the Grahamstown Musical Society, Glennon started a brass band for the Grahamstown Yeomanry. — Probably the name Grahamstown Brass Band which was referred to above was a remnant of a group known by this name, which had been started in 1837 by the organist of the Cathedral, J.G. Franklin, with the support of Birkenruth, Barber and Dell. From the scanty references it appears that the band had about 25 players and that they played mainly at civic occasions. They had a notable day on April 10, 1845, when the foundation stone of the new Wesleyan Commemoration Chapel was laid. They not only played as a band, but also accompanied a choir in the singing of what must be regarded as the first local composition – an anthem by the Rev. H.H. Dugmore to words by the Rev. Thornley-Smith: "Sound ye the trumpet o'er land and o'er sea/Ye sons of Britannia whose spirits are free." — The band of the First City Volunteers, which has already been mentioned, remained responsible for the band music heard in the town. Their band leader, Glennon, resigned at the end of 1878 in favour of George Hind,** a young man of only 22 years and of a roving disposition, who was to become a well-known figure in the musical life of the Eastern Province.

Under his direction the band improved, but very soon, in June 1880, Hind exchanged Grahamstown for Graaff Reinet. His departure was regretted in view of the good work he had done in establishing, for example, open air concerts, which were regarded as an ideal way of passing the time of the day. Sergeant Rogers tried to keep the band going, but his efforts were regarded by the press as being totally inadequate. There was thus a sense of relief when Hind returned after sojourns in Queenstown and Graaff Reinet. For the next four years he was responsible for concert series in the open air and in diverse halls, afforded a musical background to sports meetings and supported important occasions with brassy sounds. These efforts were gratefully acknowledged and two benefit concerts given on behalf of the conductor were well supported by a public desirous of expressing its appreciation. His concerts were given in the Botanical Gardens, at the Drostdy, at the Grey Reservoir, and on Church and Market Squares (even during the evenings, with small paraffin lamps attached to the music stands); but also in the town hall, the Albany Hall (the Drill Hall) or the hotel. He could regularly depend on the co-operation of proficient vocalists and instrumentalists like Eberlein, elocutionists, dramatic players and choirs. During these years Grahamstown acted as host to the Prince Alfred's Guards Band from Port Elizabeth and to the Band of the Cape Mounted Rifles, conducted by Tardugno. In short, things were going well, and in 1886 it was even possible to reorganise the orchestra and to replace some of the instruments. Unfortunately Hind could not overhear the siren voice of Kimberley and in 1886 he left the town, this time for good and all. — He was again succeeded by J.O. Rogers, the same sergeant who had been in charge at an earlier stage, but this time with considerably more success. During his term as conductor the moonlit concerts held at Grey Reservoir became very popular, but the public did not take kindly to the idea that they had to contribute to the upkeep of the band. In a letter to the press Rogers complained that the upkeep of the band required between R200 and R300 per year, whilst their income seldom exceeded R50. He left in the second half of 1891 and the band acquired a dynamic leader in the person of bandleader Gilder, formerly of the Prince Alfred's Guard Band in PE. He immediately introduced regular practices and very soon the band became a feature of practically every occasion, whether of a political, sporting, entertaining, romantic or adventurous nature. Starting in December 1892 they made a point of organising concerts on stock fair days, a novelty which soon became an institution and was accorded steadily growing support. The organisers discovered that apt advertisement was an excellent way of attracting attention and within a year or two it had become publicity with the accent on humour: "The management desire to provide the Public of Albany and Grahamstown with a bright, cheerful, sparkling hour of happiness, wet or fine. (The Hall is watertight)". In March 1895 the public read about "Music and Song! Agriculture and Melody! Good luck for Spade and Furrow!" In September of the same year they advertised as follows: "Telephone talk! Are you there? Yes dear! Will you come? Where darling? To the Stocker, of course! Why certainly, love, it's all the go! I'm so glad! Stop! When is it? Toosday, at 8, as the clock strikes! But – ho! Come back! Well? You really must be early (rings off)". The programmes were judiciously varied with songs (comic as well as serious or sentimental), all sorts of solos on a variety of instruments (the piccolo being an especial favourite), excerpts from popular stage works (of the Gilbert and Sullivan variety), recitations and addresses, something for everybody in fact. It brought an element of light entertainment into the social round and sounded a happy note in the lives of the frontier people. Finally the concerts became so crowded that people had to make a point of arriving early to obtain seats. The mood started changing when the war against the Republics broke out in 1899. Many of the band members joined the forces and after 1900 the best that Gilder could supply was an "Emergency Band". The tradition of the Stock Fairs has continued up to the present day (1979), although music has ceased to sound for a considerable time.

3. **Amateur and church music**

An Amateur Musical Society existed from mid-1837 to December 1838; it was revived again in October, 1843, but had passed into oblivion by 1846. The Society held a practice each week and a meeting each month. It seems to have been an exclusive organisation. — Prof. Kirby** has delved into the history of the theatre in Grahamstown during the first sixteen years of its existence. When military players, singers and choral members were available, some of the theatre presentations could include music in some form, as interludes between short plays, or as an intermezzo between the acts of an extended play. All the presentations were staged in the Commercial Hall. Inspired by the initiative of the scenic painter and artist, F.Y.I'Ons, an amateur company calling themselves "Honi soit qui mal y pense" presented a variety of shows in 1837–1838. With the addition of comic songs, Sheridan's *The rivals* was a great favourite; *Bombastes furioso,* embellished with six musical items, was performed no less than five times during 1838. In this same year, on 12 November, the comic sketch, *Kaatje Kekkelbek,* by Captain Andrew Geddes Bain, the traveller, geologist and road engineer, was staged. In its satirical references to state mismanagement, local events and popular grievances, this little work, written in a mixture of Dutch and early Afrikaans, was an expression of a free spirit and of humourous criticism which would have been a credit to a far more mature culture. — Opera had not reached Grahamstown by 1862, but there was a movement in this direction in the performance of *Castle spectre* (27 March 1838), a melodrama in which a so-called "orchestra" and vocalists were used to give the impression of operatic continuity. More exciting was the announcement of a burlesque opera for performance on 30 July 1838, entitled *Chrononhotonthologus.* The work had had its first performance in the Haymarket Theatre, London, in 1734; it is unfortunate that no details of the Grahamstown performance are available. — The non-musical institutes and societies in Grahamstown proved to be more durable, and had a more comprehensive influence on the culture of the frontier community. They generally included music in their programmes, and provided ample scope for such musical talent as was available in the town. By some unexplained circumstance, no less than three of these organizations came into being in 1854. The Albany Institute organized its own music and singing classes, and sometimes a band would render musical items on lecture evenings. In 1858 there were two lectures on Church Music: Mr Rose spoke on *Psalmody, or singing in the congregation,* later followed by a symposium entitled *Is chanting suitable for public worship?* The Graham's Town General Institute employed either a band, or amateur soloists, to add colour and enjoyment to their meetings. The most important group however, was the Literary, Scientific and Medical Society, which had at least four lectures on music, delivered by Mr Kennelly, in August and November 1857 and again in September and December 1858. One of his themes was *Music from ancient to modern times;* the talk included ancient English music, Italian opera, Handel, Rossini and Weber. The lectures were suitably illustrated by local musicians. Mr Dowling, the organist of St George's Church, gave another music lecture in October 1859, and two weeks later the 13th Regimental Band co-operated with amateurs to provide the Society with a Musical Evening. This was so well received, that musical items became an integral part of each meeting. On a more scientific level, the Bishop of Grahamstown lectured on acoustical principles on 26 June 1862. His address was entitled *Sound and the elementary laws of music*. — The singing class of the Albany Institute fulfilled the desire for an English choral tradition cultivated among the younger generation. In support of this a Musical Class was offered in October 1861, by a Mr Von Wissel; it was, in fact, a singing class. Regular members paid 50c a month for instruction, and 15c for copies of music issued, while casual members were expected to pay R1 per annum. — The employment of music to extract money in aid of charity from the pockets of people largely unconcerned with the art, is a well-established custom, and is invariably successful. It is a musical species peculiar to Anglo-Saxon communities and was of frequent occurrence in Grahamstown. Between 1836 and 1853, there were no less than 12 concerts in aid of the different causes, such as "The contemplated erection of an asylum for the aged and decayed Freemason" (December 1836). The Library benefited in July 1845 (on this occasion the amateur Band attempted the Overture to *Figaro*); other concerts for the Library were in January 1846, and in 1853. In St George's Church (1845) an impressive sacred concert offered a programme of 17 items: a choir was accompanied by the Amateur Band in two choruses from *Messiah,* while Miss Saunders and Mr and Mrs Moore contributed vocal trios, described as "outstanding". Other charity concerts followed, for instance in 1847, "for Distressed Irish and Scotch in the Parent Country" (under the patronage of Mrs Somerset); and again in 1852, for "Children orphaned by the Eighth Kaffir War". A feature of these concerts was the contribution made by military instrumentalists working in conjunction with choral groups and soloists. — An impressive concert given by Bandmaster Willemse of the 85th Regiment on 6 February 1858, included the Overture to the *Barber of Seville* and vocal solos by Mme Willemse who sang the *Grand cavatina* from *Robert le diable* (Meyerbeer) (in French), whilst soloists and small ensembles from the band performed on clarinet, cornet, also horn and French horn. Three years later (January 1861), Wiesbecker reorganized the Amateur Society, now known as The Philharmonic and Amphion Glee Union Society. He gave two concerts during 1861, on 28 June and 23 August, but the Society declined rapidly in the first half of 1862. When the year ended, Grahamstown amateurs unconnected with this society arranged two concerts in aid of "Distressed Lancashire Operatives". An attraction at Wiesbecker's two concerts was the singing of his daughter, said to have been a pupil at the RAM. At the concert in June there were 22 players, whose names are cited as an interesting memento of the musical pioneers of Grahamstown: Barr, Armstrong, Dell, Gooch, Hume, J. Richards and S. Wright (first violins); Fletcher, Haust and Stead (second violins); Atwell, Huntley and Kensit (violas); Brislin and Tidmarch (cellos); Dowling (double bass); Coleman, McPherson and Passmore (cornets); Locke and Tydhope (flutes); Leonard (ophicleide and clarinet). — Early in 1863 the press carried notices of Mr Wiesbecker's intention to reorganize the Grahamstown Philharmonic Society. These were repeated in 1864 and again in 1865, but nothing seems to have happened until May 1877, when the Grahamstown Music Society was established, with the Rev. J. Mullins as president, Julius Gau as secretary, and C. Glennon as conductor. The Society gave a much needed stability to musical life in Grahamstown, and performed cantatas in 1877, 1878 and 1879. In the latter year an unfortunate feud developed between Gau and Glennon, which led to the resignation of the conductor. He was succeeded by George Hind. Before the new musical society came into being there had been (in 1866) a Grahamstown Choral Society, directed by the Rev. Mullins. This group sang regularly after 1874, under the title of the New Choral Society, and had a membership of 90 ladies and gentlemen, in about equal proportion. Finally, Mr and Mrs Stier had intended forming an Amateur Music Society in 1867, but its fate has not been recorded. — The music teacher, J.A. Muire, formed a String Band, first mentioned in October 1866; this seems to have performed regularly until 1879, at the functions of church communities, and for masonic, youth, literary and benevolent societies. — The Wesleyan Young Men's Society, the Total Abstinence Society, the St Patrick's Catholic Young Men's Society, and the Independent Order of Good Templars, all offered miscellaneous literary readings and musical entertainments, at which local quartets and choirs sang with pianists, harpists and other instrumentalists sharing the honours. A function of this nature was held by the Wesleyan Young Men's Society in July 1872, when there was a lecture by the Rev. Jones on *Recreation;* the Misses Dold and Stanton sang a duet and the Settlers' composition by the Rev. Dugmore for duet and chorus, called *Prospect and retrospect,* was performed. In addition, there were piano, violin and vocal solos. At a meeting in July 1878, B. Roberts conducted a chorus of some 25 voices in glees and partsongs; a variety of solos and readings filled the rest of the programme. St George's Guild was also active with readings, glees, songs and band-playing; at an entertainment in January 1869, there was a programme of pianoforte duets, consisting of arrangements of Rossini and Mozart works. — The minstrel movement of the 'sixties and 'seventies produced a few local groups such as the Amateur Christy Minstrels (1863–1867), and the St George's United Minstrel and Dramatic Society, which lasted from 1875 to 1877. Then there were the Sable Minstrels, and the Juvenile Christy Minstrels, which entertained the public at one or two concerts. The latter were treated rather harshly by the press after their concerts in October and November, 1871: they were described as "very good, except (that the) jokes (were) dull, simple and silly". — Among the 14 church denominations in the Albany area, the Methodists were noted for their singing at annual anniversary services and at concerts. At an entertainment in 1866, two choruses were sung in "magnificent style", and Mrs Stier's solo was performed "with greater effect than at any former occasion". Church functions were often supported by music societies, military bands and touring professionals. St George's Cathedral maintained the best standards. In 1867, for example, Mozart's *Twelfth mass* was performed, also Mendelssohn's *Hymn of praise* and *95th Psalm;* and the organist, Kenelly, contributed the overture to Spohr's *Last judgement.* Rossini's *Stabat mater* was sung on five different occasions between 1867 and 1879, together with selections from the standard oratorios, and 130 singers participated in a performance of *Messiah* in February 1869. Weber's *Mass in G,* Handel's *Israel in Egypt, Judas Maccabaeus,* and *Dettingen te Deum,* Mendelssohn's *Elijah* and *Athalie,* and Haydn's *Imperial mass* were all sung in this period, either as a whole or in part. Mr Glennon, the Rev. Dean, Mr Williams, and Mr Winny conducted the performances, and Kenelly generally officiated at the organ. From May 1878, the Cathedral choir was known as the St George's Cathedral Oratorio and Classical Sacred Music Association; after this change of title it gave no less than five monthly concerts in quick succession. — On 18 September 1890 the *Grahamstown Journal* wrote: "Grahamstown has been prolific in the production of choral societies . . . they have all come to an untimely end". The availability of a strong personality who is a leader musically, is important and generally decisive; so is the availability of a well-equipped hall; and finally the fate of choral societies rests with singers prepared to devote time and money to the art. Only rarely, however does a choir survive the departure of its leader. It is as though the desire to sing loses itself in gossip, schisms and the formation of new societies. The end of it all is musical impotence. — In Grahamstown a period of twenty years (1880–1900) saw the creation of eight different choral societies and a few others who seemingly did not survive the act of creation. They were The Grahamstown Musical Society (leader: Eberlein; 1881–1884); the Commemoration Choral Society (only one program); the Cathedral Oratorio Association (probably inactive); the Grahamstown Philharmonic Society (leader: Winney; June 1885–1886, or perhaps the early years of 1887); Cathedral Choral Union (leaders: Winney and Day; 1887–1890); the Grahamstown Philharmonic Society (leader: T.E. Speed; 1890–1893 or 1894); Cathedral Choral and Orchestral Union (leader: Day; 1891–1892 or 1893) and The Grahamstown Choral Union (W. Deane; 1895–1898). For the sake of completeness the Grahamstown Orchestral Society (leader: Percy Ould; 1894–1898) should also be mentioned. It is obvious from this list that the choral conductors were at the same time the organists of various churches. Without any recompense at all, these men accepted the additional responsibility of furthering the social aspects of the art. It is also obvious that each in turn became the leader of a new organisation, although the singers were evidently always the same people. And finally it becomes clear that the rise and subsidence of the various societies coincided with the arrival and departure of organists. — A few months after settling in Grahamstown, Eberlein became the leader of the Grahamstown Music Society, which, in spite of the bickering and even opposition of Winney, was responsible for 15 concerts in the space of 18 months. It should be stated, however, that quite a considerable number of these were repeats of previously studied works. The climax was the performance of Spohr's *Last judgement,* on the occasion of the inauguration of the new town hall in May 1882. The occasion hardly warranted this rather singular choice and in a future reference it was even designated Spohr's "insipidity". — Handel's *Acis and Galatea* and Mozart's *First mass* are worthy of mention; so also *The wreck of the Hesperus* by the King William's Town composer, James Hyde. Winney's opposition took the form of Haydn's *Emperor mass* and Handel's *Israel in Egypt.* In view of the fact that the same singers had in the main to sing for both conductors, it was obvious that one of the societies had to give way. The Society of the German was forced into liquidation and Winney launched a Philharmonic Society which, however, only achieved a repeat of Handel's *Israel.* — Day tried to fill the vacuum with his Cathedral Choral Union which gave a performance of Mendelssohn's *St Paul* (December 1890). Speed followed with a Philharmonic Society which sang a number of shorter cantatas and the Handel oratorio *Samson* (May 1892). During this period Day's Choral and Orchestral Union performed *Messiah,* but then both societies dissolved and were succeeded by W. Deane's Choral Union, which hardly advanced beyond the stage of less significant British cantatas. — Percy Ould's creation of an Orchestral Society in 1894 must be accounted one of the more important happenings in Grahamstown. During the four years of its existence, it advanced from an initial 12 players to 37 and the programmes grew in stature from opera melodies, dances etc. to the first *Allegro* from Mozart's *Jupiter symphony* and Schubert's *Unfinished symphony.* A feature of this brave amateur effort was the inclusion of light works by the conductor, Ould, and dances such as valses and an odd mazurka. In 1895 the members of the orchestra presented Ould with a gift to congratulate him on his approaching marriage. When he left the town in 1898 to settle in Cape Town, his orchestra faded into oblivion. — Until 1890 the Commemoration Church had a choir available which sang extracts from *Messiah* (1883), but achieved very little after that. The organists Winney, Westerby and Day often treated the congregation and other music lovers to organ recitals, but church music in these circles only came into its own when T.E. Speed (1890–1899) was appointed organist. — Speed's programmes and his choice of choral music reflect his British background and training, but also the British character of Grahamstown for which his music was intended. Over the years the works of Victorian composers formed the staple diet, with a few pieces by Mendelssohn and a little Bach as indications that the organist was capable of better things. In the traditional manner, Italian opera melodies were entwined with organ music proper as a sop to less sophisticated tastes (Wagner was the great surprise of 1899) and the organ playing was often interrupted in favour of vocal solos and ensembles, at times also instrumental pieces of an easily digestable type. Choral work does not seem to have been Speed's *forte*. Taken as a whole the church music of the Wesleyans, and of other congregations, was attuned to the unpretentious musical requirements of English-speaking South Africans. That there was a need is a major point; but its almost exclusive confinement to the simple emotional needs of the listeners must be considered typical of the time. — At St George's Cathedral more advanced listening was expected, especially after 1890, when first A.H. Day (until 1893) and after him his brother-in-law, William Deane,** presided at the organ. Deane had the privilege of inaugurating the new cathedral organ in 1894 (it should be mentioned that Cecil J. Rhodes had contributed R200 to the cost of the instrument). During his service with the church, Day created a tradition of regular organ recitals at which many standard works from the organ repertoire were heard in the company of arrangements, also of Beethoven's *Pastoral symphony,* which was given in its entirety. Day was an excellent organist who later had a fruitful career in his new sphere of activity in Pieter-maritzburg, where he conducted the Philharmonic Society. — This was even more the case with W. Deane who played a judicious selection of works by Bach, Mendelssohn and Guilmant, and varied his programmes with a choice of choral items and contributions by soloists and ensembles. The liturgical music is less enterprising and rarely departs from the round of melodious arrangements by British composers. — In Trinity Church too there was a capable organist in the person of Mr Winney who played good music until 1883, and works labouring under emotional stresses, as favoured by the congregations. His successor, Mr Howes, was probably more drawn to the choir than to the organ and placed the accent on choral work and soloists. A climax was reached in June 1890 when he had the co-operation of Day of the Commemora-tion Church in presenting a complete programme devoted to the works of Handel, with *Messiah* especially prominent. When Howes departed to Port Elizabeth there was more or less a collapse. — It would be possible to name six other churches in Grahamstown in which the *musica sacra* received due attention, although with less continuity than in the case of Speed, Day and Deane. Until 1887 the violinist Eberlein** often appears on programmes as an active participant.

4. Visiting musicians

The first group of entertainers to visit Grahamstown was the Della Casa Circus in 1848-1849; but visiting artists were rather thinly spread during the next fourteen years. The groups that honoured Grahamstown with a visit were mainly amateur organizations from Port Elizabeth itself. The following list represents all that can be ascertained: – 1850: J. Russel's Ethiopian Serenaders, who were widely imitated by local amateurs; 1857: Martin Simonsen (violin), and Fanny Quichard (soprano); 1858: Ali Ben Sou Alle (piano, clarinet, etc.); 1860: Agostino Robbio and Charles Wynen (violinists), the PE Amateur Instrumental Society and Glee Club, accompanied by Miss Kenelly, a daughter of the organist previously mentioned; 1861: C. Wood; 1862: S. Parry and Mr and Mrs Reece (violin, singing and piano), also a group of Christy Minstrels (See article on Touring Companies). — The above persons were responsible for about 26 concert evenings. As was usual with guest artists, they depended on the support of local amateurs, a service gladly rendered for the prestige of associating one's self with visiting celebrities. — It should be remembered that the amateurs of Grahamstown, because of their easy reliance on the music of military professionals, were not singularly active during the first half of the century. It is estimated that there were 1 336 concerts in Grahamstown up to 1862. Discounting amateur participation in professional entertainments, only about 153 concerts were due to amateur enterprise, about 11% of the total. — Visiting artists and companies continued to be rare until 1879. The violoncellist, Herr Feri Kletzer** played in the Assembly Room in May 1865. The Poussard-Bailey company came to Grahamstown in the mid-year of 1867 and staidly performed programmes of arias and duets by nonentities, sometimes supported by the band of the second 11th Regiment. A romantic interlude to their visit occurred when Mr Gooch ("a member of the Town Council, a director of the Albany Hall Company, and a successful caterer for public entertainment") eloped with Miss Bailey to Cradock, "in a cart and four horses". The scandal was "settled in the most satisfactory manner possible" and the company gave a Grand Farewell Concert to conclude a twelve month South African tour, during which they had presented 125 concerts. — October 1868, saw three "fashionable concerts" by the Harper-Hirst Company, which returned in 1869 as the Miranda-Harper Company. They performed Act IV of *Il trovatore,* and extracts from *Bohemian girl, La sonnambula* and other operas. A "charming" operetta or two was presented by the D'Arcy-Read Operetta Company** in 1870, and thereafter followed a long silence broken by the Harvey-Turner Company, conducted by James Hyde,** in mid-1875. In Grahamstown this Company performed three "pretty comic pieces", two operas (*Il trovatore* and *Faust*) and Balfé's *Bohemian girl.* Frank Hyde** accompanied his brother on this occasion, acting as a cornet player in the orchestra. Mme Anna Bishop** arrived with her pianist Lascelles** in 1875, and advertised for amateurs to assist them in their production of Offenbach's *The grand duchess.* The following year the Harvey-Turner Group returned on their way back to England, and in July Mr Harvey was there again with an Italian Opera and Ballet Company, which performed *Lucia di Lammermoor* and *Il trovatore.* Mr Harvey visited Grahamstown once more in 1877, with Marie Harvey, to present a "Grand Fashionable Night", at which arias from *Faust* were sung; Emily Bradshaw played piano items, W.P. Cox played the violin, and some minstrels introduced "the latest and most successful songs". In May 1879, the Kennedy family gave four concerts in Grahamstown. Other visitors were Mme Mendelssohn,** who was accompanied by Herr Eberlein** in three concerts

(1879), and the Vesalius Sisters, who sang ballads in Albany Hall during December 1879. — There were a few groups offering light entertainment as for instance, The New Christy Team from Piccadilly, which arrived in November 1868. This group seems to have offered mixed programmes, with instrumental solos sandwiched between comic and vocal items. It also organized a Monster Christy Minstrel Entertainment together with the local Christy's and the band of the Second 11th Regiment, which was very well received. During November 1870, "Sign. Raffaelo Abecco and W.W. Allen's Combination Troupe with Mlle. Julie" gave three concerts in the Albany Hall, consisting of harp solos, comic songs, dances, Negro acts and gems from the operas, in short, a "most enjoyable and varied" entertainment. — Mr Walter, in association with the "Witty Youths" of Australia, and the champion clog-and step-dancer, Tom Robson, gave a Negro and Magical Entertainment in 1877. This evening was disturbed by a commotion at the rear of the hall, where an unsteady gentleman essayed a hornpipe, and was escorted by willing hands up the steps and onto the stage at the very moment when Mr Walter was performing his wellknown Sack Trick. There was an annoying confusion which lasted until several Good Templars and a couple of policemen restored order by marching onto the stage. The entertainment proceeded with two policemen stationed close to the front. Benson's American Troupe arrived shortly afterwards, and issued a warning to all boys "not to make disagreeable noises"; they were advised: "leave your sticks at home!" — There was indeed no need for Grahamstown to feel musically neglected. Apart from the excellent leadership the town enjoyed in having capable, well-trained church organists who were also prominent in communal music-making, Grahamstown was treated to a wealth of variety concerts offered by local talent to benefit charity or some other praiseworthy goal. These *raisons d'etre* include the Chapel Fund and the inauguration of St Aidan's Chapel in November 1883; the removal of inmates of the Asylum to a new home; the erection of a new laboratory at St Andrew's School; the organ fund of the Baptist Church; to honour visiting football teams; to take leave of a personality prominent in musical circles; benefit concerts for a person or an organisation; war funds; in aid of a school; to buy an harmonium for the Sunday School; to buy vocal scores for a church choir; for the roof or tower of a church; or for visitors to the town, such as the "English Cricketers", who were treated to a smoking concert. There was always a cause deserving of support, which, instead of a futile appeal to the public, could best be served by following the roundabout way of an entertaining variety concert. — Characteristic of this almost forgotten concert genus was the readiness of available talent to serve a meritorious cause. Quite apart from questions of status or prestige, violinists like Eberlein or Ould, or singers like Miss Spoor, or pianists like Ambrose Comfort, shared programmes with persons who performed comic sketches, or sang as they could, or who performed minstrel items, or bands, or a variety of instrumental ensembles, or strings of ballads, or recitations, or lectures. — In the period 1880–1900 there was a continuance of professional touring companies, or single persons, or else simply adventurers, who all boosted their offerings with telling references to Home, or London theatres, or particular successes with some song or other, or references to "late from...", "fresh from..." etc. Most of the artists and/or groups mentioned in the article Touring Theatre Groups,** also called at Grahamstown with its flourishing musical life, admirable newspaper coverage and appreciative audiences. To mention only a few of the most prominent visitors, a selection has been made from the average of four visiting groups per year. In the twenty years from 1880 to 1900 about 90 different groups appeared in Grahamstown, and as the distances were comparatively vast and the transport slow-moving and leisurely, a few of them stayed on for a while, giving more than one concert. The selection includes: Vesalius Sisters (1881); Loftus Troupe (1882); Pauline Bredelli with Norman and Thies (1883); Anglo-American Minstrels, Julia Sydney's Opera Co. (1884); Wheeler Comedy Co. (1885); Walther and two other artists (1886); Reményi (1887 and 1888); Tregarthen (1887); Virginie Cheron, Searelle Opera Co. (1888); Walther and Clifford Hallé (1889); Black choir on its way to England and America (12 members) (1891); Zulu choir on its way to England (1892); Madame Stefani, Lyric Opera Co., Signor Foli (1893); Marguerite MacIntyre (1894); Payne Bellringers, Sir Charles and Lady Hallé, Madame Trebelli, Virginie Cheron with Avron Saxon and Signor Rotondo (1895); Ellie Marx (1897); Friedenthal, Pollard's Lilliputians (1898); Roger Ascham and Theo Wendt (1900). — The year 1895 was exceptional – no less than 11 groups and/or individuals gave concerts in the town. Remarkable is the paucity of opera companies. It seems as though these concentrated on the financially stronger centres where they had more opportunity of recuperating their often considerable expenses.

5. Music education

Information on the personalities prominent in this field is so sparse before 1862 that a summary of names and known facts will have to suffice. The earliest pianoforte teachers were Mrs Rawlinson (from 1823) and Mr Franklin (1837); the latter was said to have been a pupil of Sir George Smart in England. Mrs Geo. Gunn gave lessons in both pianoforte and singing in 1846. John Younger advertised classes in Sacred Music, and a Glee Singing Club, in 1832; Mr Birkett advertised similar classes in 1860 and is reported to have been very successful. Mrs Blackburn moved her "Ladies' School" from Port Elizabeth to Grahamstown in 1834, and advertised instruction in the harp, pianoforte, guitar, English, Italian and French, singing and dancing, in addition to the normal school education. Mrs Eades, who had similarly moved from Port Elizabeth to Grahamstown, emphasized in 1845 that music-teaching on the pianoforte and harp, as well as "dancing à la Francaise", was prominent in her school's instruction. She presented annual concerts from 1850, and added singing instruction to her list of musical subjects in 1860. — The Cathedral Grammar School was founded in 1844 by the Rev. John Heavyside, but its opening was postponed until October 1849 for financial reasons. Selected boys of this school were trained in the usual way as choristers for Cathedral services. By 1891, twelve free scholarships had been instituted, and by the end of 1892 the school had 62 pupils, of whom 20 were trained as singers. — Judging from steady advertising in the *Grahamstown Journal* after 1860, the town was well supplied with teachers of the pianoforte, strings, harp, flute, clarinet, cornet and guitar. Until 1877, Mr Wiesbecker advertised pianoforte tuition, and instruction in harmony "according to the rules of Thorough Bass and Composition". C.W.F. and Mrs Stier were teaching in Grahamstown during the years 1866–1867, and John A. Muire, "professor of music and pianoforte tuner", taught the violin, cello, clarinet, flute and guitar. This man also offered his services in the making of violins, the repairing of concertinas and harmoniums, and the re-hairing of violin bows. According to Muire's accounts, kept in the Cory Library of Rhodes University, he had done extensive repairs to a pianoforte belonging to a "Mr Hyde" in 1878, probably James Hyde, who had arrived in South Africa as conductor of the Harvey-

Turner company. Muire's memory is also perpetuated as the composer of the waltz, *Prince Alfred's farewell to Grahamstown*. Other teachers include the Cathedral organist, Frederick Griffiths, who was also a piano tuner "provided with the latest improvements in tuning instruments from England"; Herbert Winney "professor of organ, piano and singing", as well as choirmaster of St Andrew's College; Mr and Mrs Dudley, who gave pupils' concerts between August 1875, and September 1876, at which music by Mendelssohn, Attwood, Pleyel, Lindsay and Mozart was presented. Subsequent to January 1873, choral work was offered free of charge at St Andrew's and singing was included as a subject at the Grahamstown Junior Public School. A year later, the Misses Rolph and Humphreys advertised music instruction at their school at R3 per term, St Andrew's Diocesan College offered instruction in a free choice of music, and the Diocesan School for Girls announced that they offered instruction in vocal as well as instrumental music. — In 1863 Mr C. Birkett introduced the tonic sol-fa method of instruction into Black schools at Grahamstown, Cradock and Healdtown. Only 22 years after sol-fa had been developed by the Rev. John Curwen for use in Sunday Schools, Birkett used the method to teach choirs in and around Grahamstown to sing choruses like *Hallelujah* or selections from the *Hymn of praise*. The *Grahamstown Journal* referred in complimentary language to the singing of Black Sunday-school choirs which had been trained by Birkett according to this system. The choirs sang at a public concert, at which Mr Impey played the harmonium and Wiesbecker's string band assisted. After 1863 there is a silence of ten years, broken by the announcement that Chris Birkett had been appointed principal of the school at Fort Beaufort. There he resumed the good work. After Birkett's departure from Grahamstown, John Wedderburn and Mr Hawkins, who had attended classes with Birkett, formed a Tonic Sol-fa Association and ran classes in the method in the Bathurst Street School Room. On 2 July 1874, a concert was given by Black persons trained under the direction of Hawkins; the "Bantu Total Abstinence Benefit Society", formed at this time, was conducted by Wedderburn in musical selections in February 1877. — With such a gifted and well-trained variety of musicians in Grahamstown, it follows that music teaching in the period up to 1900 functioned on a high level of efficiency at the schools and in the private sector. The more prominent musicians generally taught at more than one school and accepted the responsibility of planning and preparing the programmes for the yearly prize distributions. In this predominantly English-speaking town these were important occasions, on which speeches were heard and a variety of prizes were distributed for a variety of achievements, backed by a music programme in which both talent and teaching shone. The efforts of the pupils were integrated with contributions by their teachers and only in exceptional cases did the teacher's share exceed that of the pupils. The usual subjects. offered for instruction were the piano, violin and singing, but the Convent of the Assumption distinguished itself by also arranging for instruction on the harp and guitar. — Eberlein exhibited much enterprise during his stay of six years in Grahamstown. From 1881 to 1887 he worked mainly at the Diocesan Girls' School (DSG) and at the Wesleyan High School. In 1883, for example, he arranged for performances at the prize-giving ceremony of the *Don Giovanni overture* (Mozart) and the *Scottish symphony* of Mendelssohn, both performed by an ensemble consisting of a pianoforte duet and an harmonium. In this same year he instituted an additional prize for a superior achievement in music and the newspapers published appreciative reports on the improvement noticeable in the string playing. The next year he arranged for an operetta to be performed, supplemented with works by "modern" composers such as Dvořak and Brahms (Liebeslieder Walzer). At the Wesleyan High School, where Winney was employed, he arranged and gave a series of illustrated lectures, at which the girls were expected to take notes and eventually to write an essay on the subject. The lectures concerned themselves with Beethoven (with illustrations played on violin and pianoforte, including a movement from the *Fifth symphony,* and singing), Mendelssohn, The music of France, Schubert, How music is composed, interpreted and played (with illustrations, now performed on 2 pianos, flute, violin and cello) and finally with Haydn (illustrated by the combination mentioned in the previous item). Among the other teachers at the DSG before 1900, there were Ambrose Comfort (able to give a concert performance of Beethoven's *Sonata op. 109),* Percy Ould, William Deane and for a short while, Theo Wendt. Clearly this school exerted itself to supply the best music instruction available in Grahamstown. — Apart from his engagement at the Wesleyan High School, Winney also taught at St Aidan's where in 1887 the pupils sang Hyde's cantata *The wreck of the Hesperus* under the direction of an unknown musician. Other teachers at this school were Messrs Speed, Muire and Deane. Speed's main occupation was however at Kingswood College where the pupils at times presented a programme. Percy Ould was attached to St Andrew's College which had an active Recreation Society and a Literary and Debating Society. Both made use of music in compiling their programmes. But this school advanced beyond this point when they tackled an operetta directed by Percy Ould. He also conducted an active school choir and the chapel singing showed marked improvement, advanced by the acquisition of a Memorial Organ which was blessed on 12 February 1893. At the yearly prize-giving he provided vocal and instrumental items by his pupils. In those years it was customary at St Andrew's to stage a play, for which Ould and his pupils provided incidental music – an overture or entr'actes. Ould's good work was continued by A.E. Abbott, also an excellent violinist. — The persons responsible for the music instruction at the schools, also gave private individual instruction in town. Mr Deane e.g. enjoyed an enviable reputation as a pianoforte teacher and regularly advertised that he applied the Leschetizky method and could provide physical solutions for technical problems. Mr and Mrs Day started a Grahamstown College of Music and usually held a quarterly pupils' concert in the town hall, which was well supported by parents, family members and friends. Mr Winney on the other hand concerned himself with the production of operettas in which the parts were practically all sung by children. He achieved resounding successes with both *HMS Pinafore* and *Pirates of Penzance.* The second work even achieved four performances. Finally, T.E. Speed occupied himself in the private sector too, and, between 1896 and 1898, Theo Wendt achieved good results as a teacher of pianoforte.

6. Music shops, printers and publishers

The first music warehouse was opened in 1859 by Mr Barr, who boldly claimed that he catered "for all tastes and requirements". Business in pianos must have been brisk in early Grahamstown, since the *Journal* observed in 1860: "We fancy there are few places in the world where pianos are more plentiful". This might imply not only that there was much music-making in the homes, but also that the community was prosperous. After 1856, the inhabitants of Albany could boast an *Eastern Province Monthly Magazine,* in which Edward Russel Bell published four articles on *National*

GRAHAMSTOWN

music (vol. I parts 9 & 10 and vol. II parts 13 & 14 (1857)). These were intended for
the instruction of a more enlightened public. — The visit of HRH Prince Alfred in
1860 was a stimulus to the creative powers of Grahamstown musicians, and a few of
the patriotic effusions were privileged to find publishers. W.M. Ireson (1817–1865),
bandmaster of the Imperial Cape Riflemen (1856), composed a *Prince Alfred polka
and Euryalus schottische,* which he dedicated to Col. Eustace and the officers and men
of the Cape Royal Rifles. This was published by Darters** of Cape Town. Similarly,
the bandmaster of the 2nd Battalion, 10th Regiment, J. Rupel, composed the *Prince
Alfred quadrilles,* which he dedicated to the Prince himself. It was published by the
printers of the *Grahamstown Journal,* Godlonton and Richards. The tailor, John Alex
Muire (1835–1903), who later became a music teacher, composed a valse, *Prince
Alfred's farewell to Grahamstown,* and a number of other works, which were left in
manuscript though provided with a printed title-page. At a later date, Muire wrote a
Masonic waltz, printed by T. and O. Sheffield, Music and General Printers, Gra-
hamstown. The political controversy of 1860 inspired him to write a *Separation
League quadrille.* — Godlonton and Richards (later Richards, Slater & Co.), James
Hay, A.R. Gooch & Co. (proprietors of Gooch's Musical Saloon), and T.H. Grocott,
printer and stationer, were firms who advertised pianos, mainly of British origin,
"made expressly for this climate". An interesting relic was recently discovered in the
Kingswood Preparatory Hostel – a piano built in 1829 and repaired in 1881, which
was played upon by a variety of celebrities. The Settlers Memorial Museum has a grand
piano by Broadwood, which was imported in 1836. Apart from pianos, these firms
advertised musical-boxes at from R10 to R40, harmoniums, accordions, concertinas,
violins and their accoutrements, violoncellos, double basses, cornets, clarionettes,
flutes, saxhorns, triangles, castanets and flautinas. A flautina, probably the only one
left in South Africa, is in the possession of Mr S.J. van der Merwe of Oudtshoorn, who
had it from an uncle, S.J. van Heerden of Murraysburg. It had been in use to play tunes
at the religious exercises of the family. The instrument is 45 cm long, has a breadth of
13 cm and a height of 19 cm. There are 22 white and 15 black notes, the white ones 6
cm long and the black ones 3 cm. At the back it has two little bellows, which were
operated by the left hand, or by another person, while the right hand played the tune.
The sound was produced by reeds, on the principle of the harmonium. — Organ-
building was carried on apace. In 1871 an organ of 14 stops was erected at St
Bartholomew's Church, and the Baptist Church inaugurated a new instrument in
September 1873. In 1875 an organ was installed in the Methodist Commemoration
Chapel, and in October of the same year another instrument was put into use in the
Presbyterian Church. — A large variety of sheet music was advertised, both for the
piano and for voices. An advertisement by Messrs Godlonton & Richards lists 13
major works by Handel, and individual compositions of Haydn, Rossini, Beethoven,
Mozart, Mendelssohn, etc. Albums of sacred music, popular music, four-part songs,
collections of hymns, and "moral songs" were popular. Pianoforte volumes entitled
Showers of pearls, Home circle, Silver chord, Musical garland (duets), *Pianists' album,
Melodia divina,* and songs with all sorts of quaint names, were offered for sale. There
were also music instruction-books, such as *Lily's first music book, Farmer's piano
tutor, Hamilton's instruction book* and Czerny's *101 exercises.* — The years 1880 to
1887 were meagre years in the music trade, but the firm of Richards, Slater & Co.
managed to retain the lion's share, although the demand for instruments and printed
music was rather limited. They were thus particularly sensitive to competition

132

afforded by other, short-lived firms. Pianos were for example sold by Rivenhall & Co. (1882), Castledon's Music Depot (1883–1886) and by Brister & Co. of Port Elizabeth and Grahamstown (1881). To promote sales Richards & Slater organised a music lottery and introduced a system of hire purchase. This however merely delayed their inevitable collapse, which came in August 1887. The firm of Galpin Bros. was more successful, though the music trade was a mere adjunct to their actual trade as watchmakers, jewellers and opticians. This talented family entered the trade round about 1884 and started selling pianos and printed music. Soon they were able to add autoharps to their stock, to tackle pianoforte tuning and repairs and even to act as publishers of music. Until 1900 they regularly advertised in the *Grahamstown Journal*. In 1898 the new firm of Jackson Bros.** appeared on the scene, after an important branch of their firm had been launched in PE by Percival Jackson. In Grahamstown they advertised a wide range of pianos, the erection of organs, the sale of all music accessories and of a variety of instruments including banjos, mandolines and accordions. They were also willing to publish compositions by local composers, sold pianos on the hire purchase system and were quite willing to lend instruments for important concerts. — The most important organ builder in Grahamstown was without a doubt G.W. Price, who started business in Market Street and subsequently lived and worked in Bathurst Street, on Church Square and finally at the corner of Hill and Cross Streets. Price thoroughly overhauled, enlarged and, in the case of the Cathedral rebuilt, in all, six organs in the town. They were in the Wesleyan Church, West Hill; St Bart, Trinity; St George's Cathedral; Commemoration Church and the Baptist Church. At the schools of St Andrew's and St Michael's he erected two smaller instruments. But his work was by no means confined to Grahamstown only – he actually had a national reputation. Thus his services were required by Kimberley (Trinity, St Mary's Roman Catholic Church), Queenstown (Wesleyan Church), Bloemfontein (Anglican Church), Somerset East (Presbyterian Church), Stellenbosch (DR Church), Pretoria (Wesleyan Church) and Cape Town (DR Mother Church). When this excellent organ specialist left Grahamstown in 1899 the town suffered a significant loss. — With ten years between them, two Exhibitions were held in Grahamstown during the last decade of the century. These were the exhibition in honour of Queen Victoria's jubilee year (15 December 1887–14 January 1888) and another one known as the Exhibition of Arts and Industries (15 December 1898–21 January 1899). The musical organisation of the Jubilee Show was at first entrusted to both Eberlein and Winney, but after Eberlein's departure Winney probably managed it alone. He procured the co-operation of Reményi, Virginie Richards (Cheron), the band of the Cape Mounted as well as of the First City Volunteers, Mr and Mrs James Hyde**, Tregarthen** and the bagpipe band of the Royal Scots. Reményi also agreed to exhibit a part of his collection of antiques, Africana and archaeological oddities in locked glass cases. During the first exhibition days a large choir was prominent with performances of Handel's *Coronation anthem, Dettingen te Deum* and *Judas Maccabaeus* and of Standford's *Revenge*. On two occasions a Black choir called the "United Native Choirs", sang a variety of apparently mainly British songs. Quite a stir was caused by Reményi's *Song of liberty*, which was given a number of times. As could be expected, there were a considerable number of complaints about people who walked about conversing, so that justice could hardly be done to the music. The organisers tried to surmount this problem by having a bell rung before each musical item, to signal an appeal for a respectful silence. According to the press reports, this measure did not quite come up to expectations. — The Grahamstown South African Exhibition of Arts and Crafts also had an extended musical programme, mainly devised by Percy Ould. He trained a large choir in Sullivan's *Te Deum laudamus* and an abbreviated version of *Messiah,* and assembled from various parts of the country an orchestra of more than 50 members. This "orchestra" did not have symphonic stature, but confined itself to orchestral contributions played between items sung by the vocalists Misses Currie, Bergh, Thelka Webster and Florence Fraser,** together with Messrs Lowe, Cawse and Vernon Reid. They also accompanied the choral works. Some of the pieces heard at the Exhibition were composed by Percy Ould, Theo Wendt *(Exhibition march)* and an old Grahamstonian, Basil Scholefield.** The Angelus Male Voice Quartet saw to the entertainment side with comic, frothy and sentimental songs, whilst the band of the Royal Berkshire regiment, relieved a few times by the band of the First City Volunteers, maintained the atmosphere of a jovial trade show with bright and brassy sounds. Two of the exhibitions displayed a variety of musical instruments and printed music supplied respectively by Galpin Bros. and Jackson Bros. At times Theo Wendt performed on some of the pianos and attracted considerable attention. Taken as a whole, the exhibition was a major success for Grahamstown, attracting no less than 29 850 people. — Grahamstown was so well endowed with musicians that it would have been surprising if original work had been neglected. In 1865 Mr Stier made known two new pieces which he had written: *I look up to the lattice heights* and *The hour is come.* No trace of this music has been found. In addition the names of nine persons who wrote one or more pieces have come to light. Surprisingly original these might not have been, but they were representative of the community's taste for naively emotional songs, dances and marches. Some of the composers are dealt with in separate articles: George Hind, Percy Ould, W. Deane and Theo Wendt. There remain the names of the music writers. N. Pulvermacher, Henry Hess, J.A. Muire, Charles Parsons and the Rev. Charles Raymond-Barker. — **Charles Parsons** is the author of one single song, *I love thee* (words and music by the composer; publ. by T. & G. Sheffield, Grahamstown). **Henry Hess** was an attorney and an editor who seems to have written quite a number of dances, since he reacted in the 'eighties against persons who were critical of his predilection for dance music. He points out that composers are hardly able to cover their costs if they disregard popular music, since this is the only kind able to cover costs from sales. In addition he wishes to point out that his dance music is "not despised" in London. His waltz, *Ewig treu,* is his fifteenth work, according to an advertisement. It was printed by Hay Bros. of King William's Town (1884) and must have sold well, since it had to be reprinted. There is another popular dance melody by this same person, *Come back to me, love,* based on words by W.S. Craven, which he dedicated to Mrs H.F. Blaine in 1884. The leader of Ould's orchestra from 1894 to 1897 was **J.A. Muire,** who wrote a march called *Farewell to Grahamstown.* It possibly concerns Ould's departure, since it was performed by Ould's orchestra in July 1897. This same author also wrote a *Freemasons waltz* (pr. by T. & G. Sheffield) which he dedicated to the District Grand Master and members of the District Grand Lodge of South Africa. This has no date. Next there is **N. Pulvermacher,** who had achieved a reputation as an enthusiastic singer in Grahamstown, but also ventured to write music. He composed a *Grahamstown march* (Berlow & Co., New York, 1883) and a song, *I arise from dreams of thee* (Berlow & Co., New York, 1884), to a poem by Shelley, which he dedicated to Miss E.A. Lowe. The *Eastern Star* discovered "a number of grave errors" in this song and Pulvermacher felt called upon to defend, in particular, his opening chord against their attack. For the Jubilee Exhibition of 1885 he wrote an *Exhibition march* which he dedicated to Sir Hercules Robinson. There was another attack on this in the *Grahamstown Journal*, in which the critic wrote: "In the Introduction may be seen at once the mental strain the composer has endured in search of original ideas . . . Considering the number of marches which have been composed, it is astonishing that such a combination of chords, which form the first movement, should have slept until now." Be that as it may, this march also found a printer and was published by T. & G. Sheffield in 1885. — Finally there is the Rev. **Charles Raymond-Barker,** professor of Science at St Aidan's School from 1894/5 to 1899. This science master generally had Novello of London as his publisher. The works by him which have been traced are *Hope's message,* probably a song, two pianoforte works; *The Southern cross* and *Hope's message* (for piano) and a series of *Anthems of the Blessed Virgin,* including *Alma redemptoris, Salve regina, Ave Maria stella* etc. These were published by Cary's of London during the time the composer spent at St Aidan's.

BIBLIOGRAPHY
Bromberger, K.I.: *Music in Grahamstown (1812-1862).* B.Mus. script, RU, 1967.   Radloff, T.E.K.: *Music in Grahamstown, 1863-1879.* B.Mus. script, RU, 1969.   Sparrow, M.J.: *Music in Grahamstown, 1880-1900.* M.Mus. dissertation, RU,1978.   Van der Merwe, F.Z.: *Suid-Afrikaanse musiekbibliografie, 1787-1952.* J.L. van Schaik, Pretoria, 1958.

SOURCES
Dellatola, Lesley: City of saints. *Panorama,* Dec. 1970.   Kirby, Prof. P.R.: An early organ by William Hill. *The Organ* XXXVIII/150, Oct. 1958.   Kirby, Prof. P.R.: An early Cape musical society. *Quarterly Bulletin of the South African Library* XIII/3, Mar. 1959.   Kirby, Prof. P.R.: Frederick Timpson I'Ons and the first sixteen years of theatre in Grahamstown. *Africana Notes and News* XV/2, June 1962.   *Cape Frontier Times:* 1844-1864.   *Eastern Province Monthly Magazine:* Sept. 1856 to Aug. 1858.   *Graham's Town Journal:* 1831-1862. Draft article on the early period by Dr C.G. Henning.

– J.P.M.

GRAHAMSTOWN MUSIC CLUB, THE, was founded in October, 1949, as a member of the Federation of Music Societies (Eastern Cape),** with the object of sponsoring and promoting music. The first chairman was Professor W.E.G. Louw. Since then its main task has been the organisation of seven to eight concerts each year by South African and international artists. The first of these was a recital by the singer Dorothy Clarke, accompanied by Adelaide Newman,** given in the Grahamstown City Hall on 6 March, 1950. In addition, record recitals have been arranged, and occasionally members have themselves performed. In 1953 the Club formed its own choir, and gave performances of Bach's *Peasant cantata* and Haydn's *Passion music.* In 1954 a group of members organised a series of "Song and Dance" evenings, with performances of folk songs and folk dances of different countries. At the Annual General Meeting of 1963 Prof. P.R. Kirby,** who had been Chairman since 1957, was nominated Honorary Life President. The membership of the Club stood at about 370 in 1964.

– J.C.v.H.

GRAHAMSTOWN

GRAHAMSTOWN PHILHARMONIC SOCIETY P.E. Ould, C.H. Wood

GRAND NATIONAL HOTEL Johannesburg III/2

GRAND THEATRE Port Elizabeth, E.R. Goodacre, Bloemfontein II/2, Touring Theatre Groups 7

GRANT, PROF. E. D.I.C. de Villiers, S. Grové, Higher Educational Institutions I/2, I/7(ii)b, M. Whiteman, C. Yutar

GREAT HALL, WITS UNIVERSITY Higher Educational Institutions I/4, P.R. Kirby

GREATHEAD, LUCIE A.J. Louw, Port Elizabeth II/2(iii)

GREEN, MR East London I

GREEN, EDWARD KNOLLES, *in January 1788 (or December 1787?) presumably in Preston, Lancashire; ° 19 April 1828 in Cape Town. Music dealer and co-founder of the first Academy of Music in Cape Town.

Green arrived in Cape Town on 16 April, 1814; he had been sent by the London firm, Thomas Simpson & Co., to install the new organ of the German Evangelical Lutheran Church in Strand Street. In the event, he was to remain in the country. Before the work on the organ had been completed, he had opened his own music shop in Bree Street, and established himself as an agent of the London Music House of Clementi & Company. Unlike other music dealers, Green concentrated on musical instruments and their accessories, and on sheet music only; in addition, he tuned pianos and organs. His association with the Clementi firm, as well as his association with his brother John (who was also a music dealer and publisher) enabled this enterprising young man to offer for sale in 1818, one year after the patent was granted in Paris, Maelzel's metronome. As early as 1823 Beethoven's vocal music was available in his shop. Two years later, he opened a branch of his shop in Long Street, and made space available in the Bree Street premises to start a Music Academy, in collaboration with Frederick Logier** (1826). — With the help of his mother-in-law, the widow Berning, who stood security for him, Green was given the contract for a new organ for the Groote Kerk in 1828. The organ was to be built in England, under the supervision of his brother John. Less than a month after notification had been given by his brother that the new organ would be shipped within six months, Green suddenly died after a short illness. The organ was nevertheless installed by Hitchcock, from England, and was inaugurated on 11 July 1830. — Green's widow tried to carry on the promising business, but in 1832 and again in 1834 the executors sold it by public auction. His eldest son, also called Edward Knolles Green, was organist of the Dutch Reformed Church in Suider-Paarl and in Malmesbury, before he became a wine merchant in Cape Town and established the firm that still bears his name. This son died on 28 May 1883, in Cape Town, a wealthy man.

BIBLIOGRAPHY
Bouws, Jan: *Die musieklewe van Kaapstad, 1800–1850, en sy verhouding tot die musiekkultuur van Wes-Europa.* Cape Town/Amsterdam, 1966.   Bouws, Jan: Nuwe strominge in die Kaapse

musiekonderwys in die eerste helfte van die negentiende eeu. *Suid-Afrikaanse Akademie: referate,* Pretoria, 1966. Otterman, Reino E.: *Die kerkmusiek in die Evangeliese Lutherse Kerk in Strandstraat tussen 1780 en 1880.* M.Mus. dissertation, US, 1963. Pügner, Georg: *Johan Bernhard Logier – Leben und Werk.* Leipzig, 1960.

SOURCES
Bouws, Jan: Edward Knolles Green, 'n Kaapse musiekhandelaar. *Quarterly Journal of the South African Library* XXI/1, 1966. Kirby, P.R.: Wine, women and song. *South African Journal of Science* XL, Johannesburg, 1943. *The Cape Monitor:* 1851. *The Cape of Good Hope Government Gazette:* 1828. *Kaapsche Stads Courant en Afrikaansche Berigter:* 1814–1828. *The South African Commercial Advertiser:* 1826, 1832. *Het Volksblad:* 1883. *De Zuid-Afrikaan:* 1832, 1834, 1843, 1857. File: Nieuwe orgel. Ned. Ger. Kerk archives, Cape Town. MOOC, testaments 7/104, no. 63 (1815) and 64 (1828). Archives, Cape Town.

– J.B.

GREEN, WILLIAM (VERDI) Johannesburg 1, Pretoria 1, Theatres and Concert Halls IV, Touring Theatre Groups 3, 4

GREENWOOD, HARRY, *12 May 1868 in Nottingham; °30 June 1948 in Worcester. Blind music teacher, organist and composer.

Greenwood studied at the Royal Normal College for the Blind, near London, before becoming first Head of the Music Department at the School for the Blind, Worcester, in 1894. The school only possessed a small one-manual organ, with pedals, which was unsuitable for serious study. In the decade after 1900, Greenwood and his pupils gave a series of concerts in various centres in order to raise funds for a better organ and to publicise the work of the school. Towards the end of 1908 a new hall was completed, containing a two-manual instrument by Norman and Beard, built to the specification of Greenwood. This organ hall became the centre of many of the school's musical activities. With the advent of the gramophone, Greenwood and his wife (herself an accomplished pianist, singer and teacher of music), bought an Edison Disc Phonograph and began a series of record recitals, with explanatory appreciations and illustrations, which lasted until his retirement in 1933. Harry also spent much of his time transcribing examination music into Braille, here again assisted by Mrs Greenwood. — For some years he was organist at the English services in the Dutch Reformed Church, and from 1938 until June 1948 at the St James Church in Worcester. He often acted as adjudicator at eisteddfodau in Cape Town, Pretoria and elsewhere; and in the early days of radio transmission, broadcast some of his compositions from the Johannesburg and Cape Town studios. While on a visit to England, he was invited by the BBC to broadcast. — Among his many pupils who became church organists and music teachers, are Johannes de Lange (who succeeded him at the School for the Blind), Peter Cruse of Pretoria, and Andries van Velden, a composer of hymn tunes.

WORKS
Five Songs (Thomas Moore). McKay & Co., Cape Town, n.d.: 1. Oh! Breathe not his name 2 The song of Fionnula 3. A Finland love-song 4. 'Tis not the tear 5. Echoes. I have given my heart to a flower, song (Rudyard Kipling). Novello & Co. Ltd., London, n.d. Soldier's song. Published c. 1910. Two songs (Tennyson). McKay & Co., Cape Town, n.d.: 1. Cradle song 2. Slumber

song.   Ballade, for piano. Published (?).   Canzonetta for violin and piano. Ms., n.d. Celtic song, for viola and piano. Ms., n.d.   Fairy dance, for piano. Ms., n.d.   The Office of Holy Communion. Ms., n.d.   Orpheus with his lute, song. Ms., n.d.   Polonaise, for piano. Ms., n.d.   Slumber song of the old year, for viola and piano. Ms., n.d.   Sonata in E, for piano. Ms., n.d.   Two songs. Ms., n.d.:   1. The primrose   2. If thou could'st know. Valse caprice, for piano. Ms., n.d.

SOURCES
Anon, (an ex-pupil): *As I remember him. First blind music master in South Africa.* Ms., n.d.   Greenwood, Mrs E.: *Service. A short biographical sketch of H. Greenwood and his wife.* Independent publication, n.d.   Research Centre for South African Music, HSRC, Pretoria.
– H.G.

GREGORY, J.   St George's Cathedral

GREIG, CHRISTINA, *1906 in Durban; °22 December 1966 in Dundee. Mezzo-soprano, music teacher, stage personality.

Christina Greig was the daughter of Captain Frank Greig and Mrs Florence Greig, formerly Florence Perry (died December 1949), an early member of the D'Oyly Carte Opera Company. After leaving school Christina studied music, and particularly singing, in Durban. When it became evident that she had a fine mezzo-soprano voice, she was sent to London to study with her uncle, Ben Davies, a celebrated singer and teacher. After her return to South Africa she began her long career as a concert artist and as an actress, during which she was associated with many companies and played in many radio plays. She was equally at home in comedy and in tragedy, Noel Coward or Shakespeare, Gilbert and Sullivan or grand opera. Vitality and sincerity dominated all her music making. Her last stage appearance in Durban was in 1966 at the Lyric Theatre as "The Medium", in Menotti's two-act opera of that name. — For many years Christina Greig was chairwoman of the Durban Music Society.** She was also a leading personality in the Durban Music Teachers' Society throughout her teaching career of 30 years. In May 1967 the SASMT** decided to establish the Christina Greig Memorial Trust, a fund to be used each year for giving financial assistance to a Natal boy or girl who wished to attend a summer music camp held in Europe.

SOURCES
Natal Daily News: 23 Dec. 1966; 10 May 1967.   *Natal Mercury:* 8 Dec. 1949; 24 Dec. 1966.
– G.S.J.

GREIG, NANCY   Durban Chamber Music Groups

GREY INSTITUTE   E.G. Draycott, C.J.H. Eberlein, Port Elizabeth I/2, 4(ii), Port Elizabeth Amateur Choral and Orchestral Music, Amateur Theatre Groups, Prince Alfred's Volunteer Guards Band

GREYLOCK MUSIC ACADEMY (STELLENBOSCH)   F.W. Jannasch, Higher Educational Institutions I/8

GRIFFIN, NANCY VERA (NAN) (NéE HILLIER), *30 September 1904 in Durban; at present (1978) in East London. Music teacher.

Nan Griffin was born in South Africa of English parents. Both grandmothers were brilliant pianists and one also sang very well. Nan started piano lessons with Miss Holden in Durban, but when she was sent to school in England, a Miss Norah Parker of Reading University took charge of her training. She also studied dancing, and when she returned to South Africa, she made a living as a dancing teacher until her marriage to Mr Griffin in 1928. During the next twenty years she had singing lessons with various people, including F. Lee of East London and John Booth of the RAM, acted as critic of the *E.L. Daily Dispatch* and played leading roles in musical comedies and operettas. In addition she sang with the East London Municipal Orchestra and with the Durban Orchestra and broadcast as a singer and as a pianist-singer. She has written a fair amount of music for shows, but only three items were published under the pseudonym of Glen Copeland. These were three marches which appeared during the War. On the death of her husband in 1948 she became a full-time teacher of voice training, pianoforte and organ. A number of her pupils have been successful in broadcasting and in concerts. Mrs Griffin has also adjudicated at eisteddfodau held in Natal and the Eastern Province.

WORKS

V for victory, quickstep march (own words). Ivan Joffe, Johannesburg, 1941.   The silver lining (own words). Ivan Joffe, Johannesburg, 1941.   The song of the infantry (own words). Ivan Joffe, Johannesburg, 1941.

– Ed.

GRIFFITH-VINCENT, ANNIE ELIZABETH, *26 April 1866 in Chester; °26 December 1936 in England. Contralto.

Winner of the John Thomas Welsh Vocal Scholarship in 1883, Annie studied singing at the RAM. After her marriage to the actor Edward Vincent, in 1890, she toured South Africa with her husband, finally settling in Cape Town, where she set up a teaching practice. She often gave Lieder recitals, sang in oratorios, and organised choral and other concerts by her pupils. — When the South African College of Music** was initiated in 1910 by Madame Appoline Niay-Darroll,** Miss Vincent gave her support by bringing in private pupils and herself becoming a lecturer in singing. This appointment she held until her retirement on re-marriage in 1915. Madame Griffith-Vincent was made a Fellow of the RAM in 1909.

– N.B.

GRIFFITHS, D.   Krugersdorp

GRIFFITHS, F.   Organs 5, Port Elizabeth I/2, I/3

GRIFFITHS, GENEVIEVE   Johannesburg 2, Johannesburg Musical Society, H.S. Marleyn, Touring Theatre Groups 3

GRIFFITHS, J.W.   King William's Town 5, 11, 14, E. and C. Mendelssohn

139

GRIFFITHS, R.A.   B.J. Ewins, Queenstown 2, 4

GRIFFITHS, DR TEASDALE   N.H. Mitchell

GROENEWALD, COENRAAD CORNELIUS (CON), *1 March 1927 in the district of Caledon; now (1979) in Sea Point, Cape Town. Collector of historical gramophone records.

Con Groenewald completed his high school education at the Hoërskool Caledon in 1944 and became a telegraphist in the service of the Department of Posts and Telegraphs. In 1948 he accepted a position with a well-known publishing firm in Cape Town. His hobby is collecting historical vocal recordings of international and early South African singers, a field in which he must be regarded as the highest authority in South Africa.

– Ed.

GRONDELER, FRANS CHISTIAAN, *about 1795 in Cape Town; ° in April 1856 in Cape Town. Organist, pianist and teacher of music.

F. Ch. Grondeler was a son of Hendrik Frans Grondeler (Heinrich Franz Gründeler, *1753 in Basel, Switzerland; °14 March 1818 in Cape Town) and Apollonia Wilhelmina Broodryk (°7 October 1824 in Cape Town). His father, formerly a soldier, was assistant organist from March 1791 till 1794, and subsequently until 1818 chief organist of the Groote Kerk on the Heerengracht in Cape Town. Grondeler sr also gave piano lessons. It is not known who taught Frans Christiaan music, but it was presumably his father. Later, it appears that he was sufficiently trained to instruct pupils in violin and tenor violin. In 1815 he was appointed deputy organist to his father, and from 6 April 1818 till April 1856, he was the permanent organist to the Groote Kerk. In 1821 and in 1822 he also played the organ for Anglican services held in the same church. — Grondeler was known as a conscientious musician, but he seldom gave concerts. In 1826 he made two successful appearances with an amateur orchestra in the Stock Exchange concerts, and played, *inter alia,* a piano concerto by Domenico Corri (1746–1825). Grondeler collaborated with Logier,** who was responsible for the inauguration of the new Jan Hoets organ, on Sunday, 11 July 1830, and received high praise according to a letter published in *De Zuid-Afrikaan.* To supplement his salary of R60 per annum, "this countryman of ours, born and bred in South Africa" (as the author of the letter has it), had to rely on the irregular income provided by the teaching of music and the tuning of pianos. Despite all his efforts, he was declared bankrupt in 1827, and spent many years struggling against financial difficulties.

BIBLIOGRAPHY
Bouws, Jan: *Die musieklewe van Kaapstad, 1800–1850, en sy verhouding tot die musiekkultuur van Wes-Europa.* Cape Town/Amsterdam, 1966.   Hopkins, H.C.: *Die moeder van ons almal.* Cape Town/Pretoria, n.d. (1965).

SOURCES
De Verzamelaar XXXII: 26 Aug. 1826.   *De Zuid-Afrikaan* I/17: 30 July 1830.

– J.B.

GROSE, AUDREY   Ballet V, VII, Faith de Villiers

GROVÉ, I.J.   D.J. Roode

GROVÉ, STEFANS * 23 July 1922 in Bethlehem; now (1980) in Pretoria. Composer.

On his mother's side Stefans Grové is descended from the musical and well-known Porterville family, Roode.** His father was a school principal and his mother a music teacher, who started his music education when he went to school. Because he was shy and found it difficult to communicate with other children, he would rather sit at the piano, preferably not to practise, but to compose; as a child of nine he had started writing his first music. After matriculation Stefans became the seventeen-year-old organist of the DR congregation of De Bloem. By that time his uncle D.J. Roode** had taken over the boy's training and Stefans obtained licentiates for pianoforte (performer's and teacher's) and for organ playing in 1942. In the same year he also won two gold medals, two silver medals and a cup for composition at the Johannesburg Eisteddfod. At this stage he had not yet had any formal training in composition, but he bought musical scores and analysed them carefully and laboriously. — From 1942 to 1944 he was organist and music teacher in Klerksdorp. A ballet suite for full orchestra was completed in 1944 and after he had shown it to Eric Grant he was accepted as a student at the South African College of Music** in Cape Town. During 1945, and up to the time of his death, W.H. Bell** accepted the task of steering Grove's exceptional talent and exuberant phantasy into disciplined channels. The Bells became very attached to Grové who, in those years, was a highly nervous and extremely sensitive personality, a young man who could only be guided by a friendly approach. Cameron Taylor,** who was his piano teacher (1945–1947), and after 1946, Erik Chisholm,** exercised a strong influence on his development as a musician. During these years of study, he played the organ at the DR church in Rondebosch. — In Cape Town in 1945 he became acquainted with C.H. Weich** (music critic of *Die Burger*), at that time chairman of the Oranjeklub, who was so impressed by Grove's *String quartet in D major* that he made arrangements for a performance of the work at the Oranjeklub. He wrote in the press that it was "probably the greatest and most difficult work to be written in South Africa until that time". The English press was equally enthusiastic ("his authority to write in this exacting manner is un-questioned"). In 1946 Grové dedicated it to the memory of W.H. Bell. The College of Music had devoted a programme to his works on 16 April 1946 (two days after Bell's death), including three songs, three parts of his ballet suite (performed on two pianos), for pianoforte solos and a czardas for violin and pianoforte. — During this time he often played accompaniments in the Cape Town studios of the SABC and wrote criticisms for *Die Burger,* also teaching as a junior lecturer at the South African College of Music (1950–1952). In 1953 he received the Fullbright Scholarship for study in Musicology at Harvard University, where he was awarded a degree of M.Mus.

141

in 1955. He was also awarded a bursary to continue his study of the flute at the Longy School of Music. Walter Piston guided him in composition and for two consecutive years he won the G. Arthur Knight Prize and the New York Bohemian Prize with a *Pianoforte trio* and a *Sonata for pianoforte and cello* respectively. In 1954 the Margaret Crofts Scholarship enabled him to study under Aaron Copland in Tanglewood. — After the completion of his post-graduate studies, Grové was attached to the *avant garde* Bard College in the State of New York for one year and then, in 1957, against stiff competition, he was chosen as lecturer in theory and composition at the Peabody Conservatoire in Baltimore (1957–1971). At the same time he also became organist and choirmaster of the Franklin Street Presbyterian Church, where he gave performances of lesser-known choral works dating as far back as 1450, also including more recent works and even contemporary choral pieces. — In 1960–1961 he visited South Africa on long leave and acted as senior lecturer at the PU for CHE and at the SACM. On his return to America in 1962, he gathered a group of young musicians under the name Pro Musica Rara and led them in performances of lesser-known cantatas by J.S. Bach. During the 'sixties he became a member of the American Association of University Professors and of the American Guild of Organists, but the climax of his educational work in America came in February 1972, when he was chosen as one of the Outstanding Educators of America – a choice that has to be merited by inspired teaching and is commemorated by means of a silver medal. — In January 1972 Grové returned to South Africa to accept a temporary appointment at the South African College of Music. Since July 1974 he has been a senior lecturer at the Music Academy of the Pretoria University and, in his spare time, the music correspondent of *Rapport* and *Beeld*. He has also published a volume of short stories (1975). — Since 1952 Grove's works have been performed in the USA, England and in Europe. His *Three inventions* for pianoforte were played at the Festival of the International Society for the Promotion of Contemporary Music in Salzburg in 1953, various chamber music works were played in Washington (National Gallery, 1952: *Elegy for strings)*, Cambridge (Creative Guild Concerts, 1954: *Sonata for flute and piano)*, London (Guildhall concert series 1954: *Harp quintet)*, Brussels (1964: *Partita for orchestra*) and in other centres. His *First symphony* was played by the Cincinatti orchestra under Max Rudolph in 1966 and the *Violin concerto* was performed in Baltimore in the same year with Gabriel Banat as soloist. Pierre Rampal performed the *Flute sonata* during an SABC concert series in 1968 and the *Cantata profana* was performed by the American guild of Organists in Baltimore and in Arlington, in 1962, 1964, 1970 and 1972. His *Sinfonia concertante* was played and recorded in 1973 by the Radio Orchestra of South-West Australia.

WORKS

A. Instrumental

1. Keyboard music

Four pieces for pianoforte. Ms., before 1945: 1. Scaramouche 2. Elektron 3. Berceuse 4. Toccata.   Six mood pictures, for pianoforte. Ms., before 1947: 1. Sonderlinge tweege-sprek 2. 'n Geestelike gesang 3. 'n Nagtelike minnaar 4. Vrouebeeld 5. 'n Nuwe gewaarwording 6. 'n Fantasiese droom.   Three inventions, for piano. Ms., 1951.   Three piano pieces. Ms., 1965.   Ritual, a fantasy for an organ with four manuals. Ms., 1969.   Sty-listic experiment: twelve pieces for piano in different styles. Ms., 1971.   Chorale prelude on

Ps. 42, for organ. Ms., 1974.   Tweespalt, a piano piece for the left hand. Ms., 1975.   Seven graded piano pieces for the youth. Ms., 1975.   Rhapsodic toccata, a concert piece for organ. Ms., 1977.

2. Chamber music

String quartette in D. Ms., 1946.   Czardas, for violin and piano. Ms., 1946.   String trio. Ms., 1948.   Sonata, for clarinet and piano. Ms., 1949.   Duo, for violin and cello. Ms., 1950.   Trio, for violin, cello and piano, commissioned for the Van Riebeeck Festival. Ms., 1952.   Serenade, quintet for flute, oboe, viola, bass clarinet and harp, awarded a prize by the Northern California Harpists' Assn. Ms., 1952.   Trio, for oboe, clarinet and bassoon. Ms., 1952.   Sonata, for cello and piano. Ms., 1953.   Quintet, for harp and strings. Ms., 1954.   Divertimento, for recorders. E.C. Schirmer, New York, 1955.   Sonatina, for two recorders. E.C. Schirmer, New York, 1955.   Sonata, for flute and pianoforte. Ms., 1955. String quartette. Ms., 1955.   Recorder arrangements of Bach chorales. E.C. Schirmer, New York, 1955.   Divertimento, for flute, oboe, clarinet, bassoon. Ms., 1955.   Alice in Wonderland, suite for viola, single woodwinds and strings for modern dancing, commissioned by the Peabody Institute. Ms., 1959.   Cantata profana, for two voices, flute, oboe, cembalo and cello, a parody commissioned by the American Guild of Organists. Ms., 1959.   Daarstelling, for flute, cembalo and strings. Ms., 1972.   Die nag van drie April, for flute and harpsichord. Ms., 1975.   Vir 'n winterdag, a phantasy for bassoon and piano. Ms., 1977.   Gesprek vir drie, an ensemble work for oboe, cor anglais (one player), clarinet, bass clarinet (one player) and percussion (one player). Ms., 1978.

3. Orchestra

Ballet suite, for full orchestra. Ms., 1944.   Elegy, for strings. Ms., 1948.   Overture. Ms., 1953.   Turmmusik, for brass. Ms., 1954.   Sinfonia concertante, commissioned by the SABC. Ms., 1956.   Concerto, for violin and orchestra, commissioned by the SABC. Ms., 1959.   Symphony, commissioned by the SABC. Ms., 1962.   Incidental music to *Die dagboek van 'n soldaat,* commissioned by the SABC. Ms., 1963.   Partita for orchestra, commissioned by the Belgian Radio. Ms., 1964.   Concerto grosso, for violin, cello and piano, commissioned by Oude Libertas. Ms., 1974.   Symphony for 3-part choir and orchestra. Ms., 1975.   Waratha, a ballet for symphony orchestra, commissioned by Oude Libertas. Ms., 1977.   Maya, a concerto grosso for violin, piano and strings, commissioned by the University of Port Elizabeth. Ms., 1977.   Kettingrye, a concertante work for groups of instrumentalists and symphony orchestra, commissioned by the SABC. Ms., 1978.

B. Vocal

1.Songs

Drie liedere. Ms., before 1945: 1. Dis al (J.F.E. Celliers) 2. Berusting (Toon van den Heever) 3. Weeklag (?)   Vyf liedere, for mezzo-soprano and guitar (Old Chinese poems). Ms., 1973.   Psalm 54, for mezzo-soprano, flute and harp. Ms., 1974.   Lig oor Judea, for mezzo-soprano and a melody instrument. Ms., 1974.

2. Choir

Deo gratias per solvamus, for unaccompanied ladies' choir (old English carol from *Musica Britannica),* commissioned by the Free State Youth Choir. Ms., 1974.   Parit virgo filium, for unaccompanied four-part mixed choir (old English carol from *Musica Britannica*), commissioned by the Free State Youth Choir. Ms., 1974.   Kaapse draaie, for four-part mixed choir, guitar,

GROVÉ

piano, marimba, flute, clarinet and xylophone (D.J. Opperman), commissioned by TRAMUS. Ms., 1974.   Tuin, for three-part ladies' choir, flute and viola (Louis Eksteen). Ms., 1975.   Lied van die Transvaal, for double choir, pianoforte duet, two trumpets and three tympani (F.J. Pretorius), commissioned by the University of Pretoria Choir. Ms., 1975. Music for Easter choir, organ, flute, strings and Orff instruments. Ms., 1977.   Advent music, for choir, recorder and Orff instruments. Ms., 1977.

PUBLICATIONS
Die nuwe musiek en sy tydgenote. *Standpunte* VII/I, no. 25 of 1952.   Die probleme van die Suid-Afrikaanse komponis. *Standpunte* VII/2, no. 26 of 1952.   Credo. *SAMT* 59, Dec. 1960.   Musiek word in Suid-Afrika misbruik. *SABC Bulletin*, 19 June 1961.   Huidige tendense in die musiekopvoedkunde. SASMT lecture. *Opus* IV/4, June 1973.   Metric phenomena in music from Purcell to Brahms. *Musicus* III/2, 1975.   Liturgiese orrelmusiek. *SAMT* 59, Dec. 1976.

Between the ages of 8 and 18, Grové schooled and disciplined himself by emulating traditional musical styles. He is convinced of the efficacy of this method, since stylistic sources are more or less like a dictionary of quotations which can be consulted for the solution of certain problems. In his eighteenth year he discovered the French Impressionists and his pianoforte music of the following years exemplifies certain coloristic usages of Debussy and aspects of Ravel's formal mastery. Before long, Bartók exerted an influence on Grové's rhythm, which gained in vitality. Finally, in 1947, he became acquainted with the music of Hindemith and Henk Badings and from that time onwards he concentrated on achieving a sharply contoured and athletic style of writing, which led to an unsentimental style essentially his own. The most prominent characteristics are the emphasis on colour and vital energy, with contrapuntal procedures formally conspicuous. The *Duet for strings,* the *String trio, Pianoforte trio, Harp quintet, Serenade for winds, Flute sonata, Turmmusik* and *Sinfonia concertante* are works which all exhibit, in some form or other, the tendencies of this 'neo-classical' period. — The *Violin concerto* (written in 1958) was a transitional work in which he dissociated himself increasingly from neo-classicism, but the actual stylistic change dates from 1960, the year in which he started working on his *Symphony* (completed in 1962). In this he applies the method of composing with twelve tones, without slavishly copying it or even adhering strictly to the basic tone row. As a consequence, his thematic work, rhythms and command of form became more supple and the expressive quality of his music benefited to a marked degree. The *Symphony* also dated his future practice of juxtaposing, e.g. dramatic dynamicism and lyrical nostalgia, and of combining, simultaneously, two themes of a sharply contrasting character. In this work he also freed himself from adherence to the formal dictates of sonata form. Instead he employs, in a new perspective, the binary principle of two movements as a basic order for cyclical works. — In 1966, when he wrote his *Three piano pieces,* his style became even more spare and athletic through a further advance towards economic employment of material. This can possibly best be described as a striving towards a prose-like fluidity, a tendency which is especially noticeable in much of his music written for solo instruments. The form of some of his short stories has, since 1974, stimulated him to compositional emulation: the pianoforte pieces for the lefthand *Tweespalt (Schizophrenia),* for example are based on the monologue *The young woman in Ward F12 – a schizophrenic case.* It has two

144

elements – peacefulness, centering around B flat, and nervous hysteria, which moves predominantly in the lower registers. Similar extremes also occur in *Die nag van 3 April*, for flute and harpsichord, and in the *Symphony* (1975) written for a choir of 15 members (mezzo-sopranos, baritones and basses) and a large orchestra. At times the dividedness is evident in the vocal parts and at other times in the instruments. The tension generated by these procedures is relieved by cadences on which solo instruments and/or groups of voices hover or attain a condition of relative rest. The orchestration is mainly attuned to colour: considerable use is made of timbre modulation, one tone modulating by means of orchestral overlapping to a related shade of colour.

BIBLIOGRAPHY

Baker's dictionary of music and musicians. New York, 1957.   Bouws, Jan: Stefans Grové. *Muzikale Ommegang*, Amsterdam, 1948.   *Die Musik in Geschichte und Gegenwart*. Bärenreiter, 1952 ff.   Du Plessis, Hubert: *Letters from William Henry Bell*. Tafelberg Uitgewers, Cape Town, 1973.   *Four South African Composers*. HSRC, Pretoria, 1975. *Grove's dictionary of music and musicians,* 5th ed., 1954.   Jacob, Arthur: *New dictionary of music*.   *Riemann's Musiklexicon* I. Schott's Söhne, Mainz, 1972.   *Thompson's international cyclopedia of music and musicians*. London, 1964.   Voorendyk, L.H.D.: *Die musiekgeskiedenis van Wes-Transvaal, 1838-1960*. M.Mus. dissertation, PU for CHE, 1971. Winkler Prins: *Encyclopedie der Muziek*.

SOURCES

Bouws, Jan: Stefans Grové. *Die Huisgenoot* 1639/22, Cape Town, 1953.   Cornet di falsetto: Facing the music. *Trek* X/19/22, Cape Town, 1946.   Uys, J.H.: Stefans Grové. *Die Huisgenoot*, 17 Jan. 1947.   *Die Burger:* 26 June 1953; 21 May, 1954; 8 June 1954; 28 July 1960; 13 Apr. 1961; 18 May 1961; 24 June 1961; 22 July 1972.   *Rapport:* 4 Apr. 1976.   *SABC Bulletin:* 19 June 1961; 8 Oct. 1962.   Key notes on his music, written by S. Grové.   Research Centre for South African Music, HSRC, Pretoria.

– J.P.M.

GRUBER, GEORG, *27 July 1904 in Vienna; °5 September 1979 in Grahamstown. Musicologist and educational musician; leader and conductor of the Rhodes University Chamber Choir.**

After completing his school education, Georg Gruber entered for a study of Law at the University of Vienna (1922-1923), but in 1924 he switched to music and became a student at the Vienna Staatsakademie für Musik und Darstellende Kunst in Composition, Organ, Pianoforte, Gregorian plain-song, Conducting, Church Music and Singing. These studies were completed with distinction in 1926, although he had further instruction in Conducting from Prof. R. Nilius, until the end of 1928. In conjunction with these practical studies, Gruber also attended the classes given at the Institute for Musicology of the University of Vienna by Guido Adler, Robert Haas and Robert Lach. This led in 1928 to the award of the D.Phil. degree after the completion of a thesis on *Das deutsche Lied in der Innsbrücker Hofkapelle des Erzherzogs Ferdinand.* He was then launched on a career in music and at first held the position of director of a music school for adults under the Austrian Department of Adult

Education, with the added responsibility of training a boys' choir and of directing opera productions. He also lectured on the History of Music, gave lessons in Orchestral and Choral Conducting, and led the University's chamber choir called *Waltharia*. — When Gruber became the conductor-in-chief of the Vienna Boys' Choir in 1930, his career entered the new phase of training boys' voices and undertaking tours with them in Europe and North and South America. This lasted until 1937, when he resigned from this position to found and conduct the Vienna Mozart Boys' Choir. With this group he again toured European countries, visited the United States (twice), Australia and New Zealand, and in addition, accepted invitations to conduct symphony orchestras on their itineraries. When the Second World War broke out in 1939 he was in Australia, where, until 1941, he was given permission to teach in Melbourne at the St Patrick's Cathedral and to lecture on School Music at the Teachers' Training College; following the Japanese invasion of New-Guinea, he was interned by the authorities. — After the War, Gruber returned to Austria and collaborated with Bernhard Paumgartner as an assistant-editor in producing a Jubilee-issue of Mozart's music on records. He was chosen as secretary of the International Music Festival in Bad Gastein (held in 1950) and in 1952 as secretary of the 26th International Music Festival of the ISCM held in Salzburg. — This post-war interlude ended when in 1953 Gruber was appointed a lecturer in Music at the Rhodes University in Grahamstown. When Prof. Hartmann moved to Johannesburg in 1955 to occupy the Chair of Music at the Witwatersrand University, Gruber became his successor at Rhodes as Professor and Head of the Music Department. Apart from his departmental duties he creatively concerned himself with school music in South Africa and with the training of future choral conductors. Drawing on his vast experience, he established the Rhodes University Chamber Choir** in collaboration with his wife, the singer Sophie Gruber. This choir repeatedly toured in South Africa and Rhodesia, and on four occasions with exceptional success in Europe. His was the first choir to put such ambitious schemes into effect, though there has since then been considerable emulation by other university choirs. On the musicological side he interested himself in Black music and when he finally retired from Rhodes University in 1974, he accepted the responsibility of supervising the study and practice of music among Black students at the University College of Fort Hare.

WORKS

A. Vocal

Missa in Hon. Sanct. Innocent (3 voc.). Ms., 1940.   Missa in Hon. Sanct. Soph. (6 voc.). Ms., 1948.   Proprium Missae Domin. XXIII post Pent. (3 voc.). Ms., 1956.   'n Musikale Trap der Jeugd/A musical ABC. NASOU, Parow, 1962.   Kindertjies sing toerala/Merrily, merrily let us sing. NASOU, Parow, 1963.   Terra nova, cantata for solo and a capella choir (6 voc.) (Guy Butler). Rhodes University Press, Grahamstown, 1964: 1. Praeludium   2. Passacaglia   3. Conclusio.   Ukucula Ematola (Echoes from the Amatola Mountains), cantata for solo and a capella choir, 4–8 parts (trad. Xhosa). Ms., 1965.   Prayers from the ark, song cycle for medium voice and pianoforte (Carmen Bernos de Casztold, transl. from French by Rumer Godden). Ms., n.d.: 1. The prayer of the cock   2. The prayer of the little bird   3. The prayer of the old horse   4. The prayer of the goat.   Izango Zakwa-Ntu (African scenes) for 3 soloists, choir, Bantu drums and guitar (J.T. Mtyobo). Ms., 1968: 1. Ulwaluko – initiation   2. Imiguyo – girls' initiation dance   3. Emathongweni – nightly vision   4. Igqira – the witch doctor.

Cantata brevis, for soprano and a capella choir, 4–6 voices. Ms., nd.   Menschliche Landschaften, for a capella choir (J. Weinheber). Ms., n.d.   Sophienmesse, for a capella choir, 6 voices. Ms., n.d.   Ungarische Volksweisen, for a capella choir (Trad.). Ms., n.d.   Xhosa suite for a capella choir, 4–6 voices (Trad.). Ms., n.d.   Approx. 400 arrangements of folk songs written for boys' choir or mixed choir (Vienna Boys' Choir, Vienna University Chamber Choir 'Waltharia', and Rhodes University Chamber Choir). Mss., 1929 to 1974.

B. Instrumental
Sonata, for cello and pianoforte. Ms., 1940.   Praeludium, for cello and pianoforte. Ms., 1941.   Divertimento, in D major, for strings. Ms., 1942.   Serenade, for two flutes and guitar. Ms., 1943.   Four impromptus, for pianoforte. Ms., 1944.   Suite, in C major, for strings and two flutes. Ms., 1948.   Sonatina in A, for pianoforte. IGNM, Vienna, 1951.

PUBLICATIONS
Musiekonderrig in Suid-Afrika, publ. in *Die Burger* in 1959: 12 Mar., 19 Mar., 26 Mar., 2 Apr., 9 Apr., 17 Apr., 24 Apr., 22 May, 7 Aug. There were probably more.   The position of music in contemporary life. *Res Musicae* VIII/3, Mar. 1962.

SOURCES
Anon.: Advancement of musical education among youth in South Africa. *Res Musicae* VI/1, Sept. 1959.   Anon.: The Mozart year in South Africa. *Res Musicae* III/2, Dec. 1956.   Anon.: Rhodes University choir. *Res Musicae* VII/1, Mar. 1961.   Bosman, F.C.L.: George Gruber. *Res Musicae* VII/1, Mar. 1961.   Galloway, Dave: George Gruber. *Opus I/4, 1966.   SAMT:* 65, Dec. 1963; 67, Dec. 1964; 69, Dec. 1965; 70, June 1966; 75, Dec. 1968.   *Die Burger:* 27 Apr. 1962 (W.E.G. Louw); 17 June 1962; 28 Feb. 1963; 14 July 1964 (W.E.G. Louw).   *Cape Times:* 15 Aug. 1964.   *Pretoria News:* 17 June 1956.   Research Centre for South African Music, HSRC, Pretoria.

– Ed.

GRUBER, SOPHIE, MRS G. Gruber, Higher Educational Institutions I/3, G.W.R. Nel, Rhodes University Choir

GRUJON, LUCIEN Kathleen Allster Ensemble

GRÜNBERGER, FREDA Israel (Charles W.)

GRÜNDLER (GRONDELER), H.F. F.C. Grondeler, Organs I(v), Piano Music III/1

GUILD OF CHURCH MUSICIANS. Four Johannesburg organists founded the Johannesburg Guild on 1 December 1954, in order to create an undenominational fellowship for all interested parties. The Guild was to be controlled by locally elected members. Registration was obtained on 26 March 1955, and the Guild is affiliated to the Incorporated Association of Organists (England). Members regularly receive this associations's publication, *Organists' Review,* and there has been some interchange of visits.

The activities of the GCM include: 1. bi-annual interdenominational services in the Johannesburg City Hall, in which various church choirs participate. At these services selected music is introduced, which may be sung by participating choirs in their own churches, thus exerting an influence on the choice of church music and on the standards of performance. Past services have been recorded, and a number broadcast. Valuable experience has been gained by guild members in playing the large City Hall organ, and in conducting massed choirs. During the service held in the Johannesburg Festival in 1964, a choir of 500 took part; 2. lunch-hour organ recitals from the City Hall; 3. organ recitals in the Johannesburg Roman Catholic Cathedral on Sunday afternoons. — On 12 August 1964 membership was extended to include church choirs, the constitution of the Guild being adjusted accordingly, so that the name could be changed to its present form. By May 1969 there were more than 50 members, including a number of organ builders, and church choirs joined from all parts of the Republic excluding the Western Cape, which has its own guild. — An advisory committee of the Guild is available to: 1. assist with the choice of music, organs and organists; 2. arrange visits to organs and organ factories, as well as talks and demonstrations; 3. arrange an annual all-day church musicians' workshop. — On 29 January 1969, the Guild's badge, displaying five organ pipes, was registered by the State Herald, and on 30 March of the same year the work of three founders was recognized by their election as Fellows. These are Howard Bryant, Harry Stanton** and Herbert Woodhouse, who had then together completed 124 years of organ playing.

– H.W.

GULLRIET, A.   Piano Music IV/1

GUNNING, A.L.   Pretoria 2

GÜNTHER, ROTHILDE   Windhoek 2

GUSTAV HALLÉ BURSARY   D.B. Coutts, W.M. Fine

GUTSCHE, DR HUGO, *18 July 1869 in King William's Town; °4 June 1956 in Heidelberg, Transvaal. Editor-in-chief of the *FAK-Volksangbundel* (Folk Music Album) (1931–1937); former pastor of the Evangelical (Lutheran) Church, school principal and an inspector of education (1923–1929).

Hugo Gutsche and his brother were scholars at a Gymnasium in Memel (Germany). After completing his school career he studied Theology in Halle, interrupted his studies for a year with Spurgeon in London, and then carried on with Theology for another three years in Leipzig. His first congregation was in East London where he and Pastor Schneider were active in the creation of a German school. Gutsche's early training in music came to good stead here, for he was often compelled to play the organ accompaniments at his own services and at the school he conducted the singing classes, emphasising especially the German folk song. After further study in Germany he returned with the degree of D.Phil., acted for a while as country Pastor in his father's congregation and then accepted an appointment as principal of the Primary School at Steynsburg. Eventually he became the principal of a Senior School at Christiana and finally the Transvaal Education Department appointed him as an Inspector of Education, initially with Standerton as his base before he was moved to Heidelberg. — Dr Gutsche's enthusiasm for music repeatedly found expression in the field of school music, in the compilation of vocal albums suitable for school use and in the active promotion of folk music among the South African youth. This labour of love found its logical completion when the FAK appointed him on the editorial committee responsible for the compilation of a Volksangbundel (Folk Music Album). This was two years after he had retired from his educational career. As editor-in-chief of this undertaking he guided the album to its publication stage in 1937, a timely musical provision shortly before the start of the symbolic Ox Wagon Trek (1938). In reality it indicated a new chapter in the musical history of the Afrikaans people, since the rapid growth of Afrikaans literature could in future be matched with the emotional impact of its musical complement. As chief editor Gutsche showed a marked predilection for the German folk song, although this doesn't really detract from the importance of his work.

A. Writings
Oorsprong van die Volksangbundel. *Die Huisgenoot:* 12 Feb. 1943; 10 Sept. 1943; 17 Sept. 1943.   By wie het ons geleen? *Die Huisgenoot,* 18 Feb. 1944.

B. Vocal albums
Lus en lewe, 'n sangbundel (Gutsche/Eitemal). J.H. de Bussy, Pretoria, 1932. This contains *Die lied van jong Suid-Afrika* (Eitemal).   *Die Dageraad-liederbundel vir laerskole* (Gutsche/Theo. W. Jandrell). J.H. de Bussy, Pretoria, 1933.   *Die Dageraad-liederbundel vir hoërskole* (Gutsche). J.H. de Bussy, Pretoria, 1934.   *Die Dageraad-speelliedjies vir die grade en standerd I* (A.D.E. Gutsche). J.H. de Bussy, Pretoria, 1934.   *Die Dageraad-liederbundel vir standerds I tot III* (Gutsche/Theo. W. Jandrell). J.H. de Bussy, Pretoria, 1936.   *Die FAK-Volksangbundel* (Dr H. Gutsche, Dr W.J. du Preez Erlank and Mr S.H. Eyssen). J.H. de Bussy, Pretoria, 1937.

BIBLIOGRAPHY
Bouws, Jan: *Woord en wys van die Afrikaanse lied.* Cape Town, 1961.   *Chronik der SA Familie Carl Hugo Gutsche.* J. Meinert Ltd., Windhoek, 1939.

SOURCES
Eyssen, S.H.: *Ons Skoolblad,* Hoër Volkskool, Heidelberg, 1956.   Gutsche, H.: *Memel-Erinnerungen,* 1951.   Meiring, A.M.: *Die Voorligter,* May 1953.   Contributions by Stephen Eyssen.

– Ed.

HAAGEN, XANDER, *25 May 1924 in Keetmanshoop, South West Africa; at present (1977) in Germany. Baritone, composer and author.

HAAGEN

While Xander Haagen was a student at the University of Cape Town for the degrees of B.A. and B. Com., he was trained in voice production by Rosita Silvestri and Alessandro Rota and when he left for London in 1946, it was with the intention of specialising in singing. F. Field-Hyde of Cambridge supervised the development of his voice and he was given tenor parts to sing in musicals and operettas produced in the London West End. Two of these were *Lilac domino* and *Zip goes a million*. Further theatre experience was gained on a tour with an operetta company in England and Scotland. In 1949 he moved to the Continent and was trained in singing by Gustave Sacher and Maria Hittorff in Vienna. His student days were concluded with a concert performance in the Concertgebouw in Amsterdam (19 February 1950), followed by solo tours in Holland and Germany. — In 1956 Haagen returned to South Africa, gave concerts in various parts of the country over a period of twelve months, and was then appointed a lecturer in singing at the College of Music** in Cape Town. Adelheid Armhold** became his teacher and promptly switched his training from tenor to baritone range. During his five years in Cape Town he was a member of the Opera Company of the University of Cape Town and interpreted parts in operas produced by G. Fiasconaro.** — When the University of Pretoria launched its Music Academy in 1961, Haagen was appointed lecturer in singing, a position he filled with distinction until 1969. Under his guidance, vocal students produced annual operatic performances in the Musaion** and the Aula** of Pretoria University, including one-act works such as Gluck's *Bekehrte Trunkenbold* and Arne's *The cooper,* as well as full-length productions of Mozart's *Huwelik van Figaro* and Humperdinck's *Hansie en Grietjie.* Haagen was responsible for the coaching of all the voices, for the direction and for the supervision of the decor and the costumes. Apart from his educational responsibilities, he continued his career as a concert singer in Lieder recitals and in concert engagements with the SABC Symphony Orchestra, in the Aula and in radio transmissions. As opera singer he was engaged by the Pretoria Opera Society** as well as by PACT. During the years in Pretoria he also composed and produced Afrikaans musical comedies with student singers and professionals. Among the works seen in Pretoria were *Aandster ver, Opsitkers en vonkelwyn* and *Haaipolfaai en tierlantyn.* — After his resignation from the Music Academy at the end of 1969, Haagen was a lecturer in singing at the Pretoria College for Advanced Technical Education,** but in 1972 he decided to settle in Cologne where he is a teacher of singing and a repetitor at the Opera House.

WORKS
Met liefde van Marlies (Anna Rudolph). DALRO, 1972 (Afrikaans) and 1973 (English). Lenteliefde, musical comedy (libretto and music). Ms., n.d. Aandster ver, musical comedy (libretto and music). Ms., n.d. Opsitkers en vonkelwyn, operetta (libretto and music). DALRO, Johannesburg, 1970. Frederick and Bastiana, musical comedy (libretto and music). Ms., n.d. Haaipolfaai en tierlantyn, musical comedy (libretto and music). Ms., n.d. Incidental music for the PACT productions of *Die onwillige weduwee* and *Die Italiaanse strooihoed.*

WRITINGS
Soos stof verstrooi, drama. Hier en daar, comedy. High blows the wind, novel.

SOURCES
Anon.: Xander Haagen gesels oor sy operette. *SABC Bulletin*, 2 Apr. 1962.   Anon.: Otto Bach musical play awards. *SAMT* 81, Dec. 1971.   *Die Burger:* 7 Apr. 1960; 23 Apr. 1960.   Research Centre for South African Music, HSRC, Pretoria.

–Ed.

HAAPE, HEINRICH FRIEDRICH CARL (HEINZ), *6 January 1910 in Oberhausen in the Rhineland, West Germany; ° 18 February 1976 in Krefeld, Germany. Medical practitioner, Doctor of Philosophy (Bonn), University diploma in Psychology (Strassburg), newspaper editor, producer of operas, poet, painter, author and director of companies.

Dr Haape came of a musical family which counted Wilhelm Koester, composer of church music, among its members. As a leading personality in the artistic enterprise of the CVJM in Germany during his student days, he found ample scope for his wide interest in the visual arts, as well as drama and music. At the close of the Second World War, during which he served with distinction as a medical doctor throughout the Russian campaign, he established a committee in Germany for assisting destitute artists and acted as editor-in-chief of a daily newspaper, an art journal and a popular monthly magazine. During the post-war period he also wrote a few librettos for the composers Sixt and Dünnwald, but the main emphasis was on reactivating the concert life for the benefit of relief work. — In 1952 he emigrated to Natal where he carved out a new career as an industrialist and devoted himself to the promotion of music and especially of the operatic theatre. In the latter ventures he was ably assisted by his wife, the experienced opera singer, Martha Arazym-Haape;** who had been a prominent singer in Germany before and during the war. — From 1953 to 1957 he was the leader of his own Orpheus Studio which toured in Natal giving concerts of instrumental and vocal music. This preparatory work was followed in 1958 by the founding of the Durban Opera Company, an opera workshop for singers. With complete performances of *Le nozze di Figaro* (Mozart), and *Tales of Hoffman* (Offenbach), as well as individual scenes from operas, his company achieved considerable success. In 1963 the Durban Opera Company, together with all its assets, was taken over by the newly-created NAPAC. As chairman of the NAPAC Opera Committee and as producer, Dr Haape staged *Figaro, Madame Butterfly, Tales of Hoffman, Cavalleria rusticana, Aïda* and *Zauberflöte* and he was the motive power behind NAPAC's decision to buy the Alhambra Theatre in Durban as a venue for opera and ballet. His work in this direction was guided by his ambition to establish an ensemble theatre in Natal, which could act as a stimulus for artists and promote a feeling of achievement in the musical public. — The climax of his cultural work in Natal came on 18 May 1974 when his oratorio, *May the land worship the Lord,* was sung in the Pietermaritzburg Town Hall as part of Natal's Jubilee Festival. Both the libretto and the music of this work were written by Dr Haape himself, though the music was revised and orchestrated by Stefans Grové.** In an amplified version it was again sung on 21 April 1975, during the Cape Town Festival.

WRITINGS
Specialist contributions on Medicine and Psychology.   *Moscow tramstop. War reminiscences.* Collins, London, 1957.   De profundis. Libretto for an oratorio, composed by Paul Sixt

in Germany, 1948. Apocalypse. Libretto for an oratorio, composed by Paul Sixt in Germany, 1950. Der Teufel im Glase. German comic opera in verse, composed by Dünnwald in Germany, 1951. Ludovicus. South African adaptation of Der Teufel im Glase. 1963. May the land worship the Lord. Oratorio, words and music by Dr Heinz Haape, Durban, 1970–1975. Various poems in German, some of which have been set to original melodies.

– Ed.

HAAPE, MARTHA MARIA AUGUSTA (NéE ARAZYM; STAGENAME: ARAZYM-HAAPE), *21 May 1918 in Vienna; at present (1977) in Gillitts, Natal. Soprano.

In 1936, after studying singing for three years under Alexander Kirchner in Vienna, she passed the final examination of the Vienna Conservatoire with distinction and qualified for a career in opera. In the same year she obtained a Diploma at an International Competition in singing and piano. She was then engaged by opera houses in Brünn and Reichenberg (Czechoslovakia), Duisburg (1938–1943) and Stuttgart (1943–1951) and sang in the Festival at The Hague as a guest singer (1940); also in Cologne, Düsseldorf, Wupperthal, Essen, Munich, Augsburg, Wiesbaden and Hanover. In addition she sang in symphonic works such as Beethoven's *Ninth symphony* and gave Lieder recitals. Some of the highlights of her career were her interpretations of leading female roles in the world premières of *Der Sturm* (The tempest) and *Romeo and Juliet,* both by Sutermeister, and of *Christoph Columbus* by Werner Egk. Gifted with an unusually extensive vocal compass, she has sung the following in the 64 leading operatic roles to her credit: Carmen, Mignon, Octavian *(Der Rosenkavalier),* Martha *(Tiefland* – d'Albert), Madame Butterfly, Aïda, and Gilda *(Rigoletto).* — In 1952 she joined her husband, Dr Heinz Haape,** in South Africa and played a prominent part in his musical enterprises and thereafter in the operas presented by NAPAC. The Haapes can justifiably be described as pioneers of opera in recent Natal musical history.

– Ed.

HAARBURGER, IVAN HARTWIG, *25 March 1869 in Hamburg; °18 January 1933 in Bloemfontein. Music dealer.

Trained to play the violin as well as the piano, Ivan Haarburger became a second violinist in the Hamburg Philharmonic Orchestra at an early age. Never very robust, his health deteriorated after he had turned 19, and he was sent to Bloemfontein in South Africa where relations of the Haarburgers, the family Leviseur, employed him as a shop assistant. Subsequently he became a clerk in the Bookshop of Deale Bros. and eventually Carl Borckenhagen opened a door to music when he put him in charge of his department for instruments and sheet music. He also acted as the booking agent for Bloemfontein concerts. After the death of Borckenhagen, Haarburger purchased the musical section of his shop and in 1898 he launched out on his own. In 1904, shortly after his marriage in Lübeck, Germany, he transferred to the main street and carried on the trade of a music dealer until his death in 1933. — Haarburger was actively engaged in the incipient city's musical life as a violinist, a pianist and as a conductor of their amateur enterprise. He taught music privately at schools, such as the Eunice Women's Institute and Greenhill Convent and, acted as accompanist to both local and visiting celebrities. In 1893, with the combined efforts of Bloemfon-tein's music lovers, he managed to start an Orchestral Society, which gave a few professional musicians and his own pupils the opportunity of indulging in combined playing. He trained this body until 1902. Sporadically he was also connected with the Bloemfontein Choral Society (started in 1897), which he conducted during 1898, and when they were revived in 1901 for a single performance of *Messiah,* he again consented to be their leader. As a professional musician and as a trader in music, he strongly advocated the introduction of music examinations in 1894, and more or less by way of an experiment, he also published a few original works by Bloemfontein musicians. — After 1904 he dedicated his energies to trade matters and gradually withdrew from active music making. At times he still played accompaniments, arranged musical evenings at his home and exerted himself publicly to arrange concerts and recitals on records, but he never again conducted after 1902. Haarburger was an outstanding public speaker who served on the City Council for several years and acted as Mayor of the town from 1912 to 1914. He was five times the president of the Free State Chamber of Commerce and for many years a member of the South African United Chambers of Commerce (president of this organisation in 1929/1930). For the last eight years of his life he acted as chairman of the Jewish community in Bloemfontein.

PUBLICATIONS
A South African talks with Einstein. *The Outspan,* 11 Nov. 1927.   Young South Africans and commerce. *The Outspan,* 14 Feb. 1930.

BIBLIOGRAPHY
Human, J.L.K.: *Musiek in die Oranje-Vrystaat vanaf 1850 tot aan die begin van die Anglo-Boereoorlog.* M.Mus dissertation, UOFS, 1963.

SOURCES
The Bloemfontein Post: Jan.-Sept. 1901.   *The Friend:* 1902–1932; 19 Jan. 1933 (obitu-ary).   Personal documents in the possession of H. Haarburger.

– J.L.K.H. (amplified)

HAASDIJK, P.W.   J. Luyt (sr), H.C. Marcus, K.F. Metzler

HADDON, PEGGY-ANN (MRS NEVILLE RICHARDSON), *23 March 1931 in Johannesburg; at present (1977) in Johannesburg. Pianist and music teacher.

During her childhood in Krugersdorp, Peggy-Ann Haddon accompanied her mother, an amateur violinist, and her father, an amateur singer. She was trained in pianoforte playing by Eileen Manners, who taught her for 13 years. After obtaining various licentiate diplomas, she at first acted as assistant to Miss Manners, then worked for two years at the South African Institute for Medical Research, and finally turned to music again. A pupil of Adolph Hallis** from 1951, she won the UNISA Overseas Scholarship in 1953, and studied pianoforte and singing in London and subsequently in Munich, where she gave a number of recitals under the auspices of the British Council. — Since her return to South Africa, Miss Haddon has become one of the

153

HADDON

foremost pianists in Johannesburg. She is technically well equipped to do justice to modern scores of extreme complexity. Among her South African "firsts" are Humphrey Searle's *Second piano concerto,* Menotti's *First piano concerto* and Boris Blacher's *Concerto in variable metres,* all of which she performed with the SABC orchestra. She is also an enthusiastic chamber music player who has been variously associated with the Musica Intima group of Derek Ochse,** the Overvaal Ensemble of Pieter de Villiers,** with Walter Mony** in violin/pianoforte works and with Gordon Beasley in works for two pianos. She also formed her own trio with Ralph Kastner** and Tam McDonald.** While studying singing with Betsy de la Porte** she often acted as accompanist for the other singing students. Recently she has formed a trio with Annie Kossman and Marian Lewin.

SOURCES
Anon.: A lass with a delicate air. *SABC Bulletin,* 8 July 1968.   Let us learn. *SAMT 81,* Dec. 1971.   Stookes, A.K.: Let us learn. *Opus* II/3, May/June 1971.

– Ed.

HADLOW, J.   Higher Educational Institutions I/1, S.M.E.P. Serfontein

HAESTIER, J.C.   Johannesburg III/1

HALFORD-SMITH, G.   Johannesburg 1, Johannesburg Philharmonic Society

HALL, ELSIE STANLEY, *22 June 1877 at Toowoomba in Queensland; °27 June 1976 in Cape Town. Pianist.

When the exceptional musicality of Elsie Hall became apparent in her fourth year, she was placed with a German violinist, Herr Kretschmann, for instruction in pianoforte playing. He had a direct and intuitive insight into music and laid a true and firm foundation for her career. By the time she had turned nine she had advanced to the stage where she could give a public performance of Beethoven's *Concerto no. 3 in C minor* in the Sydney University Hall. In the same year her generous parents decided that she should have a European training and so Elsie, accompanied by her mother and a younger sister, left for Stuttgart in Germany. She studied at the Conservatoire for 18 months and then her mother decided that they should move to England for schooling and music lessons, but in the event her career took a different turn. They touched at Paris, where Elsie's playing elicited the offer of a French bursary for study at the Conservatoire de Musique, and continued their journey to England where she was placed for tuition with John Farmer, the organist of Balliol College in Oxford, and attended school in Clapham. She was also accepted into the home of Victor Benecke, an enthusiastic cello player of German extraction, who was married to the eldest daughter of Felix Mendelssohn. — They were on friendly terms with the family of Robert Schumann in Germany and their home in England was the musical rendezvous of celebrities like the violinist Joseph Joachim, with whose string quartet she became acquainted there. Elsie was most impressed by the musicianship and personality of Joachim and announced her intention of continuing her studies in Berlin, to be in his vicinity. He in turn, was impressed by her youthful capabilities ("Sie hat eine Gabe Gottes und wundervolle Finger") and eased her way into the Berlin Hochschule,

154

where she became a pupil of Prof. Ernst Rudorff, a great friend of Clara Schumann. The period in Berlin lasted until 1896 and culminated in her being awarded the Mendelssohn Prize. During these years she lived in close contact with chamber music on the high level of Joachim and with first-class symphonic playing. She was also introduced to Brahms and towards the end of her stay she spent one morning in 1896 in the company of Clara Schumann. It was to be the last day of Madame Schumann's life. — After an absence of ten years Mrs Hall decided on a return to Australia with her two daughters. The nineteen year-old pianist soon left on a concert tour of Australia, accompanied for part of the way by her sister Muriel, who was a capable violinist, and then spent two years (1899–1900) teaching music at the Conservatoire in Adelaide. But in 1900 she decided to return to London to resume her concert career. She remained there until her marriage to Dr Stohr in 1913, making rapid headway due to her readiness to perform in touring groups in all parts of England and also, for example, in the Promenade Concerts of Sir Henry Wood. Without directly employing concert agents, she was continually active as a member of variously composed groups, giving concerts in all types of halls, including music halls. At various times she was a guest of members of the aristocracy. When, for example, she was forced to rest her arm, she spent two years as the guest of the Bishop of Peterborough, acting as a companion to his two daughters. She also revisited Germany as a pianist, spent holidays in Brittany and on one occasion even played for the ladies in a Turkish harem. — Dr Stohr was approached by the Belgian government to do research on the tsetse fly in Southern Africa, and so Northern Rhodesia (now Zambia) became their African home. They spent the Great War in Britain and immediately after hostilities ceased, Elsie Hall left for Berlin with her eldest son to study with the Russian-born immigrant-composer, Nicholas Medtner. In 1919 Dr Stohr resumed his work in Africa, but she was under no obligation to sacrifice her career as a concert pianist. Starting on 19 November 1919, when she played Rachmaninoff's *Piano concerto in C minor* with the Cape Town Orchestra,** she divided her time between Rhodesia, South Africa and Europe. Not only did she frequently accompany her husband on his official visits to England, but she also stayed in France for a while, studying with Gabriel Fauré and in Italy where Hermann Scherchen introduced her to his philosophy of music. On her journeys in Southern Africa and Kenya she was at times accompanied by the cellist May Mukle or by the concert singer, Percy Heming. During the last year of World War II Elsie Hall, on the invitation of the South African Army, played to the military personnel and troops in Egypt, Austria and Italy. — To make more live music available in South Africa, Elsie Hall turned impresario and, partly with the co-operation of the SABC, organised tours for the Amsterdam String Quartet, the Loewenguth Quartet and the Quintette Chigiano. After the death of Dr Stohr (1948) she teamed up with Herman Salomon to perform sonatas for violin and piano. They toured through South Africa, and then gave concerts in England, Holland, France and Switzerland. At a later stage she had the violinist of the Loewenguth Quartet, Maurice Fueri, as a touring partner in the Cape and the Transvaal. In addition to the Charles Kreitzer Quartet,** there were probably no Cape musicians of note with whom she did not engage in chamber music at some stage. Using her art for the edification of the public was not so much a professional necessity, as a form of sharing the beauty of musical sound with others. This is evidenced by her willingness to give lecture recitals at schools and educational institutions in Southern Africa, playing either the pianoforte or the harpsichord. But she was equally ready to assist at any serious musical project, be it the ordering of a new grand pianoforte, or arranging for the visit of a celebrity. It would be difficult to imagine the musical life of Southern Africa without the vital part played by Elsie Hall. — The enthusiasm for music never left her. Her ninetieth birthday on 22 June 1967, was celebrated with a piano recital in the Cape Town City Hall. At the end of the evening the Mayor presented her with the keys of the City. The programme was broadcast and later made available commercially as a disc. On the same day the German Ambassador to South Africa surprised her with a gift on behalf of Germany and Boris Blacher, the director of the Hochschule in Berlin where she had been trained, sent her a congratulatory telegram. The university of Cape Town honoured her services to music in this country by awarding her an honorary degree of D.Mus. (1957), and in 1965 the Cape Tercentenary Foundation rendered her homage in the form of a major prize.

PUBLICATION
The good die young, an autobiography. Constantia Publishers, Cape Town, 1969.

SOURCES
Res Musicae: III/2, 3, 4, and IV/4, 1957–1959.   *SAMT:* 72, June 1967; 73, Dec. 1967. *Sarie Marais:* 8 Nov. 1961.   *Die Burger:* 29 June 1957; 1 July 1957; 26 Nov. 1965; 24 June 1967; 13 Dec. 1969.   *Cape Argus:* 27 Mar. 1954.   *Cape Times:* 29 June 1957; 13 July 1957; 28 Nov. 1964; 25 June 1966; 15 Nov. 1969.   *Natal Witness:* 17 Sept. 1971.   *Pretoria News:* 12 June 1962; 13 Nov. 1962.   *Die Vaderland:* 11 June 1968.   *Die Volksblad:* 25 Sept. 1971.   Personal documents, scrap books and letters in the UCT Library, Cape Town.   Research Centre for South African Music, HSRC, Pretoria.

– J.P.M.

HALL, LEONARD DUNCAN, *22 July 1915 in Sydenham, London; °12 August 1966 in Cape Town. Lecturer and pianist.

Leonard Hall obtained the degrees of B.A. (Modern History) and B. Mus. at Balliol College, Oxford, in 1937, before becoming a student at the RCM where, as a Leverhulme scholar, he studied pianoforte, composition and orchestration. After war service in the East Surrey Regimental Band, he did some concert work and taught at Evening Institutes in London. —In 1948 he was appointed a lecturer in pianoforte at the South African College of Music** in Cape Town and taught there until his death. He practised his art in South Africa and Rhodesia, in concertos with various orchestras and in broadcast programmes. Energetic and vital, he was a fluent speaker who loved participation in symposiums and often lectured on a variety of musical subjects. He was chairman of the Cape Town branch of the SASMT from 1959 to 1960 and President of the Cape Musicians' Association from 1961 until his death. The Leonard Hall Memorial Prize Fund was set up in 1966, with the object of providing an annual award to assist in the musical education of a deserving person of any race.

PUBLICATION
The South African musician, his position and future. *Res Musicae* VI/1, Sept. 1959.

SOURCES
Anon.: Who's who. *SAMT 58*, June 1960.   Anon.: In memoriam. *SAMT 71*, Dec. 1966.   Anon.: Leonard Hall Memorial Prize. *SAMT* 71, Dec. 1966.   Research Centre for South African Music, HSRC, Pretoria.

– Ed.

HALL, MARIE   Potchefstroom 4, Touring Theatre Groups ɔ

HALL, MINNIE MARION (MRS WELCH)   E.W. Welch

HALLBECK, HANS PETER   Brüderkirche

HALLÉ, GUSTAV   Durban 6, Natal Society for the Advancement of Music

HALLER, MICHAEL   Free State String Quartette, N.E. Haller

HALLER, NIKOLAI EMANUEL, *8 April 1906 in St Petersburg (Leningrad); °6 October 1970 in Stellenbosch. Choirmaster and lecturer in School Music.

A chequered career, disrupted first by the Russian Revolution of 1917, and then by the Second World War and its aftermath, offered Haller little opportunity to develop his musical gifts. In 1918 his musical mother (née Annamarie Keltjärv) fled with him and a sister to Esthonia, where in Reval in 1923 he was able to complete his schooling. He qualified as a teacher and by means of private study and courses at the Conservatoire he learned to play the violin, viola, double bass, recorder and organ. Haller took a leading part in local concerts of chamber music and developed into a talented director of choirs and song festivals. In order to make a living, he had to undertake a great variety of activities, which included the performance of church music and the organising of wind bands. — After the Second World War, in which he served on the German side as an official translator, he and his family were in Southern Germany and he emigrated from there to South Africa to become the principal of a small German school in Philippi near Cape Town, and thereafter a teacher at the German school, St Martini, in Cape Town. Through the large repertoire of his Haller Family Choir and through other choral activities, broadcasts and his direction of courses in singing and song festivals (including those among the indigenous tribes in Paulinum, South West Africa) he acquired a reputation as a versatile and gifted choirmaster whose beautiful musical calligraphy became almost proverbial. — In 1962 he was appointed lecturer in school music and choir training at the Music Academy of the University of Pretoria** and characteristically thorough, did important work in training choral conductors and teachers of school music. Unfortunately, progressive deterioration of his health gradually imposed restrictions. In 1969 he retired and settled at Stellenbosch. Of his five children, Michael Haller chose music as a career. At first Michael was a member of PACT orchestra and thereafter a cello lecturer at UOFS and a member of the Free State String Quartet.

PUBLICATION
FAK Kerkkoorboek II, compiled by E. Haller. FAK, Johannesburg; Studio Holland, Cape Town, Nov. 1968.

ARTICLES

Nederlandse Kamerkoor; also discussion of *Skoolmusiek in Suid-Afrika* by A.W. Wegelin. *Vita Musica* I/2, June 1962.   Kurrende – sang. *Vita Musica* I/4, Dec. 1963.   Kerk en skool: wenke vir die koorleier. *Vita Musica* I/4, Dec. 1963.

SOURCES

Die Burger: 20 Dec. 1958; 6 Jan. 1962.

Research Centre for South African Music, HSRC, Pretoria.

– F.S. (amplified)

HALLIS, ADOLPH, *4 July 1896 in Port Elizabeth; at present (1976) in Johannesburg. Concert pianist, music teacher and composer.

Adolph left for Vienna with his mother when he was six years old, and had his first pianoforte lessons from Schalit, a pupil of Leschetizky. He returned to Port Elizabeth in 1904, where he became a pupil of Roger Ascham** and Horace Barton** (for theoretical subjects). After his first public performance, a sonata by Mozart, at Ascham's 277th organ recital on 18 March 1906, the *E.P. Herald* records 15 more public appearances by this young pianoforte prodigy, of which seven were at Ascham's recitals in the Feather Market Hall. With his teacher playing the orchestral parts either on the organ or on a second piano, Hallis performed works such as the *B flat concerto* by Mozart, Beethoven's *Third concerto,* and Mendelssohn's *G minor concerto.* Both the latter works and Liszt's *Concert study in D flat* were played during 1911, the year in which Hallis was awarded the Overseas Scholarship of the University of the Cape of Good Hope. — He left for England in the same year, and studied at the RAM under Oscar Beringer; subsequently privately under Tobias Matthay. At the conclusion of his scholarship tenure in 1914, he remained in England for a few months, returning at the end of 1915 to become a lecturer in pianoforte at the South African College of Music.** At the RAM, he had won no less than five prizes for excellence in pianoforte playing, sight reading and composition. The Pattison Haynes prize was awarded to him for his *Prelude and fugue,* composed probably in 1915. Before assuming duty in Cape Town, he scored a tremendous triumph in the Feather Market Hall, Port Elizabeth, where he gave a recital on 27 January 1916. He played Tchaikovsky's *First concerto* (with Thomas Robinson playing the orchestral part on a second piano), Chopin's *Sonata in B minor,* and other works. After P.E. he played with the Cape Town Municipal Orchestra** and in all the main centres in South Africa and returned to the Port for recitals in 1916 and 1919. In the latter year however, he left South Africa to attend master classes in pianoforte playing, and to launch his European concert career. — Hallis's first concert engagement abroad was in Turin, followed by performances in Paris, Berlin, Vienna, Budapest, Milan, Zürich, Geneva and other European cities. After a concert tour of South Africa in 1926, he settled in London, where he studied and taught at the Matthay School of Music. He gave frequent recitals at the Wigmore Hall, broadcast for the BBC and made recordings for the Decca Company, including the first complete recorded rendering of the Debussy *Studies.* In 1930 he again toured through South Africa and before the outbreak of War, organised three seasons in London called the Adolph Hallis Chamber Music Concerts, which were held in the Wigmore and Aeolean Halls. The programmes included first performances of several contemporary works. — Hallis returned to South Africa when the war started (1939) and inaugurated a scheme whereby music clubs were integrated into a South African Music Club Association. This was particularly successful in the Eastern Cape, where clubs started at King William's Town and Queenstown are still thriving today. Hallis was Music Master at Hilton College in Natal in 1941 and then settled in Johannesburg where he was exceptionally active as a teacher and as a performer frequently heard in broadcast recitals. After 1948, he visited Europe several times and gave recitals in London and elsewhere. He played the first performance of Hindemith's *Piano concerto* with the Hallé Orchestra conducted by Sir John Barbirolli in Manchester in 1956 and in the same year he also toured professionally in Czechoslovakia. In 1963 he assembled the Orpheus Male Quartet which for many years played a prominent part in the musical life of the Transvaal, the OFS and the Cape. — Among the pupils of Hallis who have attained prominence, are Ivan Melman,** Philip Levy,** Peggy Haddon,** Elizabeth Tomlinson, Avril Fasser, Greta Beigel, Philippa Podlaschuc, Cynthia Kloppers and John Britton, all of whom were overseas scholarship winners of the University of South Africa. Other notable pupils of a later generation have been Marian Friedman,** Nicola Magni and Neville Dove. — The Fellowship of the RAM was conferred on Hallis in 1950 and in 1966 he was awarded a gold medal of the Suid-Afrikaanse Akademie vir Wetenskap en Kuns** for important contributions to South African musical culture.

WORKS

A Vocal

1. Operettas
Jakaranda, radio operetta (Phyllis Freeman). Ms., SABC broadcast 1943.   Port of call, radio operetta (Oliver Walker). Ms., SABC broadcast 1943.   Love is gold, radio operetta (E.H. Cameron McClure). Ms., SABC broadcast 1946.   A bowl of Constantia Red, operetta. Ms., n.d.

2. Songs
All kinds of things, for male voice quartette and piano (composer). Ms., n.d.   Animals, for male voice quartette and piano (composer). Ms., n.d.   Devon maid (composer). Ms., n.d.   Dolores, tango for soprano and piano (Edmund Seagrave). Ms., n.d.   Ek hoor, for voice and piano. Ms., n.d.   Finale, for four voices (Royston Lee). Ms., n.d.   Italian love song, for baritone and piano (Royston Lee). Ms., n.d.   La chapelle, for voice and piano. Ms., n.d.   Nature, for male voice quartette and piano (composer). Ms., n.d.   Nagliedjie, for voice and piano. Ms., n.d.   Nagrit, for voice and piano. Ms., n.d.   Song of the busker, for baritone and piano (Olive Turner). Ms., n.d.   Song of the exile, for baritone and piano (Olive Turner). Ms., n.d.   South Africa, for voice, 2 violins, viola, cello and piano. United Music Publishers, n.d.   Suid-Afrika, a musical joke for male voice quartette. Ms., n.d.   The last of the Ivanoffa, for bass and piano (Lynton Hudson). Ms., n.d.   We are the stars, for male voice quartette and piano. Ms., n.d.   Wireless lullaby, for voice, 2 violins, viola, cello and piano. Ms., n.d.   Who said what? for male voice quartette and piano (composer). Ms., n.d.

B Instrumental

1. Piano
Prelude and fugue, comp. at RAM. Ms., 1915.   Twelve concert preludes. Ms., 1959–1960.   Alla marcia. Sylvester Music Co. Ltd., n.d.   A little aside. Sylvester Music Co. Ltd., n.d.   Dancing dolls. Sylvester Music Co. Ltd., n.d.   My old black briar. Ascherberg, London, n.d.   Paint and powder. Sylvester Music Co. Ltd., n.d.   Round about London

HALLIS

Town, children's suite. Ms., n.d.   Three small preludes. Ms., n.d.   Vivace ma non troppo.
Ms., n.d.

2. Chamber music
Sonata in D major, for cello and piano. Ms., 1941.   Sonata in G minor, for violin and piano.
Ms., 1941.   August bank holiday, for 2 violins, viola, cello and piano. Ms., n.d.   Fantasy on
French folk songs, for 2 violins, viola, cello and piano. Ms., n.d.   Fantasy on Hungarian folk
songs, for 2 violins, viola, cello and piano. Ms., n.d.   Fantasy on Russian folk songs, for 2
violins, viola, cello and piano. Ms., n.d.   Fantasy on Spanish folk songs, for 2 violins, viola,
cello and piano. Ms., n.d.   Fantasy on West Indian tunes, for 2 violins, viola, cello and piano.
Ms., n.d.   Five fingers for two pianos. Ms., n.d.   Trio in C minor, for piano, violin and
cello. Ms., n.d.   Variations on *Au clair de la lune,* for 2 violins, viola, cello and piano. Ms.,
n.d.   Variations on *Ding, dong, dell,* for 2 violins, viola, cello and piano. Ms., n.d.   Variations on *Oranges and lemons,* for 2 violins, viola, cello and piano. Ms., n.d.

3. Orchestra
Concerto, for pianoforte and orchestra, in E flat major. Ms., 1963.

PUBLICATIONS
Has our musical taste improved? *The Outspan,* 1 Aug. 1930.   Has South Africa grown more
musical? *SAMT 22,* May 1942.   Show your pupils how to think. *Opus* I/5, 1967.

SOURCES
Musicus: II/1, 1974.   *Res Musicae:* III/4, June 1957; V/3, Mar. 1959; VIII/1, Sept. 1961;
VIII/3, Mar. 1962; IX/1, Dec. 1962; VIII/5, Sept. 1962.   *SABC Bulletin:* 12 Aug.
1968.   *SAMT:* 40, June 1951; 81, Dec. 1971; 84, July 1973.   *EP Herald:* 1906-1919.
The Star: 3 July 1971.   *Sunday Times:* 6 Nov. 1955.   Research Centre for South African
Music, HSRC, Pretoria.

– Ed.

**HAMER, CHARLES, *30 May 1886 in Leeds, Yorkshire; °22 September 1955 in
Durban. Organist and music teacher. Brother of Alban Hamer.****

Charles commenced his musical career as a chorister at the Leeds Parish Church,
where he sang solos for over five years. At the age of sixteen he obtained his first
post as organist, and eventually became organist of the Collingham Parish Church,
Yorkshire, and conductor of the Collingham Choral Society. For four years he studied
voice production at the Leeds College of Music, and at the Yorkshire Training College.
Subsequently he sang in Wagner's *Ring der Nibelungen,* with the Denhof Opera
Company in Leeds and Manchester. — In 1921 Hamer came to South Africa as music
master at St Andrew's School in Bloemfontein, where his brother Alban had already
been teaching for some time. Shortly after his arrival, he was appointed organist to the
Trinity Wesleyan Church, a position he held until he succeeded his brother as organist
of the Bloemfontein Cathedral in 1927, after Alban had transferred to Cape Town.
Charles often appeared as a soloist in Bloemfontein, both at concerts and in
productions of the Bloemfontein Choral Society and the Orpheus Club. He was the
founder (1924) and conductor of the Bloemfontein Male Voice Choir, and he also
conducted a Ladies' Choir. Eventually he became Musical Director to the Bloemfontein
Municipality. — At the end of November 1945, he left for Durban, where he was

HAMER

appointed Master of Music at St Paul's Church in January 1946. At the same time he taught voice production at his home in Durban North. In 1946 he also became Choirmaster of the Durban Civic Choir, under the direction of Edward Dunn;** but two years later he resigned and formed a Ladies' Choir, which he led up to the time of his death. Charles Hamer was President of the SASMT in 1935, and served as Vice-President for the OFS branch from 1933 until 1945. As an adjudicator, he was a well-known figure at music festivals in South Africa.

WORKS
Droomvallei, song (Rex Ferrus). Nasionale Pers Bpk., Bloemfontein, 1945.

BIBLIOGRAPHY
Van der Merwe, F.Z.: *Suid-Afrikaanse Musiekbibliografie, 1787–1952.* J.L. van Schaik, Pretoria, 1958.

SOURCES
The Friend: 1922–June 1925.   *SAMT:* 8, Apr. 1935; 11, Oct. 1936; 17, Dec. 1939; 24, June 1943; 29, Dec. 1945; 49, Dec. 1955.

– Ed.

HAMER, JAMES ALBAN, *25 January 1882 in Leeds, Yorkshire; °22 March 1952 in Cape Town. Organist, choirmaster and music teacher.

Hamer started his musical education at the Leeds College of Music, but at a later stage he studied privately. A chorister at the Leeds Parish Church, he afterwards became assistant organist to Dr Bairstow at the same church. He obtained the ARCO diploma in 1907 and the FRCO in 1910 and was organist and choirmaster at All Souls' Church in Leeds, before he came to South Africa in 1920. — In January 1921 Hamer was appointed organist and choirmaster at the Bloemfontein Cathedral, and music master at St Andrew's School. He frequently gave organ recitals, conducted performances by the Cathedral choir, acted as Musical Director to the Orpheus Club, which produced, *inter alia,* some of Gilbert and Sullivan's operettas, and organised concerts by local artists. Six years later he succeeded Dr Barrow-Dowling** as organist and choirmaster of St George's Cathedral, and became music master at St George's Grammar School in Cape Town. In addition, he taught at the Teachers' Training College, at the South African College of Music** (1927–1949), as well as privately. His pupils include Harry Stanton,** Roger O'Hogan** and Michael Brimer.** — As in Bloemfontein, Hamer extended the range of his musical activities in Cape Town to include the training of choral groups and annual presentations of either Bach's *St Matthew Passion* or Brahms' *German requiem,* sung by the Municipal Choral Society, of which he was the leader. He adjudicated at eisteddfodau in South Africa, and acted as the official representative in this country of the Royal School of Church Music. These services received official recognition in 1937, when he became the recipient of an Honorary Doctorate of Music, awarded by the Archbishop of Canterbury.

– A.P.-J.

HAMILTON, G. King William's Town 10

161

HAMILTON-ROSS, ELLEN (MRS C.N. THOMAS)   C.N. Thomas

HAMMA, MISS   Bloemfontein I/8, F. Fraser

HAMMAN, B.M.   Higher Educational Institutions I/7(ii)(a)

HAMPSON, C.   Pietermaritzburg

HANDEL HOUSE (PORT ELIZABETH, J. KANTOR)   Port Elizabeth I/5

HANKINSON, MICHAEL NEVILLE, *23 January 1946 in Maghull near Liverpool; at present (1979) in Johannesburg. Organist and composer.

Michael Hankinson was a chorister at the Liverpool Anglican Cathedral (1953–1956) and then became a choral scholar at Hereford Cathedral (1956–1962). He commenced organ studies while still in Liverpool and subsequently continued at Trinity College in London, where he graduated LTCL (Mus. Ed.) in 1968. From 1968 to 1970 he worked as a freelance musician in London and formed the record company, Vista Records, which has become noted for its specialisation in organ music. A first visit to South Africa was made in September 1970 when he composed and conducted music for the film *Shangani patrol.* Shortly after this he settled in this country and has since scored feature films, including *Die Voortrekkers, Die banneling* and *De Wet's spoor.* In addition he arranged and conducted music for South African singers such as Mimi Coertse,** Gé Korsten,** Joyce Barker** and Diane Todd.** His recording work has been varied, including *avant-garde* electronic music and electronic realisations of classical works, such as *The classical synthesizer* and *Synthesia.* He was elected a Fellow of Trinity College in 1976 and received an appointment as Durban's City Organist in 1977. As a conductor he has been employed by PACT for their productions of *The sound of music* and *Stop the world.*

WORKS

A. Vocal
Christus vincit, for chorus, narrator and organ, composed for the St Stithian's Singers, Easter 1977. Ms.

B. Instrumental
Transitions, for orchestra and electronic instruments, commissioned by the SABC for *Adventure festival,* 1974. Ms.   With a little help from my friends, a symphonic ballet based on tunes by the Beatles, commissioned by PACT, 1978. Ms.   Theme and variations for piano, violin, cello, clarinet, bass clarinet, oboe, cor anglais, flute, alto flute, French horn, recorded by SABC television for use with the documentary series *Six women.* Ms., 1979.   Inventions, for orchestra, in six parts. MFP Music Co., n.d.   Inventions, for orchestra and electronic instruments. Ms., n.d.

– Ed.

HANN, A.H.   R. Müller (Pty) Ltd

HANSEN, DEIRDRE DORIS, *16 August 1938 in Piet Retief, Transvaal; resident in Grahamstown in 1981. Ethnomusicologist

After training in pianoforte playing in Durban and Dundee, Deirdre taught at the Newcastle Academy until she entered for the B.Mus. degree at Rhodes University (1958–1961). While teaching at the Victoria Girls' High School (1962–1964), she continued her pianoforte study under Rupert Mayr,** and became a pianoforte teacher at Rhodes University in 1964. Concurrently, she was a research assistant at the University's Institute of Social and Economic Research. Miss Hansen completed the requirements for the M.Mus. degree in 1968, and has since then applied herself to an investigation of the influence of Western music on composers of the Nguni people. After 1971 this research became a comprehensive investigation into the music of the Xhosa-people, submitted on completion (1981) to the University of the Witwatersrand for a Doctorate in Musicology (D.Phil). Thus the work which began as research into the life and work of Tyamzashe has found its logical conclusion. She has now (1981) become South Africa's leading authority on the music of the Cape Nguni and a prominent figure in South African ethnomusicology. Apart from her academic studies, she has performed as pianoforte soloist in concerts and programmes of the SABC.

DISSERTATIONS

1. *The life and works of B.J. Tyamzashe.* M.Mus. dissertation, RU, Grahamstown. Rhodes University Press, 1968   2. *The music of the Xhosa-speaking people.* D.Phil. thesis, UWits, 1981.

– Ed.

HANSEN, L.   Higher Educational Institutions II/1

HARBORNE, JOHN THOMAS, *15 May 1874 in Norwich; °5 June 1960 in Umtata. Conductor and tenor.

John began his musical training as a choir boy at Norwich Cathedral, with the ultimate aim of joining the D'Oyly Carte Opera Company, thus following in the footsteps of his parents. His father, however, stipulated that his son learn a trade before taking up a full-time musical career, in case he should develop the throat trouble that had plagued himself; and so the boy was first apprenticed to the Broadway piano company as a piano tuner. At a later date Harborne visited Italy to study singing. On returning to England he achieved his ambition and became a member of the D'Oyly Carte organisation, singing as a tenor for many years. Here he met and married Kate Storey, at that time a contralto of the company. — When his throat started troubling him, he gave up singing and emigrated to Melbourne in Australia. He eventually left Australia and settled in Durban, where he carried on his trade as a piano tuner. There he met a resident of Umtata, V.L. Klette, and the two decided to open a music shop in that town (September 1924). Soon after his arrival in Umtata, Harborne organised people interested in choral work, and founded the Umtata Choral Society, which gave performances of *The rose maiden* (Spohr), *The mikado, San Toy,* and other Gilbert and Sullivan operas and musical plays. The works were performed not only in Umtata, but also in other Transkei towns, and on a few occasions also in East London. In 1932 the name of the Society was changed to the Umtata Choral and Orchestral Society; the orchestral section had actually been in existence since 1924. — Harborne was also organist and choirmaster of the Anglican Church in Umtata, where he was responsible for the performance of several oratorios.

HARBORNE

SOURCE
Daily Dispatch: 1924–1932.

– H.N.

HARDESTY, FRED F.B.M. Moeller

HARMONIE EN EENDRAGT CHOIR L.H. Beil, J.W.C. Brandt

HARMONIUM (SERAFIJN, HUISMUSIEK OR SERFYN) South African piano music I/3

HARPER, JAMES HENRY, *1844 (1843?) in England; °7 November 1892 in Cape Town. A pioneer of opera in South Africa.

Born of a musical family, James Harper was trained in singing and cello at the RAM and in addition had vocal training under Schira and Garcia. A few years of music teaching were followed by a period of theatre activity (also in Covent Garden) during which he gained experience in Italian opera, as a singer and a cellist. His connection with South Africa starts in 1868 when he formed an "opera company", consisting of his wife, the contralto Winifred Leffler, and a soprano Annette Hirst, which gave a series of six concerts in the Cape Town Stock Exchange. The series was launched on 5 August and consisted of arias and folk songs, with the usual local support, in this case supplied by George S. Darter.** The Capetonian played his new piano composition called *Platte-Klip,* and Winifred Leffler sang one of his latest songs. Then they journeyed by sea from Cape Town to Port Elizabeth and gave concerts there from 21 September to 5 October. In November they presented three "fashionable concerts" in Grahamstown where Madame Leffler was so besieged for encores that the concert became "a double entertainment in one evening". The programmes consisted mainly of arias, duets, trios, folksongs, ballads and cello solos. On 19 November 1868 they presented their "farewell concert" in Port Elizabeth. — For the second concert series in Cape Town (December 1868), the company was reinforced by the arrival of the tenor, David Miranda. Miranda had formerly sung at Covent Garden and Drury Lane and had been attached to a music academy in New York (1859), where he was described as "the best English tenor, both as vocalist and as actor, that ever appeared West of the Atlantic". Provisionally, the composition of programmes remained unaltered and Darter again contributed two new songs created for Annette Hirst and David Miranda. The concerts in Cape Town were followed by a tour in the interior, of which the itinerary is only partly known. During 1869 they visited Bloemfontein (March), Graaff Reinet (April), Cradock, Queenstown (5 May), King William's Town, Grahamstown (June) and gave five performances in Port Elizabeth (between 15 July and 5 August) and two at Uitenhage (2 and 3 August). — During this tour there were important innovations. It appears that Miranda was taking charge, the name of the company was changed to the Miranda-Harper Company, and, above all, they began to present operas. In Port Elizabeth they performed *Il trovatore, La sonnambula, The Bohemian girl* and Donizetti's *Lucretia Borgia,* the operas of Verdi, Bellini and Balfé being repeated in Grahamstown. These were the first opera performances ever given in Port Elizabeth and Grahamstown. The company then returned to Cape Town, where operas were presented for the first time since 1834: *Maritana* (Wallace) and *Martha* (Flotow). In November they contributed to a

164

performance of *Messiah* and, with the co-operation of G.N. Thomas,** to a programme consisting of oratorio selections. A series of promenade concerts in the New Market concluded this third visit to Cape Town. Romance came into its own towards the end of 1869 when Miranda was married to Annette Hirst in the city. —In January 1870 a more ambitious journey was undertaken, which took them through the Eastern Province, over Beaufort-West, Graaff Reinet (1–10 August), Hanover, Colesberg, Philippolis, Kimberley, Potchefstroom to Bloemfontein and eventually to Durban. As in the other centres, except in Cape Town, the company made history in Durban by presenting *Il trovatore* in a full production. Unfortunately the company dissolved in Durban: in October the Harpers co-operated with the D'Arcy Reads in their successful dramatic and musical entertainments, while Miranda and Annette Hirst sang in operettas in Trafalgar Hall. The Mirandas remained in Durban when the Harpers left for the Diamond Fields via Bloemfontein, where they gave "drawing room entertainments" and an operetta, *The ring and the keeper,* in which they played and sang all the parts (October 1870). — They arrived in Kimberley towards the end of October and settled at Klipdrift. Until December 1873 they played an important and progressive role on the Diamond Fields, although their artistic success was questionable – in 1871 they had a boarding house at Bultfontein; but in that year they originated a dramatic club which performed in the Theatre Royal at Du Toit's Pan, also in shops and hotels, and started a school for the children of diggers in Klipdrift. The St James's Hall was built in May 1872 – as a result of their enthusiasm – and in 1873 a choir of 40 with soloists used it for performances of extracts from *Messiah* and *The creation.* — A notable fact regarding these years in Kimberley is that since their arrival a certain Mr J.H. Leffler is regularly mentioned in connection with their performances. He was probably a brother of Mrs Harper. They gave six concerts at Graaff Reinet between 1 and 10 August 1873, with a complete change in their repertoire to Dibden's operetta, *The waterman,* light vocal items and ten plays. After 1873 there is no further reference to the Harpers in the diamond country, but in 1874 they were on tour in the Eastern Province: Queenstown in June and Port Elizabeth and Uitenhage in August. It is likely that they met Captain Disney Roebuck** during this tour, since Roebuck was in Port Elizabeth between 5 March and 3 July, thereafter in Grahamstown and from October to December back in Port Elizabeth. There are no records of the company in 1875, but in 1876 they again played in Cape Town. Cape Town's musical life was so lively that they were relegated to the background; but when Roebuck directed his attention to light opera, Harper returned to the limelight as choirmaster and as a singer in works by Sullivan, Offenbach, Planquette, Lecocq and others. After Roebuck's death early in 1885, Harper successively hired the Exhibition Hall and the re-opened Theatre Royal, but with limited success. Between 1888 and 1889 he went on his last tour – this time to Johannesburg – in the company of Searelle.** He became involved in the projects of Edgar Perkins, but his best years had gone by and after the end of 1889 he existed as a music teacher in Cape Town. Three years later he died of an incurable disease of the throat. It may be a measure of the regard in which he was held, that Barrow-Dowling** conducted a memorial concert in the Cathedral on the day after his death. — Well-trained but inexperienced, Harper's company enterprisingly toured through South Africa, presenting variety entertainment in many guises, as well as operas and operettas, often with recourse to resourceful improvisation. They aimed not so much at artistic standards as at giving pleasure; what was lacking in the public, the halls, around the stages, even to the most elementary theatre facilities, they compensated for with youthful enthusiasm. At the very least Harper sparked some reaction even in very small villages. As a pioneer of opera, he occupies a prominent place in the musical history of South Africa.

BIBLIOGRAPHY

Henning, C.G.: *A cultural history of Graaff Reinet, 1786–1886.* D.Phil. thesis, UP, 1971. Human, J.L.K.: *Musiek in die Oranje-Vrystaat vanaf 1850 tot aan die begin van die Anglo-Boere-oorlog.* M.Mus. dissertation, UOFS, 1963. Jackson, G.S.: *Music in Durban from 1850–1900.* Ph.D. thesis, UWits, 1961. Radloff, T.E.K.: *Music in Grahamstown, 1863–1879.* B.Mus. script, RU, 1969. Wolpowitz, Lily: *James and Kate Hyde and the development of music in Johannesburg up to the first World War.* D. Mus. thesis, UP, 1965. J.L. van Schaik, 1969.

SOURCES

The Cape Times: 1887–1892. *The Diamond News and Vaal Advertiser:* 1870–1873. *Eastern Province Herald:* Sept., Oct., Nov. 1868; July–Aug. 1869; Aug. 1874. *The Knobkerrie:* 1884. *The Lantern:* 1877–1886. *Ons Land:* 1892. *Queenstown Free Press:* May 1869. *Het Volksblad:* 1868–1886. *De Zuid-Afrikaan:* 1870.

– J.B. (amplified)

HARPER, JOHN MARTIN, *3 July 1924 in Sudbury, Suffolk; resident at Botha's Hill, Natal, in 1970. A versatile musician and conductor.

John Harper's musical training commenced in 1939, when he received private tuition in pianoforte and organ. After war service as a pilot, he enrolled at St Paul's College, Birmingham University, and at Trinity College, where he obtained the ARCM and ARCO diplomas (1948–1951). In 1965 he continued his studies privately, also at the RSCM, and obtained the LTCL diploma, a Fellowship of the RCM, and the Choirmaster's Diploma of that College. In England he held positions as organist and choirmaster at churches, conducted operas and musical comedies, taught music in Birmingham (1951–1957) and at Clacton County High School (1957–1959), and acted as choirmaster of the Birmingham Grammar Schools' Music Festival. — Harper was appointed Director of Music at Kearsney College after coming to South Africa in 1959. In 1966, on his return from England where he had gone for further study, he resumed his teaching at Kearsney College and inaugurated the Private Schools' Music Festival for schools in and around Pietermaritzburg. Harper is proficient in organ, pianoforte, clarinet and flute and is often heard in chamber music groups. Apart from giving piano and organ recitals, he also acts as accompanist and plays the clarinet in the Pietermaritzburg Philharmonic Orchestra.

– Ed.

HARP SOCIETY OF SOUTH AFRICA, THE, was formed as a result of Kathleen Alister's visit to Israel in 1962, during the Second International Harp Contest, which was combined with the annual World Conference of the International Association of Harpists and Friends of the Harp. The conferences have taken place since 1959. The President of the Association, P. Pierre Jamet, invited Kathleen Alister to form a South African branch of the Association, and on 8 December 1962, the inaugural meeting of the Harp Society of South Africa was held in Johannesburg in the home of Dr and Mrs I.S. Brink. — The Harp Society of South Africa is a cultural non-profit-making society.

Its objects are to promote interest in the pedal harp and the Celtic harp; to promote the teaching of the harp; to encourage composers to write for the harp; to hold lectures and to arrange performances of live harp playing, as well as programmes of recorded harp music. Classes for the tuition of the Celtic harp were started in Johannesburg in June 1963. The Society had three harp teachers, Josephine Acres, Kathleen Alister and Desmond McCarthy.

– K.A.

HARRADEN, H.   Port Elizabeth I/2, 5, Prince Alfred's Volunteer Guard Band

HARRIES, HILDA   L.B. de Kock, Johannesburg III/2

HARRIS, BRADLEY, *1 November 1932 in Cardiff; living at Cowie's Hill, Natal, in 1971. Music teacher and tenor.

For many years Harris's mother was a professional violinist and the musical director of the Prince of Wales Theatre in Cardiff. Her son was trained in music at Cardiff University and at the Trinity College in Carmarthen. In 1956 he emigrated to South Africa and after four years as a music teacher at, respectively, the High School and Primary School in Westville, he was appointed to a similar position at the Durban High School (1960). Apart from major roles in operas, produced by the Durban Opera Group of Dr Haape,** and in operettas by Gilbert and Sullivan, he appeared with the Durban Civic Orchestra** and sang in radio recitals. Since 1961 he also acted as choral conductor of the Westville Civic Choral Society. — In September 1964 Harris decided to dedicate himself to singing and became the first singer to sign a contract with CAPAB. He sang major roles in their opera productions until August 1969, but in January 1970 he reverted to teaching and accepted a position as music teacher at the Kloof High School under the Natal Education Department. A year later he was appointed a lecturer in Music at the Springfield Training College.

– Ed.

HARRIS, G. CLIFTON, *1895 in Eastbourne, Sussex; resident in Port Elizabeth in 1970. Organist.

Harris's father, a chemist, emigrated to Port Elizabeth in 1904 in the employ of J.W. Couldridge & Co. Clifton was entered as a pupil at the Grey Institute and sang in St Mary's Choir until 1910, when the family returned to England where he was educated at Devizes Secondary School in Wiltshire (for which he composed a school song, *Our school we sing*) and subsequently at King's College, Taunton, in Somerset. — The Harris family returned to Port Elizabeth in 1912, and Clifton became an official on the administrative staff of the Telephone Engineers' Department (1914-1955). Music, however, was his passionate hobby: he studied organ-playing under Thomas Robinson** of St Mary's Anglican Church, for whom he acted as assistant organist (1912-1918) and was a pianoforte pupil of Roger Ascham,** with whom he progressed so well that he performed Mendelssohn's *Piano concerto in G minor* at Ascham's 788th Organ Recital on 25 August 1918, with Ascham playing the orchestral part on the organ. He was also assistant organist to E.R. Goodacre** at

167

St John's Methodist Church until 1918, when he succeeded Goodacre. He played in St John's from 1918 to 1933, and then again from 1935 to 1970. — In 1934 he succeeded Ascham as organist to the Holy Trinity Church. After only six months he was transferred to Pretoria, but he was back in Port Elizabeth early in 1935. Before becoming choirmaster at St John's in 1945, Harris had been associated with the performance of choral works such as Stainer's *Crucifixion* (1920), Maunder's cantata *From Olivet to Calvary* (1921), Spohr's oratorio *The last judgement* (1922) and *The holy city* by Gaul. In addition, from September 1918 to February 1923, he had been the official accompanist to the P.E. Choral Society,** directed by Thos. Robinson, and from 1919 to 1925 an accompanist to soloists appearing at concerts given by Ascham and others. — Harris's main activity, apart from his duties as an organist, consisted in directing the P.E. Amateur Operatic and Dramatic Society,** which he conducted in *A country girl* (1921 and 1932), *The Quaker girl* (1927), *The earl and the girl* and *Tonight's the night* (1928), *Our Miss Gibbs* (1929), and *Oh, oh Delphine* (1934). During 1930–1931 he was music critic for the *E.P. Herald,* and for about ten years after the death of Roger Ascham in 1934, he shared the municipal Sunday evening organ recitals with C. Pellow-White** and George Draycott. — After World War II Harris often played the organ at Robert Selley's** monthly Lunch Hour Concerts. An interesting aspect of his career was the voluntary pealing of the carillon on Sundays from 5.00 to 5.30 pm, before the Second World War, and again from 1945 to 1946. The first carillon broadcast from Port Elizabeth took place in 1945.

WORK
Behold, o God our shield, a coronation anthem. Ms., 1953.

– C.G.H.

HARRISMITH TOWN BAND, THE, was formed round about 1880 by Charles Warden, son of Major Warden, who was transferred from George to Harrismith at that time. He was the possessor of a silver trumpet which had been presented to him by the members of the George Brass Band in 1865. — The Harrismith Town Band ceased to exist in 1899, and shortly afterwards, in 1902, Charles Warden, who was Magistrate of Harrismith, died. The Band was revived in 1903 by his son, William Gustav Warden, with the help of the bandmasters of five military regiments stationed in Harrismith (the 42nd Black Watch Scottish, the King's Royal Rifles, the Staffordshire, the Yeomanry and the First and Second Mounted Brigades). They taught the townsmen with such good effect that in 1904 the Band had grown to an ensemble of 45 amateurs supported by a number of military players. The Town Council, the general public and a few business men contributed towards the purchase of instruments in England and France and the acquisition of suitable uniforms. By 1910 they had given concerts in Ladysmith, Dundee, Newcastle, Standerton, Kroonstad, Volksrust and Bethlehem and their signature tune, *Oh, listen to the Band,* had become generally known. In 1904 Willie Warden also founded the Harrismith Spes Bona String Band, combining local violinists and a few knowledgeable bandsmen into an ensemble which was often heard at dances and, at times, in concerts. In May 1908 they combined with Prof. Abendroth's** Harrismith Symphony Orchestra for the festivities surrounding the opening of the new Town Hall. — In 1910 bandmaster Warden settled in Clocolan, founding a similar band in that town. He was succeeded in Harrismith by bandmaster R.G. Wright, better known as "Oompie" Wright, a former

Major in the King's Royal Rifles. Himself a flautist, bandmaster Wright was a sound musician and under his direction the Harrismith Town Band was entered for the National Eisteddfod** in Johannesburg, coming fourth in the military band competition. In 1912 the Band lost a few men when the British regiments in Harrismith were withdrawn, but it maintained an overall strength of 40 men. Two years later (1914) bandmaster Benson succeeded Wright. He was a former member of the Royal Fusiliers Music Corps and remained bandmaster until 1921, when he was succeeded by Jack Todd, a Harrismith member of the band. The Band ceased to exist in 1926. Since then the instruments, stands and sheet music have been housed in the basement of the Town Hall. The writer of this article, Piet du Plessis (later Colonel) joined the orchestra in 1903, when he was thirteen years old, and was soon assistant to the secretary, Tom Odell. In 1913 he became Honorary Secretary and maintained this position until 1926, when activities ceased. — Beginners had to practise in Katspruit, a deep ditch on the outskirts of the town; but those who had obtained a certain standard of proficiency on their instruments, had at first the Magistrate's Office and then the Market Hall at their disposal. Concerts were given on Sundays on the bandstand at Vrede Square; this was built in 1905 and eventually demolished to make room for a bowling green. A special feature of the Band was the one female member, a schoolgirl, Gwen Lewis, who was an excellent trumpet player. She played on Charles Warden's original silver trumpet, and was considered the mascot of the Band.

– P.duP.

HARRISON, MAUDE (CONSERVATOIRE)   M. Albu, H. Barton, H. Becker, D. Boxall, L. Danza, H. Garvin, E.N. Harvey, Higher Educational Institutions I/4, Johannesburg 2, R. Kofsky, E. Mann, H.S. Marleyn, D. Mossop, P.A.G. Pritchard, S. Rosenbloom

HARRY STANTON SINGERS   H.A.C. Stanton

HART, ALICE MAUD, *17 May 1859 in Gravesend, Kent; °28 August 1944 in Durban. Composer and music teacher.

Alice Hart became a student at the RAM when she was 17 years of age and studied there for four years. In 1880 she left England to become a music mistress at Miss L. Hall's Establishment for Young Ladies in Graaff Reinet, where she described herself as a qualified medallist of the RAM. But the very next year she was in Durban where she opened her own school of music and started teaching pianoforte, singing composition, harmony and part-singing. She instituted pupil concerts at the first of which, in 1881, she led the singing of a ladies' choir consisting of seventeen voices. — Prior to Miss Hart's arrival, recitals of serious piano music had been almost unknown in Durban. As a professional pianist, she did not associate herself with amateur musical enterprise; but in 1881, and again in 1882 and 1886, she tried to stimulate an interest in chamber music concerts by giving song and piano recitals with her sister Carrie. She was also responsible for the success in 1886 of a new type of entertainment, *Tableaux vivants,* which combined visual experience with music. — After Miss Hart's first marriage to a Mr Beviss in the early eighties, she taught at the Ladies' College until 1889. When she rejoined the staff in 1897, she was Mrs Challinor. Among her prominent pupils were Virginie Cheron** and Mary Watson (Mrs Otto Siedle**).

HART

WORKS
Joyous thoughts, for piano. Ms., 1882.   Ostrich dance, for piano. Ms., 1882.   Scherzo in B flat minor, for piano. Ms., 1882.   Durban chimes, musical sketch for piano. Ms., 1885. Characteristic sketch, for piano. Ms., 1887.   Heroes of the sea, performed by Bijou Orchestra. Ms., 1900.   Waiting for the dawn, sacred song (words by composer). Weekes & Co., London, 1916: No. 1 in B flat; No. 2 in D flat.   Cuckoo song, for pianoforte duet. Jackson Bros., Durban, 1926.   Two sketches for piano. Duff Stewart & Co. Ltd, London, 1927:   1. Rigaudon 2. Venetian boat song.   Helping hand, song (Cecil N. Palmer). Edwin Ashdown Ltd, London, 1929.   O! I wonder, song (Cecil Loraine). Weekes & Co., London, n.d. Menuet and trio in F sharp minor, for piano. Weekes & Co., London, n.d.   South African Kaffir dance, piano solo. Weekes & Co., London, n.d.   South African march, for piano. Weekes & Co., London, n.d.   Sunday, song (words by composer). Edwin Ashdown Ltd, London, n.d.   The sphinx, waltz for piano. Edwin Ashdown Ltd, London, n.d.   Three sketches for piano. Edwin Ashdown Ltd, London, n.d.: 1. Minuet 2. Rustic dance 3. Minuet.   Twelve finger exercises for the piano. Weekes & Co., London, n.d.

BIBLIOGRAPHY
Henning, C.G.: *A cultural history of Graaff Reinet, 1786–1886;* publ. as *Graaff-Reinet, a cultural history.* T.V. Bulpin, Cape Town, 1975.   Jackson, G.S.: *Music in Durban from 1850 to 1900.* D.Phil. thesis, UWits, 1961.   Van der Merwe, F.Z.: *Suid-Afrikaanse musiekbibliografie, 1787–1952.* J.L. van Schaik, Pretoria, 1958.

– E.H.S.

HART, HAROLD, *30 August 1907 in Exeter, Devon; living in Cape Town in 1966. Baritone.

Harold Hart was a choirboy from his seventh year, and eventually a soloist in the choir. At the age of twenty he commenced the study of singing, and sang leading roles at the Scala Theatre in London. A business appointment brought Hart to South Africa in 1935. Here he studied under Timothy Farrell,** developing a special interest in oratorio and church music, a field in which he has gained wide recognition in South Africa. Since 1937 he has frequently sung in broadcasts by the SABC, and has been the baritone soloist at four Oratorio Festivals held in Port Elizabeth.

– Ed.

HARTMAN, ANTON CARLISLE, *26 October 1918 in Geduld, Transvaal; °3 February 1982 in Johannesburg. For many years conductor and Head of Music of the SABC. Professor of Music and Head of the Department at the University of the Witwatersrand.

Anton Hartman completed his school career in 1934 at the Monument High School in Krugersdorp and subsequently became a student for the degree of B.Mus. at the University of the Witwatersrand. He completed the requirements for the degree in 1939 and during the early 'forties continued his study for the M.Mus. at the same University. He achieved this with distinction in 1946. These years saw not only the awakening of his interest in conducting, and his first acquaintance with the technique of rehearsing small choirs and instrumental ensembles, but also the beginning of his enthusiasm for Afrikaans folk music, light music and eventually art music. — The year 1939 saw the start of his association with the SABC. In 1947 a temporary transfer to Cape Town enabled him to study conducting under Albert Coates** and when he returned to Johannesburg in the next year, he conducted amateur orchestras and rehearsed choirs for John Connell's** opera seasons. These endeavours led in 1949 to the award by the Witwatersrand University of the Melanie Pollak Bursary.** Amplified by a government bursary, this enabled Hartman to study conducting, composition, violin and piano under prominent Austrian musicians during the years 1950–51. He was especially successful at the International Summer School in Salzburg: the conductor Igor Markevitch invited him to Salzburg in 1953 and again in 1955, to act as his assistant. — In 1952 the SABC appointed him assistant-conductor of the former Radio Orchestra and during 1953/54 he had an active share in the establishment of an enlarged Radio Symphony Orchestra, coinciding with the dissolution of the Johannesburg Symphony Orchestra. Four years later he conducted a performance of *In the drought* by John Joubert,** which was produced through the combined efforts of the National Opera Society of South Africa** (est. in 1955) and the Opera Society of South Africa (OPSA)** (est. in 1956) working together as the South African Opera Federation (est. in 1957). When the Johannesburg Civic Theatre** was inaugurated in 1962 he conducted a performance of *Die verhale van Hoffman.* In the meantime the SABC had created the position of Head of Music, as part of the reorganisation which had followed on the centralisation of South African broadcasting in Johannesburg, and appointed Hartman to the new position. He continued conducting and, at his own request, was relieved of administrative duties in 1964 to become Conductor-in-chief of the orchestra. Gideon Fagan** took over as Head of Music until his retirement in 1967, when Hartman was relieved of his responsibilities as chief conductor and again became Head of Music. He remained in this position until 1977, exerting himself on behalf of South African music. He personally conducted first performances of major works by no less than 18 South African composers and extended the musical patronage of the SABC by regularly commissioning new works from South African creators of music. For the advancement of music in performance he in 1970 advocated the institution of an annual SABC Music Prize, awarded alternately for pianoforte playing in one year and for other instruments or singing in the next. This was soon coupled to a further prize donated by SAMRO** (see Gideon Roos**). — His interest also extended to the musical education of young South Africa. During the sixties and early seventies he used his connection with the FAK, of whose Music Committee he had been the chairman since 1953, to launch courses devoted to school music held in various cities and in South West Africa. On another front he associated himself with the efforts of the South African Society of Music Teachers** to train young orchestral players and acted as consultant and as musical director on some occasions. He became an Honorary Member of this Society. — Apart from his musical endeavour, Hartman was a member of various committees and councils, including the Suid-Afrikaanse Akademie vir Wetenskap en Kuns,** the Department of National Education (various bodies) and the Council of the Rand Afrikaans University. He had the honour of conducting the SABC Orchestra on a number of festive occasions (e.g. the inauguration of the Aula and Amphitheatre of the University of Pretoria) and has also been distinguished in other ways. An Honorary Degree of D.Mus. was bestowed upon Hartman by the University of Stellenbosch in 1968 and by the University of the Witwatersrand in

1975, and the Suid-Afrikaanse Akademie vir Wetenskap en Kuns awarded him their Medal of Honour in 1962. — In 1978 he assumed new duties as Professor of Music and Head of the Department in his Alma Mater, the University of the Witwatersrand.

WRITINGS

Oorsig van Europese musiek in Suid-Afrika, 1652–1800. M.Mus. dissertation, UWits, 1946. Skat van Afrikaanse volksmusiek besig om uit te sterf. *Kultuur (Filma)* III/2, June 1946. Waar staan ons met ons musiek in Suid-Afrika? *Radio Week*, 6 and 13 June 1947. Hoe word komposisies geskep? *Radio Week*, 28 Mar. 1947. Komponiste van Suid-Afrika. *Radio Week*, 12 July 1946 to 28 Mar. 1947, 14 articles. 'n Kwarteeu van S.-A. toonkuns. *Standpunte* IX/3, 1954. Waarheen Boeremusiek? *Fleur* XI, Feb. 1955. My werk as dirigent. *Res Musicae* III/3, Mar. 1957. Arturo Toscanini. *Res Musicae* III/3, Mar. 1957. Afrikaans as musiektaal, in *Die wonder van Afrikaans.* Voortrekkerpers, 1959. Die betekenis van musiek in ons volkslewe. *Justitia* III, 7 Oct., 8 Nov., 9 Dec. 1963. Die SAUK en ons eie musiek. *SABC Bulletin*, 25 July 1966. Die Nasionale Simfonieorkes van die SAUK. *Lantern* XXI/3, Mar. 1972. Die wêreldtekort aan strykers. *Opus*, new series IV/4, June 1973. Contributions to *Die Burger:* 24 Nov. 1945; 16 July 1962; 4 Aug. 1962. Programme series for the radio on a variety of topics, including a "Music Periodical", which was broadcast for 100 weeks. Translations into Afrikaans of: *Le nozze di Figaro, St John Passion, Amelia goes to the ball,* cantatas of Bach.

BIBLIOGRAPHY

Elsevier's Muziekencyclopedie. *Grove's dictionary of music and musicians,* 4th ed., 1940. *Riemann's Musiklexicon.*

SOURCES

Van der Merwe, J.: Anton Hartman. *Afrikaans-Nederlands Maandblad,* July 1957. Van der Merwe, J.: Anton Hartman. *Res Musicae* VIII/3, June 1962. Oosthuizen, J.J.: Anton Hartman musiekhoof. *Huisgenoot,* 21 Oct. 1960. Cillié, G.G.: Huldigingswoord aan Anton Hartman. *Tydskrif vir Geesteswetenskappe,* new series 2, 1962. *Res Musicae,* June 1962. *SABC Bulletin:* 12 Sept. 1960; 9 Jan. 1967; 2 Dec. 1968; 11 Aug. 1969. *SAMT* 82, June 1972. *Die Burger:* 2 Oct. 1957; 8 Aug. 1959. *Dagbreek en Sondagnuus:* 23 Oct. 1955; 10 Mar. 1963. *Die Vaderland:* 26 Mar. 1971.

– Ed.

HARTMAN, GERTRUIDA ELIZABETH (GERDA), *8 July 1943 in Nigel; now (1978) living in Paris (France). A lyric soprano who has successfully risen above the handicaps imposed by an attack of poliomyelitis in her childhood.

During her school career in Standerton and Kimberley (1949–1960), Gerda Hartman had instruction in pianoforte playing from various teachers, only starting on her singing career during the time she studied music at the University of Pretoria as a BA student entered for languages and music. She started taking lessons in singing with Xander Haagen in 1962 and completed her degree course in 1964 with a distinction in music. She continued her studies in music and in 1966 she was awarded the overseas scholarship of UNISA after an excellent examination for the Performer's Licentiate in singing. The previous year, she had obtained the Teacher's Licentiate in pianoforte of the same University. The bursary enabled her to take up singing in London, under the guidance of Mary Makower, but a further bursary awarded by the French Government for eminence in the French language at the University of Pretoria, enabled her to continue her vocal study in Paris under the guidance of Pierre Bernac (1967–June 1969). During these two years she attended two summer academies in Salzburg and in 1969 she moved to this city for voice production and guidance in Lied interpretation by Paul Schilhasky (1969–1971). At the end of this period she obtained the artist's diploma of the Mozarteum with distinction, an award as the "best foreign student in the vocal art" and a medal for the most distinctive achievement in singing. — In 1971 Gerda Hartman returned to Paris to become singing teacher to soloists connected with the youthful Maitrise de Radio France, taking up professional concert work at the same time. Since then she has advanced rapidly as a song recitalist (with both pianoforte and harpsichord accompaniments) and as a soloist in oratorios, not only in Paris and other French centres, but also in Frankfurt and Munich, as well as during her two visits (1970; 1978) to South Africa. Both the French Radio and the SABC have repeatedly organised broadcasts of her vocal art with the accompaniment of either a keyboard instrument or an orchestra. Other distinctions with which she has been honoured are the award of the first prize during an international song competition in Paris (1970), the Mozart Prize in Paris (1970), the Lilli Lehman Medal in Salzburg (1971) and the hotly contested Hugo Wolf Prize in Salzburg (1977). — Her extensive repertoire includes operas of Rameau and vocal albums by older composers (Monteverdi to Telemann), larger choral works of Bach, about ten oratorios by Handel, Haydn, Schumann, Mendelssohn, Honegger and the *Carmina Burana* by Carl Orff, as well as an extensive collection of songs by composers from Mozart to Messiaen. A representative selection of Afrikaans songs by about six South Africans should be especially mentioned. Her exceptional musicality qualifies her as an interpreter of the *avant-garde*, in a wide variety including Charles Ives, Schoenberg, Weber, John Cage, Luciano Berio, John Feritto, Hand Eisler and numerous other composers. Deserving of explicit mention is her permanent connection with the Parisian Kaleidocollage Ensemble with whom she has been prominent on festival days devoted to contemporary music held in Sweden, La Rochelle and Salzburg. This contemporary art does not only have the benefit of her distinguished musicality, it also gains by the touchingly human qualities of her expressive timbre.

– J.P.M.

HARTMAN, JOSINA WILHELMINA (JOSSIE BOSHOFF), *25 May 1918 in Philippolis; now (1979) in Johannesburg. Soprano.

Jossie Boshoff spent her early years in the Western Transvaal, but matriculated in Johannesburg (1935) at the High School Helpmekaar. Successes in eisteddfodau and radio programmes led to voice development under the guidance of Hilda Harries in Johannesburg and, after her marriage to Anton Hartman in 1944, to lessons with Eveline Fincken** in Cape Town and finally to voice training by Maria Hittorff in Vienna (1950–1952). She also attended courses in song interpretation given by Erik Werba at the International Summer Academy in 1951 and again in 1955. — In South Africa she was active in the advance made by opera during the 'fifties and early 'sixties. She had major roles and parts in four operas by Mozart, two by Menotti and one each by Puccini, Verdi, Bellini, Flotow, Humperdinck, Johann Strauss, Smetana and John Joubert** (*Die droogte*). A few highlights were Rosalinde (*Die Fledermaus,* 1957),

Queen of the Night (*Zauberflöte*, 1960) and Susanna (*Marriage of Figaro*, 1962). In addition Jossie Boshoff distinguished herself in performances of oratorios in Johannesburg, Pretoria, Cape Town, Port Elizabeth and Pietermaritzburg and in the interpretation of German and Afrikaans songs, of which she has a considerable repertoire. Overseas, she sang for radio transmissions in England and the Netherlands and in performances conducted by Malcolm Sargent (1956) and Jascha Horenstein (1962). — Ill health terminated her professional career in 1970.

– Ed.

HARTMANN, MRS A.   F.H. Hartmann, D.J. Wagner

HARTMANN, FRIEDRICH HELMUT (FRITZ), *21 January 1900 in Vienna; ° 5 January 1972 in Vienna. Professor of Music and composer who worked in South Africa at RU and UWits (1939–1961).

Fritz Hartmann was the son of Dr Eduard Hartmann, a professor at the State Academy for Music and Dramatic Art in Vienna. His musical education began at the age of four, when he had his first pianoforte and violin lessons. After matriculating, Hartmann became a student in the Law Faculty of the Vienna University and graduated in 1922 as a Dr Jur. Concurrently he was a student at the State Academy for Music, where Joseph Marx, Franz Schmidt, Max Springer (composition), Ferdinand Löwe, Clemens Kraus, Dirk Fock and Felix von Weingartner (conducting), were his more important instructors in the various branches of music. At 27, he became a lecturer in theory at the New Vienna Conservatoire and two years later he was appointed a teacher in conducting at the Volksmusikhochschule. In 1931 he returned to the State Academy as professor in composition and musical theory and achieved an estimable reputation as professor of theory and as conductor of the Vienna Chamber Orchestra. Before the Anschluss in 1938 he was chairman of the Austrian Music Circle, chairman of the Viennese musicians' trade union, and member of the State Commission for music examinations. — The deterioration in the political situation forced Hartmann to leave Austria. He chose South Africa as his new home and became Head of the Music Department at Rhodes University in 1939. He was also connected with UNISA since his election as chairman of its Music Committee (1942). He remained in this position until 1958, when UNISA instituted its own music department. The committee was responsible for drafting regulations and syllabi in music for the various university colleges and for conducting the external examinations in academic music. In 1951 Prof. Hartmann himself obtained UNISA's Doctor of Music degree for a set of compositions which were examined by Prof. P.R. Kirby** and the Swiss conductor, Ansermet. — In 1955 Hartmann left Grahamstown to accept a position as Professor of Music at the University of the Witwatersrand. He remained there until 1961 and campaigned tenaciously for a conservatoire of music under the auspices of the University of the Witwatersrand – unfortunately without success. As Head of the Music Department he firmly insisted on a musicological basis for the study of music, with the result that postgraduate research increased considerably during his tenure. — The holder of the Queen Elizabeth II Coronation medal and of the Mozart Medal, Hartmann returned to Vienna in 1962 to become Deputy President of the State Academy of Music and Dramatic Art and Professor in History of Music. From 1965 onwards he was also responsible for Composition. He held these positions until he retired because of ill-health in 1970. — Primarily a theorist and a composer, Hartmann published a book on harmony which seeks to prove that tonality is musically organic. Among his other publications is a textbook on counterpoint, in which a single cantus firmus in various shapes and variations serves to unify all the examples.

WORKS

A. Instrumental

1. Keyboard instruments
Konzertsonate für Klavier; publ. in Copenhagen, 1930.   Toccata and fugue, for organ. Ms., 1960.

2. Chamber music
Sechs Tänze für zwei Oboen und Klavier. Ms., n.d. (Nationalbibliothek, Vienna).

3. Orchestra
Symphony in D. Ms., 1923.   Symphonisches Konzert für Horn und Orchester. Ms., 1934.   Clarinet concerto. Ms., 1942 (Grahamstown).   Concerto for clarinet in Bes, with trumpet, strings, percussion instruments and 2 pianos; first performance Grahamstown, Oct. 1945. Ms., n.d.   Oster-Musik (Easter music), for three pianos. Ms., 1947 (Cape Town). The song of the four winds (Die lied van die vier winde), a South African symphony for mezzo-soprano, baritone and orchestra. Ms., 1951–1953.   Van Riebeeck festival overture. Ms., 1952.   Van Riebeeck symphonic fanfares. Ms., 1952.   Suite for string orchestra. Kriesche, 1965 (Nationalbibliothek, Vienna).   South African symphony. Ms., n.d.   Toonbeelde vir die jeug, for orchestra. Ms., n.d.

4. Incidental music
Der weisse Fächer (The white fan), music to the stage play by Hugo van Hoffmansthal. Ms., n.d.; also an independent orchestral work (J.L. 7233).

B. Vocal

1. Solo
Drei Landschafte, für Bariton und Orchester. Ms., 1926.   Rawija singt, Symphonie für Tenor und Orchester. Ms., 1927.   Songs for mezzo-soprano and chamber orchestra. Ms., 1944 (Durban).   South African triumph march, for voice and piano, also in orchestral score. Ms., 1953.   Five-fold tryst (Erscheinungen des Todes) symphonic songs for alto and baritone. Ms, 1952.   The song of the four winds, symphony for mezzo-soprano, baritone and orchestra. Ms., 1953.   Erscheinungen des Todes (The five-fold tryst), five songs for voice and orchestra, arr. for voice and piano (German words Ricardo Huch, English words Michael Roberts). Ms. dedicated to Carl Oliver Bell, n.d.: 1. Tod Schenk (Death the tapster)   2. Tod Saemann (Death the sower)   3. Tod Schnitter (Death the reaper)   4. Tod Fischer (Death the fisherman)   5. Tod Schiffer (Death the skipper); also for alto or baritone and orchestra (J.L. 7231).   Five songs, a cycle for mezzo-soprano or baritone, string orchestra and one flute. Ms., n.d.   Five songs, for alto or baritone, with flute and strings. Ms., n.d.: 1. Zueignung (Dedication)   2. Sie Spricht (Morning)   3. Sommerlied (Summer)   4. Herbstlied (Autumn)   5. Abendgang (Evening).

2. Chamber music
Ein Osterspiel aus Österreich (with Anton Missriegler). Ms., 1938 (Nationalbibliothek, Vienna).   Passion mass for solo voices, three choirs, organ, orchestra and one speaking voice. Ms., 1950.   Passion mass, for soloists, choir, orchestra and organ, dedicated to composer's wife and daughter. Ms., n.d.

3. Incidental music for voices and orchestra
Schauspielmusik zu Der weisse Fächer (Hoffmansthal). Ms., 1927.   Musik zu Goethe's *Faust*, für Solisten, Chor und Orchester. Ms., 1927.   Musik zu Falckenberg's *Ein deutsches Weihnachtspiel*. Ms., 1927 (Nationalbibliothek, Vienna).

PUBLICATIONS

Harmonielehre. Universal Edition, Vienna, 1934 (Nationalbibliothek, Vienna). *Kontrapunkt.* Der strenge Satz von Max Springer in Form eines systematisch-methodischen Lehrganges bearbeitet und für den Unterricht und Selbstunterricht herausgegeben von Dr. F.H. Hartmann. M. Springer Verlag, Vienna, 1936.

SUNDRY WRITINGS

Thoughts on the share of woman in musical culture. *SAMT 21,* Dec. 1941. Congress in Vienna. *Res Musicae* III/1, Sept. 1956.

SOURCES

Idelson, Jerry: Sketches of South African composers. *Bandstand,* Sept. 1953. *Kürschner's deutscher Musikkalender,* 1954. Prof. Hartmann to Wits University. *Newsletter* I/5, SA Council for the Advancement of Music, Nov. 1954. Prof. Dr F.H. Hartmann. *Res Musicae* VI/1, Sept. 1959. Prof. Hartmann's departure from South Africa. *Res Musicae* VIII/1, Sept. 1961. *Die Musikerziehung:* Mar. 1972. *Österreichische Musikzeitschrift:* Feb. 1972. *PE Saturday Evening Post:* 29 Jan. 1972. Linde, B. van der: In memoriam F.H. Hartmann. *Ars Nova* IV/1, June 1972. List of works in the SABC Music Library supplied by the Music Librarian. Research Centre for South African Music, HSRC, Pretoria.

– V.C. (amplified)

HARTWIG, ERNST *17 April 1874 in Marienkoog near Tondern on the border of Denmark; ° 2 May 1962 in Pinelands, Cape Town. Missionary, adapter and compiler of the hymns and songs in the volume entitled *Sionsgesange.*

Ernst Hartwig's father was a teacher and a music-lover, with the result that he grew up in a "home of music", as he used to say. Ernst went to school in Itzehoe, Holstein, and at the Gymnasium in Glückstadt; thereafter he was trained at the theological seminary in Halle and was later ordained as Pastor. After his military training he spent three years doing religious work at schools and universities and then lectured at Barmen in Greek, Latin and other subjects. In 1903 the Rev. Hartwig came to South Africa as a missionary and served consecutively in the communities of Worcester, Saron and Carnarvon. While he was in Carnarvon he started compiling the *Sionsgesange,* a volume that was taken over by the Dutch Reformed Mission Church in 1946 and published as its official hymn book in 1949. — The Rev. Hartwig wrote the following about this hymn book: "The hymns and songs of this book represent about 20 years of concentrated work. There are 402 independent arrangements of psalms, hymns and songs: a collection based on Dutch, English and German originals. In adapting these I have tried to retain, as far as possible, the spiritual content of the original poems and to present them in simple but exalted language. In regard to the settings, in so far as these have not been finalised, I myself am responsible; also for the adaptation of certain melodies and for some of the new melodies in this book." — In addition to the Alphabetical Register, an appendix contains brief references to the derivation and origins of the hymns and songs and their melodies.

WORKS

Heideblommetjies gepluk en aangebied deur E.H. Nas. Pers Bpk, Cape Town, 1946. Ons vlag/Our flag. E.H. and A. Methfessel. Distr. by Nasionale Boekhandel, 1962.

– W.F.L.

HARVEY, EVA NOEL, *23 October 1900 in Basutoland; living in Johannesburg in 1976. Prominent patroness of music, composer and violinist.

Eva Noel Harvey received her musical education in Johannesburg, where she studied violin under Violet Jameson (1912-1921), pianoforte under Maud Harrison (1914-1920), and singing under Ethel Mann** (1918-1921). She holds licenciates in violin, singing and pianoforte, and won two bursaries for violin playing and five gold medals at eisteddfodau. In 1921-1922 she continued her study under Beatrice** and Ellie Marx** in Cape Town, and appeared as soloist with the Cape Town Municipal** and the Durban Orchestras.** — After her marriage to Richard N. Harvey, a Johannesburg businessman, and especially during and after the Second World War, their home in Sandhurst became a centre where many young artists were presented to the public. Her interest not only gave them the incentive to perform, but introduced them to experienced colleagues, who could advise and guide them to suitable musical activities. During the past seventeen years (1960-1976), her private concert-room has also provided a venue for senior South African and overseas artists, as well as facilities for chamber groups, small orchestras, choirs, the Harp Society of South Africa** and the Society of South African Composers.** On one occasion the Durban Orchestra was accommodated there. Where the groups were too large, open-air performances were held in the garden. — Among the South African artists who have performed at Mrs Harvey's home are Arnold van Wyk,** Betsy de la Porte,** the De Groote Family Ensemble,** Sini van den Brom,** Nellie du Toit,** Jossie Boshoff,** Toon van Dongen,** Jean Gluckman,** Peggy Haddon,** Kathleen Alister,** Gerrit Bon,** Alan Solomon,** Betty Pack** and her Ensemble, and many others. Overseas artists include George Themeli and Pierino Gamba. — The Society of SA Composers has presented first performances of new South African compositions, either in her concert-room or at a theatre hired by Mr and Mrs Harvey. These include the *Violin concerto* (Alan Solomon), *Piano concerto* (Paul Loeb van Zuilenberg),** *Overture* (Michael Wolfson**), song cycles and choral works by Lourens Faul,** and Joyce Loots's** prize-winning entry in an SABC song competition. In 1968 the Society organised a competition for an original choral work by a Black composer. The prize-winning work by Benjamin Tyamzashe** was first performed at an open-air concert at the Harveys on 20 December 1969, by the Ionian Music Society Choir, directed by Khabi Mngoma**. — Mrs Harvey commenced composing during the war years. Her works include one three-act and two one-act operas, and vocal and instrumental compositions, of which a number have since been performed in Holland, America and Ireland. Her *Japanese song cycle* and *African tone poem suite* won prizes in SABC competitions between 1950 and 1957. Several other works have been broadcast. — Mrs Harvey has given numerous lectures on musical subjects, especially those bearing on the relationship of the arts and the influence other art forms have on music. She uses her own music "as having been inspired by any of the aforementioned arts" to illustrate the lectures, which are designed to stimulate mental, aural and visual activity. The subjects have included *The music of the spheres, The art of listening, The meaning of Christmas,* and *Greek myths.* The lectures were given to the Rare Music Guild,** the Divinity Group of the Witwatersrand University, the Rand and Pretoria Women's Clubs, the Vanguard Club, the Arts Forum and many other groups. — Since 1965 Mrs Harvey has been official auditioner of applicants for the Anglo-American Corporation's overseas grants.

WORKS

A. *Vocal*

1. *Opera*

Yugao, miniature opera in one act, based on Japanese fairy story, for voices, oboe, percussion, harp, organ and piano (E.N. Harvey). Comp. 1967, perf. 1967. DALRO, 1970.   Esther, grand opera in 3 acts, for coloratura soprano, mezzo-soprano, contralto, light baritone, 2 bass-baritones, 5 baritones, 3 tenors and orchestra. Comp. 1969. DALRO, 1970.   Ruth and Naomi, one act opera for voices, flute, clarinet, oboe, percussion, organ and piano (Biblical). Perf. 1969. Ms., 1969.

2. *Cantata, Oratorio, Choir*

To the glory of God, religious cantata for soprano, mezzo-soprano, chorus, piano and organ. Ms., n.d: 1. Make a joyful noise unto the Lord   2. By the waters of Babylon   3. My Son, forget not my law   4. The Lord is my shepherd   5. Again will I build thee.   Lift up thine eyes, oratorio for soprano, mezzo-soprano, baritone and bass, with oboe and organ. Ms., n.d.   O Lord how excellent is Thy name, for choir. Ms., n.d.

3. *Songs*

Japanese song cycle, prizewinning entry, SABC competition (trad.). Ms., 1950–1955 (?).   Aftermath (anon.). Ms., n.d.   Arise, shine (unknown). Ms., n.d.   Chinese lanterns (trad.). Ms., n.d.   Chinese proverb (trad.). Ms., n.d.   Drie nuwe liedere. Studio Holland, n.d.: 1. Salute d'amore (A.G. Visser)   2. Krulkop klonkie (C. Louis Leipoldt)   3. Bokmakierie (C. Burmeister).   Fain would I waken. Studio Holland, n.d.   Five carols. Ms., n.d.   I know that my Redeemer liveth, for mezzo-soprano or soprano (Charles Jennens). Ms., n.d.   Kom dans met my (C. Louis Leipoldt). Ms., n.d.   Later winternag (Ernst van Heerden). Ms., n.d.   A little Child shall lead them (Biblical). Ms., n.d.   The loom (anon.). Ms., n.d.   My tears will gently fall (anon.). Ms., n.d.   O Diep Rivier (E. Marais). Ms., n.d.   Oktober (W.E.G. Louw). Ms., n.d.   Ontwaak (composer). Ms., n.d.   Out of the captivity, for mezzo-soprano. Ms., n.d.   Sing, vinkie, sing (C. Louis Leipoldt). Ms., n.d.   Six religious solos. Ms., n.d.   Song cycle (Ezra Pound). Ms., n.d.: 1. Francesca   2. Dance figure   3. The white stag.   Song cycle from Greek myths, for soprano, baritone, vocal quartet, flute, percussion and piano. Ms., n.d.: 1. Venus   2. Echo and Narcissus   3. Bacchus and Ariadne.   Three gipsy songs. Ms. n.d. Toeral loeral la (C. Louis Leipoldt). Ms., n.d.   When the morning stars sang together. Ms., n.d.   Windswael (C. Louis Leipoldt). Studio Holland, n.d.   The wisdom carol (E. Willoughby). Ms., n.d.   With His truth, psalm 96 (Biblical). Ms., n.d.

B. *Instrumental*

African suite, tone poem for piano. Comp. 1952–1957. Studio Holland, n.d.: 1. Song of the Ntombazana   2. Corngrinder's lullaby   3. Old warrior "Mdala".   African tone pictures, for piano, perf. in America and Ireland. Ms., 1965.   Chanson de soir, for cello and piano. Ms., n.d.   Suite, for oboe and piano, based on African melodies, perf. in Holland. Ms., 1965.   Suite, for two pianos. Ms., 1965.   Suite, for celtic harp. Ms., n.d.

SOURCES

Sandton arts foundation. *Opus*, new series III/1, Sept. 1971.   Randse opera-eksperiment. *Opus*, new series III/2, Jan. 1972.   Sandton arts foundation. *Opus*, new series III/3, Mar. 1972.   Research Centre for South African Music, HSRC, Pretoria.

– Ed.

HATTERSCHEIDT, C.   W. Frewer, A.W. Kehrmann, Windhoek 2

HAWES, ALLEN   Ada Forrest

HAY BROS   J. Hyde, King William's Town 5, 14

HAYES, W.   Kimberley 2

HAYGARTH, J. W.   Durban, Queenstown, Kimberley, Touring Theatre Groups 7

HAZELHURST, GRACE   Barberton III/4, IV, V, VI, IX/2, F. Dillon, Israel (Charles Wilhelm), E. Leviseur

HEALDTOWN   Bantu Composers of South Africa

HEAP, H.   Port Elizabeth I/4(i), I/5

HEATH, L.   Johannesburg 1, R.H. Heath

HEATH, ROBERT HAINSWORTH *1842 or 1843 in Torquay, England; °3 February 1912 in Johannesburg. Organist and music teacher.

Heath settled in Johannesburg in the early nineties as a music teacher, with his wife and seven children, and was appointed organist to St Augustine's Church, Doornfontein (built in 1892). When the Musicians' Club was formed in 1895, he was elected Vice-President. During the Anglo-Boer War he was in Durban, where he advertised as "former organist of St Mary's Church", Johannesburg. He formed the Durban West Country Association, a choir of chiefly Johannesburg singers, that contributed the proceeds of their concerts to the Transvaal Relief Fund. Returning to Johannesburg, a published list of staff members mentions him in 1903 as a teacher of organ, serving Epstein's** South African College of Music. — Leo Heath, official accompanist to the Wanderers Club (1901), chorus master of the Lyric Club (1902), and director of the Apollo Quartette (1902), was probably Robert's son Leopold Sydney. Leopold was organist at St Mary's Church after the Anglo-Boer War, and often gave recitals there.

WORKS
Abide with me, sacred song with organ accompaniment and cello obligato. R.H. Heath, Johannesburg, n.d.   Imperial Light Horse, valse for pianoforte. R.H. Heath, Johannesburg, n.d.   Transvaal Scottish march. R.H. Heath, Johannesburg, n.d.

BIBLIOGRAPHY
Jackson, G.S.: *Music in Durban from 1850 to 1900*. D.Phil. thesis, UWits, 1961.   Van der Merwe, F.Z.: *Suid-Afrikaanse musiekbibliografie, 1787–1952*. J.L. van Schaik, Pretoria, 1958. Wolpowitz L.: *James and Kate Hyde*. J.L. van Schaik, Pretoria, 1969.

SOURCE
The Star: 1892–1895.

– L.W.

HEATLY, PHILLIS (MRS ROBERTSON)   H. McLeod Robertson

HECHT, J.   Discography

HEIBERG, MARTHA JACOBA (DOLLY; NéE SWART, THE WIDOW LIVINGLI McDONALD), *27 October 1919 in Ventersburg; living in Bloemfontein in 1976.

Dolly Heiberg obtained the ATCL (organ), LTCL (piano), and the UTLM, UPLM and ODMS (organ) diplomas at the Stellenbosch Conservatoire of Music;** in 1952 she was awarded the Gertrude Buchanan grant and in the same year she obtained a M.Mus. degree for a dissertation on F.W. Jannasch. She visited Salzburg in July 1968, and attended the Carl Orff course in school music at the Orff Institute. — Mrs Heiberg lectured at the University of the Orange Free State from 1947 to 1950; at the Stellenbosch Conservatoire (in organ) from 1951 to 1952; and then she was appointed senior lecturer in Class Singing at the Teachers' Training College in Bloemfontein (1954–1958). While at the College, she organised an annual song festival to which the public was invited. Between 1958 and 1961 she lived in the Cape Peninsula where she taught school music at two schools and adjudicated several Coloured choirs. In 1961 the University of the Orange Free State appointed her a lecturer in organ and in school music in its Department of Music, a post which she still holds (1976). Dolly Heiberg has been the organist of the Dutch Reformed Church (the "Mother Church") in Bloemfontein since 1941, with the exception of the years during which she lived elsewhere. She takes an active part in music recitals and choir performances in Bloemfontein and its vicinity, and has given organ-recitals broadcast by the SABC.

WORKS

Wysies en deuntjies vir meisies en seuntjies (Mariechen Naudé), with the co-operation of Hubert du Plessis.** FAK, Johannesburg, 1960 (2nd edition in preparation, 1970).   Settings included in three plays for children (*Die Reënboogkruik en ander toneelstukkies* by Mariechen Naudé). Nasionale Boekhandel, Parow, 1963:   1. Die Reënboogkruik (DALRO, Johannesburg, 1970)   2. Letta se soektog   3. Somme en tafels.

PUBLICATION

Prof. F.W. Jannasch en sy bydrae tot ons kerkmusiek. M.Mus. dissertation, US, 1952. Published under the name of M.J. McDonald. Sondagskool-pers, Bloemfontein, 1955.

– Ed.

HEIDELBERG (TRANSVAAL), MUSIC IN
   1. Church music
   2. Brass bands
   3. The "Studente-Orpheum"
   4. The Heidelberg Music Circle

1. Church music
When the town of Heidelberg was proclaimed on 28 March 1866, there were two congregations, of the Nederduits-Hervormde and the Nederduitse Gereformeerde

Kerk. The latter was a small group that held services about six miles to the north-west of the present town, without precentor, catechist, verger or organist. One of the members, G.D. van den Heever (later MP for Heidelberg), had been an organist in the Cape Province, but there was no instrument for him to play on and the minister had to take the lead in every liturgical act. In 1881 it was noted: "The reading is done by the Minister with due reverence, and for the edification of the congregation; the precenting is done with due reverence and for edification; both are done according to the direction of the Minister." — The Hervormde Kerk had a music-loving minister in the Rev. N.J. van Warmelo, who possessed a pianoforte and a seraphine. Provisionally, the congregation had a reader and precentor, called P.N. Slymers, the government teacher, who received R50 annually for his vocal work in the church. When he was dismissed for drunkenness and immorality, Jacobus Spruyt temporarily took his place. Spruyt found it impossible to attend every service, because he lived on a farm, and when he did turn up it was understood "that for every Sunday on which he did service, the sum of R1 shall be paid to him". This unsatisfactory arrangement lasted until 1874, when the Church Council decided that the Minister himself should act as reader. Two years later the Rev. Van Warmelo lent his new harmonium to the church, and W. van Heusden was appointed as "organist", at a "compensation of R40 as annual allowance". Van Heusden did not play the harmonium for very long, since the 23-year-old H.J. van der Linden was appointed in his place in 1878. But Van der Linden left in the same year and then the Minister's wife occupied the post, at an annual salary of R50. —The Nederduits-Hervormde and the Nederduitse Gereformeerde Churches merged in 1885, although a group of Nederduits-Hervormdes in Heidelberg maintained a separate Hervormde congregation. Mrs Van Warmelo did not feel at home in the United Church, and preferred to stay in the Hervormde Church. This resulted in her resignation as organist in 1887, but Van der Linden was again available to take over from her. The harmonium had deteriorated in the meantime, and Van der Linden insisted on a new one. Each member of the church council was expected to exert himself in the drive to gather money for a new instrument, and the undertaking was so successful that Van der Linden had his new harmonium in April 1889. He did not play for very long, because in 1891 a large stone church was completed, with a new organ (presented by Mr F.J. Bezuidenhout), which was built in the gallery behind the pulpit. The harmonium was presented to the Sunday School, where it laboured until 1937, when it was replaced by a third harmonium. The instrument of 1889 has remained in the possession of the congregation. The new church and organ were inaugurated with a festival lasting three days. It is interesting to note that a choir sang during this festival, subject to a directive of the Church Council: "that only Psalms and Hymns are to be used during the inaugural ceremony". This was the first time a choir was mentioned in connection with an Afrikaans church service. — A month later, on 15 April 1891, Van der Linden died at the age of only 36 years. His death came as a shock to the whole community, and at the first meeting of the Church Council afterwards it was decided "that provision be made to have the organ played for one year gratuitously, so that the salary of this period can be paid to the widow as a contribution to the education of her children." The person who acted in this honorary capacity was the principal of the school, P.J. Möller, who remained organist until 1894. A petition by the choir to continue its existence with Möller as leader "and precentor" was approved by the Council. In January 1892, Möller wrote, requesting the singing of other spiritual songs than psalms and hymn tunes during Church services, but this was refused by the Council, which confirmed "that the ordinary hymns and psalms are simply to be continued". Shortly afterwards the Rev. Van Warmelo died, and when the church elder, Kok, left, the Council decided to address a friendly request to the organist "to take the lead in the ordinary Sunday service". — This arrangement continued until April 1893, when the Rev. A.J. Louw came to Heidelberg as Minister. He had liturgical objections to a permanent church choir, so that until 1925 choral singing was heard only on special occasions. After some impressive singing during the Reformation Service in 1924, the elder, Liebenberg of Kafferskraal, again pleaded for a permanent church choir, and gained so much support that the Rev. Louw was moved to discuss the matter with the organist (Stephen Eyssen**). Early in 1925 the Minister was able to communicate that the discussions had progressed satisfactorily, that only devoted, selected persons would sing in the choir (when necessary, in consultation with the Minister), and that the Council would have to arrange for funds (supplemented by organ recitals) to buy the necessary choral literature. The choir was to perform each Sunday, alternately at the morning and the evening services, and to present a full programme of sacred music twice a year. From this time choral singing was a normal ingredient of the church services. — P.J. Möller left for Pretoria in 1894, and W. Rawlinson took his place. Rawlinson was a dedicated organist, who had the interest of the church very much at heart. In 1898, for example, he made a voluntary contribution towards installing benches in the organ gallery; during the Anglo-Boer War he did his work without payment, and even carried on afterwards at a very small salary. The Council was conscious of his zeal and gave him a special bonus of R50 in 1906. In 1912 the organ was in a bad condition, and a firm in Johannesburg asked R70 for repairs. Rawlinson offered the Council R100 to repair the instrument, and his offer was accepted with thanks. When he finally resigned in 1920, the Minister thanked him during a special thanksgiving service for loyal services lasting 25 years. He was offered another bonus of R50, and notified "that he could use the instrument for his own pleasure at any time when it is not occupied". — The Council had Otto Menge** in mind as a successor to Mr Rawlinson, but when he was unable to accept, the school teacher, Stephen Eyssen (later principal of the Hoër Volkskool) was appointed, at an initial salary of R120 which was later increased to R156 per annum. Stephen Eyssen played the organ until he became MP for Heidelberg in 1948, with an interruption during the Second World War, when he was interned. In 1925 Eyssen managed to introduce choral singing into the services (see above), and in 1927 he appeared before the Council to discuss the condition of the organ. The instrument was then 36 years old; repairs were necessary, and the costs would be approximately R665. An organ commission reported that the work was necessary, and the council decided to devote the proceeds of a thanksgiving service in April 1928, to this purpose. When the material arrived in November 1928 it appeared that the gallery was not sturdy enough for the extra weight, and the Council had to have the gallery reinforced too. With wood carvings on the gallery front, a design by Mr Chris Neethling, the work was finished in September 1929. The restoration had cost the congregation R1 454. Since that time the manual blowing of bellows had passed, but faulty electric wiring often left the organ without wind, to the consternation of both player and congregation. Eyssen was very active in the cause of Church music; he invited solo instrumentalists to play during evening services (e.g. Otto Menge), and did much to improve congregational singing by utilizing the choir. For the dedication of the Afrikaans Psalms and Hymns, he composed a *Bible cantata* (1943), which was heard for the first time in Heidelberg after the War. — The poet A.G. Visser officiated at the organ during an Evensong which formed part of the festivals during the quatercentenary of the Reformation. When the earth at Blood River was solemnly dedicated on 16 December 1920, the Rev. Louw, who acted as chairman, took with him Otto Menge, Lennie de Villiers, J. Langenegger (violinist), M.J. Viljoen (cornet) and A.G. Visser (pianoforte), to participate in the festival programme. Visser also acted for Eyssen at the organ, whenever the latter was absent. — From 1948 to 1954 E.W. Albertyn was the organist, and then H.J. Joubert** acted for five years. In 1954 the entire church building was subjected to restoration; the organ gallery was enlarged and provided with a concrete floor. The organ itself was rebuilt, and enlarged at a cost of R6 000, the amount being presented by Mr P.J. Potgieter and his family. Mrs W.H.S. Bogenhofer has been the organist since 1961. — Under the patronage of the D.R. Church, measures were taken to provide the pupils living in church hostels with tuition in pianoforte and organ. Practice rooms were built in 1921, and then followed a long period of growth, culminating in 1948 in the creation of a music school. The principal of the school was also the church organist. E. W. Albertyn was the first head of the school, which grew to muster 250 pupils in pianoforte, organ, violin and singing, and a staff of up to 10 members. This music school came to an end in 1959, when the hostels were absorbed by the Provincial Administration and the head, H.J. Joubert, became vice-principal of the Pretoria Conservatoire of Music (1960).

– A.E.F.B.

2. Brass bands

So far as is known, there have been three brass bands in Heidelberg, two of which were active over the same period. The only evidence found to prove the existence of the first Heidelberg Brass Band, is a photograph taken in 1891, in which can be seen a group of 17 members, five of whom are children. The only persons who can now be identified are T.H.P. Ivey, later the conductor of the Heidelberg Town Band, and a thirteen-year-old boy, Marthinus Viljoen (better known as Ouboet Viljoen), who became the founder and conductor of the "Wilhelmina Muziek Vereeniging". — The Heidelberg Town Band received financial support from the Heidelberg Town Council, and came into existence under T.H.P. Ivey shortly after the Anglo-Boer War (1899–1902). Ivey was succeeded by W.J. Ward, and while he was conductor the band at one stage had a membership of 25, of whom many were young boys. In one respect this band differed from its predecessor: it consisted not only of brass and percussion instruments, but also had three clarinets. The Heidelberg Town Band was quite active – during the summer months it regularly gave a monthly promenade concert in Graham's Garden and appeared at local shows and sports gatherings in towns such as Nigel, Vereeniging and, on one occasion, Dundee in Natal. — The "Wilhelmina Muziek Vereeniging" was established on 24 September 1904, with T.E. Dönges (teacher, first principal of the Heidelberg Teachers' Training College and later a Senator) as chairman, and "Ouboet" Viljoen as conductor. On 2 March 1905, the latter was succeeded by A. Brüllbeck, who continued in this office for some time, because Ouboet Viljoen was indispensable as a cornet player. However, Viljoen again appears as conductor at a later stage. The secretary of the society was Fred Ahrbeck, who filled this position for the greater part of the band's existence, and blew the bugle as well. — The money used for the purchase of instruments was donated by Frederick J.

Bezuidenhout, in recognition of which the society was named after "tante" Wilhelmina, his wife, and he ("oom" Frikkie) was invited to be its president. The activities of the Wilhelmina Band (as it was usually called) were much the same as those of the Town Band, except that it also performed at educational and social functions. The membership of 22 remained more or less constant. The writer Sangiro (A.A. Pienaar) was at one stage a member of this band. — In January 1910, the Heidelberg Town Band and the Wilhelmina Muziek Vereeniging amalgamated and adopted the name of Heidelberg Wilhelmina Town Band. This combination, however, did not last very long, and in March 1911, the two groups separated. Perhaps it was soon after this that the Town Band ceased to exist. The Wilhelmina Band continued a while longer, but in 1912 it also terminated its usefulness.

3. The "Studente-Orpheum" was founded on 9 March 1917, at a general meeting of staff members of the Hoër Volkskool, Heidelberg (HVH), and others who were interested. The first committee consisted of J.K. Scholtz (chairman), J.J. van Zijl (vice-chairman), R. Schulze (secretary), J.J. Langenegger and Cissie Nel. Although the principal of the school, "Meester" A.J. Louw (later professor and head of the Normal College, Pretoria), did not serve on the first committee, he was undoubtedly the driving force behind the whole enterprise. During the early years he was the double-bass player in the ensemble. — As the name signifies, the original idea was that this musical society should consist of students of the local Teachers' Training College plus pupils and teachers of the Hoër Volkskool, and any of the local residents who were interested. In practice, however, matters worked out otherwise. As early as 1918, J.J. van Zijl wrote that it was actually a school society. After 1921 the Orpheum became exclusively a musical society of the HVH, except for members of the public who assisted the group, e.g. Otto Menge, Cornelis Spruyt, Violet Long-Innes, J. Deysel, Albertus Malan and Ena Bennett. — From its inception the Orpheum boasted an orchestra and a choir. The latter, originally about 60 strong and later sometimes augmented to 120, was under the direction of B. Elbrecht, until he was succeeded by Stephen Eyssen in 1921. The original orchestra had about twelve members: teachers (both men and women), townspeople and one pupil. As the Orpheum was attached to the school, more pupils were in due course absorbed into the orchestra, and for some of them the music was simplified. Among the original members was J.J. Langenegger (violinist), the conductor; but in 1919 his place was taken by Otto Menge, who had established himself in Heidelberg as a teacher of the violin. After his departure for Bloemfontein, round about the middle of 1922, the orchestra came under the direction of Stephen Eyssen, who at that time officiated from the piano. — In 1919, for the first time, the Orpheum presented two concerts during the year, and with few exceptions this practice continued until 1947, after which there was again only one concert a year. At the second concert of 1922 there was a performance of a cantata, *The flower queen* (George Root). For many years the programme of the Orpheum was as follows: in the first half of the year, a concert by one or more visiting artists, which included contributions by the choir and the orchestra; in the second half of the year, a cantata or an operetta, mainly light works by composers such as Root, Thomas, Best, De Ridder, Preud'homme etc., accompanied by the orchestra. — After Stephen Eyssen was interned in November 1941, the activities of the Orpheum temporarily ceased. In 1942 and 1943, however, there was at least one concert a year, until Denis de Kock, a teacher at HVH, took over the direction in 1944. On his return to Heidelberg in May

1945, Eyssen once again led the performances of the Orpheum; but after his election as a Member of Parliament in Aug. 1948, the conductorship was resumed by Denis de Kock, under whose leadership the Orpheum celebrated its golden jubilee in 1967.

4. **The Heidelberg Music Circle** was founded on 21 June 1932, at the home of the widow of the poet, Dr A.G. Visser, and the Rev. J.P.W. de Vries became its first chairman. — The purpose of this society was to provide local music-lovers, amateurs and professionals, with the opportunity of meeting once a month to practise music of a serious kind. At the commencement of each year the programme for the year was drawn up by the committee and each month a portion of the scheme was presented. Usually this consisted of a paper on some prescribed topic, with piano solos or duets, violin and vocal solos and choral items to serve as illustrations. One evening a year was devoted to a discussion of a South African musical topic; a regular feature was the discussion of a popular opera. — The Music Circle flourished between 1940 and 1950, when there was a yearly average of 35 active members, and 15 associate members. On 20 September 1957, its twenty five years of existence was commemorated by a concert in the hall of the Teachers' Training College, but shortly afterwards, on 17 November 1959, the Circle held its last meeting.

SOURCES
Minutes of the Heidelberg Music Society (1932–1949).   Stephen Eyssen collection in the Research Centre for South African Music, HSRC, Pretoria.

– P.H.L.

HEIJNS, C.F.   Tierbergmanne Kwartet

HEIJNS, ELIZABETH JOHANNA, *13 October 1927 in Beaufort West; now (1979) in Stellenbosch. Lecturer in singing, concert singer.

After obtaining her Teacher's Licentiate at the South African College of Music** (1956–1958), Elizabeth Heijns lived in Parow as a piano teacher and acted as chairman of the local music society until she became lecturer at the Pretoria College of Education (1962–1964). In 1965 she left for Trinity College and obtained, in the same year, the LTCL and (at the RAM) the LRAM. In Paris she pursued specialist courses in French and the art song under the guidance of Pierre Bernac, before returning to the College in July 1966. Studying privately she had by 1968 obtained the LRSM (teacher's and performer's), the UTLM and UPLM in singing and the FTCL. In July 1968 she became lecturer in singing at the PU for CHE. Since April 1974 she is on the staff of the Conservatoire of Music** of the University of Stellenbosch. — Between July 1966 and June 1968 she organised a series of concerts in the Little Theatre for the Pretoria College of Education, in which she herself performed, singing for example in a programme devoted to French songs. She similarly often contributed to the Collegium Musicum** of the University in Potchefstroom. Well-known among her pupils are Ria Lemmer (soprano) and Cecile Kirchner (mezzo-soprano).

SOURCE
Opus, new series I/1, Dec. 1969.   – Ed.

HEIJNS, NICOLAAS GODFRIED, baptised 7 October 1725 in Cape Town; ° 1792 in Cape Town. Organist and music teacher.

This first music teacher born in South Africa had a belligerent character which led him into trouble at various times. As organist he played on the first organ of the Groote Kerk, but on 16 February 1753, complaints concerning misconduct were laid against him with the Political Board. Subsequently he slandered members of the Church Council in a public house, and was dismissed on 27 February. Nevertheless, Heijns continued to give music lessons, two of his pupils being children of the Bergh family, but in 1766 his temper again led him into excesses. On 2 December 1764 he was married to the widow Du Toit, previously known as Alida de Swart, but barely 2 years later the marriage was dissolved when he was involved in a legal suit concerning the ill-treatment of a female slave, and fined a hundred rixdollars. In later years he treated his slaves with more consideration. — On 7 May 1779 Heijns and three other delegates from the Cape were selected by Cape residents to visit Amsterdam, to protest against despotic measures of governor Joachim van Plettenberg. The delegates achieved little success in their discussion with the Council of the DEIC; instead, Heijns was reminded of his misconduct in 1753. — After his return to the Cape, he apparently enjoyed slight support as a music teacher, and it became difficult for him to make a living. With practically no income, he lived with his eldest son Hendrik Heijns after 1785. When he died in 1792 his possessions were listed as an old silver watch, a rifle, a violin, a few music books, and a heterogeneous selection of books in various languages. His total estate was assessed at 22 rixdollars and 30 stivers.

BIBLIOGRAPHY

Beyers, C.: *Die Kaapse Patriotte, 1779–1791.* Cape Town/Johannesburg, 1929.   Bouws, J.: *Musiek in Suid-Afrika.* Brugge, 1946.   Hopkins, H.C.: *Die moeder van ons almal.* Cape Town/Pretoria, n.d. (1965).   Spoelstra, C.: *Bouwstoffen voor de geschiedenis der Nederduitsch Gereformeerde Kerk in Zuid-Afrika II.* Amsterdam/Cape Town, 1907.   Van Tonder, Izak W.: *Van Riebeeck se stad.* Johannesburg, 1950.

– J.B.

HEIMES, KLAUS FERDINAND, *9 July 1930 in Deutmecke, Germany; now (1976) in Port Elizabeth. Professor of Music.

In September 1946, Klaus Heimes enrolled at the Staatliche Hochschule für Musik in Cologne, and studied there for six years. After passing the Reifeprüfung (pianoforte) with distinction in July 1952, he visited Paris in 1953 for additional study under Marguerite Long. — After his arrival in South Africa in 1956, Heimes taught music at various high schools in the Cape Province, gave radio performances and played concertos with the orchestras of the SABC and of Cape Town City. Since his naturalisation in 1961 he has obtained the qualifications of a B.Mus. degree (1963) an M.Mus. degree (1965, with distinction) and the D.Mus degree (1967) through the University of South Africa. In 1961 he qualified for the UPLM and LRSM diplomas and in 1962 he was awarded the Overseas Bursary of the University of South Africa. In 1963 Heimes was chosen as an examiner for the practical music examinations of the University of South Africa, and in 1964 he became senior lecturer in the Music Department of the same university. Four years later he moved to the University of Port Elizabeth where he occupied a similar position until 1969. In this year Prof.

Wegelin** retired and Heimes was promoted to the professorship in Music. He retired for health reasons in 1979.

PUBLICATIONS

Antonio Soler's keyboard sonatas. M.Mus. dissertation, UNISA, 1965. Middleton & Joubert, Pretoria, 1969. *Carlos Seixas's keyboard sonatas.* D.Mus. thesis, UNISA, 1967. Trends in music education. *New Nation,* June 1969. Musicology and performance. *SAMT* 76, June 1969. The uses and misuses of the "isms" in music. *Opus,* new series I/3, June/July 1970. Towards a balanced music education. *New Nation,* Apr. 1971. Carlos Seixas: Zum Quellenstudium seiner Claviersonaten. *Archiv für Musikwissenschaft* 3, 1971. Music and society. *Focus,* Oct. 1972. Matriculation in music and university requirements. *Opus,* new series IV/1, Oct. 1972. Impressionism and after: attitudes towards modern music. *De Arte,* Oct. 1972. Avant garde and artistic sincerity. *Opus,* new series V/1, Oct. 1973. The ternary sonata principle before 1742. *Acta Musicologica* 2, July-Dec. 1973. The question of Domenico Scarlatti's influence: Carlos Seixas's keyboard sonatas. *Bracara Augusta, Actas do Congresso* III, 1974. Music history in a situation of compromise. *Ars Nova* VIII/1 & 2, 1976. Carlos de Seixas; also Jacinto Frei: *Grove's dictionary of music and musicians,* 6th ed. Macmillan, London, 1978.

– Ed.

HELDERBERG COLLEGE, near Somerset West, C.P., is owned and operated by the Seventh Day Adventist Church. Its music department employs four full-time and four part-time teachers, giving instruction in piano, organ, violin, singing, brass and woodwind instruments, and choral music. The a capella choir of Helderberg College was formed in 1948 by Frances Brown of California; it toured South Africa for the first time in 1950. Under the direction of Dodds Miller, who succeeded her as conductor, the choir broadcast several sacred concerts, including a performance of *St Paul* (Mendelssohn). The next director, Robert McManaman, appointed in 1957, conducted the choir during tours of South Africa undertaken in the period 1959–1962. — The choir, which sings only sacred works, usually has about 40 voices. The members are all students following professional and B.A., B.Sc., or B.Com. courses at Helderberg College. The Helderberg College Brass Band, which was founded by Robert McManaman, comprises 30 brass, woodwind and percussion instruments, the players ranging from Standard Seven pupils to College men and women. It has given public concerts in the vicinity of the College, and in Cape Town and Bloemfontein.

– P.J.v.E.

HELY-HUTCHINSON, CHRISTIAN VICTOR NOEL HOPE, *26 December 1901 in Cape Town; °11 March 1947 in London. Composer, pianist and conductor.

Victor Hely-Hutchinson was born during the time his father, Sir Walter Hely-Hutchinson, was Governor of the Cape of Good Hope. After spending his early years in South Africa, he was educated at Eton and Balliol College in Oxford, and musically at the Royal College of Music and privately by Sir Donald Tovey, until he returned to South Africa to become a lecturer at the South African College of Music** (1922–1925). Victor had been at Eton with Leslie Heward,** at that time conductor of the Cape Town Orchestra, and a close friendship developed between the two men, which ended only with Heward's death. Hely-Hutchinson was an accomplished pianist and appeared with Heward in many duo-piano recitals. He made several appearances as guest-conductor with the Cape Town Orchestra,** directing perform-ances of his own works. — After his emigration to Britain, Hely-Hutchinson was appointed to the music staff of the BBC (1926–1934), resigning to become Barber Professor of Music in Birmingham University, a position he held until 1944. In Birmingham he renewed his association with Heward, who had been conductor of the city orchestra since 1930. After Heward's death in 1943 Hely-Hutchinson returned to the BBC in London, as their musical director-in-chief (1944). His career was terminated by his untimely death. He was married to Miss Marjorie Hugo, a South African. — As a composer, Hely-Hutchinson had a particular gift for setting humorous verse. Although he composed a number of more serious works, it is chiefly for his delightful settings of some of Lear's *Nonsense songs,* and his parody of Handel in the musical version of *Old Mother Hubbard,* that he is remembered.

WORKS
(Unless otherwise stated, the following mss. are in the Jagger Library, UCT)

A. Vocal

1. Vocal unaccompanied
A coon with guitar. Ms., n.d.   L'envoi, for unaccompanied vocal quartette (Rudyard Kipling). Ms., n.d.   Psalm 150: Praise ye the Lord, for mixed voices. Ms., n.d.   Music, thou queen of heaven, madrigal for vocal quartette. Ms., n.d.   Nunc dimittis, arr. for unaccompanied mixed voices. Ms., n.d.

2. Vocal with solo accompaniments
South African national anthem. Ms., 1909 (not in Jagger Library).   The hidden things, song (W. Beaumont). Stainer & Bell, London, 1925.   The bees' song (W. de la Mare). Elkin & Co., London, 1927.   Three songs (W. de la Mare). Elkin & Co., London, 1927.   Old Mother Hubbard, in the style of Handel. Paterson's Publications Ltd, 1929.   Adam lay I-bounden, song (old English words). Elkin & Co., London, 1931.   The jolly beggar, song (trad.). Elkin & Co., London, 1931.   The twa Corbies (anon.). Elkin & Co., London, 1931.   Castlepatrick (G.K. Chesterton). Elkin & Co., London, 1933.   The rolling English road (G.K. Chesterton). Elkin & Co., London, 1933.   The song of soldiers (W. de la Mare). Elkin & Co., London, 1933.   Who goes home (G.K. Chesterton). Elkin & Co., London, 1933.   Song from *The bad child's book of beasts* (Hilaire Belloc). Elkin & Co., London, 1935.   Cities and thrones and powers (Rudyard Kipling). Elkin & Co., London, 1937.   Cuckoo song (Rudyard Kipling). Elkin & Co., London, 1937.   The Queen's men (Rudyard Kipling). Elkin & Co., London, 1937.   Alice songs (Lewis Carroll). Elkin & Co., London, 1939.   Beautiful soup (Lewis Carroll). Elkin & Co., London, 1939.   Ruthless rhymes for heartless homes (Harry Graham). Elkin & Co., London, 1945.   Absence. Ms., n.d.   Alice in Wonderland, for voice and piano, in six scenes (E. Lewis Verne). Ms., n.d.   The battle hymn of democracy, with piano or organ. Ms., n.d.   A birthday (Christina Rossetti). Holograph, n.d.   Bravo! (F.E. Weatherby). Ms., n.d.   Christmas everywhere, carol for those at sea. Ms., n.d.   Come, landlord. Ms., n.d.   Cradle song, for medium voice. Ms., n.d.   The crown of memory (Natalie Hely-Hutchinson), comp. 22 Aug. 1910. Ms.   The daddy longlegs and the fly. Ms., n.d.   Gratiana dancing, in G (also F) (R. Lovelace). Ms., n.d.   Daniel (V. Lindsay). Ms., n.d.   Dead before death (C. Rossetti). Ms., n.d.   Dominus illuminatio mea (anon.). Ms., n.d.   Dreamland (C. Rossetti). Ms., n.d.   Vocal album, for female or boys' choir with piano (Blake, *Songs of*

innocence). Ms., n.d.: 1. The echoing green 2. The shepherd 3. Laughing song 4. Holy Thursday 5. The blossom 6. Cradle song. Heraclitus (William Covy). Ms., n.d. Home (Rupert Brooke). Ms., n.d. The horseman (Walter de la Mare). Ms., n.d. I leave this garden with a blood-red tulip. Ms., n.d. If in a throng . . . Ms., n.d. Invictus (W.E. Henley). Ms., n.d. It was a lordling's daughter (Shakespeare). Ms., n.d. Jock of Hazeldean (Sir Walter Scott). Ms., n.d. Lavender Ann. Ms., n.d. The little green orchid (W. de la Mare). Ms., n.d. The logical vegetarian (G.K. Chesterton). Ms., n.d.; also for voice and orchestra. The lost shoe. Ms., n.d. The march on Ivywood. Ms., n.d.; also for voice and orchestra. A mass, in C, in memory of his father. Ms., n.d. May dew (Sterndale Bennett). Ms., n.d.; also for voice and orchestra. The mocking fairy. Ms., n.d. More ruthless rhymes for heartless homes, 27 songs (Harry Graham). Ms., n.d. Mr Mandragon. Ms., n.d. My love, she's but a lassie girl (James Hogg). Ms., n.d.; also for voice, strings, woodwind and horn in F. My love is like a red, red rose (R. Burns). Ms., n.d.; also as four-part song with piano. Noah. Ms., n.d.; also for voice, strings, woodwind, brass and percussion. Now (Natalie Hely-Hutchinson). Ms., n.d. O love, they wrong thee much. Ms., n.d. The old stone house. Ms., n.d. A ripple song (Rudyard Kipling). Ms., n.d. The rolling road, in D. Ms., n.d. Ruthless rhymes for heartless homes, 21 songs (Harry Graham). Ms., n.d. The Saracen's head. Ms., n.d. Serenade, for voice and piano. Ms., n.d. Shir and the grasshopper, an Indian lullaby for mezzo-soprano (Rudyard Kipling, *Jungle Book*). Ms., n.d. Six Shakespeare songs. Ms., n.d. Song against grocers. Ms., n.d. A song cycle from *The follies*. Ms., n.d.: 1. Gwennie 2. Dan Everard 3. Our scene-painting brother 4. Ben 5. Morton and Burt. A song of enchantment. Ms., n.d. The song of Quoodle. Ms., n.d.; also for voice, strings, woodwind, brass and percussion. The song of shadows. Ms., n.d. The sweep and the daffodil. Ms., n.d. They would sell silks to me (from the *Arabian nights*). Ms., n.d. Three nonsense songs, with piano accompaniment (Edward Lear). Ms. (SABC music library), n.d.: 1. The owl and the pussycat 2. The table and the chair 3. The duck and the kangaroo. Two songs (Robert Herrick). Ms., n.d.: 1. To blossoms 2. Fair daffodils. The way through the woods (Rudyard Kipling). Ms., n.d. Who goes home? Ms., n.d. Wisdom. Ms., n.d.

3. Vocal with ensemble or orchestral accompaniment

The echoing green and other songs, for female chorus and strings (words from Blake's *Song of innocence*). Elkin & Co., London, 1932. Hearts and trumps, operetta (libretto by L. du Garde Peach). Elkin & Co., London, 1932. The unveiling, a play with music (Gwendolyn Downes). Elkin & Co., London, 1932. Auld Robin Gray, with orchestral accompaniment (Lady Anne Lindsay). Ms., n.d. Beggar on horseback, incidental music (G.S. Kaufman and M. Connelly), broadcast on 31 Jan. 1930. Ms., 17 items, of which the following are in the Jagger Library: 1. Jazz wedding march 2. Symphony 3-4. Pantomime 5. Cynthia 6. Jazz wedding march 7-8. Jazz symphony 16. Song 17. Pantomime The fairy flute, for mezzo-soprano, with flute, violin and viola. Ms., n.d. Deirdre of the sorrows, accompanied by chamber orchestra and harp (J.M. Synge). Ms., n.d. Dream song, in F, accompanied by strings, woodwind and horn. Ms., n.d. The house fairy, incidental music for solo voice, choir, strings and flute. Ms., n.d. I vow to thee, my country, for choir and orchestra (C. Spring Rice). Ms., n.d. Incidents in the life of my Uncle Arly, for voice, strings, woodwind, horn in F (E. Lear). Ms., n.d. The Lord is my Shepherd, for soprano, alto and strings. Ms., n.d.; also for mixed voices. The merry month of May, for 3 female voices and orchestra (T. Bekker). Ms., n.d. The mock doctor, incidental music for choir and strings (Henry Fielding). Ms., n.d. The Napoleon of Notting Hill, incidental music for choir and 4 trumpets (John Watt, from novel by G.K. Chesterton). Ms., n.d.　　On the death of Smet-Smet, arr. for choir, strings, piano and gong. Ms., n.d.　　Orchestral work with solo voice or choir (several pieces, probably from a Greek play). Ms., n.d.　　Precession, incidental music for voice, strings, oboe and 2 clarinets. (E.J. King Bull). Ms., n.d.　　The Quangle Wangle's hat, for voice, strings, woodwind and brass (Edward Lear). Ms., n.d.　　The rumour, incidental music for choir, orchestra and piano. Ms., n.d.　　Serenade, for voice, strings, brass and percussion. Ms., n.d.　　The way of love, for alto, 2 violas and cellos. Ms., n.d.

B. Instrumental

1. Solo

A field day, suite for piano. Elkin & Co., London, 1931.　　Air and variations, for piano (unfinished). Ms., n.d.　　Allegro alla marcia, for piano. Ms, n.d.　　Allegro non troppo, for piano. Ms., n.d.　　Canonic scherzo, for monochord. Ms., n.d.　　The "Early morning" polka, for piano; comp. 1908, publ. by Novello in *A child's thoughts*.　　Good shot!, for piano; comp. 1908, publ. by Novello in *A child's thoughts*.　　An impromptu, for piano, dedicated to his father. Ms., n.d.　　A little sonatine, for piano. Ms., n.d.　　Piano piece. Ms., n.d.　　Piano pieces (very early, unfinished). Ms., n.d.　　The river, for piano; comp. 1908, publ. by Novello in *A child's thoughts*, n.d.　　Sonata, for piano; comp. 1909, publ. as "Little sonatina" by Novello in *A child's thoughts*, n.d.　　Sonata for piano, dedicated to F.C. Faulkner, Esq. Ms, n.d.　　Sonate in F for piano, dedicated to his mother. Ms., 1915.　　A souvenir of Tchaikovsky, for piano. Ms., 1911.　　Spring-tide, for piano; comp. 1909, publ. by Novello in *A child's thoughts*, n.d.　　Three scherzos and a noval, for piano, dedicated to R.S.W. Dickinson. Ms., n.d.　　Vale, for piano. Ms., n.d.　　Valse caprice, for piano. Ms., n.d.　　Vivace, for piano. Ms., n.d.　　Without God we can do nothing, for organ. Ms., n.d.

2. Chamber music

Three fugal fancies, for string quartette or string orchestra. Elkin & Co., London, 1932. Bourrée, for violin and piano. Ms., n.d.　　Dance, for cello and piano. Ms., n.d.　　Three dances, for two pianos. Ms., n.d.　　Dead march, for violins, trombone and organ. Ms., n.d.　　Envoi, for violin and piano. Ms., n.d.　　Fairies' dance, for violin and piano. Ms., 1909.　　La fête joyeuse, for violin and piano; comp. 1909, publ. by Novello in *A child's thoughts*.　　Gavotte and rondo (J.S. Bach), arr. for violin and piano. Ms., n.d.　　Harvest song, for violin and piano. Ms., "in J.L.", 1909,　　Herzliche Grüsse, for violin and piano. Ms., n.d.　　Hoedown (The flop-eared mule and Redwin), for violin and piano. Ms., n.d.　　Idyll and diversions, for flutes, hobo, clarinet, bassoon, horn and piano. Ms., n.d.　　Irish lullaby, for violin and piano. Ms., n.d.　　A joyful return to home, for violin and piano. Ms., 1908.　　The Kimberley march, for violin and piano; comp. 1909, publ. by Novello in *A child's thoughts*, n.d.　　March, for wind instruments and drum. Ms., n.d.　　Zwei Menuette, for violin and piano. Ms., n.d.　　Three minuets, for violin and piano, dedicated to Miss King. Ms., n.d.　　Ombra mai fu, arr. for violin and 2 cellos. Ms., n.d.　　Piano quintet. No detail.　　Piece for two pianos, for 4 hands. Ms., n.d.　　Piece for violin and piano. Ms., n.d.　　Quartet, for piano and strings; comp. 1909, publ. by Novello in *A child's thoughts*. Quartet, for piano and strings. Ms., June 1909.　　Quartet no. 1, for piano and strings. Publ. by Novello in *A child's thoughts*, n.d.　　Romance, for viola and piano. Ms., n.d.　　Romance, for violin and piano, dedicated to Sebastian Barl. Ms., n.d.　　Romance, for violin and piano; publ. by Novello in *A child's thoughts*, n.d.　　Romance, for violin and piano, publ. by Novello in *A child's thoughts*, n.d.　　Romance, for violin and piano, dedicated to his father; comp. 1909, publ. by Novello in *A child's thoughts*, n.d.　　Rondo, for flute and piano. Ms., 1917.　　Sarabando, for violin and piano. Ms., n.d.   Scherzo, for string quartette. Ms., n.d.   A scherzo-mazurka, for violin and piano (unfinished). Ms., n.d.   Serenade, for violin and piano. Ms., n.d.   Sonate in C minor, for violin and piano, dedicated to Mr Lewis Bruce. Ms., n.d.   Sonate for viola and piano. No detail.   Sonatine, for two pianos. Ms., n.d.   Song of sleep, for violin and piano. Ms., Nov. 1908.   Swing song, for violin and piano. Ms., 1909.   Theme and variations, for string quartette. Ms., n.d.   The unknown warrior, for viola and piano. Ms., n.d.

3. Orchestra

The young idea, rhapsody for piano and orchestra. Elkin & Co., London, 1931.   Andante and variations on a French theme by Schubert, arr. for small orchestra. Ms., n.d.   Carol symphony. No detail.   Comedy overture, for small orchestra. Ms., n.d.   Concertino violino, for string orchestra. Ms., n.d.   Concerto, for violin and piano. Ms., 1909.   Concerto, for 2 violins and piano; comp. 1908, publ. by Novello in *A child's thoughts*.   Two dances, for string orchestra. Ms., n.d.   Fugal fancies, for string orchestra. Ms., n.d.   March in C minor, for orchestra. Ms., n.d.; also for two pianos.   Medley, arr. for strings and percussion instruments. Ms., n.d.: 1. The little red caboose behind the train   2. She'll be coming round the mountain.   Parnesius, overture for orchestra, in F. Ms., n.d.   Serenade, for orchestra. Ms., n.d.   Symphony, for small orchestra. Paterson's Publications Ltd., n.d.   A symphony in F major, for piano (unfinished), dedicated to E.M. Browne. Ms., n.d.

4. Incidental music

Anthony and Cleopatra, for string quartette and trumpet in C. Ms., n.d.   *Camouflage* (film music). Ms., n.d.   *Castle of the king* (at a broadcast speech). Ms., n.d.   *The city,* for orchestra and harp (A. Dunning). Ms., n.d.   *Excavators* (film music). Ms., n.d.   *Macbeth,* for strings and percussion instruments. Ms., n.d.   *St Joan,* for strings, 2 trumpets and organ, from pieces in the *Fitzwilliam Virginal Book.* Ms., n.d.

BIBLIOGRAPHY
Burke's peerage 1939 (article on Earls of Donoughmore).   *Grove's dictionary of music and musicians,* 5th ed., 1958.   Van der Merwe, F.Z.: *Suid-Afrikaanse musiekbibliografie, 1787–1952.* J.L. van Schaik, Pretoria, 1958.   – W.D.S. (amplified)

HENNING, COSMO GRENVILLE, *20 April 1932 in Uitenhage; now (1979) in Durban. Director, Documentation Centre for Indian Culture, University of Westville.

Introduced to pianoforte playing by his mother, Henning was instructed by Sydney Jackson-Lee** at the Grey High School until December 1948. The next year he entered for the degree of B.Mus. at Rhodes University, but in 1951 he interrupted his study to acquire the diplomas LTCL, L.Mus.TCL and FTCL at Trinity College. By the end of 1954 he had been successful and had also completed a part of the requirements for the degree of B.Mus. at the London University. After teaching in a temporary capacity at various schools in England, he returned to South Africa in 1956 to become a music teacher at Dale College in King William's Town. The next year he introduced Music as a school subject at Graeme College in Grahamstown and again entered for B.Mus., now at UNISA. During 1959 he taught at the Durban Boys' High School, where he created and conducted a chamber orchestra, and in 1960 to 1961 he was the teacher of music at the Dirkie Uys High School in the same city. — The year 1962 saw

Henning back in England, where he got married and started at Sheffield University on his research for a dissertation on opera buffa, but in 1963 he was appointed a lecturer at the Graaff Reinet Training College. He taught there until 1968, also conducting the College Choir, i.a. in a performance of Fauré's *Requiem* with the support of an amateur orchestra. During these years he resumed his work on opera buffa at the University of Pretoria and in 1965 he was awarded the degree of M.Mus. with distinction. Immediately after, he commenced his research on the cultural history of Graaff Reinet for which he was awarded the D.Phil. degree in 1971. He had resigned from his position in Graaff Reinet in 1968 to become a temporary lecturer at the University of Pretoria. — Cosmo Henning's connection with the HSRC started in 1970 when he was appointed research officer of the *South African Music Encyclopedia,* with the history of music in the Eastern Province (with special reference to Port Elizabeth) as a major project. In 1974 he was promoted and became Head of the former Music Documentation Centre of the HSRC. In February 1979 he resigned to take up a similar position at the Indian University in Westville. — Since 1975 he had been the organist and choir-master of the Methodist Church in Brooklyn (Pretoria), and since 1974 he had acted as vice-chairman of the Pretoria Africana Society, editing the first two Yearbooks of the Society.

WORKS

Vocal

Song cycle for soprano and pianoforte: 16 songs from *A child's garden of verses* (R.L. Stevenson), awarded a prize in the Bothner Competition, 1953. Ms.   Met elke môre van 'n nuwe dag, school song Dirkie Uys High School, Durban (P. Nel). Ms., 1961.

PUBLICATIONS AND WRITINGS

A school history of music. Juta & Co., Cape Town, 1963.   *The origin and development of opera buffa up to 1800.* M.Mus. dissertation, UP, 1965.   S. Le Roux Marais. *Lantern,* Pretoria, 1965.   *Répertoire internationale de littérature musicale* (RILM), no. 1081/1082. Bärenreiter Verlag, 1969.   Thematic metamorphoses in *Don Giovanni. The Music Review* 30/1, Feb. 1969.   Verslag en standpunt oor die FAK se opvolgkongres oor Skoolmusiek en Skoolsang. *SASMT Newsletter* 25, Pretoria, 1969.   Where comic opera was born. *Opera* 20/4, London, Apr. 1969.   Boere-krygsgevangenes in Ceylon. *Militaria* 4/3, 1974.   Jan Orrelis – die wonder van die Paarl. *Tydskrif vir Geesteswetenskappe* 14/3, Pretoria, Sept. 1974.   De Boeren muziekgeselschap in Ceylon (1900–1902). *Humanitas* 3/1, Pretoria, 1975.   Die eerste Afrikaanse oratoria. *Musicus* 3/1, 1975.   De Strever, 'n Afrikaanse koerant in Ceylon. Africana Society of Pretoria *Yearbook* I, 1975.   *Graaff-Reinet, a cultural history (1786–1886).* T.V. Bulpin, Cape Town, 1975.   Nancy de Villiers. *Musicus* 3/2, 1975.   The music and manuscripts of J.S. de Villiers. Africana Society of Pretoria *Yearbook* I, 1975.   The National Documentation Centre for Music. *Ars Nova* 7/2, 1975.   Music from the Anglo-Boer War. Africana Society of Pretoria *Yearbook* II, 1976.   Philip McLachlan (in coll. with G. Olivier). *Ars Nova* 8/1, 1976.   The introduction of the Tonic Sol-fa system into the Eastern Cape. *Musicus* IV/1, 1976.   Research on South African music history and its application to the teaching of music history in the Republic. *Ars Nova* 9/1, 1977.   Some notes on regional history research. *Contree* I/1, Pretoria, Jan. 1977.   The dawn of Union – the story of our early national anthems and patriotic songs. *Musicus* V/1, 1977.   Totius en musiek met betrekking tot die Psalmberyming en die Afrikaanse kunslied. *Africana Society of Pretoria Yearbook* III, 1977.   Contributions to the *South African biographical dictionary,* parts III & IV, HSRC,

Pretoria 1977. Contributions to the *Afrikaanse Kultuuralmanak* issued by the FAK, 1978. Contributions on South African music to various South African newspapers.

BIBLIOGRAPHY
The international who's who in music and musician's directory, 8th ed. Melrose Press, Cambridge, 1977. *The international directory of scholars and specialists in African studies,* Brandeis University, Waltham, USA, 1977. *Directory of international biography* XV (1978-79). Cambridge. Wie weet wat? *SA register of conservation and cultural history specialists.* Simon van der Stel Foundation, 1978.

SOURCES
Beeld: 17 Jan. 1974. *Daily Dispatch:* 9 Apr. 1970. *EP Herald:* 9 Sept. 1970; 23 Dec. 1974; 6 Aug. 1975. *Evening Post:* 10 Aug. 1970; 19 Dec. 1974. *Graaff-Reinet Advertiser:* 6 Mar. 1967; 16 Mar. 1967; 16 Oct. 1967. *Hoofstad:* Nov. 1974; 24 Feb. 1977. *Natal Witness:* 19 Sept. 1975. *Die Oosterlig:* 9 Sept. 1970. *Pretoria News:* 12 Nov. 1974; 29 July 1975; 12 Aug. 1975. *The Star:* 9 Dec. 1975.

– Ed.

HERMANNSBURG Evangelical Lutheran Church (Hermannsburg)

HERRICK, DEAN, * in Chicago, USA; living in Johannesburg in 1962. Organist and businessman.

Herrick played the organ in cinemas until 1930, when the "talkies" were first introduced, and only a few of the larger radio stations still had cinema organs. He first performed on the electronic organ in public at the Bismarck Hotel, Chicago, in 1935. — Two years later (1937) Herrick was sent to South Africa as solo organist by MGM, whom he left in 1940 to join 20th Century Fox. He opened his own radio production studio (Herrick-Merrill) in 1946, and has become well-known through radio broadcasts as an organist of light music. He became a South African citizen in 1948.

WORKS
With all my love (Eric Parry). L.E. Joseph & Co. Ltd, 1944. Ghost love (W. Monte Doyle). Southern Music, Johannesburg, 1953. Kathy, musical comedy with South African background. Ms., n.d. Kersfeeslied. Ms., n.d. My wintersdroom. Ms., n.d. To say goodbye to you. Ms., n.d.

BIBLIOGRAPHY
Van der Merwe, F.Z.: *Suid-Afrikaanse musiekbibliografie, 1787-1952.* J.L. van Schaik, Pretoria, 1958. *Who's who of Southern Africa.* Argus Printing & Publishing Co. Ltd., Johannesburg, 1960.

– Ed.

HERRING BEQUEST, INSTITUTE OF THE. In 1894 Miss Elizabeth Herring and her brother, William, both about thirty years old and members of a musical family consisting of 15 brothers and 12 sisters, arrived in Cape Town from England. With

193

them came a huge variety of heirlooms, such as jewels, crystal glass, Chinese porcelain, silver, antique furniture and musical instruments. Professionally William was a bank clerk, but he could give good account of himself on the viola. Elizabeth again, was a violinist who gave lessons on her instrument and was an asset to chamber music groups. Apart from teaching privately, she was employed at the Stellenbosch Conservatoire in 1912. With this background it follows naturally that their home in Green Point, called "Oakdene", soon became a popular venue for musicians wishing to indulge in their art. — Elizabeth died on the last day of 1926, but shortly before, she had decided to catalogue her share of the family treasures and to bequeath the collection to the public of Cape Town. Included in the catalogue were a cello, three violins, a banjo, four pianos, books on music and printed music. William, who survived her until 13 December 1929, added his share to her bequest and in 1930 the whole collection was officially handed over to the mayor of Cape Town, the Rev. A.J.S. Lewis. "Oakdene" became an Institute with its own secretary/librarian and has since that time been of service, not only to the musical life of Cape Town, but also to persons from far beyond its boundaries. The Institute has a number of studios available for musicians, as well as a small hall suitable for chamber music, a lending library of printed music and space for the safe storage of musical instruments at a low cost.

SOURCE
SAMT: 3, Nov. 1932.

– M.H.

HERRING, E   Herring Bequest Institute

HERRLE, HANS   Windhoek 3

HERTSLET, FRANCES (NéE LILFORD), *near Lady Grey; °26 December 1956 in East London. Composer and pianist.

During the 1914–1918 war Frances Hertslet served as a nurse. Previously she had received a gold medal for the highest achievement in nursing in the Union of South Africa while practising her profession at the Frere Hospital in East London. Already an accomplished musician, she gave a number of recitals in East London, and in 1930 went to England, where she obtained the LRAM and ARCM diplomas (1934). On her return to South Africa, Frances settled in Bloemfontein, where she formed a Philharmonic Society and gave lessons in pianoforte playing – after 1936 in collaboration with Sydney Rosenbloom.** In 1943 she returned to East London, and for twelve years gave lecture-recitals to school-children under the auspices of the Education Department; tours were undertaken with Sydney Rosenbloom, who assisted in the venture. In 1952 she in turn assisted Rosenbloom in a series of master classes in pianoforte and composition, which he presented at the East London Technical College.

WORKS
Note: Frances Hertslet composed much more music than the following list suggests, but the manuscripts of her work have not been traced.

Cradle song, for pianoforte. Bosworth & Co., London, 1938.   Lantern and moths, for pianoforte. Bosworth & Co., London, 1938.   Four sea idylls, for pianoforte. Bosworth & Co., London, 1939: 1. Seafoam and bubbles   2. Sandpipes on the beach   3. Sea murmers   4. Ebb-tide.   Polonaise in G minor, for pianoforte. Ms., 1947.

BIBLIOGRAPHY
Van der Merwe, F.Z.: *Suid-Afrikaanse musiekbibliografie, 1787–1952.* J.L. van Schaik, Pretoria, 1958.

SOURCES
Daily Dispatch: 21 June 1947; 11 July 1952; 1 Jan. 1957.   *SAMT:* 27, Dec. 1944.
                                                                              – E.H.S.

HERZ, H.   Theatres and Concert Halls IV/2

HESS, H.   Grahamstown 7, King William's Town 14

HESTER, NICOLAAS EMIL ERNST, *25 May 1882 in Amsterdam; °21 October 1918 in Pretoria. Chemist, choir-master and cellist.

Since his early years Emil Hester had demonstrated a keen interest in music, and eventually received tuition in violin, pianoforte and cello in Amsterdam. When he emigrated to South Africa in 1903, he joined the orchestra of the Johannesburg Philharmonic Society as a cellist, but by 1904 he had settled in Pretoria where he was appointed a chemist at the Koedoe Pharmacy. In later years he was also employed at the Hollandsche Pharmacy. — Emil Hester, together with Charles Israel** (violin), E. Amorison (violin), A. Wilmot (viola) and A.G. Quayle** (violin), often formed string trios and quartettes which played at concerts of the Hollandsch Mannenkoor** and the Christelike Sangvereniging Asaf.** He was the choir-master of the Hollandsch Mannenkoor between 1911 and 1915 and in 1914 he also became the conductor of the Pretoria Amateur Operatic and Dramatic Society. Under his leadership the choir and orchestra gave successful performances of *The belle of New York, A Chinese honeymoon, The silver slipper, Pinkie and the fairies* and *Snow White.* — Hester died in the influenza epidemic, four months after he had been seriously injured in a motorcar accident (June 1918).

BIBLIOGRAPHY
Vermeulen, Elizabeth: *Die musieklewe in Pretoria tussen 1902 en 1926.* M.Mus. dissertation, UP, 1967.
                                                                              – E.Ve.

HEUSCHNEIDER, K   Higher Educational Institutions I/3

HEWARD, LESLIE HAYS, *8 December 1897 at Liversedge, Yorkshire; °3 May 1943 in Birmingham. Conductor and composer.

HEWARD

At the age of eight Heward was acting as assistant to his father, an organist at the Lower Wyke Moravian Church. In 1910 he became a chorister at Manchester Cathedral, receiving his education in the Choir School, and four years later he became their assistant organist, also filling the post of organist and choirmaster at St Andrew's Church, Ancoats, Manchester. He gained the ARCO diploma at the age of 16 and in 1917 he won a composition scholarship to the RCM, after which he became music master at Eton College and organist of Holy Trinity Church, Windsor. From 1920 to 1921 he was Director of Music at Westminster School in London. His career as conductor started with the first performance of Maeterlinck's *The betrothal* at the Gaiety Theatre, London, which led to his appointment as a regular conductor for the British National Opera Company (1922). — In 1924, already a considerable figure in the musical life of England, he consecutively accepted the posts of Musical Director to a broadcasting organisation and then of conductor to the Cape Town City Orchestra** in succession to Theo Wendt,** who had occupied the position since the inception of the orchestra in 1914. In spite of its small numbers (30 permanent players), the orchestra possessed fine instrumentalists, especially in the woodwind section; and under Heward's direction music in the Mother City rose to new heights, culminating in the Beethoven Centenary Festival, organised and conducted by him in 1927. — In 1925 Heward made history by taking the orchestra on a tour of England, including a performance in the South African Pavilion at the Wembley Exhibition, and a command performance at Buckingham Palace. Although it was well received by musicians and critics, attendances were bad, and after only 25 of the 50 performances planned, the orchestra had to be recalled. Financially the tour was a great disappointment. — Leslie Heward decided to return to England in 1927, as a result of poor health and the strain of continual financial crises in the orchestra. In England he rose to eminence, rejoining the National Opera Company and subsequently (1930) becoming conductor of the City of Birmingham Orchestra, which he fashioned into a first-rate ensemble. Concurrently, from 1934 to 1939, he conducted the BBC Midland Orchestra, and was also invited to conduct in Stockholm, Copenhagen, Leningrad (1936) and the United States and Canada (1938). During the War he was conductor of the Hallé Orchestra. In his later years he found no time to exercise the considerable talent for composition which had originally brought him to the fore.

WORKS

A. Vocal

1. Songs

The rosebud, song. Ms., 1913.   Five songs, for baritone. Ms., 1916(?):   1. Requiescat   2. The death knell   3. The way that lovers use   4. From a railway train   5. The cow.   Two songs, for baritone. Ms., 1918:   1. Looking-glass river   2. There is a lady sweet and kind.   Two folksong settings. Ms., 1918:   1. John, come kiss me now   2. George Kiddler's oven.   Go, lovely rose, song for tenor. Ms., 1918(?).   Two songs, for soprano. Ms., 1920:   1. I had a dove   2. April.   The dark chateau, song for soprano and small orchestra. Ms., 1920.   Seven children's songs. Ms., 1920:   1. The owl and the pussycat   2. Polly   3. Some one   4. From a railway carriage   5. The dunce   6. The cupboard   7. A lullaby.   My flocks feed not, song for tenor and small orchestra. Ms., 1921.   Song for baritone. Ms., 1921.   Song for tenor and piano. Ms., 1925.   Trees, song with orchestra. Ms., n.d.   Two Chinese songs, with orchestra. Ms., c. 1935: 1. The little lady of Ch'ing-Ch'i 2. Plucking the rushes. A cradle song, with orchestra. Ms., c. 1937. Little Jesus, song with orchestra. Ms., 1942.

2. Choral
A morning and evening service in B flat, for SATB. Ms., 1916. Four anthems. Ms., 1916. The witches' sabbath, part song for unaccompanied voices. Ms., 1919. Two-part songs, for female chorus and piano. Ms., 1919: 1. Over hill, over dale 2. Ye spotted snakes.

3. Part songs
Bunches of grapes, part song. Ms., 1912. Hymn 699, A. & M., 2nd supplement, 1916. The return of spring, trio for soprano, baritone and piano. Ms., 1918. Two motets, for unaccompanied voices. Ms., 1919: 1. O Lord turn not Thy face from me 2. Stars of the morning. Love is a sickness, part song for unaccompanied voices. Ms., 1919.

4. Opera
Hamlet (Shakespeare), unfinished opera. Ms., 1916. Peer Gynt (Ibsen), unfinished opera. Ms., 1922.

B. Instrumental

1. Solo
Piano sonata. Ms., 1910. Sunday morning, for organ. Ms., 1916(?). Variations on an Irish theme. Ms., 1926. La mora, for piano. Ms., n.d. Two hymns without words. Ms., n.d.

2. Chamber music
Variations, for diverse orchestral instruments and piano. Ms., 1911. Variations and fugue, for two pianos on an original theme. Ms., 1915(?). String quartet in A minor. Ms., 1918. Recitative, air and scherzo, for flute, oboe, violin, viola and cello. Ms., 1921.

3. Orchestra
Irish tune, for strings. Ms., 1916(?). Two movements of a dance suite, for full orchestra. Ms., 1920: 1. Revel 2. Quodlibet. Suid-Afrikaanse piekniekliedjies, for orchestra. Ms., 1925. Elegiac rhapsody, for small orchestra. Ms., 1926. Nocturne, for small orchestra. Ms., n.d.

4. Incidental music
Music for the film *The loves of Robert Burns*. Ms., 1928.

BIBLIOGRAPHY
Blom, Eric (Ed.): *Leslie Heward – a memorial volume*. J.M. Dent & Sons Ltd, Oxford, 1944.

SOURCE
Heward, L.H.: My three years in South Africa. *The Outspan,* 25 Mar. 1927.

– W.S.

HEWARTSON, HUGH THOMAS, *12 August 1914 in Germiston; resident at Voortrekkerhoogte in 1967. Clarinettist and Director of Music to the South African Army.

Hewartson received his initial musical training from his parents, and later continued with clarinet study in East London, under W.E.H. Kealey.** During these years he was a member of the East London Municipal Orchestra conducted by Franz Moeller,** and of the combined bands of the Kaffrarian Rifles and Comrades, conducted by W.E.H. Kealey. At the East London eisteddfodau of 1930 and 1931, he was awarded gold medals for his clarinet playing. — In February 1933, Hewartson joined the South African Police Band in Pretoria, receiving instruction in theoretical subjects from Col. L.P. Bradley,** the conductor of the band, in clarinet from George Spencer and in cello from Betty Pack.** He left the Police Band in July 1938, having served as solo clarinettist and as principal cellist of the string section for the previous two years. After a period as principal clarinettist and saxophonist to African Theatres, he joined the South African Permanent Force Band in 1939, serving throughout the Second World War in North Africa and Italy as solo clarinettist and chief instructor under Capt. W.E.H. Kealey and E.A. Kealey. In October 1945, he joined the SABC Symphony Orchestra in Johannesburg as principal clarinettist. On several occasions he performed as concert soloist with this orchestra and he has a number of first South African broadcast performances of clarinet works to his credit. — On rejoining the South African Army Band in 1948, as solo clarinettist and chief instructor, he studied conducting and military band orchestration for the next seven years under the guidance of Capt. E.A. Kealey.** He was appointed assistant conductor to the Director of Music in May 1956, becoming Director, with the rank of Captain, in October 1961. He was promoted to Major in 1965, and to Commandant in 1966. Commandant Hewartson is the first Director of Music in the South African Defence Force to be awarded the Southern Cross Medal for services to music in the Army.

– Ed.

HEWITT, J.B. Potchefstroom 2

HEYMAN, PEGGY ·Johannesburg III/2

HEYNE, A.H. Evangelical Lutheran Church in the Cape, Organs 1(iv)

HIDDINGH HALL CONCERTS E. Chisholm, Higher Educational Institutions I/1

HIGGS, G.A. King William's Town 9, 10

HIGHER EDUCATIONAL INSTITUTIONS, MUSIC AT

I. UNIVERSITIES
1. Bloemfontein: UOFS
2. Cape Town: SACM
3. Grahamstown: Rhodes University: RU
4. Johannesburg: UWits
5. Port Elizabeth: UPE
6. Potchefstroom: PU for CHE
7. Pretoria: (i) Music Academy and Department of Music: UP
             (ii) (a) Department of Musicology: UNISA
                  (b) Music examinations in South Africa: UNISA

8. Stellenbosch: Conservatoire of Music: US
9. Pietermaritzburg and Durban
10. Western Cape
11. Zululand

II. TEACHERS' TRAINING COLLEGES

1. Johannesburg College of Education
2. Goudstad Teachers' Training College, Johannesburg
3. Potchefstroom Teachers' Training College

III. TECHNICAL COLLEGES (TECHNIKONS)

1. East London
2. Pretoria College for Advanced Technical Education, now called Technicon
3. Rustenburg, Conservatoire of Music

IV. PRIVATE INSTITUTIONS

Pretoria, Conservatoire of Music

I. UNIVERSITIES

1. Bloemfontein: University of the Orange Free State: UOFS

Although the Department of Music at the University College of the OFS (University of the Orange Free State since 1950) was only instituted in 1946, it had been possible to take Music as a subject in the Faculty of Arts under the aegis of the Faculty of Education. The brothers Proff. W.F.C. and J.G.A. Arndt kept such interest in music as there was alive by forming a music society for lovers of the art in 1934, and by holding musical evenings at their homes. In 1945 a committee consisting of Proff. H. van der Merwe Scholtz (Rector), Ross, Kok, Britz and Arndt was formed to consider the creation of a Music Department. The committee found that the most practical way to establish the Department was to take over completely the existing Free State Music School of Mr D.J. Roode.** Mr Roode was to act as Head of the Department with the status of Professor and as Head of the UCOFS Music School; the department was to fall under the Faculty of Arts and tuition was to be accorded to matriculated students who chose music for B.A. and B.Mus. degrees, to students who wished to enter for the theoretical, certificate and licenciate examinations of UNISA, or other institutions, and to anyone else who wished to practise music as an art. — In 1946 the Department was launched with six students who had chosen Music as a major for the B.A. degree, while the Music School could boast of 300 students of whom half were matriculated. The first student to obtain the B.A. degree in Music was Mr Gradwell of Bloemfontein. Apart from Prof. Roode, the Department had Mr F.J. van der Merwe and Mr O.A. Karstel** on the staff. Miss Henriette Roussouw, Mrs F. Roode, Mrs J. Hadlow, Mrs M. Blignaut and Mr Victor Pohl** were among those who taught at the School. — The provision of classrooms and practice facilities was initially a major problem. After much negotiation and vacillation, it was decided that the university would erect the necessary buildings on its campus. Until these were completed, the Music Department was housed in four bungalows of the President Steyn Hostel; after the completion of the Conservatoire in 1949, these continued to serve as practice rooms. Understandably, the curriculum had not yet been very clearly defined in 1946. — In 1948 the need was felt to improve the purely academic training and the following year Dr A.J.C. Koole** was brought from the Netherlands to bolster the musicological aspects . Dr Koole was not only a brilliant musicologist, but also an outstanding practical musician who did much to promote musical life in Bloemfontein. His departure for the USA in 1964 was a blow to the department. In 1950 the University awarded its first B.Mus. degrees to Mr G.W. Koornhof and Miss A. Haarhoff, and, also in that year, the requirements for the M.Mus. degree were clarified. — An important step was taken in 1954 when the Department of Music was entirely separated from the Music School, where students who were not enrolled at the University were receiving tuition. Thus reconstituted, the staff of the Department included, apart from Prof. Roode, Mr Van der Merwe, Dr Koole, Mrs Kautzky (appointed in 1951) and Mr Koornhof. Four years later Prof. Roode resigned his position and in April 1959 he was succeeded by Prof. Leo G. Quayle,** who remained in the post until 1964 when Prof. Chris Swanepoel** became the Head. —During the incumbency of Prof. Swanepoel (1965– 1977) the Department grew very swiftly: the degrees and diplomas offered by the University and the regulations governing these certificates were radically revised, in August the first part of a new building for the Music Department was inaugurated, the Free State String Quartet** was assimilated into the staff (1966), Dr J.J.K. Kloppers** was appointed to the staff on 1 May and the enrolment showed a distinct increase year by year. The facilities were eventually completed in 1977 and include a concert hall, called the Odeion, with accommodation for 400 listeners, a concert organ of 34 registers, a harpsichord and a concert grand pianoforte. The hall is used for rehearsals, choral and orchestral concerts, recitals of chamber music and by visiting and local artists. The complex also houses an open-air theatre seating 227 people, a rehearsal room for choral groups, 3 large lecture rooms each adapted to 64 students, a lecture room seating 30 students, another one for music education, 32 studios and 52 practising rooms. The lecture rooms are equipped with all the necessary facilities, pianos, overhead projectors and sound apparatus such as tape recorders, playback amplifiers and speakers and cassette recorders. Other facilities include 8 pipe organs (five with mechanical traction), 43 grand pianos, 68 uprights, epidiascopes and a slide projector. The four-year B.Mus. course is offered in four channels – Musicology, Musical Theory, Music Education and Practical Music- which lead to Honours courses with a similar division, followed by the Master's and Doctor's degrees restricted to Musicology only. Besides these possibilities, the Department also offers tuition leading to a B.A. (Musicology) with the complementary Honours, Master's and Doctor's degrees. Finally a four-year UOFS Teacher's Diploma course is offered which runs parallel to the B.Mus. course. As an essential facility the Department is equipped with a spacious library/discotheque with modern listening equipment and an extensive collection of reference works, musicological and theoretical books, periodicals, sheet music and gramophone records. — Professor Swanepoel retired from the University at the end of 1977 and was succeeded in 1978 by Prof. J.H. Potgieter** who had served on the staff since 1977. Prof. Kloppers resigned in 1976 and was succeeded by Prof. C.L. Venter in 1977.** Other lecturers who had been in the service of this department were

Jan Coetzee** (1961–1976) and Prof. Pierre de Groote**. Prof. J.L.K. Human** (1961–), Mrs Nettie Immelman, Mr Derek Ochse (1979–), Mr John Wille, Mr Ernst Conradie (also conductor of the University Choir), Mrs Dolly Heiberg** and Margaret van der Post are a number of the present members of the lecturing staff. From 1977 to 1982 Prof. G.G. Cillié** taught in the church music department. — Five students of the Department have been awarded overseas bursaries and since 1952 ten more have played concertos with the symphony orchestras of Durban, Johannesburg, CAPAB and the National Symphony Orchestra of the SABC. Of the staff members, Prof. Roode was active, from the Department's beginning, in training a choir which gave annual performances of an oratorio or a large choral work. Their performances included *Die skepping, Elijah, Messias* and parts of *Tannhäuser.* The Free State String Quartet enhanced musical life in the town with public concerts, morning concerts at schools and Sunday afternoon concerts in the hall of the Museum. After Prof. Chris Swanepoel's founding of a University Choir in 1966, Bloemfontein and the University have had the privilege of hearing a variety of oratorio performances, including the *Johannes-passie,* the *Duitse requiem, Messias,* the *Phantasy for choir, piano and orchestra* by Beethoven and Hubert du Plessis'** *Suid-Afrika: nag en daeraad.* Among the students who have excelled, are Derik van der Merwe,** G.W.F. Koornhof,** M. Koornhof,** Japie Human, Niel Immelman and Ernst van Biljon, who occupy posts at universities and conservatoires.

– J.J.K.K. and J.H.P.

2. University of Cape Town: South African College of Music: SACM

The S.A. College of Music was officially opened by the Mayor of Cape Town on 20 January 1910. The register shows that 33 students enrolled when the College opened on the first floor of the premises of The Bank of Africa, now Barclays Bank, in Strand Street. — The preliminary prospectus issued in 1909 contains an impressive list of patrons and mentions the names of the first members of the College Council. The Chairman was W. Duncan Baxter;** then follow the names of a number of university professors and of the musicians Mme Apolline Niay,** Mrs Griffith Vincent,** Dr Barrow-Dowling,** Frank Holt and G. Denholm-Walker.** Apolline Niay acted as Secretary and Treasurer. "Had it not been for her", wrote Prof. W.H. Bell,** in the *SACM Quarterly* for January 1922, "there is no doubt in my mind that the College would never have survived the year of its birth". The first council members may be said to be the founders of the College, but Apolline Niay-Darroll has always been looked upon as the prime mover in its foundation. — The first years of the College were financially difficult; the founders had considerable difficulty in raising R800, which was the estimated annual cost of running the College in those times. The position improved radically in 1912, when the Cape Provincial Administration gave the institution an annual grant, while obtaining a measure of control. The Superintendent of Education at that time, Dr (later Sir) Thomas Muir had a great deal to do with the successful conclusion of this transaction. With its financial future assured, the Council managed to obtain the services of William Henry Bell of the Royal Academy of Music, who became its first director and guided the destinies of the college for the next 23 years. Of him, Colin Taylor** has said: "There can be no doubt that Bell was the right man in the right place at the right time, for he was of the stuff pioneers are made of: bold, optimistic, tireless and resilient". By 1914, the enrolment of students had increased to 69 and new, more extensive accommodation was found in a former hotel in Stalplein. In that year Bell also formed the College Orchestra, which has been maintained since then, and eventually provided the conclusive argument for an extension of the College activities in the direction of ballet and opera. — The idea of incorporating the College in the University of Cape Town, had never really been lost sight of. A decisive step was taken by the university in 1920, when degree courses in music were instituted and Bell was appointed Professor of Music. Three more years of preparation were followed in 1923 by the final incorporation of the College in the University and the creation of a Faculty of Music with Bell as its first Dean. It is still the only music faculty in South Africa. In 1924 the University bought a number of properties, including the home of the Struben family in Rosebank and the following year the College moved from Stalplein to its new home in Strubenholme. It has remained there, with extensions, until the present time. Strubenholme was originally built as a villa, and although adapted to the needs of a music college, it had many shortcomings of which a lack of sufficient space and of a sound-proofing system were the chief. In 1974 the University completed a large extension of facilities which enabled the training to be conducted under more ideal circumstances. The new building has been designed as an extension of the existing building with which it is connected by means of a broad passage, so that the academic and practical departments still function as a unit. The new block contains 60 practise rooms and 40 studios for musical instruction, equipped with 60 grand pianos and 2 practise organs. The opera-school now has its own quarters, including separate facilities for make-up, changing rooms and a commodious rehearsal room. Then there is a small hall for recitals and a large studio for ensemble work. Finally provision has also been made for modern musical improvements in the form of a well-equipped electronic studio where programmed sound, experiments in composition and the preparation of examples for class work, acoustical lectures and school music can be carried out. The Music Library, known as the W.H. Bell Library, has also been moved to the new building and is now situated between the old and new sections in a position where it can be of service to both the academic and the practical sections. — Under Bell's direction, the College continued to grow steadily. Speech training and Elocution had been one of the brightest departments of the College in its pre-university days when it operated under the guidance of Minna Freund and a galaxy of enthusiastic assistants, including future theatre personalities such as Marda Vanne ('Scrappy' van Hulstein) and the British actress, Cassilis. After its incorporation, it was felt that speech training was a necessity, especially in the Department of Education, and the faculty was extended to include a new Department of Speech and Drama, which flourished under the guidance of Ruth Peffers (1931–1945) and Rosalie van der Gucht (1943–?). After 1931 an old chemistry laboratory in Orange Street was converted into the Little Theatre** to provide an intimate venue for this department's activities, as well as for opera. A year before his retirement, Prof. Bell invited Miss Dulcie Howes,** a London-trained dancer and choreographer and a member of Pavlova's Ballet Company, to form a ballet school in Cape Town. The University Ballet** first appeared in the Little Theatre in November 1934 and performed there regularly until 1949. — When Bell retired in 1935, the SA College of Music was a comprehensive and well-equipped music school. He was succeeded by Prof. Stewart Deas, who had graduated under Sir Donald Tovey at Edinburgh University and had been a pupil of Weingartner for conducting. During the three years under his direction, he improved the standard of the orchestra, developed chamber music, ballet and opera, but he left in 1938 to become a music critic in Edinburgh and, at a later stage, Professor of Music at Sheffield University. Prof. Eric Grant, a former piano teacher at the Royal Academy of Music in London, guided the College through the war years (1939–1945) and was in turn succeeded by another pupil of Donald Tovey, Dr Erik Chisholm.** — Prof. Chisholm was an exceptionally enterprising, widely experienced musician, and an eminent and fluent composer, who had been prominent in Scotland, Canada and the Far East. He was a brilliant organiser with a comprehensive knowledge of music and extended the activities of the College in all directions. Chisholm reorganised the College staff, creating twelve new full-time appointments; extended the faculty curriculum from 32 to 75 courses, adding new degrees and diplomas; and organised student recitals and tours of the University Opera Company which took them to other parts of the country. The first opera performed by music students had been produced by Giuseppe Paganelli in 1933, with W.J. Pickerill** conducting the Cape Town Municipal Orchestra.** After that John Andrews became responsible for opera productions and with the advent of Chisholm, the size of the orchestra was increased and opera came into its own at the College. Gregorio Fiasconaro** was placed in charge of the opera department in 1951 and when the University Opera School was created in 1954, he became its full-time director. Up to 1960, the students produced 40 different operas in 650 performances, all accompanied by the University Orchestra under the direction of Erik Chisholm, with one exception in 1949, when Albert Coates** conducted performances of Gluck's *Orpheus,* produced by Vera de Villiers.** The Opera Company toured to various parts of South Africa and to the former Northern and Southern Rhodesias and in 1957 it visited London to give the first performance there of Bartok's *Bluebeard's castle.* On this occasion College students and staff members also presented six different concert programmes in the Wigmore Hall, and toured in Scotland and England. This tour was the first of its kind ever undertaken by a South African university student group and was eminently successful in presenting South Africa's musical achievements in England and in helping to launch some outstanding students on their professional careers. Other notable landmarks are the first performances of *In the drought* and *Silas Marner* (John Joubert**) and *The Pardoner's tale, The inland woman* and *Dark sonnet* (all three by Chisholm) in the Little Theatre. — The Music Library of the SACM** is intrinsically, as well as historically, important as a completely self-contained, functionally designed music library; it forms a separate subject heading in this Encyclopedia. — When Erik Chisholm died in 1965, his position as Dean and Director of the College was taken by Prof. Gunter Pulvermacher** who had been on the staff since 1945. He directed the affairs of the College until his retirement in 1973. His successor was Prof. Michael Brimer** who acted as Dean until his departure for Australia at the end of 1979. A great many prominent South African musicians have served and are still serving on the staff. Separate articles in this Encyclopedia have been devoted to most of them. Of its students a number have distinguished themselves as composers (Gideon** and Johannes Fagan,** Stefans Grové,** John Joubert,** Priaulx Rainier** and Blanche Gerstman**), whilst a large number have become prominent performing artists, such as Lionel Bowman,** Adelaide Newman,** Manuel Villet,** Cecilia Wessels,** Emmerentia Scheepers (Emma Renzi),** Desirée Talbot,** Xander Haagen,** Albina Bini,** Nella Wissema, Yonty Solomon,** Johan van der Merwe,** Noreen Berry, Nellie du Toit,** Ernest Fleischmann,

Geoffrey Miller,** Raie da Costa,** Albie Louw,** Noreen Hastings and Antoinette Krige. — In addition to the usual degree courses in music, the College also offers a variety of diploma courses introduced mainly by Prof. Pulvermacher, including orchestral playing, opera, ballet and music librarianship, which are at present (1979) not available at another university in South Africa. The present Dean of the Music Faculty is Prof. Dr Brian Priestman (1981).

SOURCES
Souvenir programme, *Golden Jubilee Music Festival, 1910–1960.* Cape Times, 1960.   *Lantern* XII/1, Sept. 1962.

– J.P.M.

3. Grahamstown: Rhodes University: RU

There had been musical activity among the staff and students at Rhodes University College for several years – in the form of a College orchestra, a women's choir and a madrigal choir – when the possibility of lectures in Music was mooted in 1922. W.B. Collingwood B.A. (Oxon) ARCO became the first part-time lecturer in an experimental music course offering Harmony, Counterpoint and History of Music. A course in Music and Art was also suggested, "for the purpose of encouraging women to come to College". In 1924 six students enrolled for Music which counted as one course for the B.A. or B.Sc. degrees; by 1928 it had been extended to a second-year course. When Collingwood died in 1929, the first-year course consisted of History of Music, Form and Harmony and Aural Training and in the second year the growth of the symphony, Form, Harmony, Counterpoint and Aural Training. There were five first-year students and two second-year students. — Miss K. Patterson was appointed temporary lecturer after Collingwood died and in 1934 Prof. P.R. Kirby** was invited to examine and report on the Musical Department. The report was favourable and Miss Patterson was recommended for reappointment. A generous donation of gramophone records was made by the Carnegie Trust (1935–1937) which formed the nucleus of the record library until recently. In 1938 the appointment of a full-time lecturer was recommended and in 1940 Dr F.H. Hartmann LL.D. (Vienna) came on the scene as senior lecturer. — From then on the Music Department was firmly established and extended its activities to include a four-year course for B.Mus. and eventually post-graduate work leading to M.Mus. and D.Mus. During Prof. Hartmann's time (1940–1955) the Department had a variety of well-qualified teachers. Archie H. Iliffe-Higgo was appointed for pianoforte instruction in 1941 and in 1945 the staff consisted of Prof. and Mrs Hartmann, Mr and Mrs G.H.M. Whiteman,** Miss Whitaker and Miss R.L. Lany. Mrs Shuttleworth and Miss A.E. Knowles were subsequently appointed for pianoforte and violin and in 1948 Hubert du Plessis,** A.H. Graham** and U.V. Schneider** joined the staff. Dr Georg Gruber** came to Rhodes in 1954 to take up a lectureship and when Prof. Hartmann left for the University of the Witwatersrand in 1955, Dr Gruber was appointed Professor and Head of the Department. Also in 1955, Dr Rupert Mayr** was appointed lecturer in Music. He was promoted in later, successive years to Senior Lecturer, Reader in Music and Professor of Music and Musicology (1970). Other members of the staff since then have been Miss B. Biesheuvel, Dr H.B. Kurth-Grammatke, Norbert Nowotny** (since 1966), A.E. Honey** (since 1967), Dr K. Heuschneider (1968–1970) and Mr T.E.K. Radloff (since 1970). In 1973 Prof. Mayr was appointed to the Chair in Music and Mrs I. Sholto-Douglas commenced her duties as a lecturer. — Since 1970 the name of the department has been changed to Department of Music and Musicology. Practical tuition is given in pianoforte, organ, singing, stringed instruments, woodwinds, recorder, classical guitar and conducting. Theoretical subjects cover theory of music, History of Music, various courses in the field of school music, choir training and orchestration. The various licentiates enable students to get professional training in practical courses which have to be taken with a certain number of obligatory theoretical subjects. The B.Mus. degree is directed chiefly at an historical training and much attention is consequently paid to a thorough grounding in Musicology. B.Mus. students are expected to write a thesis on any topic, chosen in consultation with the staff in their final year. — At post-degree level the Music Department offers students the choice of different fields of study. There is much emphasis on the development of the piano sonata during the 18th and 19th centuries, a wide field for which an exceptionally representative collection of relevant sources in the form of printed music, microfilm copies, photocopies and reprints has been secured. Other research topics include studies in musical analyses, the history of local music-making, music education and the comparative study of Renaissance and Baroque choral music. For these purposes the music library is equipped with a variety of special collections and editions of old music. — Courses for prospective school music teachers have been given since 1975 and specialist courses for persons already in the possession of a teacher's diploma since 1980. The Department moved into its new building in 1979 and now has considerably more facilities at its disposal. Apart from the usual lecture rooms, practise rooms and teaching studios, it has ample accommodation for the library and a concert hall with an adjoining studio where students have the opportunity of becoming acquainted with professional recording techniques.

– A.E.H. and R.M.

4. Johannesburg: University of the Witwatersrand: UWits

During the early twenties wide interest in the teaching of music at university level led to the creation of music departments at three South African universities. In 1921 the University College of Johannesburg (to become the University of the Witwatersrand during the next year) inaugurated a Department of Music and the Rector, J.H. Hofmeyr, invited Prof. P.R. Kirby** to act as Professor and Head of the Department, after Theo Wendt** had refused the position. Initially housed in Eloff Street, the Department started in a small room furnished with a few desks and chairs, a blackboard and an American upright pianoforte: one student studied for a degree in Music, and a couple of others were interested in music in a general way. In 1923 Kirby reorganized its syllabuses to provide for B.A., B.A. Honours, M.A. and a four-year B.Mus. course, which remained a three year course until the early sixties. The next year a two-year course, leading to a professional diploma for pianists and teachers of pianoforte, was introduced. There was also a one-year course in History and Appreciation of Music. A further revision affecting the courses for B.A. and B.Mus. followed in 1927. — When the Department was planned, the University had given an undertaking to the music teachers of the Rand that no practical music would be taught. This proved to be an impossible curtailment, and the practice of music became a normal part of the tuition after 1923, although the University did not appoint full-time staff, but only temporary specialists drawn from the profession in Johannesburg. The first of these was C.A.O. Duggan,** who was officially recognized as part-time instructor in pianoforte in 1925. In this same year he was joined by Horace Barton** and Robert B. Lloyd** and by 1930 a number of leading music teachers were actually exerting pressure for the University to institute a proper school of music, under the aegis of the Music Department. The University consulted the University of Cape Town, to ascertain whether such a department could maintain itself financially. The reply from Cape Town came in the form of a tabular analysis of revenue which clearly proved that the College of Music** was a distinct and increasing liability to the Cape University. Thereupon the Council decided not to venture into troubled waters, dismissed the subject and the Department continued with a panel of approved practical teachers appointed on a temporary footing. — Fire destroyed the central portion of the Arts Block at Milner Park in December 1931, but the Music Department was not affected, and the collection of music instruments it housed sustained no damage. The fire had the effect however of urging on the construction of a new Arts Block, and seven years later the Department moved into its new quarters where Prof. Kirby's growing collection of aboriginal musical instruments could be housed in display cabinets. When Kirby retired in 1952, the collection contained 600 specimens, of which about 400 were instruments from South Africa. The collection is now housed in the Africana Museum in Johannesburg. — Concurrently with the new Arts Block, the Great Hall was completed as a concert hall, although it also had to do duty for lectures and the presentation of plays. Seating 1 100 people, it was inaugurated on 10 June 1940, with an orchestral programme backed by a performance of *The music master*. The Great Hall, as it came to be called, became the venue for dramas, operas and orchestral concerts. The history of the University's stage productions goes back to 1922, when the *Trojan women* by Euripides was produced with sung choruses, set to music by Prof. Kirby. This led to the founding of the University Players, who became responsible for an annual presentation of a play, usually with incidental music composed or arranged by Kirby. In 1928 the performances moved to the large hall in Milner Park, which Kirby and his assistants had adapted to the production of plays. It was inaugurated with a pasticcio compounded of various 18th century ingredients, called *An evening with Lady Anne Barnard*. This was followed in 1929 by *Robin and Marion* (Adam de la Halle), and in 1930 by the creation of a university orchestra, which regularly participated in all productions until 1952, the strength varying from 30 to 62 players. The orchestra also gave an annual concert and played for the productions of UCT Ballet** in 1942, 1943, 1945 and 1946. With an orchestra available, Kirby concentrated on opera intermezzi, small operas and choral works, choosing little-known compositions by Pergolesi, Mozart, Bach, Elgar, Handel, Offenbach and Weber. During the 'thirties the programmes had so-called triple bills, in which the Music Department and the Department of Drama combined to present a one-act opera, a one-act play, and an item combining mime and dancing with singing or declamation and orchestral accompaniment. These were continued in the Great Hall up to the time of Kirby's retirement in 1952. Kirby often had to arrange, rewrite, re-orchestrate and in some instances even to compose music for these presentations. — In 1955 Kirby was succeeded by Prof. Friedrich Helmut Hartmann** of Grahamstown, who vainly tried to create a conservatoire of music in Johannesburg, centred at the University. During his term of office post-graduate work was extended considerably, and a number of Masters' and Doctors' degrees were awarded. He left the University in 1961 to return to Vienna, where he was appointed Vice-President of the Staatsakademie für Musik und darstellende Kunst. In 1963 he was succeeded by Prof. Ulmont Victor Schneider.** In spite of many laudable enterprises, the Music Department had not developed significantly during the first forty years of its existence. This was mainly due to the policy followed by the authorities who did not acknowledge active support of the performing arts as a field of academic endeavour, a trend which was abandoned in the seventies. Plans have now been drawn up for the erection of a large Performing Arts Centre, a Drama Department was founded and provision has been made for the establishment of a Conservatoire of Music to supplement the work of the Music Department. Licentiate and diploma courses were introduced to encourage the study of practical performance and school music. These plans were given further impetus by the appointment of leading South African musicians to the staff of the Department, renamed School of Music to reflect the new approach. Dr Anton Hartman,** former Chief Conductor and Head of Music of the SABC, became the Head of the School in 1978; two distinguished composers, Carl van Wyk** and Dr Henk Temmingh,** joined the staff; and the piano and singing departments were strengthened by the appointment of Annette Kearney and Joyce Barker.** — During 1979 new, diversified courses for B. Mus. were adopted, which make provision for specialisation along five independent lines, respectively: School Music, Performance, Individual Teaching, Composition and Musicology. In 1980 the preparations were concluded for the founding of an opera studio. A string quartet and a chamber choir (led by J. van Tonder) and several other ensemble groups have been created and it was decided to specialise in the training of orchestral players. Principals of the PACT and SABC Orchestras serve as teachers and the Wits Orchestra (conductor, W. Mony**) provides opportunities for experience of orchestral practice. — During 1979 the School of Music was transferred from its former cramped quarters to the top seven floors of University Corner, a 20-storey building overlooking the campus. Practice room facilities were trebled, new pianos and orchestral instruments were purchased and the lecture rooms improved. Extensive renovations to the Great Hall were commenced, which transformed it into a fine concert Hall of 1 000 seats, with an adjacent chamber music hall and a practice room for percussion instruments. The foundations were also laid for a new drama theatre seating 350, with an experimental theatre adjoining. — The greater emphasis on practical music widened the scope of activities and did not detract from the musicological work. Between 1970 and 1978, 6 masters and 3 doctors degrees were awarded for composition and musical research, which ranged in subject matter from the music of the Shangana-Tsonga peoples and South African keyboard concertos to Baroque opera, Bartok's *Microcosmos* and contemporary string techniques. — A limited number of scholarships and bursaries for the study of music were available for many years, but since 1978 a number of large bequests and donations have radically altered the situation. Apart from scholarships for harp and organ study a considerable number of bursaries for general music study is available. A significant acquisition was the Hans Adler Library and Collection of Historical Keyboard Instruments,** which was bequeathed to the School in 1979. This large collection contains many rare books, scores and instruments and

207

transforms the Music Library into one of the most comprehensive in South Africa. — During the time that Prof. Kirby occupied the Chair for Music, W.P. Paff acted as his Senior Lecturer. The size of the staff was increased under Prof. F. Hartmann to include Dr U.V. Schneider,** Dr K. van Oostveen** and Dr G. Vitali and since 1963 Dr D.J. Reid,** Dr June Schneider,** W.A. Mony, Isobel Sholto-Douglas, Dr Peter Cohen,** Jeanne Zaidel** and G. Chew have served on the permanent staff. With the advent of Prof. A. Hartman the composition of the staff has changed considerably, to include, besides persons mentioned earlier, Mrs Mary Rörich, Mr Robin Walton, Miss Peggy Haddon,** Mrs Kathy Primos, and Mrs Joan Clarke.

BIBLIOGRAPHY
Kirby, P.: *Wits end.* Timmins, Cape Town, 1967.

SOURCES
Year Books etc., UWits, Johannesburg, 1923–1970.   Communications provided by Prof. A. Hartman.

– Ed.

5. University of Port Elizabeth: UPE

One year after the creation of this University in 1965, A.W. Wegelin** was appointed as professor, to organise and conduct a music department. He remained in this position until March 1970, when he resigned. His successor was Dr K.F. Heimes.** Since that year the Department was reorganised to comprise two separate units: a Subject Committee which is responsible for the practical and academic tuition of full-time degree students, and a Conservatoire which gives practical and theoretical tuition to children and part-time students. The Director of the Conservatoire was at first Prof. J.H. Potgieter** (1970–1976) and since 1978 it has been Prof. J.G. de Wet,** a former member of the Free State String Quartet** and the leader of the Free State Youth Orchestra.** During the period 1978–79 Prof. de Wet was also chairman of the Subject Committee. The accommodation of the Music Department was completed in December 1976. Situated on the campus, it served both the Subject Committee for Music and the Conservatoire until July 1979, but in that month the Conservatoire acquired new premises in the City. It is now known as The Music Centre and serves mainly as a training centre for orchestral musicians. The trainees are children and part-time students of the University and the endeavour has the support of the Education Department. — Senior members of the Subject Committee for Music were Virginia Fortescue,** Angeline Scholtz, D. du Plooy, Dr P.C. Stroux,** Prof. J.G. de Wet and M.J. Strümpher. Senior members of the Music Centre were T. Boekkooi, S.A. Kirman and H. Robinson. — The courses prescribed for degree and post-degree work are arranged by the Subject Committee for Music, with the emphasis on Music Tuition, Musicology and the Performing Art. Four Diplomas, respectively in Music Teaching, School Music, Orchestral Playing and the Performing Art are offered. There are regular student concerts, but the Subject Committee also organises yearly Master Concerts in conjunction with the Oude Meester Foundation. The Music Centre specialises in concerts offered by the Youth Orchestra. Professor Heimes resigned at the end of 1979.

– K.F.H.

6. Potchefstroom: Department of Music and Conservatoire: PU for CHE

The creation of the Department of Music and Conservatoire of what was then the PUC for CHE, was mainly the work of J.P. Malan,** who came to Potchefstroom in 1941 to take over Miss G.H. du Toit's music practice. — A year after his arrival he put forward the idea of introducing music as an academic subject at the University and in 1943 a one-year course for the B.A. degree was instituted, with Malan as part-time lecturer. There were no facilities whatsoever and a considerable amount of pioneering work had to be accomplished; but the first step had been taken and by 1945 music could be taken as a major subject for the B.A. degree, whilst a one-year course in Music Appreciation for interested amateurs had been drawn up and approved. A further development came in 1948 when the first two courses for the B.Mus. degree were introduced. These increased responsibilities necessitated the appointment of J.J.A. van der Walt** as lecturer. Hitherto Malan had been solely responsible for all branches of lecturing in all the courses and had to expand his private school of music with the aid of two associates. The third and fourth courses for the B.Mus. were introduced in 1950. — Throughout these years Malan had applied himself to the establishment, through the University, of a Conservatoire of Music, with the intention of concentrating and co-ordinating the somewhat scattered music teaching in Potchefstroom, of making a wider choice of practical tuition possible and of accelerating the rate of growth of the Music Department itself. After repeated attempts, more auspicious conditions were created for this project by the establishment of a choir and a music society at the University, as well as of a lively civic society in the Town. These improvements in Potchefstroom's concert life were indirectly responsible for a more congenial atmosphere and the University approved in principle the establishment of a Conservatoire. The building in Potgieter Street, where M.M. van der Bent** had formerly had his music school, was bought for this purpose. — Malan wished to see the Department of Music and the Conservatoire working as separate entities, but in close collaboration, and so the University appointed M.C. Roode,** Organiser of Music for the Transvaal Education Department, as independent Head of the Conservatoire. He started on his new duties in July 1949, completed the preparatory organisation, and was able to launch the Conservatoire on 1 February 1950. During the first year there were 307 students of all ages, taught by a staff of 14 teachers, of whom 6 had been appointed to full-time posts. Those who, under Roode, initiated the Conservatoire were D. Müller, T. Pretorius, G.H. de Wet, M.R. Coetzee and G. van Boelken-Hamm. In 1951 A.W. Wegelin** was appointed lecturer in violin and Naomi Papè** lecturer in singing, which meant that tuition was available in pianoforte, violin, singing and organ, from the lowest to the highest grades. A number of professional diplomas were introduced in collaboration with the Department of Music, which was now free to introduce post-graduate musicological work. The University's first M.Mus. degree was awarded to J.J.A. van der Walt in 1954, for his research into the Afrikaans edition of the Psalm melodies. The music section of the University had reached maturity and the further history is one of sturdy growth and the improvement of facilities. — In 1955 Malan had established a Collegium Musicum** as an extention of the historical studies in Music and in 1959 J.J.A. van der Walt created the Institute for South African Music.** After years without sufficient space, and a considerable amount of moving from one building to another, the whole music section was finally concentrated in a specially built conservatoire which has a concert hall accommodating some 350 people. These premises gradually became inadequate and in 1977 considerable extensions were undertaken, including studios for teaching purposes and practise rooms, a well-equipped laboratory for electronic music, a new hall in which a new organ with mechanical traction has been installed, and extensions to the library which has been fitted out with an adequate stock of books, scores and gramophone records. An important section of the library is devoted to a representative collection of South African music, including practically complete collections of works by South African composers. Many of these latter items are in the original manuscript form. — When Malan left the University at the end of 1955, he was succeeded by Van der Walt who had just returned from Cologne after the completion of his doctoral studies. M.C. Roode died in 1967 and the University decided to integrate the Department and the Conservatoire. Van der Walt was appointed Professor and Head of the unified Department and in January 1968 P.J. de Villiers** became the new Director of the Conservatoire with the rank of Professor. — Through the years the Music Department has become the focal point of musical life in Potchefstroom. On an average it presents some twenty concerts per year as an extension of its educational programme, including about fourteen Collegium Musicum concerts by staff members and students of the Conservatoire, and organ and harpsichord recitals in the new hall. Some of these musical events are presented by a chamber orchestra and a conservatoire choir. The other concerts are given by national and international celebrities of the musical world. In turn, a number of staff members are active in concerts given elsewhere in South Africa. The educational work also benefits considerably by master classes offered as special courses. — Alumni of the Department have become noted musical personalities in South Africa, and a number have been the recipients of bursaries enabling them to study abroad. Thus Dr H.P.A. Coetzee, Dr C.L. Venter** and Dr H. Temmingh** have been promoted to professorships at university institutions and H. de Vries, for example, has won the overseas bursary awarded by UNISA. Since Prof. Van der Walt completed his Master's thesis in 1954, the University has awarded this degree thirteen times and the degree of Doctor of Music to five candidates. — The staff has grown considerably since the early days and now includes 22 teachers of whom three have the rank of professor. The latest addition to this group has been Prof. H.P.A. Coetzee. A number of well-known musical personalities like G.W. Koornhof, S.M.E.P. Theron, H. van Babst, A.A. van Namen, G.W.R. Nel,** H. de Vries and E.A. Davey occupy positions on the staff.

– J.J.A.v.d.W.

7(i) Pretoria: Academy of Music and Department of Music: UP

The present music section of the University of Pretoria dates from 1960/1961, but the history of Music as a subject at the university goes back to the early 1920s – a time when active interest in music at university level was becoming evident at four South African universities. In 1923 the University of Cape Town went through the final stages of incorporating the SA College of Music,** thus creating a Faculty of Music with the Head of the College, Prof. W.H. Bell,** as first Dean; the University of the Witwatersrand established an academic Department of Music in 1921 with Prof. P.R. Kirby** as acting Head and from 1923 as Professor and Head of the Music Department; and in 1922 the Council of the University of Pretoria decided to initiate a similar move by instituting a one-year course in Music for the B.A. degree. — The first step was taken at UP on 11 March 1921 when the University Council decided to form a

College Choral Society to encourage cultural activities among the students (the medium of instruction has been Afrikaans since 13 September 1932). John Connell** was appointed conductor of the society at R4 a practice-session, for six sessions every quarter term. The Society was expected to maintain itself. Only a month later the possibility of introducing Music as a one-year course for the B.A. degree was put forward and after due investigation the extension was approved, with effect from 1922. Connell drew up a copious and over-loaded syllabus and in the same year began to lecture on music in premises made available by the Girls' High School. He did this work at a salary of R400 p.a., in addition to his work with the Choral Society. — Characteristically, he did not remain idle. In the same year (1922) he formed an Orchestral Society at the university and succeeded in persuading the authorities that the establishment of a school of music was a necessary extension of university facilities. Lectures would be given by a panel of approved music teachers in Pretoria. He also proposed a three-year diploma course for music teachers and the extension of the one-year B.A. course to two years, with the syllabi reduced to more realistic proportions. But the expansion did not end there: in June 1923, apparently under the influence of developments at the University of Cape Town, where Bell had been appointed Professor and Dean of the Faculty of Music, the authorities at Pretoria University decided to promote Connell to a chair and to raise the status of the School of Music and the Department, with its two degree-courses and three academic students, to a Faculty. To crown this memorable year, Connell arranged a refresher course for music teachers and music-lovers in October. Prominent musicians such as Dolores Wedlake Santanera, Sydney Rosenbloom,** Willem Gerke,** Harold Ketelbey** and Johannes Beck assisted as lecturer-performers. — In 1924 there was a further superficial extension with the institution of a four-year B.Mus. degree course, with the emphasis on composition. Composition was the only subject offered in the fourth year. Further oddities about Connell's B.Mus. syllabus were the absence of Musical Form and the inclusion of a single course in History of Music in the first year. From 1924, provision was made for training organists, and the B.A. syllabus was revised once more. In June of 1924 an inquiry into the possibility of establishing a new course in Elocution was held and it became evident that the internal administration of the Faculty and its financial standing were not sound. Among the irregularities which emerged, was the fact that non-registered students were attending lectures. Connell ironed out the offensive details and in July he persuaded the University Council to institute yet another course, Music Appreciation, which was to be offered extra-murally. Another refresher course was held in the first week of October. — After all this, matters rested for a while, but by 1926 there were only 17 students, of whom 13 had registered for practical tuition and 4 for the teachers' diploma. There were no degree students. At this stage the dis-ease concerning the Music Faculty began to assume disturbing proportions. Lectures were given in the extra-mural section of the University in Vermeulen Street, where they caused disturbance to lectures in other departments. The expenses incurred in making Connell's room soundproof, again brought the financial burden of the music section to the attention of the University Council. The Council and the University Senate reviewed the status of the Faculty, since it had remained a condition of Connell's appointment that the music section had to pay its own way. However, it was decided to give the Faculty a chance for one more year and to assess the situation again in June 1929. However, there was only one degree student, one diploma student, and eleven candidates for practical tuition at the beginning of 1929, and on 27 March Connell tendered his resignation. Nevertheless he agreed to remain on until the end of the year and to meet a combined committee of the Council and Senate, to discuss the future of the Faculty. The outcome was that it was refashioned as a Department of Music in the Faculty of Arts and Philosophy, that a part-time professor was appointed and that the department was to be supervised in future by an advisory committee. — At the end of 1929 it had one student. — Where Connell had erected an academic facade before the department's insufficiencies, his successor, Harold Ketelbey, devised an attractive screen of concerts to serve the same purpose. He was an outstanding violinist and a competent performing artist who sought to win public support by means of a concert series held on the last Saturday of every month. Quartets from the classical repertoire, violin sonatas, instrumental and vocal music were performed by staff members and other professional soloists, usually before small audiences. A climax was reached with a production of *Der Freischütz* (Weber), which Ketelbey presented, partly with the help of students, on October 2, 3, and 4, 1930. This production was a contribution to the festivities marking TUC's promotion to the status of an autonomous university on 10 October. — The concerts by Ketelbey and members of his staff created a good impression. The Rector of the university, Prof. A.E. du Toit, wrote personally to thank him: "You have established a landmark and a standard for the Department of Music and in this way you have secured a much smoother passage for the Department than could have been hoped for at this stage." Indeed, the Council extended Ketelbey's appointment for a further year, raised his salary to R900 a year and donated R50 to the department as surety against possible losses from the remaining concerts given in 1930. Meanwhile, in his annual report, the Dean emphasized the need both for better buildings for the department and for a music library. The number of students was then 82, most of whom had registered for practical tuition only. At the end of 1930 the picture the University had of its Music Department was the brightest since its inception in 1922. — After 1931 the great economic depression obliged universities to exercise drastic savings, like cuts in salaries and other austerities. The outwardly healthy Department of Music, as a part-time undertaking of the University, again came under pressure. Prof. Ketelbey was notified that the department would be allowed to carry on, but only on condition that it became completely self-supporting; that Ketelbey himself would be expected to assume the burden of all departmental work; and that he could employ assistants only on his own responsibility. Ketelbey accepted these conditions, and when, in the same year, he produced another opera, *Shamus O'Brien* and showed a deficit of R600, he had to make good the loss himself. — Another committee was appointed towards the end of 1931 to investigate the affairs of the department. The recommendation was that it should be given a chance for yet another year, that R600 should be set aside for a part-time professor and that bilingualism should be made effective. This was the year when the Council took the historic decision that henceforth the medium of instruction at the University of Pretoria was to be Afrikaans. One consequence of this decision was that the City Council of Pretoria withheld its annual capital donation and by so doing, aggravated the already pressing financial difficulties. However, the Department was able to continue, albeit without its annual opera, and in March 1933 the first and only degree student to complete her studies in this music department received her B.Mus. — Mrs Ghita Kallmeyer. At the end of 1932 the Senate again appointed a committee to scrutinise the affairs of the Department and they recommended that there should be no appointment for 1933; but at its last meeting of the year, the Council decided that the department should be maintained and that Gerrit Bon** become the Head of the Department as from 1933. — At this point Douglas Mossop** wrote to the Council, informing them that he had been giving all the lectures in the department for Prof. Ketelbey, and that he had been under the impression that he would be Prof. Ketelbey's successor; Mossop forcefully objected to the fact that it had been a student who had informed him of the latest developments. It now transpired that Mossop had lectured in accordance with a private arrangement with Ketelbey, and without the official knowledge of the University. Ghita Kallmeyer, for instance, had completed her entire degree course under Mossop's supervision. It emerged from the subsequent enquiry that the university was not responsible for this state of affairs and that Mossop had misunderstood his position in relation to the University. The Rector unequivocally stated the position in a letter to the Secretary of the Council: "I, to this moment, fail to understand how he could possibly have turned up to lecture to classes without any authority whatsoever . . . The unfortunate position in which Mr Mossop placed himself is . . . entirely due to . . . a misapprehension which probably arose out of an arrangement made by Professor Ketelbey with him, which was not completely outlined or understood by him." At the end of 1933 there was not one registered academic student of music. — The Department of Music at last began to achieve stability when it appointed Gerrit Bon as Professor Extraordinary. The syllabi in the main were left unchanged, but the number of lectures per subject was increased and from 1935 conditions of admission were laid down. Practical tuition – which students had to arrange and pay for themselves – still had to be taken outside the Department and for the first time in the history of university music, Afrikaans was used as the medium of instruction in musical subjects. What had been a school of music began to develop as an academic department. The enrolment began to rise at once and where, in 1931, there had been five degree students among 51 registered students, in 1935 there were 13 students enrolled for degrees in music. But teaching facilities were unsatisfactory and classes had to be conducted in one small room, while all demonstrations had to be held either at Prof. Bon's home or at the women's hostel, Damestehuis, where Bon had only a dilapidated piano at his disposal. Study material in the library remained inadequate, even after ten years – a gramophone and records were only purchased during Bon's time. — According to an important memorandum by Bon, dated 25 May 1935, he received no salary, only the fees paid by music students. In 1934, for example, these fees amounted to R196. His recommendation that a professor be permanently appointed at an agreed salary, is one modest item in a memo which stipulates the minimum requirements for the continued existence of the department: a more fitting lecture room with a decent piano and an allowance of R100 to buy essential equipment. While these recommendations were still being considered by the authorities, Bon was given a permanent appointment on the staff of the Normal College, where he had also been lecturing on a part-time basis. The Council, already under financial pressure and finding itself facing the actual implications of a Department of Music on the one hand and the possibility of losing Bon on the other, finally decided in September 1935 that the "Department of Music be gradually abrogated, and that no further students of music be accepted". This came about at the end of 1936 "until further notice", as the 1937 *Calendar* laconically states. — During the fourteen years of its existence the Department of Music had conferred only one degree. The University did not have the means to maintain such a department;

moreover, uncertainty about the difference between a music school and a department, and about the financial implications of musical training, led to the belief that enrolments and concerts would be able to pay for the institution. This misconception was not cleared up before Prof. Bon's appointment; by simply stipulating the basic necessities, Bon clarified the entire situation, and the Council reacted positively by putting an end to the lengthy experiment. — Twenty-five years later, in February 1961, the University of Pretoria launched its second department of music. This time the Council approached the matter with exemplary caution, establishing the department only after thorough investigation and comprehensive preparation. Under the Rectorship of Prof. C.H. Rautenbach (1948–1970), the University grew phenomenally, as much in the number of students as in buildings, courses of study and facilities for study, to become the largest residential university in South Africa. A consequence of this growth was that by 1955 it had become virtually self-evident that the University had to meet its obligations in the fine arts sector too. The completion of a large concert hall, the Aula,** which has come to play a major role in the development of the arts in South Africa, was the first step, and the building complex of the Musaion,** the Amphitheatre, and a well-equipped music school with 38 practice rooms, soon followed. J.P. Malan** was appointed Head of the new Department and Director of the Music Academy** which provides the practical training. After four months of planning and preparation, the Department started on its career in February 1961. — The Council had decided that the Department should be primarily academic, with the emphasis on university tradition. A pointer to the growth of the Department is the high percentage of post-graduate students, whose research up to 1969 was concentrated on South African music. Another is the development of training in composition, which has produced promising work at under-graduate as well as post-graduate level. Every year since 1961 the Music Academy has presented an opera or a programme of two short operas, string orchestra concerts, a variety of chamber music recitals and concerts in which students perform as soloists, and recently (1969) also in concertos with the PACT orchestra. Up to 12 student groups perform in concerts in other cities and towns of the Transvaal every year, and recital groups are made available for congresses, church bodies and other associations in Pretoria. A balance between practical and academic work is maintained at under-graduate level: the practical course at present includes training in all instruments of the orchestra, in church music and in music for schools. In addition, provision has been made for students interested in Musicology. — Among past and present members of staff are the names of Gertrud Kautzky (Austria), Chris Lamprecht,** Alain Naudé,** Xander Haagen,** Dr Johann Potgieter,** Philip Levy,** Jos de Groen,** Spruhan Kennedy,** Walter Mony,** Stefan Zondagh,** Emanuel Haller** and Inka Polic.** Former students fill a number of lecturing posts at universities and teachers' colleges, while others have gone overseas on merit bursaries to continue their studies. Important factors in departmental training are the wide-ranging arts' festivals which are arranged twice a year by the Aula Committee of the Council to take place in the university halls. Students of music are thereby given the opportunity to pursue their studies in a musical atmosphere. — A milestone in the history of the Music Academy was the historic decision of the Pretorium Trust (Co-op) Ltd to make eight bursaries available to students of music at the University of Pretoria every year, with further provision for bursaries for exceptionally gifted students to pursue their studies overseas. As far as is known, this investment in musical education is the most significant and far-reaching ever to have been made by a business concern in South Africa. Malan retired at the end of 1978 and was succeeded in 1979 by Dr S. Paxinos.

BIBLIOGRAPHY
Engels, M.M.: *Die departement van musiek aan die TUK/UP (1923/1936)*. Research for the degree B.A. (Mus.) (Hons.).
Ad destinatum, festival publication of the University of Pretoria. Pretoria, 1960.

SOURCES
Minutes of the Council and Senate. Reports by the Dean and correspondence in the archives of the University of Pretoria, 1921–1937.

– J.P.M.

7(ii) (a) Pretoria: University of South Africa, Department of Musicology: UNISA

Before the University of South Africa (Unisa) became a lecturing university in 1946, it had been an examining body, also for B.Mus., M.Mus. and D.Mus. degrees. From 1919 to 1958 students were trained privately, or at the music department of one of the University Colleges affiliated to Unisa. When Unisa was re-constituted as a lecturing university, it remained an examining body for external students of music until 1958. In that year it created its own Department of Music and began to provide music instruction by correspondence. — From 1919 to 1942 the University Senate relied on an official adviser, Prof. P.R. Kirby,** for advice on academic matters which concerned music. From 1942 to 1958 a Committee for Music, chaired by Dr F.H. Hartmann,** took over all matters pertaining to regulations, syllabi and examinations. Unisa's first B.Mus. degrees were conferred on B.M. Sullivan (Rhodes University College) and M.M. Moerane** (private student in 1941); and the first Master's Degree in Music on H.M. Oxley in 1944; Prof. F.H. Hartmann was the first person to receive a Doctorate in Music from this University in 1951, on the strength of a set of large-scale compositions. — When the lecturing Department of Music was created in 1958, the University's Director of Music, Prof. D.J. Roode,** who in that year had become responsible for organising all the practical certificate and licentiate examinations, was appointed Acting Head of the Department. He was assisted by Dr W.P. Paff, a part-time senior lecturer. Under the guidance of Prof. Roode, syllabi for B.Mus., M.Mus. and D.Mus. degrees were compiled, the standard of practical work required for these degrees was improved (in future students were required to play a practical entrance examination) and a new teachers' diploma in music was instituted. At the beginning of 1965 the position of Director of Music was made independent of the Department and when Prof. Roode retired at the end of 1966, he was succeeded as director by H.J. Joubert**. Prof. B.S. van der Linde** was appointed the first full-time Head of the Department of Music in October 1966. After his appointment syllabi were revised and given a more specific musicological bias. The practical requirements for a B.Mus. degree were maintained, but courses such as Composition and Orchestration were suspended and post-graduate work was concentrated on musicological research. — In accordance with the Department's new academic approach, it became known in 1970 as the Department of Musicology, and the designation Baccalaureus Musicae was changed to Baccalaureus Musicologiae. Since 1968, the higher degrees have been entitled Magister Musicologiae and Doctor Musicologiae. — The number of students enrolled for the B.Mus. degree has increased steadily from approximately 70 in 1967 to about 230 in 1979. Consequently, there has been a corresponding increase in the lecturing staff from 5 in 1967 to 14 in 1979. Towards the end of 1977 both Dr A.J.J. Troskie** and Dr S. Paxinos** were promoted to the rank of Associate Professor. Since the time of Prof. Roode the following have been staff members of this department: Mr R.J. Cherry** (1960–1967), Mr J.P. Malan** (1965–1969), Dr K.F. Heimes** (1965–1968), Mr T.C. Wrogeman (1967–1969), Prof. Dr S. Paxinos** (1965–1978), Mrs B.M. Spies (1967–1974), Mrs E. Roux (1969–1976), Mrs J. van Leeuwen (1969–1976), Dr R. Temmingh** (1971), Mr E. Rörich (1972–1977), Mr F.J. van der Merwe (1967–1979), Prof. Dr A.J. Troskie** (1971–1979), Dr J.D. Drury (1976–1979), Mr R.J. van den Berg (1968–1979) and Dr D.G. Geldenhuys (1977–1979). During the period 1967–1979 the Department has been responsible for 11 degrees of Master and 5 of Doctor. — It is the only Music Department in South Africa to publish its own periodical. Called *Ars Nova,* it is distributed among the students in the Department and is forwarded to some 50 libraries in other countries. With Prof. Paxinos as editor, 1978 saw the publication of the tenth edition. Since 1977 Mr F.J. van der Merwe has acted as co-editor and since 1979 Prof. Van der Linde has been the editor.

SOURCES
Year Book of the University of South Africa: 1921, 1922, 1942, 1943, 1946, 1953, 1957, 1958, 1968–1979.   Minutes of the Council and of the Senate of the University for 1958. Files of the Registrar, 1958.

– B.M.H. and B.S.v.d.L.

7(ii) (b) Music examinations in South Africa: UNISA

Music examinations in South Africa began after a memorandum had been drawn up by music teachers in the Cape Colony in 1891, requesting the Council of the University of the Cape of Good Hope to establish such examinations. A letter from A. Biden, who served as spokesman for the teachers, was considered by the Council of the University on 26 September 1891 and referred to a committee for music, which was created for the purpose. The request had the active support of Dr. J.H. Meiring Beck** who in 1891, during a visit to England, discussed the necessity for the step with Sir George Grove, then director of the RAM. On 30 January 1892, at a meeting of the University Council, he was able to report on his discussion and submit a letter from Sir George, in which Grove recommended an experimental examination. Dr Beck was appointed by the Council to their Committee for Music and thereafter matters proceeded rapidly. — The University Council, having received recommendations from the Committee for Music, decided on 28 May 1892: (1) that the institution of examinations in Theory and Practical Music was both possible and desirable (2) that the system as already applied in the United Kingdom, would meet the requirements of the Cape Colony (3) that the offer by the RCM to assist the University of the Cape of Good Hope in conducting the examinations, and in nominating an examiner for the Cape Colony, be accepted. — The advantages to be derived from the acceptance of the offer of the Associated Board were only too clear. Apart from the fact that the Board, with its tradition and experience, would give status to the examinations and deputize highly qualified examiners, the connection implied the additional advantage of enabling talented South Africans to promote their studies in England without interruption. These expectations were fully realised in the years that followed. A sizeable number of talented students was eventually drawn to London for specialised training. A change in this trend only became evident after the Second World War, when the University of South Africa assumed control of the examinations in all their aspects, and youthful talent left for countries other than England for professional study. Furthermore, the Council judged that the institution of music examinations would have a profound and permanent influence on the way of life in the Cape Colony, and that in view of this the State should be requested to subsidise the undertaking from public funds wherever necessary. At the same meeting, 28 May 1892, the Council also considered a letter from W. Coulson Tregarthen** in which Council was requested not to examine in elementary music, but rather to consider introducing university degrees in music. The Council gave due thought to this far-sighted proposal, but decided to adhere to its decision that elementary music examinations were a responsibility of the University which should be assumed according to the pattern followed in the United Kingdom. — The University Council decided at its meeting of 25 November 1893, that the first series of examinations should be held from July to September 1894. On the recommendation of the Associated Board, Prof. Franklin Taylor, who was professor at the RCM and member and examiner of the Associated Board of the RAM and the RCM, was appointed examiner. The following regulations for the examinations were approved: 1.   The examination would consist of two sections, vis.: (a) a preliminary written examination (b) a practical examination   2. The preliminary examination would contain questions on the fundamentals of music and subject to exceptions in 4. below, had to be passed by every candidate before the candidate could present himself for a practical examination   3. The practical examinations would be taken in the sections Piano, Violin, Organ, Singing. There would be two sections in Piano, Violin and Organ, a Lower grade and a Higher grade 4. There would be a separate examination on Harmony and "Grammar of Music". This examination would also have a lower and a higher grade. Candidates who entered for either grade of the practical examination and also for the examination in Harmony and Grammar of Music would be exempted from the preliminary examination 5. The written examinations would be held on 18 July 1894 and the practical examinations during August and September 1894. — In 1894 a total of 327 candidates for the written and practical examinations was tested in different centres in the Cape Colony. At its meeting on 13 October 1894, the University Council decided that for the 1895 examinations and thereafter, the written examinations would be held at all centres where candidates had entered for the University School Elementary Examinations; that centres for the practical examinations would be considered each year; that the recognition of venues beyond the borders of the Colony would be considered, should there be an application. In January 1895 the University Council approved a request of the Superintendent-General of Education in Bloemfontein that Bloemfontein should become an examination centre. Prof. Eaton Faning was appointed examiner for the 1895 examinations, for which there were 731 candidates, 433 for theory and 298 in the practical section. The University Council also decided to establish a special examination for piano teaching from 1896. Twenty-five candidates took this examination in the first year. Prof. Franklin Taylor was again the examiner. On 29 May 1897 the University Council considered a letter from the Associated Board in which the Board declared itself willing to exercise greater control over the preparation of syllabi and the appointment and remuneration of examiners, but the Council decided that it would prefer to retain control over these matters. — Thus the examination system was established in broad outline: a close association with British institutions, the advantages of expert external control over local standards and the retention of university approval and control over finances and administration. As the number of candidates increased, more examiners were appointed and the number of examinations at different levels of musical development gradually multiplied, eventually to eight grades and five licentiates. The system was maintained by the University of the Cape of Good Hope until 1918 when its successor, the University of South Africa, inherited the system and continued it until the end of the Second World War. A notable agreement with the Associated Board was the one in which provision was made for the nomination of a proportional number of South African examiners, with the understanding that not more than one third of the examiners appointed in one year would be local musicians. In practice, the accepted ratio until 1940 was five overseas and three South African examiners. In 1941 the Associated Board was forced by war-time conditions to agree to a ratio of four to four. In 1943 only one and in 1944 only two overseas examiners could officiate. — In April 1945 the Associated Board cabled to inform the University that it found it impossible to designate two examiners for the examinations of that year. The University Council decided to nominate two additional local examiners and to appoint P.J. Lemmer,** D.J. Roode,** A. Iliffe-Higgo, and Prof. M. Fismer** for the licentiate examinations, with the understanding that three of the four would officiate in two differently composed groups, to avoid the situation where an examiner would have to act in his own area. Until 1944 the panel of South African examiners consisted of: Horace Barton,** Lorenzo Danza,** Prof. Maria Fismer,** Prof. Eric Grant, Adolph Hallis,** Prof. F.H. Hartmann,** A. Iliffe-Higgo, O.A. Karstel,** P.J. Lemmer,** Ellie Marx,** Dr W.P. Paff, D.J. Roode,** Colin Taylor,** Cameron Taylor.** — In June 1945 the Associated Board wrote to inform the University Council that it had decided to discontinue its collaboration with the University as it found the arrangement unsatisfactory. The University's reaction was to invite Universities with music departments, recognized schools of music and other interested bodies to consider in conference the appointment of a representative body for the control of music examinations in South Africa. This was held in Pretoria in August 1945, and on its recommendation the Council decided to assume full control of music examinations and to delegate its responsibility to the Joint Advisory Committee for Music and a Committee for Music Examinations. — The Joint Advisory Committee was constituted to advise the Council on matters referred to them by the Council and to make recommendations to the Council on all matters relating to public music examinations, including standards, syllabi, appointment of examiners, bursaries and prizes, and other relevant business. This Committee consisted of two representatives of the University of South Africa, one of whom would be chairman; one representative of the Department of Education, Arts and Science; one representative of each of the four provincial education departments and the education department of South West Africa; one representative from each university with a department of music; two representatives from the South African Society of Music Teachers.** — The Music Committee was a committee of the Council. The Joint Committee for Music could not report independently to the University Council, only through the Music Committee. The first meeting of the Advisory Committee was held in Pretoria on 29 April 1946. Since that date all matters relating to the University's music examinations in South Africa have remained a purely South African responsibility. — In 1947 the panel of examiners for the practical examinations consisted of Horace Barton,** Erwin Broedrich,** Lorenzo Danza,** Willem Eggink, Prof. M. Fismer,** Alan Graham,** A. Hallis,** Prof. F.H. Hartmann,** A. Iliffe-Higgo, E. Joubert, O.A. Karstel, P.J. Lemmer, Ellie Marx,** Dr W.P. Paff, W. Poles,** D.J. Roode,**M.C. Roode,** Cameron Taylor,** Colin Taylor,** Cyril Wright.** The transition to full responsibility had hardly been accomplished, when in April 1948, the Associated Board wrote to the University Council proposing future collaboration of the two bodies "on a basis compatible with the dignity and the aims of both". This proposal was considered by the University Council in April 1949 and rejected by 16 votes to five. — An important development came in 1958: Prof. D.J. Roode was appointed the first full-time Director of Music, and held this post until December 1966. Hennie Joubert** succeeded him on 1 January 1967. Until 1959 examiners for the music examinations were appointed on an observer basis. New examiners wishing to be appointed, had to act as observers for a specified period under senior examiners conducting examinations at the various centres. This system was found to be unsatisfactory for a variety of reasons and was replaced by a system of tests for aspirant examiners. The observer tests are now conducted annually before a panel of senior examiners. The candidates present themselves for test examinations, their abilities are thoroughly tested, and a common standard of adjudication is established by means of discussion. Standards are also determined at an annual meeting of examiners held immediately before the practical examinations. — In September 1965 the University Council decided to transfer the control of music examinations from the existing Advisory Committee to a smaller Music Committee, which would report directly to the Council and meet three times a year. At present this Music Committee consists of eleven members: the council of the University of South Africa – two members, of whom one would be chairman; the Director of Music; three representatives of university departments of music, nominated by the Council on recommendations by different universities; two people not connected with a university, nominated by the Council on the recommendation of the South African Association of Music Teachers; three representatives nominated by the Council on recommendations received from the various education departments. — A further development followed in April 1966, when the University decided to inaugurate refresher courses for music teachers. In 1966 two such courses were arranged – one in Bellville and the other in Pretoria. These were eminently successful and thus the University has decided to hold them annually and in a larger number of centres. — The growth in the number of examination entries since 1895 is indicated in five-year periods on the attached table. Up to and including the 1925 to 1930 examinations, there was high correlation between enrolments for the theoretical examinations and those for the practical. During the 'thirties a notable reduction in the number of enrolments for the theory examinations occurred, following the introduction of elementary practical examinations, which did not require a theory examination as a prerequisite. Since 1945 the enrolment figures for theory examinations have gradually risen, reaching the approximate level of the 1925 examinations in 1965. Excluding a comparatively small drop in enrolment in 1935 – which is probably attributable to the depression – the number of candidates for the practical examinations has constantly increased from about 4 000 in 1925 to about 11 000 in 1965.

NUMBER OF CANDIDATES WHO ATTENDED WRITTEN AND PRACTICAL EXAMINATIONS OF THE UNIVERSITY OF SOUTH AFRICA IN THE SPECIFIED YEARS

YEAR	THEORY – Preliminary	Qualifying	Lower Harmony	Higher Harmony	Intermediate Harmony	Intermediate Counterpoint	Advanced Harmony	Advanced Counterpoint	Advanced Rudiments	Final Harmony & Counterpoint	General Musicianship	Licentiate H & C	Primary Harmony	Elementary Harmony	Transitional Harmony	TOTAL	PRACTICAL – Primary	Elementary	Transitional	Lower	Higher	Intermediate	Advanced	Final	Licentiate	TOTAL	GRAND TOTAL
1895	349		51	33												433				160	138					298	731
1900	370		74	22			1									467				278	212		48		15	553	1 020
1905	849		230	125	102		13									1 319				531	482	248	206		29	1 496	2 815
1910	1 235		373	257	167	27	154									2 213				627	713	525	416		44	2 325	4 538
1915	1 601		329	223	198	31	146									2 528				724	704	578	492		111	2 609	5 137
1920	2 311		490	293	235	57	212									3 598				937	891	690	458		131	3 107	6 705
1925	2 725		295	271	247	33	118	18	106	3		3				3 816				1 025	1 081	809	648	322	130	4 015	7 831
1930	2 471		279	226	179	54	82	27	186	3		19				3 525		998		877	771	732	524	441	201	4 544	8 067
1935	1 547		114	112	65	11	20	4	140			3				2 016	592	872		616	589	476	316	270	140	3 871	5 887
1940	1 412		89	87	32	8	50	7	38	10		1				1 727	842	917	688	668	506	347	338	258	99	4 623	6 350
1945	1 693		20	10	18		7				80	2	14			1 868	860	929	755	710	599	340	266		87	4 804	6 672
1950	1 408	856	39	41	39		18			2	69	3		8		2 482	1 249	1 235	1 007	649	475	281	191	203	70	5 360	7 842
1955	1 534	1 133	38	26	16		11				69	1				2 832	1 595	1 521	1 449	867	741	509	404	283	71	7 440	10 272
1960	1 905	1 240	27	31	9		3			1	80	3				3 297	2 360	2 071	1 764	1 095	856	661	434	338	111	9 690	12 987
1965	2 177	1 541	49	36	6		1			4	66				15	3 883	2 574	2 291	1 973	1 366	1 091	752	468	317	130	10 962	14 845

SOURCES
The official minutes and documents of the Universities of the Cape of Good Hope and of South
Africa.

– W.H.leR.

8. Stellenbosch University: Conservatoire of Music: US

This is the oldest existing institution for advanced musical education in South Africa.
The people who were responsible for its establishment in 1905 were Hans Endler,**
F.W. Jannasch,** Armin Schniter – a Swiss music teacher who had worked with
Jannasch – Nancy de Villiers** and Mrs Elizabeth von Willich.**[1] F.W. Jannasch was
the first principal (1905–1921). — Stellenbosch began to develop as a significant
educational centre during the second half of the 19th century, and it was Prof. N.J.
Hofmeyr in particular – the first of two professors at the Theological Seminary of
what was then Victoria College – who realised timeously that the town had a great
need for music training. It was through his endeavours that Jannasch came to
Stellenbosch in 1883. By virtue of his ability and his devotion to music teaching, this
man became, in fact, the founder of musical education in Stellenbosch, commencing at
the Bloemhof School and eventually, in 1899, starting his own Greylock Academy of
Music. Shortly after 1902 the sisters Nancy de Villiers and C.J.H. von Willich,
daughters of J.S. de Villiers,** opened the second music school in Stellenbosch and
called it Villieria, and in 1903 the able Austrian musician, Hans Endler, appeared on
the scene. Several people had by that time already suggested that these educational
endeavours should be combined and it appears that the leading figures themselves had
come to some kind of an agreement as early as 1904, because an impressive
advertisement for a proposed South African Conservatorium of Music was published
in the November 1904 issue of the *Student's Quarterly*. — When they realised the
need of an own specially-built conservatoire, the founders did not hesitate to buy a
portion of Charlie Neethling's vineyard on the north side of Van Riebeeck Street and,
with the financial assistance of A. de Waal, erected the building which remained in use
until 1978. It was completed by the end of 1905 and a series of festival concerts on 3, 4
and 5 May marked the inauguration. These were given with the co-operation of staff
members, an orchestra consisting of 30 players, a choir of 100 singers and a number of
advanced students. The participation of the choir and the orchestra, for which Hans
Endler was largely responsible, added lustre to the occasion. The rapid growth of the
College's reputation was in the main also due to his exertions: he advertised their
educational work, often at his own expense, and imbued the musical life of this
educationally important centre with much of his own zeal. The Conservatoire issued
certificates and diplomas which enhanced the status of their work and the quality of
the training, especially in Jannasch's department of church music, soon established a
tradition; but it was mainly Endler's large-scale, regular presentations of oratorios and
operettas (mostly by Gilbert and Sullivan), involving as they did hundreds of students
through the years, that contributed largely towards the fame of the institution. Close
collaboration with W. Pickerill,** who was conductor of the Cape Town City
Orchestra** at the time, led in subsequent years to repeat performances in Cape Town
of the presentations that had been rehearsed for Stellenbosch. Similarly, Endler also
took the lead in bringing chamber music to the fore. — At the end of 1906 Mrs Von
Willich left the Conservatoire. She was followed in 1907 by Armin Schniter, who
resigned because of ill health, and in 1910 by Nancy de Villiers, who left Stellenbosch

with her husband in 1912, two years after their marriage. By 1921 Jannasch was too old to continue regular teaching and he also retired; so that only Endler was left to carry the burden until April 1934, when he sold the Conservatoire to the University of Stellenbosch for R13 000. During the last thirteen years of the institution's existence as an independent, private organisation, Endler associated himself with it to such an extent that he even lived there. He extended its activities and introduced a Department of Speech, Elocution and Drama and courses in Dalcroze Eurythmics, Classical Gymnastics and Painting. — When the University took charge, a new phase in the history of the Conservatoire was introduced. The studies were re-organised on an academic basis by the institution of university degrees and diploma courses in Music and the University Council approached Maria Fismer** to join the permanent staff. She relinquished her flourishing music practice in Robertson and came to Stellenbosch where, in 1938, she became the first Professor and Principal of the Conservatoire of Music. Endler remained on the staff until shortly before his death in 1947. During the seventeen years under the direction of Maria Fismer, the Conservatoire consolidated its new status; the departments of Organ and Music Teaching flourished and a course in School Music was introduced. When she retired in 1951, the University acknowledged her zeal by conferring on her an Honorary Doctorate in Music. George van der Spuy** was her successor and remained principal until 1960, when he resigned. After this, the administrative side of the Conservatoire was placed on a new footing – the principalship was replaced by a new post, that of Director, to which Richard Behrens** was appointed. In 1965 he was promoted to a chair. — The Conservatoire has always been the centre of musical activities in Stellenbosch and because of the many organists and music teachers that have been trained there, it has played its part in shaping the church and educational music of the Afrikaans-speaking people. Among its former students who have become well-known as composers, are Arnold van Wyk,** Hubert du Plessis** and O. Cromwell Everson. Leading university personalities such as Johan Potgieter** (Bloemfontein), Chris Swanepoel** (SABC in Bloemfontein up to 1979), Pieter de Villiers** (Potchefstroom), H. Joubert** (UNISA) and Stefan Zondagh** (Pretoria)** also received their training at the Stellenbosch Conservatoire. Other students of the Conservatoire have excelled in the fields of church music, choral work, music teaching and music in performance. — The University of Stellenbosch entrusted the task of designing a new Conservatoire to the firm of architects, Colyn & Meiring, in 1971 and the actual building operations started in 1975. A festival to mark the completion of the project took place in May 1978. As a whole, the complex can be seen as a functional unit consisting of four distinct sections: 1. the central portion, embracing the administrative offices and the larger localities (2 halls, larger studios, lecture rooms) 2. the part devoted to the practice of the art (studios covering two storeys; practice rooms covering three storeys) 3. the library 4. the concert hall, named after Hans Endler. — The facilities of the building are designed to cope with an optimum number of 220 students. Proper provision has been made for research, sound recording, ensemble work, sound experiments and the various types of musical performance. Exceptional characteristics of the construction are the high level of sound proofing which has been achieved, and the effective system of adjustable acoustics in all rooms where music is practised. This makes it possible to adjust the acoustics to the requirements of every type of musical activity. — Pride of place should be accorded to the concert hall (the Endler Hall) with 556 seats, equipped with all the usual facilities, and with a three-manual organ built by the Danish firm of Marcussen. This hall is suitable for solo recitals, chamber music, and choral and orchestral performances. In addition there are a rehearsal room (the Fismer Hall) with 200 seats, which, apart from its use for rehearsals, can be adapted for intimate concerts and recording sessions; a main lecture room (the Jannasch Hall) with 180 seats; studios for teaching and performance; lecture rooms; a recording studio with control facilities; a sound laboratory; a studio for electronic music; a studio for church music, with a two-manual organ built by Paul Ott of Germany; 57 practice studios; a library with books, scores, sheet music, gramophone records, spacious reading desks and listening facilities. — Apart from the Music Department the building also houses the Department of School Music. When the building was inaugurated in 1978 the departmental heads were: Prof. Richard Behrens (Department of Music) and Prof. Philip McLachlan** (Department School Music). The rest of the staff includes two assistant professors, five senior lecturers, thirteen lecturers and ten part-time teachers. The composers Arnold van Wyk,** Hubert du Plessis** and Roelof Temmingh** are members of the staff. The Department of School Music has two lecturers in addition to the professor. — The electronic facilities form part of the recording studio. It is equipped with an 8 track 8 channel tape recorder, a 4 track 4 channel tape recorder and a number of 2 track 2 channel tape recorders. This equipment, as well as the microphones, a complete mixture board (16 to 8), echo chamber etc. are all of high quality. A medium ARP and a portable EMS synthesizer complete the equipment which includes a number of smaller items. Considerable extensions are envisaged. The studio is mainly used   1. as an extention to the study of acoustics   2. to fabricate electronic sound-illustrations used in school music, studies of form etc.   3. for original compositions   4. for conventional recording and editing. Mr John Bannister, principal technical officer of the Conservatoire, is responsible for the recording section of the studio, and senior lecturer Dr Roelof Temmingh is in charge of composition with technical media.

BIBLIOGRAPHY
Behrens, R.H.: Die ontstaan en ontwikkeling van die Konservatorium. *Gedenkblad van die Konservatorium vir Musiek van die Universiteit Stellenbosch, Goue Jubileum, 1905-1955.*
K., W.H.: The Stellenbosch Conservatorium of Music. *The Arts in South Africa.* Knox Printing & Publishing Co., Durban, 1933.

SOURCES
Information made available by Prof. R.H. Behrens and Dr R. Temmingh.
— J.P.M.

1. Her own spelling.

9. Pietermaritzburg and Durban: NU

The first step towards the founding of a Department of Music was taken in December 1965, when the University of Natal decided that trust funds bequeathed to it by the daughters of the late L.G. Joël for the purpose of creating a Chair, would be used as a contribution to the establishment of a Chair of Music. It was not, however, until 1970 that a decision was taken to proceed with the founding of the Department. The first Professor of Music, Michael Brimer,** took up his position in January 1971, and used the year to begin planning for and equipping the new Department, as well as for recruiting staff; the first students were registered in February 1972. Professor Brimer resigned during 1973, and by the beginning of 1974 the fledgling Department had a new incumbent of the L.G. Joël Chair of Music: Professor Christopher Ballantine.** — At present (1979) the Department has ten full-time teaching positions. These are held by three musicologists, a composer, a music educationist, two pianists (one also a harpsichordist), an oboist (who also teaches other woodwind instruments) and a cellist; the position of violinist is currently being advertised internationally, and upon his arrival the Natal University Piano Trio will be formally launched. The full-time staff are: Christopher Ballantine (Professor and Head of Department); G. Bon,** Moira G. Kearney, Elizabeth D. Oehrle and Alfredo Stengel (senior lecturers); G.A. la Pierre, David Allen, Beverly L. Parker and Isabella Stengel (lecturers). — The Eleanor Bonnar** Music Library, housed in the Department of Music, contains a representative collection of books, journals, scores, tapes and gramophone records. Much of the world's music is represented in the collection of 7 000 LP's; and in addition there is an archive collection of 78 r.p.m. discs numbering 4 500. Students have access to all these recordings by way of twenty-three listening booths, each equipped with a turntable, tape-deck, amplifier, and earphones. — The Department is equipped with an electronic music studio. Its central feature is a large studio-model ARP synthesizer (ARP 2500) with four keyboards and two wing panels. Also available are a bank of tape-decks with recording facilities for quarter-, half-, and four-track tapes, as well as a 12-in and 4-out mixer, a quadrophonic playback system, and various testing equipment. The Department also possesses a large number of all the usual western musical instruments. — Five types of B.Mus. degree are offered, each distinguished by a different area of emphasis. They are: Composition, Music Education, Performance, Musicology and Ethnomusicology. The University of Natal is, incidentally, at present the only university in South Africa offering a degree in Ethnomusicology. In addition, the Department offers some of these latter academic courses as units leading towards the B.A. degree. Arising out of the Department's commitment to progressive ideas in education, students are permitted – and indeed encouraged – to exercise numerous choices both in the construction of the curriculum for their degree, and in the contents of that curriculum. They are also constantly involved as active – rather than passive – participants in the educational process, by means of a teaching system that lays great emphasis on seminars. Presently (1979) about 85 students are registered in the undergraduate programmes, and about 14 students are working towards master's or doctoral degrees. Moreover, many students are accepted for instrumental study only, and work under the tuition of the performing staff; such students need not necessarily be registered for any degree or diploma. — The Department presents public concerts throughout the academic year on a weekly basis, at which artists visiting from abroad as well as musicians residing in South Africa are featured. The performing members of the Department's staff take a prominent part in this series. The main student performing groups in the Department are the University Singers, the University of Natal String Orchestra and the University of Natal Wind Band. — Plans for the future include the further development of the Ethnomusicology programme, leading ultimately to the establishment of a sub-departmental research centre for the study of African music; a substantial collection of African instruments is now being built up for this purpose.

– C.B.

10. The University of the Western Cape

The Music Department of the University of the Western Cape commenced in a small way in 1974 when Mr Jan Fredericks was appointed to conduct a Preliminary Course in Music for students who considered taking up music elsewhere; but in the next year a proper Department was initiated with Bruce Gardiner as its Head. He had the assistance of Wilfred Foster. Two courses were immediately introduced: a course leading to the degree of B.A. (Mus.) and another one to a Diploma in Music Teaching. The Preliminary Course has continued to cater for students who are not sufficiently qualified to start on their first year in either of the courses mentioned above. — Nick Basson joined the permanent staff in 1976 and Mrs Nancy Hofmeyr in 1977 and, as the Department continued to expand, the part-time teaching of instruments other than the pianoforte became a necessity. By 1979 there were four part-time assistants: J.S. Buis for recorder, A. Vigeland for guitar, J. Stott for trombone and Mrs C. Holmes for singing. The enrolment has been increasing steadily during the past five years. At present there are, in all, 29 students of whom 14 have enrolled for the Diploma, 11 for the Degree and 4 for the Preliminary Course. In addition the Department also offers music as a subject for students who have entered for a Senior Teacher's Diploma in the Department of Education. At concert level at least 6 instrumental concerts are offered each year and the University choir conducted by Nick Basson has sung in various parts of Cape Town. Vivaldi's *Gloria* was performed on two evenings in May 1979 and in 1980 the Department tackled *The mikado* as its first major production.

– B.G.

11. The University of Zululand

The Music Department was instituted in 1976, the year in which student unrest forced the University to suspend its activities. Fifteen students had entered for music study leading to the Bachelor of Arts degree in Music (B.A. (Mus.)), a course which takes three years to complete. It is an adaptation of Western models to the needs of Black musicians. Thus there are three academic subjects – Music Theory, History of Music and Practical Music – coupled to a language course, the choice of language including Zulu or Sotho. Practical Music is at present limited to Choral Technique, Pianoforte and Violin. An interesting feature of the course structure is that each year of the study in each subject is divided into two semester units of which the first is orientated to Western music and the second to African music. Students who are being prepared for a career in music teaching also have to do a Method course. — The staff consists of a Senior Lecturer (Mr Khabi Ngoma), who is the Acting Head of the Department, and a lecturer. The Head of the Department is responsible for History of Music, Choral Technique and violin instruction and the lecturer for Music Theory and instruction in pianoforte. Khabi Ngoma also acts as Director of Research into African music and as Director of the University of Zululand Choir, a first-class ensemble which has performed at numerous functions and has issued its first long-playing record. Acting realistically, he has also instituted a Children's Music Education Programme in which 32 children are instructed in the playing of orchestral instruments (mainly strings) and about 40 are taught the rudiments of music to develop their musical literacy. Apart from these educational and academic efforts much attention is paid to music on the campus, where the music students are provided with a platform for their own performances, and artists from elsewhere are invited for concerts. Among those who have appeared there are Joseph Dubazana (singing to his own auto-harp accompaniment), the Durban Male Voice Choir conducted by Dr John Pauw, the Natal Instrumental Group of H. de Villiers, the Frommener Dorfmusikanten from Western Germany, the Pretoria Youth Choir and others. There are also jazz and pop concerts, performances by youthful string players and choral singers trained by Ngoma, and Finalist Concerts. Each year in September the Music Department organises its own Music Festival for the promotion of University music. — Since 1977, when there were 10 students, the enrolment has increased to 18 in 1979, distributed over the three years of the academic study. At present the Department is still housed in three prefabricated structures with facilities for lecturing, practising, rehearsing and administration.

– Khabi Ngoma

II. TEACHERS' TRAINING COLLEGES (UP TO 1970)

1. Johannesburg College of Education

Until 1957 there was no music department at the Johannesburg College of Education, although music was taught as part of the training for the various teachers' diplomas. Miss Dorothy Boxall** did the lecturing, and directed the main part of her attention to the organization and conducting of non-competitive school music festivals. She had an orchestra consisting of pupils of various schools in the vicinity of the Training College, and of students of the College itself. During the Royal visit to South Africa in 1947 a massed choir sang under her direction, and she was presented with a gold medal by the King for her educational work in music. — Miss Boxall remained in charge until serious illness interrupted her work in January 1951. Miss M. Starke and Miss Wilkinson were welcomed at the beginning of that year as new music lecturers at the college. Miss Starke trained her students in the use of Orff instruments, keeping them up-to-date with developments abroad, and in 1957 became the first Head of the newly-established Music Department. She remained in this position until 1960, when she transferred to the University of Cape Town, and Derek Lewis** took charge of tuition in this Department. During his term, which lasted until 1968, he also instructed choirs for the SABC and the College, trained and conducted the National Youth Orchestra, and conducted the Johannesburg Symphony Orchestra.** — When Lewis became Vice-Rector of the College in 1968, he was succeeded by Dr Lourens Faul**, who has devoted his attention to the benefits to be obtained from mechanical and electronic aids to tuition, in harmony and aural work. As a result of his pioneering efforts, the Education Department is now equipping Music Centres with Music Laboratories, and is considering the establishment of a Programming Centre where teachers will be trained in the methods required in these Music Laboratories. Besides Dr Faul, the Music Department had six senior lecturers in 1970: Mrs M. Peterse (since 1959); L. Hansen (since 1960); R. Winchester (since 1962); E. Quirke (since 1964); Miss L. McKenzie (since 1965) and H. Ahlers (1966–1973).

– L.F.

2. Johannesburg: Goudstad Teachers' Training College

In 1961, the year in which the Goudstad College was established, a one-year general course in music was offered under the direction of Mr. H.R. Steel. He was departmental head of Junior Work, Physical Training, and Music. The music syllabus was the responsibility of one lecturer, Dr R.E. Pienaar,** who also taught pianoforte to 11 students and trained the College choir. In 1962 another lecturer was appointed and the syllabus was extended to offer courses in Junior and Senior Primary School Music which could be taken at either a specialised or semi-specialised level. The number of students increased to such an extent during the following years that the Department of Music became independent in 1964. Miss Pienaar became Head of the Department with four lecturers on her staff. A year later the courses were further extended, taking in a specialised course for the High School, a semi-specialised course for the Primary School (either Junior Primary or Senior Primary), a course in Music for nursery school teaching, and, for those students who were interested, a course in piano accompaniment. — The first two public appearances by students were presented jointly by the Music and Drama Departments. In 1963 it was a week-end trip to Witbank and Bethal with a programme of theatre music, and in 1965 a performance of *Kalulu, die slim hasie,* with original music and libretto by the two departments. After this the Department of Music presented the operetta *Die minnesangers* (J. Esterhuysen and J.P. Malan**) (1966) and in 1969 the *Stabat mater* of Schubert. The choir has taken part in massed choir performances (1966), and in 1970 and 1971 it undertook tours through the eastern and northern Transvaal and Rhodesia, and through the Free State and the Cape respectively. — In 1971 the staff consisted of the departmental Head, Dr R.E. Pienaar; three senior lecturers, Mrs A.M. Viljoen, Miss E. van der Merwe and Mr P. Roos; and two lecturers, Mrs R.F. Joubert and Miss C. Kok.

–R.E.P.

3. Potchefstroom: Teachers' Training College

On 23 April 1919 the Potchefstroom Normal College was opened as a preliminary training centre with J.S. van Heerden as principal and on 5 May the TED appointed Mrs F.L. van der Bent as part-time teacher of singing at the College. From 1920 she was assisted by Miss A.F. Marks (at the time teacher of singing at three high schools). The classes in "singe" (singing) were held at the Preliminary Training Centre, but when this was closed Mrs Van der Bent was appointed lecturer in singing at the College (25 July 1923). Students could choose between singing and cardboard modelling and the available seven hours a week of the one-year course in singing were divided into four periods. The text books (also used initially at the Preliminary Centre) were *Paam liederen* (Juta); *Glee singers* (Juta); *School songs* (Koomans); and *The Snow tonic sol-fa* (Juta). — The 86 singing students of 1928 had become 100 by 1929, but they did not take their studies very seriously, as appears from the criticism of the examiner Alan Howgrave-Graham on 20 June 1930. According to him the students lacked knowledge of notation and sol-fa. They were also inclined to sing flat and their breath control was inadequate. "In one batch, the chief means of getting breath control seemed to be in the opinion of the candidates to sing the song *All through the night."* Prof. Gerrit Bon** was the examiner in November 1931, when each of the 73 candidates was examined for 10 minutes in practical music ("singe"). Bon recommended an additional "Endorsement Course" since there was such a great shortage of well-trained class music teachers. — From 1934, one weekly period of 2 to 3 hours was used for musical theory and in 1935 the remaining 4 to 5 hours devoted to singing were increased to 8 a week. Instruction in pianoforte was added to the curriculum and the course was amended to give second and third-year diploma groups the benefit of the addition. Four classes were given at the College every week and one demonstration class was conducted in a school. However, in June 1938 the TED forbade instrumental music on the College premises and arranged for College students to make use of the facilities at the High School for Girls. — In January 1939, M.M. van der Bent,** Mrs Van der Bent's husband, was appointed head of the department. His influence was immediately evident and in his ten years of service he appreciably influenced the teaching of music in Transvaal schools. The Education Commission (1939) recommended in its report that talented students in the Junior Primary group receive additional training free of charge and, on Mrs Van der Bent's insistence, piano lessons were included in the scheme. The course began in 1944 with the students the Misses J. Botha, M. Potgieter, W. Botha, C. van der Merwe and N. Naude: *Section A:* Afrikaans and English; *Section B:* School teaching subjects; staff notation and sol-fa notation; percussion band; music appreciation; breathing and voice exercises; singing lesson, with and without piano; conducting; *Section C:* Rudiments; theory; harmony; composition; musical form; history of music. *Section D:* Practical: instrumental; singing. — Van der Bent's successors were Dr Wöhler** and after him Dr Y. Huskisson.** In 1971 there were 8 members in the Department of Music under A. de Klerk: D.W. de Beer, T.C. de Villiers and Miss H. van der Wateren (senior assistants), P.J. van der Westhuyzen, Mesdames M. Albertyn, J. Breitenbach and A. de Bruin (assistants). Each week, ninety seven hours in all are devoted to the following courses: a basic course in school music; junior primary and senior primary work with specialisation in music (two four-year courses); secondary courses in school music and in instrumental music (both four years). These courses embrace the following subjects: piano (practical); method of piano teaching; recorders; percussion work; melodic percussion work; harmony; history of music; score playing; musical form; theory of music; choir training and conducting; the methods of school music; aural training; voice training. As an extra-mural activity, students present a large scale musical performance annually and spend a considerable amount of time on choral works, operettas and cantatas.

III. TECHNICAL COLLEGES (TECHNIKONS) UP TO 1970

1. East London Technical College

The Music Department was established in 1949, when two classrooms at the College were set aside for the teaching of music. When, in 1950, the city built a new museum, the College purchased the old museum and by partitioning the great hall on the ground floor, created a number of studios for a Department of Music. The first Head of the Department was Alan Salmon. Under his direction the Department had by 1954 grown to 100 students with two full-time teachers and two part-time assistants. Petrus Lemmer** became the Head in 1956. In 1957 he presented the operetta *Lilac time* with such success that it was described as "East London's musical event of the year". Lemmer was also responsible for the acquisition of an organ for the school hall. Bruce Gardiner** took over in 1958, and by 1970 there was a staff of two full-time teachers and fourteen part-time assistants. The school provides tuition in organ, singing, violin and pianoforte. Serious as well as light music (syncopation) is provided up to and including diploma standard for those studying piano. Every year the College presents highly popular recitals known as *Piano parade,* at which the main item is a piano group recital with as many as 18 students playing on nine pianos.

– B.G.

2. Pretoria College for Advanced Technical Education, now Technikon

This School of Music was started in 1960 (with Mrs Henriette Pauw as part-time principal) in one of the houses formerly used as a men's hostel in Edward Street. By 1962 there were 76 students and during the following two years this number increased to 165, so that it became necessary to increase the staff. By the end of 1963 there were eight lecturers. After the retirement of Mrs Pauw in 1964, Miss Diana Brooke was appointed her full-time successor and when Miss Brooke was succeeded by J.W. van der Merwe** in January 1968, he started with 209 students, 3 full-time and 10 part-time lecturers. From 1968 until today (1971) this school has passed through a period of phenomenal growth. There are now about 1 000 students, 22 full-time lecturers and 31 part-time. — Tuition is given in piano, organ, singing, all string, woodwind- and brass instruments, recorder and classical guitar, and also in speech and drama. Although there is a high percentage of part-time students, some of the facilities offered to full-time students are: tuition on a principal instrument, a second instrument, history of music, musical form, harmony and counterpoint, general music theory, choir training, teaching method for the principal instrument, repertoire and aural training. The School of Music does not have its own examinations, but enters its pupils for the examinations of UNISA, the Royal Schools of Music and the Trinity College of Music. — Since 1966 it has been housed in the East block of the College and at present 8 studios and three administrative offices are in use. However, tuition still continues in the house in Edward Street which has five studios, and in a house in Proes Street where there are seven studios. To meet the needs of students living in the suburbs there were studios in Annlin, Arcadia, Brooklyn, Danville, Irene, Lynnwood, Lynnwood Glen, Menlo Park, Meyerspark, Queenswood, Riviera, Silverton, Sinoville, Valhalla, Villieria, Waverley and Wonderboom-Suid. — In 1970 a string orchestra was formed from members of the student body. (Also read Couzyn, Dawie).

SOURCE
SASMT News Letter, Oct. 1970.

– J.W.v.d.M.

3. Rustenburg Technical College, Conservatoire of Music

In 1958 Derek Ochse** established this institute as a private Conservatoire of Music. Its rapid progress, especially in the face of a dire shortage of teachers, induced the Department of Higher Education to take over the Conservatoire in 1969 by incorporating it as a Music Department of the Technical College. Derek Ochse was appointed Head of the Department and two more full-time and eleven part-time teachers were added to the staff. At present (1970) the Conservatoire instructs between 230 and 360 students in pianoforte, violin, cello, organ and in theoretical subjects. Students are examined by the University of South Africa.** In 1970 Derek Ochse directed the introduction of a course in choir singing. As a final preparation for examinations, candidates perform at public concerts. The original Conservatoire building is still in use (1970), but the envisaged new Technical College building includes lecture rooms, studios for practising and a concert hall for recitals. (Also read Ochse, Derek.)

– J.P.deL.

IV. PRIVATE INSTITUTIONS

HIGHER EDUCATIONAL INSTITUTIONS

1. Pretoria: Conservatoire of Music

In 1959, at the suggestion of the Administrator of the Nederduitse Hervormde Kerk of Africa, Mr A.B. van N. Herbst, and the Chairman of the Finance Council, the Rev. A. Ras, a Committee of the General Synod decided to proceed with the establishment of an institution for the teaching of music. Since 1952 this Church had maintained a school of church music in Krugersdorp, with Willem Mathlener** as Principal. In January 1960, the new institution was opened in temporary premises in Lynnwood Road, Pretoria, with Willem Mathlener as the first Director, and a staff of five, including Erwin Broedrich** (violin) and Nellie du Toit** (singing). The Nederduitse Hervormde Kerk provided the temporary premises free of charge, and also the necessary instruments. — The institution afforded proof that it was providing for a need, and it developed so rapidly that by July of the year of its foundation it became necessary to appoint six more members to the staff. In March of the same year an official meeting was convened at which future control of the Conservatoire was handed to a Council of Trustees, chosen on a broad basis, to give representation to the Church, the State and the music profession. The first official recognition of the Conservatoire came from the City Council of Pretoria, which granted it a subsidy of R10 000 in June 1960. Meanwhile the building of a permanent abode for the Conservatoire proceeded in Jacob Maré Street and in October 1960, it was possible to move into the new building which is the property of the Nederduitse Hervormde Kerk of Africa and is rented by the Conservatoire. — During the first eventful year of its existence, the Conservatoire's policy regarding musical training was clearly outlined. The emphasis was on the spiritual value which music has for everyone, each according to his capacity; this was to be the point of departure for education, rather than a system of examinations or competitions. Instead of the latter, there were to be public performances by the students. — In January 1961, the Conservatoire's three-year Diploma for Music Teaching was instituted, with two practical subjects and the additional requirements of a background of theory and musical history. At the same time the Conservatoire inaugurated a Higher Diploma for students who had obtained the Teacher's Diploma. This required two further years of study. In 1963 these diplomas were recognized by the Department of Education, Arts and Science, as full qualifications for the music-teaching profession in South Africa. At the end of 1963 the first students for the Teacher's Diploma submitted themselves for examination before a board of overseas and local examiners. The examination for the first award of the Higher Diploma was controlled by a similarly constituted board of examiners at the end of 1965. Since 17 April 1964, the diplomas have been awarded at a special ceremony with some distinguished personality in public life as the main speaker. At the Diploma ceremony of 1966 the main speaker, Mr J. de Klerk, at that time Minister for Education, Arts and Sciences, announced that the diplomas of the Conservatoire would henceforth be granted recognition by all four Education Departments in the Republic. For salary purposes they would be equivalent to similar qualifications issued by the Universities. On the strength of this, since 1969, full-time training by the Conservatoire has also been subsidized by the Government. — Over and above its function of providing individual tuition, the Conservatoire actively promotes the practice of music in ensembles and in the community itself. Under the direction of Willem Mathlener a students' choir and an orchestra have performed cantatas by J.S. Bach and annually, since 1964, the *St John Passion* by the same composer. In 1969 these efforts reached a peak when the *St Matthew Passion* was performed in its entirety by the musical forces of the Conservatoire. Other great occasions were the performance of the Brahms *Requiem* (1965) and the *B minor Mass* by J.S. Bach (1967). As an additional service to the community the Conservatoire has, since December 1961, presented free Sunday-evening concerts; thus, not only guest artists, but students of the institution are provided with the opportunity of performing in public. — The various branches of study in music-teaching were extended during the first 10 years to all the usual orchestral instruments, and to other special fields of training. From the second half of 1967, there was offered a Junior Professional Course for the specially talented over the age of eight; they receive a balanced musical education at half the usual cost. Today (1969) there are 20 full-time and part-time musicians on the staff.

- W.M.

HILL, DANIEL (DAN), *11 July 1923 in Lithuania; now (1976) in Johannesburg. Dance band leader.

Resident in South Africa since 1928, Hill took lessons in pianoforte playing and, while at school, played in its orchestra and led a group in the SABC's *Calling to youth* programme series. As a student at the Witwatersrand University, he organized a jazz group with the pianist Archie Silansky. Dave Kitai played violin and bass. This group played at dances and clubs, and marked the beginning of the Radio Rhythm Club. After obtaining the B.Sc. (Elec. Engin.) degree in 1948, Hill devoted himself to music, concentrating on clarinet and saxophone. His was one of the first bands to play on commercial radio, and in 1957 he was awarded the first "Golden Record" presented in South Africa, commemorating his long-playing record, *Happy days are here again;* but his band also achieved its national reputation through broadcast programmes such as: *The Al Debbo show, The B.P. supershow, Stars of tomorrow.* Hill has written numerous commercial jingles, as well as music for films, and accompanied most of South Africa's leading singers of light music. He was appointed Musical Director to Gallo (Africa) Ltd in 1957. His wife is the vocalist, Artemis, who formerly appeared with his dance band.

- Ed.

HILLIG, RUTHILDE   Windhoek 3

HILTON, H.   Organs, I(v)

HIND, DOROTHY AND HIND, H.   Durban 10, Durban Light Orchestra

HIND, GEORGE, *6 March 1852 in Canterbury; ° 28 December 1905 in Oudtshoorn. Bandmaster.

George Hind succeeded C. Glennon in Grahamstown, where the latter had achieved much as bandmaster to the 32nd Light Infantry and previously as conductor of the Prince Alfred's Guard Band (1877–1879). Until the diamonds of Kimberley enticed him away, the young Hind was variously employed as bandmaster in the Eastern Province, in Grahamstown, but also in Queenstown, Graaff Reinet and East London.

Whilst he was in Grahamstown, from January 1879 to June 1880, his name also turns up in Queenstown. It has been recorded that during his first short term as conductor the standard of band playing by the First City Volunteers improved noticeably and that up to 300 people turned up at the Drostdy, even in rainy weather, to listen to their playing. A noteworthy fact is that his programmes included a few of his own compositions (*Kiss and make it up, Voyage of the Conway Castle*) and some arrangements. As far as is known only two of these were printed. — From June 1880 to June 1881 he earned his living in Graaff Reinet as a "professor of music who was prepared to give lessons on violin, cornet, flute, clarinet etc, and to tune pianos". As a conductor he made no progress at all, as the very experienced and doughty James Saunders commanded the band forces in that town. Graaff Reinet was experiencing a boom period musically, which makes it all the more remarkable that Hind is only mentioned for his co-operation with a touring company. In any case, he left Graaff Reinet for Queenstown, where he succeeded Pogson as leader of the Volunteer Band. This group usually performed at public functions and at dances. His popularity in this place is testified to by the fact that a benefit concert was arranged for him at which Mme. Mendelssohn** appeared as a vocalist. Supported by a number of strings, the band offered an interpretation of Verdi's Miserere from *Il trovatore.* — In the meantime, however, he had again in July 1882 become the bandleader of the First City Volunteers in Grahamstown who had been without a proper conductor for two years. The efforts of Sergeant Rogers to keep them going were not treated very respectfully by the press. During his second period of four years, Hind was particularly successful in this town, at times giving practically a weekly concert and then again subsiding into silences which sometimes lasted for months. Significant again is the fact that two benefit concerts given for the conductor were quite successful, an indication that the community approved of his orchestral efforts. It should also be noted that a considerable variety of local talent assisted at both his in- and outdoor concerts. — There is at present no factual knowledge about his career in Kimberley and after, until his death occurred in Oudtshoorn. He left Grahamstown in the first half of 1887.

WORKS

The battle song of Lobengula, South Africa, with refrain (J.F. Sewell). Pr. C.G. Röder, Leipzig, n.d.   The Grahamstown reveries waltzes, dedicated to Lady Barry. B. Williams, London, n.d.

BIBLIOGRAPHY

Bromberger, K.I.: *Music in Grahamstown, 1812-1862.* B.Mus. script, RU, 1967.   Henning, C.G.: *The cultural history of Graaff Reinet, 1786-1886.* D.Phil. thesis, UP, 1971.   Radloff, T.E.K.: *Music in Grahamstown, 1863-1879.* B.Mus. script, RU, 1969.   Sparrow, M.J.: *Music in Grahamstown, 1880-1900.* M.Mus. dissertation, RU, 1978.   Van der Merwe, F.Z.: *Suid-Afrikaanse musiekbibliografie, 1787-1952.* J.L. van Schaik, Pretoria, 1958.

SOURCES

Graaff Reinet Advertiser: 20 Oct. 1885.   *Graaff Reinet Herald:* 26 June 1880; 5 Nov. 1880.   *The Grahamstown Journal:* 1831 to 1900.   *Queenstown Free Press:* 25 July 1879 to 15 Apr. 1880; 12 July 1881 to 25 Apr. 1882.   Estates, Cape Colony: MOOC 6/9/539, DN 295.

– Ed.

HIRSCHLAND, HEINZ, *1901 in Essen; °18 April 1960 in Munich. Pianist and composer.

According to available information, Heinz Hirschland studied music at the Berlin Hochschule für Musik, where he was a pupil of Artur Schnabel for pianoforte, and of Franz Schreker for composition. He gave his first recital in Heidelberg, Germany, in 1920, and subsequently went on a concert tour with the singer Lotte Leonard, which took them through Germany, Italy, Spain and Switzerland. — Hirschland came to South Africa in 1934, as a result of the political upheaval in Germany, and after a period in Cape Town, moved to Johannesburg in 1935. There he established a studio for pianoforte teaching, and advertised in *The Star* (10 Aug. 1935) that he was the "only teacher of Artur Schnabel's method" in South Africa. He performed as pianist at John Connell's** organ recital on 16 March 1936, and a recital was broadcast on the 30th of the same month. Soon he came to be regarded as one of the most versatile and proficient concert pianists in Johannesburg, and frequently appeared at meetings of the Johannesburg Musical Society,** thus in June and November 1936 and in February 1937. He was also engaged in Connell's Music Festivals for the performance of pianoforte concertos with the Festival Orchestra. — Active as a composer, Hirschland often included his own works in his programmes (March 1942 and July 1949; first performance of his *Concertino* at the concert conducted by Jeremy Schulman** in March 1942). On occasion he arranged programme series in which a whole evening was devoted to one composer. In 1945 he became the founder of the Society of South African Composers, and launched a series of subscription concerts in the Library Lecture Hall, at which South African composers presented their own compositions. On 19 May 1945, his *Bulgarian suite for pianoforte* was introduced to a Johannesburg audience and at the next concert in June, Nella Wissema played his *Violin sonata,* with the composer at the piano. — After the war, in 1947, Hirschland visited Brazil on a recital tour, and in 1952 he played in London. There he spent much time studying harpsichord with Christopher Wood, a pupil of Arnold Dolmetsch, and had lessons in composition with Humphrey Searle. Several of his compositions were performed in London during this visit. After his return, the South African Composers' Society was reorganized to offer regular concerts. Hirschland's *Bantu suite for piano, xylophone and voices* was performed, the composer participating personally, at a concert held in Durban on 15 May 1954. In February 1958, a whole evening was devoted to his music in the ATKV Hall, with Walter Mony,** Betty Pack**, Ileana de Jongh, Gert Potgieter** and Hirshland himself participating. — In 1959 Hirshland decided to leave South Africa and resettle in Germany; he was given a farewell concert at the home of Mrs E.N. Harvey.**

WORKS
(All works exist in ms. only. It was not possible to trace the present custodian of the collection).

A. Vocal

1. Songs
Cinque duetti Italiani, for mezzo-soprano, tenor and piano.   Five songs, for soprano and piano.   Huit chansons d'enfants, for soprano and orchestra.   Huit chansons polyglottes, a song cycle for medium voice in Spanish, German, French, Portuguese and English.   'n Kinderhandjie, song cycle by Lorenz Schultz for a mezzo voice and piano.   Preghiera alla

Madonnina, a mass for soprano, flute, oboe, bells and piano.   Seven nocturnes, an Afrikaans cycle, for bass-baritone, oboe, violin and piano.   Sewe Afrikaanse liedere, for soprano and piano.   Sing, vinkie, sing! (C.L. Leipoldt).   Spanish songs from South America, for voice, clarinet and piano.   The tender songs of David Dainow, for soprano and piano.   Twaalf Afrikaanse liedere, for a mezzo voice and piano: 1. Die antwoord (E. Eybers)   2. Maartmaand in Johannesburg (E. Eybers)   3. Die gebed van verstarrende siele (E. Eybers)   4. O koele water van die spruit (C.M. v.d. Heever)   5. Die wrak (C.M. v.d. Heever)   6. Die waaiende fontein in die park (C.M. v.d. Heever)   7. Slaap (D.F. Malherbe)   8. My hondjie (H.J.F. Lochner)   9. Die dwergie (H.J.F. Lochner)   10. Kat en muis (H.F.J. Lochner)   11. Die aandete (H.J.F. Lochner)   12. Slampamperliedjie (C.L. Leipoldt).   Veertien Afrikaanse liedere, for medium voice and piano: 1. Die boodskap van Maria (N.P. van Wyk Louw)   2. Renboot (N.P. van Wyk Louw)   3. Blommeprag (I.D. du Plessis)   4. Stilte (I.D. du Plessis)   5. Branders (I.D. du Plessis).   6. Die duif (I.D. du Plessis)   7. Gebed (I.D. du Plessis)   8. Minneliedjie (I.D. du Plessis)   9. Rus en stilte (I.D. du Plessis)   10. So ja, seuntjie (B.J. Dreyer).   11. Sagte aandreën   12. Die middag van die Uniefees   13. Herfsskemering (L. de Swaan)   14. Eerste sneeu (L. de Swaan).

2. Choral works

Die Dieper Reg, a dramatic Afrikaans oratorio on words by N.P. van Wyk Louw, for five soloists, choir and orchestra.   Ngoma, a Bantu serenade for male voice choir and orchestra.

3. Opera

Johannesburg – Park Station, a dramatic opera in three acts.

B. Instrumental

1. Piano

A Bantu suite (piano version).   Fantasia on Spanish themes.   Fourteen short pieces with 12 tones.   La Madonna del Salvador Dali.   My doll Martha, ten children's pieces. Piano suite for little Anelja.   Seven preludes, in the twelvetone style.   Sonata.   Suite, in the old style.   Three sonatinas.   Two Bulgarian suites.   Various piano pieces.

2. Piano duets and works for two pianos

Ten Bulgarian dances, for piano duet.   Waltzes, for piano duet.

3. Chamber music

A Bantu suite, for piano, xylophone and voices.   Bulgarian dances, for 2 pianos and clarinet.   Five pieces for cello, piano or harp.   Five sonatas, for violin and piano. Novoseltzi, Bulgarian dances for 2 pianos and clarinet.   Serenade, for violin and piano. Sonata, for flute and piano.   Sonata, for cello and piano.   Sonata, for oboe and piano.   Sonata, for clarinet and piano.   Sonata, for bassoon and piano.   Sonatina, for clarinet and piano.   String quartet no. 1.   String quartet no. 2 on Zulu themes.   String quartet no. 3.   String quartet in the twelvetone style.   Trio, for piano, violin and cello.   Valley of a Thousand Hills, for 6 woodwinds and piano.   Variations on an Italian cradle song, for violin and piano.

4. Piano and Orchestra

Bulgarian rhapsody, for piano and orchestra.   Concertino I "In the old style", for piano, 2 flutes and strings.   Concertino II, for piano and orchestra.   Concertino III, for piano and orchestra.   Four peculiar pieces, for piano and orchestra.   Three fantasies, for piano and orchestra.

5. Orchestral
Concerto grosso.   Sarie Marais variations.

ARTICLE
What makes a great composition? *Lantern* IV/3, Mar. 1955.

SOURCES
Idelson, Jerry: Sketches of South African composers. *Bandstand,* July 1935.   "Hirschland Recital", programme dated 22 Feb. 1958.

– L.W. (amplified)

HIRST, ANNETTE   James H. Harper
HIRST, IRA   Mackay Bros, South African piano music 1(i), 2(ii)
HITCHCOCK, T.J.   Bloemfontein, Organs 1(i), 1(v), South African piano music III

HOBDAY, MISS   King William's Town 6

HOBY, CHARLES, *in London: °circa 1938 in England. Conductor, music teacher, composer.

Hoby studied violoncello, organ and pianoforte at the RCM and instrumentation for military bands under Charles Godfrey, before being posted to India as bandmaster of the Punjab Frontier Force. His health failing, he returned to England, and became a candidate for the bandmastership of the Royal Engineers, but was rejected because he had not qualified at Kneller Hall. He was appointed organist to the Royal Military Asylum, Chelsea, and at the same time engaged on the staff of the *Orchestral Times* (later the *British Musician*), to which he contributed articles on the violoncello and other subjects. — In 1891 Hoby came to South Africa as assistant to Dan Godfrey,** Musical Director of the Standard Opera Company, which inaugurated the new Standard Theatre** in Johannesburg. After an extended tour, he settled in Durban as Bandmaster of the Natal Royal Rifles; he was also a music teacher at the Durban High School, and conductor of the Durban and Berea Choral and Orchestral Union (1893–1894). In 1894 he organized amateur musical theatricals in Durban, producing *Erminie* (Jakobowski) and *The old guard* (Planquette), for which he reorchestrated the whole opera, and composed music for an opening chorus, as well as dances and two songs. Three years later he formed the Diamond Jubilee Opera Company with J. Ferguson Brown.** As an organist, Hoby often gave recitals during his tenure at St Paul's Church (1894–1897). — During the first five years of this century Hoby was a prominent musical personality in Durban, having succeeded Frank Proudman** in October 1900 as conductor of the Durban Orchestral Society,** in which he had previously been a cellist. He also succeeded R.H. Macdonald** in 1902 as conductor of the Durban Musical Association** and Ernest Lezard** as conductor of the war-time Bijou Orchestra at the end of 1901. In 1903 he became conductor of a choir of twenty male voices, the Gleemen of Durban. — In 1906 Hoby left Durban "on a short trip", but he never returned to South Africa. He eventually became bandmaster of the First Division of the Royal Marines at Clapham, with the rank of major in 1912, after obtaining the Mus. Doc. degree at Oxford University with a set of compositions.

WORKS

Sonata, for cello and organ. Ms., 1893.   Andante and allegro commodo, for violin and organ. Ms., 1894.   Scenes of childhood, suite for orchestra. Boosey & Hawkes, London, 1896. Scenes from Venice, suite for orchestra. Ms., 1898.   Britannia's flag, song (Lynn Lyster). Vause, Slatter & Co., Durban, 1899.   Britannia's piccaninny, song (Lynn Lyster). Jackson Bros, Durban, 1899; also P. Davis & Sons, Durban, n.d.   Brown, Bonnie Brown, military song (Lynn Lyster). P. Davis & Sons, Pietermaritzburg, 1899.   Lord Roberts' own march. Ms., 1900.   On active service, for orchestra. Ms., 1900.   Pretoria! Pretoria!, military song (Lynn Lyster). Jackson Bros, Durban, 1900.   Barcarolle, two-part song (words by composer). Novello & Co., London, 1903.   Under the greenwood tree, two-part song (Shakespeare). Novello & Co., London, 1903.   The South African junior song book. Longmans Green & Co., London, 1904.   The South African school sight-singing method. Longmans Green & Co., London, 1904.   The old spinet, morceau rococo for orchestra. J. & W. Chester Ltd., 1928.   Album of duets, for violin with pianoforte accompaniment. Augener & Co., London, n.d.: 1. Romance 2. Bourrée 3. Fairy tale 4. Alla mazurka.   Come closer, waltz. Ascherberg, Hopwood & Crew Ltd., London, n.d.   The lads of the Carbineers, song (Lynn Lyster). Vause, Slatter & Co., Durban, n.d.   A Russian wedding, for orchestra. Hull, Bromley, n.d.   The South African school song book, edited and arranged as two-part songs. Longmans Green & Co., London. The following songs by Hoby are included: 1. His Majesty the King (words by composer) 2. Raise the flag (words by composer) 3. The Englishman (Eliza Cook) 4. Stand for the King (Lynn Lyster).   The Southern Cross barn dance. Ms., n.d.   The twilight serenaders, for orchestra. Hull, Bromley, n.d.

BIBLIOGRAPHY

Brown, James and Stratton, Stephen: *British musical biography*. Birmingham, 1897.   Jackson, George: *Music in Durban from 1850 to 1900*. D.Phil. thesis, UWits, 1961.   Van der Merwe, F.Z.: *Suid-Afrikaanse musiekbibliografie, 1787–1952*. J.L. van Schaik, Pretoria, 1958. Additional information supplied by Dr Jackson.   Research Centre for South African Music, HSRC, Pretoria.

– E.H.S.

HODDERSON, JOHANN LUD(E)WIG, *in Oldenburg, Germany. Organ builder and piano tuner.

Hodderson came to the Cape in 1779 as a soldier in the service of the DEIC, but from 1780 he was an independent organ builder and the inspector and renovator ("opziender en repareerder") of the Groote Kerk organ. After repairing the organ of the Lutheran Church in Strand Street in 1782, he was also employed there, from 1783, as organ builder ("orgelmaker"). In 1786 he was commissioned to enlarge the organ of the Lutheran Church, but he only completed the work in 1788, to the dissatisfaction of his employers, who complained about his behaviour and lack of attention to his duties. A new organ which he had to build for the parish in Paarl was similarly delayed; it was not ready for use until 1791. The Lutheran Church Council broke its association with him in 1790 but were obliged to re-appoint him in 1793. He remained their organ tuner until 1809. — Hodderson also provided organs for places beyond Cape Town, in the country districts. Lichtenstein relates how he heard one of these organs being played on the farm of Hilgard Muller; he also mentions (in 1803) that Hodderson made a reasonable living in Cape Town from his organ building and piano tuning.

BIBLIOGRAPHY
Bouws, Jan: *Musiek in Suid-Afrika.* Brugge, 1946.   Hoge, J.: *Personalia of the Germans at the Cape, 1652-1806.* Cape Town, 1946.   Lichtenstein, H.: *Reizen in het Zuidelijk Gedeelte van Afrika in de jaren 1803, 1804, 1805 en 1806, I* (Uit het Hoogduitsch vertaald door W. Goede). Dordtrecht, 1813.   Moorrees, A.: *Die Nederduitse Gereformeerde Kerk in Suid-Afrika, 1652-1873.* Cape Town, 1937.   Ottermann, R.E.: *Die kerkmusiek in die Evangeliese Lutherse Kerk in Strandstraat, Kaapstad, tussen 1780 en 1880.* M.Mus. dissertation, US, 1963. Schmidt-Pretoria, Werner: *Der Kulturanteil des Deutschtums am Aufbau des Burenvolkes.* Hanover, 1938.

– J.B.

HOGG, CYRIL   Port Elizabeth II/5

HOLLANDSCH MANNENKOOR, THE, owes its origin to the social club or "sociëteit", De Hollandsche Klub, which came into being in Pretoria on 14 March 1895, with C. May as chairman. Shortly afterwards its members appreciated the desirability of meeting with a definite purpose in view. Since the club had male members only, their thoughts inevitably gravitated to the idea of a male voice choir. Barely five weeks after the club had been founded its choir was launched with C.H. Maas as chairman and Dirk Balfoort** as musical director (25 April 1895). This choir, which was to become a significant force in the cultural life of Pretoria, and in 1915 was called "een zieraad voor de Hollandsche Gemeenschap" (an ornament of the Dutch community) by the Dutch Consul, Dr Verschuur, fulfilled a patriotic function throughout its history (celebrations of Queen Wilhelmina's birthday) but without ever losing its original convivial character. The "rookavondjes" (smokers' evenings), frequently made practicable by the donation of a keg or two of Dutch beer, tobacco and cigars, constitute a leading characteristic of its history. — As early as 31 August 1895, the choir gave its first performance to coincide with Queen Wilhelmina's birthday celebrations, and the first social gathering took place shortly afterwards. On 1 January of the following year J.A. Schallies became chairman, and under his leadership (which continued until 28 April 1898), the choir built up a substantial reputation. In February 1896, the choir was able to play an important role during a festival gathering in the President Theatre – a gathering which, although the President was not present, had the character of a State function. According to press reports, those present included Commandant General P.J. Joubert, the Director of Railways, G.A.A. Middelberg, the State Attorney, Dr E.J.P. Jorissen, Judge Dr Schagen van Leeuwen, officers of the State Artillery, the Consul General of the Netherlands, and the Consuls of France, Germany and the Congo. The concert was given in aid of a memorial fund for burgers killed in the Malaboch war. The programme included the *Transvaal anthem* and *Transvalers ontwaakt,* played by an orchestra (presumably with choir and community singing)

Avondlied for male quartette by Verhulst, and songs by a German double quartette. Other participants were E. Amorison, who featured in almost all musical programmes of the time, and Messrs Luttig and Landgraf. Other performances took place on 27 November of the same year, and on 30 April 1897. — On 3 August 1897, the choir gave Dirk Balfoort's cantata, *De haringvisschers,* its première and on 29 January 1898 they repeated the performance with great success. This second performance had its place in another concert which bore the character of a state function. The conference held by the two republics of the Transvaal and the Orange Free State, with a view to possible confederation, took place in Pretoria, and the Free State delegates were invited to the performance. The Transvaal Government was represented by the State Secretary F.W. Reitz, the Under Secretary for Foreign Affairs, C. van Boeschoten, and by the State Attorney, Mr Gregorowski. An unknown orchestra played the *Free State anthem,* and M. de Groot conducted in a performance of a *March, nocturne and caprice* by A.E. Matt. The composer Balfoort, together with the soloists, H.W. Casteleins and J.H.A. van Bakeren, received flattering tributes in the columns of *De Volksstem* and *De Press.* Other participants in the variety programme were Messrs Knoll, Reepmaker van Belle, and Susan and T. van Noort. Of Balfoort the press said that he was "de aangewezen man . . . om ook onze Afrikaansche gedichten op muziek te zetten" (the obvious man to set our Afrikaans poems to music). — On 28 April W.H. Nijenes was appointed chairman, and on 13 May the choir officially received its own standard. On this occasion they sang a new *Banierzang* of which the music has since been lost, although the words still exist. In expressing the aims of the choir, the words of the unknown poet also vindicate the Dutch language:

> Door naar 't edel doel te streven,
> zingend eerend Hollands taal . . .
> (By striving for the noble cause, to
> honour, singing, the Dutch language).

The year 1898 also witnessed an official visit of high-ranking officers of the Dutch Navy to Pretoria. They were entertained at a State social gathering when the choir offered musical tributes to the guests. In April 1899 the choir-master, Dirk Balfoort, left for Belgium, and was succeeded by M. de Groot, who remained in charge until the outbreak of the Anglo-Boer War, which drastically crippled the choir. Some of the choir members emigrated, while others joined the Boer forces. In August 1900 only seven members remained. At a leave-taking ceremony Balfoort was presented with an album and when the train departed the choir sang *Mijne moedertaal.* — The choir was revived in 1903, with Nijenes still in the chair, and in May of the same year the first gathering of old and new members could take place. Choir practices were resumed on Friday evenings at the Imperial Hotel under the direction of Hendrik Visscher.** Under his guidance the choir was able to give a public performance as early as 7 July. Once again it played a role in the commemorations of Queen Wilhelmina's birthday, and the Rookavondjes were resumed; the choir arranged its own independent concert evenings, its successful programmes consisting of choral items varied by song solos and instrumental items, occasionally classical string-quartettes performed under the direction of Amorison (as in March 1906). An interesting facet of the programmes at this time was that works by Dutch composers like Verhulst, Richard Hol and François Gevard were performed fairly regularly, and that chamber music items were regularly chosen to vary the choral numbers. Instrumentalists whose names frequently appear were Charles Israel,** Aubrey Wilmot, A. Quayle,** E. Amorison and Emil Hester.**

— In 1905 the choir consisted of 33 active members, 134 ordinary members, 12 patrons and one honorary member. The director at the time was J.J. de Visser and the rehearsals took place in the Royal Café. In this year the choir celebrated its tenth anniversary in the Empress Theatre with the co-operation of the Apollo Choral Society and members of the band of the Christelijke Jongelieden Vereeniging. — Under Petrus van den Burg's** guidance from February 1907 to 1909, the choir attained an even greater reputation which was maintained by his successor, Pierre de Beer,** between 1909 and 1911. The fifteenth anniversary was celebrated on 25 April 1910 at the Opera House.** On this occasion De Beer, and the conductors J.J. de Visser, Petrus van den Burg and Mrs Bal van Lier,** conducted the choir in turn. With Emil Hester as choirmaster the Hollandsch Mannenkoor began to give performances outside Pretoria in Johannesburg and neighbouring towns. After their successful performance at the Carlton Hotel in Johannesburg (December 1911), the choir was described in the *Pretoria News* as one of the best in the country. — During World War I its public appearances were less frequent and chiefly restricted to contributions to so-called Neutral Concerts, held in aid of war funds. It would seem that the choir suffered a setback at that time, because in July 1918 it had become necessary for J.J. de Visser to reorganise the choir "sodat deze oudste vereeniging van Hollands-sprekendes te Pretoria weer met nieuwe kracht zal opstaan" (so that this oldest society of the Dutch people in Pretoria may rise with renewed strength). After a brief period under De Visser's leadership, Henri ten Brink** became the new choir-master and remained in office until his death on 8 November 1920. In May of that year he conducted the choir on the occasion of its 25th anniversary. Public performances again diminished after his death, and in 1926 this first Hollandsch Mannenkoor eventually ceased to exist. During the last ten years of its life, it had gradually lost its unadulterated Dutch character due to an increasing number of Afrikaans members. The musical role which the Hollandsch Mannenkoor had maintained for almost a quarter of a century was taken over by larger mixed voice choirs like ASAF** and the English-speaking Pretoria Male Voice Choir,** at first called the Apollo Male Voice Choir. The termination of the Hollandsch Mannenkoor concluded a highly characteristic chapter of Dutch cultural activity in Pretoria.

BIBLIOGRAPHY
Vermeulen, Elizabeth: *Die Musieklewe van Pretoria tussen 1902 en 1926.* M.Mus. dissertation, UP, 1967.

SOURCES
Ploeger, Jan: Die Sangvereniging "Hollandsch Mannenkoor", *Pretoriana* 39/40, Aug.–Dec. 1962.   *De Volksstem:* 15 Feb. 1896; 29 Jan. 1898; 31 Jan. 1898; 17 Apr. 1899; 29 Apr. 1905; and 3 May 1910.   *De Press:* 31 Jan. 1898.   Information provided by the late D.J. Balfoort of Den Haag, son of the first choir-master.

–J.P.

HOLLINS, A.   R. Ascham, J. Connell, Durban 5, H. Greenwood, Johannesburg 2, R. Lees-Ingles, Port Elizabeth, Organs 10, 11

HOLMES, D.   U. de Villiers, E.M. Slatter

HOLMES, SAMUEL PATRICK, *17 December 1932 in Nottingham; at present (1979) Director of Music, South African Police, Pretoria, with the rank of Colonel. Military bandmaster.

Colonel Holmes joined the British Army as a boy musician at the age of fifteen and in 1948 was registered as a student at the Royal Military School of Music (Kneller Hall) for one year's training as a flautist under Robert Murchie, flautist of the London Philharmonic Orchestra. After rejoining his regiment, he remained with them in West Germany until 1960, when he was chosen to attend a full four-year course at Kneller Hall. During this time he had instruction on all band and orchestral instruments and was trained in orchestration, choral techniques, conducting and other musical subjects. The diplomas testifying to the efficiency to which he attained at the Military School are A(Mus)LCM, ARCM, ALCM. He completed his studies in 1964 and received an appointment as bandmaster to the Royal Highland Regiment (the "Black Watch") and saw service in Europe, South America, the Far East and North Africa. — By 1972 Holmes had become a senior bandmaster of the Scottish Division and was appointed a Senior Lecturer in Music at the Scottish Military School of Music in Edinburgh. He remained in this post until December 1974 when he was chosen to become Director of Music to the South African Police in Pretoria. With characteristic energy he revised the working schedule of the Police Band to include section and group practices, combined rehearsals of scales and chords, full band rehearsals and playing in brass and woodwind chamber groups. The practical work is supported by individual instruction in theoretical subjects and promotion examinations are held twice yearly to examine the candidates' proficiency, for classification to the status of 3rd, 2nd or 1st class musicians. — Despite his manifold duties, Colonel Holmes still performs as a flute soloist, an instrument which he instructs in the Transvaal Education Department. He is also associated with the South African National Youth Orchestra and accompanied them on their 1978 overseas tour. In South Africa he has added to his qualifications by obtaining the FTCL, and LTCL, and the UPLM of UNISA.

– Ed.

HOLT, C. South African piano music IV/1

HOLTZHAUSEN, JACOBA SUSANNA (NUNEZ), *22 May 1886 on the farm "Die Post", near Port Elizabeth; ° 30 April 1974 at Middelburg, Transvaal. Coloratura soprano.

Nunez Holtzhausen was a direct descendant of the first Holtzhausen who emigrated from Germany to South Africa in 1730. Just before the Anglo-Boer War her father trekked from the Cape to the Transvaal and although technically a British subject, he joined the Boer forces. Her mother was interned in a concentration camp at Germiston during the war. Her sporadic education was resumed after the war and in 1905 she studied in Stellenbosch for a music teacher's diploma at the newly-created conservatoire of F.W. Jannasch.** Properly equipped in 1908, she taught on the Witwatersrand where she became interested in voice production. After 1915 Aimée

Parkerson** was in charge of her voice training and at a later stage she also had lessons from Burns-Walker. When she had completed her 37th year (1924), she spent two years at the Kochen School of Singing in Berlin, made her debut there in 1926 in the Schiller Hall and also sang in the Netherlands. In this same year she considered the possibility of an opera career, but and returned to South Africa where she immediately went on a tour of the Western Province, accompanied by the elocutionist, Stephanie Faure, and received glowing press notices. The *Burger* wrote: "She must sing, sing often and sing culture into South Africa" (quoted by Louise Behrens in *Sarie Marais, 3 Aug. 1960*). After a further concert with the Durban City Orchestra,** she toured in Natal with them and also visited Johannesburg and Pretoria for a few concerts. Shortly afterwards she organised her own tour in South African centres and in Rhodesia, where she typically included the Daisyfield Afrikaans orphanage on her itinerary. — Complete identification with the historical development of the Afrikaner nation had been a pronounced motive of Nunez Holtzhausen's career since her return to South Africa. For the fortieth birthday celebrations of Johannesburg in 1926, she trained a children's choir which participated in the historical pageant clothed in Voortrekker costume; and she herself often preferred the same costume during the thirties, when she had to sing in public. She was similarly enthusiastic about Afrikaans folkdancing, among children at first, but eventually extended to include adults. In 1933 she trained an adult group for a demonstration given at a cultural meeting in the Pretoria City Hall. Pollie Roberson (spelled thus), her pianoforte accompanist, acted as her advisor in this work. From the same patriotic motive rose her enthusiasm for an Afrikaans Music Club** (1941), of which she became the first musical director, and for the incipient Afrikaans art song. She recorded Lettie Joubert's** *Lentesang* for HMV at the request of the FAK,** including other songs, interpreted by herself and Stephen Eyssen,** on the reverse side of the record (see Discography). Lacking suitable Afrikaans songs, she had the poet A.G. Visser translate some of her repertoire pieces into Afrikaans and included these with traditional Afrikaans "picnic songs" on her concert programmes. She did, in actual fact, use her talent "to sing culture into South Africa", notably among her Afrikaans compatriots. — Besides coloratura favourites from *Norma, La traviata* and *Zauberflöte,* Nunez also included Ophelia's "mad scene' from *Hamlet* (Thomas) and extracts from *Ariadne auf Naxos* (Gluck) and *Rosenkavalier* (Strauss) in her programmes, combining coloratura exhibitionism with genuine drama and songs. An obvious choice were the songs about nightingales, which displayed her coloratura abilities to advantage. An interesting novelty at the time was her practice of singing opera arias in appropriate costumes. — For a period of nine years she taught singing at the primary school Pretoria-Oos (1940–1949) and produced a children's operetta almost every year. One of her successes was *Boernooientjie* (an Afrikaans translation of *The milkmaid*) which she produced with a choir of 400 children, all dressed in Voortrekker costumes. On other occasions she arranged children's concerts, with the assistance of Lettie Joubert and Judith Brent-Wessels. Her other activities include lecturing to HED students on school music (one year only) and adjudicating at eisteddfodau. — From 1949 to 1953 Nunez Holtzhausen bred Ayrshires on the farm "Mizpah" in the Belfast district, but during the latter year she returned to Pretoria. From her first marriage to G.A. Hattingh two sons were born, of whom the eldest became a farmer in the Middelburg (Transvaal) district. She resided on his farm until her death.

HOLTZHAUSEN

SOURCES
Behrens, Louise: Die Transvaalse Nagtegaal. *Sarie Marais,* 3 Aug. 1960.　Stegmann, Frits: Nunez Holtzhausen. *Die Burger,* 6 July 1961.　Correspondence with Dr G. Hattingh, Pretoria.

– J.P.M.

HONEY, ALBERT EDWARD, *29 April 1919 in Torquay, Devon; at present (1978) in Grahamstown. Flautist, composer and lecturer in music.

After completion of his education at the Simon Langton School, Canterbury, Albert Honey studied organ and counterpoint (1937–1939) and during the war learnt to play the flute in the band of the Royal Dragoons. In 1945 he was appointed principal flautist to the Coldstream Guards Band in London, and during the four years of his service he won a composition scholarship tenable for two years at Trinity College (1946–1948). In 1948 he was awarded a French Government Scholarship to study flute at the Conservatoire National de Musique in Paris (1949–1950). — On his return to Britain, Honey became principal flautist to the Scottish National Orchestra in Glasgow (1951–1954), subsequently serving for ten years as principal flautist to the BBC Revue Orchestra, London. Continuing his studies, he obtained the LGSM, with a silver medal for achieving the highest marks in the British Isles, and also the LRAM and ARCM diplomas, all in 1961. In 1965 he terminated his contract with the orchestra, became a free-lance flautist and accepted engagements with TV, films and recording companies. In addition he taught music in the service of the London County Council and was a music teacher at the Goldsmith's College of the London University. Until he left for South Africa in 1967 he was in charge of the wind ensemble of this College for five years. — Honey was appointed lecturer in Music at Rhodes University in April 1967. He continued his study of music at Rhodes, obtaining an M.Mus. degree with distinction (1969–1970), for a dissertation on *Woodwind instruments at the crossroads.* Since that time his thesis for the degree of Ph.D. has also been accepted. He formed and trained a wind band and an orchestra at the University and in June 1971, a youth orchestra was established under his guidance. Since 1976 he has been the bandmaster of the Prince Alfred's Guard in Port Elizabeth and conductor at band concerts in the Eastern Province.

WORKS

A. Vocal

1. Songs with piano or guitar accompaniment
To England (A.E. Honey). Ms., 1941.　April (W. Watson). Ms., 1944.　Summer night (Margery Agrell). Ms., 1944.　Shed no tear (Keats). Ms., 1946.　The cherry tree (A.E. Housman). Ms., 1947.　Twelfth night, for voice and guitar. Ms., 1967.　Fair land of Erin (A.E. Honey). Ms., 1969.　Psalm 34, for two sopranos. Ms., 1973.

2. Choir, SATB
Wee brown man, with orchestra (Kathleen Doran). Ms., 1968.　Bredon Hill (A.E. Housman). Ms., 1971.　Home thoughts (R. Browning). Ms., 1971.　My true love hath my heart (Sir P. Sydney). Ms., 1971.　The Redcoat (A.E. Housman). Ms., 1971.　When daisies pied (Shakespeare). Ms., 1971.　When music sounds (W. de la Mare). Ms., 1971.　Vita brevis, a madrigal (A.E. Honey). Ms., 1972.

242

B. Instrumental

1. Orchestra

Canterbury bells. Ms., 1968.   Rustic dance, for children's orchestra. Ms., 1971.   Original compositions based on Grieg's incidental music to Ibsen's play *Peer Gynt*, for bass saxophone and piano. Ms., n.d.: 1. Rustic dance 2. Morning 3. Anitra's dance 4. Dance of the Trolls.

2. Band

Suite in F major. Ms., 1945.   The promise of victory. Ms., 1945.   Fantasia on Tallis's canon. Ms., 1964.   Passacaglia. Ms., 1964.   Rondo for reeds. Ms., 1965.   Brave banner, march. Ms., 1972.   Bockbierpolka and Kegelgalop, for Deutsches Klub in PE. Ms., 1972.   Tin Hats, jubilee march for MOTHS. Ms., 1977.

3. Woodwind quintet (2 flutes, oboe, clarinet, bassoon)

Wind quintet in E flat. Ms., 1960.   Theme and variations. Ms., 1964.

4. Incidental music, 1967–1976

Dr Faustus for wind band, percussion and piano (play by Christopher Marlowe). Ms., 1968.   Menaecumi, for 2 flutes and 2 clarinets. Ms., n.d.   Noah, for percussion, harpsichord, cello and piano (play by André Obey). Ms., n.d.   St Joan, for flute, clarinet, harpsichord and piano (play by George Bernard Shaw). Ms., 1967.   The silent woman, with cello, double-bass and harpsichord (play by Ben Jonson). Ms., n.d.   Toad of Toad Hall, with three violins and piano. Ms., n.d.

C. Arrangements

1. Choral, SATB

Art thou troubled (Handel). Ms., 1971.   Sally in our alley (trad.). Ms., 1971.

2. Band

1820-jubilee march (Rev. H.H. Dugmore), performed during the 1820 festival, 1970.   Band and barrel, English, Afrikaans and German folk tunes. Ms., 1970.   Deutsche Weisen. Ms., 1970.   Radetzky march (J. Strauss). Ms., 1971.   Evergreen, popular dance melodies. Ms., 1974.   Italia mia, medley. Ms., 1976.   Prince Alfred's Guard regimental march (R. Tardugno). Ms., 1976.

3. Woodwind quintet (2 flutes, oboe, clarinet, bassoon)

Three English songs. Ms., 1964.   Three Afrikaans songs. Ms., 1968.   Three Scotch songs. Ms., 1968.

4. Operetta

Dear friends and gentle hearts, operetta based on songs of Stephen Foster with original overture and ballet music (R. Holderness). Ms., 1969.

WRITINGS

The art of flute playing, textbook written in 1960.   *The history, organisation and training of wind bands*. Ph.D. thesis, RU, 1972.

BIBLIOGRAPHY

Burke's peerage, London, 1969.   *Who's who in music*, 5th ed. London, 1969.

– Ed.

HONORÉ, JASMINE (MRS HERBERT), *20 July 1924 in London; living in Ireland in 1966. Ballet dancer, teacher and choreographer, who specialised in Spanish dancing.

Jasmine was brought to South Africa in December 1927, and was eventually trained by Dulcie Howes** at the University of Cape Town Ballet,** dancing with the UCT Ballet and the Cape Town Ballet Club** before leaving in 1946 for further study in London with Brunelleschi, Volkova and Craske. In London she became a member of the Ballet Rambert. After her return to South Africa in 1948, she joined the staff of the University of Cape Town Ballet School and produced a number of ballets for the Company. For family reasons, she resigned in 1950 and in 1961 she moved to Ireland, to stay there permanently. Among her pupils were Joy Shearer** and Marina Keet.** She performed *Pliaska* and *Fête galante* for the UCT Ballet and choreographed five ballets, including *Amor eterno* and *Ancient lights*.

– M.G.

HOOGENHOUT, IMKER FRANÇOIS MARAIS, *20 March 1919 in Bethal; °14 October 1974 in Wellington. Wine farmer, journalist and active protagonist of popular music.

After the completion of his school career at the Afrikaanse Hoër Seunskool in Pretoria, Imker Hoogenhout studied at the University of Pretoria and served as a Captain during the Second World War. In 1945 he returned to the family farm "Optenhorst" in the Wellington district. As a schoolboy he had pianoforte lessons in Pretoria, but at the age of 16 he turned to vocal ditties, accompanying himself on the guitar. His association with radio broadcasting started in his seventh year (1926), and was at a later stage continued in Pieter de Waal's weekly Afrikaans features. After settling at the Cape, Hoogenhout became prominent in broadcasts of Boeremusiek (Afrikaans dance music) and came first in a Boeremusiek competition organized by the SABC. He composed several songs of his own and collected the ditties of the Coloured community, which he adapted for his broadcasts.

– Ed.

HOOPER-REES, LOUISE *11 August 1869 in England; °11 July 1954 in Johannesburg. Music teacher and choral conductor.

After her marriage to Sydney H. Rees,** who like herself was a Licentiate of the Victoria College of Music, London, the couple lived in Cardiff, where Louise taught piano and singing, was organist at Wood Street Chapel, and conducted a ladies' choir that won two Bardic Chairs at Welsh National Eisteddfodau. On settling in South Africa in 1901, Mrs Rees founded the Kimberley College of Music with her husband and started the Kimberley Ladies' Choir. In 1906 this choir amalgamated with the Kimberley Choral and Orchestral Union, which had also been established in collaboration with her husband. At the end of 1910 the family settled in Johannesburg, where Mrs Rees again opened a singing studio and formed another ladies' choir; it is known to have given performances and broadcasts until the early forties. The years between 1919 and 1929 were spent in England. — Louise's sons, **Percy Harcourt Rees**

(*21 November 1893) and **Walter Rees** (*29 July 1895) came to South Africa with their parents in 1901. After a period as cellist in the Cape Town Municipal Orchestra,** Percy Harcourt played in cafe ensembles and eventually settled in Johannesburg, as cello principal in the Colosseum Orchestra, conducted by Charles Manning. In 1930 he was a member of the Danza** and Ferramosca ensemble, which performed at the Regent Restaurant. Walter was well-known as a ballad singer in Johannesburg, where he settled in 1910, and became one of the first singers to broadcast from Johannesburg. He was also a member of the Melodians, a vocal quartette which enjoyed great popularity during the 1920s and 1930s. He played the piano professionally at home entertainments.

SOURCES

Programmes of the Kimberley Choral and Orchestral Union and other material housed in the Public Library, Kimberley.   *The Outspan:* 2 Aug. 1929; 30 Oct 1931.   *Diamond Fields Advertiser:* 5 Aug. 1942.

– D.R.

HOPWOOD, MRS M.   Bloemfontein I/2, 8, E. Leviseur

HORNBURG, DR F.   Windhoek, 3

HOSKYN, MARGARET, *11 June 1899 in Torquay, Devonshire; now (1979) in Stellenbosch. Music teacher and author.

After her father's death in 1913, Margaret Hoskyn and her mother decided to emigrate to Grahamstown in South Africa, where she had a sister who was a student at the Training College and an uncle, Peter van Braam, who lectured in Classics at the University College. She went to school at the Diocesan School for Girls and had her music lessons at the same place. After her matriculation, Messrs Taylor and Jackson and Mrs Streatfield attended to her instruction in piano and violin for a while, but in 1920 the family moved to Cape Town with the object of enabling Margaret to attend classes at the College of Music.** Mrs W.H. Bell** took charge of her pianoforte playing and Miss Winifred Loeffler trained her in violin playing. A visit to a brother living in the Philippine Islands and a prolonged indisposition interrupted this work for a few years, but eventually she resumed her lessons in Cape Town, now travelling to Stellenbosch for violin instruction given by Ivy Angove.** In 1926 Miss Hoskyn obtained a Teacher's Licentiate in pianoforte and taught successively at the Girls' High School in Malmesbury (1930), at St Cyprian's in Cape Town (1931–1939) and at the Rhenish Girls' High School in Stellenbosch (1940–1953). For two years after her retirement she was partially responsible for the pianoforte teaching at the Training College in Stellenbosch; until 1967 she taught privately at home and finally, until 1973, she was a part-time teacher of pianoforte at the College of Music in Cape Town. — Margaret Hoskyn was prominent in the musical life of Stellenbosch, where in 1946 she helped to establish the Stellenbosch Music Society. She acted as chairwoman of this group from about 1963 until 1978 and served the Stellenbosch branch of the SASMT in a similar capacity. She had been a member of this organisation since 1931 and became their National President in 1958. In addition she occupied herself in the writing of four books, the preparation of talks for the English service of the SABC (on subjects like Music Appreciation, British Music and Women in Music) and in writing for the English press. For the *National Biographical Dictionary* she prepared and wrote four articles on academic personalities in Stellenbosch.

PUBLICATIONS
All kinds of music. Maskew Miller, Cape Town, 1946. *From sackbut to symphony.* Juta & Co., Cape Town, 1950. *A Britisher in the Philippines* (letters written by a member of her family in the 19th century). Education Department, Manila, 1964. *Stellenbosch Village.* Tafelberg Uitgewers, Cape Town, 1979. *SAMT:* 37, Nov. 1949; 39, Nov. 1950; 54, May 1958; 56, June 1959; 69, Dec. 1969.

SOURCES
SAMT: 40, June 1951. Research Centre for South African Music, HSRC, Pretoria.

– Ed.

HOTCHKISS, MR Organs 4

HOUGHTING'S MUSIC HALL (DURBAN) D'Arcy Read Operetta Co., Durban 3

HOUWERT, PIETER S.P. Naudé

HOUZÊT, MILLICENT (MRS LEMMER) P.J. Lemmer

HOWES, DULCIE (MRS G. CRONWRIGHT), *31 December 1909 in the Mossel Bay district; living in Cape Town in 1972. Director of CAPAB Ballet and founder of the University of Cape Town Ballet.**

Dulcie Howes studied ballet dancing with Helen Webb,** before leaving for London in 1927 to be trained by Margaret Craske (classical ballet, Cecchetti method), Derra de Morode (national dancing), Karsavina (mime), Ruby Ginner (Greek dancing) and Brunelleschi (Spanish dancing). She was a member of a Pavlova Company which toured on the Continent. On her return she first taught pupils of Helen Webb in Cape Town, later those of Pearl Adler in Johannesburg and Pretoria and then opened her own school in Rondebosch at the Cape. She was invited by Prof. W.H. Bell** to join the staff of the University of Cape Town College of Music** in 1934, and launched the University of Cape Town Ballet School,** out of which the UCT Ballet Company was formed. This Company, of which she is the Director, undertook annual tours as far as Rhodesia; in 1965 it became professional, CAPAB taking over the financial side. — Dulcie Howes has trained many dancers of international standing, such as Desmond Doyle,** David Poole,** Pamela Chrimes,** Patricia Miller,** Petrus Bosman** and Johaar Mosaval.** Two internationally famous choreographers, John Cranko** and Alfred Rodrigues,** received their basic training at the UCT Ballet School. She has prepared the choreography for many ballets, most of them also seen in other parts of South Africa. She was Director of the Little Theatre** in Cape Town in 1936, and is an Honorary Life Member of the Imperial Society of Teachers of Dancing. In 1952 the Cape Tercentenary Foundation made her an award for her exceptional services to ballet in South Africa.

SOURCE
Dulcie Howes. *SAA* X, 1970.

– M.G.

HUDDLE, T. H.   Durban 7, 8, Durban Orchestra

HUGO, GLADYS ELIZABETH (NéE LIESCHING; MRS G. ZONDAGH), *8
January, 1896 in Victoria-West; living in Cape Town in 1964. Soprano.

Gladys Hugo's tuition in singing, which started when she had lessons from Gladys van
Niekerk and Giuseppe Paganelli, was completed in Rome when she and her husband,
Dr C.J. Hugo, resided there temporarily. After her return to South Africa she was
appreciated as a concert and radio singer. The series of concerts she held in the
Western Cape as a member of a trio formed with Joan van Niekerk** and Dr Con de
Villiers** was an important cultural factor of the 1930s. She was one of the first
singers to dedicate herself to Afrikaans as a vocal medium. This was achieved with
artistic results and afforded her considerable popularity.

BIBLIOGRAPHY
De Villiers, C.G.S.: *Musici en mense.* Nasionale Boekhandel Bpk., Cape Town, 1958.

SOURCES
Stegmann, Frits: Die Afrikaanse vrou as sangeres. *Kultuur,* under the editorship of *Filma,* Nov.
1945.   Stegmann, Frits: Gladys Hugo. *Die Burger,* 3 Aug. 1961.   Steyn, J.C. de W.: Gladys
Hugo. *Die Huisgenoot,* 22 Mar. 1946.

– F.S.

HUGO, JAPIE   South African Society of Music Teachers II/3

HUGO, P.   J.S. de Villiers, Organs 10

HUGUENOT COLLEGE   D.I.C. de Villiers, A. Joubert, Wellington

HUGUENOT SEMINARY   H.W. Egel, Wellington

HUGUENOT UNIVERSITY   K.F. Metzler, Wellington

HULLEBROECK, EMIEL, *20 February 1878 in Ghentbruges, East Flanders,
Belgium; °26 March 1965 in Liedekerke, Belgium. Flemish composer and singer.

Hullebroeck was educated in music at the conservatoire in Ghent where in 1898 he
won the first prize for organ playing. This youthful musician dedicated himself
enthusiastically to the revival of the Dutch Renaissance choral music, using for this
purpose the excellent Ghent a capella choir; this, however, did not mean that works by
contemporary composers were debarred from their programmes. His campaign for
sound folk singing was initially based on old Dutch folk songs, but he later extended
this repertoire by composing new songs in the folk style. As a singer he himself

interpreted a wide variety of these songs at numerous vocal concerts. Some of his own efforts became so popular in the Dutch language, that individual lines such as the following were often quoted as proverbs: "Hy die geen liedje zingen kan, die moet er maar eentje fluiten" (He who cannot sing a song must try to whistle one). — At a later stage, when he became a school music inspector, he exerted himself in text books to advance the cause of the Dutch language in Flemish musical education. Furthermore, he took the initiative in creating a society for the protection of copyright (NAVEA), which was eventually extended to become the foundation SABAM. In 1922 he also launched the periodical *Muziekwarande*. — While on a concert tour in South Africa (Sept. 1920–1921), he visited 64 cities and towns and evoked considerable enthusiasm with his settings of poems by A.D. Keet, Jan Celliers, C.J. Langenhoven and C.F. Visser, which he introduced at his concerts. In their published form as *Zes kunstliederen*, some of these added authority to the advance of the art song in Afrikaans. Although they are numerically not important in Hullebroeck's complete works, their influence on Afrikaans music at the time of their publication should not be underestimated. A few, like *Lamtietie-damtietie, Trou* and *Vryheidslied* are still sung today. — In his book, *Zuid-Afrika,* Hullebroeck betrays considerable concern about the adverse influence which study abroad may have on young South African musicians. He feared that our music students by studying in foreign centres – particularly in London – may become estranged from their own people. In 1959 his contributions were acknowledged by the Suid-Afrikaanse Akademie vir Wetenskap en Kuns** by the award of a medal of honour.

WORKS

114 Unison songs with pianoforte accompaniment, published in nineteen volumes. Of these, the sixteenth series, *Zes liederen* (G. Alsbach & Kie, Amsterdam, n.d.) has Afrikaans words: 1. Afrikaanse wiegeliedjie (C.J. Langenhoven) 2. Sonnedaal (A.D. Keet) 3. Die sterretjie (C. Louis Leipoldt) 4. Uit pure pret (A.D. Keet) 5. Studentelied (C.F. Visser) 6. Trouw (Jan F.E. Celliers); and from the eighteenth series: 6. Vryheidslied (J.F.E. Celliers).   A number of individual unison songs, of which the following have Afrikaans texts: Verlange (A.D. Keet) and Suid-Afrika (M.J. Vorster-Van Straten), dedicated to the Voortrekker movement. J.L. van Schaik Bpk., Pretoria, n.d.   Twaalf Maleise liedere (with Malay and Dutch texts), in four volumes.   Twenty four two-part songs and songs arranged for choir.   Two cantatas for children.   Six instrumental works.   Ten operettas, i.a. *Sepp'l,* performed in Pretoria by Gerrit Bon** (in Afrikaans) on 10 December 1938.

PUBLICATIONS

Theoretical works. Zuid-Afrika. *Cultuur en Wetenschap* 23, Brugge, 1928.

BIBLIOGRAPHY

Bouws, Jan: *Woord en wys van die Afrikaanse lied.* Cape Town, 1961.   Nuten, Piet: *Hullebroeck en zijn beteekenis.* Antwerp, 1939.

SOURCES

Bouws, Jan: Emiel Hullebroeck sewentig jaar. *Die Huisgenoot,* Cape Town, 1948.   Bouws, Jan: Sanger van Vlaandere sterf op hoë ouderdom. *Die Burger,* Cape Town, 7 Apr. 1965. Bouws, Jan: 'n Eie styl in die Suid-Afrikaanse musiek. *Standpunte* 69, XX/3, Parow,

1967. *De Automobilist:* Emiel Hullebroecknummer XIX/7, Antwerp, 1966. Hartman, A.: Emiel Hullebroeck, huldigingswoord. *S.A. Akademie Jaarboek* 19 (ou reeks), 1959.

– J.B.

HULME, GEORGE A. King William's Town 8

HUMAN, JACOB LOURENS KRIEL (JAPIE), *18 December 1932 in Winburg; at present (1978) in Bloemfontein. Pianist, lecturer and specialist on the musical history of the Free State.

After initial musical training in Winburg, Japie Human obtained a B.Mus. degree (1950–1953) and a B.A. degree (1954–1956) at the University of the OFS, where his pianoforte instructors were D.J. Roode,** Arend Koole** and Gertrud Kautzky. In 1957 he continued his studies under Frank Merrick in London and took the ARCM performer's examination within a year. Back in Bloemfontein he placed himself under the guidance of Dr Arend Koole and obtained the degrees of B.Mus. (Hons) in 1960 and of M.Mus. in 1963. This was followed in 1976 by further research into the musical history of the Free State which was rewarded with the degree of D.Phil. Throughout these academic studies Human maintained his pianoforte playing at concert standard and performed as soloist with the orchestras of the Free State's Regional Council and the SABC, as well as in a two-pianoforte combination with Henrietta Pauw. In the meantime he had also developed an interest in the jazz idiom on which he gave lecture recitals. From the same source he drew the idea of *revues* which emphasize pianoforte jazz, such as *The story of ragtime, The piano jazz of the 'twenties* and *Vintage 'thirties,* all three performed in Bloemfontein. Human has specialised in Music Education, a subject to which he applied himself especially in 1968 during a visit to the Northwestern University in Illinois (USA). — Before becoming a lecturer in Music at the Free State University (1961), he acted as a music teacher at high schools in the Free State. Among these were Grey College and the Volkskool Wilgehof, both situated in Bloemfontein.

WORK
Cupido op die campus, musical comedy. Ms., 1961.

WRITINGS
Musiek in die Oranje Vrystaat vanaf 1850 tot aan die begin van die Anglo-Boere-Oorlog. M.Mus. dissertation, UOFS, 1963. *Die musieklewe in Bloemfontein, 1900–1939.* D.Phil. thesis, UOFS, 1976. The Montessori method as an aid to piano teaching. *Opus,* new series II/4, July 1971. The importance of creativity and rhythm in music education. *Musicus* IV/1 & 2, 1975.

– Ed.

HUMEWOOD BEACH, HOTEL Pietermaritzburg, Port Elizabeth II/4, II/7

HUMPHRIES, WALTER J.K. Pescod

HUMPHRIES-JONES, J. East London I

HUNTER, MONICA   Port Elizabeth Male Voice Choir, Port Elizabeth Salon Choir, R.E. Selley

HUS, MONSIEUR   South African piano Music II/1

HUSKISSON, YVONNE, *13 January 1930 in Johannesburg; at present (1980) in Durban. Ethnomusicologist.

Yvonne Huskisson commenced playing the pianoforte before she went to school, and while at the Forest High School became the leader and pianist of a concert party which visited hospitals and other institutions on the Reef on Saturday evenings. This activity continued for twelve years, past matriculation and into her time as a music student. At the University of the Witwatersrand she obtained the B.Mus. degree in March 1951, and subsequently the B.Mus. (Hons). While still a student, Yvonne organized and presented musical productions. In 1952, while serving as a part-time lecturer on the staff of the Music Department, she attended the Johannesburg Teachers' Training College, obtaining the Teachers' Training Diploma in both Primary and Secondary teaching methods. Subsequently she was appointed by the Witwatersrand University as a full-time lecturer on the History of Music. An interest she developed in ancient and eastern musical systems resulted in a tour of the Middle East. On her return to South Africa, she taught for some months at the Rhodesian College of Music and then, intermittently, for short periods at various high schools in the Republic. — In October 1954, Miss Huskisson founded a college of music in Vereeniging, where she gave tuition in pianoforte, theory of music and voice production. She also assembled and trained a Bach Choir which she conducted in performances of *St Matthew passion, Elijah* and *Messiah*. An appointment on the staff of the Music Department of the Potchefstroom Teachers' Training College in 1960 led to a senior lectureship and eventually to promotion as Head of the Department. Here she presented student productions of Gilbert and Sullivan operettas, oratorios and concertos; she also accompanied the Transvalia Students Choir on their overseas tour in April 1961. Miss Huskisson frequently visited the Sterkfontein Hospital where she applied music therapy to selected patients. — During the years at Vereeniging, Yvonne developed an interest that was to shape her future career. She visited Black schools and Training Colleges in the Transvaal to study the methods, policies, musical systems and syllabuses in use in teaching music; and she completed a thesis on *Music in the Native schools in the Transvaal,* for which she received the M.Mus. degree of the University of the Witwatersrand in March 1956. As a result of this comprehensive survey, she was approached by the newly-formed Department of Bantu Education to draft the syllabuses for music teaching in the Lower and Higher Primary Black schools. With the aid of a Government grant and other awards she next undertook research among the Northern Sotho tribes in the Transvaal, and was awarded a doctorate by the Witwatersrand University for a thesis on the *Social and ceremonial music of the Pedi* in 1959. — In January 1962, she was appointed by the SABC to organize the musical programmes of the newly-instituted Radio Bantu. Since then, she has travelled extensively in the Republic and neighbouring territories, generally accompanied by her husband, a specialist in recording techniques, to record the traditional music of the Blacks. These were in due course returned to the educational authorities of the countries concerned in the form of recorded transcriptions. At the same time she was responsible for the smooth functioning and extension of the Black services, for the inclusion of traditional music in these programmes and for the recording and broadcasting of musical works by the growing number of Black composers of light as well as serious choral music. In this manner she paved the way for the radio as prime factor in the cultural consciousness of the Blacks, encouraged their emerging creative talent by presenting them with interpretations which could be heard wherever a radio was available, and served the cause of preserving their musical folk traditions. Dr Huskisson has been continuously active in writing about Black music in South Africa, not only for the SABC but for numerous radio services in foreign countries. She has lectured on the subject in various centres in South Africa and has gathered source material for her major opus – the book on Black composers (see list of publications). By utilizing the possibilities of Radio Bantu in an imaginative manner, Dr Huskisson has in many respects become the pivot of Black music in South Africa. It is hardly possible to overlook her contribution towards preserving the identity of the Black peoples whilst helping to ease their transition to a White civilization

PUBLICATIONS

Dr Huskisson has contributed numerous programmes, brochures and articles to Radio South Africa, and to a variety of journals; they deal with aspects of instrumental, vocal and ceremonial Black music, and include the following: A survey of the musical practices of a Swazi tribe resident at Hoepakrans in Sekekhuneland, 1960.   Series for the *Radio Bantu Music Bulletins* I & II, 1965–1966.   Compositions of Black composers for Radio Bantu, 1965–1969.   Publications of the SA Department of Information, including: Singing through life. *Bantu,* Sept. 1966.   Folksong of the Bantu.   Traditional instruments of the Bantu.   Modern Bantu composers are inspired by own traditional music. *Bantu Educational Journal,* Oct. 1962 and *Digest of SA Affairs,* July 1962.   Bantu music, how it has been affected by involvement with Western civilisation and modern progress. *Bantu,* 1968.   Music of the Bantu. *Sovenga.* Univ. College of the North, 1973.   Indigenous music and radio. *SABC Bulletin,* Oct. 1966. Radio Bantu's role in fostering Bantu music. *SABC Bulletin,* Apr. 1963.   Township Bantu evolve a music all their own. *Data,* Autumn 1968.   Bantu choirs and their history in South Africa.   *Standard encyclopedia of Southern Africa.* Nas. Pers Bpk., Cape Town, 1970–1976.   *Bantu composers of South Africa.* Published by the SABC, 1969; Supplement, HSRC ISBN 0 86965 121 8, 1974   *Marimba* (or *The Hare and the Rain);* a folk-tale about the origin of the marimba.

Dr Huskisson has written numerous programme series on Black music for the internal, external and school programmes of the SABC and for radio corporations in Australia, Belgium, Japan, France, Iowa (USA), Germany, Switzerland and Austria.

SOURCES

Anonymous: Musiekreis na Mosambiek. *SABC Bulletin,* 11 Aug. 1965.   Van der Westhuizen, Vincent: Lied van Oos-Caprivi. *Bantu,* Feb. 1974.

– Ed.

HUTCHINGS, AUGUSTUS WILFRED, *6 January 1900 in Lamorna, Cornwall; living in Johannesburg in 1970. Bass.

Wilfred Hutchings commenced his study of voice production and singing in Johannesburg under Mme Hodgson-Palmer in 1926, continuing under Hayden Matthews** two years later. During his career he won a University exhibition for singing in 1927, and sang the bass solo in various oratorios in Johannesburg, Port Elizabeth and Pietermaritzburg, as well as the principal parts in operas such as *Boris Godounov* (Moussorgsky) and *Don Giovanni* (Mozart). He also appeared in many Gilbert and Sullivan operas and musical comedies. He was the bass of the Melodians, a male quartet that became well-known in broadcasting, and recorded Afrikaans numbers for Columbia. — Hutchings was until recently still heard in oratorio and other vocal works.

– Ed.

HYDE, FRANK, *24 January 1858 in Birmingham, a twin; °15 January 1917 in England. Music teacher and conductor; brother of James Hyde.**

His father, James Hyde, a violinist and piano teacher in Birmingham, was Frank's first pianoforte teacher. Somehow, he also learned to blow cornet and when his older brother, James Hyde jr., conducted the Harvey-Turner Opera Company on their South African tour in 1875, Frank shared in the adventure by playing solos on this instrument. He probably played quite well because the few reviews on his performances are favourable. The tour completed (1876), Frank returned to England where he was associated with various opera companies, but ten years later (1886) he turns up in Kimberley. It is a remarkable fact that, though his brother James Hyde was then in King William's Town, and remained in South Africa for 43 years, there is not the slightest reference to Frank either in his diary, or in his wife's memoirs or in their letters. — For thirteen years (1886–1899), Frank Hyde conducted a Roman Catholic Church choir in Kimberley, but he was also a music teacher and a piano tuner. In addition he had a so-called Quadrille Orchestra and massed 300 voices from various schools for the Kimberley Exhibition held in August 1892. He may have been a music teacher at these schools. He also played a leading part in a Kimberley opera company and works like *Patience, HMS Pinafore* and *Maritana* were performed with his co-operation, probably as conductor. — Early in 1899, his wife (Sarah Juded Wilkin) died and Frank Hyde left Kimberley. He turned up in East London in the same year, and advertised himself as a piano tuner (11 April 1899) and as a piano, cornet and singing teacher (10 January 1901). Up to 1902 his musical activities in East London were numerous and varied. He was associated with the Grand Challenge Shield Competitions held between the schools of East London and King William's Town under the guidance of Fred Farrington.** He not only acted as an adjudicator, but in 1899 and again on 26 May 1900, he conducted the East London Orchestral Society in the accompaniment of juvenile choirs of up to 100 voices in performances of prescribed programmes containing excerpts from *HMS Pinafore, Dorothy* and *Il trovatore*. In 1900 *Maritana* was performed under his baton by a cast of fifty and, when the KAMADS of King William's Town brought their production of *The gondoliers* to East London, he conducted the show. In addition there were concerts for the benefit of the Roman Catholic Church, at which Charles Israel** and J. Tryal Beaven** co-operated, and variety concerts for St Patrick's Day in 1901 and 1902. Haydn's *Imperial mass* was performed at one of the church concerts. In 1902, while preparations for a performance of *The mikado* were under way, he left East London and this production became the responsibility of Theo Wendt.** — For unknown reasons, probably on the recommendation of Charles Israel, Frank Hyde settled in post-war Bloemfontein. There he helped to establish an opera society which produced *Maritana* in 1904 and *The mikado* in 1905. He also conducted his own string orchestra (Hyde's orchestra) at Sunday evening concerts to which the band of the 5th Dragoons contributed brassy items (1904). — According to the late Miss Rupert, Hyde settled in Graaff Reinet in approximately 1908 and practised at 112 Cradock Street as a piano tuner and a music teacher. The only documented fact about his stay in Graaff Reinet is that he trained a choir for the opening of the Victoria Hall (the Graaff Reinet Town Hall) on 5 September 1911 and that the choir sang his anthem, *The sons of South Africa*. — Hyde returned to England probably before the beginning of World War One.

WORKS

Moonlight on the Vaal, vocal waltz. Frank Hyde, Graaff Reinet, n.d.   Sons of South Africa (Henry Heugh). De Ville & Co., Graaff Reinet, 1911.   Vat jou goed en trek Ferreira, arr. as vocal barn dance. Beare & Son, London, n.d.

BIBLIOGRAPHY

Henning, C.G.: *A cultural history of Graaff Reinet, 1786–1886*. D.Phil. thesis, UP, 1971; published as *Graaff-Reinet – a cultural history*. T.V. Bulpin, Cape Town, 1975.   Van der Merwe, F.Z.: *Suid-Afrikaanse musiekbibliografie, 1787–1952*. J.L. van Schaik, Pretoria, 1958. Wolpowitz, Lily: *James and Kate Hyde and the development of music in Johannesburg up to the First World War*. J.L. van Schaik, Pretoria, 1969.

SOURCES

The Bloemfontein Pelican: 28 Jan. 1905.   *Diamond Fields Advertiser:* 1886–1898.   EL *Daily Dispatch:* 11 Apr. 1899–25 Aug. 1902.   *The Friend:* 28 Jan. 1904–1905.   Programme of the inauguration of the Victoria Hall in Graaff Reinet, Sept. 1911.

– E.H.S. (amplified C.G.H.)

HYDE, JAMES, *1 June 1849 in Birmingham; °8 August 1939 in London. Conductor and composer.

The fourth of that name, James Hyde came of a long line of musicians. His father was a violinist, pianist and teacher; his grandfather a trumpet player and composer of ballads; while his great-grandfather was trumpeter to the Duke of York and the reputed inventor of the slide-trumpet. James Hyde was first taught the violin and piano by his father; then he had violin lessons with Henry Hayward and organ and harmony lessons with Andrew Deakin. On 24 February 1862, at the age of thirteen, he made his debut as violin soloist at the Monday Evening Concerts in the Birmingham Town Hall. Apart from his ability as a violinist, he gradually became recognised as a teacher, musical director and composer in the city of his birth. — In 1870 Hyde moved to London, where he relinquished his appointment as conductor at the Royalty Theatre to join the Carl Rosa Opera Company, as first violinist and chorusmaster. One of the principal singers of the company was Kate Leipold, who later became his wife. When James W. Turner decided to take a small opera company to South Africa, Hyde was chosen as his conductor. The Harvey-Turner Opera Company sailed for South Africa in 1875, and after touring through the Cape Colony, returned to England in

1876. This experience led to the formation of Hyde's own operetta company, which toured Lincolnshire, Warwickshire and the Hunting districts for six months, performing ballad-operas such as *The Quaker* and *The waterman,* as well as excerpts from serious opera. — However, Hyde soon decided to return to South Africa, and arrived in King William's Town in 1877, opened a music store in Maclean Street, and established himself not only as a music dealer, tuner, publisher and teacher, but also as organist and choirmaster of the Catholic Church of the Sacred Heart. The King William's Town Choral Union, which performed for several years under his direction, was formed in 1879. In 1882 Hyde returned to England to marry Kate Leipold. — When they were back in King William's Town, these versatile musicians began to play at concerts in their home town, and elsewhere in the Eastern Province. They adapted their talents variously, performing on the organ, piano and violin, or singing and playing on the English concertina, or conducting a choir; thus they served the community and were completely happy in doing so. At a sacred concert in Queenstown (August 1888) Kate sang whilst James played the organ, including a *Carnival march* of his own composition in the programme. During the Jubilee Exhibition in Grahamstown the organisers obtained the artistic co-operation of the pair to give two concerts on 27 and 28 December 1887. Mrs Hyde sang and Mr Hyde played the violin "and other instruments". His *Wreck of the Hesperus* had an adult performance in this town, and another by a school, and Mr Hyde was able to express himself "satisfied with the standard" they maintained. — In 1889 the Hydes undertook a concert tour of towns in the Eastern Cape, on their way to Johannesburg, where they gave three concerts and James became Musical Director to the Edgar Perkins Opera Company (August, 1889). The Company, with Hyde as conductor, undertook an exacting tour of the country, visiting Port Elizabeth, Kimberley and Cape Town before returning to Johannesburg for a final season. When the company dissolved at the end of July 1890, the Hydes returned to King William's Town, but only temporarily, for in 1891 Hyde was offered the conductorship of the Military Band and Orchestra of the Wanderers Club in Johannesburg. During their last two years in the Eastern Cape, Hyde also served as conductor of the East London Choral Society in addition to his duties to the King William's Town Choral Union. The latter group gave its seventy-seventh concert under his direction on 25 March 1892, as a farewell tribute to the Hydes. — From 1892 until the outbreak of the Anglo-Boer War in 1899, Hyde was conductor of the Wanderers bands, and untiring in his efforts to raise the standard of music in Johannesburg. His ability as composer, orchestrator and versatile musician was called upon for much of the music provided at the weekly orchestral and military concerts. Besides the usual Sunday Evenings, he introduced a winter series of popular and classical concerts given by the Wanderers Amateur Orchestra. The highlight of his year in Johannesburg was the formation of the Wanderers Choral Society, which he conducted publicly for the first time on 29 September 1892, in a performance of Sterndale Bennett's *The May queen.* Concurrently, he acted as conductor of Edgar Perkins' Lyric Opera Company, which opened at the Globe Theatre in November 1892, for two seasons of opera. — During the Anglo-Boer War Cape Town provided a temporary home, not only for the Hydes, but for many who had been members of the old Wanderers Orchestra. He gathered the refugees together in an orchestra which had H. Garvin** as leader, and conducted several concerts in aid of churches and war funds. In addition he conducted the choir at the Wynberg Catholic Church. — Soon after his return to Johannesburg in January 1902, Hyde was informed that his conductorship of the Wanderers Bands had been terminated, since the resident military bands could provide music for the club concerts. On 23 March 1902, Hyde resumed his series of weekly Sunday-evening concerts with a small orchestra of his own in the Masonic Hall, which very soon could not contain the audiences. So he took his musicians to His Majesty's Theatre** in July 1903, and then to the Caledonian Hall for the third series of concerts (14 July to 18 August 1907). The programmes of all Hyde's orchestral works after 1902 are characterised by progressive planning. They include many romantic and a number of classical works, together with a representative variety of compositions by British composers. The critic of *The Star,* Lissant-Collins,** was enthusiastic about Hyde's programmes, although he was less complimentary about the selections, especially from the operas of Wagner. Unfortunately, disputes with the Musician's Union caused the abandonment of the concerts, of which the fifth and last series was given from 18 May to 21 June 1908. In 1909 Hyde's orchestra ceased to exist. Two years later he conducted two ambitious programmes for the Philharmonic Society in Pretoria, who had lost their conductor, Galeffi,** in 1910. The interest was, however, too meagre for a third concert, and this series too came to an end. — After this Hyde conducted in Johannesburg on invitation only. At the opening of the new Town Hall on 7 April 1915, he was the director of ceremonies; he conducted a small orchestra that played the accompaniments to *Cavalleria rusticana* and *Pagliacci* for Signor Terassi at the Palladium Theatre; and finally he was in charge of the Johannesburg Orchestra of Theo Wendt** at the Orpheum Theatre in October 1926, when he and Dave Foote** were decorated with laurel wreaths to honour their pioneering work. — Resigned to the prospect that his days as an orchestral conductor were over, Hyde continued teaching at home, and acted as singing master at several schools in Johannesburg (Marist Brothers' College, the Convents of the Holy Family in End Street and Yeoville, and the Johannesburg High School for Girls). After his wife's death in 1935, he left Johannesburg (June 1936) for England, where he stayed for a while with his sister, Mrs Thwaites, in York. On 2 November 1936, he was admitted to the Twyford Abbey Nursing Home, Park Royal, London, where he remained until his death in 1939.

WORKS

A. Vocal

1. Cantatas
King Dodo's choice.   The wreck of the Hesperus. C. Jefferys, London, 1883.

2. Songs
Our fair colonial maid. Hay Bros., King William's Town, 1882.   The frontier land. Hawkes & Sons, London, 1884.   The land of Good Hope (E.J. Byrne). Beare & Sons, London, 1886.   The Wanderers vocal waltz. Wickins & Co., London, 1897.   Come joyous spring (Dora Greenwell). Wickins & Co., London, 1906.   Under the fragrant mimosa (words and music by J. Hyde). J.R. Glynn & Co., London, 1921.   A wet sheet and a flowing sea. C. Jefferys, London, n.d.   All the world to me. Ms., n.d.   Noloti (E.J.B.). Beare & Son, London, n.d.   Sons of the South, arise! (E.J.B.). Mackay Bros., Johannesburg, n.d.   Spells of evening, vocal duet. Ms., n.d.   Stars of the summer night. Ms., n.d.   The lonely kittens, vocal duet. Ms., n.d.   The Swiss toy girl (Philomel). C. Jefferys, London, n.d.   Together (R.A. Nelson). R. Müller, Cape Town, n.d.   United. Ms., n.d.

B. Instrumental

1. Pianoforte

The Gonubie galop, 1882. Ms., n.d.   The carnival march. Ms., ca. 1888, perf. Queenstown 30 July 1888.   Caprice and melody, duet for violin and pianoforte. Beare & Son, London, 1908.   South African rhapsody. J.R. Glynn & Co., London, 1921.   Grandmother's story. W. Paxton & Co. Ltd, London, 1923.   All aboard. Alfred Oliver & Co., London, n.d.   Dora waltz. Ms., n.d.   Fantaisie grotesque. C. Jefferys, London, n.d.   Oom Paul polka. Kaffrarian Music Warehouse, King William's Town, n.d.   The pixies. Alfred Oliver, London, n.d.   The rêve du Montagnard. C. Jefferys, London, n.d.   The rivulet. C. Jefferys, London, n.d.   The tiger hunt. Ms., n.d.   La Toupieaérienne. Ms., n.d.   African melody. Ms., n.d.

2. Orchestral

Floreal. Hawkes & Son, London, 1899.   Flying spray. Reid Bros Ltd, London, 1915. Southern Cross, valse. Darter & Sons, Cape Town, n.d.   The Rand rifles. Ms., n.d.   Transvaal Volunteers. Ms., n.d.

3. Organ

Wedding march. Ms., n.d.

4. Gymnastic and cadet music for military band

(All in manuscript, undated)   Flourish for gymnastic exhibition.   The football polka. The giant's polka.   The gym valse.   Flourish for gymnastic exhibition and double step for gymnasium.   Our Empire.   School marches, no. 1, 2, 3 and 4.   The Marist's cadet march.   Music for dumb bell exercises.   Transvaal Volunteers' march.   Swanee river march.   Ta-ra-ra-boom-da-ray march.   Music for squad exercises.   The holiday valse. Vat jou goed en trek, Ferreira.   The land of Good Hope.

C. Arrangements

1. National anthems for military band

National Anthems of various countries, perf. King William's Town, 23 June 1886.   The Volkslied, 1895.   God save the King.   God save the Queen.   National anthems of America (arranged for voice and orchestra), Austria (arranged for voice and orhcestra), Belgium, Denmark, France (arranged for voice and orchestra), Old France, Germany, Holland, Italy, Old Portugal, Orange Free State, Russia (arranged for voice and orchestra), Transvaal.   The "Old Hundredth".   The star-spangled banner.

2. For orchestra

Irish Jig, 1897.   America, fantasia by Winterbottom.   Auld lang syne.   Caution. Cavatina, from *Nitroci* (Mercadante).   C'est l'Espagne (Offenbach).   Chinese march. Columbia, the pride of the ocean.   Combat march.   Coronation march by Meyerbeer. Country dance, no. 2.   Dance, introduced in *Falka*.   Dead march in *Saul*, by Handel. Esmeralda, Spanish dance by Halêvy.   For he's a jolly good fellow.   For he is an Englishman, from *HMS Pinafore*.   God bless the Prince of Wales.   Graceful music and trumpet call.   Hot time in the Old Town tonight.   Kaffir song.   King Charles (Maud V. White).   Melody, by Rubinstein.   Railway galop.   Rule Britannia.   Swanee river.   Tell me pretty maiden, from *Floradora*.   The refrain, from *Soldiers of the Queen*.   The Campbells are coming.   The College hornpipe opening.   The ladies' battle, no. 1.   The roast beef of Old England.   The Roman carnival.   The Union Jack of Old England.   'Tis the day, from *The beggar's opera*.   White wings.   Yankee doodle.

3. Operatic music
Blue-eyed Susan, a musical extravaganza for small orchestra. *Faust* (Gounod). *Il trovatore* (Verdi). *I Pagliacci* (Leoncavallo). *Peter Spyk* (Planche). Spoiling the broth (Offenbach). *The blind beggars* (Offenbach). *The Bohemian girl* (Balfé). *The gondoliers* (Sullivan). *Trial by jury* (Sullivan).

BIBLIOGRAPHY
Brown, J.D.: *Biographical dictionary of musicians.* Alexander Gardner & Paisley, London, 1886. Brown, J.D. and Stratton, S.S.: *British musical biography.* Chadfield & Son Ltd, Derby, 1897. Grove, G.: *Grove's dictionary of music and musicians.* Vol. III, 1954. Kirby, P.R.: South Africa, in *Grove's dictionary of music and musicians,* Vol. VII, 1954. Kirby, P.R.: *Saint Cecilia goes South.* Musical Association, London, 1937. Leyds, G.A.: *A history of Johannesburg.* Nasionale Boekhandel Bpk., Cape Town, 1964. Sparrow, M.J. *Music in Grahamstown, 1888-1900.* M.Mus. dissertation, UP, 1978. Wolpowitz, L., *James and Kate Hyde.* J.L. van Schaik, Pretoria, 1969.

SOURCES
Original papers
Hyde, K.: *Recollections - English - Bavarian - South African - of an unimportant musician* (D.M. Seggie, Johannesburg). Cuttings and programmes, J. Hyde: 1839-1908 (The Strange Library of Africana, Johannesburg Public Library). Lezard, E.: *Memories, 2 November - 28 December 1945* (Mrs V. Lezard, Johannesburg). Seggie, D.M.: *Memories of a godchild, 12 August 1965* (L. Wolpowitz). Minutes of the Wanderers Club. 13 Mar. 1889-26 Nov. 1892, 26 Feb. 1898-2 Oct. 1899, 1 Nov. 1901-31 Dec. 1910 (The Strange Library of Africana, Johannesburg Public Library).

2. Letters
The Librarian, Birmingham Public Library, Reference Library, Ratcliffe Place, Birmingham. The town clerk, Borough of Ealing, London W.5. The principal, Johannesburg High School for Girls. Dr W. Burton, King William's Town. The librarian, King William's Town Public Library. Other letters and documents in the writer's possession.

3. Periodical
Mr and Mrs James Hyde. *South African Lady's Pictorial,* Apr. 1915.

4. Newspapers
The Eastern Star: July 1889-Dec. 1889. *The Standard and Diggers News:* Jan. 1892-Dec. 1893. *The Star:* July 1889-May 1915.

– L.W.

HYDE, KATHERINE CECILIA CLARA (KATE, NéE LEIPOLD), *17 December 1856 in Birmingham; °25 January 1935 in Johannesburg. Contralto, pianist and music teacher.

The daughter of Johann Leipold, a German organist, choirmaster and music teacher, Kate Hyde received her musical education in Munich, where she appeared as a child prodigy at the age of eight. Until she was old enough to start singing lessons in earnest, she studied piano with Bärmann and harmony with Peter Cornelius at the

Munich Conservatorium. The Leipold family settled in London in 1872, where Kate had singing lessons with Manuel Garcia; two years later she joined the Carl Rosa Opera Company, of which James Hyde** was the chorus master. Later she belonged to another English opera association, the Mapelson, appearing as a contralto at the Haymarket Theatre, and in Madame Blanche Cole's opera company at the National Standard Theatre, Bishopsgate. Her repertoire included the roles of Azucena in *Il trovatore*, Sibel in *Faust* and Mrs Cregan in *Lily of Killarney*. — After her marriage to James Hyde in June 1882, the couple sailed for South Africa and settled in King William's Town, where Hyde had established a music business. Husband and wife combined well as a team, and proved themselves versatile musicians when they appeared at concerts in the Eastern Cape. In 1892 Hyde was appointed conductor of the bands of the Wanderers Club. During the forty-three years she lived in Johannesburg, Mme. Hyde-Leipold trained some of the best singers and instrumentalists in the town. She performed as singer or pianist at almost every concert of consequence until 1903, appearing thirteen times as soloist at Hyde's Orchestral Concerts between March 1902 and November 1903. In 1892, when her husband was on duty at the Wanderers, she deputized for him as conductor of the Lyric Opera Company at the Globe Theatre. She toured with the Company to Pretoria and Cape Town, returning to Johannesburg for their "second annual season" in 1894. — As a teacher, Mme. Hyde trained both singers and instrumentalists, and organized concerts with her pupils in the Masonic and Caledonian Halls. She also adjudicated at eisteddfodau, and continued to act as accompanist after her performing days were over.

SOURCES

Hyde, K.: *Recollections – English-Bavarian-South African – of an unimportant musician*. D.M. Seggie, Johannesburg, n.d.   Seggie, D.M.: *Memories of a godchild*, 12 August 1965. (In possession of L. Wolpowitz).   Lezard, E.: *Memories, 2 November – 28 December 1945* (In possession of Mrs V. Lezard, Johannesburg).   Mr and Mrs James Hyde. *South African Lady's Pictorial*, Apr. 1915.   *The Eastern Star:* July 1889–Dec. 1889.   *The Standard and Diggers News:* Jan. 1892–Dec. 1893.   *The Star:* 1894–1915; 26 Jan. 1935 (obituary).   Cuttings and programmes, J. Hyde: 1839–1908 (The Strange Library of Africana, Johannesburg Public Library).   Sundry letters and documents in the author's possession.

– L.W.

HYLTON-EDWARDS, STEWART, *6 June 1924 in London; at present (1979) in Trinidad, West Indies. Composer, university and college music director, music critic and poet.

Stewart Hylton-Edwards received his musical education at the Guildhall School of Music in London (1940–1942 and 1946–1947) where he obtained the FTCL (honoris causa) and the LGSM. A talented composer, he became Wainwright Memorial Scholar in 1941, and won the Lady Mayoress of London's Prize for composition in the same year and again in 1947. For his *First symphony* he was awarded the Royal Philharmonic Society's Prize in 1948. — In the same year Hylton-Edwards came to South Africa to become Assistant Director of Music at St John's College in Johannesburg, a position he held until his departure from South Africa at the end of

1956. From 1950 he also lectured extramurally at the University of the Witwatersrand and acted as an examiner in musical theory to UNISA. Among his most prominent pupils was Stanley Glasser.** Hylton-Edwards frequently broadcast for the SABC; generally he gave discussions during the intervals, of works performed in symphony concerts. His forthright views often gave rise to lively discussions in the press. Some of his own compositions were broadcast by the SABC Symphony Orchestra. Between 1950 and 1957 he was music critic for the magazine *Forum*. — Many of his symphonic, vocal and chamber-music works, a number originating in South Africa, have been performed on the concert stage. In 1952 the central committee of the Cape Van Riebeeck Festival commissioned his *Fanfare* for performance in Cape Town. During the celebrations his *String quartet no. 1* was awarded a first prize and the *Easter symphony* a second prize. His *Union Day cantata* received first prize in the SABC competition of 1954. During a talk on *Music in Africa* for the BBC Third Programme in 1954, his arrangement for violin and pianoforte of an African tune, *Nimuze*, was broadcast from London. Incidental music was commissioned for and performed at theatrical productions by the National Theatre, the Experimental Theatre and other companies. He wrote the incidental music for the National Theatre production of *Twelfth night* (Shakespeare) in 1952; this enjoyed over 100 performances in South Africa and Rhodesia; there was a Royal Command performance before the Queen Mother and Princess Margaret in Salisbury. —Appointments as senior lecturer in the History of Music at Dalhousie University, and head of the theoretical department of the affiliated conservatoire in Halifax, Nova Scotia, caused him to leave South Africa at the end of 1956. He was Director of Music at St Mary's College, Port of Spain, Trinidad, from 1959 to 1962.

WORKS

A. Vocal

A Union Day cantata for solo, chorus and orchestra. Ms., 1955.   A dream of fair women (Five Victorian portraits), a song cycle for SATB. Ms., 1951.   Three carols, for treble voices. Augener Ltd, London, 1950.   The birds, carol for SATB and organ. Ms., 1945.   Good morrow to the day so fair, song. Ms., 1949.   Remember me, song. Ms., 1949.   Come away death, song. Ms., 1952.   O mistress mine, song. Ms., 1952.   Sweet day, song. Ms., 1949.   Trust not too much, song. Ms., 1949.   Krymekaar, song. Ms., 1951.   The vision, song. Ms., 1953.   You and I, song. Ms., 1953.   Three Easter carols, for soprano and oboe. Ms., 1953.   Why should there be two? Song, for performance during *The firstborn* (Christopher Fry). Ms., 1954.   I have desired to go, song. Ms., 1956.   Wys my die plek, song. Ms., 1956.   Descant to *Lord of all being* (Sir Percy Buck), Saccerdos et Pontifex. Ms., 1960.

B. Instrumental

1. Solo

English country scenes. Augener Ltd, London, 1950.   Introduction, pastorale e allegro, for unacc. oboe. Ms., 1953.   Suite for piano. Augener Ltd, London, 1954.   Two aquarelles. Augener Ltd, 1954.   Two etudes. Augener Ltd, 1954.   Variations on an African theme (1953, for reed trio; rewritten for pianoforte, 1954). Augener Ltd, London, 1960.   Three etudes (1954, sonata for viola and violin, rewritten for pianoforte). Ms.   Sonata for piano. Ms., 1960.   Sonata for piano. Ms., 1961.

HYLTON-EDWARDS

2. Orchestra
Symphony no. 1. Ms., 1947.   Symphony no. 2. Ms., 1948 (since withdrawn).   Easter symphony. Ms., 1951 (since withdrawn).   Adagio for orchestra. Ms., 1950.   Fanfare. Ms., 1951.   Four Shakespearian characters. Ms., 1956.   Trivia, scherzo for orchestra. Ms., 1951–1956.   Bank holiday, concert overture. Ms., 1956.   Chiaroscuro, concert overture. Ms., 1957.

3. Works for soloist and orchestra
Concerto for viola and orchestra. Ms., 1952.   Four folk idylls for oboe and strings (also arranged for oboe and piano). Ms., 1953.   Fantasy for harmonica and strings. Ms., 1955.   Concerto for piano and orchestra. Ms., 1957.

4. Chamber music
String quartet no. 1. Ms., 1951.   Variations on an African theme, for reed trio (since rewritten for piano). Ms., 1953.   Sonata for violin and viola (since rewritten for piano). Ms., 1954.   Sonata for cello and piano. Ms., 1954.   Nimuze (an African Tune), for violin and pianoforte. Ms., 1954.   Contrasts, for reed trio. Ms., 1955.   Three airs, for cello and piano. Ms., 1958.   String quartet no. 2. Ms., 1958.

C. Incidental music
Twelfth night. Ms., 1952.   *Abraham my love.* Ms., 1953.   *Prometheus.* Ms., 1953. *Nativity masque.* Ms., 1954.   *Hamlet* (1). Ms., 1956.   *Hamlet* (2). Ms., 1956.

PUBLICATIONS
Music in Africa. Royal Society of Arts, London, 1954.   *Ralph Vaughan Williams – a tribute.* Dalhousie University Press, 1958.   Volumes of poetry, 1956–1980.

– Ed.

HYMNBOOKS   Afrikaans Church and Mission Music I/2, I/4, H. Bodenstein, Brüderkirche, G.G. Cillié, Evangelical Lutheran Church (Hermannsburg), E. Hartwig, C. Murray, Sacred songbooks with Dutch words.

IAN RAINSFORD McHARRY SCHOLARSHIP   D.J. Reid

IBACH, R.   Piano Manufacturing Co. of South Africa

IDELSON, A.Z.   Idelson, J.

IDELSON, JEREMIAH (JERRY), *12 December 1893 in Liepaya, Latvia; now (1977) in Johannesburg. Composer, conductor and viola player.

Jerry Idelson was trained in violin, pianoforte and musical theory at the School of Music in Liepaya. He was partial to viola which, at the age of 14, he played in chamber ensembles and in an orchestra which performed at operas and in symphonic concerts. Two years later, in 1909, he made his first solo appearance. His brother, A.Z. Idelson, had spent about a year in Johannesburg (1906), composed a few songs and choral pieces, and then moved on to America and Jerusalem, where most of his research and creative work was done. Jerry's sisters had also settled in Johannesburg and in 1912 he came out to join them. The rest of the family eventually followed. — He was very active in a number of branches of music, even playing in a tea-room (where he tried his hand at the saxophone and the banjo) and was engaged as a theatre conductor by J.C. Williamson & Co. to enliven silent films shown in His Majesty's Theatre** in Johannesburg. In 1916–1917 and again in 1922–1923 he played viola in the Cape Town Municipal Orchestra** and at the same time studied composition with Prof. W.H. Bell.** In Johannesburg he was musical director for African Theatres from 1923 to 1926 and a member of chamber music ensembles in Johannesburg and Pretoria during 1917 and later. — In 1926 he joined the "orchestra" of the African Broadcasting Company, later the SABC, primarily as viola player, but eventually as librarian, programme compiler and orchestrator. This connection lasted until 1946 when he resigned to devote himself to composition and journalism. He has conducted the orchestras of Cape Town, Durban and Johannesburg and in 1954 he conducted the Israeli Radio Orchestra in programmes which included some of his own compositions. – Jerry Idelson is Director of Music to the United Jewish Progressive congregations of Johannesburg, Honorary Director of Music to the South African Union for Progressive Judaism and in 1942 he became the founder and Honorary Secretary of the Society of South African Composers,** retaining that position until 1949. He married the violinist Anne Sacks, a winner of the Overseas Scholarship of UNISA, in 1940.

WORKS

A. Vocal

1. Sacred
Israel is marching, cantata. Ms., 1943.　　Remember thy Creator, for solo, choir and organ. Ms., 1965.　　45 liturgical choir items. Ms., n.d.　　Three psalms. Ms., n.d.

2. Operetta
The Rajah's treasure. Ms., 1943.　　The Pied Piper. Ms., 1944.　　Jacaranda. Ms., 1956–1957.

3. Radio
The song of songs, radio musical. Ms., 1942.　　The story of Betar, radio phantasy with voices. Ms., 1945–1946.　　The wanderer's return, radio phantasy with voices. Ms., 1946.　　A Hanukah festival, radio phantasy with voices. Ms., 1947.　　If I forget thee, O Jerusalem, radio phantasy with voices. Ms., 1947.

4. Songs
Freedom troops (A. Shepherd); publ. 1942.　　Ask me never (L. Sowden). Ms., n.d.　　A tear (D. Dianow). Ms., n.d.　　A vision (H. Heine). Ms., n.d.　　Bantu chief (L. Sowden). Ms., n.d.　　Baron of bees (C.S. White). Ms., n.d.　　Die bosveld (F. Burgers). Ms., n.d.　　Die lied van die Karoo (L. Kamson). Ms., n.d.　　Ek smeek (R.A. Moll). Ms., n.d.　　In die maanskyn (I.D. du Plessis). Ms., n.d.　　In memoriam (L. Tobias). Ms., n.d.　　I wish I were content (L. Sowden). Ms., n.d.　　Mabalel (E.N. Marais). Ms., n.d.　　Miracles (L. Picardie). Ms., n.d.　　My dearest own (J. Parry). Ms., n.d.　　O dreamy, gloomy, friendly trees (A. French). Ms., n.d.　　Pagan death (L. Sowden). Ms., n.d.　　Paratroopers (C.S. White). Ms., n.d.　　Per Aspera ad Astra (P. Baneshik). Ms., n.d.　　Prospectors (C.S. White). Ms., n.d.　　Rosie (L. Sowden). Ms., n.d.　　Salute to freedom (A. Shepherd). Ms., n.d.　　Slampamperliedjie (R.A. Moll). Ms., n.d.　　Slapies my kindjie (W. Venter); publ. by FAK, n.d.　　Song of the land (L. Sowden). Ms., n.d.　　Staan, poppie, staan. (E.N. Marais). Ms., n.d.　　There's victory in the

air. (A. Shepherd). Ms., n.d.   The road to better days (C.S. White). Ms., n.d.   The sparrow
(L. Sowden). Ms., n.d.   The universe (L. Picardie). Ms., n.d.   Throw away thy rod (A.
French). Ms., n.d.   Two Bantu school songs, for choir. Ms., n.d.

5. Hebrew songs
Hebrew song (J.L. Peretz); publ. 1945.   Eleven Hebrew songs (M. Hoffman); publ. in Israel,
1950.   Ten Hebrew songs (M. Hoffman); publ. in Israel, 1950.   Complete Sabbath eve
service (in Hebrew), for choir and organ. Ms., 1958.   Hebrew song for choir (M. Hoffman).
Ms., n.d.   Hebrew song (J.L. Peretz). Ms., n.d.   Hebrew song (S. Tchernichovsky). Ms.,
n.d.   Hebrew song (N. Datt). Ms., n.d.   Yiddish song, for choir (M. Hoffman). Ms.,
n.d.   Seven Hebrew songs (J. Kamson). Ms., n.d.   Two Hebrew songs (N. Pines). Ms., n.d.

B. Instrumental

1. Orchestra
Overture in D, for orchestra. Ms., 1922.   Incidental music to the pantomime *Aladdin*. Ms.,
1941.   The bad business of Bozzy, radio phantasy. Ms., 1941.   The sad story of Sullivan,
radio phantasy. Ms., 1941.   Rhapsodic paraphrase, for cello and orchestra. Ms., 1942.   Has-
sidic suite, for orchestra. Ms., 1943–1961.   A pageant of the land, radio phantasy. Ms.,
1946.   Moorish dance, for orchestra. Ms., 1946.   Mabalel, symphonic poem. Ms.,
1951.   Overture on Afrikaans themes. Ms., 1959.

2. Chamber music
Fantasy, for string quartet. Ms., 1940.   Jeansa, for two violins and piano. Ms., 1944.   Mielie-
stronk-polka, for small orchestra. Ms., 1945.   Plaasjoligheid, for small orchestra. Ms.,
1945.   Variations on a Hebrew theme, for violin, cello and piano. Ms., 1946.   Improvisation, for violin and piano. Ms., 1951.   Duet, for two violins. Ms., 1960.   N'ila, violin solo.
Ms., 1962.   Perpetuo mobile, violin solo. Ms., 1962.   Humoresque, for flute, violin and
harp. Ms., 1964.   Polka and variations, for flute, violin and harp. Ms., 1965.

3. Piano
Farewell. Ms., 1911.   Two pieces (valse and etude). Ms., 1914.   Wedding march. Ms.,
1916.   Three animal sketches. Ms., 1954.

PUBLICATIONS
History of symphonic music in South Africa. *Bandstand,* Jan. 1952.   South Africa grows in
musical prestige. *Musical Courier,* New York, 15 Jan. 1952.   South Africa features Van
Riebeeck festival. *Musical Courier,* New York, June 1952.   Sketches of South African
composers. *Bandstand,* July 1952 to Feb. 1954.   They helped to further music in South Africa.
Supplement to *The Zionist Record,* 21 Nov. 1958.   Jewish music and its particular
characteristics. *Res Musicae,* Mar. 1960.   Jewish musicians in South Africa. *Africa Jewish
Newspaper Issue,* 1964.

BIBLIOGRAPHY
Jerry Idelson's part in South Africa's music story. *Bandstand,* Dec. 1951.   Jerry Idelson: music
maker. *Southern African Jewish Times,* 8 July 1960.

SOURCE
Davis, Anne: Jerry Idelson. *Opus,* new series I/2, Mar. 1970.

– Ed.

IGNEFF (IGNEV, IGNATIEFF, IGNATIJEV), BORIS, *26 June 1895 in St Petersburg (Leningrad); °March 1976(?) in Graaff Reinet. Composer and pianist.

Boris Ignev studied pianoforte and composition at the St Petersburg Conservatoire until the Revolution (1917) and then fled to Eastern Asia. He lived there for three years. In 1921 his career was resumed in Yugoslavia, where he acted as repetitor to the Wurmzer orchestra in Zagreb and to Arpad Bachi. He also accompanied Russian singers. In 1925 he joined the Yugoslav ballet company as choreographer and repetitor, and eleven years later he accompanied the Yugoslav team of ballet dancers to the Berlin Olympic Games (1936). This team included Masha Arsenieva,** whom he had married in 1933. In 1941 he became a member of the Roman Societá Autori e Editori, under whose auspices eleven of his compositions were published. In South Africa since 1946, he assisted his wife in her ballet ventures by playing the piano for her ballet classes and by composing ballet music for her concert tours and for the concerts given by her pupils.

WORKS

Instrumental

1. Orchestra
Bosna (Bosnian rhapsody). Ms., 1935; performed in Berlin, 1936.   Oro (Montenegriner folk dances). Ms., 1935, performed in Berlin, 1936.   From the merry village (Croatian folk dances), a potpourri. Ms., 1935, performed in Berlin 1936; also in piano score.

2. Pianoforte ballet music
Valse caprice; composed 1935, publ. 1941.   Bagatelle; composed 1934, publ. 1941.   Arlequinade; composed 1934, publ. 1941.   Valse triste, opus 18; composed 1934, publ. 1941. Danza del diavolo (The devil's dance); composed 1942, publ. 1943.   Valse intermezzo; composed 1933, publ. 1943.   Dopo di ballo (Ritorno dal ballo); composed 1933, publ. 1943.   Polca sentimentale; composed 1942, publ. 1943.   La campana (Holiday bells); composed 1940, publ. n.d.   The magnificent lie; composed 1940, publ. n.d.   Coquette; composed 1940, publ. n.d.   Chopiniana. Ms., 1929.   Al lavoro (Song of work). Ms., 1929.   Polonaise aus dem Ballet Schneewittchen. Ms., 1939–1940.   Wiener Lied. Ms., 1942.   Prima della vita: 4 pezzi di una pantomima (Circle of life), ballet for two dancers. Ms., 1942: 1. Allegro – infanzia 2. Moderato – gioventu 3. Andantino – maternita 4. Andante maestoso – la fine.   Ragazza della strada (Song of the street). Ms., 1942.   The blind, solo dance. Ms., 1949.   Salome, a solo dance. Ms., 1949.   Three women, a group dance. Ms., 1949.   Serenade. Ms., 1949.   Prologue, a group dance. Ms., 1950.   Diamonds in the sands, three-act ballet based on S.A. theme, performed during Van Riebeeck festival. Ms., 1952.   Grand valse. Ms., 1952.   Gypsy wedding, a solo dance. Ms., 1952.   Last waltz. Ms., 1952.   March, a group dance. Ms., 1952.   Two masques, a duet. Ms., 1952. Around the fire, a short gypsy ballet. Ms., 1953.   Ballade. Ms., 1953.   Evening, a solo dance. Ms., 1954.   Mazurka in e minor, duet. Ms., 1953.   Little pizzicato. Ms., 1953.   Ouma se tjalie, one-act ballet on a S.A. theme. Ms., 1953.   Preludium, a dance solo. Ms., 1953.   Pizzicato, duet. Ms., 1958.   Satanie, solo male dance. Ms., 1958.   Intermezzo, solo dance. Ms., 1958.   Going West, ballet burlesque. Ms., 1957.

3. Pianoforte compositions for children's ballet
The unfaithful pierrot. Ms., 1949.   The magic shop. Ms., 1951.   Princess caprice. Ms., 1951.   The enchanted cave. Ms., 1952.   Tales of the forest. Ms., 1953.   Christmas

dream. Ms., 1963.   The healing tears. Ms., 1963.   The cheated canary. Ms., 1964.   Kiss of the snow. Ms., 1966.   The pearls. Ms., 1966.

4. Pianoforte compositions for infants' ballet
Ballet mozaique. Ms., 1964–1966.   Ons eerste dans. Ms., 1964–1966.   Passies en ritme. Ms., 1964–1966.   Snow flakes. Ms., 1964–1966.

5. Piano solo
Valse impromptu. Ms., 1958–1964.   Valse in B minor. Ms., 1958–1964.   Valse lento e dolce. Ms., 1958–1964.   Valse melancholic. Ms., 1958–1964.

– C.G.H.

ILIFFE-HIGGO, ARCHIBALD   Aronowitz, C.G. Feros, Higher Educational Institutions I/3, I/7ii(b)

IMMELMAN, NIEL, *13 August 1944 in Bloemfontein; at present (1977) assistant professor in pianoforte at the RCM.

Niel Immelman's training in pianoforte playing started in 1950 under the guidance of his mother and was continued after about twelve years by Prof. Leo Quayle.** In 1964 the Royal Schools of Music awarded him a bursary which enabled him to continue his studies at the RCM under Cyril Smith. Apart from various other distinctions, he climaxed his career at the RCM by winning the Chappell Award for Pianoforte at the end of his studies in 1969. Subsequently his playing was shaped by Ilona Kabos and Maria Curcio. Whilst still a student at the RCM, Niel Immelman performed the *Paganini rhapsody* (Rachmaninov) with the London Symphony Orchestra and has since then played concertos with the English National Orchestra. As soloist he has played in most of the London concert halls, also in various parts of England and Scotland. On the Continent he has played in the Concertgebouw in Amsterdam, and subsequently in Italy, Greece and Cyprus (all in 1974). His repertoire embraces more than 40 concertos and quite often he also participates in chamber music, notably with the Chilingirian String Quartette.

– Ed.

IMPERIAL RUSSIAN TRIO   A. Cherniavsky

IMRIE, JOHN MURDOCH McGREGOR, *18 January 1911 in Durban; now (1976) in Simonstown. Director of Music to the South African Navy.

Commander John Imrie studied in Pretoria with Rosita Gooch, Col. L.P. Bradley** and others from 1935 to 1956 and became a licentiate of the Trinity College of Music. His career had begun in Bloemfontein as principal clarinettist in the OFSVA Band in 1928 and was continued four years later in the band of the Regiment President Steyn. In 1935 he was transferred to Pretoria and joined the South African Permanent Forces Band as principal clarinettist and First Band Sergeant, becoming Assistant Director of Music to the South African Air Force in 1946. He became the first South African-born Director of Music in the Permanent Force when he was appointed Director of Music to the South African Navy in 1956 and he was the first to attain the rank of Commander.

PUBLICATION

The military band in South Africa. Struik, Cape Town, 1973.   – Ed.

INDEPENDENT ORDER OF GOOD TEMPLARS (IOGT)   Barberton, Potchefstroom, Pretoria 1, Queenstown 2

INDIGENOUS MUSICS OF SOUTH AFRICA

I. INTRODUCTION: INDIGENOUS MUSIC OF SOUTH AFRICA

"Indigenous" seems to be the best word to describe the musical practices which are discussed in the following pages. "Musics of the Bantu-speaking peoples" would exclude the music of the Bushmen and Hottentots, and "Black Music" is a term more appropriate to Afro-American music which has not yet been generally used to refer to the musics of Africa. "Native" is neater than "indigenous" and would be acceptable in many other countries, but it has connotations in South Africa which must be avoided. "Unwritten music" would exclude the music of composers which is aesthetically and structurally closer to African than European musical traditions; and to use the adjectives "popular" or "folk" would be confusing, as there is "art" in most African musical traditions, and by no means all music is shared by everyone in a society. — The terms "art" and "folk" are irrelevant and inaccurate, both as descriptions of musical styles and as classifications of different types of society and culture. In particular, they tend to conceal the social origins of musical experience *and* of musical sound in all cultures. All music is folk music, in the sense that music cannot be transmitted or have meaning without associations between people. And all music is art music, in the sense that it is humanly organized sound, and that its structures are not arbitrary but reflect the organization of the societies, cultures, and minds of its creators. (This argument is developed and illustrated with musical examples in J. Blacking: *How musical is man?* University of Washington Press, 1972.) All human beings are bound in culture by different systems of relationships to their natural environment, and so the term "ethnic" is also unsatisfactory, because it lays more emphasis on the kind of men who create the music, rather than on the *systems of relationships* between man and fellowman, and man and his natural environment, which are the real sources of musical creativity. Finally, "indigenous musics" is chosen, because although there are some features that these different systems have in common (see chapter III), each must be viewed as self-contained and logically interrelated with the social and cultural organization of the people who make the music. — The descriptions of indigenous musics which follow are hopelessly inadequate, but they constitute a first step and should be regarded as such. It is to be regretted that reports on the music of the Bushmen (by Dr Nicholas England), the Xhosa (by Miss Deirdre Hansen), and the Sotho of Lesotho (by Dr Charles Adams) could not be ready in time for publication, and that no detailed studies have yet been made of the music of the Tswana and of urban "folk" music. Still more regrettable is the fact that all reports are by Whites who are either South Africans or have come to do fieldwork in South Africa. Ethnomusicology is a luxury which Black African teachers and musicians can as yet ill afford, but it is to be hoped that some will soon come forward to fill the gap and produce studies of their musics that can compare with those of men like Prof. Kwabena Netkia of Ghana. — Verbal descriptions of the music without gramophone records are hardly adequate for appreciating sounds and systems which are unfamiliar. The reader is referred to Alan Merriam's discography, *African Music on LP* (Northwestern University Press, Evanston, 1970), and to the magnificent collection of records available from the former International Library of African Music, Roodepoort. These recordings were made by Dr Hugh Tracey,** who for forty years devoted his energies to the study of African music, and was responsible for founding the International Library, The African Music Society, and the journal, *African Music,* as well as writing a number of books and articles on the subject. Another collection of recordings has been built up by the South African Broadcasting Corporation under the direction of Dr Yvonne Huskisson,** but these are not publicly available. Finally, recordings have been made of traditional music by South African recording companies, but some of the best are out of print or not easily available. — Dr Tracey shares the honour of chief pioneer in the recording and study of South African indigenous music with the late Prof. P.R. Kirby,** whose chapter appears posthumously. If some of his information is repeated in subsequent chapters, it is partly because it seemed a good plan to include, say, a discussion of instruments in general as well as a description of the use of particular instruments in context, and partly because the editors felt that it was best to leave Professor Kirby's contribution as near as possible to the original. For the same reason, his views on the evolution of music, musical stratification and the origins of scales from natural harmonics, and his contention that four-part music is not genuinely Black African, have been presented without comment, although there is evidence for different interpretations. Prof. Kirby's conclusions are based on many years' fieldwork in all parts of Southern Africa where indigenous music was made, as well as an exhaustive study of all written and other records of musical practices made in the past. — The chapters describing the musics have been grouped partly according to cultural and linguistic affinities, and partly geographically, from south to north. The writers of the chapters on the musics of the Zulu and Swazi, the Pedi, the Shangana-Tsonga and the Venda, speak the indigenous languages with varying degrees of fluency, and all have done intensive fieldwork for periods ranging from twelve to twenty-two months. They are, respectively, specialists in linguistics and Bantu languages (with musical training), in music, again in music, and in social anthropology (with musical training), and all have relied heavily on transcriptions and analyses of tape-recordings made in the context of the situations in which the music is normally performed. The editors neither prescribed a rigid format for the contributions, nor attempted to iron out the differences of style and emphasis which reflect the different interests and fieldwork strategies of the writers. — It will be years before we have anything approaching a complete account of even one indigenous musical system of South Africa. Chapters VII and VIII are inevitably inadequate, but it is hoped that the other chapters give a fair and adequate summary of what is at present known about some of the remarkably varied and complex indigenous musics of South Africa.

– J.A.R.B.

II. THE MUSICS OF THE BLACK RACES OF SOUTH AFRICA

1. Introduction
2. The musical practices
   a. What is African music?
   b. Relationship to African music in other parts of the continent
   c. Music of the Bushmen
   d. Music of the Hottentot peoples
   e. Musical instruments of the Black peoples
      (i) autophones
      (ii) membranophones
      (iii) idiophones
      (iv) aerophones
      (v) chordophones
3. References

1. Introduction

The musicologist in South Africa is in an exceptionally fortunate position, for he is in an area in which the musics of different stages of man's development may still be studied. It is particularly important to realise that the aborigines of South Africa, especially those living to the south of the Vaal River, would appear to have largely escaped the overwhelming influence of great eastern civilizations which have for centuries strongly affected, and even in some cases dominated, the central and northern areas of the continent. And the influence of European civilization has only been brought to bear upon the inhabitants of the South African hinterland in relatively recent times. — A considerable number of the Bushmen, Hottentot and Bantu-speaking peoples are still living as their ancestors did. The Bushmen, who have always been nomadic hunters armed with clubs, spears and bows and arrows, are still to be found in remote areas. Their dancing is similar to that which Curt Sachs attributes to the most ancient cultures. It is "extrovert" in style and is characterised by animal dances, loose dances (the participants never joining hands) and choral dances, the last-named predominating. This kind of dancing is the type also practised by the pygmies of Central Africa. — The Hottentots, on the other hand, were originally semi-nomadic pastoralists, armed with only clubs and spears. As far as we can discover from written records, they did not acquire the shooting-bow until the beginning of the 17th century, and it was from the Bushmen that they derived it. There are comparatively few Hottentots living today, and most of those who still exist have been profoundly influenced by neighbouring and more "advanced" civilizations; nevertheless some of them until recently were still able to revive the practices of old, including those of music. — The Bantu-speaking peoples, unlike the Bushmen and Hottentots, are widespread throughout the Republic, and they have always tended to settle in particular areas, in which they not only tended their herds but also tilled the soil, for they were both pastoralists and horticulturalists, though they practised hunting also when the occasion offered. Their weapons were clubs and spears, though the shooting-bow was used by one branch of them, the Venda of the Northern Transvaal. — The great differences between the modes of life of these three groups, Bushmen, Hottentots and Bantu, is, of course, reflected in their musics, since the art of music is always closely bound up with the social life of the people who practise it. And as the impact of modern civilization is causing the original musics to be modified and, in some instances, almost completely replaced, we are able, like the geologist, to apply the principle of stratification to our study, and to observe the evolution of the art of music from some of its very earliest stages right up to the present time. No such possibility exists, as far as I am aware, in any other part of the world except, perhaps, in parts of the Americas. Moreover, the instrumental music of the aborigines seems to have been conditioned by natural law, and their vocal music by certain linguistic phenomena. But both the natural law and the linguistic phenomena involved also operated in Europe in bygone ages though more recent developments have tended to diminish their direct influence and even to cause them to be lost sight of. — The Bushmen, who appear to have come from the north in remote times, were at one period inhabiting practically the whole of South Africa, though scattered over it in small groups in the pleasantest places that they could find. But today, having been driven thence by the pressure of dominant cultures, they are found chiefly in the central and northern parts of the Kalahari Desert. Relics of their former dwelling-places, however, are found all over the country in the form not only of skeletal remains but also in rock paintings and engravings. One of the paintings, discovered more than 50 years ago by George William Stow, but now apparently no longer in existence, is one of the most significant documents in the history of music. Fortunately Stow made an accurate copy of it before it was destroyed by vandals. It will be discussed later. — The Hottentots, who also appear to have come from the north, were likewise at one time fairly widespread over South Africa, though they principally inhabited the coastal areas. The three main divisions of them were the Namaqua, who lived in Namaqualand, the Korana, who seem to have been in the neighbourhood of the Cape when Van Riebeeck arrived there in 1652, but who, in the opinion of the present writer, were at Mossel Bay when Vasco da Gama called there in 1497, and the Gonaqua, who were the most easterly branch, who dwelt along the south coast between Algoa Bay and the Great Kei River. Although a fair number of Namaqua are still to be found, only isolated small groups of Korana have survived. These are to be found at Upington, along the Vaal River, and in the neighbourhood of Bloemfontein. The Gonaqua, however, have entirely disappeared, only traces of their language remaining in the names of rivers and of a few places along the south coast. — The Bantu-speaking peoples of South Africa arrived in the country in more recent times. They may be broadly classified as (1) Sotho-Tswana (2) Southern Nguni, (3) Shangana-Tsonga and (4) Venda. The word "Bantu" is a linguistic term, applicable to all those peoples speaking allied languages who inhabit the southern two-thirds of the continent. There is a similarity of general principles in their musics, but considerable variety of regional styles, which are probably related to linguistic and cultural differences. The rhythmic complexity of Central African music is transformed into vocal polyphony in Southern African music. — The Sotho-Tswana group, which consisted of many related tribes, was originally spread, though probably sparsely, over the greater part of the country north of the Orange River, and to the west and north of the Drakensberg. They include the Tswana of Botswana, the Sotho of Lesotho and other near-by areas, and the Pedi of Sekhukhuneland in the Transvaal. — The Venda of the north-eastern Transvaal are more akin to the Karanga of the Zimbabwe area of Rhodesia than to the Sotho, though they have customs and music in common with the Northern Sotho. — The Southern Nguni include the Swazi, the Zulu and the Xhosa. It must, however, be remembered that our political boundaries do not define ethnological-al areas; for Swazi are to be found in the Republic as well as in Swaziland, and Tswana are met with in many districts apart from Botswana. — The Zulu were originally a relatively small accumulation of Nguni clans which were welded into a powerful military nation by Shaka (1787–1828). They are closely related linguistically and in other ways to the Swazi and the Xhosa, but whereas the Zulu lived in the northern districts of Natal, the Xhosa tribes inhabited the coastal districts from the southern Natal border nearly to Algoa Bay. The Southern Nguni, the "spear-point" of whom consisted of Xhosa tribes, appear to have penetrated South Africa from the north, migrating along the east coast at least before the close of the 16th century. They were well settled to the east of the Great Kei River by 1686, in which year the survivors of the wrecked *Stavenisse* found both Pondo and Xhosa proper in that neighbourhood during their wanderings before their eventual rescue. The Shangana-Tsonga live in Mozambique and also in the Northern Transvaal. — Finally it is essential to know that the Sotho of Lesotho consisted of members of various Sotho-Tswana tribes who in the early eighteen-twenties migrated into their present territory. They were refugees from hordes of Nguni who had been harrying them for years past. They, joined by a number of Nguni refugees who had escaped from Shaka's country, had been welded into a powerful nation by the wise ruler Moshoeshoe (c. 1793–1870), who had been born at Lichtenburg in the Transvaal. Moshoeshoe welcomed all refugees, whatever their origin, and some of these were actually Zulu. — The map will give the reader an idea of the general distribution of the various peoples referred to.

2. The musical practices

a. What is Black African music?

The question, "what is Black African Music?" has not been satisfactorily answered. There are, indeed, some scholars who even go so far as to say that there is no such thing. What they really mean is that there are throughout the continent so many different kinds of musics made by so many different kinds of Black Africans, that no single one of them may be considered to be the typical music of Africa. And this is quite true. There are many African musics. — The early missionaries who set up their stations in various parts of South Africa had many difficulties to contend with, not the least of which was their lack of musical instruments with which to lead the praise in their churches. However, the invention and wholesale manufacture of instruments of the harmonium and American organ type, which date from the early years of the nineteenth century, soon eased the instrumental side of the problem, but the vocal aspect remained. The missionaries, on hearing the music performed by Africans during their own ceremonies, must have rapidly realised that whereas the ordinary "domestic" music generally consisted of a simple one-"line" melody of rudimentary rhythmical structure, the "ceremonial" songs were usually rendered in a kind of polyphony, two or more of the voices proceeding in a parallel progression in which certain intervals used in European harmony were prominent, though the whole was

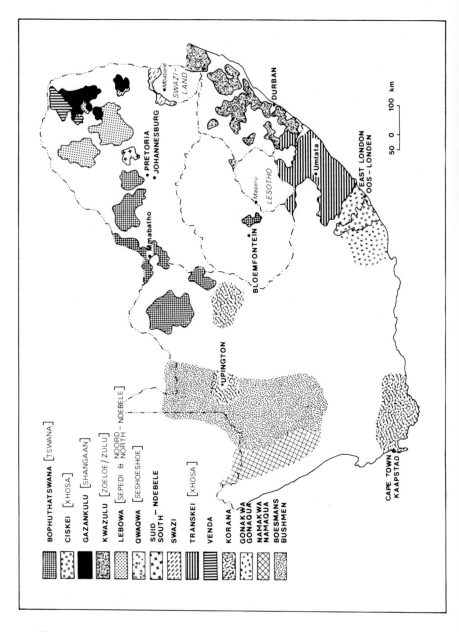

very different from that to which they themselves had been accustomed. What intrigued them still more was the power and resonance of the male voices of their African converts. This led them to endeavour to teach them to sing their hymns in four-part harmony, generally with organ accompaniment. — As it happened, Africans were for the most part, at the same stage of musical development as were Europeans, ecclesiastically speaking, in the tenth century. It was therefore possible for the missionary to assist his pupils to "short-circuit" the centuries, and to lay the foundations, chiefly through the medium of the Tonic Sol-fa notation, of what has become in little over a hundred years an ecclesiastical tradition among many Black Africans of "four-parts-at-any-price". This tradition, however, is not genuinely African, but has been imposed upon Black Africans from without. — It was while touring Natal officially that the writer first encountered a Black African musical instrument, which opened his eyes to what he considers to be the basis of most of their instrumental music. This was the *ugwala* of the Zulu, which, both by name and nature, betrayed its Hottentot origin; for it was obvious that this instrument was none other than the celebrated *gorá,* which had been adopted by the Xhosa people of the south-eastern coast, and passed on by them to the inhabitants of Natal. The importance of the *ugwala,* as of its immediate ancestor, the *gorá,* lies in the fact that from it the performer can elicit several sounds which form part of the "harmonic series", and no others, since those which he does produce are controlled by natural law. The sounds heard when a military bugle or trumpet is played belong to the same series, which explains what Lady Anne Barnard meant when she said of a Hottentot whom she heard performing upon the *gorá,* "he played the dragoons' music". — It was also among the Zulu people that I was first struck with the essentially musical character of their language. Every sentence seemed to me to have a melody of its own, and the fact that most words ended with vowels, or "voiced" sounds, emphasised the point. Apart from curious "clicks", defined by Doke and Vilikazi as "injected consonants produced by a rarefaction between tongue and palate", which were incorporated into their languages by the Nguni peoples through contact with Bushmen or Hottentots, the Zulu tongue seemed to me to be as musical as Italian, and for similar reasons. It was very different when it was spoken by the average European, for the "melody of the sentence" was far less apparent, and was sometimes even non-existent. — In 1852 Captain Robert Garden, an officer of the 45th Regiment, was "exploring" Natal with a view to writing a scientific work about it. Although primarily interested in the natural sciences, Garden was also attracted by the life of the Blacks whom he encountered, and in his unpublished diary he wrote thus about the Nguni tongues: "The missionaries speak the language grammatically without applying themselves to learn the idiom pronunciation or rather intonation of it as spoken by the native. Missionaries speak and learn the language in the manner white men learn a language, but they do not strive to acquire the peculiar intonations which the Caffirs give words and sentences or the idioms which exist as used by the natives. The Caffirs say we hear them speak but their words do not penetrate our ears. We cannot understand what they would imply. A word pronounced one way has one meaning but giving it a peculiar intonation or altering the prefix a totally opposite meaning may be given to it".[1] It is quite clear from this that Garden fully realised that Zulu was a tone-language, and that it was inherently musical. Thus the European practice of writing several verses to be sung to a tune must appear to a Zulu to be quite unnatural. — The music syllabus prescribed by the Natal Education Department of those days for use in Black schools had been inherited from those in use in Britain. Pupils were taught to read simple music from the Tonic Sol-fa notation, and they were expected to learn a few unison songs. But this, though sound enough from an educational point of view, was completely opposed to the ecclesiastical requirements of the missionaries who wished their converts to be able to sing hymns in four-part harmony, and had encouraged them to do so from the earliest days of missions. And not only did they do this, but they even translated the verses of many hymns into the Bantu languages, completely regardless of whether the rise and fall of the melodies corresponded, even generally, with those of the syllables of the translated words. What was possibly even worse, they forced the vernacular texts into the rhythmic patterns of the European tunes, often with disastrous results. — That my view was shared by thoughtful Black Africans who were aghast at hearing their beautiful language thus maltreated, is proved by the words of one of their number, the Xhosa composer, John Knox Bokwe** (1855– 1922), who summed up the position in these words: "The author's knowledge of music was self-acquired. Departing from the usage his own people had grown accustomed to in their religious hymn-singing, he composed his tunes so as to preserve *in singing* the correct accentuation followed in speaking the Xhosa language. The practice in church praise had hitherto been to adapt English tunes to Kafir words, but the different usage of the two languages in placing the accent made the accentuation fall quite out of place on the Kafir words in most of the hymns".[2] It will be noticed that Bokwe emphasized only the matter of *accentuation,* and did not mention that of *intonation.* The fact, however, is that Bokwe himself had been brought up in an atmosphere of four-part hymn-singing, and since this had become natural to him he accepted the departure from linguistic intonation as having been inevitable, though naturally regrettable. — It was, of course, impossible when writing in four-part harmony for the voices to preserve the relative rise and fall of speech-tones in hymn-singing, particularly as regards the bass part. For one of the chief tenets in writing four-part harmony in the European style is to cause the bass part to move, as far as possible, in contrary motion to the melody, and this alone was sufficient to destroy all sense of tone in a language so treated. — While listening to many Black choirs and conducting not a few of them, I was always struck by the fact that the intonation of several notes of the scale was not in accordance with what was acceptable to the educated European ear. Moreover, the singers displayed a tendency to alter the notes of a melody when they involved the interval of a semitone, and to change the harmony whenever it went beyond the simplest chords. Further, it was remarkable that they disliked "inversions" of chords, and would, whenever possible, replace them by chords in "root" position. As for the "natural harmony" of the Nguni peoples, I observed that a cardinal feature of it was the tendency for the voices, when not singing in unison, to proceed in parallel fifths or fourths, with the occasional introduction of a sixth or third, which latter were bound to be present when such parallelism is the result of singing in a pentatonic scale or mode (see ex. 1).

Example 1

Parallelism of this nature is, of course, totally opposed to the general practice in Europe, though it was common in the religious music of the tenth century, in which the system of choral singing in parallel fifths or fourths, known as "organum" or "diaphony", was universal. But in those days heptatonic, or seven-note, scales were in regular use in Europe, and therefore parallel singing within them did not involve the use of the intervals of the sixth and third. Writers on the musical history of Europe have regularly described this practice, but none of them has been able to give a satisfactory reason for its origin. To me, however, it has always been apparent that here in South Africa "parallel singing" was the natural and inevitable result of tone in language. My final pronouncement on the matter was published in my article on "Primitive Music" in Vol. VI of the fifth edition of *Grove's dictionary of music and musicians* (London, 1954). — My suggestion that song has thus developed from speech has not been universally accepted by scholars, some of whom have found in various parts of the world musical systems that appear to have a different basis. But as far as South Africa is concerned the principle which I have stated would appear to be fundamental to the music of the Blacks and may have in very early times governed the development of that of primitive man, however much it may have become differentiated in later periods and in different regions. — In this connection it is both interesting and important to note that in the article on "Greek Music (Ancient)" in the fifth edition of *Grove's dictionary,* the author states that: "By virtue of its pitch-accent the spoken language (of the Greeks) possessed an inherent melody. In setting words, Greek composers tended to follow, or at least to avoid conflict with, this speech-melody. The tendency is less pronounced in pieces written when the pitch-accent was giving way to stress". The present writer goes further than this, and suggests that it was precisely because of the presence of pitch-accent in ancient Greek as a determinant of meaning that these artistic people were unable to evolve harmony as we know it today, and were obliged to content themselves with "magadizing", or singing in octaves. — At this point one may well ask what brought about the change from pitch-accent to stress-accent. Although there is a danger of being dogmatic on a question of this nature, I would nevertheless suggest as a possible reason a phenomenon which is known to have produced this very result in the case of at least one African language, Swahili. Swahili is a composite language, in which Bantu speech has been infiltrated by other tongues, particularly Arabic. Today it is not a tone-language, for in it semantic tone had yielded to stress-accent. In my opinion this is what one should expect when two or more languages, each with its individual speech-tones, become fused, as in the case of Swahili. And when Black Africans learn European languages, their semantic tone must first tend to become diluted, and may finally disappear. — Of the "other phenomena" to which I have alluded, the most important is the recognition and practical use of the harmonic series, doubtless originally observed when the string of a shooting-bow was plucked, when an open reed was blown across by the wind, or in other simple natural ways. I consider that the first of these was in use in the Magdalenian period (between 20 000 and 30 000 years ago), as shown in a cave-painting at Ariège, in the south of France, in which a man wearing an animal mask is depicted using a shooting-bow as a musical instrument.[3] This very practice is still to be observed among certain of the Kalahari Bushmen;[4] and the majority of the stringed instruments made and played in Southern Africa are manifestly derived from their ancestor, the shooting-bow. The practice of producing harmonic sounds by blowing across open reeds can also be observed among the Nguni

273

peoples who, however, use the lower open end of the tube as a single "finger-hole", thus adding several of the harmonics of a "stopped" pipe to those of the open tube.[5] — But the most important deduction that can be drawn from these practices is that both string and pipe (the latter when it is "fingered") yield a form of pentatonic scale, which is controlled solely by natural law. Since it is commonly stated that the origin of the pentatonic scale is unknown, it is intriguing to find this natural form of it still in use in South Africa; and one is tempted to think that the many varieties of this type of scale now known in Europe and elsewhere had a similarly simple and natural beginning. — The influence of this elementary form of scale or mode, as produced by rudimentary musical instruments, upon the vocal music of early man was naturally profound, and its effects can still be observed in the singing of the Bushmen and, to some extent, in that of the Hottentots. For the choral songs of the Bushwomen that I have heard and recorded in the Kalahari Desert were based solely on several "partials" of various harmonic series, manifestly derived from those elicited from the string of the shooting-bow of the men; while the songs of the Korana Hottentots heard by Heinrich Lichtenstein near the Sak River in 1804 were as clearly based upon the harmonic sounds yielded by their national *gorá*.[6] — It used to be believed that the South African peoples had few musical instruments, and that they made little artistic use of those that they had. The erroneous generalisation was chiefly due to ignorance on the part of those writers who made it, who either failed to recognise them as musical instruments when they saw them, or did not comprehend the true nature of those that they did observe. As a matter of fact the aborigines had a surprising variety of instruments, including "autophones" or self-vibrating instruments (rattles, etc.), "membranophones" or skin-vibrating instruments (drums, etc.), "chordophones" or string-vibrating instruments (musical bows, etc.) and "aerophones" or wind-vibrating instruments (horns, flutes, whistles, etc.).

b. Relationship to African music in other parts of the continent
The greater part of northern Africa, from Egypt to Morocco and as far south as the Sudan, has been for centuries past subjected to the domination of invaders from the Near East; while the eastern coast and the vast areas in its hinterland have likewise been powerfully influenced not only by Near-Eastern peoples, but by others of the Far East. Most ethnologists and archaeologists, to say nothing of historians, have with few exceptions ignored the evidence provided by musical instruments, many of which remain either in their pristine condition or in a state of degeneration, though still recognisable as legacies from the "foreigners" who first brought them to our shores. To the ethnomusicologist, on the other hand, they are of the utmost importance, since from such instruments or from what I regard as their "vestigial remains", not only can he deduce the ethnic origins of the men who bestowed them on Africa, but he may even hazard approximate dates for their acquisition by African peoples. One of the most significant of these musical instruments, nowadays found spread widely over the central areas of the continent, is the resonated xylophone, commonly called by Europeans the *marimba,* or, vulgarly, the "Kaffir piano". The Blacks themselves, however, have their own names for it, among them being *mbila,* the name by which the instrument is and was known in East Africa since at least the sixteenth century, and by which it is still called by the Venda of the Northern Transvaal, whose ancestors brought it with them from north of the Limpopo river many years ago. I have no doubt whatever that this instrument originated in Indonesia, and I believe that I have

succeeded in tracing the manner of its invention there, and how (and possibly when) it came to Africa.[7] — We have, of course, comparatively little evidence of the nature of the culture of the earliest inhabitants of South Africa, and particularly of their music. A few fossilised animal bones have been found here and there, which were surely used as signal whistles, the opening at one end being doubtless plugged with some appropriate material such as animal fat mixed with ashes, or, if not so plugged, the lower opening may have been temporarily closed by a finger. My reason for coming to this conclusion is twofold. In the first place a short tube (and the two existing specimens are both short) cannot be readily sounded, if at all, by being blown across one end if the other is left open; and in the second place similar bone whistles made by some of the present-day Blacks are almost invariably plugged in the manner and with the materials that I have described. — In the University of Stellenbosch are preserved six bones of narrow bore, which may have been used as whistles and are much longer than the former two, varying from about 7 cm to 17 cm. Four of them are beautifully ornamented with carefully incised designs. They were found in a cave near Knysna. These whistles, if such they are, were made and used by the so-called "strandlopers", but of what ethnic group these people were, or when they lived in the Knysna district, is not known. If these bones were actually used as whistles, they would have been converted into "stopped" pipes by being plugged at one end and being blown across the other.

c. Music of the Bushmen

The South African Bushmen were a nomadic people, living by hunting and by gathering edible plants. The earliest written record of them will be found in the journal of Simon van der Stel's expedition to Namaqualand in 1685. It is worth remembering, for comparative purposes, that it was in this year that both Bach and Handel were born. By great good fortune the journalist of Van der Stel's expedition described the singing of the Bushmen as it sounded to him as "resembling nothing so much as a herd of yearling calves just turned out of the cowshed".[8] No mention of musical instruments was, however, made by him, so it is possible that the Bushmen whom he met did not play any at that time, or that he did not consider what he may have seen as musical instruments. Doubtless also Van der Stel's party were unacquainted with "yodelling", which is characteristic of Bushman singing, and regarded it as mere animal noise. Incredible though it may seem, this is the only reference to Bushman music prior to the nineteenth century! — But in 1800 the Rev. J.J. Kicherer, of the London Missionary Society, endeavoured to convert to Christianity the Bushmen living near the Sak River. In this he had little success, and was driven to inducing them to attend his services by bribing them with tobacco.[9] We may, however, assume that the Bushmen picked up the tunes of the hymns they were taught with comparative ease, for they were, and are, great mimics. By this time, however, the Bushmen had become "neighbours" of the Hottentots, particularly the Korana. From the latter some of them acquired the *gorá,* to which they gave the name of their shooting-bow, *ǀha.* It is because of this that more than one ethnologist has fallen into the error of regarding the *gorá* as an original Bushman musical instrument. This was certainly not the case, as I shall hope to show. — When William John Burchell, the scientist-explorer, was travelling in the vicinity of what is now Griquatown towards the end of 1811, he fell in with a group of Bushmen, one of whom performed on the *gorá* for him. Burchell, however, recognized that the instrument had been "borrowed" by the Bushmen from the Hottentots, and was punctilious in noting the fact, although this has often been overlooked or ignored by writers who have quoted from him. Burchell's transcriptions of the music that he heard played upon the instrument are, unfortunately, unreliable. Since he himself was an amateur flautist, he noticed in the Bushman's performance several passages which sounded to him rather like similar passages which were typical of the flute. As a result he included in his transcription much that cannot be played upon the *gorá,* controlled as it is by natural law.[10] The history of the *gorá* will be discussed with the music of the Hottentots. — On a second occasion Burchell witnessed a Bushman "solo" dance, the music being provided by a companion, who sang a strongly rhythmical tune while marking the time on a primitive drum. The scientist, who must have been amazed at the novelty of the strange vocal sounds he was hearing, did his best to transcribe them, writing down the queer little tune in musical notation, but adding below it what at first sight appears to be a mere meaningless jingle, expressed by him by the syllables "Aye O, Aye O, etc." Not until 1936, when I myself was in the Kalahari Desert, was I able to understand what Burchell and the later explorer Alexander (who noted down similar syllables as "Ei-oh, Ei-oh,") intended to convey. For the Bushmen were "yodelling", and as the word "yodel" had not then been incorporated into the English language, they had to indicate the nature of the phenomenon as best they could. In common with other European researchers I had imagined the practice to be confined to Switzerland and the Tyrol. The discovery that the Bushmen also yodel and other findings in this connection was published at the time in *Bantu Studies.*[11] — The Bushmen, however, had also songs with words. The texts of over twenty of them were taken down phonetically by the Bleek family of Cape Town between 1870 and 1876, the singers being prisoners from the northern border of the Colony who were serving their sentences at the Cape. These texts, however, were not published until 1911, when they were included in *Specimens of Bushman folklore,* by the late Dr W.H.I. Bleek and his sister-in-law, Miss Lucy C. Lloyd. But the music to which the songs were sung was not given, although a musician of Cape Town, Mr Charles Weisbecker, made an attempt to transcribe them in musical notation. To enable him to fit the notes to the appropriate syllables, Miss Lloyd wrote the words of the songs below the staves in two manuscript music books. Weisbecker did his best to note down what he heard, but considered that he had failed. By great good fortune the late Miss Doris Bleek, daughter of the celebrated philologist, presented the precious books to me. I was able to divine Weisbecker's intentions, and to reconstruct and publish the songs together with their texts, so that my reconstructions and conclusions could be checked and challenged by anyone who might care to do so.[12] — My examination of these songs showed that they had a pentatonic basis, and that the harmonic chord was present in all. Other notes, foreign to a pentatonic mode, occurred but rarely, and may have been due either to the singer "overshooting the mark" or to European influence. Most of the songs were embedded in folk-tales, where they were used, as similar songs were wont to be used in Europe, to heighten the effect of the stories. In several of the songs the moon was personified; in others, animals. Some again were definitely dance-songs, and one, strangely enough, was a song about the Korana, who were preparing for a raid on the Bushmen. This was unusual, since people like the Bushmen, who had no tribal organisation, had no need for war songs. All these songs, however, were performed by individual singers. Nothing of a "choral" nature, such as the performances heard by Burchell and Alexander, was recorded by Miss Lloyd and Mr Weisbecker. The singers, moreover, all belonged to the /Xam group of Bushmen. — From my examination of this material, together with the scattered allusions to Bushman musical practices which were to be found in the writings of various nineteenth century missionaries and travellers, I came to the conclusion that Bushman solo songs were closely related to Bushman speech, and that they were pentatonic in character. Their subject-matter was principally concerned with domestic topics, hunting and the heavenly bodies. War and historical songs were absent. The form of the songs, as of their texts, was clearly strophic, though very simple. Their extent never exceeded a single musical sentence. Rudimentary part-singing was indulged in occasionally, and the songs in general were closely connected with dancing. — My analysis of the songs was published in *Bantu Studies* in June 1936, together with one recorded by means of an Edison phonograph on a wax cylinder by Miss Doris Bleek in 1921. The singer of this last song was at that time living on the Lower Nossop River. The transcription revealed that it appeared to be pentatonic, based upon partials of the harmonic series, including the seventh, which is not normally used in European music. In 1936, I took with me to the Kalahari a set of six specially made brass pan-pipes, which were tuned to partials of the harmonic series, these being Nos. 4, 5, 6, 7 and 8, and also No. 9, pitched an octave lower than it would naturally occur in the series. This gave a pentatonic scale derived exclusively from the harmonic series, which could be roughly represented in ordinary musical terminology as the notes *C, D, E, G, B flat* and *C¹*, the *B flat* (the seventh harmonic) being flatter than it would be in the European scale system, and the *D* (the ninth harmonic) being an octave lower than in its usual place in the series. On hearing a group of Bushwomen executing one of their strange choral songs, in which they yodelled, I found that I was correct, and that their "mode" matched that of my pan-pipes, being indeed pentatonic, and derived directly from the harmonic series. — My suggestion that the Bushman pentatonic scale was derived from the harmonic series has not yet been generally accepted. This is doubtless due to the fact that most scholars who have studied the question have based their conclusions chiefly upon pentatonic modes which have survived among peoples who have developed what we regard as advanced civilisations. But the Bushmen have never so developed, and their music would appear to represent one of the earliest stages in the evolution of the art. — The Bushwomen's choral songs, as heard in 1936, were all associated with the dance.[13] One woman, selected by common consent, or possibly self-elected, would act as leader or "precentor" and would begin a rhythmless "tune-pattern", which was invariably based upon the pentatonic scale. She sang this "pattern" to vowel sounds, deliberately chosen so as to favour the production of alternate "chest" and "falsetto" notes, resulting in yodelling. Having established the "tune-pattern" the leader would break into a simple rhythmical strophe in triple time, and the other women would join in, attempting to follow her in unison, at the same time clapping their hands in time to the music and executing little dance steps. The latter in some songs duplicated the rhythmic pattern of the hand-clapping; in others they did not, but established a different, though still simple, pattern. In a few songs there were two sets of hand-claps of different patterns, while the dance steps were also independent. All, however, were very simple. — The "form" of these songs was sometimes what would be called a four-bar sentence, and at others a six- or even an eight-bar one. Such units would be repeated over and over again with little variation, except for the occasional substitution of one "harmonic" melody-note for another. But in one song, the first "sentence" would be repeated several times, and then another would replace it for a while, after which a return to the original "sentence" would be made. A little later a third, and even a fourth "sentence" would appear, giving the impression of a "rondo". I could discover no system whatever in the occurrence of the various "sentences". It was obvious that the Bushmen not only preserved unity in their music, but demanded a certain amount of variety in it, though they had not succeeded in organising any extended musical forms. Modulation, of course, was non-existent. — Several songs performed by men were, like those of the women, based upon the mode derived from the partials of the harmonic series. This was especially noticeable when a man sang to the accompaniment of a stringed instrument. — The capacity of Bushman girls for imitating foreign music was considerable. I heard them sing a couple of European hymn tunes, in which they employed, without hesitation, the ordinary western diatonic scale, including the two semitones.[14] Some of them even added a lower part, and in one of the tunes two such parts were added. But it was quite obvious that these girls had picked up the hymn-tunes from listening outside some church or other, for they would begin them at any point, and not at the real commencement. — In addition to these hymn-tunes, I heard them sing a number of songs of European origin, all with Afrikaans words.[15] They had picked up no fewer than eleven of these, among which were "So lank soos die lepel in die jam pot staan, roer Maria, roer.", and "Die Boesman meid, die koringkop". All of these songs were harmonised by the girls in European fashion, though crudely. It was of exceptional interest to see how they were able to discard their own age-old musical idioms, and to assume those of Europeans, without confusing either. Their mimicry extended even to a vocal imitation of a European or Coloured dance band of violins and guitars, including the bass part. The girls had apparently seen such a band play at some remote farm, for they occasionally imitated the movements of performers on the instruments. One girl actually produced deep bass notes by bringing her pharynx into action! — Although I had been told that I would not find any musical instruments in use among these particular Bushmen, I succeeded in discovering no fewer than eight types, several of which were of the most rudimentary description.[16] Two types of percussion instrument were used: ankle-rattles made from dried cocoons filled with fragments of ostrich-egg shell, and a dried skin of a buck laid over a hollow in the sand. On the latter one or two men danced, the skin serving both as a dancing platform and as a rudimentary drum. Nothing was known by these Bushmen of the celebrated ankle-rattles made from the ears of the springbok, and filled with hard dried berries, which were observed by the traveller Burchell in 1812, and by the Bleek family in the late eighteen-seventies, who also secured a description of their manufacture in the vernacular. They are now no longer made. — Nor did these Bushmen know the "bull-roarer", with which the /Xam Bushmen used to attract the bees. The drum observed by Miss Lloyd at that time, which the /Xam women used to make from a pot covered with springbok skin, was also unknown to these /Auni. This was not surprising, since the pot drum was essentially a Hottentot instrument, and was, in my opinion, imitated by them from the drums of the Tswana. — Among the /Auni I found only one wind instrument, a primitive "ocarina" made from an empty dried gourd of small size. It had only two openings in it, the upper serving as an "embouchure" and the lower as a "finger-hole". From this instrument the woman who played upon it elicited two notes, the pitches of which were naturally fortuitous. Of the signal whistles of horn, bone or ostrich quill, which were and doubtless still are in use among the Bushman people to the west of the Kalahari Desert, I found no trace. There was, however, a kind of temporary "jew'sharp" which consisted of a length of stiff dry grass held across the mouth and twanged by the fingers. It yielded two tones of rather indefinite pitch, which were supposed to suggest the sound of a hartbees escaping from a hunter. — The first of the stringed instruments had never before been observed and described. This instrument, which was called /ka/kanasi, was said by the /Auni Bushmen to have been played in the olden time by old women. The performer had provided herself with a long string of twisted sinew, a man's knobkerrie, a cocoon from a set of dancing rattles, a roll of dry hide from the belly of a buck, and a length of *riem*. She stuck the knobkerrie in the sand, and sat down in such a position that the kerrie was immediately in front of her outstretched legs. She then looped the string of sinew round the knobkerrie, passing one half of it between the toes of her left foot, and the other half between those of her right foot, thus keeping the two halves apart. She tied the ends of the two halves of the string to the tip of the cocoon rattle, and threaded the *riem* through the other tip. The *riem* was then passed round her body and tied behind her back. Finally she inserted the roll of hide between the cocoon rattle and her chest to serve as a resonator. By leaning backwards she could tighten the two strings which now stretched from her breast to her toes, and thus raise their pitch; conversely, by leaning forwards, she could slacken them, and thus lower their pitch. To produce sounds from them she plucked them with thumbs and fingers, and the result was more rattle and buzz than musical tone. Nor could I detect any systematic rhythmic or melodic scheme in the "music", which was in the nature of the case very faint; and the pitch of the various notes produced was completely fortuitous. Nevertheless the instrument is of considerable interest, for it shows how music may be extracted from a string without its being supported by a frame, as in the case of the majority of musical instruments that have evolved from the shooting-bow. — The other three stringed instruments that these Bushmen possessed had all been evolved from the shooting-bow, and were all called by its name, /khou. The simplest of these was an actual shooting-bow, used temporarily as a musical instrument. The player held the bow in his left hand, with the middle of the stave across his open mouth. He either tapped the string with a twig or plucked it with the forefinger of his right hand, when it yielded its fundamental note and also several harmonics which were both isolated and reinforced by the player's buccal cavity. The pitch of the bow-string when tensioned for shooting is such that the Bushman can readily isolate and resonate partials Nos. 4 to 9 of the harmonic series, while the fundamental, which is produced by the string as a whole, serves as a "drone". The player can thus extemporise little tunes from the harmonics, which with the "drone" results in one of the most primitive types of two-part polyphony. This phenomenon is of very great importance, since recently several distinguished musicologists have stated categorically that the harmonic series has never given rise to anything in the nature of scales and melodies, and also that the "drone" appears relatively late in the history of civilisation. Further, the late Dr Curt Sachs refused to entertain the idea that the musical bow evolved from the shooting-bow, and even maintained that it was the other way about. — The second form of the /khou consisted of a slightly modified shooting-bow, both longer and lighter than the regular weapon, with a wire in place of the string of sinew when it can be obtained. The performer takes an empty tin, if he can procure one, and places it upon his bare chest, the open end next his skin. He then places the stave of the bow, which he holds vertically in his left hand, against the closed end of the tin which serves as a temporary resonator. With a light twig he strikes the lower end of the string, and elicits from it a clear ringing tone, in which both the

279

fundamental and several harmonics can be distinctly heard. But by drawing the bow-stave downwards, the player can rock the tin away from his body, thus exposing more or less of the open end of it. The result of this procedure is remarkable, for by utilising it the performer can isolate various harmonics, while the fundamental is also heard. And by pinching the string against the stave near its lower end he can raise the pitch of the fundamental, and thus bring into action a second set of harmonics. By combining the two series he can execute simple tunes in rudimentary two-part polyphony, the whole being the result of the application of natural law. — The third form of the _/khou_ consisted of a completely modified bow, of such a nature that it could never have been used for shooting, but had manifestly been designed for musical purposes only, although derived from the weapon. It consisted of a pliable bow, the string of which was strained to such an extent that the stave was bent into the form of a semicircle. The performer sat down on the ground and placed the lower end of the instrument either on the ground or upon any convenient hollow vessel, such as a skin milksack or any empty tin, while the upper end rested against his left shoulder. His right leg, passing between the string and the stave, held the instrument firmly in position. Taking a light twig in his right hand, he would tap the string with a _staccato_ action, thus producing its fundamental note. But by touching the upper part of the string lightly at the appropriate "nodes" with his left hand, he could elicit several harmonics. Further, by bending his head over the instrument, he could press on the upper part of the string with his chin, thus raising the pitch of the fundamental, and from this second fundamental he could elicit a second set of harmonics. This instrument made it clear that the Bushmen had at some time or other been in close contact with Korana Hottentots; for this instrument was characteristic of them, and had also been passed on by them to the Tswana, to whom the shooting-bow was unknown.

d. Music of the Hottentot peoples

The Hottentot peoples, who were the first to be encountered by Europeans when they arrived in South Africa, were, unlike the Bushmen, semi-nomadic pastoralists. And they do not seem to have known the shooting-bow until the early years of the seventeenth century, when they first came into serious conflict with the Bushmen. There were three main branches of the Hottentot race: the _Gonaqua,_ the _Korana_ and the _Namaqua._ – The _Gonaqua,_ appear to have inhabited the area along or near to the southern coast from about Algoa Bay to the Umtata River. They are now quite extinct, though traces of their heritage can still be observed in the countenances of many individuals of obviously mixed race in those districts, and of their language in the names of these South Coast rivers which begin with a "K", which represents one of their "clicks". — The _Korana,_ as far as one can now judge, originally lived near the coast from the neighbourhood of Mossel Bay westwards, until they were driven northwards. Today only a few scattered remnants are to be found along the Vaal River, at such places as Bloemhof and Christiana, with several in the Bloemfontein area. A good deal, however, has been discovered about the Korana and their movements, and also about their music. — The _Namaqua,_ of which a fair number still exist, originally inhabited the western districts, from the Cape itself up to the Orange River, and even beyond it. Their mode of life and their language have been studied by many travellers and several scholars, and their cultural connection with the other Hottentots is quite well known. — It is with the Hottentots that the history of known music in South

Africa may be said to begin. When on 2 December 1497, Vasco da Gama anchored in Mossel Bay, and landed on the beach near the present-day lighthouse, he and his men were welcomed by the "blacks" as he called them, who were, in my opinion, Korana Hottentots. These men greeted the Portuguese with music played on their "reed-flutes". Each of these flutes was a single "pan-pipe", a "stopped" tube of reed, which yielded but one sound, so that each player contributed only one note to the ensemble. Da Gama's log-book informs us that there were four or five of the flutes, but adds that they were sounded "in harmony", a fact that greatly surprised the Portuguese. Fortunately for us, the original tuning of the four principal flutes has been retained, unaltered, by the Namaqua Hottentots, and also the memory of it by the Korana. The latter, who came into conflict with the Tswana towards the end of the eighteenth century, long after they had been driven from their original home near the coast, passed their reed-flutes on to their conquerors. To this day several of the Tswana tribes still knew the reed-flutes when I visited them in the nineteen-thirties, and one, the Bamalete of Ramutsa, have retained the original Hottentot four-note scale, and play in harmony just as did the Korana of the fifteenth century.[17] — A number of old men of the Namaqua group also remembered the flutes, and in 1931 I was just in time to assemble a group of them and to record the sounds of the original tuning. Their four-note scale, undoubtedly the oldest in our country, is also possibly the oldest organised musical scale in the world (see ex. 2).

Example 2

The Hottentot people, as I have said, did not make use of the shooting-bow, and consequently had no stringed instruments until they clashed with the Bushmen, and from them acquired the "long-distance" weapon. They soon imitated the Bushmen practice of using it not only for defence and offence but also as a musical instrument. — The two principal types of "musical bows" which I described as being used by Bushmen were also played by the Korana. The first of these was in every respect similar to a shooting-bow, though of lighter construction. The Korana called it *!gabus,* and in its technique it corresponded exactly to that form of the */khou* of the Bushmen which, as we saw, was an actual shooting-bow used temporarily for musical purposes. — The second type, which the Korana called by the name of their own shooting-bow, */kha:s,* was identical with the more elaborate type of Bushman */khou.* In my opinion this form of musical bow was originated by the Korana, from whom it was later acquired by both the Bushmen and the Tswana. — The Hottentots went further than the "little people". Being a race of flute-players, they invented a method of causing their bow-string to vibrate by air, by interposing between one end of it and the stave a short spatulate piece of flattened quill (see plate 8, p. 360).[18] By holding the bow thus altered transversely, with the quill between the parted lips, and by drawing in their breath with varying degrees of force, the string vibrated and yielded several "partials" of the harmonic series, with, in the hands of an expert player, a clear, ringing trumpet-like tone. Thus was born the famous *gorá* during the seventeenth century. It was so named after the bird whose feather was the soul of the instrument. The *gorá* provides us with one more example, and a particularly striking one, of the practical use in music of the harmonic series. The *gorá* was passed on by the

Hottentots in the Cape to the Xhosa towards the end of the eighteenth century, by the Xhosa to the Sotho and Zulu, and thence to the Swazi and, via Mzilikazi, to the Venda, who retained it for about eighty years. Some of the Tswana, who had come into contact with the Matabele, also imitated it, together with its Zulu name. Likewise some Bushmen copied it, and the instrument was being played by a Bushman when William J. Burchell heard it and described it. He was, however, careful to point out that it was a Hottentot instrument. It is now rarely met with, and then chiefly among the Sotho of Lesotho. There the herd-boys play upon it while herding cattle, and they call it *lesiba,* which simply means "a feather". — From time to time travellers have tried to describe Hottentot music. One of the best of these was the German Lichtenstein, who recognised the true nature of the *gorá,* and who realised that the songs of the Korana were based on the sounds which they could produce from that instrument, including the strange seventh harmonic. But the influence of Europeans in more recent times has tended to eradicate the original music of the Hottentots. Early in the eighteenth century they begin to make crude imitations of the stringed instrument used by the Cape Malays, and called by them by various names from which the present one, *ramki,* was evolved.[19] In similar fashion the drum of the Cape slaves was copied by the Hottentots. In making it they used either a *bambus,* or milk-container of bamboo, when they could get it, or a clay pot, as the "shell" or body of the instrument, covering it with skin, which they tightened by heat from the sun or from a fire, and they played it by beating it with their hands, and not with a stick. Peter Kolb, in his description of the Cape which was published in Nürnberg in 1719, depicted a Hottentot playing upon such a "pot-drum", the pot of which is clearly of Tswana origin; and he compares the instrument with the *rommelpot* of Flanders. Careless readers and writers have frequently assumed that this was the real name of the Hottentot drum, but this is quite wrong. The *rommelpot* of the Low Countries is a form of "friction drum", and the true name of the Hottentot drum is */kha:s.*[20] —In Namaqualand, the "German" concertina, which is diatonic, became popular from about the eighteen-thirties, with the result that a whole series of more or less diatonically tuned high notes were added, in the form of loose pan-pipes, to the original four-note reed-flute ensemble. The Korana, who were directly influenced by German missionaries who had established a mission on the banks of the Vaal River near Bloemhof, absorbed European musical practices to such an extent that they have lost almost everything of their own music.[21] — In the old songs, as I have heard them performed by the older men, the "scale" was manifestly pentatonic, and the texts were concerned with the customary domestic topics.

e. Musical instruments of the Black peoples of South Africa
(i) Autophones
All the South African Black tribes make use of dancing-rattles, some of which are worn on the ankles as in the case of those of the Bushmen, while others are shaken in the hand.[22] The ankle-rattles of the Sotho-Tswana are made from cocoons, large numbers of which are filled with small stones and attached to long *riems,* which are then wound round the ankles of the dancers and secured (see plate 10, p. 364). In Lesotho, however, the people nowadays make their anke-rattles from goat-skin, in imitation of cocoons, since the trees on which the cocoon-forming insects used to live have been practically eliminated. — The Nguni, particularly the Zulu, who also use cocoons for their ankle-rattles, arrange them in thick clusters instead of in long strings, and in this

form they may still be seen worn by the few remaining ricksha-haulers of Durban. Finally, in Pondoland one occasionally meets with ankle-rattles made from woven strips of ilala palm. This is curious, since similar woven ankle-rattles are found in Madagascar. With the Venda the ankle-rattles are made from dried hollow fruits of a globular form, filled with small stones, and fixed in parallel rows to light wooden frames. They are worn like cricket-pads, to which they have a considerable resemblance (see plate 11, p. 365). — The hand-rattles to which I have referred are generally oval in shape, being made from calabashes of suitable size containing small stones. At each end of the calabash is a circular hole, through which is passed a stick. This projects from the lower end and serves as a handle. This type of instrument is used by the Shangana-Tsonga and the Venda, and to some extent by the Swazi and Zulu (see plate 12, p. 366).

(ii) Membranophones

Several varieties of drum are met with, though curiously enough the indigenous types are confined to the Sotho-Tswana, Venda and Tsonga peoples, that is, to those whose tribal names begin with the prefix "Ba". The Nguni group, who almost all use the prefix "Ama", do not have indigenous drums except for one of a most unusual nature.[23] Among the Zulu this drum, which is called *ingungu,* consists of a clay beer pot over the opening of which a piece of goat-skin is secured by means of thongs. The *ingungu* is never struck like an ordinary drum, but is sounded by means of a reed which is held vertically over the skin, and caused to vibrate by being stroked downwards by the moistened hands of the player. The vibrations of the reed are communicated to the skin, and the result is a roaring sound, not unlike the roar of a distant lion. This instrument is only made for and used in the *omula* ceremony, the initiation of a Zulu girl to womanhood. It is a true friction drum, and therefore the most southerly representative of that type of musical instrument. Its real nature has until recently been invariably misunderstood by lexicographers. — The Swazi had a similar drum, called by them *intambula,* a name which strongly suggests the Portuguese word *tambor,* or perhaps the Afrikaans word *tamboer.* It is, however, a true friction drum, though made for temporary use only. One man, kneeling on the ground, holds a piece of goat-skin tightly over the opening of a clay beerpot, while a second man, the player, holds a reed vertically upon the skin, and strokes it downwards with his moistened hands in the same manner, and with a similar result, as the performer upon the Zulu *ingungu.* – The Southern Nguni, however, have for long employed their military shields of ox-hide as substitutes for drums, either striking them with their assegais or knobkerries, or actually dashing them down upon the ground. The effect of the latter method, when performed by a large number of men, is barbaric in the extreme. Among the Xhosa an analogous drum, substantially derived from a practice similar to that of the Zulu just described, is the *ingqongqo.* This is a stiff ox-hide which is either supported upon several upright sticks or held round its edges by a number of women who are the performers. It is prepared and beaten by the women on the occasion of the initiation of manhood of their sons. There is no doubt that the hide represents the shield which was formerly used, and the engraved sticks with which it is beaten (and which actually bear the name) a particular type of Xhosa assegai, these articles having in the past been given to the successful initiates to set them up in life. — The Southern Nguni nowadays occasionally make and play a two-headed drum upon which they beat with two padded drum-sticks. This drum, called *isigubu,* is unquestionably an imitation of the bass drum used by the European military in relatively recent times. The general appearance of the instrument, the padded sticks, the position in which it is held, and the swagger of the performer, all testify to this. — Among the "Ba" peoples true drums are universally found, all of them, with the exception of one or two "imported" types, being singleheaded instruments with hemispherical or conical "shells". — The Sotho-Tswana, who make and use the latter, call them *moropa* (see plate 9, p. 363), which is philologically connected with the name of a similar drum used by the Venda, who call it *murumba*. These drums are always played by women, who beat them with their bare hands. The Sotho-Tswana beat theirs while seated, but the Venda while standing, the drum being held between the performer's legs. The Sotho of Lesotho, whose country, formerly well-wooded, is now largely bereft of trees suitable for drum-making, manufacture a substitute *moropa* from a clay pot with a skin laced over the opening. They use it at the initiation of their young women. It is now extremely rare. — The Venda of the Northern Transvaal, who are connected with more northerly tribes, have another and very distinctive type of drum, which is made in various sizes, and used regularly in pairs. These drums have large hemispherical shells carved out of a solid tree-trunk. The opening at the top is covered with a stout hide, and the instrument is beaten with a single wooden beater. The larger size is called *ngoma,* a term that is applied to drums in many parts of the African continent for either a drum or for a dance in which drums play a part. The smaller is called *thungwa*. These drums are played as a rule by women and girls, although the large *ngoma* is beaten by a man when the drums join with reed-flutes in the performance of the national dance known as *tshikona*. This dance will be discussed later. — One very significant feature of these Venda hemispherical drums is that at the four "cardinal points" round the upper part of the instruments interlaced "handles" are carved, which are known to the Venda as "the frog's knee", or "Mrs Frog." This is the more curious since in the Far East, particularly in Tonkin, but also at one time in the Malay Archipelago, large cylindrical drums were made from metal, with a circular disk of metal replacing the usual skin head; and at the four cardinal points round this circular plate were soldered four metal figures of frogs. It is therefore not unlikely that the Venda drums provide evidence of a former connection with the Malay Archipelago, a suggestion that will be dealt with more fully when the African resonated xylophones are discussed. — There remain the "frame-drums" of the Tsonga people, which consist of circular hoops of wood over one side of which skins are tightly stretched, in a manner exactly similar to that of the familiar tambourine, though the skins are kept in position by thongs which are secured at the back of the instrument. This drum, called by the Tsonga, *mantshomane* (cf. chap. VI, plate 13), is held in the left hand by the male performer and struck with a wooden beater held in his right. It is used in the *gongondjela* ceremony, in which an attempt is made to exorcise the evil spirits that are supposed to be possessing some unfortunate individual. It has been taken over to some extent by the Swazi. None of the other peoples have it.

(iii) Idiophones

Instruments usually classified as "idiophones", in which the sound is produced by the vibration of the material of which the instrument is made, are rare in South Africa.[24] The most important of these is the resonated xylophone, called *mbila mutondo*, of the Venda people. This superb instrument, which is rapidly becoming obsolete, if it has not already become so, consists of between twenty-two and twenty-four carved slabs of hardwood, carefully tuned to a seven-note scale. These slabs are hung from a wooden frame, and vertically beneath each is secured an elongated calabash, open at the upper end, so chosen and tuned that the air-column contained in it vibrates with exactly the same frequency as the slab above it. Two players provided with rubber-headed beaters are required to perform upon the instrument. But whereas the player at the "treble" end of the instrument has but one beater in each hand, the one at the "bass" end has one for his right hand but two for his left, which are held so as to form a Y (see plate 17a, p. 435). — This type of resonated xylophone, with a similar number of slabs, was seen and heard at Sofala near Beira, in 1586, by the Portuguese priest, Dos Santos. He stated that the performers were "Mocaranga" (i.e. Karanga), who were distant connections of the Venda. There is no doubt whatever in my mind that the instrument originated in the Malay Archipelago, and that it was brought to the shores of Eastern Africa either by Indonesian traders or by Africans who had by some means or other, whether as slaves, traders or even ambassadors, visited the Archipelago and picked up a good deal of information about the culture of the Far East. Many features displayed by the *mbila* testify to this, not the least of which is the use of two beaters in the left hand, which is undoubtedly a survival of the ancient forked beaters of the Malay Archipelago. — The music played by the Venda on their resonated xylophones is rhythmically complicated. At times two different rhythmical schemes are opposed, the resulting combination being quite different from any to be found even in European music of the ordinary kind, although modern compositions reveal practices of an analogous nature, which might be described as "counterpoints of rhythms". — The Venda, too, possess the well-known little iron-tongued *mbila,* commonly though erroneously called *sansa,* a name that is not used for the instrument in South Africa. This type of *mbila* was also observed by Dos Santos among the "Mocaranga" in 1586. Since that is so, and since the iron-tongued *mbila* is unknown in the Malay Archipelago, it would appear that the resonated xylophone arrived in East Africa long before this date, and most probably before the cessation of Indonesian trade with the African continent, which occurred about the beginning of the thirteenth century, and that the invention of the iron-tongued instrument took place in Africa itself rather later than this, the new instrument being given the name of its predecessor. — The Chopi of Mozambique also have resonated xylophones which are, however, furnished with resonators made from globular fruits. They are to be seen on the Rand mines, where "orchestras" consisting of many players upon three different sizes of *timbila* (the plural of *mbila)* are a regular feature of the social life of the Chopi mine workers. The organisation of these "orchestras' and, indeed, the sound of them, is strongly reminiscent of that of the *gamelan djoged,* or ensemble of resonated xylophones, of the island of Bali in the Malay Archipelago. The Balinese instruments are, however, made from bamboo, both as regards the slabs and the resonators. Bamboo of sufficiently wide diameter was, however, not available in Africa until relatively recently, hence the substitution of wood for the slabs and calabashes for the resonators. But that the instruments of the two cultures are related there can be no question.

(iv) Aerophones

The wind instruments of the Southern Bantu consist of horns and trumpets made chiefly from the horns of animals, and of whistles and flutes of various kinds. No wind instrument sounded by a vibrating reed after the manner of the European oboe and clarinet class, is found. This alone would appear to rule out direct Arabian or even Indonesian influence, and although the resonated xylophone came to Africa from Indonesia, it did so before the Muslim period in the Archipelago, which began about 1500 A.D., and it was the Muslims who introduced the oriental "oboe" into both Indonesia and Africa. — One solitary exception to the general statement about reed-vibrated instruments is a kind of "squeaker" in which a narrow membrane, or strip of elastic material, is secured between two small hollowed out pieces of wood, bound together. When blown the membrane vibrates, producing a curious squeaking sound, which is supposed to be the voice of a spirit. The player, who is called *nonyana*, is disguised as a spirit, and he blows his *sitlanjani*, as the instrument is called, during the initiation of Venda girls. A precisely similar instrument, made from tin and rubber, is sometimes found in Christmas crackers.[25] — All the Sotho-Tswana peoples and the Venda use animal horns as signalling trumpets, especially those of the sable antelope.[26] The horns of this animal were probably the oldest variety made use of for this purpose, since the Tswana name of that antelope, *phala*, has for centuries been used for the name of the instrument, even when not made from the horn of that animal. These horns are called *phalaphala*, and they were observed and heard by Dos Santos in 1586, though he spelt the name *parapandas*. To convert such a horn for musical purposes, the maker removes the interior of it and makes an opening, frequently rectangular, in the side just below the solid tip. By applying his lips to the opening thus made, and by blowing as a trumpet is blown, at least two sounds can be elicited, the fundamental note and the first harmonic of the tube, which are either exactly or approximately an octave apart (see plate 1, p. 349). In the case of signal horns made from the horns of the *kudu*, four, and sometimes even five, partials of the harmonic series can be elicited, the resulting music being similar to that produced from an ordinary military bugle. — Among the Southern Nguni, however, the use of antelope horns for making such instruments appears to have died out. The Zulu, for example, use simple ox horns, the name of such a horn being *upondo*. Nevertheless they sometimes call an instrument made from an ox horn by the name *mpalampala*, as if it were made from the horn of an antelope. In more recent years the Zulu have developed a kind of endblown trumpet made from a length of hollow reed to which an ox horn has been attached by way of a "bell". From this instrument several notes can be elicited, though they are irregularly "spaced". The Zulu name for this instrument is *icilongo*, and it may possibly have been imitated from the military trumpets of the British army in comparatively recent times, especially since a specimen in the Africana Museum, Johannesburg, has a detachable mouthpiece of horn, manifestly modelled upon a European one, which fits into the end of the tube of reed. A precisely similar instrument is to be found in Madagascar, which is called by a name which means "the horn of the white people". And although it is unlikely that the Zulu variety came thence, the possibility cannot be completely ruled out. But in either case it is obvious that the instrument was copied from a European prototype. — There is considerable variety in the whistles and flutes made and played by the Southern Bantu.[27] The simplest are little "stopped" pipes of reed or bone. If made from the former material, a natural "node" frequently forms the stopping; but if from the latter, a paste of ashes mixed with fat is often used. These little instruments yield only a single shrill sound. Among the Pedi of Sekhukhuneland stopped whistles of bone, known as *lengwane*, are used by herd boys. They were observed in that country by Louis Trichardt in 1837 near the place where the village that bears his name is located in the Transvaal. —

Rather longer whistles of wood, with a conical bore burned out by a red-hot wire, and with a large opening at the upper end which serves as a mouth-hole or embouchure, and a tiny one at the lower which acts as a finger-hole, are common among the Venda. These are played by small boys. There is a still larger variety, in which the tube is made by splitting a conically shaped piece of wood down its centre, hollowing a half-conical channel down either half, and then fastening the two pieces together again by covering them with a piece of wet intestine which, when dry, draws the two halves of the instrument together and seals it effectively. On such an instrument it is possible, with an effort, to elicit quite a number of different sounds by overblowing and fingering; but in practice Africans make use of only one or two of them, these being the lowest and therefore the most easily produced. I have found whistles of this type among the Venda, Pedi, Swazi and Zulu, among whom it is always played by men, especially while hunting. Special varieties, sometimes made from horn, are used by traditional doctors. These instruments are themselves usually "doctored" by being anointed within by the fat of various animals. The fat serves to lubricate the interior, and thus to cause the whistle to sound more readily; and a feather, supposed to have come from the plumage of the "lightning bird", is often kept in the tube, ostensibly to add to its magical properties, but actually to distribute the fatty ointment evenly. — No actual sets of "pan-pipes", fashioned like the *syrinx* of the ancient Greeks, are to be found among the peoples of South Africa. They are, or were, however, in use along the Zambesi and in Rhodesia. But the Venda, Tswana and Transvaal Sotho all make and play upon sets of "stopped" pipes made from reeds, exactly as the Hottentots of old used to do.[28] In the ensembles, as in their older Hottentot prototypes, each player is responsible for only one note, which he contributes to the ensemble at the appropriate time. This ensemble of reed-flutes would appear to represent a stage in the evolution of the pan-pipes anterior to the *syrinx* of the ancient Greeks. And whereas the Tswana admittedly acquired their reed-flutes from the Hottentots, whose performance upon them has already been described, the Venda seem to have brought theirs with them from the north when they crossed the Limpopo River several centuries ago. Moreover, the Tswana reeds are stopped by plugs of fibre, exactly as those of the Hottentots were, and can be tuned by means of a "plunger" of wood; whereas those of the Venda are stopped by natural "nodes" of the reeds, and are of fixed pitch. In addition, the Tswana have retained the old Hottentot four-note scale intact, but the Venda scale is heptatonic, and strongly suggestive of one of the ancient Greek "modes". Curiously enough, the Transvaal Sotho, though they acquired the reed-flutes from the Venda, discarded the heptatonic scale to which they were tuned and substituted their own vocal pentatonic scale. — Among the Swazi, Zulu, Pondo and Xhosa a simple oblique flute of reed, or, in the case of the Swazi, the axis of the inflorescence of the *umsenge* or cabbage-tree, was at one time in regular use during the celebration of the *umkosi,* or feast of the first-fruits. Indeed among the Zulu, the making and sounding of the instrument, which was called *umtshingo,* was strictly prohibited until the chief had given the people permission to partake of the new crops. The tube of reed or *umsenge,* cleared of all interior obstructions, was about three feet in length, the upper end being cut at an angle of forty-five degrees, and the lower end similarly being either cut or else sheared off at right angles to the axial line of the reed. By applying the embouchure to the mouth, and directing the breath obliquely across it, the performer could elicit several partials of the harmonic series of the open pipe, though not the fundamental, since the tube was too narrow to permit this. — By stopping the lower end of the tube with the forefinger of the right hand, a second series of harmonic sounds could be produced, these being the odd-numbered partials of the harmonic series. By combining these two sets of sounds, a definite pentatonic scale resulted, which was brought about by natural law. And since it is still frequently stated that the origin of the pentatonic scale is unknown, it is particularly interesting to find that in South Africa there is one such scale which has a natural physical explanation. An equally important point is that the ancient Pharaonic oblique flutes of Egypt were similar in every respect but one to those of the Southern Nguni. For the ancient Egyptian oblique flutes were furnished with several finger-holes, frequently three, whereas the Nguni instruments were not. It is specially important to realise that such an open pipe as that of ancient Egypt, if supplied with three finger-holes, must yield a heptatonic scale, whatever the pitch of the notes which constitute it, whereas the Zulu type of instrument, which has but the lower end hole available for fingering, must yield a pentatonic scale, and no other. Finally, the Egyptian hieroglyph for flute was ⟨image⟩ , which represents the obliquely cut embouchure, and the hieroglyph for a fluteplayer was a seated figure of a man, holding in position for playing an oblique flute, which suggests that this was the earliest Egyptian form of the instrument. Yet in South Africa there is an even earlier one! — Another Zulu whistle or flute associated with the same ceremony of the first fruits consists of a pair of instruments of peculiar construction, known as *igemfe*. For each of the pair a suitable length of fairly wide-bored reed is selected, one end of which is sheared off on both sides at an angle of about forty-five degrees. Into the lower ends of these are inserted suitable lengths of a thinner type of reed, the complete instrument measuring about 35 cm. in length, though one unit of the pair must always be slightly shorter than the other. Two performers are required for the instruments. Each lays the semicircular opening of the top end of his instrument against his lower lip, thus forming a "fipple" or whistle mouthpiece, such as is seen on the wellknown "penny whistle". "By blowing across this rudimentary "fipple" each man can elicit a single note when the lower end of his instrument remains open; but if he closes the lower end with his forefinger, a second sound, of different pitch, can be produced, rather lower in pitch than the first. By alternating these four sounds antiphonally a not unattractive musical "figure" results. The great importance of this instrument lies in the fact that the true "fipple" is of very ancient lineage. Specimens of whistles made from reindeer horn and provided with true "fipples" have survived, which date from the Ice Age. Yet in South Africa we can still see the process by which the "fipple" was discovered and adopted. — Hitherto I have made no mention of a transverse flute, because such are only met with among the Venda, the Tsonga and the Swazi. The Venda name for the transverse flute is *tshiṭiringo*. The ancestral home of the transverse flute was certainly India, where the Lord Krishna is always depicted playing upon one. From India the instrument spread eastwards to China and westwards to Persia, and eventually to Europe. But the transverse flutes of all these peoples are always furnished with at least six finger-holes, whereas the African specimens have but three as a rule, though in two unusual specimens that I have obtained, there are four. Moreover, the transverse flutes of the northern hemisphere are closed at the embouchure end only, while the South African types are closed at both ends. The result of this is that whereas the latter act as stopped pipes when all the fingerholes are covered, they act as open pipes when one or more of them are opened. The resulting scale is irregular in character, but on all instruments of this type, whatever their pitch, the general scales are "similar" (in the Euclidean sense), although not identical, the large intervals of one corresponding in position to those of another and the small intervals also corresponding. There is, moreover, no standard pitch to which these instruments are made, the basic pitch being entirely fortuitous. The effective length of the tubes selected depends on the air-column between the nodes which stop it at either end, and the finger-holes are bored so as to suit the hand of the performer. The nature of the scale of the *tshiṭiringo* therefore depends upon a botanical attribute and a physiological one! — That unique stringed-wind instrument, the *gorá,* has already been discussed. Its migration through South Africa can now be readily traced from its invention by the Hottentots in the seventeenth century.[29] The pentatonic scale produced by the *gorá* is identical with that elicited from the *umtshingo.* Can anyone doubt after this that the harmonic series has definitely played a very important part in the development of man's music, even though the influences of it may not be readily perceived in Europe today?

(v) Chordophones

The stringed instruments are of eight distinct types, though all are obviously derived from the shooting bow.[30] This, however, is somewhat curious, considering that, with the exception of the Venda, who are comparatively late-comers into the country, none ever used the bow as a weapon. It is therefore reasonable to assume that they all derived their "musical bows" from neighbouring peoples who did possess the weapon. — The one characteristic feature that is common to all of the indigenous stringed instruments is one which we have already noted in those of both Bushmen and Hottentots, namely, that the music played upon them invariably involves the unconcious or deliberate use of the harmonics of a string. These harmonics are utilized in one or other of three ways; sounded together as a chord, isolated for melodic purposes, or used in conjunction with their fundamentals to produce rudimentary polyphony. In all of the instruments a resonator of some sort is used to amplify the feeble sounds produced by the bow-string, and this resonator may be either the mouth of the performer or a hollow object, such as a calabash, which may be temporarily or permanently attached to the stave of the bow. — There are two varieties of these "musical bows" which produce one or more harmonic chords, of which the fundamental and a few of its harmonics are audible to the performer, who can, and does, use them as "focal points" for the melody of his songs. Both look very much alike, and have frequently been regarded as one and the same by superficial observers. The first consists of a fairly long bow, to which an open calabash is attached near the lower end of the stave to serve as a resonator, being insulated from it by a pad of fibre or similar substance (see plate 6a, p. 357). The player holds the bow in his left hand, near its lower end, with the opening of the calabash against his bare chest, and with a twig held in his right hand he taps the lower end of the string, his action being as we should say, *staccato.* Sometimes a length of stiff grass is used instead of a twig. By doing so the performer causes the string to yield a clear harmonic chord, and by altering the position of the calabash relative to his chest, he can modify the "colour" of the chord. He can also, with the fingers of his left hand, press on the string at its lower end, thus shortening its length. The result of this rudimentary "fingering" is to raise the pitch of the string, a whole tone being the interval by which the string is generally raised, and the new fundamental thus produced yields a second harmonic chord. This instrument was generally, though not invariably, played by men. It was formerly the "classic" instrument of the Swazi, but is now practically obsolete in their country. It

289

was also typical of the Zulu, the Sotho of Lesotho and the Xhosa. Among the last-mentioned people it was invariably played by women.

Indigenous names: *segwana* (Tswana); *tshitendje, dende* (Tsonga); *sekgapa* (Transvaal Sotho); *thomo* (Lesotho Sotho); *ligubu* (Swazi); *ugubu, ugumbu, gubuolukhulu, inkohlisa* (Zulu); *uhadi* (Xhosa).

The second instrument of this type consists of a rather shorter and generally lighter bow, of which the string is tied back near the middle by a loop of sinew. At the point where this loop surrounds the stave of the bow an open calabash is secured, and is insulated from the stave by a pad of fibre. The player, holding the instrument vertically near the middle in his left hand, can tap either portion of the string with a twig or grass stalk, and as they are of different lengths they yield two different harmonic chords. And by stopping the lower portion of the string, near the loop, with the knuckle of the hand holding the instrument, a third harmonic chord can be produced. The interval between the lower and the upper portions of the string varies, but is usually a whole tone or a minor third. That between the upper part and the "fingered" part is usually a semitone. This type of instrument was used by Venda, Transvaal Sotho, Swazi and Zulu, but not by Tswana, Sotho of Lesotho or Xhosa. As far as I can discover it was not played by the Zulu in the time of Shaka. Both men and women were the performers. Among the Tsonga the instrument is sometimes of large size, the stave of the bow being much longer than that of the average weapon. This, however, is unusual.

Indigenous names: *tshikala, dende* (Venda); *tshitendole* (Chopi); *nkaku, nkoka, dende* (Tsonga); *sekgapa* (Transvaal Sotho); *umakweyana* (Swazi); *unkoka, umakweyana, isiqwemqwemana, uqwabe, imvingo, inkohlisa* (Zulu).

Of the stringed instruments in which harmonic sounds are used purely for melodic purposes, there are two kinds. The first of these is identical with the Korana */kha:s,* which in its Bushman form has already been described. It is played only by the Tswana, who undoubtedly acquired it from the Korana, since they themselves never used bows as weapons. The Tswana name for this instrument is *nokokwane.* — The second type consists of a hollow tube of reed, or a bar of wood hollowed along one side, which is fitted with a string, preferably of wire, the pitch of which can be raised or lowered by a tuning peg. The string is made to vibrate by means of a miniature friction bow of wood strung with hair from the tail of a cow, resin being applied to the hair. The mouth was originally used as a resonator, and is still so used in Vendaland. More recently, however, a one-gallon paraffin tin would be hung over the upper end of the instrument, which was then held against the left shoulder, and in this manner it was used by Sotho, Zulu and Xhosa. By a kind of circular motion of the bow the harmonics of the string could be isolated, and a simple tune based upon them could be played. This practice, I believe, is unique. The use of a friction bow for setting the string in vibration, must have been acquired from some superior civilisation, though when and whence is a question that is difficult to answer, for the earliest mention of a bow is in Persia of the ninth century. It would therefore seem that the Blacks of South Africa acquired the practice from either peoples who had been in contact with men from the Malay Archipelago, who received the friction bow from the Arabs after about 1500 A.D., or directly from the Arabs themselves. On the instrument we have been describing, however, the fundamental sound of the string is never used.

Indigenous names: *tshidzholo* (Venda); *sefinjolo, segankuru, setinkane* (Tswana); *sekgobogobo, setsegetsege* (Transvaal Sotho); *sekatari* (Lesotho Sotho); *pone* (Ndebele); *isikehlekehle* (Swazi); *ubheli'indhlela* (Zulu); *uhadi* (sic) (Xhosa).

There are four stringed instruments in which harmonic sounds are combined with fundamentals to produce rudimentary polyphony. The first of these is a plain bow, exactly like a Bushman shooting-bow, but much lighter in construction, and quite useless as a weapon. But by using it as the Bushman uses his actual shooting-bow, the performer can also, by employing his mouth as a resonator of variable size, isolate several of the harmonics of the string, while the fundamental serves as a drone. But the Black peoples improve upon the Bushman method of performance, for they "stop" the string near one end, thus obtaining a second set of harmonic sounds, with their new fundamental as a second drone. By combining the two a kind of simple polyphony results, of which, however, the intervals used are the result of natural law. This type of stringed instrument is used universally in South Africa, being generally played by women and girls, though occasionally by boys.

Indigenous names: *lugube* (Venda); *umqangala* (Tsonga); *lengope* (Tswana); *lekope* (Transvaal Sotho); *umqangala* (Swazi); *umqangala, umqengele* (Zulu); *inkinge* (Pondo); *inkinge* (Xhosa).

The second type is a bow of special construction, being either of solid wood thinned towards the tips of the stave, or with a thick central portion into either end of which thin pliable pieces of wood are fitted (see fig. 3, p. 353). The string is now usually of wire, but in some parts in olden times a giraffe hair, or a string of twisted sinew, was employed. The string, however, was always drawn back towards the middle of the stave by means of a loop of sinew, though the two portions of the string were always of unequal length, and therefore of different pitches. The instrument is similar to the second of the "calabash bows" previously described, except that the mouth is used as the resonator. As on the first type of instrument described in this group, the performer could, by plucking the string with a plectrum of thorn or other suitable material, produce a fundamental sound and its harmonics from each portion of the string, and, by stopping it, a third fundamental and its harmonics. Again the result was rudimentary polyphony controlled by natural law.

Indigenous names: *tshihwhana* (Venda); *lekope* (Transvaal Sotho); *setolotolo* (Lesotho Sotho); *penda* (Chopi); *sekgapa* (Tsonga); *isitontolo* (Swazi); *isitontolo, isiqomqomana* (Zulu).

The third instrument in this group consists of a short bow of solid wood, the two ends of which are thinned down to such an extent that they can be bent up sharply. A series of notches is cut along one side of the thick central portion of the stave. A flat strip of ilala palm is wetted and stretched from tip to tip of the bow, and when dry becomes quite taut. The performer holds the instrument in his left hand, in such a manner that the right-hand end of the palmleaf "string" lies across his opened mouth. In his right hand he holds a kind of rattle, made by thrusting a stick through one or more small globular dried fruits containing small stones, and this he rubs to and fro along the notches, thus causing the string to vibrate, yielding its fundamental sound (see fig. 12, p. 394). But by varying the capacity of his buccal cavity he can isolate several of the harmonics of the string, which sound•with great clarity simultaneously with the fundamental. And by stopping the string with the fingers of his left hand he can shorten it and produce a second fundamental and its harmonics, usually a whole tone higher than the first. He is thus in possession of sufficient sounds to enable him to perform little tunes in simple two-part polyphony, with a delicate tone-colour that I can only describe as "fairy-like". Only the Tsonga and the Venda play upon this instrument, though I have found a crude imitation of it in the hands of a Bushman, who must have acquired it from some Black performer. This type of stringed instrument is quite rare; it has, however, been found in northern India!

Indigenous names: *tshizambi* (Venda); *xizambi* (Tsonga).

The fourth and last instrument of this kind is very curious, and has been usually regarded as an aberrant form by musicologists who have only come across isolated specimens of it. It was however, in fairly common use among Swazi, Zulu and Xhosa, and also in a degenerate form among the Pondo. It consists of a length of hollow river-reed or soft wood, into the upper end of which is secured a thin and pliable rod. To the tip of this rod a string of fibre or of rush is attached, the other end of which is secured to the lower end of the instrument, which assumes more or less the shape of a "lacrosse" racquet. The instrument is held with the upper part of the main rod against the cheek and mouth, the latter acting as a resonator. The string is "bowed" with a piece of thin maize stalk. The musical results are similar to those yielded by the three previously described instruments, but are far less effective.

Indigenous names: *utiyane, ipiano (sic)* (Swazi); *umrube* (Zulu); *umqunge* (Pondo); *umrube* (Xhosa).

I have gone into considerable detail in discussing these African stringed instruments because I feel that there is a most important deduction to be made from them. To begin with, they have all had a common ancestor, the shooting-bow, and all make use of the harmonic series, which has not only provided "focal points" for their vocal music but also originated a system of simple polyphony, the course of which has been controlled by natural physical law. In this latter respect the Southern Bantu would appear to have developed their instrumental music beyond their vocal music. This may well have been due to the fact, to which I have already drawn attention, that Bantu speechtone compelled their vocal music to retain a large measure of parallelism, and thus prevented, or rather delayed, the development of the independent movement of parts until European influence broke down the linguistic characteristics chiefly by inducing Black Africans to adopt Western practices and ideals and to abandon their own. — There is an even more important deduction to be made from a study of the rudimentary polyphony that is performed on these simple stringed instruments. A careful analysis of this polyphony reveals that certain definite principles govern the movement of the two parts involved, and that only certain intervals are made use of. These intervals are the unison, octave and fifth. If one tabulates the progressions used on these instruments by the Blacks, one realises at once that they are controlled by natural law, and that they correspond in large measure with the similar principles that controlled the "new organum" of the 12th century.[31] May we not therefore dare to suggest that the European medieval practice referred to was likewise originally controlled by physical law? No satisfactory explanation of it has hitherto been vouchsafed by musical historians, and here we have what seems to be a perfectly rational one.

3. References

1. Ms. in the Natal Society's Public Library, Pietermaritzburg.
2. Bokwe, J.K.: *Amaculo ase Lovedale* (third edition). Lovedale, 1910, p. iii.
3. Breuil, Abbé H. and Bagouen, Comte: *Nouvelle gravure d'homme masqué, etc.,* Paris, 1930. The authors, however, originally interpreted the instrument as some kind of flute, but the present writer convinced the Abbé by practical demonstration that it was a bow.
4. Kirby, P.R.: The musical practices of the *!?auni* and *!khomani* Bushmen. *Bantu Studies* X/4. Johannesburg, 1936, pp. 378–382, in which the methods of performance and the musical results are fully described.
5. Kirby, P.R.: *The musical instruments of the native races of South Africa.* London, 1934 (second edition, Johannesburg, 1965), pp. 112–120.
6. Lichtenstein, H.: *Reisen im südlichen Africa.* Berlin, 1812, pp. 379–380. Translated and fully dealt with in Kirby, P.R., op. cit. pp. 174–175.
7. Kirby, P.R.: The Indonesian origin of certain African musical instruments. *African Studies.* Johannesburg, March 1965.
8. Waterhouse, G.: *Simon van der Stel's journal of his expedition to Namaqualand, 1685–6.* Dublin, 1932, p. 35 (original Dutch) and p. 128 (English translation).
9. Kicherer, J.J.: *Transactions of the Missionary Society* I. London, 1803, p. 335.
10. Kirby P.R.: The *gorá* and its Bantu successors. *Bantu Studies* V/2. Johannesburg, 1931, p. 99.
11. Kirby, P.R.: The musical practices of the *!?auni* and *!khomani* Bushmen. *Bantu Studies* X/4. Johannesburg, 1936, p. 390 et seq.
12. Kirby, P.R.: A study of Bushman music. *Bantu Studies* X/2. Johannesburg, 1936, pp. 205–252, and plates 1–32.
13. Kirby, P.R.: The musical practices of the *!?auni* and *!khomani* Bushmen. Op cit., 1936, pp. 390–399.
14. ibid., pp. 400–402.
15. ibid., pp. 302–417.
16. ibid., pp. 374–389.
17. Kirby, P.R.: The reed-flute ensembles of South Africa, etc. *Journal of the Royal Anthropological Institute* XIII. London, 1933, pp. 313–388; and plates XVIII–XXVI, in which the complete history of these ensembles is dealt with. See also Christopher Ballantine: The polyrhythmic foundation of Tswana pipe melody. *African Music* III/4, 1965, pp. 52–67.
18. Kirby, P.R.: The *gorá* and its Bantu successors. Op. cit. 1931, pp. 89–109, and plates I–VII.
19. Kirby, P.R.: The musical instruments of the Cape Malays. *South African Journal of Science* XXXVI. Johannesburg, 1939, pp. 477–488.
20. Kirby, P.R.: *The musical instruments of the native races of South Africa.* etc., pp. 14–19.
21. Kirby, P.R.: The music and musical instruments of the Korana, *Bantu Studies* VI/2. Johannesburg, 1932, p. 203 et seq.
22. Kirby, P.R.: *The musical instruments of the native races of South Africa:* etc., Chapter I: Rattles and clappers.
23. ibid., Chapter II, Drums.
24. ibid., Chapter III, Xylophones and sansas.
25. ibid., pp. 132–134.
26. ibid., Chapter V, Horns and trumpets.
27. ibid., Chapter VI, Whistles, flutes and vibrating reeds.
28. ibid., Chapter VII, Reed-flute ensembles.
29. Vide Note 10 supra.

293

30. Kirby, P.R.: *The musical instruments of the native races of South Africa,* etc. Chapter IX: Stringed instruments.
31. ibid., pp. 241–242.

– P.R.K.

III. SOME PRINCIPLES OF COMPOSITION OF THE INDIGENOUS MUSICS OF SOUTHERN AFRICA

Prof. Kirby's classic study of the musical instruments of the Bantu-speaking and Khoisan peoples of Southern Africa was published in 1934, and it was followed by analyses of the music of the Bushmen; before he died in 1935, Erich von Hornbostel had published seven papers on Black African music, which, though based on recordings rather than fieldwork, showed remarkable understanding and insight; two of the Rev. A.M. Jones's important studies of African music had already appeared by 1937, and Hugh Tracey had been working for nearly a decade in Southern Rhodesia and South Africa, and had begun to accumulate the unique collection of recordings which is now (1970) housed in, and published by, the International Library of African Music, RU. — In spite of the range and quality of this pioneering work, it was only after about 1950 that the study of Black African music gathered impetus and attracted the attention of scholars in Europe, Africa and the U.S.A. On the whole, more support for research came from anthropology than from music, but most students began with musical interests and training, and in many cases with a special concern for jazz and Afro-American music (or Black music, as it is now more commonly called). Two important stimuli to research were the development of the tape-recorder and the growing interest in Africa. — Because of this bias, there was more attention to the social background of the music and the subject-matter of songs than to principles of communal music-making and patterns of melody, more concern with music as a means of communication than with the musical structures by which communication is achieved. For instance, in an article in the *African Studies Bulletin,* May 1962, Prof. Willard Rhodes quotes the Zulu words of certain South African freedom songs as examples of "music as an agent of political expression". But Zulu is not the language of many who sang these songs, nor is it well understood by all. The impact of the songs stems not so much from their particular words, as from the general *sound* of their music, whose syncretic elements express the values and interests of townsmen and "the new Africa". Similarly, when I was transcribing traditional Venda songs in a Zulu rural area, local workers passed my window scores of times without comment. But one day, when I began to play some of the modern music of schools and separatist churches, they stopped and listened with pleasure, although they did not understand a word of the Venda language. It is by the *sounds* of different musical styles, by their patterns of rhythm and melody, that a Venda can explain what is happening in his district on a clear, moonlit night when sound carries far. It is the *sound* of *tshikona* music which becomes the ultimate arbiter in a Venda political dispute (see chap. X, 6), and it is the expansion of *musical* sound which brings the greatest pleasure in communal performances. — Because of the prevailing interest in jazz and Black music, there was also a tendency to select as most typically African those elements which seemed to be most un-European. Thus the main features of Black African music were often said to be the use of predominantly pentatonic modes, with "blue" notes; strong, explicit rhythms; antiphonal singing, with call/response patterns and part-singing in parallel motion which does not disturb the melodic patterns set by the speech-tones of words. All these elements exist in Black African music. But no less common are hexatonic and heptatonic modes; tone is as important in drumming as rhythm; and harmony and four-part music are as "genuinely African" in some parts of the continent as they might be called "genuinely European". Some of the so-called European elements of Afro-American music, and especially of spirituals, could therefore have come as easily from Africa as from Europe. — Concern with the social background of the music and the subject matter of the songs has to be extended to include their effects on the music itself. The social functions of different music affect its forms not only by prescribing certain instruments, vocal ensembles, and kinds of song (i.e. to accompany specific work tasks and ritual actions), but also by determining the structures of the variations within each form as they are created by the situational interaction of performers and audience. Examples are given in chapters V, VI, IX and X. The words of the songs affect patterns of melody not descriptively but formally in ways which are described generally in chapter IV. More details of formal relationships between the speechtone of words and melodic contour are given in chap. IX and in the rules 3.0.0. and 3.4.2. at the end of Chapter X (see also ex. 58, p. 422). — Although performances of Black African music may appear spontaneous, they are in fact systematic and predictable, and accuracy is a fundamental requirement of any good interpretation. Performers and audiences alike are careful listeners, and wrong notes and faltering, or irregular drumming, are immediately criticized. Improvization follows certain set patterns, and it is the sequence chosen and the appropriateness of the selection which provide the novelty and excitement. The addition of topical, new words to an existing melody is another source of interest, as is the composition of a new tune. — The composing process has not been adequately studied in Southern Africa, but it is safe to say that most of the music is, and presumably has been, composed by individuals, and then perhaps modified during the course of trial performances. Eventually, a version crystallizes to the satisfaction of audience, performers and composer. In some cases, songs are known to have been composed by a particular composer, but more often than not their creators are anonymous, though the period, or even the precise year, of their composition may be known from a reference to events made in the words. — Certain rules of composition may be derived from analyses of the music, but they are not always apparent in the surface structures. In particular, it seems that tonal and harmonic models are always in the mind. Whether or not they are generated by alternating movements of the body or of dance steps, they consist of regular shifts of tonality in such a way that neither "pole" really dominates. The intervals commonly used vary from one culture to another: for instance, the tonal "poles" may be a semitone apart, as amongst the Swazi and Zulu (see chap. V), or separated by a whole tone, a minor third, or a major third (as in *//!Kung* bow music in Angola). In the music of the Venda, a chief-note, or tonic, is specified in the reedpipe ensembles (see chap. X), and it might be argued that many melodies have the equivalent of shifting tonic/dominant tonality. Ex. 3 shows the sequence of root-progressions and harmony for the ocarina duets given in exs. 64a,b,c, p. 434, but none of the roots is really a tonic (see ex. 3, p. 296). Much Black African music seems to be derived from a conceptual framework of chords rather than single tones. Evidence of this is provided by the principle of "harmonic equivalence": if alterations in melody are precipitated by changes in speech-tone, or if other singers are "filling out" a song with extra lines of melody, the tones must be systematically selected from tones which occur in the "chords" that implicitly

Example 3

accompany each shift of tone in the basic melodic pattern (see ex. 77, p. 460). This feature of Black African music probably accounts for the enthusiasm and ability with which urban Blacks harmonize new melodies "spontaneously". This is *not* an imitation of Western music, but a continuation and adaptation of traditional Black African practice. It also spread to America, and emerged in the harmony of spirituals and the close harmony of jazz. — In some cases the impact of tonal shifts is balanced by corresponding harmonic shifts, as in fig. 1, which should be compared with ex. 56, p. 420 and ex. 105, p. 494. The harmonic progression in fig. 1 occurs in the Venda system, where harmony gives tones extra power: thus a tone is strongest when accompanied by its companion tone, a fifth below. Harmonic and tonal forces combine to give the music movement.

Figure 1

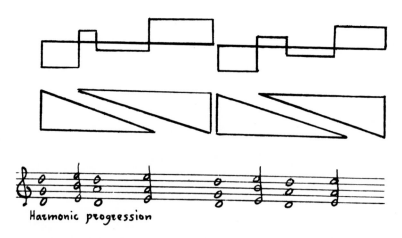

The harmonic and tonal progressions of the Venda *tshikona* and *khulo* (see chap. X, exs. 56, 105) showing the shift of maximum tonal power from "tonic" (D) to "leading note" (E), and back to "tonic": the rectangles symbolize shifts of tonality, and the changing thickness of the "wedges" illustrates the decrease and increase of the tonal power of the "tonic" and "leading note", which is achieved by the harmonic progression of the chords.

If "blocks" of tonality and harmony provide the basic force in much Southern African music, it is by building up patterns of tempo, metre and rhythm that composers "chip away" at these blocks to capture force with form and produce melody. But again, apparent differences in tempo and metre may be reduced to one or two basic tempi and a few interrelated metrical patterns for all the music in a single society. — The unity of tempi may be compared to a classical *Adagio*, where the presence of demi-semiquavers need not make its movement any faster or less relaxed. Interrelationship of metrical patterns exists when polymetric models have much the same function as harmonic models. Thus three crotchets may occupy the same span of time as two dotted crotchets, and vice versa; and so a metrical pattern of four dotted crotchets at ♩. = 90 is the same as six crotchets at ♩ = 135, and several different patterns may be generated by adding or combining "units" of two or three that are linked by a single tempo, which may be implicit or explicit. A common basic metrical unit in central Black African music, which is found in the Northern Transvaal but does not seem to be much used further south, is that of twelve quavers grouped as in ex. 4a, b, c. When one considers an alternative arrangement of the same figure (see ex. 4b), the relationship to an implicit 2:3 framework (ex. 4c) becomes clearer.

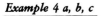

Example 4 a, b, c

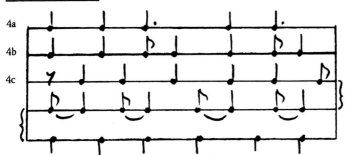

Apart from the music of the Shangana-Tsonga and a little Venda music the tempo of most South African music is slow, especially in comparison with the music of central Africa. But although vocal music predominates, the organizing principles are similar. One even finds the same metrical patterns, but at a much slower speed. For instance, the pattern in ex. 4a sets the pace on the drum *gogogo* for the *makuntu* dance songs and *nyele* music of the Gwembe Tonga of Zambia, at twice the speed at which it is normally used by the Venda of the Northern Transvaal. — Rhythm is the feature of Black African music which has attracted the most attention, and in particular the use of added metres and polyrhythmic techniques. Polyrhythm may be envisaged as a horizontal, linear embellishment of sound, in much the same way that harmony is a vertical elaboration. It expresses symbolically the principles of movement and process, and of individuality in community which underlie much Black African music. Although performances in unison are common and desirable, the addition of a second part in counterpoint emphasizes the presence of a second person, and hence of a larger group of people and of potentially greater social solidarity. Thus polyrhythm expresses in sound what is desired at every ritual and social gathering – the presence of a larger number of people co-operating harmoniously. Co-operation in work situations may be similarly expressed in rhythm: for example, two women may produce alternate strokes of a $\frac{2}{4}$ rhythm as they pound maize in a single mortar; the addition of a third person using a winnowing tray may be heard as a $\frac{3}{4}$ rhythm against the $\frac{2}{4}$ of the pounding of the pestles. — It should not be forgotten that although rhythm is very important in Black African music, the *tonality* of drumming is of equal importance. Drums "speak" and may even produce melodies; and although, as in melodies, exact pitch may not be required, observance of the relative pitch in patterns of rhythm is an essential feature of performance. Polyrhythmic principles are not, of course, applied only to drumming. They are applied to performances on xylophones, *mbiras* and reedpipes, and even to the use of voices. — An essential concept in understanding South African music is the idea of *process* rather than progress. The image of the waterfall is apt: at a distance, a waterfall is frozen, apparently static and monumental, but in reality it is always changing, always moving. This is almost dramatically illustrated in the widespread use of the hocket technique, in which each performer produces one or two notes of a total pattern – on reed-pipes amongst the Tswana, the Venda, the Transvaal Sotho, and the Hottentots of former times (see chap. II) and with voices amongst the Bushmen and the Venda (see ex. 105, p. 494). At a distance, the hocket music sounds like a shimmering block of sound; but as one approaches the players or singers, who are usually dancing in a circle as they perform, the sounds become more and more varied and a variety of melodies can be extracted from the total pattern. In those societies where hocketing is practised, it seems as if these extractable patterns generate a variety of compositions for voice or solo instruments (see, for instance, J. Blacking, *Venda children's songs*. Witwatersrand University Press, Johannesburg, 1967). — Ballantine's study of Tswana pipe melodies (in *African Music* III/4, 1965, pp. 52–67) suggests that the hocketing technique may in some cases be a transfer of polymetric principles of drumming to instruments that produce more precise tones of longer duration. Thus, for example, given a combination of four metrical patterns always played together in the same way (see ex. 5) and four different tones on which any one of them can be played, one has the possibility of at least 24 different melodies. Some of these may have to be rejected because their tonal or harmonic sequences are unsatisfactory; but when it is considered that the relationships between the entry of the metrical patterns can be changed, still further possibilities are open.

Example 5

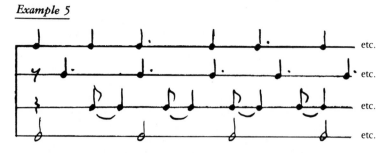

A sample combination of four metrical patterns, combined polyrhythmically. Different melodies can be produced by assigning differently pitched one-tone pipes to each of the metrical patterns.

Some of the vocal music of the Pondo and Baca of the Transkei, and especially that which is used to accompany dancing, suggests that a transformation of principles of drumming to voices has been made. But more precise distinctions between what is hocketing and what is "applied polymetre" must await further research. In many respects, there is conceptually little difference between the two techniques; but it may be important to distinguish between melodies which are produced incidentally by systematic combinations of given tonal and metrical patterns, and those which are broken up into parts by the application of a hocket technique of performance. — A similar analytical dilemma exists in cases of vocal polyphony. Sometimes the filling out of parts follows the pattern of a pre-conceived framework in which every tone is conceived harmonically (see ex. 42, p. 403 and ex. 77, p. 460). In other cases chords seem to arise from the overlapped antiphony which can be a consequence of the call/response pattern which is a fundamental form in vocal music and often replicated in solo instrumental music. "A fundamental principle of Zulu and Swazi multi-part vocal music is the non-simultaneous entry of voices. In any choral song, there are at least two voice-parts, singing *non*-identical words. These parts never begin together" (see chap. V). The sequence of "overlapping phrase-pairs" contributes to the idea of process which is so important in Black African music, and it has led Rycroft to represent such music in terms of two or more concentric circular musical staves (see D.K. Rycroft: Nguni vocal polyphony, *Journal of the International Folk Music Council* XIX, 1967, pp. 88–103). As in hocketing and similar practices, it seems that there are two different conceptual approaches to vocal polyphony. Further research will be needed to find out whether there are two significantly different systems and if, perhaps, they are related to differences in Nguni and Sotho-Tswana social organiza-tion. — It has been suggested that Black African melodies are generated by a variety of factors, some of which are extramusical, and that they can rarely, if ever, be regarded as independent creations. Broader tonal and harmonic structures affect their shape no less than in scores of the melodies of European "art", "folk" and "popular" music. Their tone-rows may be selected not so much from scales as from total patterns of sound which may have been composed without too much concern for any scale foundation. — Nevertheless, the tunings of instruments and the patterns of vocal music suggest that concepts of mode exist, even if they are not precisely stated. Many different modes are used, most of which resemble those found in folk music in other parts of the world – e.g. the Dorian mode. There are varieties of pentatonic scale, and it is a mistake to think that all Black African pentatonic scales resemble that which can be played on the black notes of a piano. Naturally, in individual melodies composers do not use all the notes of the modes available to them. It is sometimes said that Blacks cannot sing chromatic music or semi-tones. In their traditional music the Swazi and Zulu very commonly use modes containing two semitone intervals, though they never occur in the leading-note/tonic relation. — Each musical system has its own body of theory, which is understood by its performers, acquired partly by learning and partly by osmosis, and passed on from generation to generation. Each system is partly related to other Southern African systems, and partly self-contained, logically interrelated with associated cultural themes, and affected by its own language patterns. In general, there are two types of variation on themes, which may tentatively be called "explicit" and "implicit". — *Explicit variation* is that which occurs within a single piece of music, as for example the variations in speechtone which are discussed in chapter IV and elsewhere. Variations in the social situation will precipitate variations in the music. In the Venda girls' dance, *tshigombela,* there are two phases: a communal circle dance is followed by a series of "solo" dances in which girls come out in twos, threes, and fours, and execute a variety of steps, each of which has a different rhythmic pattern. The length, variation and form of the music will therefore depend on the number and excellence of dancers present. If there are only a few older, experienced girls, there will be few volunteers for the "solo" dances, and hence fewer variations. Similarly, in possession dances, although the same songs are repeated, there is an audible difference between the music before all the members of the cult group have been taken by the spirits, as well as sudden breaks when someone falls to the ground, and the music played on the two or three days following, when the possessed are virtually dancing out a ritual and interest tends to centre round the visitors who dance. They may become very excited, but they cannot be possessed by their own spirits in the home of members of another lineage. In all these cases, there is close rapport between dancers and drummers, and especially the master drummer. Explicit variation is therefore intended and recognized as such by performers and audience, and it adds lustre to any performance. It is also present in arrangements of communal music which are made for solo instruments such as *mbiras* or musical bows. — *Implicit variation* is not consciously intended by the musicians and dancers. It exists between different pieces of music and is something observed by the musicologist. Examples of this are given on p. 420–21, exs. 56 and 57. Thematic unity underlies the apparent variety of many melodies. Moreover, it is not a figment of the musicologist's imagination: for example, certain distinctive patterns of melody in Venda children's songs can only be derived from the *tshikona* pattern, and they can be explained in no other way. From a sociological and psychological point of view, such explanations make good sense. Composers draw on remembered sound. Is it therefore surprising that the thematic basis of many Venda songs should be the most important and exciting music in Venda society, their national dance? Many other examples of implicit variation could be given. It can be shown that variations in melody and style within the musical tradition of a single society are in fact variations on a number of themes which permeate the entire musical tradition, in much the same way that Rudolph Reti has shown that the themes of, say, a symphony of Beethoven are "contrasting on the surface but identical in substance". — The music of *tshikona* incidentally illustrates another important feature of Black African music, which may be compared to what a number of African writers (e.g. J. Nyerere and L. Senghor) have said about an "African personality". It epitomises the principle of individuality in community: in order that the total pattern may be correctly performed, each individual must hold his part and at the same time keep in perfect time with his neighbours. Each individual conducts himself for the good of the community; and without adherence to this principle, vocal and instrumental polyphony (or polyrhythm, or hocketing) could not be achieved.

BIBLIOGRAPHY

Further information on Black African musics can be found in the periodical *African Music,* published since 1954 by the International Library of African Music. The following are also useful: England, Nicholas: Bushmen counterpoint. *Journal of the IFMC* 19, 1967, pp. 58–66.   Gaskin, L.P.J.: *A select bibliography of music in Africa.* International African Institute, London, 1965.   Jones, A.M.: *Studies in African music.* OUP, London, 1959.   Jones, A.M. and Kombe, L. *The Icila dance, old style.* African Music Society, 1952.   Jones, A.M.: African rhythm. *Africa* XXIV, January 1954.   King, Anthony: *Yoruba sacred music from Ekiti.*

Ibadan University Press, 1961.   Merriam, Alan: *African music*. Bascom W.R. and Herskovits, M.J. edit.: Continuity and change in African cultures. University of Chicago Press, 1959. Idem: *The anthropology of music*. Northwestern University Press, Evanston, 1964.   Idem: *African music on LP, an annotated discography*. Northwestern University Press, Evanston, 1970.   Nketia, J.H. Kwabena: *Folksongs of Ghana*. OUP for the University of Ghana, London, 1963.   Idem: *African music in Ghana*. Longman's, London, 1962.   Idem: The interrelations of African music and dance. *Studia Musicologica* 7, 1965: pp. 81–101.   Thieme, D.L. *African music*. Library of Congress, 1964.   Tracey, Hugh: *Chopi musicians: their music, poetry and instruments*. OUP, London, 1948; 2nd ed. 1971.   Von Hornbostel, E.M.: African negro music. *Africa* I, Jan. 1928.   Wachsmann, K.P.: Musical instruments of Uganda. Trowell, M. and Wachsmann, K.P.: *Tribal crafts of Uganda*, part II.   Idem: *Essays on music and history in Africa*. Northwestern University Press, Evanston, 1971.

– J.A.R.B.

IV. THE RELATIONSHIPS BETWEEN SPEECH-TONE AND MELODY IN SOUTHERN AFRICAN MUSIC

1. Introduction
2. Speech-tones
   a. Sentence intonation as against essential word tone-patterns
   b. Other linguistic factors affecting tone in different languages
3. Interaction of words and melody
   a. Close conformity with speech contours
   b. Stylised speech contours as a replacement for melody
   c. Pseudo-melodic features in praise-poetry
   d. Melodic contours in place of sentence intonation
   e. Alternative essential tone-patterns
   f. The effects of syllable elision and length distortion
   g. Partial melodic violation of speech-tones
   h. Differing interpretations
   i. Total violation of speech-tones
4. Bibliography

1. Introduction

In folk song and in most of the vocal "art music" of Europe (apart from operatic recitative) the rise and fall of the melodic line generally bears little relation to the pitch contours used for a spoken rendering of the text, yet this causes no confusion of meaning. But melodic freedom has been found to be curbed, to some extent, in the case of certain languages in which words have their own inherent "tunes" or tone-patterns, and where the substitution of a different sequence of pitches may often produce a totally different word, with an unrelated meaning. — The languages of all the indigenous peoples of Southern Africa may be referred to, in a linguistic sense, as tone languages (cf. Pike, 1948) in that the pitch contours of speech are semantic. By altering the pitch of one or more syllables a change of meaning may often occur, e.g. Zulu: *inyanga*, "doctor", *inyangá*, "moon" or "month" (high speech-tones being marked here by an acute accent sign). In Xhosa verb constructions a sixfold contrast is occasionally found, as in the following six meanings for *uyasindisa*, distinguished solely by *tone* (though opinions differ as to whether the third pattern can really be differentiated from b.; the latter generally serves for *either* meaning) (see fig. 2).

Figure 2   *Uyasindisa:* six Xhosa sayings distinguished by sound only.

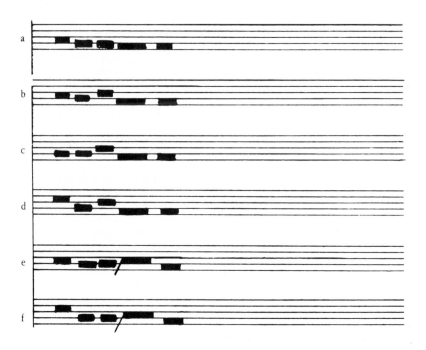

a you help to smear
b he/she helps to smear
c you rescue
d he/she rescues
e you cause to weigh down
f he/she causes to weigh down

Five relative pitch levels are shown here, but more would be needed in longer utterances. The lowest level (occurring finally) represents the lowest pitch in the speaker's normal range. Each step above this might be roughly a wholetone higher, or all intervals could be expanded, as for instance when "raising the voice" for greater audibility. Absolute pitch is unimportant, but the *relative* pitch of a syllable, whether it is higher or lower than each of the others, is significant. Extra *length* occurs on the penultimate syllable in all cases, but *intensity stress* comes on the first and third syllables. Assimilatory *on-glides* have been ignored here, but the rising on-glide shown in patterns e and f is conditioned by the preceding consonant *d.* The effects of such tone-lowering consonants in some languages will be discussed later. (For tonal studies see, *inter alia* Lanham, 1960; Cope, 1966; Rycroft, 1960 and 1963.) — When words in such languages are set to music, the speech-tone patterns of the text usually exert some influence on the melody. The degree to which melodic movement is affected differs in different languages, and in different types of song within the same language. This kind of tone/tune relationship has been noted to some extent in the music of various other peoples (cf. von Hornbostel, 1928; Herzog, 1934; Schneider, 1943 and 1961; Jones, 1959). For Southern Africa there is some published information about the position for Venda music (Blacking, 1967) and for Zulu, Xhosa and Swazi (Dahle, 1927; Starke, 1930; Rycroft, 1957, 1960 and 1970), but this subject has attracted very little detailed attention from linguistic and musical scholars and it is not yet possible to speak authoritatively about each of the many different languages in this area. — P.R. Kirby has made the general observation that, in any language in which speech-tones determine meaning, whenever speakers use the same words simultaneously, *"their voices must proceed in parallel motion,* rising and falling together". In song, if speech-tones are strictly observed, only parallelism of the *organum* type would presumably be possible (Kirby, 1954). Such parallelism does in fact occur to some extent in Southern African music; but it is often avoided, through such measures as the use of antiphony, non-simultaneous entry of voices, and the assigning of different lines of text to different voices (see Rycroft, 1967). — From available information, Bushman songs appear to be mostly wordless, and to employ yodelling (cf. Schapera, 1930, pp. 202–7; and Kirby, 1934, p. 390) thus falling outside the scope of our present study. Nevertheless there are verbal texts in twenty-two Bushman songs transcribed, in 1879, by Lloyd and Weisbecker (published in Kirby, 1936, pp. 205–252). Kirby considers that these songs "seem to be very closely connected with Bushman speech, melody being largely determined by speech-tone, and rhythm by verbal emphasis" (ibid., p. 249). No detailed study of the relationship was made, however. — Among the Hottentots, verbal texts occur in some of their music (cf. Schapera, pp. 400–5; and Westphal, 1962) but no information concerning speech-tone influence on melody appears to be available. — All other indigenous languages in Southern Africa belong within the Bantu language family, which extends over most of Africa, south of the Sahara (apart from West Africa) and is distinguished principally by prefixal gender-agreement and a stock of related wordroots. (Regarding the classification of Bantu languages, see Doke, 1954; and Guthrie, 1948, 1956 and 1967.) On criteria of closeness of mutual relationship, the principal Bantu languages of Southern Africa can be grouped as follows:

Nguni group:	Xhosa (Eastern Cape and Transkei)
	Zulu (Natal and Zululand)
	Swazi (Swaziland and Eastern Transvaal)
	Ndebele (Rhodesia-Zimbabwe)
	Transvaal Ndebele (two separate dialects, Northern and Southern, both influenced by Sotho)
Sotho-Tswana group:	Southern Sotho (Lesotho and OFS)
	Pedi or Northern Sotho (Transvaal)
	Tswana (Botswana and Western Transvaal)
Tswa-Ronga group:	Tsonga, Tswa-Ronga, Gwamba (Moçambique and North-Eastern Transvaal)
Venda group:	Venda (Northern Transvaal)
Shona group:	(Rhodesia-Zimbabwe)
Herero and Ndonga groups:	(South West Africa-Namibia)
Yeye group:	(Botswana)

Chopi group: (Moçambique).

Languages listed under the same group name are to some extent mutually intelligible, while those from different groups are far less so.

2. Speech-tones

In Bantu languages, spoken utterances display a great many variations of pitch. However, just as in English, there is no fixed scale of absolute pitch values like that expected in music. The multiplicity of pitches used in speech has often made it difficult for investigators to isolate essential, meaningful tonal contrasts from the total contour. For Zulu, for example, Doke in 1926 postulated nine different levels of pitch, which he numbered 1 to 9 in descending order when marking the tone patterns of words.

a. Sentence intonation as against essential word tone-patterns

Variation of pitch seems to be a universal feature in all languages; but it may serve totally different functions, or even serve more than one function in the same language. In English, raised pitch on a syllable may optionally accompany extra intensity, as an ingredient of stress, especially for emphasis; but the overall "tune" of the sentence for which the linguistic term is "sentence intonation", is more important and may override this. We use different types of sentence intonation, like a "carrier wave", to convey different nuances. In normal statements the voice generally drops at the end, while for questions the pitch tends to rise. This can be done freely, whatever words are employed. Our words have their own fixed patterns of stress and vowel length, but they do not have fixed inherent tone patterns. — In tone languages there is usually no correlation between high pitch and intensity stress. The various syllables of a given word must rise or fall, relative to each other, in a particular way, though alternative patterns may be required in different contexts. However, besides these inherent word patterns there is also an overall "carrier wave" of "sentence intonation". In most Bantu languages this follows a gradually descending contour for normal statements. The patterns of individual words in the sentence cause momentary higher and lower deflections in the descending intonation contour, from syllable to syllable; successive high and low tones, respectively, take progressively lower actual pitch, especially towards the end. In consequence, a high tone at the end may come to be rendered at equal, or even lower actual pitch than an early low tone. Questions, as against statements, usually take a different overall intonation contour. In some Bantu languages this amounts to suspension of progressive "downdrift", so that successive high tones take equal pitch, instead. The general multiplicity of speech pitches thus appears to result from at least two interacting factors in such languages: (i) an overall "carrier wave" of intonation, which may vary to convey different nuances; this might be viewed as "intermodulating" with (ii) the "essential" tone-patterns of the constituent words. — Since Doke's earlier postulation of 9 levels for Zulu, it has later proved feasible to distinguish only two "essential" relative tone levels or "tonemes" for any syllable, plus glides combining both – all further variations in actual pitch being accounted for by the interaction of other predictable factors, such as overall sentence intonation, context and position of word or syllable in sentence, assimilation to adjacent tones, and the effect of "tone-lowering" or "depressor" consonants (which, in the south, seem to be peculiar to Nguni languages and, to a lesser extent, those of the Shona and Tswa-Ronga groups). — For the majority of Bantu languages it nowadays appears that recognition of two contrasting levels for any syllable is generally sufficient (e.g. compare all third syllables, or all penultimate ones, etc., in the six Xhosa patterns shown earlier); but significant falling and rising glides combining both levels can also occur (besides non-significant assimilatory on-glides and off-glides); and upstep or downstep movement between adjacent high tones, as against equal pitch rendering, may also be semantically distinctive. — It has been demonstrated by Carrington, from his investigation of drum language in the Congo, that only two drum pitches are required for message transmission. The "talking" drums do not reproduce the exact pitch contours of spoken utterances. Only the essential tone-patterns of the individual words are abstracted; additional modifying factors such as sentence intonation are discounted (Carrington, 1949, pp. 44–5). The Xhosa do not use drum language, but the essential word-tones in the six examples given in fig. 2 could nevertheless be abstracted as follows, by discounting descending "sentence intonation": pattern *a:* all low tones; patterns *b* and *c:* syllable 3 high; pattern *d:* syllables 1 and 3 high; pattern *e:* syllable 4 high; pattern *f:* syllables 1 and 4 high (all others counting as low, in each case). — Though widespread depth studies would be needed for confirmation, it seems that an extention of this principle, i.e. of abstracting only the essential tones, might perhaps prove to be fairly general in Black African music – these essential tone-patterns serving to intermodulate, not with the normal sentence intonation of speech (as their "carrier wave") but with overall contours that are musically determined, instead. This would confirm Von Hornbostel's earlier, very general impression, that "the pitches of the speaking voice indeed appear to determine the melodic nucleus; but they have no influence upon its inborn creative forces. These, and not any qualities of speech, direct the further course of melodic development" (Von Hornbostel, 1928, p. 37). However, even within the repertoire of one and the same speech-community, there may be considerable variation between different categories in the matter of conformity to speech features, as will be discussed later.

b. Other linguistic factors affecting tone, in different languages
No two languages are identical in their choice of tone patterns, or in the operation of their tonal system. To some extent this is due to other linguistic factors. Languages differ in their noun prefixes: these are monosyllabic, and normally low in tone, in the Sotho-Tswana, Venda and Tswa-Ronga groups, among others; but in the Nguni group there is an extra initial vowel. This either takes high tone itself, or confers high tone on a later syllable, depending on the tonal category of the stem (see Rycroft, 1963). — In some languages there appears to be a process of tonal repetition whereby, after one high tone, the same pitch is also taken by a certain number of following syllables. In Nguni languages this tends to occur in non-final words, in quick speech, on syllables coming between two structural high tones; but it cannot occur if there is a "tone-lowering" consonant. In Zulu and Swazi song there is some latitude in the melodic realisation of such intervening syllables. — Languages differ considerably in the complexity and variety of their word-tone patterns, and in how these are employed and modified. Verb tones vary for different tenses, and in negative usage. Patterns may also differ according to the position of the word in the sentence, or the company it keeps: in Tsonga, for example, noun tone patterns become syntactically modified, varying when serving as subject or as object, etc. This does not happen in Nguni languages, but different patterns are often required for non-final, as against final

position. In song, position is sometimes disregarded, and *either* variant may serve. — Especially in the Nguni group, "tone-lowering" consonants interact with high speech-tones, resulting in a great number of variant patterns, conditioned by particular types of consonantal sequence. A similar correlation between voiced consonants (*d, d, z*, etc.) and the lowering of pitch has been observed in Chinese, and also in German. Forschhammer (1921) noted a pitch-lowering effect from initial voiced consonants, which produced rising on-glides in German song. He prescribed exercises to counteract this "undesirable" feature. — In spoken Zulu, and other Nguni languages, the consonants concerned comprise all voiced fricatives, clicks, and plosives (excepting implosive *b*), and all compounds containing these sounds. High-toned syllables beginning with such consonants commence with a brief rising on-glide (or the high tone may be displaced to the next syllable in some cases, if this has a non-lowering consonant – though this does not occur in Xhosa). Likewise, descending off-glides from high tones are conditioned by a succeeding consonant of this type. — Such features are automatically carried over into song, where these consonant-induced phenomena, in addition to true duel-tone glides, account to a large extent for the prevalence of stylised *portamento* in Nguni music. However, there are also further types of *portamento* glide which are not directly taken over from speech. A descending glide of a 4th or 5th quite frequently occurs on the last syllable of a phrase, often serving as a compromise between word-tone and melodic requirements – as for instance for the realisation either of a final high word-tone, when melodically the modal *finalis,* which may happen to lie lower, is required, or *vice versa.* Such treatment seems to be equally permissible for a final high, low, or falling word-tone. Nevertheless, it does sometimes happen that a final high word-tone is rendered indistinguishably from low; even elsewhere within a phrase, melodic forces occasionally override word-tone patterns in many dance-songs (see Rycroft, 1962, p. 81, for an example).

3. Interaction of words and melody

It follows from the above discussion that Bantu languages, although genetically related, nevertheless differ markedly in the matter of their speech-tone systems. They may also differ, possibly just as widely, regarding rules for setting words to music. This cannot at present be tested without far more widespread research; but it should be stressed that, without some understanding of underlying factors in the individual language, it may often prove misleading merely to make a direct comparison between a song melody and the sequence of pitches used in a spoken rendering of the same text. From existing studies (though I have not seen Starke's work on Xhosa) it seems that exact melodic imitation of the pitch contours of speech throughout an entire song is of very rare occurrence. Also, the degree to which linguistic features influence the music tends to vary considerably, both within one and the same speech-community, and beyond this, even among different items from the same category of song.

a. Close conformity with speech contours

Among the Zulu, it is in personal solo songs that one finds speech contours most closely reflected. Often, not only the essential word-tones, but also the overall sentence intonation appears to be imitated in such songs. The transcription below shows the first phrase of an example of this kind. It is a nostalgic song by Princess Magogo, of the Zulu royal house, in which she recalls memories of her late husband, and her love for him. Besides following the *pitch* contours of speech, the singer here also follows natural speech rhythms. The vocal phrasing is only very loosely correlated with the steady metre of the *ugubhu* musical bow, on which she accompanied herself (see ex. 6).

Example 6   Zulu solo song (excerpt).

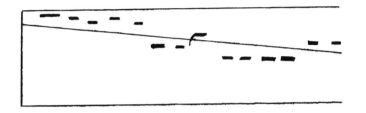

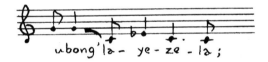

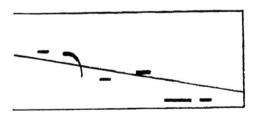

Below the musical score there is a representation of the relative pitch sequence typical for a spoken rendering of the same text. The sloping line represents the general trend of overall "sentence intonation", causing progressive lowering of the word-tones. The melodic line matches the total speech contour almost exactly. A minor difference occurs where the melody descends to *G,* for the onset of the fourth word, whereas the speech pattern ascends for a high tone with a rising on-glide, conditioned by "tone-lowering" consonant *ng.* This melodic deviation appears to result from a *change of range* in the tonality, notes *G* and *E flat* thereafter serving for high and low speech-tones, respectively, until there is a further change to *E flat* and *C,* for high and low, from the fourth-last syllable. Melodic descent to the lowest note, C, on the fourth-last syllable, is also a slight departure. In speech lowest pitch is usually not reached before the second-last syllable. Nevertheless, this example shows perhaps the closest reflection of speech values, of all songs so far encountered.

b. Stylised speech contours as a replacement for melody

Apart from personal solos, perhaps the only other Zulu song categories in which there is *close* correspondence with speech contours are the marginal ones, of war-cries (*izaga*, singular, *isaga*), and some items used for the *isigekle* recreational dance. Here, pitch movement consists entirely of stylised and exaggerated speech contours, rendered in a "sing-song" manner like choral recitation, without any fixed musical notes, but with a strictly imposed metre which often causes great distortion of syllable-length. Unstressed, normally short, syllables are frequently prolonged unnaturally, while ones that are usually long may be shortened and placed on off-beats. Though a complete reversal of normal length values may occur, root syllables still tend to retain a form of syncopated dynamic stress, contrary to the metre. Blacking gives examples of a similar vocal style used by Venda children (Blacking, 1967, pp. 78, 91 and 153–4). Among both the Zulu and the Venda (and also the Swazi) this form of choral recitation still falls within the concept of "singing", apparently by reason of its imposed regular metre. On the other hand, praise-poetry, which is non-metrical but, in Zulu, certainly tends to sound more "melodic" to European ears, is not classed as music at all.

c. Pseudo-melodic features in praise-poetry

Styles of delivery for the widespread Black African art of praise-poetry differ considerably; but for Zulu *izibongo*, four recurrent levels of pitch resembling Sol-fa notes *doh'*, *te*, *soh* and *Doh* appear to predominate and serve as a basic tonality in the musical sense. But these are used mechanically, for essential tones, rather than melodically. The upper two notes take all non-final high and low syllables, respectively, except low tones when preceded by a "lowering consonant": these take *soh;* and any low syllable in *final* position takes low *Doh*. (For detailed analysis, see Rycroft, 1960.) — Here it is to be noted that normal descending sentence intonation becomes replaced by sustained, equal levels of pitch for all high, low, and consonantally lowered syllables, respectively (until the final low tone). Linguistically, this might be seen as constituting a specialised form of overall "intonation", possibly comparable with some forms of monotonic chant in other cultures (see George List, 1963).

d. Melodic contours in place of sentence intonation

While pitch movement in Zulu praise-poetry is activated solely by speech values, additional non-linguistic factors are evident in all vocal styles accepted as "true song". For "choral speech" of the war-cry type, the imposed element is strict metre. In melodic songs it is tonal flexibility. In contrast to praise-poetry, high speech-tones, for example, are never confined to only one note. They may often be set to almost any note, provided one or more lower notes remain available for low speech-tones, as may be seen from the previous transcription of a Zulu item. This is not entirely arbitrary, however. There are commonly one or more changes of range in any song: a musical phrase or section using a higher range is balanced by at least one other, using a lower range, so that high speech-tones in the latter often take notes previously assigned to low tones. — The Xhosa dance-song shown in ex. 7 clearly demonstrates this principle. Notes A–F are used alone in the first section. Thereafter, the range changes to G–(F)–D, and finally to F–C, as indicated above the score. In the three sections, high speech-tones take A, then G, and then F, respectively – although F originally served for low tones in the first section.

Example 7   Xhosa dance song (as rendered by Mrs. L. Nongobo Whyman).

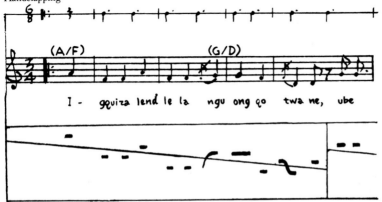

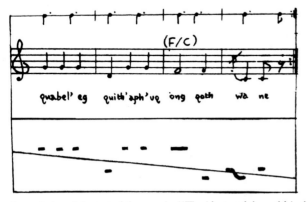

A translation of the text of the song is: ''The 'doctor of the path' is the black beetle; he came over yonder hill, did the black beetle.'' It refers to a certain type of beetle, often encountered on paths, which is said to resemble a doctor.

Although there is some apparent resemblance between the overall melodic sequence, and the spoken contours, it should be noted that the points where "change of range" occurs in the music appear to be musically determined, and are not directly conditioned by spoken pitch changes. For example, although the spoken pitch drops on the fourth syllable (compared with the first), this is not reflected in the song. Likewise in the *G–D* section of the melody, the last two high tones continue to take *G,* despite a drop in pitch for these syllables in speech. This illustrates the observation made earlier, that "essential tone" patterns of words are abstracted from sentence intonation, and serve to intermodulate with overall contours that are musically determined, instead. — In both occurrences of the word *uqongqothwane,* the syllable *ngqo* takes the note *F.* Since this syllable has low tone in speech, *G* and *C,* respectively, might have been expected. Among other possible explanations, it may be that (a) the change of range from *A–F* to *G–D* is gradual: although high syllables have already changed range, *ngqo* still takes *F,* which served for previous low tones, before *D* is adopted for subsequent ones; (b) in the second use of the word, *ngqo* assimilates to high realisation, presumably on musical grounds; (c) both cases represent latitude, allowable at the end of a line, where musical requirements have priority: there are also many instances of this in other languages. This hypothesis, of latitude at line or phrase endings, seems to be the only possible one in the case of the final syllable of *uqongqothwane* which takes low melodic realisation on both occasions, but is normally high in speech (although, as with many final vowels, it is often devocalised and almost inaudible). — Regarding the rhythm of this Xhosa song, the transcription shown here is a "broad" one. In actual practice there is a slightly syncopated or "near miss" relation between word-syllables and metre, as if – instead of the vowel – it is the onset of the preceding consonant that coincides with the beat (see Rycroft, 1962, p. 82). In passing, it might be observed that this traditional song is the one popularised in America in recent years by Miss Miriam Makeba. Her arrangement of it, entitled *The click song,* is set against a slow rumba rhythm and has "Scotch snap" syllable grouping. Essential speech-tones are nevertheless still respected. The rhythm of the original version, in ex. 7, may at first sight appear rather simple compared with Miss Makeba's rumba version; but we must not overlook the inherent "click" rhythm of the text. The spacing of the click consonants yields a subtle counter-rhythm which contrasts with the 6/8 hand-clap pattern. In future studies, the roles of consonants and of other textual features besides speech-tones need to be given closer attention if we are to make a really adequate evaluation of vocal music. — The extract from a Northern Sotho song, shown in ex. 8, suggests that a somewhat similar relationship between speech-tones and tune might be found to occur, in at least some of the vocal music of the Sotho-Tswana group. Additional changes of range do in fact occur in later phrases. I am not sufficiently conversant with this material to make adequate comment, however.

e. Alternative essential-tone patterns

In Zulu and Swazi antiphonal dance-songs, "essential" tones are reflected to a varying extent, but possibly less closely than in many Xhosa dance-songs. However, it is sometimes the case that conformity with speech is not immediately evident from direct comparison with a spoken version of the text. In speech, many words take one tone pattern when occurring finally (or before a pause, or in isolation) but a different one when non-final, and there are associated syllable-length features also, mainly on the penultimate vowel. In song, it seems that either of these patterns may be adopted,

Example 8   Extract from a Northern Sotho girls' initiation song. (Singer: D. Mokonyane).

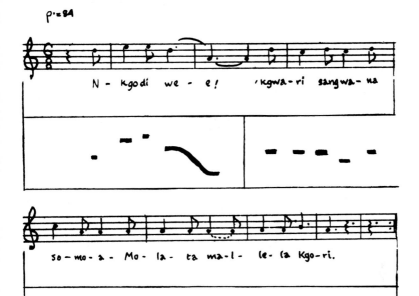

The translation of the text is: "Little river-bird, come! Miss 'Tidy-one', daughter of Somo the commoner, one who yearns for the *Kgori bird* (the mythical 'devourer')".

regardless of the position of the word. If this latitude is taken into account, some apparent divergences may be seen to be justifiable (for an instance of this in Swazi music, see Rycroft, 1970).

f. The effects of syllable elision and length distortion
Considerable mutilation of words seems to be tolerated in many Zulu communal songs and dance-songs. Vowels, or even whole syllables may be elided, to a greater extent than is usual in speech; or several syllables may be "run together" on an off-beat, while others are unnaturally prolonged, whether or not they are prominent in speech. By this means, a particular word can be twisted to fit a number of different melodic and rhythmic configurations; yet despite such treatment, "essential tone" patterns are nevertheless quite often still dimly recognisable. — The following line, sung by the leading voice in a certain three-part song, with *ugubhu* bow accompaniment, has 16 syllables when normally spoken: *ngizawulimpayiza ngilishonisephi na, Mama?* (I

311

shall roam about, and where shall I cause (the sun) to set, Mother?). When sung, it has only 9 syllables (see ex. 9).

Example 9   Extract from a Zulu 3-part song (as sung by Princess Constance Magogo and her grandchildren).

Besides syllable elision in this example (which is a tongue-twister, even for Zulus) there is also some length distortion: the penultimate syllable of each word should take extra length, but in the first word this syllable is in fact elided altogether. The word *na* should also have double length, but is rendered short. Despite these "distortions", the position of intensity stress, on root syllables, is still correctly observed; and "essential tone" patterns are broadly followed – though the falling tone on *na* is lost. (A recording of this song is available on Rycroft, 1970, no. 2. For a fuller transcription of the music, see Rycroft, 1967, p. 97.)

g. Partial melodic violation of speech-tones

Blacking, in his work on Venda children's songs (Blacking, 1967, pp. 167–171, and 199–203) provides many instances of partial conformity with speech-tones, and also a few cases where "speech patterns are sacrificed almost entirely for musical considerations". In some cases he suggests that the initial few words tend to "shape the melody and metre of the rest of the song", so that subsequent words, whatever their tonal requirements, are forced to adopt such a sequence. Even for initial words, however, similar speech-tone patterns do not always receive the same melodic treatment. He finds that this is sometimes correlated with differences in the position of the word syllables in relation to the basic beat of the song. In the majority of the Venda items he studied, Blacking considers that speech-tone patterns influence only certain parts of the song, chiefly the beginnings of phrases, while musical characteristics predominate elsewhere, particularly at phrase endings. — In other Southern African languages too, it seems to be general practice for musical forces to control particularly the ends of phrases, in song. Usually a particular note serves as a melodic *finalis*. This note may have to be approached by way of some accepted terminal or cadential interval progression, and the resultant melodic sequence tends to take precedence over speech-tone requirements. A clear example of this may be noted from the transcription of a Zulu dance-song from the Buthelezi tribe (published in Rycroft, 1962, p. 81, where accompanying diagrams show the pitches used in a spoken rendering of the same text). Of the four short phrases, all except the first conclude with the descending sequence *E–B–A*. In normal speech, the final words in the three phrases taking this sequence require, respectively, speech-tone patterns high-low-low, falling-low, and high-low-high. The first of these fits the melody quite closely, though in speech the two low syllables would be at equal pitch. In the second, the falling tone is spread over the two notes E and B, connected by *portamento,* so that a realisation very close to that of speech is obtained. In the third, however, the pattern for the last two syllables is entirely reversed. From a perusal of other Nguni songs, it appears that similar word patterns requiring final high tone quite commonly suffer such treatment in final position in a song phrase. — Phrase-final distortion of speech patterns may possibly be very widespread in Africa. A.M. Jones, in his analysis of a West African Ewe song (though Ewe is a non-Bantu language) reports similar latitude with speech-tones at the ends of phrases (Jones, 1959, chap. X).

h. Differing interpretations

Where deviations seem to occur between vocal melody and a spoken rendering of the text, several alternative interpretations are sometimes possible. For an example of the kind of controversy possible in this field, reference should be made to A.M. Jones's criticisms (Jones, 1959, pp. 230–251) concerning earlier analyses of 20 songs in the Ewe language, made by Marius Schneider (Schneider, 1943). Schneider had concentrated on "essential tones" – following Westermann's 3 tone-level system for Ewe – and disregarded "intonation", explaining deviations by means of "the rhythmical process". Jones, in his own analysis of an Ewe song, is not concerned with "essential tones" but makes direct comparison with the actual relative-pitch contours of speech, and explains deviations in terms of "seven rules for tone/tune behaviour". These include: initial and final latitude, assimilation, and use of "harmonic alternatives". In Schneider's subsequent rejoinder to Jones's claims, further detailed comparisons are made between their two systems of interpretation (see Schneider, 1961).

i. Total violation of speech-tones

In southern Bantu music there do not appear to be a great many indigenous examples of songs which disregard speech-tones altogether. But this does happen in certain children's game-songs and jingles, in which words are used for their sound rather than their meaning, or may be entirely nonsensical. Such items have been noted among various Nguni peoples, and Blacking describes a number of examples among Venda children's songs (Blacking, 1967). In Zulu and Swazi *imilolozelo* jingles, there is generally a fixed repetitive form of imposed melodic and metrical patterning, bearing no intentional relation to speech-tone requirements. — There are also a few very ancient Nguni anthems and dance-songs in which the text consists partially, or even wholly, of emotive syllables. The Zulu *uhawu* victory song is among these. Here it is not always possible to know for certain whether the words have always been meaningless, from the start, or if the melody might not originally have been influenced by speech patterns from real words, which may since have become distorted and lost. But in many less ancient dance-songs, sequences of the "fa-la-la" type quite often occur, particularly within chorus phrases, and these allow complete freedom of melodic movement. — In modern church, school and popular music in all Southern African Black languages there is generally complete disregard for speech-tones, probably inspired in the first place by the application of vernacular words to European hymn tunes, and in the adoption of various Western stylistic features.

4. Bibliography

Blacking, J.: *Venda children's songs.* Witwatersrand University Press, Johannesburg, 1967.   Carrington, J.F.: *Talking drums of Africa.* Carey Kingsgate Press, London, 1949.   Cope, A.T.: *Zulu phonology, tonology and tonal grammar.* Unpublished Ph.D. thesis, University of Natal, 1966.   Dahle, P.B.: *Eine Siegeshymne der Ama-Zulu.* Festschrift Meinhof, Hamburg, 1927, pp. 175–195.   Doke, C.M.: *The Southern Bantu languages.* OUP, London, for International African Institute, Handbook of African Languages series, 1954.   Guthrie, M.: *The classification of Bantu languages.* OUP, London, 1948.   Idem: *A revised classified list of Bantu languages,* (cyclostyled list) SOAS. University of London, 1956.   Idem: *Comparative Bantu* I. Gregg Press, London, 1967.   Herzog, G.: Speech melody in primitive music. *The Musical Quaterly* XX/4, 1934, pp. 452–466.   Von Hornbostel, E.M.: African Negro music. *Africa* I, 1928, pp. 30–62.   Jones, A.M.: *Studies in African Music* I. OUP, London, 1959, chap. 10.   Kirby, P.R.: A study of Bushman music, and musical practices of the Bushmen: *Bantu Studies* X, 1936, pp. 205–252, 373–432.   Idem: Primitive music. *Grove's dictionary of music and musicians* Vol. VI, 1954, pp. 921–926.   Lanham, L.W.: *The phonology of Nguni.* Unpublished Ph.D. thesis, UWits, 1960.   List, G.: The boundaries of speech and song. *Ethnomusicology* VII/1, 1963, pp. 3–6.   Pike, K.L.: *Tone languages.* Ann Arbor, Michigan, 1948.   Rycroft, D.K.: Linguistic and melodic-interaction in Zulu song. *Akten des XXIV internationalen Kongresses.* München, 1957, pp. 726–9.   Idem: Melodic features in Zulu eulogistic recitation. *African Language Studies* I, 1960, pp. 60–70.   Idem: Zulu and Xhosa praise-poetry and song. *African Music* III/1, 1962, pp. 79–85.   Idem: Tone in Zulu nouns. *African Language Studies* IV, 1963, pp. 43–68.   Idem: Nguni vocal polyphony. *Journal of the International Folk Music Council* XIX, 1967, pp. 88–103.   Idem: The national anthem of Swaziland. *African Language Studies* XI, 1970.   Idem: *Zulu, Swazi and Xhosa instruments and songs* (monograph with L.P. disc). Musée Royal de l'Afrique Centrale, Tervuren, 1970.   Schapera, I.: *The Khoisan peoples of South Africa.* Routledge, London, 1930.   Schneider, M.: Phonetische und metrische Korrelationen bei gesprochenen und gesungenen Ewe-texten. *Archiv für vergleichende Phonetik* VII, 1943–44.   Idem: Tone and tune in West African music. *Ethnomusicology* V/3, 1961, pp. 204–215.   Starke, Anny: *The relation between the intonation of song and speech of the Amaxosa.* Unpublished thesis, UCT, 1930.   Westphal, E.O.J.: Some observations on current Bushmen and Hottentot musical practices. *RAI symposium: Music and history in Africa and Asia.* London, 1962. Unpublished.

– D.K.R.

V. THE MUSIC OF THE ZULU AND SWAZI

1. Historical outline
2. Musical terms and concepts
3. Musical ecology
   a. Ceremonial performances
   b. Marriage ceremonies
   c. Other kinds of songs
4. Principal musical instruments
5. Structural, formal and stylistic features

a. Tonality
b. Rhythm
c. Vocal polyphony
6. Bibliography
7. Zulu and Swazi musical examples

The two closely related languages, Zulu and Swazi (or *siSwati*, to use their own term) belong to the Nguni group of Bantu languages, which also includes Xhosa and the Ndebele languages. They are all "tone languages", in the sense that the pitch contours of speech are semantic. Speech-tone requirements tend to influence the direction of the melodic line in song, and speech-derived *portamento* is also common. Besides ordinary consonants, Nguni languages have "clicks", adopted from the Bushmen or Hottentots, and also a range of "tone-lowering" consonants which affect vowel pitch in both speech and song.

1. Historical outline

Broadly speaking, the Nguni peoples have much in common in their music, as also in other branches of culture. They share the same range of traditional musical instruments for individual performance – notably musical bows and flutes (now largely displaced by Western instruments). But their communal music-making, usually linked with dancing or other bodily movement, appears always to have been predominantly vocal rather than instrumental. They dance, or work, accompanying their actions with their own singing, and have specialised in developing vocal polyphony rather than complex instrumental rhythms. Compared with more northerly Black African peoples, drums and instrumental ensembles are conspicuously lacking – though war-shields used to be used percussively, and nowadays singing is accompanied by improvised percussion instruments in certain new art-forms, like modern Zulu *ingoma* dancing. — The separate but interweaving histories of the numerous Nguni tribes and clans over the past three or four centuries are certainly reflected, however, in stylistic differences in their music, and particularly in the variety of scale systems employed. The Xhosa-speaking peoples appear distinct from the rest in several respects and are excluded here, but differences are also noticeable between tribes or clans within the same language community. This is particularly true in the Zulu-speaking area. With the rise to power of Shaka's small Zulu clan in the early 19th century, a Zulu-speaking nation was compounded from various neighbouring tribes. It seems that it is now "impossible to discover what changes actually resulted from the amalgamation of these tribes" (Krige, 1936, p. 22). Nevertheless, north of the Tugela river, in Zululand, the present-day descendants of the orginal Zulu clan, and others connected with them, still regard themselves as culturally distinct from "those *amaLala* south of the Tugela" – by which they mean various, though not all Zulu-speaking tribes settled elsewhere in Natal, whose ancestry is reputedly from the Tsonga, of the Delagoa Bay area. Certainly some musical differences are discernable, especially in the matter of tonality. — In Swaziland, traditional culture remains largely intact. Annual ceremonies are still held on a national scale, and Swazi music is more homogeneous. Despite the fact that the ruling Nkhosi Dlamini clan claim that they are descended from the Tsonga, and that many Sotho clans were incorporated into the nation early in the 19th century, there seems to be little trace of non-Nguni influence in their music. The style of Swazi choral songs is unmistakeably distinctive, but in many respects their music resembles that of Zululand – more closely, in fact, than does the music of some of the Zulu-speaking tribes of southern Natal. Although the Swazi were never conquered by the Zulu, they admit to having adopted various cultural traits from them. An Ndwandwe princess from Zululand who became the main wife of King Sobhuza, is said to have been influential in this respect. A striking feature of Swazi song texts, including those of their most important ceremonial dance-songs and anthems, is that almost all of these are in the *Zunda* dialect, spoken in southern Swaziland near the Zululand border, which employs the consonant "z" in place of the normal Swazi "t" and more closely resembles Zulu.

2. Musical terms and concepts

The traditional Zulu word for "singing" is *ukuhlabelela,* from the verb *hlabelela,* "sing" (Swazi *hlabelela* or *hlabela).* However, this term does not exactly match the Western concept of singing or vocal music. It excludes *izibongo* "praise poetry" (Swazi *tibongo)* although, to European ears, this often resembles a form of song rather than speech (ex. 10, p. 327; see also Rycroft, 1960); but it includes what Europeans would call "choral recitation". The latter style of rendering (Swazi, *kwekhuzela)* follows a regular metre but uses only an exaggerated kind of "sing-song" rise and fall of pitch, without exact musical notes. This occurs in several (but not all) items in the repertoire for the Zulu *isigekle* "recreational dance" (see ex. 11, p. 329). — In distinguishing *ukuhlabelela* from all other forms of vocal expression, one important criterion therefore appears to be the presence of regular metrical organisation, while the melodic use of fixed pitch values is not absolutely essential. Regarding regular metre, however, vocal phrasing often flouts this rather than expressing it directly: word-stresses frequently do *not* coincide with the physical downbeat of the dance-step, etc. In consequence, it can be entirely misleading to analyse songs without taking accompanying physical movements into account. — When a musical instrument yields sound, it is said to *khala,* using the verb normally meaning "cry" (as humans or animals). The verb *shaya,* normally meaning "strike", is used for playing an instrument. In Zulu, another alternative is *betha,* also normally meaning "strike". — In Swazi the word *ingoma* (plural *tingoma)* serves as the general term for any kind of song. Different categories of song are distinguished, mainly on grounds of function, e.g. *ingoma yebutimba:* "hunting song"; *tingoma yekuhlakula:* "weeding songs", etc. But many other types of song and dance have specific names, such as *umgubho* (a form of solemn, ceremonial dance-song), or *ummiso* (a variety of women's dance-song). — In Zulu the term *ingoma* (plural *izingoma)* formerly implied a "royal dance-song" performed by the king on important occasions, particularly at the annual first-fruits ceremony, but it is now applied to a modern form of neo-traditional dancing. The old Zulu word *igamu* (plural *amagamu)* may be used for a song or tune, but more commonly the borrowed Xhosa term *umculo* is now employed for "vocal music" in general, and *iculo* (plural *amaculo)* for any song. The English-derived word *umnyuziki* serves for the general concept of music. Traditionally, specific rather than generic terms were used. The most important traditional choral songs of the Zulu come under the term *ihubo* (plural, *amahubo).* There are three varieties: (1) principally, *ihubo lesizwe* (or merely *ihubo),* a solemn ceremonial anthem pertaining to the nation, or to an individual tribe, clan or sib, each of which have their own and hold it in great respect (see exs. 12, 13, p. 330); (2) *ihubo lempi,* a war song or chant; (3) *ihubo lamabutho,* a regimental song, pertaining to a particular regiment. Numerous further categories each have their own specific names.

3. Musical ecology

Music plays an important part in the life, not only of the individual, but also of the community. There are songs for different age-groups, related to numerous different activities and occasions. Many songs are directly functional, either regulating bodily actions (as in dancing, or some common task); or educative, serving to regulate behaviour; or they may express group ideals, or popular or personal opinion – sometimes critical of authority, which is permissable in song; or they serve as an essential constituent of some ceremony or social event. — Outstanding composers, singers and dancers are admired, but there are no professionals who make their living solely by that means. For praise-poetry there were formerly professional praisers or bards. But the composition of songs, often self-accompanied on a musical bow, was something almost everybody attempted from time to time. The "best" songs tend to become adapted for choral use, as dance-songs, and remain in the general repertoire. The composer's name is often remembered among the Zulu, but less so among the Swazi. Before a Zulu wedding, an acknowledged *ingqambi* (composer/arranger) may be asked to devise or arrange suitable dance music and conduct rehearsals. Sometimes old items are rearranged, to serve in a different category and context. When this is done, the question as to whether the words are appropriate or not appears to be immaterial. — Regarding the content of song texts, these often convey very little direct meaning, by comparison with *izibongo* praise poetry, where words, chosen for their imagery and aptness, are paramount. The texts of many choral songs consist only of a few short phrases, constantly repeated, and there are often meaningless emotive syllables. — The greatest living authority on Zulu music is (1967) Princess Constance Magogo kaDinuzulu. Her earliest teachers in this field were her grandmothers, the widows of King Cetshwayo (1829–1884). The following condensed account, drawn from a personal interview with her in 1964, may serve to illustrate the social role and context of some types of Zulu music: "In traditional Zulu life, music begins in early childhood, with *imilolozelo* (rhythmical 'nursery' rhymes, with or without fixed pitch values, in which words are used for their sound rather than their sense). For slightly older children, there are songs with a purpose. For example, we have a custom that boys and girls should not play together, and there is a taunting song to ridicule any child who disregards this. When a girl reaches puberty, her father arranges a party in her honour. It is said that she is being 'helped to bear the milkpail' - *ubelethiswa ithunga*. Neighbours gather, and a type of song known as *ingcekeza* is sung, accompanied by hand-clapping with cupped palms. This style of clapping, known as *ukunqukuza*, is reserved expressly for ceremonies concerning girls of that age. After this, a girl may fall in love. If she does so, she is likely to sing about the fact, making up her own songs and accompanying herself on her *umakhweyana* musical bow. Older girls in the neighbourhood will take note, and see to it that proper courting procedures are followed. — They will brew beer and arrange a secret party, unknown to their parents. Young men arrive, moving in a line and chanting an *umvumo* chorus song, such as this one:

> What will you consume at bed-time, O child of ours?
> All cattle have tails, O maiden! Do they not all have tails?
> > (i.e. our bride-price cattle are as good as anyone else's!)
> The girls choose popular fellows!
> Who shall be the 'cross-grained maize-cob' and succeed?
> > (i.e. the odd one who stands out from the crowd and draws her love).

317

"There are set forms of address, and formal ways of thanking the girls. Then the cry goes up: 'please strip for us!' The girls respond by singing:

> Look at my 'bowl for holding millet'! (i.e. stomach)
> Ha, Ha, Ha, Hawu!

"They do indeed remove some of their clothing, while singing. Then the youths dance energetically, while singing an appropriate *umvumo* song. The merry-making proceeds, but the girl who has fallen in love (for whom the party was held) must secretly disappear and go home. The older girls then express great concern and go off on the pretext of finding her. But they do not come back, and the young men find themselves left in the lurch. At young people's parties many different dances can be performed, such as the *indlamu*, the *umgqigqo*, or the old *umchwayo* dance which is sometimes done in the sitting position, inside a hut."

a. Ceremonial performances

Communal music, with dancing, forms the essential basis of traditional weddings and other important social or ceremonial occasions. The dancing is accompanied principally by the singing of the dancers themselves, but rhythmic expression is often enhanced with ankle-rattles, hand-clapping (normally with flat palms, and with the finger-tips meeting), or with the wielding of real or symbolic weapons, implements or regalia. One of the most important gestures is that of pointing, known as *ukukhomba*. These actions, and the steps and postures of the dance, are normally considered inseparable from the music: music and movement are blended to produce a larger artistic whole. Beyond this, the performance may itself be felt to be inseparable from the total context of a particular ceremony, and the ceremony to be essentially a part of some sacred or seasonal event, like the impressive *incwala* first-fruits ceremony of the Swazi. Certain *incwala* dance-songs are in fact forbidden in any other context or at any other time. The corresponding Zulu ceremony, known as the *umkhosi* or *uk-weshwama*, is no longer held on a national scale, but a small version of it is still annually re-enacted by a branch of the *amaNgcobo* clan, near Elandskop, Natal. — At such ceremonies, group solidarity appears to be reflected through total involvement, despite the fact that participants are grouped separately according to age, sex, regiment, etc. The solemn dance-songs are essentially a performers' art-form – a means of collective expression, with national and religious motivation. For their full appreciation, what is required is not a passive audience, but direct experience through participation. An onlooker gains the impression of something like real-life opera or dramatic pageant, for which no audience is really intended but only performers.

b. Marriage ceremonies

As distinct from the total co-operation exhibited in national ceremonies, there is often an element of rivalry at social gatherings, parties and weddings, reflecting group differentiation on the basis of locality, family, age or sex. The central feature of a wedding, held at the bridegroom's home, is an elaborate programme of dances. As if expressing artistically the essential two-family contractual basis of marriage, the bride's party and that of the groom dance in turn, quite separately, each seeking to assert themselves as a distinct group, worthy of social recognition. Marriage proceedings commence in the evening, with *umgqumushelo* dance-songs, in which the two parties taunt and insult each other, sometimes grossly, before retiring to their respective huts to drink beer and perform *ingadla* dancing. Next day the festivities begin with *umgqigqo* dances by young girls. Then the bride's party come on, singing first the solemn *ihubo* anthem of their clan before performing their opening *inkondlo* dance and a number of further items. An interlude then follows, during which other teams, comprising visitors or young people, have their turn to dance. Then the groom's party sing their *ihubo,* dance their opening *inkondlo* (see ex. 14, p. 331), and perform many further items such as *imphendu* and *isigekle* dances (see ex. 11, p. 329), striving to surpass all previous performers. On the following day there are again many further musical activities. (For fuller description of traditional dances, consult works by Bryant, Krige, Reader, Kuper and Marwick, listed below.)

c. Other kinds of song
Besides dance music there are songs associated with various other physical activities. Among the Swazi, for instance, communal *tingoma tekuhlakula,* or "weeding songs", are sung by groups while tilling a field, to regulate the rise and fall of the hoes; or "lifting chants" are used when concerted efforts are required. Teams of Zulu labourers in towns may frequently be heard singing while digging a trench in the street, or moving heavy loads. — Zulu regiments formerly each had their respective battlecries *(izaga)* and regimental songs and chants, some of which are still remembered today. In some battlecries there is alternation between metrical yelling, and melodic "singing" (in the European sense) (see ex. 15, p. 332). — Among the Swazi the traditional *emabutfo* age-grade regimental system still operates, and many categories of song and chant are associated with different activities, both while drilling and parading, and when going on route marches through the country. Regimental songs and chants in general are known as *tingoma temajaha.* Often the same song text may be rendered in several ways: in quick duple time, as an *ingoma yekuhlehla,* for running or jog-trotting in crescent formation; or in slower triple time, as an *ingoma yekushuca,* for walking or loping, which can serve also as a hoeing song, *ingoma yekuhlakula;* or in slow duple time, as a *ligubhu,* sung while stationary, with gestures and leg movements (see ex. 11, p. 329). Another, less melodic form of chanting, known as *indlaliso,* is used for regimental drilling. The verb used here is not *hlabela,* "sing", but *dlala* which normally means "play". — In both Zulu and Swazi society there are many further contexts in which music is found. There are hunting songs, and walking songs; songs occur within many folk-tales; there are game-songs and lullabies, and many mothers compose a personal song (Zulu, *isihlabelelo*) for a child. — Musical bows and flutes were formerly played, individually, for diversion, or while walking (see 4: Musical instruments). Certain types of musical bow were used for self-accompaniment, serving to encourage self-expression and the composition of personal songs, but these practices are rarely pursued today.

4. Principal musical instruments
Instruments used by Nguni have been described in detail by P.R. Kirby (see Kirby, 1934). Traditionally, the Zulu and Swazi (and other Nguni) seem to have used instruments mainly for individual music-making. Their communal music, involving group participation, appears nearly always to have been essentially vocal rather than instrumental. Though there is no evidence that they ever used drums, traditionally, many earlier writers have described seeing Zulu warriors emphasize the rhythm of their war songs through striking their ox-hide shields with weapons, or beating them

forcibly on the ground. This practice was known as *ingomane.* While there were no beaten drums, however, an indigenous Zulu friction-drum known as *ingungu* was formerly used to accompany girls' dance-songs at coming-of-age ceremonies. The distinctive *ukunqukuza* style of hand-clapping, with hollowed palms, or sometimes with a stone held in each palm, was also reserved for such occasions. Normal clapping (Zulu, *ukushaya izandla,* or *ukushaya ihlombe*) is performed with flat palms, and with the fingertips meeting. This is still done, by women only, as an accompaniment to certain dance-songs, among both Zulu and Swazi, and they sometimes use ankle-rattles (Zulu, *amafohlwane;* Swazi, *emafahlawane*) in some wedding dances. Metal referee's whistles, blown by girls, are the only other instruments nowadays used while dancing. "Medicine men" have traditionally used short whistles (*imbande* or *impempe*) and sometimes small struck drums for exorcism, but the latter appear to have been borrowed from other peoples. Nowadays improvised drums, often made from oil-drums, and also wooden clappers, are used for modern Zulu *ingoma* dancing, and numerous separatist religious sects use drums and sometimes improvised metal lip-blown wind instruments to accompany dancing at their services. — For individual music-making, several varieties of instruments – notably horns, flutes and musical bows (now largely supplanted by Western instruments) – were formerly used. These have been described in detail by Kirby (see under Zulu and Swazi, in index to Kirby, 1934). Side-blown horns yielding a single note were used by men as signalling instruments in war, or at ceremonies or hunts or to summon companions. The *mpalampala* was made from sable antelope horn; the *uphondo* from ox horn. The Zulu also used an endblown bamboo trumpet with ox-horn "bell" yielding two or more notes. — Flutes were played by men and boys and were mainly associated with cattle-herding. The long obliquely held flute without finger-holes (Zulu, *umtshingo* or *ivenge,* Swazi, *umntshingozi* or *livenge*) was sounded by shaping the tongue to serve as an air-channel. Notes representing partials 4 to 12 of the harmonic series could be produced through overblowing, and by alternately stopping and unstopping the end with a finger. The making and playing of these instruments, and of the smaller *igemfe,* was formerly forbidden until the time of the annual *umkhosi* festival of the first-fruits. The *igemfe* or *igekle* was used for duet playing, two such flutes usually being tuned about a semitone apart. — Several types of mouth-resonated musical bow were used for solo playing, though these are very rarely found today (see Kirby, 1934). In playing such instruments, the stave is held against the mouth. The fundamental of the string, or of one of the two segments if the string is divided, can be varied by left-hand finger stopping, but not more than two or three fundamentals are generally used. Different harmonics, usually partials 3 to 6 of the two or three fundamental tones, are selectively resonated by varying the volume of the mouth cavity in a manner similar to that with the jews-harp, and these harmonics are used melodically. (The commercially made jews-harp has in fact become popular, the Zulu name coined for it being *isitolotolo.*) The principal plucked mouth-bows are the *umqangala,* with a stave of reed, and an undivided string; and the *isitontolo,* with threepiece wooden stave and divided string, drawn in towards the stave by a loop, near the centre. — The Zulu *umhubhe* (or *umrube*) and the Swazi *utiyane* are sounded by friction, through "bowing" the string with a stalk. Similar instruments are used by the Xhosa and Mpondo (see Rycroft, 1966). The *ugwala* or *unkwindi* was a stringed-wind instrument resembling the Hottentot *gorá.* It was sounded by blowing on a piece of quill which connected the string to the stave. — The "classical" Zulu instrument for solo song accompaniment is the *ugubhu* (Swazi, *ligubhu*). This is a large musical bow with a stave about one and a half to two metres long, obtained from a tree such as the *uthathawe* (Acacia ataxacantha), *umbangandlala* (Heteromorpha arborescens), *umbonjane* (Acacia kraussiana), or *iphahla* (Brachylaena discolor). A calabash resonator, about 18 cm. in diameter, is attached near the lower end. The single undivided string is usually made from twisted cow-tail hair and is struck with a piece of thatching grass. The instrument is held vertically, in front of the player, so that the circular hole (about 8 cm. in diameter) in the calabash resonator is close to the left breast. The instrument was formerly played either by men or women, but today the last remaining Zulu performer appears to be Princess Constance Magogo, who has been recorded and filmed (see Rycroft, 1970). No remaining Swazi players of the *ligubhu* are known. — The open string of the *ugubhu* yields a rich fundamental note. A second note, usually about a semitone higher, is produced by pinching the string near its lower end, between the left thumb-nail and index finger. Partials 2 to 5 of either of these fundamentals (see ex. 25, p. 344) can be selectively resonated by moving the mouth of the calabash resonator closer or farther away from the player's breast. These harmonics are used to provide a simple *ostinato* melody below the vocal line, but they are scarcely audible to a listener if he should stand more than a metre or two away from the instrument. The basic "semitone" interval varies freely, in different performances between about 90 and 150 cents (compared with a Western equal-tempered semitone of 100, or a "just" semitone of 111 cents). — Songs accompanied on the *ugubhu* usually employ five or six notes per octave. Of these notes, four always bear the relation of fifth or octave to the fundamentals of the bow, corresponding with partials 3 and 4, as shown in ex. 25b. In some songs the additional vocal note or notes correspond with one or both of the 5th partials (marked x and y). But in many other songs neither of these notes is used, and the note z occurs instead. Although not derived directly from any of the resonated harmonics of the bow, this note is commonly sung with the lower fundamental, to which it bears the relation of minor third. Ex. 25c shows which fundamental is normally used to accompany each of the vocal notes in this mode. From a study of songs sung with the *ugubhu*, it is clear that a dual system of tonality is employed, based upon the two "roots", roughly a semitone apart, supplied by the instrument. In most songs the lower note serves as principal root, or "tonic", with the higher one as subsidiary root (analogous, in function though not in interval distance, to our dominant). In some songs, however, the order is reversed. — Another form of resonated bow is the *umakhweyana* (Swazi, *makhweyane*), also known by several other names (see ex. 17, p. 334). This instrument is reputed to have been borrowed from the Tsonga of Moçambique in the 19th century. It is still used to a limited extent by young men and unmarried girls. The string, made from copper or brass wire (or unravelled chicken wire) is divided near the centre so that it yields two "open" notes. These are generally tuned so as to lie about a whole-tone or sometimes a minor third apart. Absolute precision in tuning this interval is not regarded as particularly important. What is more important is that the calabash should resonate the required harmonics of the fundamentals: partials 3, 4 and 5 (see ex. 26a, p. 344). An additional fundamental though its tone quality is somewhat duller, can be obtained through "stopping" the string with a knuckle of the left hand, just below the dividing noose. For some songs, this "stopped" note is roughly a semitone above the higher "open" note, but sometimes an interval closer to a whole-tone is used. Alternatively, some players omit this note in certain songs and, instead, use the flesh of the left forefinger to "damp" the string intermittently in order to produce contrasting *staccato* effects. — Songs accompanied on this type of bow generally employ five or six notes per octave, related either to all three fundamentals of the bow plus their fifths (i.e. third partials), or to the two open notes only (generally a whole-tone apart) and to the major triads based on these (i.e. their third and fifth partials, see ex. 26b, p. 344). It is more usual for the higher of the two open notes to serve as principal root (see ex. 18, p. 335; for recordings, see Rycroft, 1970).

5. Structural, formal and stylistic features
Voice quality among the Zulu and Swazi is generally of the "open" variety. Women's voices most commonly keep to mezzo-soprano or alto range rather than soprano. Old men, particularly among the Swazi, often employ a slow, tremulous "diaphragm vibrato", and younger men sometimes emulate this when singing ancient solemn songs, such as the Swazi *lihubo* anthem, *Incaba kaNcofula* (see ex. 13, p. 330). — Some explosive, *fortissimo* yelling occurs in Zulu regimental war-cries and chants, as also in a style of modern male-choir singing favoured by both Zulu and Swazi in towns, known as *umbholoho*, in which high *falsetto* is also cultivated. The tune *Wimoweh,* popularised by The Weavers and Louis Armstrong in America in the 1950s, was borrowed from a pre-war recording of a Zulu "town song" of this kind, called *Mbube.* – In the singing of traditional choral dance-songs, a very common tendency is for the pitch to rise, very gradually, becoming sometimes as much as a fourth sharper by the end of a long performance. It is not unknown, in such circumstances, for the singer of the leading part to find it necessary to drop his range to an octave lower, if he is to continue. Tempo also has a tendency to increase as enthusiasm warms up. In choral songs, generally, there is considerable distortion of syllable length. Linguistic values, apart from those of relative pitch, which do influence the direction of the melodic line, are mainly subservient to musical demands. In improvised solo songs, however, linguistic features of the text usually play a larger part in determining the melody: length and stress values, as well as speech-tones, and even overall sentence intonation contours, are often fairly closely reflected in the musical setting.

a. Tonality
In considering "scales", abstracted from various songs, there appears to be considerable diversity, not only between the scale system used by different Nguni peoples, but also within single language communities. It may perhaps be broadly stated that perfect fourths and fifths appear to be important structural intervals in a great deal of Nguni music, and that in many of the various scales or modes, larger, unbridged intervals such as a fourth or third tend to lie near the bottom, and closer intervals towards the top. This suggests affinity with partials of the harmonic series, as has often been affirmed by P.R. Kirby. But not all Nguni scales allow this inference to be made. — Scale systems are not completely homogeneous among the Zulu and Swazi, nor even within the Zulu-speaking area itself. As previously outlined, this is consistent with history, though the sources of different scales or modes cannot as yet be clearly traced. It seems necessary, however, to distinguish broadly between Swaziland, Zululand, and the rest of Natal – though a far more comprehensive survey of the latter area would be desirable. — In Zululand itself, among the descendants of the original Zulu clan and those clans most closely connected with them, a few dance-songs and anthems still sung today, reputedly from the 18th and 19th centuries, employ only three notes,

which could be represented as $c' - g - f$, plus the octave of one or more of these (e.g. $c' - g - f - c$, or $f' - c' - g - f$), the only intervals being the major second, fourth, fifth, and octave (Rycroft, 1959, ex. 1). But many other songs, some clearly older, as for instance the archaic, wordless *uhawu* victory song (see ex. 23, p. 341), use penta- and hexa-modes containing two semitone intervals. The commonest of these modes in choral music, and in solo songs with the *ugubhu* (see ex. 17, p. 334) musical bow, could basically be represented as $c' - b - g$ (or g-*sharp* $- f - e$ plus octave extensions). The Swazi also employ this mode, but more commonly a variant of it, containing a instead of g ($c' - b - a - f - e$), or a hexatonic extension of this, with added "g" (sometimes varying with g-*sharp;* see ex. 20, p. 337). In solo songs with the *ugubhu* bow (or Swazi *ligubhu*) the instrument yields two roots roughly a semitone apart, e.g. f and e, plus their resonated third partials c and b. In keeping with the accompaniment, the $f - c$ and the $e - b$ tonalities are used contrastively in such bow-songs, and a similar principle of hemitonal "root-progression" underlies all Zulu and Swazi choral music using these modes (see exs. 20, 22, 24, pp. 337, 340, 342; also Rycroft, 1967). — The above scale systems are less common among Natal Zulu speakers south of the Tugela River, particularly those of reputed Tsonga origin – as also their neighbours further south, the Bhaca and Hlubi, and the Mpondo and others of the Xhosa-speaking group. Use appears to be made either of the anhemitonic "common pentatonic" (see ex. 15, p. 332) or of an incomplete "diatonic fifth" (g-f-e-d-c, plus duplicated "g" below), or of hexa-modes resembling diatonic hepta but in which either the 7th or the 3rd degree is absent, or sometimes of a full diatonic hepta. One hexa-mode, representable as $d - c - b - a - g - f$, is often associated with musical bow playing in that area, where roots commonly differ by a whole-tone instead of a semitone (Rycroft, 1966). Above roots g and f, for example, contrasting triadic tonalities $g - b - d$ and $f - a - c$ are used. Borrowed dance-songs (reputedly from the south of this area) using these modes, are nowadays widely used throughout Natal (including Zululand and Swaziland). Among the Swazi such music is known as *siBhaka,* implying reputed derivation from the Bhaka people.

b. Rhythm

Compared with the music of more northerly African people, Nguni music is noticeably lacking in rhythmic complexity but, conversely, very rich in the development of vocal polyphony. This may perhaps be correlated with the dearth of Nguni percussion instruments, but the reason why drums and polyrhythm should have remained unexploited by these peoples remains obscure. — The tempo of Zulu and Swazi choral "anthems", and of some of the older ceremonial dance-songs, is generally very slow: 50–100 beats per minute, in duple or triple grouping. Beats are often sub-divided irregularly, depending on the number of syllables ascribed to them. A "Scotch snap" rhythm within the beat is very common, with prefix syllables uttered very quickly and the root (or some other) syllable prolonged (see ex. 10, p. 327); or a single syllable may be sustained for two or more beats, or several syllables rendered in quick succession. Syllable lengths do not, however, conform strictly to normal speech values. Their treatment appears to follow traditional musical conventions. Syllables with inherent dynamic stress frequently do not coincide with the initial, strong point of the beat, which accompanies each dance-step. This off-beat relation between word accent and bodily metre seems to be deliberately cultivated (see Rycroft, 1971). — In recreational dance-songs, especially those for young people, the tempo may be much faster, with duple or triple metre. Where hand-clapping accompanies the singing, the claps are always evenly spaced and grouped, unlike the more intricate additive patterns used in much Central and West African music or in Bushman dance-songs. Likewise, when a musical bow is used to accompany solo songs, beats are almost always evenly spaced. But additive grouping, like $3+2+3$, occurs in some bow-songs (see ex. 22, p. 340), although regular triple, and simple or compound duple metres are more common. Sometimes the last quaver in each bar is lengthened to approximately a dotted quaver however, so that $\frac{3}{8}$ is virtually rendered as $\frac{7}{16}$, or $\frac{3}{4}$ as $\frac{13}{16}$ etc. Often the relation between vocal rhythm and the metre of the bow is an extremely loose one, and here the natural speech/rhythm of the text appears to be retained to some extent (see ex. 17, p. 334). — In work-songs for digging or lifting (see ex. 19, p. 336), it seems noteworthy that the voices commonly bear an off-beat relation to the moment of greatest physical exertion. This may well have a natural physiological foundation: in performing strenuous activities it appears to be an instinctive human reflex to tense the diaphragm and hold the breath, by closing the glottis at the actual moment of maximum exertion – in fact babies do it in defacation. At the actual moment of this glottal closure, vocal sound is of course impossible. But immediately before or after (or both: "huk – aaah") sound is not only possible but probable (for examples see Rycroft, 1962, p. 83; and idem, 1967, p. 92).

c. Vocal polyphony

A fundamental formal principle of Zulu and Swazi multi-part vocal music is the non-simultaneous entry of voices. In any choral song there are at least two voice-parts, singing non-identical words. These parts never begin together. In some items, the relation between leader and chorus is one of simple antiphonal alternation – first one, then the other. But overlapping phrases are more common, where the leading part re-enters before completion of the chorus (see ex. 20, p. 337). Often this re-entry takes place very soon after the chorus starts, so that the overlap is almost total. Or the overlap may be "double-ended": the solo part may commence midway through one chorus phrase, and end and restart midway through the next one, so that the phrases are completely interlinked (see ex. 21, p. 339). These techniques give rise to some fairly complex forms of polyphony. In a few Zulu songs there are *more* than two off-set parts of this kind (see ex. 22, p. 340). Among the Swazi, a *divisi* rendering of the chorus part is more usual, giving added textural enrichment. In its simplest form this involves some parallelism, mostly in fourths. But involved chording occurs in some of their ceremonial songs (see ex. 20, p. 337). — In most songs a fixed sequence of overlapping phrase-pairs, usually between two and seven pairs, makes up the single overall strophe, and this is repeated *ad infinitum* – though variations may occur in the upper part, depending on the inventiveness of the leader. In most cases no definite sense of finality attaches to the completion of the strophe. Immediate recommencement is obligatory, and perfect balance is maintained between the parts. Owing to the fixed, repetitive nature of the strophe, and the fixed (though staggered) relationship between leading and chorus parts, it is convenient to represent such music in terms of two (or more) concentric circular musical staves, instead of conventional straight ones (see Rycroft, 1967). These songs are conceived as consisting, not of separate complete parts, but rather of mutually interacting voices which are inseparable. An isolated singer, if asked to demonstrate a choral song, will usually not complete first one part and then the other, but will attempt to present the essentials of both parts, by jumping from one to the other whenever a new phrase-entry occurs (see ex. 13, p. 330). In the score, letters a, b, c, at various points indicate which of the three original voice parts is being sung. Subsequent to my adoption of circular scoring, I was interested to find that H.F. Fynn, writing in the 1830s, had noted that certain Zulu wedding songs were always "sung on the principle of a coach wheel, which is going round. One performer commences and at each repetition another joins in, till the singers are ten in number" (H.F. Fynn, p. 296). — The development of these formal techniques is particularly interesting when one notes the fact that, in tone-languages like Zulu and Swazi, a simultaneous rendering of a single text by all voices must inevitably result either in unison or parallelism. This is almost completely avoided through non-simultaneous entry and non-identical texts, so that greater independence of part-movement is possible, with frequent contrary motion and continuous change of chording. Occasional thirds and sixths, both major and minor, occur in addition to fourths, fifths and octaves. The former seem usually more transitory in use than fourths, fifths and octaves but, beyond this, no functional hierarchy of "discords" and "concords" seems to operate consistently. Since the two or more voices do not begin or end their respective phrases together, there are no coincident points of prolongation analogous to collective "resolution" or "cadence" in the Western sense. Rather than the resolution of discord by concord, the artistic intention here seems to be that of maintaining an ever-changing balance between the constituents, through contrastive chording, in addition to other features of their relationship. — Systems of "root progression" provide the harmonic scheme in all Zulu and Swazi choral music. Principal and subsidiary roots, analogous in function to our tonic and dominant, are most frequently either a whole-tone or a semitone apart, depending on the mode employed. It seems likely that musical bow-playing may at least have encouraged the development of this principle. Some Zulu choral songs, though always sung unaccompanied, are in fact reputed to have been composed by one or another ancestor "to the accompaniment of his *ugubhu* bow". An *ostinato* played on the bow can to some extent fulfil the role of a fixed vocal chorus part, above which the soloist is inspired to extemporize, and close parallels can be noted between the voice-to-bow relationships in bow-songs, and voice-part interrelations in many choral songs (for further analysis, see Rycroft, 1967). — Regarding structure, form and stylistic features it is apparent that both relatively simple, as well as considerably more complex features are to be found in different items of Zulu and Swazi music. Is there evidence, here, of historical development from the simpler to the more complex? — In the matter of part-relationships, a number of types can be distinguished, ranging from simple antiphony (without overlap) to fairly complex polyphony. Songs employing simple antiphony – though these are in the minority – do occur in most categories and repertoires. However, when the actual examples are examined, it appears that none are consistently archaic in all other respects, nor are they usually the oldest items. Similarly, Zulu dance-songs employing a rudimentary three-note scale will generally be found to have a relatively sophisticated polyphonic structure. Furthermore, despite their simple tonality, all examples so far encountered appear, from their textual content and attributed composers, to date back no further than the early 19th century. — One consistent characteristic of the oldest Zulu songs, known to date from before the 19th century, is the use of wordless "texts", containing only onomatopoeic or emotive speechsounds (later songs contain these also, but they are usually interspersed with meaningful words). Besides vowel sequences, the "French j" (as in "measure"), which is not used in spoken Zulu, is of frequent occurrence, often being used syllabically. But once again, all these songs have at least one structural feature that is not simple – like polyphonic part-relationships, or complex tonality, such as a hemitonic penta scale system. The wordless *uhawu* "victory song", which is reputedly the most ancient of all Zulu items, appears to contain both these relatively "advanced" features (see ex. 23, p. 341). — Through oral transmission, ancient songs might, in the course of time, have become transformed or modernized through the grafting on of "more advanced" features. This seems likely here, though in the absence of any documentation it can neither be proved nor disproved. But why, in some cases, should "archaisms" of scale, or of part-relationship, not only still survive, alongside "more developed" examples, but even be cultivated in songs of comparatively recent origin? — From the as yet incomplete body of Zulu and Swazi material so far examined, only a confused picture emerges, from the point of view of music history. If any particular feature is abstracted and viewed in isolation, speculation about successive stages of development, represented in various examples, seems feasible. But when due account is taken of other contradictory evidence from the same examples, no sound basis for valid historical reconstruction has so far emerged.

6. Bibliography

Bryant, A.T.: *The Zulu people.* Shuter & Shooter, Pietermaritzburg, 1949. The *Sound of Africa* series (LP discs containing Zulu and Swazi music). International Library of African Music, Grahamstown, South Africa.   Fynn, H.F.: *The diary of Henry Francis Fynn,* ed. by Stuart, J. & Malcolm, D. McK. Shuter & Shooter, Pieter-maritzburg, 1950.   Kirby, P.R.: Old-time chants of the Mpumuza chiefs. *Bantu Studies* I, 1923–26; pp. 23–34.   Idem: *The musical instruments of the native races of South Africa.* OUP, London, 1934; reprint Witwatersrand University Press, 1953.   Krige, E.J.: *The social system of the Zulus.* Longmans Green, London, 1936.   Idem: Girls' puberty songs and their relation to fertility, health, morality and religion among the Zulu. *Africa* XXVIII/2, 1968, pp. 173–197.   Kuper, H.: *An African aristocracy: rank among the Swazi.* OUP, London, 1947.   Marwick, B.A.: *The Swazi.* Cambridge, 1940.   Mayr, F. A.: A short study on Zulu music. *Annals of the Natal Government Museum* I/3, 1906.   Reader, D.H.: *Zulu tribe in transition.* Manchester University Press, 1966.   Rycroft, D.K.: Linguistic and melodic interaction in Zulu song. *Akten des XXIV Internationalen Orientalistenkongresses.* Munich, 1957, pp. 726–9.   Idem: Melodic features in Zulu eulogistic recitation. *African Language Studies* I, 1960, pp. 60–78.   Idem: Zulu and Xhosa praise-poetry and song. *African Music* III/1, 1962, pp. 79–85.   Idem: Friction chordophones in S-E. Africa. *Galpin Society Journal* XIX, 1966, pp. 84–100.   Idem: Nguni vocal polyphony. *Journal of the International Folk Music Council* XIX, 1967, pp. 88–103.   Idem: *Swazi vocal music* (monograph with L.P. disc). Musée Royal de l'Afrique Centrale, Tervuren, 1968.   Idem: *Zulu, Swazi and Xhosa instrumental music and songs,* (monograph, with L.P. disc) Musée Royal de l'Afrique Centrale, Tervuren, loc. cit., 1970.   Idem: Stylistic evidence in Nguni song. Wachsmann, K., ed.: *Essays on Music and History in Africa.* Northwestern University Press, Evanston, 1971.

– D.K.R.

7. Zulu and Swazi Musical Examples

1. Recited Zulu praise-poetry (extract from recording on Gallotone disc (GE967 A). This has melodic features but is not accepted as *ukuhlabelela* ("singing"). Pitch is determined by interaction between "essential speech-tones", "tone-lowering consonants", and position in stanza. High speech-tones take the note shown here as *F*. Low speech-tones normally take *E*, but middle-*C* if preceded by a "tone-lowering" consonant, and low *F* when stanza-final (see ex. 10 a, b).

Example 10a   Extract from Izibongo zikaShaka.

Upper transcription : Recited pitch levels (Mr. J. Mgadi)
Lower transcription : Spoken pitch levels (Mr. S. Ngcobo)

(Continued overleaf)

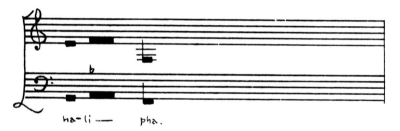

1. One who strikes but cannot be struck,
2. One who rumbles while sitting still—son of Menzi,
3. Hoe which surpasses all other hoes by its sharpness!

Example 10b

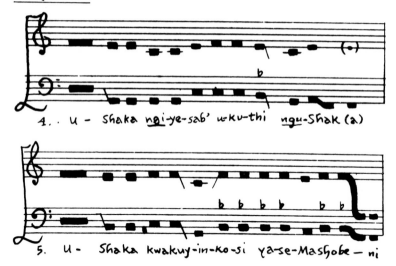

4. Shaka! I am afraid because it is Shaka,
5. Shaka, it was the chief of the Mashobeni!

Note.—In recitation, lines 1, 2 and 3 were rendered with only a very brief pause between them. Lines 4 and 5 were likewise treated together. In the spoken version there was a break after each line, with consequent lengthening of the penultimate syllable and dropping to final low pitch.

2. A zulu *isigekle* ''dance-song'' of the choral-recitation type. Performers: members of the Buthelezi clan, led by Chief M.G. Buthelezi, 1964. Triple time is characteristic for this category, but in different items the length of phrases varies widely.

Example 11   *Simthi wakla*

He showered applause over him!
We applaud him!
We pour the clapping into the ear;
We applaud him!

3. Ihubo likaCetzshwayo: a Zulu national choral song *(ihubo lesizwe).* A solo version is presented here, being a resumé of several voice parts, as sung by Sub-inspector Langa at Pietermaritzburg, 1964.

Example 12   *Uzithulele*

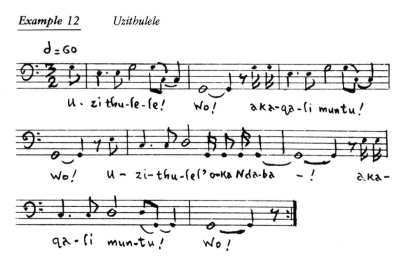

The Peaceful One! Wo! He provokes nobody!
The Peaceful One, son of Ndaba, provokes no-one!

4. Swazi *lihubo: Incaba kaNcofula.* The solo version in ex. 13 is a resumé of main phrases from three overlapping parts, as sung by Prince Clement Dumisa Dlamini, in 1969. The 'click' consonant 'c' is pronounced as Zulu 'q' in this song. Formerly a war song, this item is sung when soldiers set off on a mission, and also at the end of the annual *Incwala* ceremony.

Example 13   *Nans' incaba kaNcofula*

330

Here (indicated with a pointing gesture) is Ncofula's fortress!
You of the wild beast (who is fearsome!)
It is our bull! Heya heya hee! Hee!
You will say you never saw him;
The Son of Ndaba, (how) will he attack?

5. A zulu *inkondlo* dance-song, the most important of wedding dances, as sung by Princess Magogo and Chief M.G. Buthelezi, 1964. Example 14 is an adaptation of an older item from a different category, as commonly happens.

Example 14   *Uyaliwa*

(Continued overleaf)

Chorus: We are stabbed without reciprocating, (repeated three times)
         And we must bear the pain!
Solo: He (our chief) is rejected, he is unloved everywhere!
         Alas! O Zulus! We have nothing to say!

6. An *isaga* (battle-cry) of the amaNgcobo clan (Natal). Alternate use is made of *parlando* and melodic styles. Performers: Chief Mlungisi Ngcobo and clansmen; at Elandskop, 1964.

Example 15   *Asikashayi*

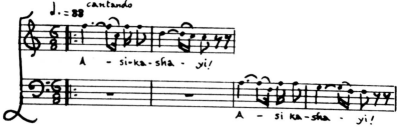

Qha-bo!   Phin-de!   A - si-ka-sha - yi!

We have not struck yet!
No! Just repeat (your provocation)!

7. Two versions of the first phrase of a Swazi regimental song: a) for running; b) for walking. Singer: Mr. J.S.M. Matsebula, 1965.

Example 16   *Wang' phos'*

a. 'Yekuhlehla' version

Wang'- phos',   wang²-phos' en - jo - be - ni,

b. 'Yekushuca' version

Wang'- phos',   wang' phos' en - jo - be - ni,

He (the King) takes me and puts me in the tassel (i.e. regiment).

8. Extract from a Zulu solo song from the early 19th century, self-accompanied on *ugubhu* musical bow, as performed by Princess Magogo, 1964. (For recording, see Rycroft, 1970). In the bow part, upper notes represent harmonics, selectively amplified by the resonator. Pause signs over bar-lines indicate prolongation of the final quaver, to approximately dotted-quaver duration. The first four stanzas, out of 73, are shown in ex. 17.

Example 17   Maye babo

Voice

Ugubhu
musical bow

resonated
harmonics

Ma - ye ba-bo -! Ye buya Noma-gundwanebo!

Ma - ye ba-bo ---! Ngi-phathel'u-ghubhu Iwami ekhaya lapho,

(ugubhu as before)

Refrain repeated
each time

Mi - na ngi hambi-le m-

Nga--ye nga-fik' em-

Alas! Oh what sorrow, Nomagundwane! (''woman-of-the rats'')
Bring me my *ugubhu* bow here in the house, O my younger sister!
I have been travelling, O sister!
I eventually reached the homestead.

9. A Swazi solo song, self-accompanied on *makhweyane* musical bow. Singer: Mazinyo
Mavuso, 1964 (recorded by Rycroft, 1970).

Example 18   *Ye lutsandvo luphelile*

(Continued overleaf)

Love has ended, O daughter of Ndzimandze!
Love has ended, O child of the people!
The one who sleeps out in the wilds, O daughter of Ndzimandze.

Order: Bow solo (two-bar phrase repeated five times);
      Voice and bow: A, A, B1, B1, B1;
      Bow solo (seven repetitions);
      Voice and bow: A, A, B2, B2;
      Bow solo (eight repetitions).

*Bow technique: The second note in each duplet is damped with the left forefinger. Variant accentuation occasionally suggests $3/4 + 2/4 + 3/4$ barring of the phrase. In addition to the selectively resonated harmonics which have been indicated, other harmonics (up to the 5th partial) are faintly audible.

10. Trench-digging song Southern Natal style (recorded in Smith Street, Durban, 1964).

Example 19   *We, Majola*

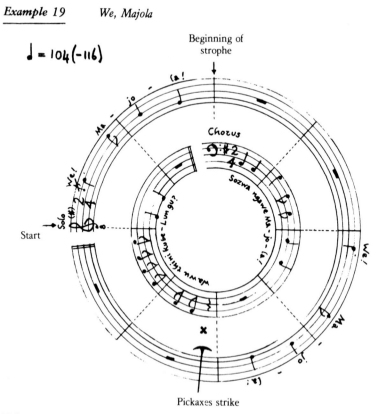

Leader: Hey, Majola!
Chorus: We shall hear about you, Majola!
What have you been saying to the Europeans?

11. A Swazi *sibhimbi* (Royal wedding dance-song) as sung by princes and princesses at Lobamba, 1964 (recorded by Rycroft, 1968). Pitch rises progressively during performance.

Example 20   Swazi *sibhimbi* anthem. *Ngayizal' indvodzana*

(Continued overleaf)

337

*Variant

Solo: Ngayizal' indvodzana, ngawuzal' umbango! Ngawabon' emadvodza.
Ya — ! Ngizal' indvodzana, ngawuzal' umbango! Idla 'madvodza!
Ya-o! Maye! Ingwe idla 'madvodza! Ya-o! Ingwe, ingwe, ingwe!

Chorus: Ya-i-a-o! Idla 'madvodza! A-yá-o-ye! Ingwe yabo!
Ingwe! Idla 'madvodza! Ya-o! Ingwe, ingwe! Ya!

Translation:

Solo: I bore a son; I begat a family feud!
I saw the men (i.e. those who met to discuss my child, born before
payment of my bride-price);
The leopard devours men (i.e the king takes the cattle of commoners)

Chorus: The leopard devours men! Leopard of theirs!

12. King Shaka's Royal dance-song: *Ingoma kaShaka,* as sung by Princess Magogo and Chief M.G. Buthelezi, 1964.

Example 21   *'Sibhunkuli samadoda*

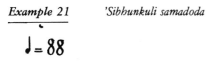

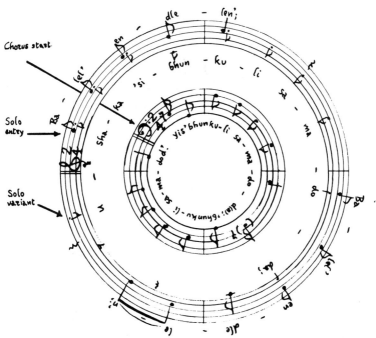

Chorus: He is the one who girds up the loins of men!
Solo: They sleep out in the wilds!
        Shaka is the one who girds up men's loins.

13. Zulu part-song with *ugubhu* musical bow accompaniment, as sung by Princess Magogo, with her son and grandchildren, 1964 (recorded by Rycroft, 1970).

Example 22   *Siqom' abant' abahle*

$\int = 192(-200)$

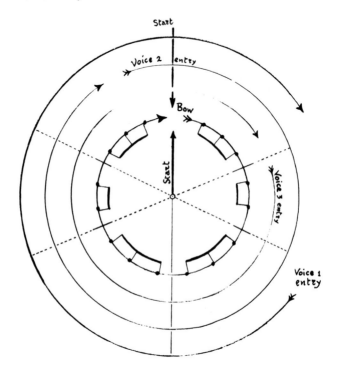

Voice 1: Ngizaulimpay'za ng'lishon' sephi na mam'?
(I shall go wandering, but where will the sun set for me, mother?)

Voice 2: Siqom' abant' abahle; siqom' amageza!
(We choose good-looking lovers; we court the handsome ones!)
Intomb' ebengiyithanda yinqam'la-juqu!
(The girl I would love is one who cuts things short!)

Voice 3: Yithathe mfan' yemuka!
(Take her, boy, she is escaping!)

14. Extract from the ancient Zulu Victory Song: *Uhawu,* from solo version, as rendered by Princess Magogo, 1964. The text contains no actual words.

Example 23　　　*Uhawu*

15. A Swazi women's communal tilling song, as sung by princes and princesses at Lobamba, 1964 (recorded by Rycroft, 1968).

Example 24   *Kulezon taba*

Transposed a Major Third higher (approx.)

Nga ba-ga-na ja-ha; Baſ tsa - tsa ſa-jo yi - na e - Man

Nji! 'Zi - nta ba! Nji! Nye - nye!

kai - a - na; Mi - ne sen-go-na-ke - le.

Nye - nye! Nye - nye! Nye - nye! 'Zint aba!

Variant renderings

- ſwa ye ſa - kha - ſeſwa; Mi-ne...

Mi-ne sen-go - na

Solo: Over those distant hills, catch the sun you crave before it sets!
         I am now just a common song (i.e. an object of ridicule)!
         Over yonder hills! You who are bewailed!
         I was betrothed to "them", O young man!
         "They" took him — he signed his work contract at Mankaiana;
         Now I am ruined!

Chorus: Nye-nye! O hills! Nji!

16. Diagrams showing a common tuning for the Zulu *ugubhu* musical bow (funda-mentals, and selectively resonated partials 3, 4 and 5), and the relation of vocal notes to bow 'roots' in several songs.

Example 25

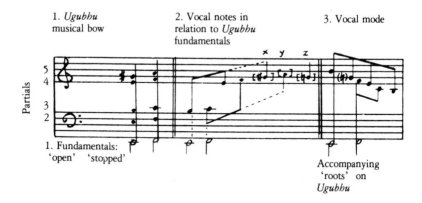

17. Diagrams showing commonest tunings for Zulu *umakhweyana* and Swazi *makhweyane* musical bows, and vocal modes used in several songs, in relation to bow 'roots'.

Example 26

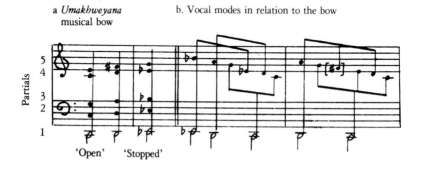

VI. MUSIC OF THE PEDI (NORTHERN SOTHO)
1. Pedi music in its social setting
  a. The annual cycle of musical activities
  b. Music and an individual's life cycle
  c. Formal traditional education and marriage
2. Categories of Pedi music
  a. Solo song
  b. Instrumental solo
  c. Solo song with instrumental accompaniment
  d. Song in ensemble
  e. Song and dance with instrumental accompaniment
  f. Instrumental ensemble
3. General features of Pedi music
4. Additional notes on Pedi instruments

1. Pedi music in its social setting
The habitat of the Northern Sotho peoples, the Pedi, Tau, Koni, Kwena and Roka, is the vast Sekhukhuneland valley in the Northern Transvaal and the areas which radiate out from it. The Pedi established a supremacy, hence the collective nomenclature by which these tribes became known. Of Sotho origin, they are classified as Northern Sotho to differentiate them from the Southern Sotho of the O.F.S. and Lesotho, and from the Tswana of Botswana and the W. Transvaal and N.W. Cape. In surveying Pedi musical practices, one has to regard their music not as an isolated cultural entity but as an integral part of their whole pattern of living, both social and ceremonial.

a. The annual cycle of musical activities
The Pedi accompany every phase of this orbit with song, which is interwoven into the fabric of their life. The Pedi year is heralded by the first sighting of the lustrous Southern Canopus star which the Pedi know as *naka*. The day following, tribal doctors throw their bones. Should the year's forecast be unpropitious, the chief orders small girls to draw water for a special brew which boys, brandishing long pliant sticks, anoint on doorways and with which they medicate fields to divert malevolent influences. Both the girls and the boys have their respective single-phrase repetitive ditties. When meaningful, the words are usually allied to the occupation of the moment, e.g. *Nke le sware kala* (hold the branch). When apparently meaningless, such as *Mawelele, wee* or *Shae makarakara,* they are mainly onomatopoeic, the essential being a rhythmic correlation with the action of the feet. — The agricultural activities of the Pedi are not based on calendar months but depend on the arrival of rain. If the rains are late, the ploughing and planting is correspondingly so. Drastic measures are however taken, each with its own song repertoire, should drought prevail. Following a basically similar procedure, the magical efficiency of the vital ingredients of the tribal rainpot is restored, the land is doctored, adverse influences are eradicated, rain-fires are lit to attract the clouds, intercession is made to tribal ancestors and spirits whose wrath is perhaps responsible, rainmakers whose powers are renowned are called upon and their chief is implored in song to come to his people's aid: *O rrare-re nyaka pula ya nape kgosi* (We ask you again, Chief, to give us rain). When rain does fall it is greeted by animated traditional rain-songs, of which

there are many, e.g. *Pula e nele Boroka,* (Rain has fallen at Boroka), *Ga-gabagaba-pula!* (the sound of falling rain). — A period of dawn-to-dusk agricultural activity follows the advent of the rain. After the men have ploughed, the women repair to the fields early in the day, making considerable headway before the heat becomes unpleasant. Meals are brought out to the fields by women appointed to cook. A Pedi chief or a private individual can have his lands worked in no time at all by inviting all those interested to "till the ground with beer", that is, he provides a quantity of beer to quench the thirst and gives a reward of meat at the completion of the allotted task. For these work-parties (*letsema*) all bring their own hoes. They hoe together in long rows: lift, strike, rest, their singing sets the pace and maintains harmony of action, while promoting social atmosphere and *esprit-de-corps.* A shrill trill on a high note, executed by one of the women, periodically inspires the others to renewed efforts. With gay beads and brightly coloured turbans offsetting blue-grey denim smocklike dresses, they are a picturesque sight, and their songs emanate from the work on hand: *Bo-mme ba-lema kgole* (Our mothers plough very far . . . the frog sings rain.). — In song, diligent workers are praised and lazy ones berated: *Bobohadi ba re "U a leme"* (My people-in-law say "I am lazy"); *Meriti ge o bona re reta matjema* (We praise hard workers). — In January, when the first crops have ripened, the year is "bitten in" before any person is permitted to partake of the green maize or vegetables from their gardens. *Chide,* a type of anti-ill-effect medicinal preparation, is distributed from the headkraal to be cooked with a vegetable, usually pumpkin (*letwatse*). In accordance with the Pedi saying, *Kosa e tswa mosate batseta re latela* (the song of the dance comes from the head-kraal), the Chief's family eats and the people follow suit. The following day is a proclaimed tribal holiday with the Chief greeted and praised in a song, *Mmakgwane.* — Once the main crops of sorghum, millet, or maize have been reaped and stacked on wooden platforms (or heaped into enormous funnel-like mounted baskets erected behind the homesteads, or even placed in huge grain-baskets buried in the cattle-kraal), the long work hours resolve themselves into a daily round of domestic duties for the women, often performed communally, accompanied by songs, while the men ply their crafts. In convivial mood, in the evenings and at the weekends, songs rise round pots of beer prepared in turn by the various homes. — The close of the Pedi agricultural year is marked by a harvest celebration, a time of revelry, eating, drinking, singing and dancing. The Chief is again praised (*mogobo*) for leading his tribe yet another year, and often not only his praises are sung but those of past chiefs: *Bogologolo bya Mamabolo* (Long, long ago the Mamabolo people) *ba dutje Byatladi ba dutji ga Kopi* (lived at Byatladi, they lived at Kopi). *Wena kgoshi Sello koana tje ke tja gago* (You, Chief Sello, these lambs are yours), *O di hlokomele di duleka kgotso* (look well after them, let them live in peace). — These are occasions on which the past and the exploits and deeds of tribal ancestors will be recounted by the tribal bard in a recitative style with a male chorus in a slow, strongly marked rhythm. The elderly women will also reminisce in song, with narrations of long ago when young warriors returned victorious from conquering their enemies, or mothers and wives mourned those who would never return. *Thabelana Bagale!* (Welcome the brave!) *Sengolo-ngolo batho ba ile kae?* (Oh, the quiet, where are the people?)

b. Music and an individual's life-cycle
From birth, every phase of a Pedi child's life is accompanied by music, singing and dancing. It is customary for the Pedi woman's first child to be born at her "maiden"

home and for subsequent births to take place at her married home, i.e. that of her in-laws. Ten days after the event a feast is held by the baby's namesake. Presents are given to the new-born infant and, amid singing and dancing, the new life is ushered in. — In its earliest years a child is soothed by the lullabies of the mother or a daughter of the household: *Ngwana wa bo-mma homola!* (My mother's child, keep quiet!) *Wa le la ngwana Mme* (My mother's child is crying). — It is a familiar sight to see a Pedi toddler on the outside of a circle of dancers, stamping his feet and twisting his body in imitation of the performers, or la-la-ing a tune with the odd word here and there. Pedi children grow up in a musical atmosphere which they cannot help but absorb. As a result, songs feature in almost every adolescent activity. At an early age Pedi boys begin to look after the calves at home. Later they take over the job of herding their fathers' sheep, goats and cattle. An early morning task is to water the animals and to milk the cows. This will be done to song, *Sjwara-sjwara-sjwara,* or a similarly expressive phrase, recurring as the milk flows and often accompanied by improvised assessments of the cow's behaviour set to the usual "milking" tune. — When they are out herding Pedi boys have many songs, some about the dreaded consequences of cattle straying into cultivated fields and the punishment that will be meted out: *Basumanyana, Basumanyana, ba bone phudi tsa esho?* (Small boys, small boys, have you seen our goats?). *Tsike,* stabbing imaginary "aloe leaf" cattle (*dikgopha*) with thorn "spears" (*motako*), is a favourite singing game of theirs. Much of their time out in the fields is also spent hunting field mice, which are lulled by song so that the boys may close in quietly and pounce, and trapping hares and other small animals and birds. — *Kuru we Nthsare,* (Come, please, Nthsare), *Nthsare a bo-dikilana,* (Nthsare of the gizzard people), *Se apara matankana* (dressed up in tatters). *Diboko si tsiwe, Nthsare* (Here are worms, Nthsare), *Mpotse xe o sa di rate* (tell me if you don't want them), *Keiphele Manthlekwa* (so that I can give them to the Manthlekwa (bird)). — These are cooked on an open fire, and in Sekhukhuneland the boys firmly believe that unless they sing *Ka fehla mollo, Ke ya le kgwale gae* (I drilled the fire . . . I shall carry the partridge home) the fire-sticks will not co-operate to produce a spark. — The action games of smaller children and girls are invariably accompanied by singing. For *makapa-makapa* they sit in a circle beating stones on the ground. They pass them round, and those that fumble and drop theirs are "out". Their song (translated) is: *Makapa – makapa* (the stone goes past); *Makapa – makapa* (the stone is going to stay here); *Makapa – makapa* (the stone is yours); *Makapa – makapa* (take it and be quick about it) (ex. 33, p. 380). — A moonlight game loved by Pedi teenagers is *liketa* or follow-my-leader, with boys and girls alternating in line and singing as they sway in imitation of the leader. Another game is *Kgetha kgarebe.* Boys and girls range themselves on opposite sides of a circle; girls break from the ranks to choose themselves a boy, and dance hopping, skipping steps in the centre, arms twined round each other's waists. Singing rises to a crescendo as the choice is made. On moonlit evenings, teenagers congregate to sing and dance through the night. Theirs are not elaborate vocal compositions but spontaneous songs made up from a single word, e.g. *Mmamasianoka* (the secretary bird), a catch phrase, e.g. *Dikgaka di a fata di a ye tshwenya* (Guinea fowl are scratching), or vocal play on some object that has taken their fancy, e.g. *Pompela, pompela re e kele* (Train . . . let us go). With natural musical creative ability one girl will sing a phrase, setting it to a simple, four-note tune. When repeated, a few more will join in, experimenting with one rhythm, and then another. Gradually others will add their quota, alto, tenor, bass, until a new song is being sung in 4-part harmony. It will consist only of a few notes, those that give most resonance, in the middle register, e.g. *E flat, F, A flat,* and the harmony will move in basic chords. The whole is sung, after a few trial runs, with freedom.

c. Formal, traditional education and marriage

As Pedi boys and girls are prepared for the transition from one stage of their lives to another, inducted to take their place as fully-fledged members of their tribal community, their instruction in both puberty and initiation ceremonies is largely through the medium of song. — The initiation of the boys involves two distinct ceremonies: the *bodika* (or *koma*) and the *bogwera* are both held in the winter months, a year apart, the *bodika* being held in the mountains and the *bokwera* at an enclosure at the headman's home or in veld huts. Formerly of three months' duration, today they are curtailed to fit into a school holiday period. The *phalafala* horn (see plate 1) summons the *bodika* novices (*badikana*); the sound of the *phalafala,* sharp blasts of the *makoditsane* or *phatola* (flute of the men – see plate 2) and a drum tattoo accompany their single file procession into the mountains. The actual circumcision is dominated by the song of men: *Tshikhi-tshikhi ga mufaga, khove jia* (Sever, sever with the knife, let the fish take). In Sekhukhuneland, once circumcised, the novices listen to the song of the young men (*mediti*): *Kgau, Madikana!* (Follow me, you initiates!) *Madika, le be le!* (Initiates, listen!) *Le bé le nkoago* (Listen and hear me,) *Tshoto maregere!* (You who are our children!) *Ke sishu sa bo noko* (The grisly gland) *Madipa, kudupa* (is only a festering sore of the loins). — Their days are spent hunting and wood-carving; in the early mornings and evenings at the circumcision lodge they receive instruction and learn formulae in the form of *Koma* songs, among them the song of the salt and the song of the lightning which contain the laws of the school. These are transmitted by imitative and repetitive methods in the form of solo and chorus, the lead taken by the master of the school (*rabadia*) or a graduate (*moditi*) with the harsh, throaty singing of the novices in 4th/5th, 2-part (tenor-bass) "harmony". The *bogwera* is characterised by the whistling language of the dancers (*bagwera*), who wear their grass costumes as they dance each morning and evening. A third initiation is practised only by the baGanawa, called *komana*. It consists of tattooing the face and revealing certain tribal secrets in connection with the *komana* drums and flutes of the ancestors. — Two rituals signify the nearing of completion of the *bogwera* school: the presence of alternating fires to denote the death of childhood ignorance and the kindling of the wisdom of manhood, and the elephant ritual whereby the young men's bodies are painted in zebra fashion with ash. And they remain with their hands raised above their heads until their mothers each contribute a basket of grain to the graduates for a "welcome home" reception. On this occasion their farewell song (*matsha*) is: *Re hlaba tlou ka diloka* (We stab the elephant with assegais); *marope re tloxa re hlaba dithaka* (make friends wherever you go). — With hair shaven, bodies clean, and arrayed in traditional dress, they will march triumphantly to the royal village as men (*banna*). — A Pedi girl is known as *lethumasa* before initiation, as *ngwale* during initiation, as *mothepa* after being initiated, and as *mosadi* when she is married. The *byale* (or *koma*) girls' initiation is of a year's duration, a month of which is spent in the mountains with the rasping *mosupiane* drum continuously warning off any who might approach. The girls return from their mountain retreat with facial incisions, smeared red with ochre, wearing blanket skirts and carrying grass mats which are quickly unfolded to counter prying eyes. Much in the nature of a fertility cult, with the

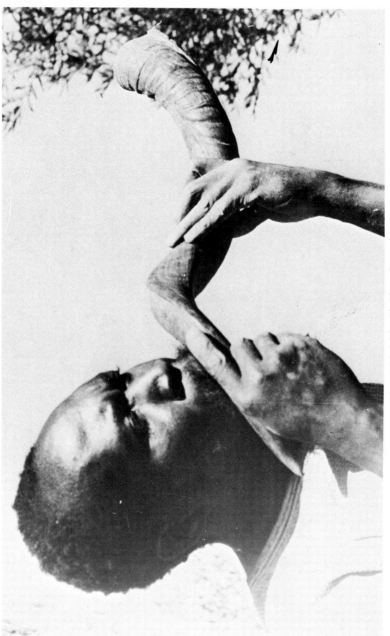

Plate 1. Phalafala, side-blown horn.

Plate 2. Phatola, wooden signal whistle.

days spent working in the Chief's fields, the mornings and evenings find the girls in their specially erected grass-enclosure, near the royal village, being prepared for aspects of marriage and its domestic and marital demands, mainly by means of song and mime. — All initiation schools are concluded by a feast of honour. After this, young women are acknowledged as having attained marriageable status and the songs sung in welcome by the women are in this vein: *Aga gosele* (Yes, it has dawned). — Pedi betrothal can evolve from the *sego* (calabash or watercup) formality in the case of an early agreement by parents regarding the nature of their son/daughter's future. This is an inoffensive way of plumbing the situation, with the boy arriving at the girl's home and asking for a drink of water, singing: *Mphisana, mphe mphemetse ke nwe kenwe ka lefiso* (Mphisana, give me water in a calabash to drink). Should she bring it herself, this is a favourable omen. The boy, on the other hand, can either take a mouthful or spit it on the fence to show his feelings in the matter. — Whether or not the *sego* test is applied, however, the Pedi marriage system basically involves agreement by the fathers of the two parties concerned. Every stage of the lengthy bride-price (*lenyalo*) negotiation between the two households has songs associated with it, e.g.: *Agee ngwana wa rena o yaya kemavumo a kgomo* (Alas, our child is going; we've accepted the cattle). The wedding itself, usually scheduled for a weekend, is a social event which is eagerly looked forward to. It has its further quota of wedding songs e.g. when the guests enter the bride's home they sing: *A re koko koko, re a kokota re re re buleleng* (When we knock, we knock; open for us.). Supporting the groom, who pretends to be drunk, the bride is lauded: *E le ngwetsi ya rena e le mosadi wa rena e le moSotho mphela* (Our bride is a proper Sotho). In song she is advised: *Nke le tshware kara mmapula ngwana nka* (Get hold of the tree-branch, my daughter . . . i.e. stick to your husband). Even after marriage a periodic exchange of gifts maintains the good relationship established between the two homes. Bringing their pots of beer, the party of women ululate. Setting them down they sing in anticipation of the meal that will be set before them in recognition of their gift: *Mushiji khi le gi* (I don't eat blackjacks), *y'o sheva ha nama* (I'm going to have meat as a relish). — In song, the Pedi openly reveal details of their private and marital lives, impotency, importunate women and unseemly behaviour, without transgressing any sense of propriety: *Ele we taba di botha* (Things are difficult), *tabaka, mathari bo u ke yisane* (young women, come to my rescue), *le nkadime madibana e* (and lend me *madibana* (a man)) *hare ka masa a boe* (to come back at dawn). *Ke rekile mokokolome wa hloka le pheo* (I've got a cock with no feathers (impotent man)). — A clay pot is dashed to pieces at a grave side. There is general lamentation but no singing or dancing. Once death has made its presence felt, everything is said to be "dark". A year of tribal mourning follows the death of a chief or important member of a Pedi royal family. During this time no official communal singing or dancing is allowed. The drums are "black" and the instruments have their "faces" to the ground. A feast is needed to reopen the drums. This often takes the form of a major tribal celebration with the installation of a new chief. The tribal fire will be extinguished and rekindled to usher in a new era. Amid the general jubilation songs abound.

2. Categories of Pedi music

a. Solo song

The word *-ipinela* means "to sing for oneself". This applies to a song which accompanies milking, the song which a child sings as he bewitches the lands, the song sung by a woman as she pounds maize with her long heavy stamper in the wooden mortar, the song of a Pedi man as he digs in his garden or busies himself with basketmaking or some other craft. It consists of a single phrase repeated *ad infinitum,* allied to the job on hand, making it congenial rather than onerous, with an occasional tonal lift following the intake of breath. A lullaby (*kuruwetso*), however, has several melodious phrases which form a much more complete *kopelo/kosa* (song).

b. Instrumental solo

A solo instrumentalist *(moletsi)* among the Pedi is the girl or woman who plays the *lekope* or *setolotolo* (the equivalent of the Jew's harp – see fig. 3, p. 353) while out walking, or the little boy who amuses himself blowing the one note of the reed flute *(naka ya lethalaka* – see plate 3, p. 354) which he has cut and fashioned himself. Found played throughout baPedi, today, by girls and young women is also the *dipela (mbira* – see plate 4, p. 355), the metal "keys" arranged basically to follow the tone quality of the four voices. It has a counterpart in the zither or auto harp *(harepa* – see plate 5, p. 356), played by men, which has wire strings stretching from nail tuning-pegs at the sides across metal bridges, on a wooden soundboard. Solo herding instruments, which used to be the prerogative of the men but are now played by boys, are the *sekgapa* (see plate 6a, p. 357), the *botsorwane* or *segobogobo* (see plate 7, p. 359) and the *lesiba* or *kwadi* (see plate 8, p. 360). The *sekgapa,* literally meaning "calabash", consists of a wooden hunting bow with an open calabash resonator attached near the lower end of the bow stave, or in the centre, with the string tied into two segments. Held vertically, the segments are struck with a firm piece of grass in a quick sharp action to yield two fundamental tones. Further fundamental tones are obtained by pressing the knuckle of the hand holding the instrument against the string. The intervals between these tones vary with the way in which the instrument is made and the string tensed. The one-string fiddle (*botsorwane*) rests on the shoulder and is played with a small ox-tail friction bow. Either the open string is used or two fundamentals, a tone apart, can be produced, each with its own harmonic series. By choosing certain parts of the string to play on, the choice of harmonic overtones is also varied. Saliva or honey is put both on the hair of the bow and the string in lieu of resin, and the string itself can also be roughened with sand. A little resin is usually found ready for use on the wooden shaft near the peg. The *lesiba* consists of a long, slightly-curved piece of wood with a quill attached to one end of a string of sinew which is at either end of the "bow". The string is vibrated by expiration and suction on the quill. Two tones are produced: a laryngeal "pedal" as the air is breathed out, and a melody note as the air is sucked in. — The traditional drum plays a solo role at certain stages of initiation. Always a solo instrument, however, the *moshupiane* of the girls' *byale* initiation, a pot-like friction drum, emits a weird, "roaring" sound when the drumhead is rubbed (counter-clockwise) with stalks of sorghum. — Similarly, the "flute of the ancestors" is heard at initiations and on any tribal occasion of note. The vertical wooden flute known as *mokudietane* or *phatola* (see plate 2, p. 350), formerly the property of a Pedi warrior, is sounded occasionally when boys are escorted up the mountains, or at an important tribal feast to give the dancers courage. The far-reaching note of the *phalafala* horn (see plate 1, p. 349) is heard in similar fashion. An uninitiated boy (*masoboro*) also has a bone flute, the *lengwane,* essentially his own, which is sounded by blowing across the embouchure hole. In Sekhukhuneland groups of boys deliberately challenge each other with these flutes, and a duel of blowing develops between two parties as they advance

Figure 3   *Lekope,* musical bow.

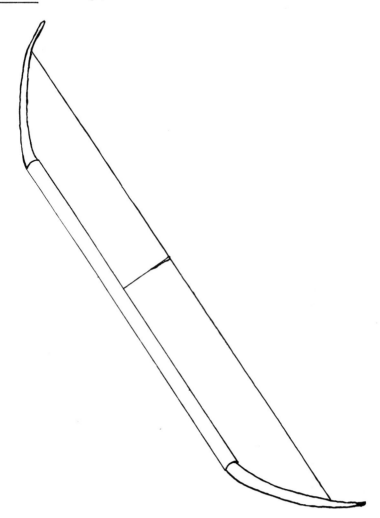

on each other. This is regarded as swearing, and the "insults" of the leaders' flutes give the cue for a stick-fight (see plate 18, p. 443).

c. Solo song with instrumental accompaniment
The *mbira (dipela* – see plate 4, p. 355) might accompany a waling song, the *sekgapa* bow (see plate 6b, p. 358) and the *botsorwane* (one-string fiddle – see plate 7, p. 359) might be heard supplying the accompaniment for a song sung to soothe the cattle as

Plate 3. Naka ya letblaka, reed pipe.

Plate 4. Dipela, mbira.

Plate 5. Harepa, zither.

Plate 6a. Sekgapa, musical bow with calabash resonator.

Plate 6b. Sekgapa, bow without resonator.

Plate 7. Botsorwane, one-string fiddle.

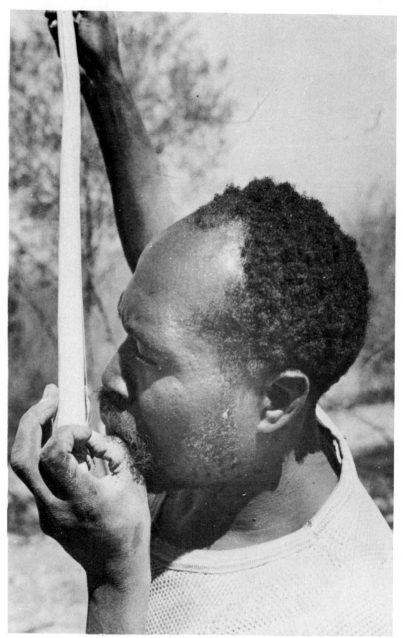

Plate 8. Lesiba, stringed wind instrument – the *gora*.

they graze. The Pedi *mbira* consists of about 11 metal tongues secured in position under and over 2 metal bar "bridges" on to a small wooden frame about the size of an exercise book. The lengths of the tongues are in accordance with the wishes of the maker and yield a note series to which he is partial. Usually it subscribes to a basic soprano – alto – tenor – bass tonal range. The player will push the tongues backwards or forwards to produce the notes he desires. The instrument is held in both hands with the thumbs free to strike the tongues at their free ends. A tin is often suspended near the soundboard, or the whole instrument placed in a tin (which might even have an array of bottle-tops for additional percussive effect) to amplify the tinkling sounds normally produced. Tones produced by two 10-note *dipela* are, for example, from left to right on the instrument (see ex. 27 a, b).

Example 27 a & b

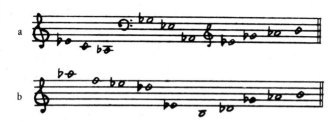

a

b

d. Singing in ensemble

After an animal has been slaughtered at a wedding, men gather to soften the skin, which will be used as a kaross in the winter. They squat in a circle, the skin in the middle, singing as they work, and periodically passing the skin around from one to the other. The theme of this type of song is always interrupted at regular intervals by a word or phrase, often onomatopoeic, e.g. *"sjwa-sjwa-sjwa-sjwa"*, sung by the men in chorus to denote the repetitive muscular movement executed at this juncture. For the rest, the rhythm usually matches the action of the hands, with a melody of four or five notes rendered by solo and chorus, the usual form of Pedi singing. — April–May are the months in which the main crops are harvested. In the maize fields the women walk between the rows picking off the cobs, and cutting off the stalk-tops with their sickles. Back at their homes de-cobbing and threshing is done communally. The maize-pips are rubbed off the cobs with a few brisk movements. The husks are loosened as the corn is threshed on a specially constructed, dung-smeared piece of ground just outside the homestead. Each woman has her own grinding stone but they often prefer to congregate at the village where, with the labour of years, numerous little hollows have been worn in a huge flat stone. Here they kneel, early in the morning or late in the afternoon. Commencing at one side of the hollow they throw some grain down on the rock and then pound it with flat stones, held in both hands, gradually working their way down the rounded depression, the composition of the grain becoming finer and finer and the thud-thudding more and more sharp until the end of the hollow is reached. With a quick, expert sweep of the hand, the flour is pushed to one side and the process repeated. — From the end of February to early April, when the ground beneath the Marula trees is covered with the golden fruit, the women gather in groups in the shade to make beer. In these activities while one woman leads, the others sing together (*-akgola*) in chorus, keeping pace with their hand-movements. These songs contain the local gossip and provide an opportunity for the women to air their views, safe from male retribution: *Agee, Tumedi, saka letlo swa mosate* (You, Tumedi, you'll burn at the chief's kraal). Unaccompanied responsorial singing is also found in the songs of the men round the fire in the evening, and in the women's memory-testing games like *mma-nthadile-a-tsela* (the one who leads the way). After the evening meal the older women keep the children busy with story-telling; the young join in with a ritual response or a choral interpolation on cue as the story unfolds. The tales usually have a moral ending so that the children receive much of their training in this way.

e. Song and dance with instrumental accompaniment

In 1874 Endemann, a German missionary working among the Pedi commented on the fact that their dancing is always accompanied by choral singing (K. Endemann: Mittheilungen über die Sotho-Neger, *Zeitschrift für Ethnologie* VI, 1874). The Pedi word for "singing", *-bina*, has its origin in singing and dancing praise-songs to the tribal totem; *-binela* is associated with singing and dancing for joy. Both *-tila* and *-phepela* are used when dancing and singing at a wedding, with a stick held aloft to express joy to the newly-married couple. Singing and dancing are always associated, and there is one who is responsible for leading (*-gobela*). He is the dance-leader and is known as *sefoko* or *sephoko* (this refers to a type of ostrich-feather headdress formerly worn by him). *Kgeleke* can refer to a good dancer or singer. Traditional wooden drums (*meropa*), and today, their tin substitutes, are used to accompany all singing and dancing. — In 1874, Endemann wrote: "Popular entertainment is especially the dance. The dancers face each other in rows, stamp their feet, hop about and make various body movements, all to the rhythm given by the feet, the clapping, the song or the drums". Women, who are the chief exponents of their percussion instruments, play the *meropa* (see plate 9, p. 363) with a sharp staccato action of the tips of the fingers, palm or heel of the hand, or in the case of their large wooden "timpani" bowl-type drums with a stick with a flattened beating end. Each dance has its own tempo. The rhythms of the dances do not, however, vary considerably. It is within the drum ensemble that the beats, each distinct one from the other, fuse into a complex cross-rhythmic whole. The pressure exerted by the fingers alters the tone quality at will. The Pedi, furthermore, build their drums in sets to correspond to the four voices; although not consciously tuned, a sub-conscious pitch sense is satisfied. In inclement weather a fire will be made to tighten the drum-skin, or wads of a rubbery substance are fixed to the drum-head to deepen the tone. In the puberty ceremony (*bokgarebe*) the women gather nightly at the hut of seclusion to sing and dance to the steady beat of the *moropa* drum. During the entire initiation of the girls, different patterns of rhythm convey certain specific meanings, and the drum accompanies the *byale* singing both morning and evening. Leg rattles (*thlwahlwadi*) made from the cocoons of worms (see plate 10, p. 364) and *mathotse* made from the fruit of the *mathotse* tree (see plate 11, p. 365) with fine seeds or pebbles inserted, are strung on thongs and twined round the calf or ankle. They supply a pleasant "shoo-shoo" accompaniment to the foot movements of the dances. Hand rattles (*ditshela* – see plate 12, p. 366) supply additional rhythmic accompaniments to singing and dancing. Tambourine-like hand drums (*mantshomane* – see plate 13, p. 368 and fig. 5, p. 385) and rattles provide the standard form of accompaniment for the hectic dancing of the *malopo* doctor and the

Plate 9. Meropa drums.

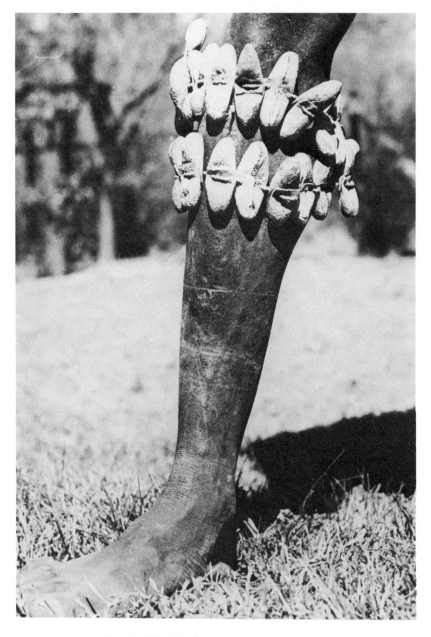

Plate 10. Thlwahlwadi, leg rattles made from cocoons.

Plate 11. Mathotse, leg rattles made from fruits.

Plate 12. Ditshela, hand rattle.

"possessed", to urge the spirits either to leave or enter the patient's body. Women flock to *malopo* gatherings on moonlit nights, and form the singing-clapping chorus: *Ruri ka mmaga MaSekana, moja nna a ye Bophoka a hlabje ditshonokela* (Verily, by your mother, MaSekana, one who attacks me must go to Bophoka and get strengthened with medicine). They regard it all very much as a social entertainment.

f. Instrumental ensemble

The best known traditional Pedi instrumental ensemble is that of the *kiba* drum and flute band (*dinaka* – see plate 3, p. 354). In the past, transverse reed flutes (*nai* – see plate 14, p. 369) were also played in sets (*mothaba*) of melody and harmony pipes with varying numbers of finger-holes. Nearly every Pedi village possesses a drum and flute ensemble of 12 to 30 players which can be hired to entertain. The dance sequence in vogue, is known as *kiba* (formerly as the *tibu/thipu*) and consists of 4 associated tunes: 1. *Monti* (dancer) 2. *Lerago* (buttocks) or *Fesa – Pesa* (verse) 3. *Kiba* (beat) 4. *Legowa* (Whites), or *Madikoti*, or *Mogobo*, or *Dinope – Dinotse* (bees), or *Dikoloi* (wagons), or *Mmope* (a heap), or *Makomane*. — Although heard by Endemann as early as 1874 and described by him as "martial marches played by drums to the accompaniment of shrill pipes – made of reed, and hollow, each with a different note and combining in a type of pan pipes", this ensemble is claimed to be an importation of the Venda reed flute ensemble. — The number of pipe players in a Pedi band depends on the number the tribe regards as a set (*mothaba*). The bands conform, numerically, either to the number in the set or multiples of it. The maker of the pipes begins with the principal pipe (*phalola* or *tsusi*) and cuts each piece of reed until he is satisfied with its pitch. Today, lengths of metal tubing, their ends beaten flat to provide stopped pipes, are matched in length and bore to an existing set as easily obtained substitutes. — Each pipe produces one note. The player grips his flute in the palm of the hand, resting thumb and first finger against the chin to steady it. The open end of the flute is placed against the lower lip with the tongue, noticeably depressed, touching it. The player blows over the top of the flute with an audible escape of breath. The free hand cupped over the ear increases his definition of the sound he produces. — The Pedi pipe melody can be heard in many Pedi festive songs, from which it must have emanated. These melodies are fixed. Through assiduous weekly practice each flautist learns his part. The harmonies arise as a concomitant to playing the tune at different tonal levels and from polyrhythmic coincidence. The performance commences with the flute leader (*malogwane* or *makokwana*) sounding his *phalola* and then each player sounding his flute as the tune arrives at his particular note in the 3–5 note, recurring phrase. Dancing with systematic foot stamping and a periodic forward shuffle, the flautists move slowly from block formation into a counter clockwise circle round the centrally positioned drums, acquiring added zest the longer the performance continues. The higher (and easier to sound) pipes retain their notes for approximately $1^1/_2$ beats until the player hears the succeeding note. This causes an overlap of sound. A lower-sounding (more difficult to play) pipe note is held for 2–3 beats which gives a type of sustained "pedal" effect. The flautists adhere strictly to the tempo of the drums in order to ensure their exact flute entry. The principal set carries the melody (see ex. 28a, p. 370), with their smaller (*lana*) and larger (*golo*) editions amplifying their notes as in an organ. It is evident that the players do not regard themselves as individual, independent units, but feel their notes as an intrinsic part of one revolving tonal pattern as a whole. There are, for example, different chordal

Plate 13. Mantshomane, tambourine.

Plate 14. Nai, transverse, three-holed reed flute.

Example 28 a

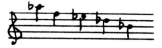

Example 28b

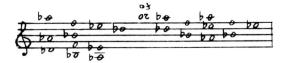

structures in two tunes (see ex. 28b). The *Kiba* tunes consist of different melodic re-arrangements of a single 3-5 note series. Their basic "hocket"-like structure was written down by Kirby (see ex. 29, p. 371). Pedi pipe harmonies are based on the intervals of the 8ve, 5th and 4th. The occurrence of other intervals is the result of a cracked pipe, an erratically or poorly sounded note, or coincidence, just as the tonal sound of discordant bells to which the reed-flute ensemble has been likened, is brought about by the subtle and complex interaction of the polyrhythmic structure on the harmonic interrelationship. — Peculiar to Sekhukhuneland, too, is a *lekope* ensemble. The *lekope* is a musical bow which has its string tied back in the centre on to the shaft and tensed to yield two fundamentals a fifth apart (see plate 3, p. 354). It is held horizontally, in line with the mouth, with the shaft placed just off centre between the lips but not touching them, so that the mouth-cavity acts as a resonator and generates harmonics. — This was the Pedi "love" bow without which no young man went courting. According to legend a certain father flatly refused to part with his daughter even after the bride-price had been fully paid. He only capitulated, worn out and weary, after being serenaded with this instrument, without halt, for days and nights on end by the prospective husband and his friend. Thereafter, success in love was associated by Pedi male suitors and girls alike with the ability to play this instrument well. In addition it was often charmed to ensure its success in love; anointed with a special medicine compounded from the first white flower of spring, the flesh of the "blind" mole, the flesh of the "pairing" doves and the sweetness of honey. Formerly a solo instrument, the bow is now used in ensemble. At Sekwati, for instance, six *lekope,* tuned in unison, made up an extraordinarily effective polyphonic combination.

3. General features of Pedi music

Pedi music was described by Endemann (in 1874) as "Verses made up at will by the singer; the lines torn apart sometimes or repeated over and over again. Sometimes two accompanying choirs, one starting with a low note and the second with a higher note, the solo starting while the choirs continue. When the solo singer pauses the choirs go on singing, a sort of inter-mezzo". — Pedi melody grew up in association with words, which have influenced the way in which it is constructed. The melodic

Example 29

outline has, to a large extent, evolved to conform with the speech-tone patterns of the language. The Pedi originally had only one word, *segalo,* which applied to all three elements, "accent", "pitch" and "tone", and another *tuma nnosi* to the "vowel sound". The predominating form of Pedi singing is responsorial, with no gap in the line of singing and the solo-chorus parts overlapping. A verse can take the form of a recitative-like spate of words, delivered at high speed, with the chorus maintaining a legato continuity. This is essentially a form used in the singing of praises by the Sotho peoples. More usually, however, while the refrain remains fixed in form, the sequence of episodes is treated with the utmost elasticity by the song-leader, who is not bound by the expressions used by the person from whom he/she learned the song. Much charm lies in the occasional introduction of elements which suit the immediate environment and in *ad libitum* improvisation. The Pedi love word imagery and have an acute sense of onomatopoeic sound together with the gift of eloquence. Song-leaders excel in these qualities. Words are chosen which allow the melodic outline to remain more or less constant. It is usual for the Pedi to sing one note to a syllable. However, at the end of a phrase, notably on a descending motif, they can be heard to sing more than one note on the last or last two syllables. Should the word-line of a phrase be lengthy, the singers also glide two syllables into one in the middle of the phrase. An extra note may also be interpolated, when necessary, into the middle of the phrase, maintaining the basic rhythm. Subtle variations of rhythms are legion. Scarcely any two phrases are sung in precisely the same manner, either rhythmically or melodically. In the melodic structure we thus do not find broad changes of melody but subtle variation within a repetitive (*maboeledi*) pattern. — The general outline of a Pedi traditional tune could be described as following the succession of the teeth of a ripsaw, the tendency being for the tune to start on a high pitch-platform and gradually work its way down with steep rises (not exceeding a 5th) and gentle slopes, from tension to rest. There is no key change in the course of the tune, but a distinct feeling of the tune hovering round a central pivot note. Broadly speaking, the music is pentatonic, with no interval smaller than a tone. The Pedi have no conscious or organised theory of music: their music-making is undivided, as if conceived "at one stroke". The polyphony arises as an accidental concomitant of the parallel singing of the melody at different tonal levels or of "subjects" and "counter-subjects" combined in a natural progression. The Pedi do, however, automatically feel a single tone as within an assumed chordal framework. In the Pedi vocabulary of old we already find words such as *-potla* – to sing low/bass, *moakgoli* – a harmoniser, *-saetsa* or *swele leleme* – to sing out of tune, which reveal the trend of their musical thinking. — Pedi music seems to have a free rhythmic basis. The complexities of the free rhythms of their singing, clapping and drumming in combination, dovetail into one another to produce a well-shaped whole. In duple/triple measure (*mosito*), this is coupled in Pedi thought with *-kiba* (to keep time with the foot in the dance), the tempo, in accordance with the Pedi language, being *allegretto* to *allegro* in all but their "classical" song-repertoire (i.e. of tribal historical significance). In these, however, the *andante* to *marcato/maestoso* chorus is offset by the *vivace* praises. — It must in conclusion, be remembered that the Pedi comprise twenty-five dialect groups. They have a saying: *Ngwana wa tadi o tsebja ka mereto* (Each bird is known by its own song). Certain work-songs and lullabies tend to be universally sung. But on the whole, there is a large measure of dissimilarity in song repertoires which, if anything, is in the present era being cultivated rather than allowed to fade away.

4. Additional notes on Pedi instruments

PLATE 1: The *phalafala* horn (also known as *phalaphala, lepatata* or *patata*). These antelope horns often have their ribbing pared away to leave a completely smooth exterior and an instrument lighter in weight. Blown through a lateral blow-hole, this was formerly an instrument of inter-tribal war, taken by the Pedi warriors to battle. It is still used today to summon the tribe, or at tribal gatherings to add prestige to the occasion and spur the dancers on to renewed efforts. It is also sounded while escorting initiates up into the mountains and as an alarm should anything untoward happen. It is blown at girls' initiation schools by a woman member of the chief's family, but otherwise sounded by men and considered to be a tribal instrument, with the chief or one of his headmen as its official owner. Tribal doctors, however, often possess a horn to "summon the rain'. The note of the Pedi horn is resonant and far reaching. It usually tends to waver, only very few players are able to hold a consistently full note. Before use, it is lubricated with water or beer.

PLATES 2 and 3: One of several *dinaka* (sing. *naka:* end-blown, stopped pipe – see plate 3, p. 354), *naka ya phatola* or *naka ya makoditsane* was made of wood and originally used in inter-tribal warfare. Its shrill signal-like notes sounded in jubilation when an enemy had been slain or victory won. It was the exclusive possession of the fully-fledged warrior and passed down from father to son. Today there are few such flutes still to be found. They are, however, still blown by a male escort of boy initiates on their way to the mountains or occasionally at a tribal feast to give the dancers additional strength and courage. The flute is of conical shape tapering slightly from upper to lower end. It is made from two hollowed-out blades of hard wood which form a tube, so closely applied as to almost fuse. The whole pipe is encased in the skin taken from the tail of a cow or leg of an antelope, pulled over while wet and, when dry, contracting to pull the two halves firmly together. This is covered with an elaborate design wrought in silver, copper or brass wire, or all three. This pipe will only produce the correct "piercing" sound after the wood has been moistened, usually with beer. Even then it is difficult to sound. It was formerly anointed by the doctor with special ingredients in keeping with the qualities desired in the warrior, i.e. the fat of the badger, celebrated for its toughness; the eagle, always in a position of power; the mamba, notoriously dangerous; young bees from the comb, with their power to sting. — Pedi doctors possess a number of pipes which they blow on certain occasions either to lend a dramatic touch to proceedings and to create a spine-chilling atmosphere with shrill blaṣts, or whose powers of persuasion they wish added to their magical incantations and entreaties. These usually consist of small natural animal horns, slung round the neck. Special medicine is placed in each and a feather inserted to lubricate and clean it. — There are also pipes (*sitlanjani*) through which, according to Pedi tribal belief, the ancestral spirits of royal lineage make known to the tribe their wants and will. During their initiation period, the mysteries of the pipes are one of the tribal secrets revealed to Pedi boys. The players are elderly tribesmen or a doctor, and the pipes are sounded at initiation ceremonies and on tribal occasions of note, in which the tribal ancestors would be expected to show a special interest. The pipe is made from two pieces of grooved wood/reed about 160 mm in length, tapering from approximately 40 mm at one end to 27 mm at the other. A thin vibrating sinew is fixed halfway down the inner tube and the whole pipe encased in a strip of skin. The sound is that of a weird "bird-whistling", a peculiar sound which is intended to fill all who hear it with awe.

PLATES 9 and 13: The traditional Pedi drum (*moropa*, plural *meropa*) has a wooden resonating shell, about 2 cm in thickness. Of varying size, it is shaped basically on the pattern of the Greek vase with a wide upper opening narrowing towards the base, closed only at the upper-end with a skin drum-head held in position by wooden pegs and thonging. For transport purposes there is often a protruding ear of wood carved as part of the shell. There are **two** distinct methods of playing these drums: (1) the woman player squats on the ground, encircles and steadies the drum with one arm, while striking the drum-head in a sharp *staccato* action with the tips of the fingers, palm or heel of the other hand, or steadies the drum against something and strikes the drum-head with both hands. (2) In the case of a drum of smaller dimension and more elongated shape, the player stands astride the drum, which is held in position by the legs, and beats the drumhèad with both hands. — The timpani-type traditional drum (in the right foreground of plate 9) is a bowl-shaped drum hollowed out of a single wooden block 60 to 90 cm in height, with its upper skin drum-head pegged into position. These drums are heavy and have, as part of the drum shell, wooden projections by which they are carried. Their beating stick has a broad, flat, rounded end. The tambourine-type drums (see plate 13) resemble their Western counterpart in all respects, but vary considerably in size. Usually beaten with a fairly long, thin stick, these instruments are seen and heard at dances of the possessed, where the spirits are either exorcised or welcomed. — There is a friction drum (*moshupiano*) which is pot-like and essentially associated with the girls' initiation ceremonies. By scraping the drum-head, in circular motion, with maize or sorghum stalks, a weird, screaming sound is emitted which the girl initiates believe to be the spirit of the hills. The men and boys are told it is a lion roaring. Primarily it is intended to warn off intruders from the initiation terrain. — Playing the drum is traditionally regarded by the Pedi as the prerogative of the women, unless in the all-male compounds at the mines, at boys' initiation schools or in the accompaniment of the men's reed-flute ensembles. The makers of the traditional drums, however, are men, skilled wood-carvers who have specialised in the art, now a dying industry.

PLATE 14: It used to be common to find groups of Pedi youngsters playing transverse reed-flutes (*nai*). These flutes, held transversely across the face in line with the mouth, consisted of naturally stopped reed pipes with an embouchure hole through which the flute was blown at the one end, and one, two or three finger-holes, spaced to suit the player's fingers, at the other. A combination of these flutes, e.g. three, one with one finger hole, one with two and one with three, yielded a series of notes and produced tunes and harmonies. There was also a double transverse flute with nodes at either end and centre, and mouth and fingerholes in both sections, which gave added "note" possibilities. The tone of these flutes depended on the maker, who would often cut and test very many reeds before being satisfied. Occasionally one finds this type of flute played in vertical position, but this is the modern penny-whistle influence. Among the Pedi, penny-whistle combos have mainly replaced the transverse reed groups. — Further information on Pedi instruments can be found in P.R. Kirby, *The musical instruments of the native races of South Africa* (1934) and in the present article by that author.

– Y.H.

VII. A NOTE ON THE MUSIC OF THE SOTHO

The chief characteristic which distinguishes the vocal music of the Sotho-speaking peoples from that of the Nguni (Zulu, Xhosa, Swazi, Ndebele, Tsonga), is the interpolation of the praise (*sereto*) within certain songs of tribal or historical import. The tempo of the Sotho-Tswana languages, moreover, is rapid in comparison to those of the Nguni group. The praise takes the form of a recitative-like spate of words extolling the virtues of an outstanding figure in Sotho history (e.g. Moshoeshoe, founder of the Sotho nation), or tracing a sequence of events of historical significance. It is occasionally recited against a background of song but more usually interrupts the singing. In deference to this rôle, the Sotho Praise Poet will always don a pyramid-shaped finely-plaited grass Sotho hat (*modianyewe*). The singing is essentially pentatonic and in solo-chorus form. While the chorus remains static, the solo is flexible, song-leaders being chosen for their ability with words. — The Sotho men have their songs, *mehobelo* (sing: *mohebelo*). It is their *mekorotlo* songs, however, belonging essentially to the regiments and the tribe, which include the praise. When singing, the men, in long khaki trousers and white shoes, form up in a long L-shaped line, stamping their feet in periodic rhythmic emphasis, at the same time bringing the knobkerry sticks, held aloft in the dance, down to the level of the body. The songs of the men are characterised by their deep bass setting, the Sotho ear loving a deep bass sound which he compares to the sound of thunder before the rain. A Sotho man who has a deep bass voice is very highly thought of. — The praise is also heard in the Sotho songs traditionally belonging to the women, i.e. the *mokgibo* or "knee" dance-song, the reciting done by one of the elderly women present. Kneeling on the ground, in semi-circular formation (this is standard for the women), the women sing in the basic solo-chorus manner, taking it in turn to do their most exhausting "knee" dance with its shaking of the breasts in deliberate up-, forward-, down-and-back movements, while periodically raising the knees and knocking them down on the ground. A high ululation (*modiatsane*) from this woman and then that one, sustains the dancers in their hectic efforts. The accompaniment to the song is hand-clapping. — Other Sotho song-types include the *diphotha*. This is the men's step-dance. For this they wear gumboots, knocking them together and slapping them with the hands in synchronised rhythm to various "step" movements executed to the rhythm of a lively concertina tune. The concertina is an instrument that Sotho men have taken to their hearts. Sometimes as he plays a man will let strings of unallied ideas follow each other in songs consisting of a 4 to 5 note melody with slight variations that may be required only by semantic tone structure. Occasionally, for example in the *lehahlaula* walking song, there will be more sequence of thought. Walking for miles, accompanying himself on his concertina, his long stride at strange variance with the speed of the language he is employing, a Sotho will describe in song the course and cause of his journey and elaborate on details of wayside interest. — A favourite pastime of Sotho boys is to lure field mice with song. The youths crouch on their haunches, in a circle to cut off an escape route, then lull the mice into a feeling of security with their solo-chorus singing while other youngsters busily forage in the grass and pounce on them. — Sotho girls, with a leader and chorus, have action/dancing songs accompanying simple foot movements. These they call *lialolo* and *metjekong*. Often some dance as others stand and clap in accompaniment. Cross-rhythm clapping is a feature of the lively *mokokopelo* dance-song of the women on festal occasions. — The circumcision of all Sotho boys takes place in seclusion near a mountain stream, with the period following spent in hunting guinea fowl and similar pursuits. In the throes of their preparation for manhood, the emphasis in the *lengae* (initiation) songs of the Sotho boys follows the pattern set in the songs of the men with a deep bass melodic line. In much the same way that Tswana men have come to regard the *serankure* one-string fiddle (see plate 7, p. 359 for the Pedi equivalent) as their own special instrument, so Sotho men are expected to acquit themselves well on the *lesiba* (lit. feather), which has become their national instrument. It is described in detail by Kirby in Chapter VIII of his study, *The musical instruments of the native races of South Africa (1934)*.

– Y.H.

VIII. NOTES ON THE MUSIC OF THE TSWANA

1. Music in society
2. Tswana musical concepts
3. Instrumental music
4. Examples
5. References

1. Music in society

The Tswana were among the first South African tribes upon which European influence was brought to bear, and many traditional songs have been replaced by mission songs. Where the former survive, indigenous harmony at the 8ve, 4th, and 5th is frequently found to be supplemented by 3rds and 6ths learned from school music (see ex. 30, p. 378). Tribal ritual keeps certain music alive, for, during a 1959 recording tour near Disaneng, Hugh Tracey noted that "a party of over sixty young men had just completed their period of isolation out in the veld . . . the singing was the best we experienced from any Tswana group".[1] — The Tswana classify their vocal music (*dipina*) according to its social function. Songs used during initiation ceremonies are called *moama* (see exs. 31 and 32, pp. 378, 379). In the boys' circumcision school (*bogwera*), such songs are taught to the initiates (*makatla*) by the overseer (*kake*) and his attendants (*bokgayane*), during dancing by the god-impersonator (*nape*). Further circumcision songs occur during the whipping dance (*segho*), the penultimate procession (*thalalagae*), and the final procession (*ditime*). The initiated male is then known as a *lekoloanyane*, and his family greet him with gifts of new clothing, a formality known as *alosa*. — In the girls' puberty school (*boyale*), the initiates (*bonwale*) sing as they don a special skin (*peeledi*) and perform a dance called *radikgaratlane*, during which a god-impersonator (*kupe*) wears clay horns (*thana-kana*). Memorization of the secret formulae is called *rupa,* and as this is mastered each girl receives incisions on the thigh, denoting graduation. After a final night-long ceremonial dance (*thojane*) the initiate is regarded as marriageable (*moroba*), and is greeted by her family with songs of return (*megolokwane*). — Further ritual music occurs at wedding feasts (*potsa*), where oxen are slaughtered and guests perform a dance known as *setapa*. Even illness can call for music, and the exorcist (*ngaka ya sedupe*) requires his audience to sing and clap during cures. Burial feasts (*magoga*) involve ritual music, as does the rain rite known as *go rapelela metsi*. — Non-ritual vocal music includes the counting rhyme (*pinapalo*), the nursery rhyme (*tlhaletso*), the singing game (*tshameko ya pina,* see ex. 33, p. 380), the contemporary jingle (*tsirimanya*), and innumerable work songs and beer songs (see ex. 34, p. 380). Although the ancient Tswana praises (*maboko*) are usually recited rather than sung, they contain many interesting musical allusions, such as when the Tlhako people are described as "those who dance to the elephant",[2] or when the age-set of Chief Isang is described as the "rhythmic movers" (*machechele*).[3] Another of these examples of oral literature mentions how womenfolk of the Kwena Chief Sechele "dance before the council",[4] and yet another mentions the traditional Tswana reed-pipe dance.[5] — The performance of much Tswana communal vocal music is related to the agricultural seasons of the year, for a period of minimum toil (such as that which occurs after the harvest) lends itself naturally to a period of maximum musical activity (such as the performance of songs and dances at beer-drinks). The seasons are as follows: *letlhafula* (autumn – from *tlhabolola,* to renew life; a time for hoeing songs and work-party songs); *mariga* (winter – from *mariba,* shade; a time for children's fireside story-songs); *dikgakologo* (spring – from *gakologo,* to melt away; a time when women and children chase birds from crops by singing shrilly in the fields); *selemo* (summer – from *lema,* to salvage fallen cobs from loose soil; a time for beer-brewing, beersongs, and beer-dances).

2. Tswana musical concepts

Tswana songs are either *mainane a segologolo* (folklore of great import) or they are contemporary, in which case they originate from a known *motlhami* (composer). They may be sung in unison (*pina e e kodunngwe*) or in two or more parts (*pina e e mantswe mabedi*), multi-part singing generally occurring during the response (*tumathulamo, tuma*) meaning "to be heard from afar" and *thulamo,* meaning "falling away". Where part-singing occurs, the upper part is known as *segalodimo* and the lower part as *segalo tlase.*

3. Instrumental music

The Tswana reed-pipe dance (*kubina dithlaka*) is the best-known form of Tswana instrumental music, and its study has revealed important compositional principles that may extend to other Tswana music. Christopher Ballantine** states that "the Tswana, in the creation of at least some of the their pipe pieces, do not proceed from melodic considerations – do not first think of a melody and then play it, with the addition of a few 'harmonies' on their pipes – but begin with one, or in some cases, two rhythmic schemes, which are then played by the pipes in a polyrhythmic way: but by their interrelation and points of coincidence are such that, apart from occasional exceptions, the canons of 'harmonic' acceptability are not offended."[6] — The drum, antelope horn, and leg-rattles (*moropa, lepapata,* and *mathlo* respectively) often accompany group dancing, as do various types of whistle known as *lengwane, lethlaka noka, mothlatsa, naka* or *palallo* according to their construction. — Four types of bow are in use among the Tswana, and they are used mainly for song accompaniment. The *lengope* consists of a curved length of cane strung with nylon fishing cord. It is mouth-resonated, fingered with the left hand, and plucked with the right forefinger. The *segwana* is a much larger bow, calabash-resonated, stick-struck, and has its cord divided unequally so as to produce two tones a minor 3rd apart (see plate 6a, p. 357). The performer may vary tone quality by raising and lowering the calabash-opening against his chest, all the while singing and dancing to his own accompaniment. The *setinkane* is similar to the *segwana* but possesses no resonator (see plate 6b, p. 358). The *nokukwane* bow was obtained from the Korana, and the Tswana are the only Bantu-speaking people to use it. The bow is crudely fashioned, and its arc is more pronounced than in the aforementioned examples. It is stick-struck, and resonated by means of a skin milk-container (*lukuku*) which has been blown up and dried.[7]

377

4. Examples

Example 30   Let the honey bear dig out the ant bear

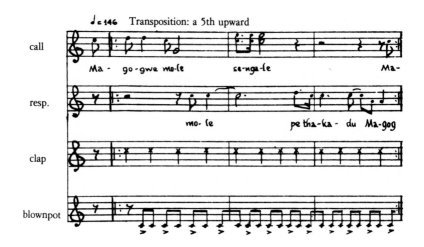

This beer song (ex. 30) was sung by four women and one man of the Tlharo group near Disaneng. They took their pitch from the sound of the blown pot, into which a woman grunted as she crawled around in imitation of the honey bear. Note that the song consists of an overlapping call and response accompanied by handclapping. The latter provides a rhythmic grid against which the lyrics are placed. Such a grid is generally consistent throughout each repetition of the song, and in this case consists of twelve equi-spaced "crotchets". An interesting counter-rhythm is provided by the pot-blower, each performer considering her *own* beat to be the main beat. This substantiates Ballantine's theory of polyphonic rhythmic schemes.

Example 31   Now we are clean for we have eaten clay.

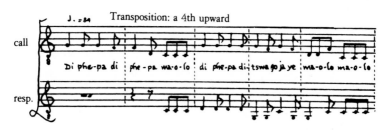

di phe-pa di | phe-pa ma-o-lo | di phe-pa di-|tswa go ja | ma-o-lo ma-o- lo

This circumcision song (ex. 31) was performed by men of the Ngwaketse group near Kanye. Its cycle occupies twenty dotted "crotchets", and the predominant harmony is 8ves, 4ths, and 5ths.

Example 32   We are lean, take this tortoise to the big men.

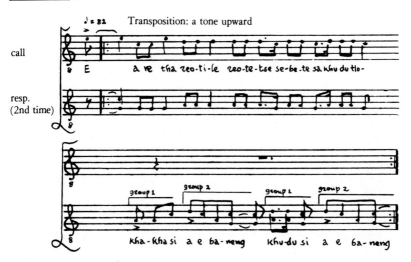

call

resp.
(2nd time)

This circumcision song (ex. 32) was performed by men of the Ngwaketse group near Kanye. Its cycle occupies eighteen "crotchets", and the predominant harmony is 4ths. Note the antiphony provided in the last half by opposing singing groups, and how the phrasing of this antiphony ignores the basic crotchet beat. In Tswana music, as in most African music, not only do speech-tones influence melody, but speech-stress influences musical phrasing.

Example 33   We are from Saulspoort. We see the buyers.

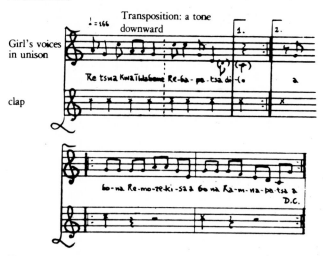

This singing game (ex. 33) was observed near Kanye, when girls of the Ngwaketse group sat in a circle and passed stones from side to side, in imitation of market transactions. The song's cycle occupies thirty-two crotchets, only the first sixteen of which are emphasized by regular claps, the last sixteen being emphasized intermittently. Note that the scale used is based on the common pentatonic *c-a-g-e-d*, the *f* being employed here merely in passing.

Example 34   The fowl is trapped by the dog, Manonope.

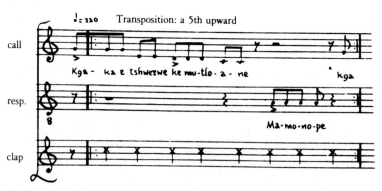

This beer song (ex. 34) was performed by men of the Kwena group near Malepolole. Normal Tswana speech-stress gave birth to the interesting rhythmic phrasing of the melody, to which, for the Tswana, the unchanging grid of eight crotchets provides a point of reference. Note once again the descending pentatonic scale, which appears to be present in much Tswana music.

5. References

1. Tracey, Hugh: ILAM Bechuanaland recording tour. *African Music* II/2, 1959, p. 65.   2. Schapera, I.: *Praise poems of Tswana chiefs*. Clarendon Press, Oxford, 1965, p. 85.   3. ibid.: p. 106.   4. ibid.: p. 176.   5. ibid.: p. 135.   6. Ballantine, Christopher: The polyrhythmic foundation of Tswana type melody. *African Music* III/4, 1965, p. 55.   7. Kirby, P.R.: *The musical instruments of the native races of South Africa*. OUP, 1934, pp. 213–214 and plate 57a.   Transcriptions are derived from recordings of the International Library of African Music (Hugh Tracey). Items are respectively: AMA TR-109 A1, A2, A3; AMA TR-109 B5; AMA TR-110 B1. — Further information on Tswana instruments and music in Kirby, P.R.: *The musical instruments of the native races of South Africa*. OUP, 1934 (2nd edition, Witwatersrand University Press, 1965). — Tracey, Hugh: *African dances of the Witwatersrand gold mines*. African Music Society, Johannesburg, 1952.

– T.J.

IX. MUSIC OF THE SHANGANA-TSONGA

1.　Instruments
　　a. *Ndzumba* drum
　　b. *Ncomane* drum
　　c. *Ngoma* drum
　　d. *Xigubu* drum
　　e. Leg rattles *(marhonge)*
　　f. Sideblown antelope horn *(mhalamhala)*
　　g. *Mbira (timbila)*
　　h. Ten- and twelve-slat xylophone *(mohambi)*
　　i. Three-hole transverse flute *(xitiringo)*
　　j. Notched friction bow *(xizambi)*
　　k. Braced gourd bow *(xitende)*
　　l. Fingerplucked hollow cane bow *(mqangala)*
　　m. Braced thick-handled musical bow *(xipendana)*

2.　The influence of speech-tone upon melody
　　a. Musical forces limiting the influences of speech-tone on melody
　　b. Musical forces limiting the impact of speech stress on song rhythm
　　c. Programmatic musical settings
　　d. Formal structure

3.　Tsonga vocal music styles

4.　Transcription of some Tsonga songs
　　a. An *ngoma* song
　　b. A beer song
　　c. A *muchongolo* song
　　d. A work song
　　e. A children's song
　　f. A *xigubu* song
　　g. A *khomba* song
　　h. A *mancomane* song

1. Instruments

The Tsonga have a considerable variety of vocal and instrumental music. A description of thirteen of their musical instruments is given below, followed by twenty-two transcriptions illustrating the influence of language on melody formation.

a. Ndzumba drum

The Tsonga *ndzumba* drum is a fairly large goblet-shaped drum used mainly in the girls' puberty school *(khomba),* and it is often paired with a smaller model called *ndzumbana* (see fig. 4, 383). The two most important rhythms played upon the *ndzumba* drum are *nyanyala* and *xisotho* (see ex. 35, p. 384), which derive from the Tsonga core pattern

Drum-making is a dying art among the Tsonga. Existing *ndzumba* drums are treasured relics of former times and are usually communal property. They are subject to many taboos, one of which is that women are forbidden to peer within the round hole in the foot of the drum.

b. Ncomane drum

The Tsonga *ncomane* drum is a hand-held stick-played tambourine used exclusively in the exorcism dance to which it gave its name – *mancomane*. It is usually the private property of a doctor-diviner *(dzwavi)* for whom it constitutes a symbol of authority. Four drums of equal size but disparate tuning are used together at one time, in conjunction with a large hemispherical drum *(ngoma)* which provides the bass (see figs. 6 and 9, pp. 386, 390). The exclusiveness of the use of the *ncomane* drum is emphasized in fig. 6 and the role of women-drummers in "exorcism" dancing and in all music for adults, is emphasized in figs. 7 and 8, pp. 388, 389.

c. Ngoma drum

The *ngoma* used by the Tsonga is obtained by purchase or barter from the neighbouring Venda, who still boast craftsmen who manufacture it. Possessing artistically-carved handles which frame the shell, these drums come in a 'family' of large, medium, and small *(xingomana).* When available, the three sizes are used simultaneously to provide rhythmic accompaniment at beer-drink dances (see fig. 9, p. 390).

d. Xigubu drum

The Tsonga *xigubu* drum is a double-membraned cylindrical drum made from discarded canisters of all sizes, and it is used in the boys' drumming school *(xigubu,* to which it gave its name), at beer-drink dances and mine dances, and at *khomba* and *mancomane* dances when other drums are not available. All Tsonga drums may be

Figure 4   Tsonga *ndzumba* initiation drum.

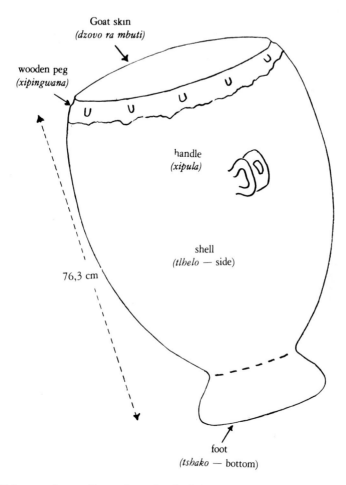

Goat skin
(dzovo ra mbuti)

wooden peg
(xipingwana)

handle
(xipula)

shell
(tlhelo — side)

76,3 cm

foot
(tshako — bottom)

Notes: In most Tsonga drumming, flat fingers are used near centre of drum; heel of palm used for accents near edge.

either hand-played or stick-played, depending upon the song and upon the function (see fig. 6 and 10, pp. 386, 390).

e. Leg-rattles (marhonge)
Tsonga women- and girl-dancers attach rattles to their calves, especially in dances of the puberty school and of the exorcism rites. These rattles are called *marhonge* and their characteristic sound *(chaka-chaka)* serves for step-emphasis during intricate movements (see fig. 11, p. 391).

Example 35   The core drum pattern in most Tsonga music.

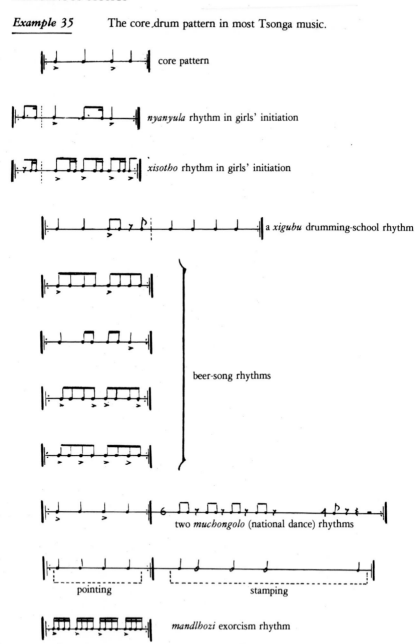

core pattern

nyanyula rhythm in girls' initiation

xisotho rhythm in girls' initiation

a *xigubu* drumming-school rhythm

beer-song rhythms

two *muchongolo* (national dance) rhythms

pointing   stamping

mandlhozi exorcism rhythm

 *xidzimba* exorcism rhythm

Figure 5   Tsonga *ncomane* — drum, rear view.

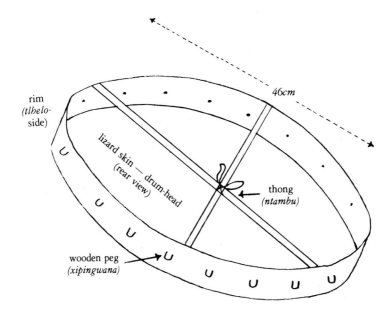

f. Side-blown antelope horn (mhalamhala) see plate 1, p. 349)
The Tsonga *mhalamhala* is a long hollowed antelope horn in which a square embouchure has been bored in the narrow (closed) end. It yields the 2nd and 3rd partials (8ve and 5th) with ease and the 4th partial (2nd octave) with some difficulty. Used exclusively in the girls' puberty school, the antelope horn is communal property in the custody of a school's supervisor (usually the chief's wife – *nkulukumba*), for it constitutes a symbol of authority.

g. Mbira (Timbila)
The Tsonga of Maputo play a 26-key *timbila* which they say came from the Ndau. It utilizes a hollow cowbell-shaped soundboard made of wood, and possesses three banks of keys played by the thumbs and forefingers. The keys of a specimen obtained from Daniel Muphahlo of Maboti (Maputo) in March, 1970, were manufactured from hammered-out umbrella spokes, and arranged in the tuning-layout of ex. 36, p. 392. The Tsonga of the Northern Transvaal play a 17-key *timbila* which they say came from the Pedi and the Lovedu. Dr Huskisson photographically reproduces a 17-key

Figure 6   Tsonga dances and the drums used for them *(ncomane's* use is very specific; other drums, less so).

DANCE	DRUM (not to scale)	OFFICIANT

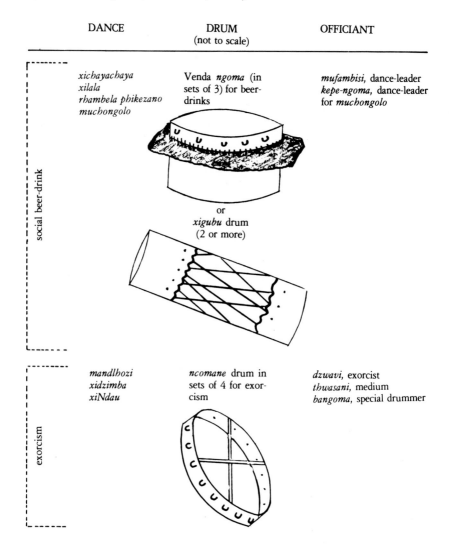

xichayachaya
xilala
rhambela phikezano
muchongolo

Venda *ngoma* (in sets of 3) for beer-drinks

mufambisi, dance-leader
kepe-ngoma, dance-leader
for *muchongolo*

social beer-drink

or
xigubu drum
(2 or more)

mandlhozi
xidzimba
xiNdau

ncomane drum in sets of 4 for exorcism

dzwavi, exorcist
thwasani, medium
bangoma, special drummer

exorcism

girls' initiation school	*ku khana* *nanayila* *managa* *ku thaga* *ku rhwala tingoma*	*ndzumba* in sets of 2 for *khomba* 	*nkulukumba*, supervisor *bangoma*, processional drum-carrier *mufambisi*, dance-leader *ndzabi*, schoolmother
boys' drumming school	*ku wamikapa* *xifase*	*xigubu* drum in sets of 2 for drumming-school 	*muqambhi*, instructor
circumcision school	*mayiwayiwane* *ku nenga*	NO DRUMS in order to keep secrecy	*n'anga*, doctor *madhlala*, shepherds

Figure 7   The role of women-drummers in Tsonga music for adults.

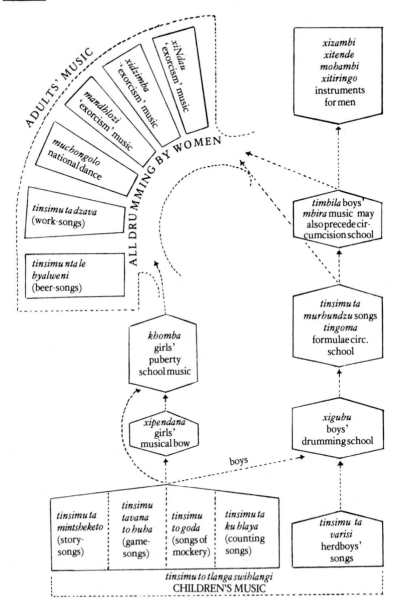

Figure 8   The learning process in Tsonga drumming.

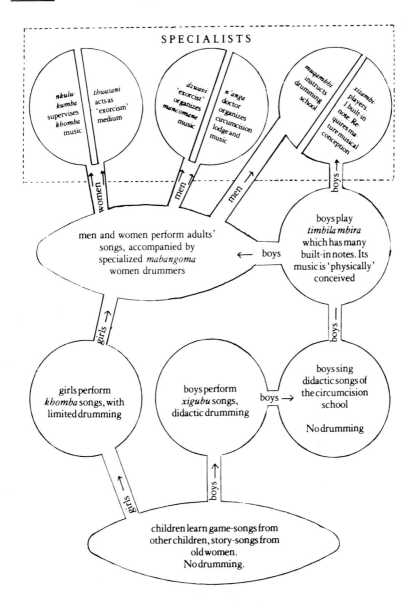

Figure 9   Venda *ngoma* drum with Tsonga names of parts.

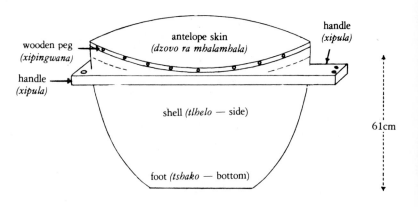

Figure 10   Tsonga *xigubu* drums (may be almost any size from 30,5 cm to 91,5 cm).

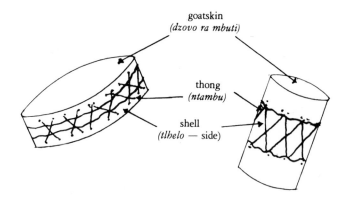

Figure 11   A *marhonge* leg rattle. Twelve of sixteen small fruitshells *(masala)* containing seeds are threaded in rows on to a square framework *(rihlanga)* to which tying cords are attached. The rattles are rarely sold, discarded, or replaced.

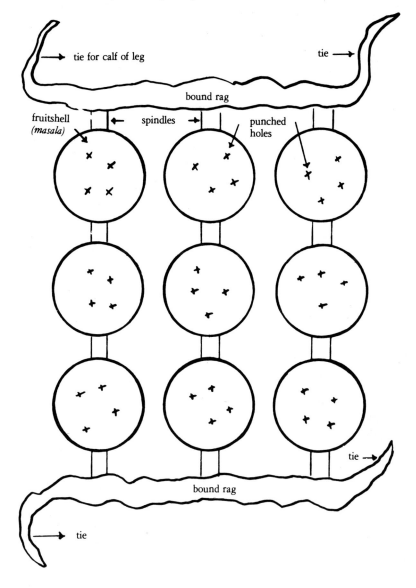

Example 36   Tuning of a Tsonga *timbila*

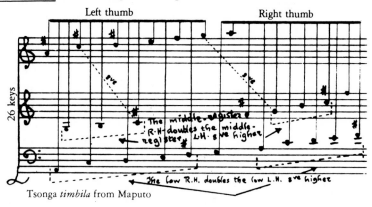

Tsonga *timbila* from Maputo

Lovedu instrument which in appearance exactly resembles the Tsonga instrument[1] (see plate 4, p. 355). The Tsonga 17-key *timbila* is said by the Tsonga to have been passed on to the Venda, where it is called *mbila tshipai*.[2] The present writer obtained many Tsonga *timbila* in various areas of the Northern Transvaal, 1968–70, and the tuning-layout (carefully verified by the owner) in most of them shows a consistency sufficient to warrant naming it a "standard" Tsonga *timbila* tuning-layout, as in the example shown in ex. 37. Music for the *timbila* is frequently polyrhythmic, each thumb independently following a separate rhythmic pattern. The player's sung melody is a composite of the constituent tones of which emerge from the whole. Although *timbila* melodic patterns are generally governed by the standard tuning-layout shown below, players occasionally rearrange individual keys to suit desired tunes.

Example 37   Specimen tuning of Transvaal Tsonga *timbila*.

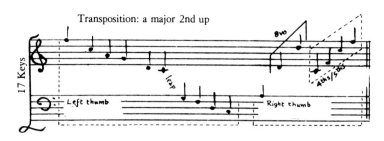

In the above tuning the 10 left-hand keys form a gradually-descending pentatonic scale terminating on low *D-C*. After this descent the pitch of the keys rises again in the right hand, a factor which gives the Tsonga key-arrangement its characteristic V-shape. Note, however, that the ascent in the right hand is not a gradual one, but consists first of sharply-rising adjacent (or almost adjacent) octaves followed by a group of 4ths and 5ths.

h. Ten- and twelve- slat xylophone (mohambi)
Mohambi is the name applied by the Tsonga to Chopi and Ndau calabash-resonated xylophones. While not manufactured by the Tsonga, the *mohambi* has long been played by them, for Junod reported its widespread use in 1897.[3] — In the smaller instrument, five wooden separators *(swiwawani)* divide adjacent pairs of slats, causing the Tsonga to regard them as *swa tirhisana* – little "spouses", i.e., little "husband and wife". The *mohambi* is supported off the ground (or braced against the abdomen) by a curved wooden frame known as *xipula,* and the slats are lightly struck with two mallets *(timhandze).* The name of the resonators varies according to the type of calabash used, but the most common name is *masala,* this being Tsonga for the monkey-orange fruit (Strychnos spinosa Lam).

i. Three-hole transverse flute (xitiringo)
The *xitiringo* is generally made from scrap metal piping or a length of river-reed, and the position of its three holes *(machayele)* is determined solely by the maker's placing his first three right-hand fingers across the pipe at a comfortable angle. Either the lower or upper end is plugged by a maize-cob, and in the case of the former the player additionally opens and closes the upper end with his cupped left palm, humming and grunting loudly *(ku xipfumisa,* see plate 14, p. 369).

j. Notched friction-bow (xizambi)
Little has been written about the notched, mouth-resonated friction-bow, yet it is the bow at which the Tsonga, of all the Bantu-speaking peoples, excel the most. The Tsonga *xizambi* is a 35 cm to 43 cm bow activated not by plucking or striking, but by rubbing its notched arch *(mphonwani,* cut from the *mphata* tree, Brachylaena discolor DC.) with a 35,5 cm rattlestick *(fahlwana).* The latter is of particularly interesting construction, as shown in the diagram (see fig. 12, p. 394). The string of the *xizambi* bow is a strip of palm leaf *(nala,* Typha capensis), and in addition to its open tone it may be stopped one to four times by the fingers. The vibrating *nala* emits the fundamental. This fundamental sounds continually below the resonated tones during playing. The buccal cavity, although it cannot affect the continually sounding fundamental, adds penetrating 3rd, 4th, 6th or 7th harmonics above. The 2nd is generally too low for buccal resonation, and the 5th is discarded in favour of fingering. Simultaneously, divisions (see fig. 13, p. 395) indicate by approximately how many cents finger-stopping can increase the frequency level of a given harmonic. The commonly-used harmonic combinations are given here. Only the "open" position (non-fingered) is shown, and it should be realized that by the use of fingering each combination can be raised from two to five semitones (see ex. 39a, p. 397). Appropriate fingering can produce the commonly-used tone-row given here, and it will also be seen that by a lateral handshift the E–D fingering 4–2 can produce F and E *flat* (see ex. 39b, p. 397). Bow tension is dictated by two factors: if the *nala* is too taut it will snap; if too slack its harmonics will be false. Thus various limitations – *nala* fragility, finger-reach, etc. – all combine to quasi-standardize *xizambi* pitch, and a correctly-adjusted instrument generally emits the fourth harmonic (two octaves above the faint fundamental and one octave above the unused second harmonic) at a frequency level of between 800 and 1100. Certain players re-adjust the bow tension slightly for particular tunes, and others change to a smaller or larger *xizambi.* This does not constitute mere register selection, for the altered string length-buccal cavity

393

Figure 12   *Xizambi* rattle stick with fruitshells

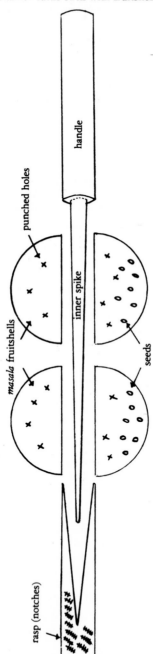

Figure 13   *Xizambi* notched friction-bow

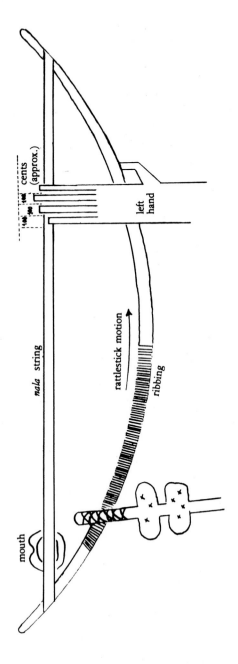

Example 38   Tsonga utilization of those *xizambi* characteristics which coincide with vocal music principles.

Many children's songs, and *khomba,* beer, *muchongolo,* and *mandhlozi* songs use this type of 'harmonisation'

top row: customary 'harmonic' equivalents (arrived at by span process)

Tsonga common melodic pattern: *g-e-d-c-a-g*

bottom row: true melody-tones

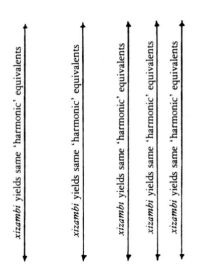

examples

response in beersong

Du-ma-li-zwe

Span process

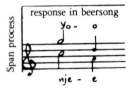

response in beersong

Yo - o

nje - e

xizambi yields same 'harmonic' equivalents

xizambi yields same 'harmonic' equivalents

xizambi yields same 'harmonic' equivalents

xizambi yields same 'harmonic' equivalents

xizambi yields same 'harmonic' equivalents

top row: resonated tones Tsonga common *xizambi* pattern *g-e-d-c-a-g* bottom row: 2nd harmonic of fingered/unfingered *nala* 'string'

Transvaal *xizambi*-players Johannes Mathye, Wilson Zulu, Elias Khosa, and Njaranjara use this type of resonation

Example 39a   Friction bow partials.

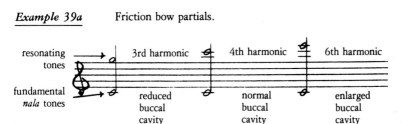

Example 39b   Friction-bow fingering.

ratio favours some intervals at the expense of others – to achieve an interval of a 3rd at the top, one may intentionally sacrifice an interval of a 4th at the bottom. — Asked to demonstrate a sustained tone, the *xizambi* player will oblige with a tone of any desired length, for there is no breath required. This sustained tone will emerge as a series of rhythmic pulses corresponding to the motion of the rattlestick. These rhythmic pulses contribute to the effectiveness of a performance, for they may be equidistant or uneven, dynamically punctuated or unaccented, of restricted sweep or following the full arc of the bow, grouped in two's or three's and combining any of the aforegoing. — *Xizambi* players often sing solo to their own accompaniment, but, because mouth-resonation must cease, this accompaniment consists solely of the rasp, the rattle, and the continuously-sounding second harmonic of the open "string". The player resumes resonation upon completion of the song, and thus the performance consists of alternating instrumental and vocal versions. In other types of performances, the player accompanies group singing or plays in duet with another *xizambi* player. — *Xizambi* players do not necessarily learn the instrument from their fathers or serve an apprenticeship. Promising aspirants are generally taught (*ku yimbisa:* to teach a musical instrument) to construct and play the *xizambi* by another player, during the period when they have ceased to tend goats but have not yet commenced herding cattle. They learn by the use of rhythmic nonsense syllables such as *hlawa-hlawa,* from which the rattlestick *(fahlwana)* derives its name. Typical learning-rhythms are shown in ex. 40. A *xizambi* player is often the musician/composer connected with a chief's inner circle, and provides music to entertain distinguished visitors. On the other hand, but less frequently, he may be a wandering minstrel (*xilombe*) who makes his way from village to village, dancing, singing, and playing in return for food, drink, and shelter. Less frequently still, he may be a recluse (*nwarimatsi*). Literally, this term

Example 40   *Xizambi* friction-bow learning rhythms.

means "child-of-the-left-handed-one", but it may refer to *social* attitudes toward left-and right-hand functions. There is a Tsonga saying which runs thus: *Ku senga homu hi rimatsi* (To milk a cow on the left side (wrongly)).

k. Braced gourd-bow (xitende)

The *xitende* braced gourd-bow is the earliest-mentioned stringed instrument of the Tsonga, having been described in 1897 by Junod.[4] A "kaffir" braced gourd-bow was described by a Jesuit priest in 1723.[5] This may have belonged to the Tsonga rather than to the Zulu, Swazi, or any other South African coastal people, for Rycroft states that the *umakhweyana* braced gourd-bow of the Zulu and Swazi "was reputedly borrowed from the Tsonga of Mozambique in the nineteenth century."[6] — The Tsonga *xitende* is cut from the *maloha* tree, and its copper wire *(ritsaninga)* is divided by a movable wire-loop to which is attached a calabash *(xiphaphani)*. The string sections are tuned a minor 3rd apart and struck with a maize stalk *(rihlangi)*, the player additionally opening and closing the calabash against his preferably bare chest. The tuning is accomplished by twisting the knotted ends of the wire-loop within the interior of the calabash, and by sliding the wire loop and calabash up or down the bow as required, these two actions being known as *ku gwimba* (see plates 6a and b, pp. 357, 358). The two open tones of the braced gourd-bow are everywhere supplemented by an additional fingered tone, but whereas some Southern African groups finger the longer string-section, thus filling-in the open tones, the Tsonga finger the shorter string-section, thus placing the additional tone outside and above the open tones (see fig. 14, p. 399). The *xitende* does not require mouth-resonation, and the player is therefore free to sing to his own accompaniment. The physical manipulation of the instrument is simple, and this leaves the player free to dance – Tsonga *xitende* players are often wandering minstrels who dance and sing. They are usually extrovert types, and in this connection it has been commented that "the dancing-singing shaman probably owes his position as much to his forceful, possibly para-psychological personality traits as to his musical talents".[7] The arrival of the minstrel in a village attracts a group of boys, some of whom come carrying a *xitende* with which to practice the *xitende* learning rhythms, some of which are given in ex. 41, p. 400.

Figure 14   *Xitende* braced gourd-bow of the Shangana-Tsonga.

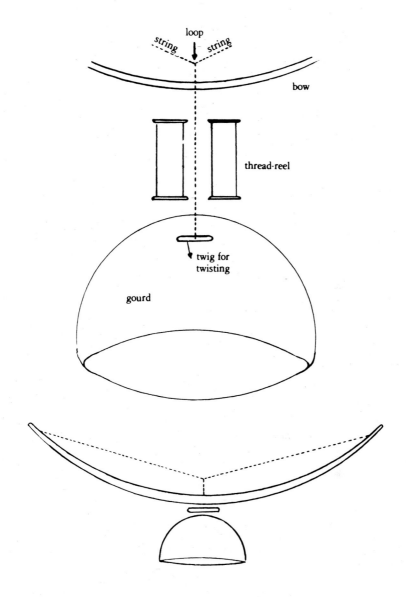

Example 41   *Xitende* gourd-bow learning rhythms.

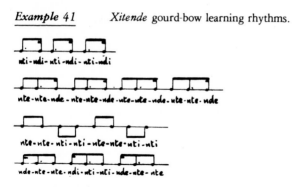

l. Finger-plucked hollow cane-bow (mqangala)

The Tsonga *mqangala* is a mouth-resonated, finger-plucked bow made from hollow river-reed and strung with discarded fishing-cord. The name itself is a "click" word, and the instrument may have been obtained from the neighbouring Zulu or Swazi, both of whom use "clicks", use a similar instrument, and apply the name *mqangala* to that instrument. Among the Tsonga it is generally played by old men who alternately sing and play during performance. The fingering (*machayele*, from the Zulu verb *chaya*, to play an instrument), extends to three positions in which the cord is depressed against the side of the bow, the *mqangala* being the only Tsonga bow whose lateral plane serves as a "fingerboard". The three positions – *sasankambana, mapokonyole,* and *matiringisi* – are named after the first, second, and third fingers respectively (see fig. 15).

Figure 15   Tsonga *mqangala* hollow-cane bow.

l.h. fingering occurs
here, pressing cord
against the wood

r.h. index finger
plucks here

this end
inserted
into
right cheek

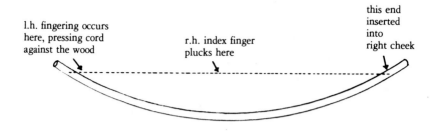

m. Braced, thick-handled musical bow (xipendana)

The Tsonga name for the mouth-resonated, braced, thick-handled bow is *xipendana* (same as the Karanga name for it), and not *sekgapa*, as stated by Kirby.[8] This latter name is used by the Pedi for their braced gourd-bow (an entirely different instrument), but not at all by the Tsonga. The Tsonga *xipendana* is played mainly by girls and is often tuned in pairs. The name is similar to the name used by their neighbours the Chopi of Maputo (*penda*) and the latter is similar to that used by the

Rhodesian Karanga, with whom the Chopi are suspected of being related by virtue of their xylophone playing. — The Tsonga-constructed *xipendana* is flat-cut except for a thick centre portion (*xipula*) forming the handle. It is cut from the *muluwa* tree (*Acacia ataxacantha*), a thorn tree whose wood splits easily into thin strips. *Muluwa* is also used for making Tsonga winnowing baskets and, in heavier thicknesses, for Tsonga axe-handles. The "string" is a length of thin copper wire, pulled in near its centre by a loop of thread. The latter is never tied to the bow-centre, but is held by the left-hand thumb and adjusted when retuning becomes necessary. — Plucking is achieved by the use of a safety-pin held in the right hand, the left hand supporting the bow. The longer string-length is uppermost and toward the player's left (facing the audience), an intermediate tone being produced from this half by the left-hand index finger (see fig. 16).

2. The influence of speech-tone upon melody

Tsonga is not strictly a tone language, as are, for example, certain Asian languages. Its speech-tone patterns may have both syntactical and semantic significance, though correct tone is not essential to understanding, which can usually be gathered from the context. The meaning of similar words may vary according to speech-tone pattern, thus:

$('$ = high, $`$ = low, $^$ = falling)
báva = to be bitter
bàvá = father
bòfù = blind person
bòfú = pus
bvímbá = an aromatic shrub
bvìmba = to seal with a lid.

These tone-patterns are not absolute but may also vary according to context. In the following different versions of a song, speech-tone markings were supplied by C.T.D. Marivate, linguist at the University of South Africa, Pretoria (see ex. 42a, b, c, d, pp. 403, 404). The musical characteristics of the initial "statement" of a Tsonga song are considerably influenced by the rise and fall of Tsonga speech-tone, and by the length and rhythmic stress of the syllables. Once melody and rhythm are set, subsequent "statements" may be a product of both linguistic *and* purely musical forces. The relationship between Tsonga song-words and their musical setting generally involves more than mere imitative processes. There are musical forces limiting the influence of speech-tone on *melody*, and musical forces limiting the influence of speech-stress on *rhythm*.

a. Musical forces limiting the influence of speech-tone on melody
There exists in Tsonga communal vocal music a phenomenon which might be termed "pathogenic" descent. An analysis of Tsonga "pathogenic" descent reveals that 24% of the songs exhibit a first-to-last-tone descent of a 5th; 20% exhibit a first-to-last-tone descent of an octave; 13% exhibit a first-to-last-tone descent of a 4th; and all exhibit a first-to-last-tone intervallic descent of one kind or another. These descents are neither sharp nor gradual, but occupy a series of plateaus, and exert a limiting counter-influence against speech-tone domination, particularly at sentence endings where a musical drop is desirable. The Tsonga have a special vocabulary of melismatic syllables, such as *huwele, welele, hayi-hayi, yowe-yowe,* etc., during the singing of which a melody is released from any possible obligation to obey speech-tone rise and

401

Figure 16   _Xipendana_ mouth-resonated braced bow.

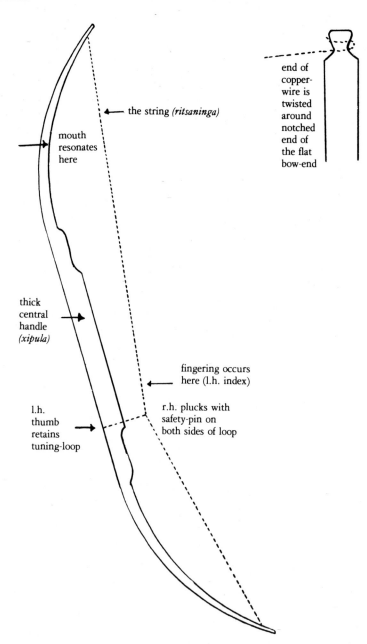

the string *(ritsaninga)*

mouth
resonates
here

end of
copper-
wire is
twisted
around
notched
end of
the flat
bow-end

thick
central
handle
(xipula)

fingering occurs
here (l.h. index)

l.h.
thumb
retains
tuning-loop

r.h. plucks with
safety-pin on
both sides of loop

Example 42 a, b, c, d

Version a (sung by a chorus of men at Samarie)

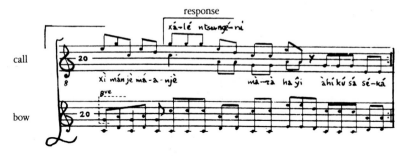

Version b (sung by Wilson Zulu)

Version c (sung by a chorus of women at Ribola)

(Continued overleaf)

Version d (sung by Joel Mashava)

Of the above four versions (ex. 42 a, b, c, d) all melodically observe the various speech-tones of the word *ximánjèmánjè*, two observe the "high-low" at *ngéni*, and all observe the "falling" at *haŷi*. Two of the versions exhibit a melodic "high-low" at *sáséká* that is not indicated by the speech-tone markings, but *sáséká* is the song's concluding word, and a cadential drop in pitch is considered (by the Tsonga) musically desirable.

fall (see chap. IV, and chap. X: rule 5.5.2). — A principle of "harmonic equivalence" allows tones distant a 5th (inverted 4th) from one another to be used interchangeably. This system of tone-substitution results in otherwise inexplicable melodic "highs" and

Example 43

The word *hlàmbyètwànà* which contains exclusively "low" speech-tones, is melodically represented by D's during the first cycle, and by A's during the second cycle, D and A being "harmonically equivalent".

"lows" during unchanging speech-tones (see ex. 43, and fig. 17, p. 406). When word-changes occur during successive cycles of a song, a choice of new words often seems to be made so that their speech-tone approximates the old words, and could, should the singers so desire, be sung to the same melody. Where the melody changes, it does so according to an implicit "harmonic" framework which could be considered as the real control. However, musical considerations may completely overrule speech-tone considerations, as in the following melody. — The speech-tones are *téká tá wèná ú fúngèngéta hí mbítá*, but the melody is:

Example 44

té - ká tá wè - ná ú fún-oèn-oé -ta hí - m - bî - ta

b. Musical forces limiting the impact of speech-stress on song-rhythm

Of particular use to the Tsonga in the relaxation of speech-stress controls is vowel elision, terminal-syllable contraction, and terminal-syllable prolongation. Vowel elision permits the singer (i) to execute one long tone instead of two short tones, and (ii) to fit a long word into a relatively short musical space. Terminal-syllable contraction permits the singer to utilize, on the concluding single tone of his song, an otherwise trochaic bisyllabic word. Terminal-syllable prolongation permits the singer to utilize, on the concluding two tones of his song, an otherwise-monosyllabic word. — In Tsonga vocal composition, many musical factors combine to limit speech-tone domination, not the least of which is perhaps a desire for musical contrast between call and response. Concerning the resultant "distortion" of word-meaning, the present writer sought the opinion of Tsonga linguists in ascertaining to what extent speech-tone may be ignored within a vocal composition. The consensus was that context is as important as speech-tone, and where, for musical reasons, the latter is dispensed with, recourse to context adequately clarifies meaning.

c. Programmatic musical settings

Onomatopoeias such as *dluva-dluva* (jump), *vula-vula* (gossip), *cele-cele* (carousing), and *ngomu-ngomu* (ogre) receive programmatic treatment at the hands of Tsonga composers, being set to reiterative, motional, or accelerative tone-patterns (see exs. 45, 46, 47).

Example 45   The reiterative setting of *dluva-dluva* (jump).

Figure 17   Distribution of "harmonic equivalents" among the parts.

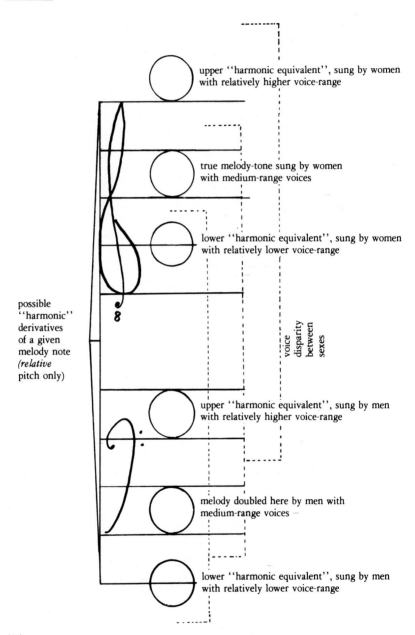

possible "harmonic" derivatives of a given melody note *(relative* pitch only)

upper "harmonic equivalent", sung by women with relatively higher voice-range

true melody-tone sung by women with medium-range voices

lower "harmonic equivalent", sung by women with relatively lower voice-range

upper "harmonic equivalent", sung by men with relatively higher voice-range

melody doubled here by men with medium-range voices —

lower "harmonic equivalent", sung by men with relatively lower voice-range

voice disparity between sexes

Example 46   The motional setting of *vula-vula* (gossip).

Swi-vu-la-vu-la nka-ta mi-na swi na nwa-Gwav'-na-ne-

Example 47   The accelerative setting of *cele-cele* (carousing)

He ny na xi nga vu-yi-i ha he nu na xi nga w-wi-i ce-le-ce-le

d. Formal structure

Tsonga communal vocal music, when compared to Venda and other Southern African musics, appears to have a predilection for longer metrical periods. These periods contain interesting proportions of call to response, and multiple reappearances of call and response within any one cycle:

		Total
Song A:	(call = 9 ♩ + response = 3 ♩	
	+ call = 9 ♩ + response = 9 ♩	
	+ call = 3 ♩ + response = 3 ♩)	= 36 ♩
Song B:	(call = 4 ♩ + response = 4 ♩	
	+ call = 4 ♩ + response = 14 ♩)	= 26 ♩
Song C:	(unison chorus = 2 ♩ + call = 4 ♩	
	+ unison chorus = 2 ♩ + call = 4 ♩	
	+ divided chorus = 4 ♩)	= 16 ♩
Song D:	(call = 6 ♩ + response = 3 ♩	
	+ call = 6 ♩ + response = 9 ♩)	= 24 ♩
Song E:	(call = 4 ♩ + response = 4 ♩	
	+ call = 4 ♩ + response = 8 ♩)	= 20 ♩
Song F:	(call = 10 ♩ + response = 4 ♩	
	+ call = 4 ♩ + response = 4 ♩	
	+ call = 4 ♩ + response = 4 ♩)	= 30 ♩
Song G:	(call = 4 ♩ + response = 7 ♩	
	+ call = 1 ♩ + response = 12 ♩)	= 24 ♩.
Song H:	(call = 6 ♩ + response = 10 ♩	
	+ call = 6 ♩ + response = 10 ♩	
	+ call = 5 ♩ + response = 27 ♩)	= 64 ♩
Song I:	(call = 2 ♩.+ response = 3 ♩.	
	+ call = 2 ♩.+ response = 11 ♩.)	= 18 ♩.

(Continued overleaf)

Song J: (call = 18 ♩ + response = 18 ♩
+ call =   2 ♩ + response =   4 ♩
+ call =   3 ♩ + response =   3 ♩
+ call =   3 ♩ + response =   3 ♩
+ call =   3 ♩ + response =   3 ♩)   . . . .   = 60 ♩

Song K: (call =   6 ♩ + response =   4 ♩
+ call =   6 ♩ + response =   4 ♩
+ call =   2 ♩ + response =   4 ♩
+ call =   2 ♩ + response =   4 ♩)   . . . .   = 32 ♩

3. Tsonga vocal music styles

Tsonga beer-songs, work-songs and *muchongolo* songs, all belonging to one main stylistic complex within Tsonga music (the beer-drink complex), are the most frequently performed songs. An estimated frequency of their use is given in fig. 18. The work-song sub-style within this complex is particularly dependent upon the changing seasons of the horticultural year, as is shown in the top half of fig. 19, p. 409. Apart from comprising three distinct sub-styles, beer-drink music possesses an "overlap" relationship with five other Tsonga musical categories, as is shown in fig. 20, p. 410.

Figure 18

beer songs 18%

work songs 4%

muchongolo 18%

beer drink music 40%

mandhlozi 12%   *xidzimba* 5%
                     xiNdau   3%

exorcism music 20%

khomba assembly, dispatch, and coming-out songs 14%

secret songs 1%

khomba music 15%

children's songs 10%   10%

solo instrumental playing 10%   10%

xigubu songs 2%

xigubu didactic formulae 1%

xigubu voice + drum conversations 1%

drum-school music 4%

circumcision *tingoma* ½% circ. *tinsimu* ½%   circ. sch. music 1%

Figure 19

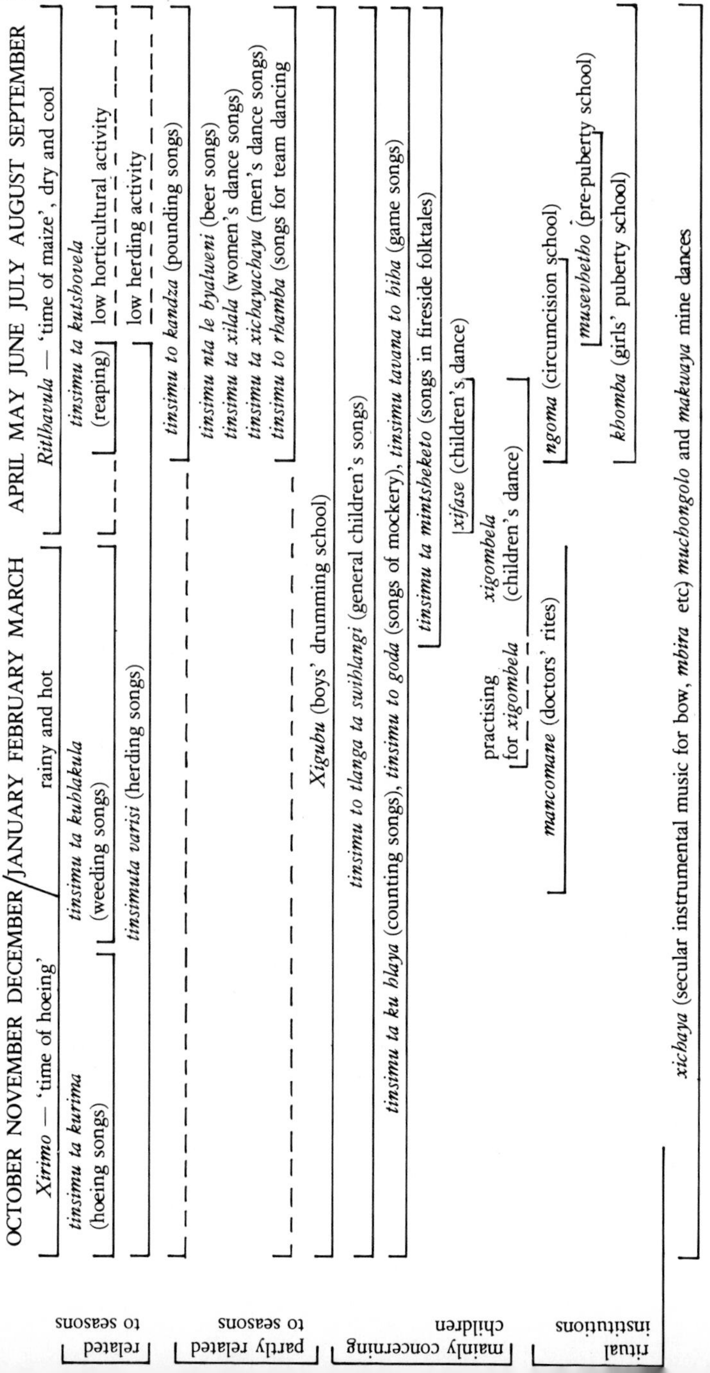

OCTOBER NOVEMBER DECEMBER / JANUARY FEBRUARY MARCH APRIL MAY JUNE JULY AUGUST SEPTEMBER

Xirimo — 'time of hoeing' / rainy and hot

Ritlhavula — 'time of maize', dry and cool

tinsimu ta kurima (hoeing songs)

tinsimu ta kublakula (weeding songs)

tinsimuta varisi (herding songs)

tinsimu ta kutshovela (reaping) low horticultural activity

low herding activity

tinsimu to kandza (pounding songs)

tinsimu nta le byalweni (beer songs)
tinsimu ta xilala (women's dance songs)
tinsimu ta xichayachaya (men's dance songs)
tinsimu to rhamba (songs for team dancing)

Xigubu (boys' drumming school)

tinsimu to tlanga ta suvihlangi (general children's songs)

tinsimu ta ku blaya (counting songs), *tinsimu to goda* (songs of mockery), *tinsimu tavana to biha* (game songs)

tinsimu ta mintsheketo (songs in fireside folktales)

xifase (children's dance)

xigombela (children's dance)

practising for *xigombela*

mancomane (doctors' rites)

ngoma (circumcision school)

musevibetbo (pre-puberty school)

khomba (girls' puberty school)

xichaya (secular instrumental music for bow, *mbira* etc) *muchongolo* and *makwaya* mine dances

related to seasons

partly related to seasons

mainly concerning children

ritual institutions

409

Figure 20   The beer-drink complex of substyles — Tsonga vocal and instrumental music.

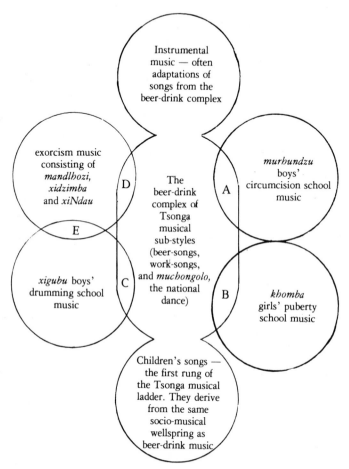

A. This area represents circumcision school coming-out songs sung at the final day beer-party with the relatives.

B. This area represents puberty school coming-out songs sung at the final day beer-party with the relatives.

C. This area represents beer-drink rhythms taught in the boys' drumming school.

D. This area represents *muchongolo* danced in an "exorcism" context.

E. This area represents "exorcism" rhythms taught in the boys' drumming school (included here for the sake of completeness).

4. Transcriptions of some Tsonga songs

Example 48   An *Ngoma* song: *Whe tsori te ki mulayo* (The laws of the circumcision school). The text is not in regular Tsonga.

Transposition: a dim. fifth higher

Example 49   A beer song: *Byala hi lebiye maseve* (Here is beer). ''Muting'' of the drumhead is effected by pressing down with the palm.

Transposition: a maj. third higher

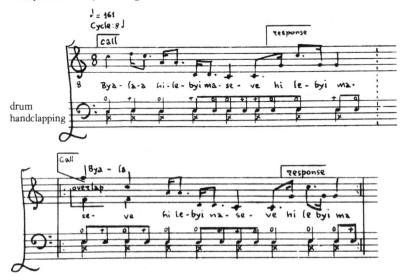

411

Example 50   A *muchongolo* song: *I nhlampfi bak' mabomu* (The fish twists like this). Sung as the dancer points a baton here and there.

Transposition: a min. third higher

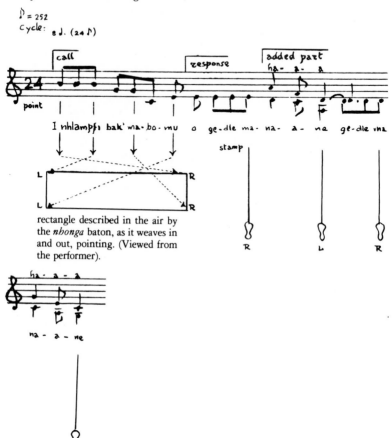

rectangle described in the air by the *nhonga* baton, as it weaves in and out, pointing. (Viewed from the performer).

Example 51   A work song: *Mavele N'wana manane* (Pounding maize, child-of-my-mother). The blow of the pestle sounds on every alternate dotted crotchet.

Transposition: a maj. ninth higher

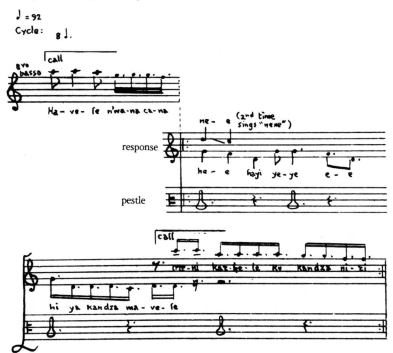

Example 52   A children's song: *Ni na makvavo xifufununu* (Wake up, brother beetle). Note the broken clap-rhythm.

Transposition: a min. seventh higher

Example 53   A *xigubu* song: *Va ni loyi kumile* (They have bewitched me). Note the broken clap-rhythm.

Transposition: a maj. second higher

Example 54   A *khomba* song: *Rhambu ra N'anga* (The divining bones). These bones are thrown during the final coming-out rites.

Transposition: a min sixth higher

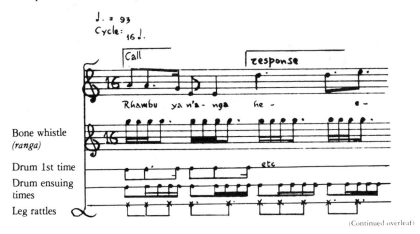

(Continued overleaf)

Example 55   A *mancomane* song: *Hayi nyoka leyo vimbha mlomo.* (I fear the snake which blocks my mouth — Tsonga ''ancestor-spirits'' are thought to sometimes assume the form of small green snakes).

Transposition: a maj. third higher

5. References

1. Huskisson, Y.: *The social and ceremonial music of the Pedi.* Ph.D. thesis, UWits, Johannesburg, 1958, plate 22.   2. Venda tunings differ from those of the Tsonga. See chapter X, ex. 37.   3. Junod, Henri: *Les chants et les contes des ba-Ronga.* Bridel & Co., Lausanne, 1897, p. 24.   4. ibid.: p. 22.   5. Bonanni, F.: *Gabinetto armonico.* Rome, 1723, p.

175.   6. Rycroft, D.: nGuni polyphony. *Journal of the International Folk Music Council* XIX, 1967, p. 96.   7. Brandel, Rose.: *The Music of Central Africa.* Nijhoff, The Hague, 1961, p. 37.   8. Kirby, P.R.: *The musical instruments of the native races of South Africa.* Witwatersrand University Press, 1965 (reprint of the 1934 edition), p. 228.   9. The principles are similar to those described in chapters IV and V and for the Venda in chapter X. See especially the list of rules 3.0.0 to 3.4.2.

6. Bibliography
a. Books

Cabral, A.A.P.: *Racas, Usos e Costumes dos Indigenas da Provincia de Mocambique, Lourenço Marques.* Imprensa Naçional, 1925.   Earthy, E. Dora.: *Valenge women.* Oxford University Press, London, 1933.   Jacques, Alexandre A. and Henri-Phillippe Junod.: *The wisdom of the Tsonga-Shangana people.* The Central Mission Press, 1957.   Junod, Henri: *Les chants et les contes des Ba-Ronga.* Georges Bridel & Cie, Lausanne, 1897.   Idem: *The life of a South African tribe,* I and II. Macmillan & Co., London, 1927.   Junod, Henri-Philippe: The Bantu tribes of South Africa (an introductory article on the Vathonga, with a bibliography, and descriptive notes on the plates). Duggan-Cronin: *The Bantu tribes of South Africa* IV. Deighton, Bell & Co. Ltd, Kimberley, 1935.   Idem: *Bantu heritage.* Hortors Ltd., Johannnesburg, 1938.   Idem: *Fifty Shangana-Tsonga fables in Tsonga verse.* Wallach's, Pretoria, 1940.   Marolen, D.P.P.: *Mitlangu ya vafana va Vatsonga.* The Swiss Mission in South Africa. Central Mission Press, 1954.   Idem: *Garingani-wa-garingani.* Beter Boeke, Pretoria, 1966.   Mkhombo, J.F.C.: *Leswi na Leswiya.* J.L. van Schaik Ltd, Pretoria, 1968.   Ntsanwisi, H.W.E.: *Tsonga idioms: a descriptive study.* The Swiss Mission in South Africa, Johannesburg, 1968.   Paiva e Pona, A.: *Dos Primeiros Trabalhos dos Portuguezes no Monomotapa, O padre Dom Goncalo da Silveira.* Lisboa Naçional, 1892.   Shilubana, R.P.M. and H.E. Ntsanwisi: *Muhlaba.* Published by the Nkuna tribe, New Shilubana Muhlaba Location, P.O. Letaba, N. Transvaal, 1958.

b. Essays, articles and papers

1. Cole-Beuchat, P.D.: Notes on some folklore forms in Tsonga and Ronga. *African Studies* XVII/4, 1958.   2. Guye, The Rev. H.: Des noms propre chez les Ba-Ronga. *Bulletin de la Société Neuchâteloise de Geographie,* 1920.   3. Johnston, Thomas, F.: Xizambi friction-bow music of the Shangana-Tsonga. *African Music* IV/4, 1970A.   4. Idem: Letter and photograph of Shangana-Tsonga nanga whistle. *Society for Ethnomusicology Newsletter* IV/5, Sept. 1970B.   5. Marivate, C.T.D.: Some traditional Tsonga songs. *Bantu Educational Journal,* Aug. 1959.   6. Ramsay, T.D.: *Tsonga law in the Transvaal.* Unpublished manuscript in the University of the Witwatersrand Library, Nov. 1941.

– T.S.

X MUSIC OF THE VENDA-SPEAKING PEOPLE
1. Introduction
2. Musical terms and concepts
3. Musical instruments (*zwilidzo*)
   a. Drums
   b. Sets of endblown pipes
   c. Whistles, horns, flutes and ocarinas
   d. Xylophones and *mbiras*
   e. Stringed instruments

4. The variety and functions of Venda music
5. Development of musical ability and transmission of the musical tradition
6. Varieties of Venda communal music
   a. Beer songs
   b. Music for children and play-dances for boys and girls
   c. "Amusements" (*mitambo*) for boys and girls
   d. *Mabepha* musical expeditions
   e. and f. *Murundu* and *Sungwi:* privately-owned initiation schools, subject to a degree of control by the rulers
      (i) *Nyimbo dza u sevhetha*
      (ii) *Nyimbo dza vhahwira*
      (iii) *Nyimbo dza dzingoma*
      (iv) *Nyimbo dza milayo*
   g. *Ngoma dza midzimu* and other types of possession dance
   h. and i. *Vhusha* and *Tshikanda,* the girls' initiation schools
   j. *Domba,* the premarital initiation school for boys and girls
   k. *Tshikona,* the national dance with heptatonic reed pipes and drums
   l. Sacred and secular music that has been added to the Venda musical tradition as a result of European influence
7. Some general rules of Venda music
   a. Social and cultural factors
   b. Tempo, meter and rhythm
   c. Speech-tone and melody
   d. Harmony and tonality
   e. Musical development of songs
   f. Transformation processes
8. References

1. Introduction

Functional analyses of musical structure cannot be detached from structural analyses of its social function: the function of tones in relation to each other cannot be explained adequately as part of a closed, purely musical, system without reference to the structures of the socio-cultural system of which the musical system is a part. Just as music is heard, learned and performed in a variety of social and cultural contexts, so its tonal structures reflect, at different levels of abstraction, the experiences and capacities of individuals in society. Variations in the form, texture, harmony and surface melody of a Venda girls' dance-song are generally a function of the number of girls present and good soloists amongst them, their experience of the music, the response of the audience, the time of day, and so on. Any description of a performance which treated the tonal organization independently of its social antecedents, would misinterpret the musical system. — Even with an identical group of performers, two social situations are unlikely to be exactly the same; and so the probability of two identical performances of communal music is rare. However, the models on which these performances are based remain the same, and they may be used for different songs in the same category, or even for different categories of music within the same tradition. They are extraordinarily flexible, because they are not so much sets of musical rules as general cultural models which reflect the organization and values of Venda society. Thus girls sing at their initiation what men play on pipes in the national dance; but their music is a transformation of the men's music, using the "female" companion of the men's keynote as their own keynote (see ex. 56). The patterns which both the men and the women perform in hocket style require at least twelve different pitches of a heptatonic scale, but the models by which they are produced also generate four-, five-, and six-tone children's songs (see ex. 57, p. 421). The models are capable of other transformations, and the ways in which they are used depend on the social context of the music required. Like the models which relate speech-tone patterns to changes in melody (see ex. 58, p. 422), I do not think that they can be used really creatively by someone who is not deeply involved in Venda society, because they are acquired unconsciously as part of the maturation process (see ex. 56). The continuity and vitality of Venda musical styles depend on a balance between cognitive consistency and continual changes in social interaction. The oral tradition, of which the musical system is a part, is a behavioural *model* of continuity, which can only be maintained by the changes which its constantly ageing transmittors make in their patterns of social interaction. Venda women do not re-learn the *music* of their *domba* initiation dance when they come together every four or five years to assist the novices: they re-live a social situation, and the *domba* music emerges when the experience is shared under certain conditions of individuality in community. This is why repeated performances of *domba* are at the same time intellectually difficult and emotionally stimulating. Though the music may *sound* similar to an outside observer of two successive initiations, it is in fact new to the performers, because of the new social situation, which required cognitive re-adjustment. That is, to re-create the music, the performers had to overcome the potential social and cognitive barrier suggested by the observation: "These are not the people I sang with before". Every performance of Venda communal music therefore demands re-creation of a special social situation as

Example 56

Illustration of the transformation process by which *khulo*, sung by girls, is related to *tshikona*, played on pipes by men, and summary of modes and basic chord sequence.

a. The upper tones of the basic repeated pattern of the music of *tshikona*, transposed down a semitone.

b. The basic pattern of *khulo*, sung by girl novices with the same hocket technique that men use with tuned pipes for *tshikona*.

c. Transposition of *tshikona*, to the same pitch as *khulo*. Note the *f* natural and the position of the tritone.

d. Transformation of *tshikona*, rewriting *d''* as *phala* (keynote) instead of *a''*. Note how the position of the tritone differs from *tshikona* in c, but agrees with *khulo* in b.

e. The three modes used in *tshikona* and *khulo*, rewritten without accidentals. The figures indicate the number of semitones in the intervals.

f. The harmonic basis of *khulo*. The sequence of chords also fits the *tshikona* pattern, regardless of the different modes used.

Example 57   Relationship between the melodies of three children's songs (exs. 75, 78 and 80) and the music of *tshikona*, the Venda national dance. Each player of *tshikona* blows one tone of the total pattern. Only part of *tshikona* is given, and it is transposed.

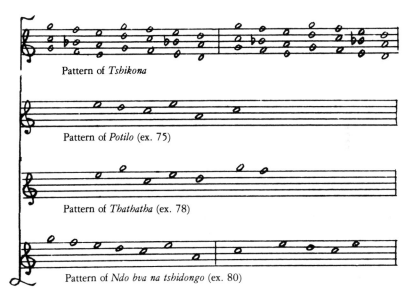

Pattern of *Tshikona*

Pattern of *Potilo* (ex. 75)

Pattern of *Thathatha* (ex. 78)

Pattern of *Ndo bva na tshidongo* (ex. 80)

Example 58

Parts of two Venda children's songs, illustrating some effects of changing speech-tones on the patterns of melody:

á = high speech-tone.
ā = secondary high.
â = falling high.
à = low.

much as a repetition of learned skills. If there is an important difference between Venda music and European written, or "art", music, it is that the "art" composer freezes a particular improvization and its corresponding social situation, or produces a composite, statistical model of several different performances of the same song. This is a consequence of changes in the division of labour in society, and it does not signify any radical change in the sensitivity and performance of Man as Music-Maker. — A basic function of music is to reinforce, or relate people more closely to certain experiences which have come to have meaning in their social life. In the Venda experience, as in the experience of the total population of any European country, there are many kinds of music, ranging from tonal experiences related to people to shared experiences related to tones. No matter how abstract the sounds may seem to be, their organization is always a function of the human experience of their composers; and however crudely functional a song may seem, it is in a sense no more or less artificial than a symphony. — Not all unwritten, so-called "folk" music survives simply because it is functional or peasants are generously uncritical. The Venda do no accept a sincere desire to express feeling as an excuse for incompetent performance or a poor composition: they expect technical brilliance and originality, and they assess the sounds produced, rather than the way a musician may roll his eyes or throw his body about. Anyone who troubles to perfect his technique is considered to do so because he is deeply committed to music as a means of sharing some experience with his fellows. — Venda music is overtly political in that it is performed in a variety of political contexts and often for specific political purposes. It is also political in the sense that it may involve people in a powerful *shared experience* within the framework of their cultural experience, and thereby make them more aware of themselves and of their responsibilities towards each other. *Muthu ndi muthu nga vhathu,* the Venda say: "man is man through his associations with men". Venda music is not an escape from reality: it is sometimes an adventure *into* reality, the reality of the world of the spirit. It can be an experience of becoming, in which individual consciousness is nurtured within the collective consciousness of the community, and hence becomes the source of richer cultural forms. For example, if two drummers play exactly the same surface rhythm, but maintain an individual, inner difference of tempo or beat, they produce something more than their individual effects. Thus, a combination of a straight-forward beat played by two people at different tempi produces the pattern in ex. 59.

Example 59

A combination of two iambic rhythms with different main beats can produce the pattern in ex. 60. These are not gimmicky ways of producing surface rhythms which could be more easily produced by one performer. They are musical expressions of concepts of individuality in community, and of temporal and spatial balance, which are found in other features of Venda culture. Such rhythms cannot be performed correctly in this way unless the players are their own conductors and yet at the same time submit to the rhythm of an invisible conductor. — There is space for only a brief description of some of the social and cultural institutions which generate Venda music, and for a few representative samples of the rich and varied sounds which may be heard in the Louis Trichardt and Sibasa districts, where most of South Africa's 300 000 Venda live, and in Soweto (chiefly in Meadowlands and Chiawelo) and the other Transvaal cities and

Example 60

towns where some have migrated or settled. — Venda-speaking people have lived in and around the Zoutpansberg, just south of the Limpopo river, for many centuries. The ancestors of some Venda clans were there long before Whites landed in the Cape, and they managed to retain their identity even after they had accepted the rule of Black invaders from the north about two hundred years ago. Although the Venda allowed the first Berlin Lutheran missionary to settle amongst them in 1872, it was not until 1899 that they finally submitted to the authority of the Transvaal Republic. They were thus the last of the Bantu-speaking peoples of South Africa to be seriously affected by contact with Europeans. There are now churches, schools and hospitals in the Sibasa district, and more recently the government has subsidized other services, such as a wholesale association for Venda shopkeepers, and launched forestry and agricultural schemes. In spite of many changes that have taken place, traditional musical activities and many traditional cultural institutions are still vigorously pursued. — The Venda have a culture which distinguishes them clearly from other Bantu-speaking people in South Africa, and a language which is classed on its own, though it has some affinities with Sotho and Karanga. They were originally shifting cultivators and hunters, but later adopted a more settled economy; they also took to keeping cattle as well as goats. They used to live in large villages which were often sited on mountain slopes and difficult to reach, and every village was administered by a chief or headman and his council. In the first part of this century, people tended to move away from the villages of their rulers, and live in homesteads scattered all over the hills and mountains. In many areas, they are now being regrouped into villages. — The Venda are a patrilineal, virilocal people, many of whom still practise polygamy and worship their families' ancestors. Members of the different patriclans can, and do, live in any of the tribal territories, because the tribe is an administrative and territorial unit, consisting of people who choose to owe allegiance to a particular dynasty. It is, of course, quite common to find a ruler attracting round him members of his own patriclan after his accession. There is no paramount chief: each tribe is ruled by an independent chief, who has under him headmen and petty headmen respectively responsible for the government of districts within the tribal territory. Most of the chiefs belong to lineages of the same clan which crossed the Limpopo river and subdued those whom they found living in the Zoutpansberg about 150 to 200 years ago. Thus there is an important social division in Venda society between commoners (*vhasiwana*) and the children of chiefs and their descendants (*vhakololo*). In the Sibasa district there are twelve Venda chiefs: some are the descendants of brothers, who were the sons of a ruling chief but broke away and established independent chiefdoms elsewhere; and others have been appointed by the government in recent years. There are a number of differences in the customs of the various patriclans, especially in religious ritual, but there are no essential cultural differences between the tribes. — Although administration of the Venda people has recently been formalized by the creation of tribal, regional and territorial authorities, these institutions had not radically altered the traditional political system in 1956–1958, when the basic information on Venda music was obtained. Music played an important part in the political process, and although much of it was sponsored by rulers, it was performed chiefly by commoners. In fact, historical and musical evidence suggest that the core of the Venda musical tradition, and especially the use of the heptatonic scale, was well established before the ancestors of the ruling clans crossed the Limpopo (see Blacking, 1971B).

2. Musical terms and concepts

The term "songs of the Venda-speaking people" *(nyimbo dza Vhavenda)* includes all tunes that are "sung" or "played on instruments", as well as patterns of words that are recited to a regular metre. It is its rhythm, therefore, that distinguishes "singing" *(u imba),* from "talking" *(u amba),* from "reciting praises" *(u renda)*, or "narrating" *(u anetshela)*. Nevertheless, although it may have no rhythm and is sometimes called *u ṱavha mukosi* (raising the alarm with a long, loud yell), a single tone blown on a stopped pipe or horn comes into the Venda category of music: the performer "plays" it *(-lidza)*, or more literally "makes it cry", since *-lidza* is the causative of *-lila* (to weep, cry). Musical instruments are thus known as *zwilidzo,* "things that are made to cry". A soloist "plants" *(-sima)* his song, and the chorus "thunder in response" *(-bvumela)*. The verbs *-sima* and *-bvumela* are used in non-musical contexts, and the latter commonly describes the way in which a person grunts to show that he is following a conversation, or responds formally when evidence is being led in a court case. — A dance-leader *(maluselo)* "shows the step" *(-sumbedza mulenzhe,* lit. shows a leg), and the others "pour it out" *(-shela mulenzhe)* after him. Great importance is attached to team-work in dancing, and the word *u tshina* (to dance) generally refers to communal dancing, in which all follow the same steps, as distinct from *u gaya,* which is "to dance a solo". Other more individual styles are *u ṱanga* which is "to dance in a stately fashion", as old women and important people do on special occasions; *u pembela,* "to dance excitedly," especially at the end of an initiation school or the installation of a chief; *u ṱhaga* "to dance *ndayo*" at the *vhusha* girls' initiation school (see plate 15); and *u dabela,* "to dance independently" of, and often in the opposite direction to, members of an initiation school, as a sign that one has graduated. The dancing of the masked youths *(vhahwira)* in the girls' initiation school *(sungwi* or *musevhetho)* is called *u vhina:* the school has been borrowed from the Sotho, and *-vhina* is simply the Sotho word for "to dance". Most Venda communal dances are basically circular and counter-clockwise: the dancers "go round" *(-mona)* and make "a cattle kraal" *(danga)* (see plate 15). Singers can indicate the metrical patterns of songs by clapping their hands, and they can sing either the solo or the chorus part alone and know exactly where to come in. They cannot isolate a pattern, nor do they seem to appreciate that there are points in time when a pattern is repeated. People simply refer to the correct melody or rhythm of a song as "the way in which it is sung" *(kuimbele)*, or "the way in which it is played" *(kulidzele)*. Mistakes in performance are recognized, though critics rarely state precisely what is wrong: they just know that it does not sound right. For instance, people said "you have gone astray" *(yho khakha)*, both when I did not observe the speech-tone patterns of children's songs, and when I failed to maintain a metrono-mically accurate tempo while playing one of the drums at a possession dance. In the first case, I had to find out for myself why I was wrong, and why I sang "like a Tsonga", and in the second, they eventually qualified their criticism by saying that I was "hurrying" *(-ṱavhanya)*. Although there is a distinction between "hurrying" or "delaying" *(-lenga)* the tempo during a performance, the tempi of the dances *tshigombela* and *tshikona* are not classified respectively as fast or slow: they "are different", and "go in opposite directions" *(-thambana)*. Time signatures and note values are not recognized, though the word *-kokodza* (to drag, pull) describes a tone that is prolonged, especially at the end of a song. — Because music is conceived as repetitions of basic patterns, there can be no concept of rests in performance, since a rest would immediately destroy the special world of time which music is meant to

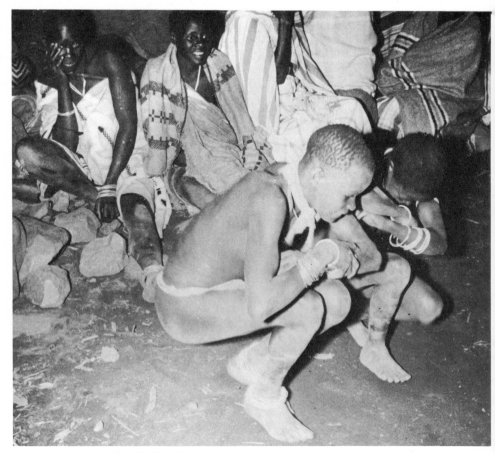

Plate 15. Two girls dance *ndayo* at the end of a *domba* initiation.
The style of dancing is called *u ṱhaga.*

create. Thus ex. 61 is a children's song, and the metrical beat does not fall on the syllables -*ḓu*-, -*tsha,* and -*nga*-, which are stressed in performance. If people clap to the song, they clap on the syllables *tshi*- -*la,* -*si,* and *ḓi,* so that there is not a rest on the fourth beat, but a total pattern of four beats. Venda music is not founded on melody or on metre, but on a rhythmical stirring of the whole body, of which singing and metre are but extensions. When a rest is heard between two drum beats, it must be understood that for the player it is not a rest: each drum beat is the part of a total body movement in which the hand or a stick strikes the drum skin. — The words -*ṱuku* (small, young) and -*hulwane* (important, senior) are generally used to refer respectively to tones that are high and low in pitch. The word -*hulu* (big, visibly large in size) is more often used to describe the number of performers and the

Example 61

1. Tshi - ḍu - ḽa tshaMu - si - nga - ḍi!
2. Vha - ko - ma vha tshi ya Dza - ṱa,
3. Vha fhi-zi sa mu - ḍi - n - ḍa pha-n-ḍa,
4. Mu - ḍi - n - ḍa ndi Ra - mu - deu - ḽi,

corresponding loudness of the sound, probably because intensity of tone is not recognized in musical terms: a performer either plays or sings with confidence, and hence with uniform loudness, or indifferently because of shyness, laziness, or ignorance of the music. Thus, assuming that the performers are doing well, loud music is at the same time "big", and vice versa, because there are many or few performing it. A few people distinguish the sound of female and male voices by calling the former "thin" (-*sekene*) and the latter "thick" (-*denya*); and pitch within the female and male ranges is further subdivided into high, which "closes the throat" and low, which "snores". — Quality of tone and phrasing, which is invariably *legato,* are not specifically taken into account: people either "play well" and "sing well", or they do not. Great vigour and energy, precision and virtuosity, are expected of the good performer: a person may sing so well that he "nearly bursts his diaphragm" and dance so that he "digs a hole in the ground", "licks the clouds", or leaps so high that "three people can crawl underneath him". People like to see and listen to a dynamic, almost destructive performance, when hand-rattles are "shaken so that they nearly break". Quite often a drumskin is torn and a ritual postponed for some hours while it is replaced, or until another drum has been borrowed; leg-rattles disintegrate during a dance, the leather supports of xylophone keys break, and people grow hoarse and lose their voices. Such accidents during a performance do not upset people, since they are usually evidence of good, vigorous playing and the intense excitement that goes with it. — The Venda have no word for "scale". They have the word *mutavha,* which is used for a complete set of divining dice, of metal amulets, or of reed-pipes, and also for a row of keys on a xylophone or *mbira.* Thus a *mutavha,* may include more than one octave of a heptatonic or a pentatonic scale, since reed-pipes and *mbiras* may be tuned to either of these scales. The Venda recognize that heptatonic and pentatonic sets sound different, and they appreciate the interval of the octave; but they do not express the difference in terms of the division of the octave into seven or five intervals. Venda melodies employ anything from two to seven different tones, but the Venda themselves are not concerned with such aspects of their musical tradition: *they prefer to classify their music on the basis of its social function,* which may indirectly affect its structure and especially its rhythmic pattern. — Most adult Venda know what is happening from the sound of the associated music. No less than sixteen different styles of music are distinguished, with different rhythms and combinations of singers and instruments; and within these styles are further subdivisions of style, as well as many different songs within each subdivision. There are scores of beer-songs, over seventy of one type of initiation song, and thirty of another, and there are always new words being added to existing songs, and often entirely new songs being composed. — Musical instruments that are used for communal performances are played only for rituals, ceremonies, and entertainments sponsored by rulers or prominent people, or during rehearsals for such events. Solo instruments may be played at any time, and generally for personal amusement. The most important communal instruments are drums and reed-pipes, which are played respectively by women and men.

3. Musical instruments (*zwilidzo*)
Venda instruments have been described in detail by P.R. Kirby (Kirby, 1934), and only brief descriptions will be given here. Fig. 21, p. 444 shows their place in Venda musical life.

a. Drums (see plate 16 a and b, pp. 429, 430)
Ngoma is a large, pot-shaped drum with a hemispherical resonator carved out of solid wood, and it is always played with a stick. — *Thungwa* is the same shape as, but smaller than, *ngoma* and is also played with a stick. — *Murumba* has a conical resonator of wood, is held between the thighs and played with the hands. — Most sets of drums are kept in the homes of chiefs and headmen, and comprise one *ngoma,* one *thungwa* and two or three *mirumba.* Sets without *ngoma* may be found in the homes of certain commoners, such as the doctors who run girls' initiation schools (*sungwi*). Drums are often given personal names. Venda in urban areas make their instruments out of old petrol and paraffin drums of various sizes: on one end they fasten with wooden pegs a piece of ox-hide in the traditional fashion. — Drums are always played by women and girls, except in possession dances, when men may play any of the drums, and especially *ngoma,* and in performances in urban areas, where men live together in compounds without their womenfolk. — For the sake of musical understanding, *ngoma, thungwa* and *murumba* will be henceforth described as bass, tenor and alto drums respectively. *Tshigubu* is a double-sided drum modelled on the European bass-drum; it is usually played in the military style with two rubber-ended beaters, and is used by schools and Separatist Churches, whose members wish to show that they have made a break with tradition (see fig. 10, p. 390).

b. Sets of end-blown pipes (similar to dismantled panpipes, see plate 3, p. 354)
End-blown pipes (*ņanga*) are tuned in two ways and made of different materials: *Ņanga dza musununu* (*ņanga,* made of a species of bamboo tuned to a heptatonic scale) and *ņanga dza luţanga* (*ņanga* made of river-reed) to a pentatonic scale. A set (*mutavha*) of the former may number more than twenty pipes and extend over three octaves, whilst a set of the latter usually numbers twelve and covers just over two octaves. Nowadays, especially in urban areas, the pipes are often made of an odd assortment of pieces of metal tubing, hose pipe, curtain rods, or even pram handles. The river-reed is found in many parts of Venda, but *musununu* bamboo is chiefly concentrated in a grove at Tshaulu, in Eastern Venda, and it is cut exclusively by the male members of one family. The first pipe to be tuned is *phala,* which is the chief tone of every set of heptatonic pipes and should be of the same pitch in the sets of all the headmen of a tribe. Not all tribes have the same chief tone, however, and people will

Plate 16a. A child plays on the *ngoma* bass drum whilst novices rest during a *domba* initiation.

Plate 16b. Two *domba* novices sway from side to side and rub the drumskins with one hand, in order to keep good time as they play the *mirumba* alto drums. The length of their hair, which was shaved at the beginning of the initiation, is a sign of their seniority in the school.

comment that certain rulers' pipes can be played together, and others cannot. For instance, in 1957 the tunings of *phala* at Makonde, Dzimauli, Lufule, and Thengwe were respectively 284, 244, 240 and 236 v.p.s. After *phala* has been cut and tuned, smaller pipes are made to provide the ascending scale, and then larger pipes for the descending scale. The pipes are tuned adjacently, and sometimes tested in groups of three, but I never heard tunings tested by intervals of the octave, fifth, or fourth. The final adjustment of the tunings takes place only when the pipes are tested by a team of players: the sound of the total musical pattern reveals errors of tuning that were not evident when the pipes were tested separately. — Each reed-pipe has a name according to its place in the scale, but the names do not seem to be used to identify notes, like the sol-fa system; in fact, I found few experts, and still fewer performers, who knew the names of all the notes, and none who could explain the significance of all of them. The pipes *thakulana, phalana, dangwana* and *kholomwana* play the same melody as *thakhula, phala, dangwe* and *kholomo*, but an octave higher; and the ending *-ana* is a diminutive, so that *thakhulana* means "little *thakhula*". *Thakhula* means "the lifter", a name which may refer to its position in the *tshikona* melody: it is the last note of the phrase, and is one tone above the chief tone (*phala*), with which the repetition of the melody begins; the rhythm halts slightly on this note, which might therefore be said to "lift" the phrase back to its tonal centre (see ex. 109, p. 498). Similarly, *tshiaravhi* means "the answerer", and it follows *phala,* which is always the first note played. *Thakhula* and *tshiaravhi* are sometimes called respectively *mvusi* (the raiser) and *mbidzi* (the caller), names which are also related to their function in the music; but the other names of the pipes, such as *kholomo* (head of cattle) are obscure. — The names of the pentatonic pipes are different, and the words show a greater affinity with Northern Sotho, the language of the people from whom they are supposed to have been borrowed.

c. Whistles, horns, flutes and ocarinas
Kirby has described in detail the various types of signal horn and whistle (*tshihoho, phala, dzwio* and *ṅanga*) used by Venda herdboys, and the whistles that doctors use (*ṅanga ya ḍanga*, made of vulture's leg). Manufactured police-whistles (*ndwevha*) are now used to signal a change of step in communal dances, and to add a simple, vigorous cross-rhythm to solo dances, especially in the girls' *tshigombela*. — Side-blown horns are most often made of the horns of kudu, gemsbok, and sable antelope: the straight are called *khwatha,* and the curved *phalaphala* (see plate 1, p. 349). They are used to summon people to the court of a ruler for a work-party, to announce an important event, to herald a special gift of beer (*murula*), or simply to express excitement during a musical performance. — Herdboys still play melodies on *tshiṭiringo* (see ex. 62, p. 432 and plate 14, p. 369), a three-holed transverse flute, made from a piece of river-reed closed at both ends by a natural knot, though many now prefer the penny-whistle, which can be bought at stores. This became particularly popular when the craze for penny-whistle bands was spread from Johannesburg in 1958 through gramophone records. *Ḍilitili* is played by herdboys, but is not often seen today. The nodes of a length of river-reed are burnt out, and an oblique embouchure is cut: by opening and closing the reed with the first finger at the distal end, the player is able to blow notes of the harmonic series of both the open and closed tube (see ex. 63, p. 433). Herdboys apparently played *zwipoṭoliyo* (sing: *tshipoṭoliyo*) ocarinas more often in the past than they do today. They are made of the hollowed-out shell of the *thuzwu*

431

Example 62

Example 63

^XIndicates audible regular beat made by the sound of the finger being placed on the hole.

Example 64 a, b, c

a

b

c

Plate 17a. Two men play the *mbila mtondo* xylophone. Note that the bass player uses three beaters.

Plate 17b. The *mbira* called *mbila dza madeza*, without calabash resonator.

Plate 17c. Mbila tshipai, mbira without resonator.

fruit, with a small hole for blowing and two for stopping with the fingers. The method in which pairs of ocarinas are selected for duets (see ex. 64 a, b, c, p. 434) and the structure of the music played on them has been described in Blacking, 1959B.

d. Xylophones and mbiras (see plate 17a, b, c, pp. 435, 436, 437)
The word *mbila* refers to the notes of xylophones and of *mbiras*. The notes of the heptatonic xylophone (*mbila mutondo*) and the large *mbira* (*mbila dza madeza*), which have about twenty-one and twenty-seven keys respectively, are called by the same names as the reed-pipes. The xylophone requires two performers: one plays the theme with two beaters on the top ten or twelve keys, and the other plays a complicated cross-rhythm on the bass-notes with three beaters, two of which are held by the left hand. Most tunes begin on the key-note (*phala*), which is the third or fourth note down from the smallest note on the keyboard (see ex. 65, p. 439). The *mbira* seems to have been brought to Vendaland by the Lemba, an endogamous clan of craftsmen who came across the Limpopo with the present ruling clans; whilst the xylophone was made and used by those whom they conquered. Nowadays, the xylophone is almost obsolete, and several non-Lemba men play the *mbila dza madeza mbira,* which is often used to accompany songs at a beer-party (see ex. 66, p. 440). A *mbira* not reported by Kirby, and apparently of recent origin, is *mbila tshipai,* which has from eleven to eighteen notes and is basically pentatonic: players add an extra note or two in order to play melodies that require hexatonic or heptatonic scales (see ex. 67, p. 441). Some say that the instrument and the scale were borrowed from the Tsonga, who live in the south, whilst others maintain that the layout of the central eleven notes was borrowed from the Northern Sotho, who live in the west and south, and that additional notes were added by the Venda (see plate 4, p. 355).

e. Stringed instruments
Dende is a wooden bow, with a string of copper wire which is tied back to it near the centre, where a small gourd resonator is attached. The string is struck with a thin stick and produces two basic tones, usually a minor third apart, which can be varied by stopping with the back of one of the fingers of the hand holding the bow. The tone can be varied by placing the resonator on or away from the body (see plate 6, pp. 357, 358). — *Ngwala* is the Venda version of the *gora* stringed-wind instrument, but it seems to be extinct. Kirby reported in 1934 (Kirby, 1934, p. 187) that it was becoming obsolete, and noted that it had only been used by the Venda for about eighty years. In 1956, I met a few old men who knew of it, but had lost their teeth and could therefore play it no more. When at last I met one who still possessed a set of teeth, I found that he had lost his arm in an accident on a forest plantation. He said that he would make an instrument and devise some way of playing it with one arm; but shortly after that he died (see plate 8, p. 360).— A few Venda play *tshizambi,* but it is really a Tsonga instrument (see fig. 13, p. 395). — *Tshidzholo* is a one-stringed fiddle, usually with a tin resonator, which is supposed to have been introduced to the Venda by the Northern Sotho. It is rare, and I met only two players of it, both of whom were Sotho (see plate 7, p. 359). — All these instruments are played by men or boys. *Lugube,* on the other hand, is for girls or young married women. It is made of a piece of river-reed about two feet long, with a string stretching from one end to the other. The player usually holds the instrument to her left, plucks the proximal end of the string with the forefinger of her right hand, and stops it with the backs of the second, third and fourth

Example 65

Example 66   Layout of *mbira* keys and approximate pitch.

The thumb plucks the keys downwards and the forefinger upwards from under the key.

Example 67   Layout of *mbira* keys and approximate pitch.

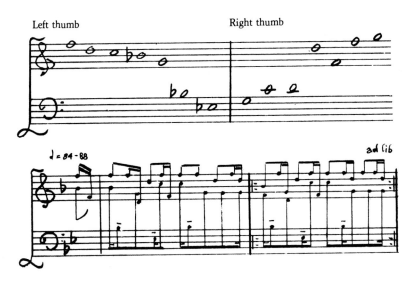

fingers of the left hand; she uses the mouth as a resonator, and by varying the size of the cavity she can produce a variety of harmonics, as well as the fundamental, fingered tones. Metal jews harps, bought at stores, are tending to replace *lugube,* and are called by the same name. — *Tshihwana* is a musical bow played by men and boys, and sometimes by girls. Its basic shape is similar to the *dende,* but it is plucked and resonated like *lugube.* Kirby compares it to "the hunting-bow of India with its thick hand-grip" (Kirby, 1934, p. 229; see fig. 16, p. 402). The string is drawn back towards the centre of the hand-grip by another string, which is always left loose and only wound round the grip for tuning and playing. The tunings of the two parts of the bow string are varied according to the requirements of the melody, which is produced by resonating the fundamentals with the mouth. — Guitars are not used in the Sibasa district as often as in other rural areas of South Africa, and hardly ever as solo instruments. They are strummed to provide rhythmic accompaniments for jive and other types of modern dancing.

4. The variety and functions of Venda music (see fig. 21 and 22, pp. 444, 446)

The styles of Venda music vary according to their social function. The metrical pattern of work-songs is regular and depends on the nature of the work; but that of beer-songs may be irregular and emphasized by handclaps or by the steps of solo dancers. The girls' dance, *tshigombela,* and the boys' reed-pipe dances are not sufficiently important to merit the use of the bass drum, which is reserved for the music of the *domba* initiation and the national dance. Similarly, only the tenor and alto drums are used in the girls' initiation schools, *vhusha, tshikanda* and *sungwi.* No drums are used for the music of boys' circumcision schools, because they are held in secret in the bush. When the bass drum is needed for the music of possession dances, it is played in an entirely different way, and by a man, so that common use of the bass drum need not imply a close functional relationship between the possession cult and those institutions in which it is played in the traditional manner by women – the *domba* initiation and the national dance. The differences between these styles both in tempi and in drum techniques express the different social interests that the institutions represent: the possession cult is practised chiefly by commoners, whereas *domba* and the national dance are sponsored by rulers. Musical styles that show various degrees of assimilation of Western techniques, express the extent to which their performers have aligned themselves with the Western way of life. Thus traditional drums are taboo to all educated Christians of European-organized churches, not because their musical sound is objectionable but because as objects they are symbols of pagan associations. Those who belong to the Salvation Army tolerate the use of a Western-type bass drum, and of course jazz drums are acceptable in a secular context. Members of Separatist Churches, who seek a compromise between European-organized Christianity and traditional Venda culture, are happy to use a drum that is a copy of the Western bass drum and sing music that is related both to traditional Venda and Western Christian styles. — The performance of most communal music is regulated by the rules of the social institutions which it accompanies, but solo instrumentalists may perform at any time of the year without special permission. Some who play the xylophone or *mbira* may accompany singers at a beer-party; others become semi-professional musicians (*zwilombe;* sing. *tshilombe*), and from time to time compose new songs, or variations on old ones, accompanying themselves on an *mbira* or a musical bow (usually *dende* or *tshizambi*). They are expected to amuse their audiences, and are admired for their wit, their mastery of technique and handling of words, and for their ability to clown as well as to protest effectively against any injustice that may need attention. Rulers like to have such men around them because, although they run the risk of being criticized publicly in songs, they gain prestige from the music they sponsor and incidentally information about public opinion. Nothing is slanderous, so long as it is said with music. In turn, minstrels like to hang around rulers' homes, where there is always plenty of food and beer, as well as visitors, and it is easier to make a living as an entertainer. The presence of a minstrel in a district seems to have an effect on the distribution of certain instruments: for instance, "clusters" of players of the *dende* musical bow may be found in districts where a minstrel lives, and most of them are young admirers, who wish one day to emulate him. — Others play instruments purely for their own pleasure. Between 1956 and 1958, young men and boys were particularly fond of the small *mbira (mbila tshipai):* I often came across a lad sitting on a rock, gazing out over the hills, singing a song of love or loneliness, or strolling along with his friends and strumming a repetitive "walking song". Some youths like to increase the volume of an instrument by using an old paraffin tin as a resonator. They may attach a flag to the tin as a decoration, and go on cattle dipping days to encourage with slow music the teams of herdboys who take part in "boxing" matches by the dipping tanks (see plate 18). While their animals graze, herdboys may play rippling ocarina duets that sound like bird song, or shrill tunes on transverse flutes. Girls play the jews harp or its prototype, *lugube,* as they go to fetch water, wild vegetables, or goods from a store, or while they sit in the sun and gossip after an afternoon bathe. The sound of the Venda stringed instruments does not carry far, and so it is virtually impossible to annoy one's neigbours; boys' signal whistles, and flute and ocarina music, often sound like an integral part of the countryside; and if xylophone music is heard, it usually

Plate 18. Two youths play *mbiras* (*mbila tshipai*) resonated with old paraffin tins, as they encourage enthusiasm at an informal boxing tournament between two teams of herdboys on cattle-dipping day.

Figure 21   The interrelationship of the functions and sounds of Venda music.

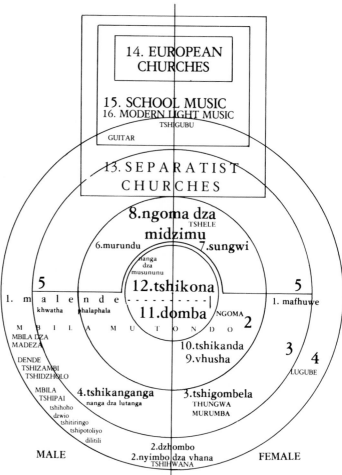

EXPLANATION OF TYPE:

music with mirumba, thungwa, ngoma drums
music with mirumba and thungwa

music without drums
STRINGED AND OTHER INSTRUMENTS
wind instruments
CIRCLES ENCLOSE TRADITIONAL, AND RECTANGLES NON-TRADITIONAL, STYLES

1. THE MOST IMPORTANT MUSIC, CONTROLLED BY RULERS (ngoma khulwane)

2. MUSIC OF A SERIOUS NATURE, SPONSORED OR PERMITTED BY RULERS (ngoma)

3. AMUSEMENTS (mitambo) SPONSORED BY RULERS

4. INSTRUMENTAL MUSIC (zwilidzo), AMUSEMENTS ETC. NOT SUBJECT TO CONTROL

5.5. MARKS DIVISION BETWEEN MUSIC MAKING GROUPS THAT ARE COMPLETELY ORTHODOX
AND THOSE THAT ARE UNORTHODOX TO VARYING DEGREES
THE GROUPS IN RECTANGLES PARTICIPATE IN ORTHODOX MUSIC OFFICIALLY TO THE EX
TENT THAT THE RECTANGLES PENETRATE THE CIRCLES: IN FACT MANY PENETRATE
CIRCLES 1 AND 2

draws a small and appreciative audience, even when the players are merely practising. The rather monotonous and disjointed sound of girls practising drums in or near the council hut of their headman, is tolerated and even encouraged, because it is a necessary stage in the preparation for communal performances, which please everybody. — Fig. 21 illustrates the interrelationship of the sounds and different functions of Venda music. Music in the traditional style is contained in concentric circles symbolic of Venda houses and dances, and non-traditional music is in rectangles, similar to the European house designs that many have now adopted. The central line divides the music of men and women, and progress from the bottom of the diagram to the centre approximates the sequence of learning the music. — Fig. 22 shows the relationship between performances of communal music and the cycle of seasons and associated activities. The twelve traditional lunar months of the Venda are approximately equal to the European months, because one year of thirteen lunar months was always allowed to every two years of twelve, and *tshimedzi,* the first month of the Venda year, was adjusted according to the position of the stars. The Venda and European terms for the seasons are not exactly equivalent, and in any case the onset of each season may vary from year to year. Both the frequency and conditions of performance of Venda communal music depend to a great extent on the cycle of seasons and the existence of an economic surplus. During the period of planting and weeding, for instance, only important ritual music and work-songs are performed regularly. Towards the end of the weeding season, when the first green maize cobs are appearing, girls begin to practise for their dance *tshigombela,* which they would find difficult to dance in the mud of the rainy season, even if they were not required at that time to help with the weeding of crops, the collection of food, and other domestic duties. Circumcision schools are held during the winter, and possession dances and boys' communal dances take place chiefly during the period of rest between harvest and planting. Communal music is never performed without some kind of reward, either to the performers or to the organizers, so that in a lean year none but the more important items are played. If the countryside resounds with music, especially at night when it is cool, it is a sign of good times. — Communal dances also introduce young people to patterns of tribal authority: the music is sponsored by rulers, and one ruler sends his dance teams on expeditions to other rulers, either to confirm his relationships with them, or, if he is a chief and they are headmen, to exact tribute. The musical expeditions *(mabepha;* sing. *bepha)* consolidate both the lineage ties of rulers, who are separated spatially because of their responsibility for district government, and the neighbourhood ties of clansfolk living in different districts, and hence the bonds between these people and their district headmen (Blacking, 1962). — The music of the boys' and girls' circumcision schools advertises the power of the doctors who sponsor them, and possession dances enhance the prestige and influence of the families who belong to the different cult groups. Within the traditional music system, ambitious men are able to attract a following and further their interests by means of the music that is performed under their auspices. **Music is therefore an audible and visible sign of social and political groupings in Venda society, and the music that a man can command or forbid is a measure of his status.** When a ruler holds a *domba* initiation, all other music in his district is banned, except for his own *tshikona* (the national dance), beer-songs and personal instrumental music. Nobody is compelled to perform music or to observe these bans, and indeed many Venda Christians ignore them altogether. Music has meaning for the Venda only in so far as its social contexts

Figure 22   Venda communal music, in relation to the cycle of seasons and associated activities.

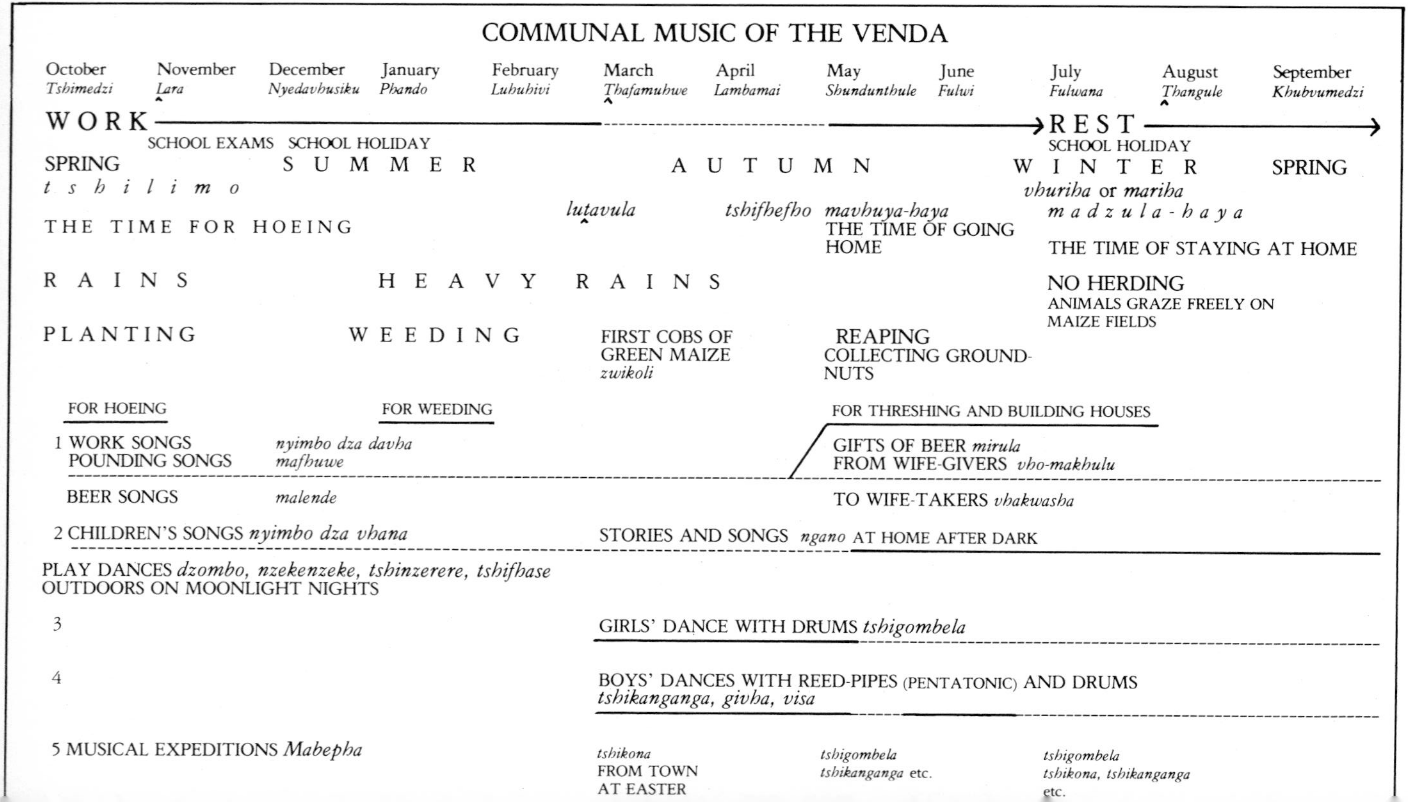

COMMUNAL MUSIC OF THE VENDA

October *Tshimedzi*	November *Lara*	December *Nyedavhusiku*	January *Phando*	February *Luhuhi*	March *Thafamuhwe*	April *Lambamai*	May *Shundunthule*	June *Fulwi*	July *Fulwana*	August *Thangule*	September *Khubvumedzi*

WORK ————————————————————————————————→ **REST** →

SPRING *tshilimo* — SUMMER ———————— AUTUMN —————— WINTER — SPRING

SCHOOL EXAMS / SCHOOL HOLIDAY (Nov–Jan) ... SCHOOL HOLIDAY / W I N T E R (July–Aug)

THE TIME FOR HOEING ... *lutavula* ... *tshifhefho* *mavhuya-baya* THE TIME OF GOING HOME ... *vhuriha* or *mariha* *m a d z u l a - b a y a* THE TIME OF STAYING AT HOME

R A I N S — H E A V Y   R A I N S — W E E D I N G — A U T U M N   R A I N S ... NO HERDING ANIMALS GRAZE FREELY ON MAIZE FIELDS

PLANTING — WEEDING — FIRST COBS OF GREEN MAIZE *zwikoli* — REAPING COLLECTING GROUND-NUTS

FOR HOEING — FOR WEEDING — FOR THRESHING AND BUILDING HOUSES

GIFTS OF BEER *mirula* FROM WIFE-GIVERS *vho-makhulu*

TO WIFE-TAKERS *vhakwasha*

1 WORK SONGS / POUNDING SONGS *nyimbo dza davha* / *malfhuwe*

BEER SONGS *malende*

2 CHILDREN'S SONGS *nyimbo dza vhana*

STORIES AND SONGS *ngano* AT HOME AFTER DARK

PLAY DANCES *dzombo, nzekenzeke, tshinzerere, tshifhase* OUTDOORS ON MOONLIGHT NIGHTS

3 GIRLS' DANCE WITH DRUMS *tshigombela* — *tshigombela* / *tshikanganga* etc. — *tshigombela* / *tshikona, tshikanganga* etc.

4 BOYS' DANCES WITH REED-PIPES (PENTATONIC) AND DRUMS *tshikanganga, givha, visa*

tshikona FROM TOWN AT EASTER — *tshigombela* / *tshikanganga* etc. — *tshigombela* / *tshikona, tshikanganga* etc.

5 MUSICAL EXPEDITIONS *Mabepha*

6

BOYS' CIRCUMCISION SCHOOL
m u r u n d u

7 GIRLS' CIRCUMCISION SCHOOL *sungui* or *musevhetho* TERMS OF ABOUT THREE MONTHS THROUGHOUT YEAR WITH PERIODS OF REST

8 POSSESSION DANCES *tshele*: (lit. HAND RATTLE) DANCED INDOORS WHEN SICKNESS IS ATTRIBUTED TO SPIRIT'S DESIRE TO ENTER SUFFERER'S BODY

ngoma dza mi̧dzimu ng dza malombo: (lit. DRUMS OF THE ANCESTOR SPIRITS etc.) PERFORMED OUTDOORS FOR 4 TO 6 DAYS

9 GIRLS' INITIATION SCHOOL *vhusha* HELD WHEN A GIRL'S PUBERTY IS REPORTED TO HEADMAN. EACH SESSION LASTS 6 DAYS

GIRLS' INITIATION SCHOOL *tshikanda*

10 HELD ONLY BEFORE BEGINNING OF *domba* IN A DISTRICT. LASTS A MONTH

11 BOYS' AND GIRLS' PRE-MARITAL INITIATION SCHOOL *d o m b a*

HELD BY CHIEFS AND HEADMEN AT INTERVALS OF ABOUT 5 YEARS IN EACH DISTRICT, AND AFTER ACCESSION OF NEW RULER

12 NATIONAL DANCE WITH REED-PIPES (HEPTATONIC) AND DRUMS *t s h i k o n a*

FOR INSTALLING, OR COMMEMORATING DEATH OF A RULER. FOR *thevhula* SACRIFICIAL RITES AT GRAVES OF RULERS' ANCESTORS FOR ANY IMPORTANT OCCASION

13 MUSIC OF SEPARATIST CHURCHES *n y i m b o   d z a   z i o n*

14 MUSIC OF EUROPEAN-RUN CHURCHES *n y i m b o   d z a   v h a t e n d i*

15 SCHOOL MUSIC *n y i m b o   d z a   t s h i k o l o*

16 MODERN SECULAR LIGHT MUSIC, JAZZ etc. *nyimbo dza tshikhuwa, dza dzhaivi,* etc. FOR WEDDINGS, BIRTHDAY PARTIES, SOCIALS, etc. LEARNT THROUGH URBAN CONTACTS. FROM RECORDS etc.

NB. THE UNBROKEN LINES INDICATE DAILY, OR AT LEAST REGULAR, PERFORMANCES DURING THE PERIOD MARKED. THE BROKEN LINES INDICATE IRREGULAR PERFORMANCES.

447

concern them. It can only express emotions and attitudes that have already been experienced: it reaffirms and enhances the social meaning of the institutions that it embellishes. — A chief, his subjects, the master of initiation and the initiates, all appreciate the music of the *domba* initiation for a variety of reasons that are related to the meaning of the institution in their lives. And yet there is a level where the music means the same to all of them: it expresses the spirit of brotherhood. Obviously chief and subjects, master and initiates see in different ways the means to expressing the brotherhood. However, when Venda work in town and talk of initiation music with feelings of nostalgia, there is no trace of the differences in appreciation that are apparent in Venda, because in the urban situation the regional social conflicts are of less concern than the more general spirit of Venda brotherhood. — Conversely, a particular style of music may evoke the same response and yet signify a division of social groups. Music may settle peacefully a political dispute: the volume of sound of communal music is an indication of the number of its performers, and hence of the supporters of its sponsor. On one occasion, a chief withdrew his candidate for a headmanship when he heard that the music of his dance team was not as loud as that of the rightful incumbent.

5. Development of musical ability and transmission of the musical tradition

From the evidence so far presented, and especially that summarized in fig. 21 and 22, it should be clear that everyone who is born a Venda is expected to identify and perform different patterns of music with almost as much ease as he or she understands and speaks the Venda language, and that a person who could not do this would be socially at a disadvantage. If we accept the common European view that some people are born unmusical, Venda society would seem to be grossly unfair to demand of its members musical competence as a basic requirement for socialization. However, the situation as observed between 1956 and 1958 was not affecting any Venda adversely, and it raises several important questions about human musicality which have been discussed elsewhere (Blacking, 1971B, 1972). (There is, of course, no evidence that the Venda are biologically different from other peoples who hold contrary views about human musicality; and even a cursory study of Venda musical practices shows that the processes involved in their creation are neither essentially different in kind nor substantially simpler than those which generate music in, say, England.) — The Venda assume that every Venda is capable of musical performance, unless he is totally deaf; and even then, he ought to be able to dance. In fact, people with physical disabilities, such as hunchbacks, seemed to excel in music and dancing. (It is hard to say to what extent this was psychological or physiological, a cultivated compensation for disability or the expression of an exceptionally robust constitution which had survived infancy against heavy odds.) Dancing is an integral part of Venda communal music, and it cannot be ignored in a discussion of their particular musical competence. What distinguishes Venda song from speech, and music from other activities, is not tone but metre. With his body man creates a special world of time, distinct from the time cycles of natural seasons and of cultural events. Just as rhythmical bodily responses to the sounds of music are regarded as the first signs of children's interest in music, so participation in communal dancing is generally recognized as the first stage in acquiring *musical* skills. Small girls copy the dance movements before they participate in *tshigombela* and sing the choruses of the songs. They master the dance-steps before they attempt to lead a song. Girls usually play the different dance rhythms on the alto drums, before they try the straightforward beat of the tenor drum, because it is more difficult to maintain a steady beat than to play complex rhythms – just as conducting an orchestra may be more difficult than playing first violin, although on the face of it the latter would seem to require more musical ability. — Venda dancing consists almost exclusively of rhythmical movement of the lower limbs. One might say that in dancing the ground is used as a musical instrument. When the upper limbs are moved, it is invariably for hand-clapping, drumming, or playing a musical instrument. They are also used in dancing, and sometimes very vigorously, but chiefly to maintain good balance whilst the legs are moved. Dancing is inseparable from most musical performances. A performance of the *domba* initiation song is inconceivable without the physical movements of the dance; and a man who cannot perform the often intricate dance-steps of *tshikona,* the national dance, as well as play his part of the melody on a stopped pipe, would not be considered musically able, even though performance is described more commonly as "blowing (sounding) *tshikona,"* rather than "dancing *tshikona".* — In saying that people "learn music from the breast", the Venda recognize that social factors play the most important part in realizing or suppressing it. For instance, a boy of noble birth *(mukololo)* might show great talent, but as he grew up he would be expected to abandon musical performance for the more serious (for him) business of government. This would not mean that he would cease to listen critically and intelligently to music. Conversely, a musically talented girl of noble birth would have every encouragement to develop her abilities, so that as a woman she could play an active role in supervising the girls' initiation schools, which are held in the homes of rulers, and for which music is an indispensable adjunct of their didactic and ritual functions. During two months of daily rehearsals of the girls' dance *tshigombela,* young relatives of a headman have been seen to emerge as outstanding performers, although at first they did not seem to be more talented than their age-mates. Their development as musicians was surely generated by the praise and the interest shown in them by the women in the audience (see plates 19a and b, pp. 450, 451). In Venda society, musicians are not born, but made according to their birth. Exceptional musical ability is expected of people who are born into certain families or social groups, in which musical performance is essential for maintaining their group solidarity. Just as musical performance is the central factor which justifies the continued existence of an orchestra as a social group, so a Venda possession cult group, or a *domba* initiation school, or a *sungwi* girls' school, would disintegrate if there were no music. The development of musical ability is a part of every Venda's experience of growing up, and because the sequence of learning is socially and culturally regulated, music is not necessarily learned in the order of its surface *musical* complexity. Thus, although boys' and girls' play-dances *(dzhombo)* in fig. 21 and 22 could be said to introduce the added metres and style of dancing common in adult beer songs, and many children's songs are derived from the music of the national dance, *tshikona,* and acquaint children with the principles that relate melody to speech-tone, some young people's music may be technically more difficult than adult music, and children often learn five- and six-tone songs before three- and four-tone songs, simply because these songs are more popular or socially more appropriate. — Venda children have many opportunities to hear all the different styles that make up their musical tradition, but they do not perform music that rightfully belongs to senior groups, although they have more direct contact with adult music-making than children in Western societies, who may perform concertos by Mozart or Beethoven. In fact, the only events at which

Plate 19a. Girls wear waistcoats, towels, bead-skirts and leg rattles, as they dance round the tenor drum during the *tshigombela* dance. Notice the age of the little girl who is beating the basic rhythm on the alto drum.

Plate 19b. Small girls stand close to the rhythm section of a *tshigombela* dance, whilst older women help them to keep time. The larger "conductor" drum is the most important of the four.

children seriously attempt to perform adult music in Venda are possession dances, when young members of the family of the organizer may venture into the dance arena for a few minutes. Also in recent years, because of migrant labour, boys have been allowed to take part in the national dance. There is little doubt that Venda children could perform adult music, but they do not do so because each social group has its associated style of music, its audible badge of identity, and it would be pointless to divorce musical sounds from their appropriate social context. — At the boys' circumcision and the girls' schools (nos. 6, 7 and 9 in fig. 21 and 22) music is transmitted chiefly by *midabe* (sing. *mudabe*) graduates of previous schools who help to instruct the neophytes. Boys' circumcision schools *(mirundu)* are run in different districts by doctors under the auspices of local headmen, and the graduates who come to help are usually relatives of the owners, or men who are particularly interested in the schools and are perhaps thinking of becoming doctors. At the *sungwi* girls' school, the graduates who help regularly are usually female relatives of the owner of the school, who are readily available because they live near the school enclosure or even stay with the owner's family while terms are in progress. At *vhusa*, the girls' puberty school, each initiate is given a ritual "mother", who sees her through the school, helps her learn its laws, and demonstrates its songs and dances (see Blacking, 1959). At *tshikanda* (section 6i), most of the instruction is in the hands of old women, and except for certain ritual songs, there is no new music to learn, since it is the same as that of *vhusha*. — The process of learning could be described further in detail; but since the transmission of music is an integral part of the transmission of social and cultural institutions, brief descriptions of those institutions and their associated communal music will cover both the different styles of music and how they are learned.

6. Varieties of Venda communal music

The different categories of communal music recognized by the Venda will be numbered and described in the order given in fig. 21 and 22.

a. Beer-songs (malende) are performed throughout the year, whenever beer is provided; they are sung for pleasure, though their performance may arise from the execution of social duties that can be irksome. Some are designed for special occasions: for instance, songs that lighten the labour of communal work-parties (*nyimbo dza davha*) generally have a simple metre which enhances, but does not interfere with, the rhythm of the work. Each time the workers hoe or weed one length of the field, they pause to drink some of the beer provided by the owner. Then someone may begin one of the many beer-songs which have an irregular metrical pattern, such as ♩ ♪♩ ♩ ♪♩ which is clapped by those who sing the chorus; those who wish to dance come out singly or in pairs, and stamp and leap to the rhythm. When songs are sung at a work-party, dancing is usually deferred until the work is finished and the last pots of beer are drunk at the home of the sponsor. Many people prefer the type of work-party called *davha ḽa mafhungwi* in which the workers are not rewarded on the same day: thus they can look forward to a day with no work, but with plenty of drinking, singing and dancing. — In the past, beer was usually brewed and drunk in the same home only when it was required to celebrate a family event, such as the return of a member from initiation school; nowadays, many women make and sell it throughout the year, and there are profit-making clubs, called *zwitokofela* for drinking, eating and fellowship, opportunities have arisen for informal performances of beer-songs. —

There is an element of formality, however, in the sequence of songs sung when wife-givers *(vho-makhulu)* bring to the wife-takers *(vhakwasha)* one of the many gifts of beer *(mirula,* sing. *murula)* which are sent both before and after marriage, as long as the relationship between the groups lasts. There are several *malende* songs whose texts are specially suited for these occasions. If the wife's people want clothes from their son-in-law, they may start the song:

Example 68

Although I am wearing a sack, I look quite smart in my sack.

If this does not strike home, they can sing another in the same vein:

Example 69

(Continued overleaf)

kwa- sha ndi fu-ka-'ni?
khu-lu ndi fu-ka-'ni?

ngu - vho.

What am I wearing, you who took one of our women?
I am making an old sack serve as a blanket.

There is a song which the son-in-law's people often sing:

Example 70

These givers of wives are takers of property!
They want pounds, these takers of property;
They want shillings, these takers of property;
They want soap, these takers of property.

They may also criticize with a song the beer that has been brought:

Example 71

This fruit-juice that our in-laws bring,
you've got to drink it;
Although it tastes like salt water, you've got to drink it.

Beer-songs are sometimes adapted for solo performance on an instrument, for the girls' dance, *tshigombela,* or for the music of the *domba* initiation, where they are called *nyimbo dza mitambo* (songs for amusement). At the *domba* initiation they are accompanied by drums, and the girls dance in a circle, as for the ritual *domba* song, but at a far greater speed. As the beer-songs contribute to the music of initiation, so the initiation enriches the beer-songs: many soloists borrow words from the ritual *domba* song. When they do this, they may use them exactly as at *domba,* or they may change a few words of the original, which may please the audience more than completely new words. The success of a session of beer-songs depends on both the beer and the presence of at least one good song-leader *(ṋambi). Mukukumedzi wa davha* (the man who cheers on the work-party) and *tshivia-mbudzi,* the "skinner of the goat" for *murula* parties, are also men who are expected to lead songs well. A good singer should have a loud, confident voice: his knowledge of words is his most important asset, and if he is able to improvise topical words or introduce an entirely new song, he will be all the more appreciated. — In comparison with other Black African musical traditions, especially some in Central Africa, the Venda have few topical songs. Topical additions rarely extend to more than two of three "lines" and merely state the facts of the case, rather than comment on it. Well-known phrases are used as symbols with a variety of meanings, and a singer does not have to labour his point. Exs. 72–74 give the outlines of the call and response sections of three beer-songs. As in all transcriptions of songs, extra vocal parts may be added at will, provided that they follow the rules of harmonic equivalence given at the end of this article.

Example 72   The country is very pleasant

1. We are going to our homes.
2. We are going to *Makonde.*
3. Let me have some snuff to prepare in my hands.

Example 73   Do not quarrel

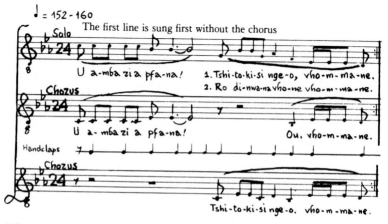

1. There is a prison over there, wife of my brother.
2. We have been troubled by you, wife of my brother.

This song is about conflict that may arise between a woman and her husband's younger brother.

Example 74   You are friendly with him!

1. Hi, kind man!
2. Hi, spoiler!
3. Hi, generous!
4. Hi, stingey!

This song is about a person who has no friends; he cares neither for good nor bad people. Notice that the shift of tonality in the melody coincides with the change of topic.

Pounding-songs *(mafhuwe)* are related to beer-songs but classified separately by the Venda. They are work-songs, but not communal in the way that *davha* songs are: women usually pound maize (or millet in the drier areas in the north) in the cool of the night with a few companions, so that there is a small chorus to embellish their solos. Although today there are few women who sing them well, pounding-songs are still important, because they provide an outlet for criticism, which is particularly effective when sung loudly in the still of the night.

b. Music for children and play-dances for boys and girls

Venda children begin to participate in music-making when they spend less time with their mothers and more with other children; they sing the musical games and songs called *nyimbo dza vhana* (children's songs). Within this broad category are two main types: *nyimbo* (sing. *luimbo)*, which are generally sung by day and at any time of the year; and *ngano* (sing. *lungano)*, which are sung in the evenings in late autumn and winter. — The Venda further subdivide *nyimbo* into "songs for boys", "songs for girls", and "songs for girls and boys"; this arises from the separation of boys and girls during a good part of every day; the boys go out herding, and girls help their mothers around the home. However, boys know and sometimes sing girls' songs, and vice versa, so that the categories should not be regarded as rigid. Some songs are further classified into "songs of mockery", in which girls may deride a boy who plays with them, or boys laugh at one of their number who has gaps in his teeth, "songs for nursing a child", and "counting songs", which are often used to select someone for an unpleasant task, and may be sung by boys and girls. The term *nyimbo mpfufhi* (short songs) is sometimes used to refer to the jingles, that consist of short musical phrases repeated over and over again, usually accompanied by a game, such as hopping, standing on the head, or playing Ring o' Roses. "Long songs" are not complete in the way that jingles are; they vary in length according to the number of words that a singer knows. A few songs are sometimes called "songs of instruction", and "songs for calling loudly to one another". — In the following three examples the first is a complete counting song (see also ex. 57, p. 421); the words of which are obscure but accompany the counting of fingers and thumbs of both hands, the second is an excerpt from a song for girls, and the third is for boys and girls. The two melodies in ex. 77 are described as the same, because of the principle of harmonic equivalence in which every Venda tone has a companion tone (see list of rules at the end of the article). Translations of the words are given below. Continuations of exs. 76–80, with notes, may be found in *Venda children's songs* (Blacking, 1967). The word *lungano* may refer to a story which is narrated formally and includes a song; to the song itself, in which the audience sing chorus to the story-teller's solo; or to a number of songs of similar structure that are sung without a story to accompany them. In all three cases, they are always performed in the evenings, when boys and girls are together at home, but not during hoeing time, when people are supposed to go to bed early, in order to be fresh for work on the following day. Stories are generally told by adults or older children, but small children join in the spoken response, *Salungano!* which follows each sentence of the story, and in the chorus of the song. *Ngano* songs, however, are generally sung by boys and girls together; the meaning of their words is often obscure, but their sequence suggests that they are stories set to music, which have become corrupted with the passage of time. There is only one commonly recognized subdivision of *ngano,* and that is *ngano dza bune* (lit. songs of the game of touch), in which the responsibility of singing the solo is passed from one member of the group to another. — Exs. 78–80 are parts of independent *ngano,* and ex. 81 is part of a Pygmalion-like story about a lonely man who carved a verandah-pole, which turned into a beautiful woman. When a chief tried to take the woman away from him, he played his *dende* musical bow, plucked a feather from the girl's hair, and she became a verandah-pole once more. Only when the chief gave in did the man convert his pole into a woman once more. Ex. 82 is from a story about a bird and an antbear who failed to build a shelter for themselves because they would not co-operate and did not want to work alone. On moonlit nights during

Example 75

Example 76

1. My head aches, Mbengeni.
2. Why does it ache, my cousin?
3. It aches because of what happened last night, Mbengeni.
4. What happened last night?
5. I don't know what happened last night, Mbengeni;
6. Ramatsheka knows what happened.

Example 77

1. Fú-ngú-vhú, ʈa-nzwá mú- lô - mò!

2. ʈà - nzwá mú- lô-mō. Ri kò-nè ʑi tshi ʃà ʑō-ʈhē;

3. Rí tshi ʃà ʑō - ʈhē. Vhó- ḿ-mé vhá' ká é - ndá pi?

4 Vhà ká è - ndà pi? Vhó li - má dà-vhá ʃà khô-mbè.

1. Crow, wash you mouth!
2. Wash your mouth, so that we can eat together;
3. We eat together. Where has your mother gone?
4. Where has she gone? She has gone to help a bachelor hoe his land.

autumn and winter, and especially during "the time of staying home" (*madzula-haya*), unmarried people of both sexes come together to dance on an open piece of ground. The dances are known by different names, according to the areas in which they are performed: they may be called *dzhombo, nzekenzeke, tshinzerere* or *tshifase* (a Tsonga word). It is not surprising that they are most popular in areas where Tsonga live amongst Venda, because the Tsonga prefer to settle in flat, open country, which is

460

ideal for this type of dance. One is inevitably reminded of the similar scene depicted by the song, *Boys and girls come out to play.* — Drums are not used: songs are accompanied by hand-claps and the footstamps of the dancers. Boys stand opposite girls and at some distance from them; one of them dances out and touches a girl, who then dances back with the boy and touches another boy; this boy dances out with the girl, whilst the first boy takes his place with the other boys. The dance continues in this fashion and girls and boys naturally like to touch a partner in whom they are interested, as they can dance provocatively close to each other while moving from one group to the other. — The songs are rhythmically and melodically more complex than the children's songs proper, though their "texts" are brief and repetitive. Their brevity gives young people an opportunity to try improvising new words to the basic pattern: they may attempt no more than repeating the names of persons and places, but it is good training in the art of fitting words to a given pattern. When they dance, they must stamp and jump in time to the rhythms in the same way that adults dance to beer-songs. Thus the play-dances lead a Venda child towards mastery of the techniques, and appreciation of the ethos of adult music. — An evening of dancing is sometimes enlivened or terminated by a musical game: there are little songs that accompany the antics of people in various types of disguise, or a game in which boys tie embers to their limbs and then dance in the dark (see exs. 83, 84, pp. 466, 467).

Example 78   (see ex. 57)

1. Thathatha! The pumpkin pips are burning, I say, they are burning:
2. They are burning with Mr Wild-oranges and Mr Hammer.
3. Mr Hammer said: Where are we going? We are going to the smithy.

Example 79

1. Child of my child!
   Child of my child, Blow up the fire!
2. Blow up the fire!
   Blow up the fire, Your daddy's coming home.

Example 80   (see ex. 57)

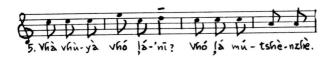

5. Vhà vhù-yà vhó ʃá-'nī? Vhó ʃá mú-tshè-nzhè.

1. I walked out with a small (earthenware) dish of meat.
2. With whom shall I eat? With Sese.
3. From where does Sese come? Vhutwanamba.
4. There at Mukwai's they fought the good people.
5. What did the good people eat? They ate white ants.

Example 81   I wander about

(Continued overleaf)

bo-mbo-zo.   Ka- mbu-le!   Ka- mbu-

Nda te-nde-le-ka.   Nda te-nde-le-ka.

le!

Nda te-nde-le-ka.

1. Spin round, little top!
2. I am hoeing the chief's field with the others.
3. My child stands over there.
4. I can pull out a feather from it,
5. And it's only a long pole that stands there.

Example 82   The bird of Musenzhe

Tshi- no-ni tsha Mu-se-nzhe. Tshi- no-ni tsha Mu-se-nzhe!

Tshi- no-ni tsha Mu-se- nzhe!

Tsha Mu-se-nzhe. 1. Vho-li-gwe de vho di-a-mba,
4. Nne thi nga m li-ndi a-nga.

Tsha Mu-se-nzhe! 2. A zi fha-ţe na dzi-n-ndu.

Tsha Mu-se-nzhe! 3. Ndi la la ndo ho-li.

I. The bulbul said to himself,
2. "Let us build houses".
3. I lay down and would not work,
4. And now I have nowhere to shelter.

Example 83   Choose!

(Continued overleaf)

1. A man is to be chosen.
2. Choose those who are beautiful! (refers to character as well as looks).
3. Leave those who are ugly.
4. Those with white eyes,
5. And long, thin legs.
6. Mine is here.
7. He is wearing shorts,
8. And he has a belt made of string.

Example 84

1. Good evening, my lady with the thin waist and waist band!
2. I will give without paying dowry.
3. The old people will be pleased to scold me.

c. "Amusements" (mitambe) for boys and girls
Tshigombela is an "amusement" *(mutambo)* for unmarried girls, which is danced in late autumn, when weeding is finished and the first maize cobs are available. It is

usually dropped for a few weeks during the harvest season, and sometimes resumed during the following period of rest. *Tshikanganga,* the boys' dance, is also an "amusement", which takes place in late autumn, but more commonly during the period of rest when there are no herding duties. — The melodies of *tshigombela* are sung by the girls but those of *tshikanganga* are played on sets of end-blown pipes, with each player contributing one tone to the total pattern. In both dances girls play the basic beat on the tenor drum, and a regular cross-rhythm with variations on two or three alto drums. The form of the dances is similar: after moving for about ten minutes counter-clockwise round the drums, the dancers gather near the tenor drum, while the alto drums are taken a few yards away to accompany the soloists, who come out to dance in two's and three's *(u gaya).* In both dances, many different abstract steps are performed together by the whole group, as well as by the soloists. The tempo of *tshigombela* is rapid and the girls' dancing is sharp and earthbound with feet kicking the ground, in marked contrast to the graceful, airborne dancing of the boys in *tshikanganga,* the tempo of which is more leisurely. Special dancing clothes are worn even at rehearsals: youths wear girls' salempores over their trousers and shirts, and girls wear hats, waistcoats, ties and shirts, with skirts of beads, and towels (see plate 19). — *Tshigombela* melodies begin with a straightfoward call-and-response pattern, but quickly develop into multi-part choruses. As their pitch rises and groups of singers can no longer reach the highest notes, they transpose tones down an octave. Thus, throughout a single performance of even ten or fifteen minutes' duration, several different tunes come out on top. Exs. 85–88 show the nuclei of three tunes *(I have already made my bet, There's an earthenware pot,* and *We are going to be old enough to marry)* and the basic drum rhythms. The use of phonemes such as *ee, ahee, yowee, io,* allows free melodic movement without any restrictions imposed by speech-tone. *Givha* and *visa* are similar to *tshikanganga,* but differ in rhythm and manner of performance. The dances seem to have been imported, at least to the Sibasa district, only in the last thirty or forty years. They are substitutes for the now obsolete *matangwa,* many functions of which have been taken over by the partially secularized national dance, *tshikona,* which is always played on heptatonic reed-pipes. Teams of men perform the music at weekends in the urban townships. Exs. 89–91 are outlines of harmonic sequences played on sets of twelve reed-pipes. The "tonic" *(phala)* is g'.

d. Mahepha musical expeditions
These have been analyzed and described in detail in Blacking, 1962. *Tshigombela* and *tshikanganga* are agreeable pastimes whose performance is partly regulated by the passage of the seasons. But they are more than this: they introduce young people gently to patterns of tribal authority. If girls want to dance *tshigombela,* they must ask their headman's permission and practise as often as possible at his kraal. The same applies to *tshikanganga,* though this may also be sponsored by a senior official, or councillor of the headman. Thus the performers learn that music may be a symbol of political powers. — The chief object of practising *tshigombela* and *tshikanganga* is to prepare for a *bepha* musical expedition, in which a team of young dancers, managed by four to six responsible adults, is sent by one ruler to another for a variety of reasons, the most common of which is to express sympathy *(u imela)* for the death of a member of his lineage. A team dances at the home of the other ruler for "as many days as there are legs of the beast" (that is slaughtered for them) and returns home on the fifth. Chiefs periodically send *bepha* teams round to their headmen to exact

Example 85

Example 86

Example 87

Example 88

Basic rhythm for all melodies and steps

Alto drum 1
Tenor drum

Variations for alto drum 2
Left-hand: tails of the notes down. Left and right hand parts may be reversed.

Tenor drum

(Continued overleaf)

alto 2 a.

b.

c.

d.

Example 89

Mutshaini

Example 90

Givha

Example 91

Visa

tribute, and on these occasions they dance at each place for only two days: each headman gives one beast to the dancers and sends another back to his chief. After such a visitation many headmen send expeditions to their own petty headmen, to make up their losses! The expeditions thus consolidate both the lineage ties of rulers and their families, whose responsibility for district government scatters them over wide areas, and the neighbourhood ties of the various clansmen living in each district, most of whom are commoners. — When they go to another district, members of teams have little or no contact with its residents, unless some of them happen to be relatives; on the other hand, the situation arising from a visit stimulates closer friendship within the team. The pleasures of these associations, of the music itself, and of eating extra meat, are enough to ensure that every ruler has a loyal and enthusiastic band of young ambassadors who can represent his interests, and in doing so grow used to the idea that these interests are of paramount importance in the district. In this way, the institution of *bepha* reinforce the solidarity of the rulers and their families, and their right to rule. — Nevertheless, *bepha* expeditions are subordinate to the demands of the seasonal cycle, and do not allow rulers to interfere with the economic life of commoner families. Their frequency varies according to the economic surplus, so that few, if any, are sent out in a bad year; and they are always sent out towards the end of the work season, and do not involve the parents of team-members in any extra expense. If girls choose to buy, rather than borrow, dancing clothes, that is their own affair, since there is no compulsion to wear them for *tshigombela*. — In recent years, some chiefs have sent out teams playing the national dance *tshikona* to exact tribute during the school holidays in July, when boys are available. This is an unusual use for *tshikona*, which was normally reserved for solemn and important rites (see section *k*); but it is partly due to the secularization of a number of Venda institutions which has arisen from contacts with urban life and European administration. Many of the men who should normally play *tshikona* are absent in town, and the available schoolboys are not well acquainted with *tshikanganga*, which would otherwise have been used for this purpose. Venda townsmen rarely lose contact with their rural homes, however: they form *tshikona* teams in town, and since 1953 many of these have gone back to the Sibasa district over the Easter weekend. These annual expeditions of urban teams began in commemoration of the death of the deposed chief, Ratshimphi Tshivhase, but they are now sent for any of the reasons which normally prompt *bepha*. — Finally, it should be mentioned that there is an interesting relationship between the structure of the music and the work that is often done by members of a team for their headman, before he sends them out on *bepha*. After a practice, the boys are told to take their reed-pipes home and return with them early the following morning; the sound of the music that is played will indicate immediately if anyone has failed to turn up for the work-party. For anyone with a good musical ear, this is a most efficient way of taking a roll-call, and particularly useful if the organizer does not write.

e and f. Murundu and Sungwi (or musevhetho): privately-owned initiation schools subject to a degree of control by rulers
The boys' and girls' initiation schools are not traditional Venda institutions, and many rites and songs are derived from similar Northern Sotho schools. According to Stayt (Stayt, 1931), both schools were well established in the 'twenties, and the boys' school had first been introduced to the Venda of the Louis Trichardt district, west of Sibasa, in the latter half of the nineteenth century; but even today, these schools have not been fully accepted into the main stream of Venda culture. They are privately owned, always by commoners and chiefly by doctors, who pay an annual fee to the local ruler for permission to hold them in his territory. The rulers support the owners of a boys' school by insisting that no other communal music (except beer-songs and children's songs) is performed while the school is in progress, and that people keep the peace; since the penalty for ignoring these taboos, for quarrelling or disputing, is a fine, the rulers stand to gain as much as the owners. Most rulers stipulate that no attempt should be made to force circumcision on men of ruling clans, because it is not a Venda custom, and by rights no circumcised man is allowed to rule, or to attend the important *thevhula* sacrificial rites at the graves of the rulers' ancestors. Once again, this arrangement clearly suits the rulers as well as the owners of the schools; and the

471

upshot of it all is that potential rivals, especially powerful men such as doctors, are pleased to work within the political system instead of in opposition to it, and many of them become councillors, and even headmen, of the rulers. — The boys' schools are run in specially-built enclosures in the bush, which are strictly taboo to all women and uncircumcised men. They are held in winter, and schoolboys are able to attend during the holidays without detriment to their studies; as long as they pay their fees, are circumcised in the proper way, and learn the laws (*milayo*) of the school, they do not have to stay for the full three months. The songs of the schools are kept secret, and no drums are used. Many of them contain Sotho words, which mean little to the initiates, and only the school song, *Hogo*, is heard outside, especially when the school is "burnt" and the initiates are welcomed home. — The girls' schools are less secret and serious, and only a relatively painless token operation is performed. They are generally held near the owner's houses, and only initiates coming from afar at the weekends live on the premises. Some owners build further enclosures near the homes of relatives, so that they can institute branches of the original school in other districts. The schools are run through the year, with terms of about three months, followed by similar periods of rest. The songs are accompanied by the tenor drum, which is called *ngoma khulu* (big drum), and by three alto drums, two of which (*mirumba ya u tenga*) play the fundamental cross-rhythms to the basic beat of the tenor drum; the other (*khedebu khulwane*) is the master-drum, responsible for the rhythmic variations. The songs are much more typically Venda in form and spirit than those of *murundu*, probably because the school is more open and it is easier to introduce new music into the repertoire, without infringing on the demands of the ritual. Four main types of song are recognized: (i) *Nyimbo dza u sevhetha* (songs for dancing round) are sung by the girls as they dance anti-clockwise in a circle round the drums. Their tempo is rapid and they are sung more often than any other type of song (see ex. 92, p. 473). Classed with them are two songs with special rhythms, a "song of dismissal" *(luimbo lwa u edela*, lit. song for sleeping) which always terminates a session of dancing and a "recruiting song" *(luimbo lwa u wedza*, see ex. 93, p. 476), which is sung when senior members go round encouraging people to join the school.

(ii) *Nyimbo dza vhahwira* are sung when the masked dancers (*vhahwira*) perform in front of the girls (see plate 20, p. 475). The tempo varies, with fast and slow episodes to accompany different phases of the dance, and distinctive rhythms to mark the various steps. Ex. 94 illustrates these rhythms.

(iii) *Nyimbo dza dzingoma* are the songs that accompany certain ordeals that the initiates must undergo when they are in the second stage of initiation (*u hwala dzingoma*, lit. "to carry the drums"). Each one has a distinctive rhythmic pattern; for instance, the initiates are made to move along on all fours, holding, wedged between their thighs, sticks sharpened at either end and called *phephenyane*. The accompanying song begins *phephenyane yo nduma tswaroni* (*phephenyane* has bitten me in the thighs), and has a rhythm of $4 + 5$, or $(2 + 2) + (2 + 3)$ quaver beats. *Mutsha* is a name given to one of the masked dancers (see ex. 95, p. 479).

(iv) *Nyimbo dza milayo* (songs of the laws of the school) are sung by the initiates and any graduates present; they kneel on the ground by the drums, whilst *muluvhe*, the girl appointed to be in charge of the initiates and to assist the masked "mother" of the

Example 92   We are dying of cold at Maguvhulele's

(Transposed down a semitone)

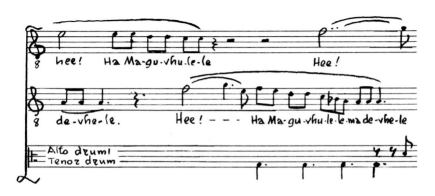

(Continued overleaf)

school (*nonyana*), leads the singing. In time with the basic beat of the tenor drum, which is slower than for the *sevhetha* songs, the girls place both hands on the ground in front of them, alternately to the left and right of their knees. Ever so often the speed of the music is doubled, and the girls sit up on their haunches, clap their hands on their knees and shake their heads from side to side in time with the half-beats of the music. — When the *nonyana* speaks to the initiates or leads the songs, he uses a voice disguiser made of a reed-pipe, one end of which is closed with a mirliton made of a spider's nest covering. The masked *vhahwira* dancers communicate only by whistling; both their conversation with the girls and the songs they intone are perfectly intelligible to the initiates after they have grown used to the idea, because the youths whistle recognizable speech-tone patterns of words. The relationship between the boys' and girls' schools is further emphasized by the fact that the youths who act as *vhahwira* and assist the owners of the schools must be graduates of the boys' school (see ex. 96, 481).

g. Ngoma dza midzimu (lit. "drums of the ancestor spirits") and other types of possession dance

In theory any person can be told that an ancestor-spirit wants to enter her, or his, body; but in fact people are possessed, and belong to cult-groups, according to a distinct pattern. A woman, or occasionally a man, becomes ill and is told that her illness is spiritual rather than physical: the ancestor-spirit wants to enter her, and she must be helped to receive him into her life. An older woman called *maine,* who has herself been possessed by the spirit of one who was a doctor, is asked to help the patient. She summons the members of her group to the home of the sick person; these are her

Plate 20. A masked *mabwira* dance by night at the girls' *sungwi* initiation school.

Example 93

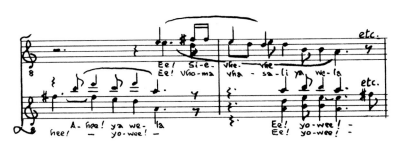

1. Ah! The girls have joined *sungwi*.
2. It's a rite for women.
3. Men may come only at night.

Example 94:   a. to g.

In the rhythms of *vhahwira* songs given below, the double bars enclose one complete call/response cycle. The basic drum beats are given: alto with tails upwards and tenor with tails downwards.

(Continued overleaf)

477

The same rhythm (d) is used in songs with different call/
response cycles, e.g. of 12 x d beats.

A cycle of 4 x d beats is also used.

"children", the *malombe,* who have been brought to knowledge of their spirits by her;
and they are generally female relatives – her daughters and daughters' daughters, and
her sisters and their daughters – who seem to be most susceptible to possession by the
spirits of males of her own patrilineage. In this way, she is able to publicize her lineage
in the home of her husband, where it normally does not count. — The preliminary
session, which takes place indoors, is called *tshele* (lit. hand-rattle, see plate 12, p. 366)
and the singing is accompanied only by hand-rattles shaken to a metronomic beat.
When the patient begins to respond to the music by swaying her head and body, they
increase the sound and vigour of the music, until she falls forward in a state of total
collapse, possessed by the spirit. The spirit is then identified, and talks through the
patient in a strange language, which is a mixture of Venda and Karanga, the language
of the group in Rhodesia from whom the cult seems to have been derived. The spirit
expresses a desire to dance in public, but is told to wait until a suitable time, usually
during the period of rest, when there is sufficient leisure and food surplus. The spirits
of the other *malombe* come, as each member of the group is possessed, and the music
continues until dawn, when the spirits depart again. The public dance, which usually
follows some months later, is held at the home of *maine's* husband or brother. The
songs are accompanied by hand-rattles and drums; the alto and tenor drums are, on
these occasions, respectively called *tshitutulu* and *dumbula* and played with one and

Example 95   It has torn my flesh.

(Continued overleaf)

1. The sharp stick has bitten me between the thighs.
2. They say it has bitten me. Mutsha has bitten me strongly.

two sticks by men or women. It is the only music in which men play the drums (see plate 21a, p. 485), and both this and its unusually rapid rhythm distinguish it from other styles of Venda music (see ex. 97, p. 483). One of the chief functions of the music is to help cult members to achieve the state of trance which allows the spirit to enter them, and therefore the rhythm must be metronomic. Even when the rhythm is perfect, however, members of the cult do not fall into a state of trance unless they are dancing with their own home group, with whom their ancestors are familiar. — Other types of possession dance, such as *ngoma dza matsogodo* and *ngoma dza malombo,* are associated with the different types of spirit by which a person can be possessed, and each one has a distinctive rhythm. The Lemba clan worships its ancestors with the *mbila dza madeza mbira,* and its possession dance is called *ngoma dza madeza.* — Apart from the basic drum rhythms, the music and the dancing are complex, since their chief function is to induce trance. Spectators and dancers usually form a semi-circle facing the drums; only one person dances at a time, and however possessed she may be, her steps are systematic; she pirouettes for sixteen repetitions of the basic rhythmic pattern, and then dances in front of, and facing, the drums for another sixteen patterns. Whenever a dancer shows signs of collapse, the rattle-players converge on her, in the hope that the spirit will enter. Some spirits are shy of entering a cult member in the dance arena, and so the players retire into a hut and continue the

Example 96

♭ = muffled beat on alto drum

♪ = right hand
           } on alto drum
♭ = left hand

(Continued overleaf)

481

1. It presses down on my shoulders.
2. It am eaten up by the drums.

song without the drums until the spirit comes. — A possession dance generally continues day and night for a week, with regular pauses between about midnight and dawn, and again between eight o'clock and midday. A woman who has been entered by a spirit wears a special dancing costume and cannot speak to ordinary mortals. People who have never been possessed by a spirit, or who are not members of the cult-group holding the dance, are allowed to dance if they wish. There is often a certain amount of rowdiness amongst spectators, especially if there is a large crowd; but as soon as things begin to get out of hand, one of the cult members enters the arena and dances, immediately setting the tone of seriousness. The organizer of the dance, or her deputy, always ensures that cult members and serious dancers predominate in the arena: her wishes can be enforced, because dancers must approach her formally for the dancing staff which must be held by all who enter the arena.

h and i. Vhusha and tshikanda, the girls' initiation schools
These important girls' schools are always held in the council huts of rulers, and supervised by senior women, who are generally closely related to the ruler. A session of *vhusha* lasts six days, and may begin at any time of the year, when a girl's puberty is reported to the headman of the district in which she was born. For a number of reasons, girls often do not attend the school for some months, or even years, after they have attained puberty. Each girl must attend three sessions of the school before she graduates, and she is given a "mother of initiation", a ritual companion who assists her at every stage in learning the rituals, music and dancing. — The ritual song of *vhusha*, accompanied by one tenor and two or three alto drums, has a characteristic beat and is danced in a slow, stately fashion (see ex. 98, p. 487). There are certain ritual songs

(*nyimbo dza vhusha*), such as those for "seeking out" the initiate, making her cry, or decorating her body with clay and red ochre; and there is *muulu*, which announces that the school has begun and warns the uninitiated to keep away; this is an unusual type of unaccompanied singing, peculiar to *vhusha*, in which the lower lip is flapped with the forefinger (see ex. 101, p. 490). *Ndayo* songs (*nyimbo dza ndayo*, derived from *-laya* = instruct) are accompanied by drums, and their rhythms are generally multiple. There are numerous *ndayo* dances, many of which are designed to teach lessons; there is a basic step in which the girls dance with their arms folded in front of their breasts, alternately standing up and squatting, kicking and shuffling their feet forward in time to the rhythm (see plate 15, p. 426). *Tshikanda* lasts a month, and is only held before a *domba* (see next section). If a chief intends to hold a *domba* for his tribe, he first has *tshikanda* for all girls of noble birth, and then each headman has one for the commoners in his district; otherwise *tshikanda* is held for both nobles and commoners alike by any headman who plans to start *domba*. The music of *tshikanda* is the same as

Example 97

* (Pitch is varied by pressing the left elbow on the right-hand side and centre of the drumskin respectively). The player does not enter until alto and tenor parts are established.

(Continued overleaf)

The big bass drum is called *ngoma khulwane* and is played by a masterdrummer, who is specially summoned for the occasion and rewarded for his services. He is called *matsige*, because he employs a special technique of muffling and altering the pitch of the drum by pressing on it with his elbow (*-tsiga,* see plate 21b).

Plate 21a. A possession dance (*ngoma dza midzimu*). Members of the cult-group who have already been possessed wear distinctive dress and shake hand-rattles (*tshele*).

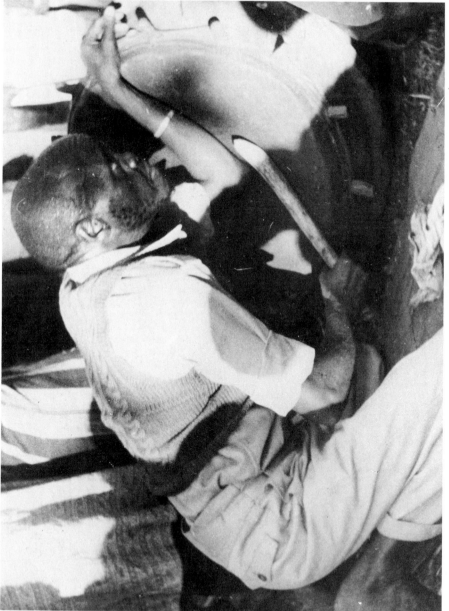

Plate 21b. A master-drummer *(matsige)* presses against the drum-skin with his elbow, and so varies the pitch and intensity of the beats.

Example 98

$\downarrow$ = muffled beat on center of skin $\downarrow$ = clear beat on edge of skin

This vocal pattern is repeated for as much as a minute or more, and then the chorus changes to the style of singing known as *khulo*. As soon as this is established the B flat is usually abandoned. Notes sung to *ou* or *oo* are falsetto, in yodel style.

(Continued overleaf)

487

Example 99   We do not seek her, seek a plant that is good to eat

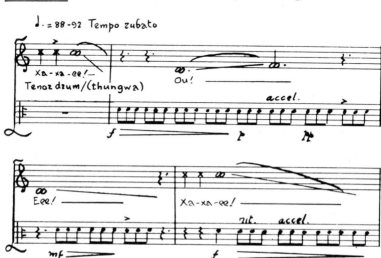

Speech-tone markings are given as follows: á = high tone; à = low tone

1. We seek a novice.
2. We seek one who has not yet gone to *vhusha*.

Example 100   Ah! The redness is going.

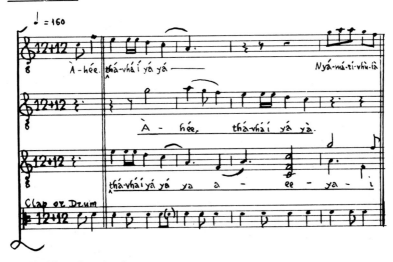

1. Ah! The redness is going.
2. *Nyamarivhula* is going.
3. The redness has gone away, *nyamarivhula*.

(The redness of the sky is compared to the redness of menstrual blood).

489

Example 101   *Muulu.* (rhythm produced by flapping the lips).

Example 102   Avheani, we are going home.

Example 103

1. Scandal-monger.
2. They should treat her with medicine.
3. Just for today.

Example 104   He has dressed himself in his finery.

1. Thovhela has come out

that of *vhusha*, except that instead of the ritual songs of *vhusha* there are songs for the rituals of *tshikanda* (*nyimbo dza tshikanda*), especially those which take place during the last night of the school and at the dramatic presentation of the story of the culture heroes, Thovhela and Tshishonge, which is held on the following afternoon (see ex. 104,). A full account of *vhusha, tshikanda, domba* and their music is given in Blacking, 1969A, 1969B and 1970A.

j. Domba, the pre-marital initiation school for boys and girls
After a period, from the age of about five years onwards, during which many of the activities of boys and girls are separate, they are brought together for *domba*, the most important Venda initiation school. Although its music is similar to that of *vhusha* and *tshikanda*, there are a number of significant changes that are related to its social and symbolic functions. The bass drum is added to the tenor and alto drums; most of the songs are "planted" by a man, the master of *domba* (*nyamungozwa*); the girls dance almost naked in the open space where court-cases, dances, and other public events are held, and not in the council hut, unless it is wet; and they move in a long chain (see plate 22, p. 493) instead of in small groups of two and three. — The ritual *domba* song is performed at least once every morning and evening, as long as the school is in progress (see ex. 105, p. 494). Over four hundred different "lines" of the song are presented in Blacking, 1969B. "Line" 3 is the signal for the dancers to move, and "line" 4 for them to stop. There is a song for dismissal in the evening (*ri a humbela tshilalelo,* "we ask for our supper"), which is accompanied by the same rhythm. Different rhythms accompany the songs of the numerous rituals and lessons of *domba* (*nyimbo dza dzingoma,* see ex. 106, p. 497), and also those which pertain to the spectacles, (*nyimbo dza matano,* see ex. 107, p. 498) that are arranged by the master. Some of these are a feature of every school, such as that in which two people appear disguised as very obviously male and female locusts, and others are invented by various masters of the schools who wish to attract more initiates by the promise of novelties. Interspersed between performances of the great ritual song are songs for amusement (*nyimbo dza mitambo,* see ex. 110, p. 499), which may be arrangements of beer-songs and *tshigombela* melodies, or songs designed specially for *domba*. *Domba* may last for anything between three months and two years. The final rite is a musical, as well as a ritual, farewell to youth. The initiates dance all through the night, so that it is called *tshilala ndo ima* ("I slept the night standing"), and on the following day they take part in several other rites, concluding with a performance of the *domba* dance, in which they are joined by married women and men who have graduated before, and for which they wear a special graduation uniform. During the night of dancing, in which there are a few moments for sleep, the girls sing and dance the *ndayo* songs of the *vhusha* puberty school, songs of the girls' dance *tshigombela,* and the songs for amusement that they have performed frequently throughout the year's initiation. Thus they perform a representative selection of all the communal music of their childhood and puberty, and are reminded of the past which they must now put behind them, as they are entering the world of adult responsibility and marriage. The end of *domba* is a very moving occasion, and the music makes it all the more so when one knows the full significance of every item that is performed.

k. Tshikona, the national dance with heptatonic reed-pipes and drums
Tshikona has been described in detail in Kirby, 1934, pp. 155–163; and Kirby, 1933. It is danced on all important occasions, such as the installation of a new ruler, the commemoration of a ruler's death (*dzumo*) and the *thevhula* sacrificial rites at the graves of a ruler's ancestors. — It is also played on Sundays in the urban areas by Venda who have organized themselves into dance-teams, with managers, musical directors, and other officials. — The men move in file anti-clockwise round the women, who play bass, tenor and alto drums. As in the boys' dance, each dancer produces one note of the total pattern on an end-blown pipe, so that a good performance depends on the

Plate 22. The *domba* initiation dance at Thengwe in 1958, with Jack Makumbila as Master of Music. Both the music and the choreography express symbolically a central theme of the school: the importance of marriage, childbirth, and institutionalized motherhood. Each performance depicts the sex act, and successive performances "create a baby" in the circular "womb" which the line of dancers makes. The bass drum is "the head of the child", and the place where the stick strikes is "the baby's fontanelle".

Example 105

$\dot{b}$ = 'muffled' beat on centre of skin with left hand.

$\underset{>}{d}$ = 'clear' beat on edge of skin with right hand.

ρ ⌐ = beat with stick on wooden edge of drum.

⌐⌐ = indicates notes that are yodelled.

(Continued overleaf)

Dance steps of novices

L R R L L R R L L R R L

Alternative pattern of basic melody:

Steps of *midabe*

L R L R R L R L L R L R

Forwards .... Backwards .... Forwards ....

1. It burns, and burns completely;
2. Young men (dancing *domba*), raise the alarm!
3. The river-reed unfolds.
4. *Gudu* has stirred the entrails.

Example 106   *Luimbolwa ngoma.* You will see that it gives you something
beautiful.

Details of interrelationship of drum parts in *domba* songs.

The use of L and R hands is shown by the direction of the tails of notes.

●   =   'muffled' beat on centre of skin

❯   =   'clear' beat on edge of skin

Basis of drum rhythms in Ex. 106   (Continued overleaf)

497

1. Sexual union changes things.

As this song is performed, girls in turn dance on and off an upturned drum, which represents first a girl when she goes to her husband; then, when she dances on it, the girl in the hut with her husband; and then, when she jumps off, her pregnant womb.

Example 107   *Luimbolwa tano.* Ah, Mr Vulture

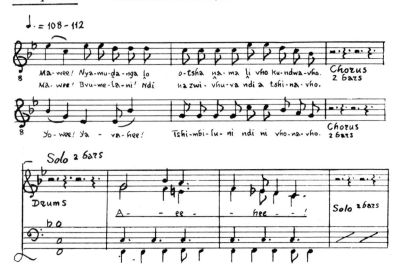

1. Ah! Mr Vulture has fried his meat, but he cannot get it back again.
2. Ah, sing up! I have some good things and I dance.
3. Oh yes, Tshimbiluni! I saw you.

co-operation of a whole team. The national dance is performed only with the sets of heptatonic pipes. The full score is given in Kirby, 1933 and 1934.

Example 108

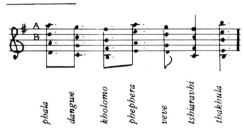

Ex. 108 is a short score of fifteen individual parts, and the names of the basic row of pipes are given. *Phala* is the chief tone. The rhythmic patterns are based on four slow dotted crotchet beats and one of the most characteristic is:

Example 109

This accompanies the "walking" step with which the dancers move round in the circle; but other rhythms may be required to accompany the different steps that are "shown" to the dancers by the musical director (*maluselo*). Some of these steps are representational and others are abstract, and most are difficult to master: as with all Venda music, nothing is done in a haphazard fashion, and the sight of a team dancing in perfect accord is very impressive. Representational steps such as *u kumbuludza*

Example 110   *Luimbolwa mitambo.*

1. When are the visitors coming back, Nyamulenzhe?
2. Aa! Come here, Mr. Lutanga

nduhu (gathering ground-nuts), *u zwala mbeu* (sowing seeds) and *mapfene* (baboons) are clearly related to horticultural aspects of the first-fruit ceremony at which *tshikona* is played. The ceremony is also a sacrifice to the spirits of the ancestors of the chief's lineage, and some of the abstract steps may remind people of their illustrious ancestors, as do the sacred spears (*mapfumo*) which serve as a "register" of ancestors; for these abstract steps are often named after a deceased chief who either invented the step himself, or in whose honour it was named. *Tshikona* is equally effective, whether it celebrates the installation or the death of a chief, the return of townsmen at the Easter weekend or a solemn sacrifice to the ancestors (*thevhula*). One of the functions of the music is to raise performers and audience above the differentiated emotions of daily experience, by absorbing them in a common undifferentiated experience of excitement. — *Tshikona* "makes sick people feel better, and old men throw away their sticks and dance", it "brings peace to the countryside", both because people leave their hoes and let the earth rest, and because it brings everyone together in fellowship and co-operation. It is *lwa-ha-masia-khali-i-tshi-vhila,* "the time when people (rush off and) leave their pots to boil over", because they are captivated by the descending scales of the reed-pipes and the stately beat of the drums. *Tshikona* is usually played when something important is happening, so that everybody wants to rush and see what it is. Then again, the players may be strangers, with some novel dance-steps, costumes and emblems, or there may be some relative amongst their number. Above all, *tshikona* is the musical embodiment of the Venda ethos: it is festive and social, and should be accompanied by beer-drinking; it is decorative, leisurely, dignified and highly systematic, and it gives free rein to self-expression and individual clowning within a disciplined structure; it has religious associations without being aggressively serious; it is a symbol of the power of chiefs and a sonorous emblem of national pride. It is communal music *par excellence,* because the participants cannot merely gratify themselves, but must submit to the strict discipline of the dance. *Tshikona* is a graceful and orderly movement of people who are united and voluntarily overwhelmed, for the time being, by a force greater than themselves.

l. Sacred and secular music that has been added to the Venda musical tradition as a result of European influence
Although European missionaries have done some admirable work in Venda, they have not been very successful in the field of music. Their ears seem to have been deaf to the subtleties of Venda traditional music, and their appreciation of European music has generally amounted to little more than a dutiful and unimaginatively conventional lip-service to their own heritage. Their sublime confidence in the superiority of their own music would not have been so unfortunate if it had been accompanied by some genuine knowledge of music. As it was, they were automatically regarded as experts by the Venda, who assumed that they were being introduced to the best, instead of what was very often the worst, of European music. Worse still, they transmitted styles and ideals of performance that were accepted unquestioningly as correct, so that the new music in Venda is often sung *staccato,* chiefly because it was taught note by note, rather than phrase by phrase; patterns of words and music conflict, because the inappropriate setting of Venda words to European melodies created a tradition that will die hard; and intonation is often faulty, because many of the Europeans who taught the music, and African teachers who have carried on the work, have been as uncertain about the correct reading of the scores as those they have taught. Furthermore,

Europeans seem to be quite unaware of the fact that the Venda have developed their own technique of harmonizing European hymn-tunes: they preserve the perfect and plagal cadences at the ends of lines, but in between they tend to accompany the melody with common chords in parallel motion. This produces a pleasing effect, which is often an improvement on a dreary melody; but it should not be taken as evidence that the Venda cannot sing European music correctly, if required to do so: when taught properly they can, for instance, sing a chromatic or contrapuntal passage as well as anyone. — Venda choir-masters cannot be blamed for these inaccuracies, since schools cannot afford such luxuries as a piano, on which to play over difficult passages. Moreover, they have no criteria of performance: even if someone has a record-player, the music that is set for the annual Eisteddfod is rarely, nor ever likely to be, available on gramophone records. (One suspects that there is a correlation between old or available stocks of music and the items chosen by the committee). The choir-masters have no specifically musical training, and the advice they receive from European "experts" can often do more harm than good, especially when such folk act as adjudicators and are asked to give their opinions. — Most school children have some experience of their traditional music before they go to school and learn music in the European tradition. While at school, there are few boys who do not, at one stage or another, join a team of reed-pipe dancers during the holidays, or play traditional instruments when they are herding. But girls rarely participate in traditional dances; they have to make a more complete break with tradition, partly because those who stay on at school are very much in a minority. In recent years, however, school girls have been attending the *vhusha* puberty school, though they rarely go to *domba*. — The African songs learned at school have been mostly compositions by Xhosa, Zulu, Sotho and Tswana composers, or Venda versions of popular urban songs. Venda teachers have begun to compose their own music, but their culture and language has not yet exerted on it any influence to distinguish it from other urban music. During recreation hours, the most popular music is jazz and modern dance music of the type recorded by urban Black African bands, or European pop music that has a vigorous tempo; they learn these tunes from records or from friends who have been to town. — Many educated Venda complain of the monotony of their own traditional music in comparison with the new music. Such remarks must either be intended as a handsome, and perhaps not altogether sincere, compliment to European music, or they reveal a lack of musical sensitivity and a tendency to identify music with prestige and power; for rhythmically, melodically, and even harmonically, most of the "new" music in Venda is more monotonous than the old. Traditional Venda music explores novel sonorities and employs patterns of rhythm, melody and harmony in a way which may be compared with good musical craftsmanship in any culture. The craftsmanship has, of course, been acquired as part of their cultural heritage; but the tragedy is that although it is a feature of traditional Venda music, it is noticeably absent in most of the European and European-derived music that is performed in Venda today. And this is certainly not due to insensitivity or lack of musical ability peculiar to educated Venda. — I heard many Venda complain that the services, and particularly the music, of European-run churches are dull and send them to sleep. The same could not be said of the Separatist Churches which have been active in Venda for over forty years: sermons are generally delivered with great panache, and the congregation punctuate them with cries of "Amen!" and "Hallelujah!" Any member of the congregation may start one of the hymns of European origin, which are sung antiphonally like traditional Venda songs, or one of the special hymns which precede a period of public prayer; these are accompanied with a distinctive beat on the bass-drum (*tshigubu*), and they sometimes sound rather like a beer song with a chorus-part in semi-harmonic style. Some of the congregation may dance as they sing, and at the end of the services there is usually a hymn to accompany the laying on of the hands of the ministers of the congregation. — Healing is an important feature of Separatist Church activities, and it is significant that several ministers have been, or still are, connected with the world of traditional Venda medicine. Others are shop-owners or business men who have had a certain amount of education and often some experience of life. And yet, like the doctors who run the circumcision schools, but unlike those who have pinned their faith solely on the pursuit of Christianity and Western technology, they see little future in making a complete break with Venda tradition and are generally anxious that rulers should approve of their churches, and that members of their families should join them. Recruitment of the congregations of Separatist Churches is often based on family ties, and it may be said that they represent a new group of influential families within the traditional political system. — Music plays an important part in the life of a Separatist Church member. Births, marriages, deaths, the opening of a new shop belonging to a minister or official, and any important occasion affecting a member of the church are all marked by services and festive gatherings at the homes of the people concerned. A lorry is hired, and the congregation travels to and from the ceremony, singing hymns and popular songs. Many services are held at night, because people are busy and unable to come during the day; some of these last all night and conclude with breakfast in the morning. All services are referred to as "work" (*mushumo*), and most Separatist Church members regard Europeans as very lazy about their worship of God. They also insist that one should kneel when praying, and express disapproval of other customs by kneeling down rather noisily if they happen to be attending a Lutheran church service.

7. Some general rules of Venda music

a. Social and cultural factors

1.0.0.   Music is performed as part of a social situation.

1.0.1.   The Venda classify different musical styles according to the social events which they accompany.

1.1.0.   Performers are recruited according to their roles in social situations (i.e. master, novice, graduate etc.).

1.1.1.   Their performing roles are a function of their social roles (i.e. the master is soloist, the novices are the chorus, the graduates (*-byumela*) and senior and experienced novices play the drums).

1.2.0.   The form of the music reflects the social situation.

1.2.1   The choice of instruments (if any) is never arbitrary (e.g. the bass drum is used for *tshikona* and *domba*, because it is music of national importance).

1.2.2.   The style of dancing (if any) is relevant to the social situation (e.g. the novices dance anti-clockwise in a chain, but graduates dance clockwise and independently).

1.2.3.   The basic form of the music expresses both the social situation which it accompanies and the intended content of the situation (e.g. the call-and-response pattern reflects the teacher/pupil situation; and the development of the *domba* song expresses the growing participation of the novices in their society, as well as the pattern of sexual communion which the dance symbolizes).

1.2.4. The length of performances depends on social conditions (thus, regular performances of *domba* are of standard length, depending on the habit of the master, but special performances, as on the last night of the school, may be much longer).

1.3.0. Ideals and variations of performance are social rather than musical.

1.3.1. Distinctions between rehearsal and performance depend on the social background of performance (thus, girls rehearse their *tshigombela* dance, but the worst performance of *domba* cannot be a rehearsal because of its ritual significance).

1.3.2. Performances are subject to the competence and experience of the performers (e.g. at the beginning of a school, *domba* is performed incorrectly, or at least badly; the extent of musical variation depends on the performers' experience).

1.3.3. The dynamics of performance are a function of the social and physiological condition of the performers (i.e. *domba* becomes louder as the number of novices and their confidence increase: unless they are tired, sick, or discontented, they perform "flat out" all the time. If some parts of the chorus sound softer than others, it is only because they lie at the bottom of the vocal register).

1.3.4. Variations in the words of the soloist, which affect the pattern of melody, primarily express aspects of the social situation.

b. Tempo, metre and rhythm

2.0.0. Metre and rhythm vary considerably within different categories of music, but tempo remains more constant. There is a tempo characteristic of Venda music which is common to several categories.

2.0.1. The general aim of performance is to establish and maintain an almost metronomic tempo.

2.0.2. The basic tempo is expressed implicitly by accented performance or explicitly by a time-setter, such as the tenor drum.

2.0.3. In many songs, a basic tempo of between 276 and 336 quavers per minute is crystallized into groups of dotted crotchets, crotchets, or combinations of all three time values.

2.0.4. A "pulse" group equivalent to 12 quavers is a fundamental unit in many songs.

2.0.5. The minimum repeated patterns of many songs are metrically based on multiples of the "pulse" group of 12 quavers.

2.0.6. In the songs of *domba*, preferred multiples of the group of 12 quavers are 1, 2, 3, 4, 8. Also found are $7, \frac{3}{2}, \frac{7}{2}, 3 + \frac{2}{3}$ and $6 + \frac{2}{3}$.

2.0.7. In the songs of *vhusha* and *tshikanda* two basic tempi of between 252 and 300, and 304 and 396 quavers per minute are crystallized into groups of dotted crotchets, crotchets, or combinations of all three time values.

2.0.8. In the songs of *vhusha* and *tshikanda*, preferred multiples of the group of 12 quavers are 1, 2, 3/2. Multiples of groups of 8 quavers are 2 and 4. (Note: groups of 24 quavers are usually 8 × 3 and rarely 3 × 8).

2.1.0.   Metre consists of the repetition of total patterns of movement (a drum beat is part of a total movement of the body).

2.1.1.   The elaboration of patterns is the result of the addition of social elements (e.g., the combination of a tenor and alto drummer, each playing a self-contained pattern, can produce a more elaborate pattern).

2.1.2.   If the social elements are different, the patterns must be combined polyrhythmically (thus, two alto drummers may play in unison, but an alto and a tenor drummer may not).

2.1.3.   If, however, a polyrhythmic pattern has been established, different social elements may combine musically, each following different parts of the total pattern (thus the feet of the dancers follow the tenor drum, whilst their voices follow the alto in *domba*).

2.1.4.   When vocal parts are added, the entry of both call and response may coincide with the basic metre.

2.1.5.   The entry of both call and response may coincide with a counter-rhythm of the basic metre.

2.1.6.   The entry of the response may coincide with the main beat, whilst that of the call coincides with a counter-rhythm.

2.2.0.   New metrical patterns may be created by combining existing patterns in canon.

2.3.0   New metrical patterns may be created by combining or subdividing existing patterns in the ratio of 2:3. Variations in the rhythm of melodies are included in this rule.

2.4.0   New metrical patterns may be created by combining or subdividing existing patterns both in canon and in the ratio of 2:3.

2.5.0.   Drums are assigned different musical roles according to the number used and the nature of the social event they accompany.

2.5.1.   In all but "foreign" music the tenor and bass drums are played with a stick, and the alto with the hands.

2.5.2   The tenor drum is the "time-keeper," announcing the basic metre of the song.

2.5.3.   If the bass drum is played, it is used to add polyrhythmic variations to the tenor.

2.5.4.   One alto drum may reinforce the time-keeping of the tenor, either by playing with it or between its beats.

2.5.5.   A second alto drum may reinforce the rhythm of the bass drum.

2.5.6.   In special cases, such as in *tshikona* and *domba*, alto drum(s) may unite to add a third pattern to those of the tenor and bass drums.

2.5.7.   One or more alto drums may improvise a rhythm which stresses in groups of two or three quavers the underlying quaver pulse.

2.6.0.   The entry of voices may create further rhythmic counterpoint.

2.6.1.   The entry of both call and response may be in strict canon with the main beat.

2.6.2.   The entry of the call may be in canon with the main beat, but the response coincides with it.

c. Speech-tone and melody

3.0.0.   The speech-tone patterns of the initial words of a song may provide the germ of its rhythm and melody, but ultimately they are subordinate to musical factors.

3.0.1.   Melodies are rarely, if ever, an exact replica of speech-tones.

3.1.0   Once the musical pattern of call and response has been established, the words and melody of the response remain constant, though additional parts may be added as harmony.

3.1.1.   Variations in the speech-tone patterns of words of the call, or solo, bring about variations in its melody.

3.1.2.   Variations affect only the first part of each phrase. The melody of the second part, like the melody of the response, remains constant.

3.2.0.   Variations in speech-tone may create rhythmic variations in the metrical pattern by means of agogic accents (i.e. accents caused by a rise or fall in tone, especially in places where the melody is not normally accented).

3.3.0   Descents in speech-tone and melody need not coincide, but a rise in speech-tone is generally accompanied by a rise in melody.

3.3.1.   When a high speech-tone occurs at the beginning of a word-pattern, the accompanying melody usually begins on the highest tone of the tone-row on which the song is based.

3.3.2.   In songs whose tonal nucleus is equivalent to $e' - d' - c' - a$ a low speech-tone at the beginning of a word-pattern is almost always set to c', where the high speech-tones are sung on g' or e'. (Thus, high-high-secondary high may be sung $g' - e' - d'$, but in the same song low-high-secondary high would be sung $c' - e' - d'$ and not $e' - g' - e'$.)

3.4.0.   All changes in melody are subject to an underlying tonal and harmonic framework.

3.4.1.   If there is a shift in tone centre in the middle of a melodic phrase, or a predominantly descending pattern of tones, high speech-tones may be accompanied by lower tones of the tone-row than in the first part of the word-pattern.

3.4.2.   Many alterations in melody which follow speech-tone patterns are regulated by the principle of harmonic equivalence (see rules 4.4.). (Thus a may be sung instead of e' or d', and c' instead of g', in order to suit the requirements of the speech-tone patterns).

d. Harmony and tonality

4.0.0.   The Venda have no word for "scale," but the word *mutavha* refers to a set of twenty-four heptatonic reed-pipes, twelve pentatonic reed-pipes, or a row of keys on the xylophone or hand-piano.

4.0.1.   The tones of each *mutavha* are named.

4.0.2.   In the *mutavha* of heptatonic reed-pipes used for the national dance, *tshikona,* the keynote is called *phala,* and the tone above it, which acts as leading note, is called *thakhula,* "the lifter".

4.0.3.   In *tshikona* the keynote begins each pattern and the leading note ends it. Thus, tonality moves from tonic to leading note and then directly back to tonic at the beginning of the new pattern.

4.1.0.   There is a relationship between the scales of reed-pipes and the modes on which Venda melodies are based.

4.2.0   There is a relationship between the tonal and harmonic systems of music played with the fixed scales of reed-pipes and that sung by voices.

4.2.1.   Certain chords are accepted in instrumental music but avoided in part-singing (e.g. the tritone: see ex. 56).

4.3.0.   Melodies may be called bitonal, in the sense that they shift from the influence of one implicit or explicit tone-centre to another.

4.3.1.   In antiphonal music, or music modelled on the antiphonal situation of solo and chorus, tonality shifts regularly between solo and chorus sections.

4.3.2.   Since the chorus is constant, its tonality is more fundamental than that of the solo (i.e. in terms of *tshikona* it has *phala* tonality, the tonality of the keynote).

4.4.0.   Every tone may be conceptualized as having a companion tone in harmony with it.

4.4.1.   Any melodic line may consequently be conceptualized as a stream of chords.

4.4.2.   Melodies may therefore be as much selections of tones from "hidden" patterns of chords as the generators of patterns of chords.

4.4.3.   Two melodies which are harmonically equivalent are regarded as the same even though their melodies may sound different.

4.5.0.   *Tshikona* serves as a model for tonal and harmonic principles in heptatonic music; or at least *tshikona* and other heptatonic music follow the same, unstated model.

4.5.1.   Chorus sections of melodies should begin on the tonic or its related tone.

4.5.2.   In a sequence of seven descending tones the first may be taken as the tonic of that tone-row. It may also be the final of the mode of the whole melody.

4.5.3.   The closest companion to any tone is the tone an octave above or below it. This relationship is often expressed in terms that resemble the grouping of people by age. For example, the tone an octave above *phala* is called *phalana* (little *phala*).

4.5.4.   The second, and perhaps more intimate companion of any tone is that which is one fifth below it, or its octave a fourth above.

4.5.5.   The third related tone is that one fifth above it, or its octave a fourth below.

4.6.0.   Harmonic variation and shifting tonality are achieved both by melodic movement and by changing the companions of tones.

4.6.1.   Harmonic cohesion and "direction" may be reinforced by repeating tones, but with different and related chords. Thus, in ex. 56 the tonic is heard firstly with its own primary companion, but secondly with its secondary companion, which in turn is the primary companion of the leading note of the tonic.

e. Musical development of songs

5.0.0.   Once a song has been established, its sound may be embellished by expanding its basic structure.

5.0.1.   There are purely musical variations which do not depend on changes in personnel or words as described in *a* and *c* above.

5.1.0.   Rhythmic variations must follow the established basic pattern.

5.2.0   The improvisation of melodic variations and harmonic additions should emphasize the existing tonal and harmonic progression (e.g. *u bvumela* in bars 15–18 of *domba*).

5.2.1   The choice of tones in improvisation is guided by the principles of harmonic equivalence, incorporated in rules 4.4.0., 4.5.0. etc.

5.3.0.   Passing-notes may be used between the main notes or chords of a melody.

5.4.0.   The soloist may improvise (*-bvumela*), while the chorus is singing (e.g. bars 16b and 17b of *domba*).

5.5.0.   The chorus may add chords to their basic melody.

5.5.1.   The chorus may develop a new and more elaborate melody on the foundation of their basic response (e.g. *khulo*).

5.5.2.   The chorus may reduce the melody to its tonal and harmonic essentials, and then develop these (see *u bvumela* in *domba*, bars 15–18), abandoning words for vocables such as *hee, ahee.*

f. Transformation processes

Some transformation processes have been mentioned in the previous sections, but it is thought worthwhile to group them here with others. The second digits are related to previous sections, so that 6.4.1., for example, covers harmonic and tonal transformations. Only radical *transformations* of musical sounds are considered. I do not include variations in the quality, quantity, dynamics, duration of performance etc., which are affected by changes in social situations.

6.1.0.   Music designed for one social situation may be adapted for another (e.g. *khulo* is a vocal adaptation of the instrumental *tshikona*).

6.2.0.   The tempo of the most frequent rapid notes (marked as quavers in the transcriptions) is relatively constant in many songs. Thus a song with four dotted crotchet beats may also be heard with six crotchet beats. Either rhythm is a transformation of the other, since both are aspects of a "hidden" 2:3 rhythm.

6.2.1.   Techniques of polyrhythm may be applied to melodic instruments (as in *tshikona*) or to voices (as in *khulo*).

6.3.0.   Changes in patterns of speech-tone, arising from the addition of new words to an existing melody, may transform its sequence of intervals and even its rhythm. Thus, as in 6.1.0., a musical variation is precipitated by a nonmusical process.

6.4.0.   The harmonic equivalent of any melody may be sung as the melody, either alone or with its own new harmonic equivalent, or with the original melody accompanying it in a subordinate role (see ex. 58). This is not a straightforward transposition, nor necessarily a regular inversion process.

6.4.1.   Just as several different melodies may be described as *tshikona* (see J. Blacking, 1967, fig. 9, p. 177), so a melody's pattern of intervals may be transformed by selection of a different mode and/or different tones harmonically associated with the "original" mode.

6.4.2.   The melodic, tonal and harmonic patterns of many songs are transformations of the music of *tshikona*, the national dance with reed-pipes tuned to a heptatonic scale (cf. 6.1.0).

8. References

Blacking, J.: Fictitious kinship amongst girls of the Venda of the Northern Transvaal. *Man* 243, 1959A.   Idem: Problems of pitch, pattern, and harmony in the ocarina music of the Venda. *African Music* II/2, 1959B, pp. 15–23.   Idem: Musical expeditions of the Venda. *African Music* III/1, 1962, pp. 54–78.   Idem: *Black background, a study of Venda childhood.* Abelard-Schuman, New York, 1964. Idem: The role of music in the culture of the Venda of the Northern Transvaal. M. Kolsinki, ed., *Studies in Ethnomusicology,* Oak Publications 2. New York, 1965, pp. 20–53. Idem: *Venda children's songs: A study in ethnomusicological analysis.* Witwatersrand University Press, Johannesburg, 1967.   Idem: Initiation and the balance of power – the *tshikanda* girls' initiation of the Venda of the Northern Transvaal. *Ethnological and linguistic studies in honour of N.J. van Warmelo.* Government ethnological publications 52, Pretoria, 1969A, pp. 21–38.   Idem: Songs, dances, mimes and symbolism of Venda girls' initiation schools. *African Studies* 28, parts 1–4, 1969B, pp. 1–35, 69–118, 149–199, 215–266.   Idem: Tonal organization in the music of two Venda initiation schools. *Ethnomusicology* XIV/1, 1970, pp. 1–56.   Idem: Music and the historical process in Vendaland. K.P. Wachsmann, ed., *Essays on music and history in Africa.* Northwestern University Press, Evanston, 1971A, pp. 185–212. Idem: Towards a theory of musical competence. E. de Jager, ed., *Man: Anthropological essays presented to O.F. Raum.* C. Struik, Cape Town, 1971B, pp. 19–34.   Idem: *How musical is man?* University of Washington Press, Seattle, 1972.   Kirby, P.R: The reed-flute ensembles of South Africa. *Journal of the Royal Anthropological Institute* LXIII, 1933, pp. 313–388. Idem: *The musical instruments of the native races of South Africa.* Witwatersrand University Press, Johannesburg, 2nd ed. 1965. Stayt, H.A.: *The Bavenda.* Oxford University Press, 1931.

– J.A.R.B.

INGLEBY, NINIAN RUSHTON, *14 February 1874 in Didsbury, Lancaster; ° 17 November 1944 in Durbanville. Organist and choral conductor.

After the completion of his school days, Ingleby registered at the RCM for organ and theoretical subjects. After obtaining the Fellowship of the RCO, he continued his study at the Conservatoire in Dresden under Ernst Pauer and Edward Dannreuther and in 1900 he accepted an appointment as organist and choral conductor of St Andrew's Presbyterian Church in Gardens, Cape Town. In 1918 he became City Organist of Cape Town and in September of that year, he was also appointed organist of the Groote Kerk in Adderley Street. He retained these two positions until he died in his 71st year. — Shortly after his arrival in Cape Town he accepted an offer to become conductor of the Sea Point Choral Society, and in 1904 he became Musical Director to the Cape Town Amateur Operatic and Dramatic Society which mainly performed the works of Gilbert and Sullivan. He directed the Choral Society for six years but the Opera Society he served practically until the end of his life. His reputation as choral conductor grew and the Cambrian Male Voice Choir was also placed under his direction. His own society, the Orpheus Male Voice Choir, became very well known in Cape Town and achieved much success in the Cape Eisteddfodau. With the establishment of the South African College of Music** in 1910, Ingleby was an automatic choice as principal organ lecturer, but he continued his private teaching of pianoforte, violin, singing and theoretical subjects. In 1918 a Municipal Choral

Society, closely associated with the Municipal Orchestra** conducted by Theo Wendt,** came into being and was conducted by Ingleby until 1920. — On 20 September 1906 he was married to Miss Elizabeth Scott of Observatory. Three children were born from this marriage.

COMPOSITION
Sea Point Boys' High School song. Ms., n.d.

SOURCES
Golden Jubilee, SACM. Cape Town, 1960.   Olivier, Gerrit: *Die orrel in die stadsaal van Kaapstad.* B. Mus. script, UP, 1967.   *Cape Times:* 18 Nov. 1944 (obituary).   Information supplied by Mr G.A. Ingleby of Cape Town.

– E.H.S. (amplified)

INKOSI SIKELEL' iAFRIKA   Khabi Mngoma

INSTITUTE OF FOLK MUSIC, STELLENBOSCH   Jan Bouws, Centenary Trek songs, FAK

INTERNATIONAL ARTS LEAGUE OF YOUTH, FESTIVAL OF   W.E. Dunn, Durban 8, 10, Durban Orchestra, C. Wright

INTERNATIONAL LIBRARY OF AFRICAN MUSIC   J.A.R. Blacking, Indigenous Musics of South Africa (bibliographies), T.F. Johnston, H. Tracey

IONIAN CHOIRS   E.N. Harvey, K. Mngoma

IRESON, W.M.   Grahamstown 6

ISCOR ORCHESTRA   O.C. Gafner, P.C. Rorke, J. Trauneck

ISRAEL, a talented Bloemfontein family who became known in various centres of South Africa between 1895 and 1940 as a chamber music group and as individuals. The father, **George Israel,** was a competent musician of German-Lutheran descent who could play piano, harmonium and violin. His name appears for the first time in 1867 when he presented the Dutch Reformed congregation of Boshof with a "melodium" (harmonium) on condition that they appoint an organist and pay him a salary of R300 per annum. The church council could not afford to do this at the time and whether George Israel was still prepared to donate the instrument is unknown, although, in 1874, an instrument is mentioned in the minutes of the council. Israel's connection with this small 11 year-old town came through his marriage with the widow Coetzee, a daughter of the first magistrate of the Western Free State, P.S.Z. Fourie. From this marriage four sons, George, Rudolf (sometimes also Rudolph), Ferdinand and Charles, and two daughters were born. For a while the family resided in Hamburg where the violinist, sculptor and violinmaker, Otto Schünemann, gave the two eldest sons lessons in music, but in 1885 they were all back in Bloemfontein and playing chamber music. From then on their home in Monument Road became a popular venue for the town's musicians. Apart from musical evenings in the family circle, the four Israel boys formed a string quartet which toured in the Free State, Natal and the Cape. According to one newspaper report they had a repertoire of 150 string quartettes. **George** Israel was the eldest of the four brothers and the leader of the quartet. Not much is known about his career. Towards the end of the 19th Century he was a member of several chamber music groups in Cape Town and the leader of an orchestra, probably that of the Cape Town Musical Society. On 15 November 1903, he made his debut in Port Elizabeth at the 181st organ recital given by Roger Ascham** and in January of the next year, he offered his services in PE as a teacher of violin, mandolin and zither. In February and again in July of that year, he performed at Ascham's concerts; in September he and Horace Barton** were members of trios who played works by Arensky and Mendelssohn; in November he played a few solos at a benefit concert for Barton; and in 1905 he performed at concerts given by Sara Lachmann and Pellow-White.** He was never really a soloist but happiest in groups or when contributing items to concerts arranged by others. Between 1905 and 1914 there is no mention of him but he is again named as a participant in a concert given for war funds in Port Elizabeth. — **Rudolf** Israel was a cellist, who died in Johannesburg on 1 August 1892. He had been resident in the city, where he owned a shop, from 1889. Rudolf sometimes played a solo at concerts or contributed to chamber music arranged by Otto von Booth** and Fräulein Kiescke. At various times he is mentioned as a cello player in Bloemfontein. He died of pleurisy. One work of his has been preserved: *The prayer* (Das Gebet), for violin, viola and cello with pianoforte accompaniment, Jackson Bros., Durban n.d. — **Ferdinand** Israel, *23 June 1869 in Bloemfontein; °29 June 1938 in Vereeniging. This violin and viola player left Bloemfontein in 1893 to become a violin teacher in Durban. He also represented the London College of Violinists. According to Dr G.S. Jackson, he contributed more than any other musician at the time to the propagation of chamber music in Durban: he arranged a series of chamber music concerts in 1894 and often participated in chamber music groups, sharing a concert with the German pianist Friedenthal in July 1898. During the Anglo-Boer War he was a member of the Bijou Orchestra of Ernest Lezard.** — Ferdinand visited England and Germany in 1903 taking with him a new invention: a very special mute about which there is a notice in the *Violin Times* of April 1904 and which was exhibited in a museum for musical instruments in Marktneukirchen, Saxony. On a visit to this town the mayor presented him with a violin made by a local violin builder. He was back in Bloemfontein in 1906 selling pianos and sheet music, tuning pianos and organs and teaching violin. Until the early 'twenties he was still playing solos at concerts, his wife accompanying at the piano. He sold all his business interests in Bloemfontein in July 1934 to settle in East London. Probably for the last time, he appeared as a soloist with the East London Municipal Orchestra in February 1936. Shortly after leaving East London, he died in Vereeniging. — **Charles Wilhelm** Israel, *1871 in Bloemfontein; °3 July 1940 in Pretoria. Charles became the best-known violin player of the family and even in his youth a great future was predicted for him. Reményi** was so impressed by the boy that in 1887 and again in 1889 he took him along on his tours from Bloemfontein to the Witwatersrand and Pretoria to give him lessons. He worked in the shop of his brother Rudolf in Johannesburg for two years, starting on New Year's Day 1890, but when his brother died in 1892, he returned to Bloemfontein. Charles Israel became the leader of the New Bloemfontein Orchestral Society created by Ivan Haarburger** in October 1893 and played solos with this "orchestra". He made a living by teaching the violin at Eunice High School. This did not last very long and in 1896 he moved to Pretoria to practise his profession there. In October 1899, shortly before the outbreak of the Anglo-Boer War, he took part in a Barberton concert given by the singer J.L. Wintle and the pianist Ethel Fainsinger to welcome back the local singer, Grace Hazelhurst, who had recently returned from vocal studies in London. While the War was on, he left the Transvaal and stayed in the harbour cities of Durban, East London and Port Elizabeth. In Port Elizabeth he played at Roger Ascham's** 120th organ concert during the last months of 1901 and also at the Queen's birthday concert. At the end of 1901 he was in Uitenhage. — After the War Charles probably stayed with his brother Ferdinand in Durban until 1904, when the singers Signor and Madame Pasquali** arrived in South Africa for a tour. The couple engaged Angelique de Beer and Charles Israel to assist them at concerts: in June they were in Barberton and in November they gave a concert in the new Opera House** in Pretoria. After this tour, Israel was more or less permanently settled in Pretoria, although he was always available for concerts at other centres such as Bloemfontein, Potchefstroom and Port Elizabeth, where he played at the first concert given by the singer Marie Dona Lloyd who had just arrived back from Paris (October 1905). Before their marriage in 1907, Charles and Freda Grünberger often played together at the German Club in Pretoria as a violin and piano combination. Until 1920, he also combined with Emil Hester,** Aubrey Wilmot,** A.G. Quayle** and others to form string trios and string quartettes which played works by Haydn, Mozart, Beethoven and Mendelssohn at concerts given by the Hollandsch Mannenkoor** and the Christelike Zangvereniging Asaf.** Naturally, he also collaborated with the orchestras of Galeffi** (1908–1909) and the Pretoria Philharmonic Society (1907–1911). When he appeared on stage as leader, he was usually welcomed with jovial remarks and applause which he elegantly acknowledged with his bow. Quite possibly, he was a member of later orchestras created to accompany the choral works conducted by, for example, G. Bon,** or for the concerts of W. Gerke,** although his name is not mentioned again. At a charity concert given by the Apollo Male Voice Choir** in the Town Hall, he contributed solos on 3 August 1923. In the early 1920s he led a group of players which acted as an *ad hoc* orchestra in the Opera House until the advent of the talkies. Apart from his private pupils, he taught at Ellen Norburn's** Pretoria College of Music from 1910, though the staff list of 1920 does not mention his name.

WORKS BY FERDINAND ISRAEL
Violin album. Ten violin solos, composed and arranged by Israel. Augener & Co., London, n.d.   Souvenir de Hamburg, for violin. Ms., 1904.   Lied aus Oberon, for violin. Ms., 1904.   For you, song. Ms., n.d.   Five pieces (and one song) to be kept in memory of me, illustrating South African scenes. Ms., Durban and Bloemfontein, 1906/7: 1. Homeward waltz 2. Leben und ein Traum 3. Fantasie Natalia 4. Free State native dance 5. Jubelklänge 6. Lullaby baby, song "composed" by his eight year old daughter, Olive, and arranged by Ferdinand Israel for voice or violin.   Plantation song, for violin and piano. Ms., 1936.   A few arrangements of popular melodies for violin and pianoforte.

BIBLIOGRAPHY
Human, J.L.K.: *Musiek in die Oranje-Vrystaat vanaf 1850 tot aan die begin van die Anglo-Boereoorlog.* M.Mus. dissertation, UOFS, 1963.   Jackson, G.S.: *Music in Durban from 1850 to 1900.* D.Phil. thesis, UWits, 1961; publ. Witwatersrand University Press, 1970.   Polonaski: Mr Ferdinand Israel. *The Violin Times.* London, April 1904.   Van der Merwe, F.Z.: *Suid-*

Afrikaanse musiekbibliografie, 1787–1952. J.L. van Schaik, Pretoria, 1958.   Vermeulen, Elizabeth: *Die musieklewe van Pretoria tussen 1902 en 1926.* M.Mus. dissertation, UP, 1967.   Wolpowitz, L.: *James and Kate Hyde and the development of music in Johannesburg up to the First World War.* D.Mus. thesis, UP, 1965; publ. HSRC, Pretoria, 1969.

– J.P.M.

SOURCES
Daily Dispatch: 1900–1901 and 1934–1936.   *Diamond Fields Advertiser:* Aug. 1892. *Eastern Province Herald:* 1901–1920.   *The Friend:* 1906–1934.   Information supplied by Franz Moeller,** Gatooma, Rhodesia.

IVANOFF, VICTOR, * 2 July 1909 in Vilnyus, Russia; now (1979) in Johannesburg. Singer and political cartoonist.
Victor Ivanoff's father was a former general of the Don Cossacks in Vilnyus and his mother was a gifted lady who very early taught him the elements of singing, dancing and playing musical instruments. After the Revolution in 1917, Ivanoff was sent for further education to Zagreb in Yugoslavia with a Don Cossack cadet school. There he was eventually trained as an architect and two Russian painters, Karpoff and Krisogonoff, gave him art classes. In 1930 he joined the Don Cossack Choir and accompanied them on a world tour. At times he sang solos, but he regularly participated in the Cossack and Caucasian folk dances. — After touring South Africa with the choir in 1936, he settled here permanently and, for the next 36 years (since 1937) he was employed as cartoonist by *Die Vaderland* in Johannesburg. He achieved international recognition as a political cartoonist in 1958 when he received third prize in The World Challenge Exhibition held in London, and in 1967 when he received the sixth World Prize in Montreal. — From 1944 to 1953 he collaborated with John Connell** and sang leading baritone roles in Connell's annual municipal operatic season. Performances in which he participated include *The snow maiden* (Rimsky-Korsakov) (1944), *The barber of Seville* and *Rigoletto.* Together with Alessandro Rota he founded the National Opera Association of South Africa**. For the SA Opera Federation** Ivanoff sang the baritone role in *Don Pasquale* (Donizetti) (1961). — Since 1950 he has held several exhibitions of paintings in South Africa. During the years 1957 to 1960 he studied painting in Germany, Austria and France. Since his teens a number of his Russian poems have been published in various European centres.

SOURCES
Bender, Anna: Die vurige sanger. *Rooi Rose,* Sept.1954.   *Die Volksblad:* 9 Mar. 1956.   *Die Oosterlig:* 9 Mar. 1956.   *Die Burger:* 10 Mar. 1956.

– Ed.

IVERSON, NOEL, *18 October 1904 in Cape Town; °18 April 1962 in Johannesburg. Music master and leader of school choirs.

Noel Iverson had a fine soprano voice as a boy and was awarded a scholarship to enter the choir of Christ Church, Kenilworth, Cape Town. In addition to the musical training he received in the choir, Dr Barrow-Dowling** took charge of his instruction in organ to such good effect that he was organist of St Mary's Cathedral in Cape Town for five years. By the end of these 5 years he had also achieved the UPLM of UNISA and then became a student at the RCM in London where he qualified as an ARCM (organ). During his time in London he was organist and choirmaster of St Luke's Church, Hampstead, and from 1928–1929 he was on the music staff at Brighton College in Sussex. — Noel Iverson returned to South Africa in 1930, to take over a music school in Malmesbury, but in January 1931 St John's College in Johannesburg appointed him director of music. He remained in this position until the time of his death. At St John's he was responsible for the College Choir and produced an operetta by Gilbert and Sullivan each year from 1934 to 1940. He resumed the series in 1949, but then offered an operetta each alternate year until 1955. In 1956 he established an Old Johannian Choir, consisting of old boys of the College.

SOURCE
The Johannian: May 1962 (obituary).

– M.W.C.

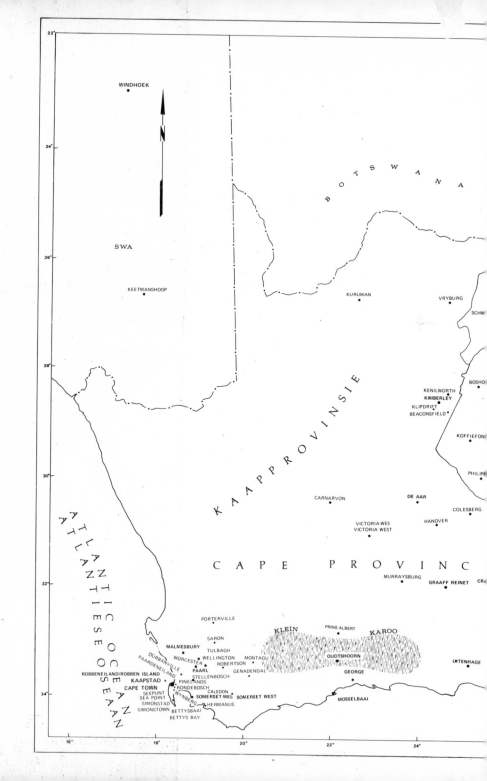